Strategic Management in the Regulatory Environment

Strategic Management in the Regulatory Environment

Cases and Industry Notes

Richard H. K. Vietor
Harvard Business School

Prentice Hall, Englewood Cliffs, New Jersey 07632

Library of Congress Cataloging-in-Publication Data

Vietor, Richard H. K.(date)
  Strategic management in the regulatory environment.

  1. Industry and state—United States—History—20th
century—Case studies. 2. Trade regulation—United
States—History—20th century—Case studies.
3. Strategic planning—United States—History—20th
century—Case studies. I. Title.
HD3616.U46V54 1989   338.973   88-6010
ISBN 0-13-851726-6

Editorial/production supervision
and interior design: **Eleanor Ode Walter**
Cover design: **George Cornell**
Manufacturing buyer: **Ed O'Dougherty**

 © 1989 by Prentice-Hall, Inc.
A Division of Simon & Schuster
Englewood Cliffs, New Jersey 07632

Printed in the United States of America

10 9 8 7 6 5 4 3 2 1

ISBN 0-13-851726-6

Prentice-Hall International (UK) Limited, *London*
Prentice-Hall of Australia Pty. Limited, *Sydney*
Prentice-Hall Canada Inc., *Toronto*
Prentice-Hall Hispanoamericana, S.A., *Mexico*
Prentice-Hall of India Private Limited, *New Delhi*
Prentice-Hall of Japan, Inc., *Tokyo*
Simon & Schuster Asia Pte. Ltd., *Singapore*
Editora Prentice-Hall do Brasil, Ltda., *Rio de Janeiro*

Contents

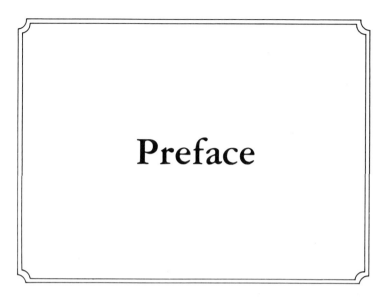

Preface

This text, in its choice of cases and organization, is designed to study the regulatory environment from a managerial perspective. It has three objectives:

1. to help develop a nonnormative concept of business-government relations, sufficiently dynamic and sophisticated to be useful to business managers;
2. to build a framework for organizing and analyzing the complex interactions between government regulation, markets, and the firm;
3. to illustrate, by example, the extraordinary challenges of managing successfully in politically salient environments.

This framework, and most of the case studies from which it is derived, were developed for a course on strategic management in regulated environments taught at the Harvard Business School. It is designed for students of business administration and public policy, or for anyone seriously interested in developing a better understanding of the American political economy.

The cases and several industry notes introduce and explore the business environment in which government regulation shapes competition and significantly alters conventional principles of business management. The perspective offered is usually that of a manager, and occasionally a regulator.

The fabric of this text is woven from several intellectual threads, the first being institutional history. The cases and industry notes, organized chronologically within each section, summarize the historical development of government regulation and regulated industries in the United States during the twentieth century.

The second thread is industrial organization. The data on industry and market structure, the grouping of cases by structural characteristics, the orientation towards competitors and the external environment, and some of the framework's conceptual elements, are derived from this extraordinarily rich subfield of economics.

Regulatory theory, from economics, political science, and history, is a third part of the pattern. Public-interest and capture theories, pluralism and corporatism, bureaucratic forces and ideologies, market failures and mismatches, can all be found between the lines, and are explored in the various cases and notes.

Business policy, and the concept of strategy, is the thread that pulls together the other three into a useful framework for management students. Business policy turns the environmental analysis inward to the organizational structure, capabilities, and motivation of the firm, and drives the analysis towards strategic action.

Two pedagogical considerations underlie the choice and organization of cases. First, the number of business contexts is limited to five: toxic substances, energy (gas, electric, and nuclear), transportation (airlines, trucking, and railroads), telecommunications, and financial services. This is to minimize superficiality, to limit start-up costs to substantive discussion, and to encourage a process of building, on content as well as ideas. Second, the materials provide three different perspectives: of the manager, the industry analyst, and the regulator. Following the principle of "where you stand depends on where you sit," this should encourage students to think about problems and controversial issues from a practical standpoint, from an intellectual perspective, and from a position of responsibility for the "public interest."

This text is organized in six parts: (1) an introduction to the scope of regulation and a framework for analysis, (2) environmental externalities, (3) natural monopoly and problems of rate-base regulation in the energy sector, (4) excess competition and transport deregulation, (5) the public goods aspects of telecommunications and the transition to mixed regulation and competition, and (6) mixed rationales for the regulatory segmentation of financial services.

Acknowledgments

Several colleagues, researchers, and MBA students contributed to the preparation of cases that appear in this book. Louis Banks directed the original case on Boston Edison, Joseph Bower directed the case on Ruckelshaus, and George Lodge and Joseph Badaracco directed the Allied case. The case on Marginalism in New York is based on excerpts from books by Douglas Anderson and Thomas McCraw. I am grateful for their contributions.

For many of the other cases, I relied on several talented researchers: William Bunting and Carl Rickertsen for the IT case, and Helen Soussou for CSX and the note on Freight Transportation. I am especially grateful to Dekkers Davidson, who not only researched and coauthored the cases on telecommunications and financial services, but helped me develop the conceptual framework of this text.

A number of corporations made it possible for me to do the field research on which most cases are based. Among these are American Airlines, AT&T, CSX, Commonwealth Edison, El Paso Natural Gas, General Telephone of the Northwest, and IT Corporation. Their support includes the time of many executives, documentation help from managers and staff, and a commitment to management education. To all those individuals who took the time to educate me, I am immensely grateful.

The Harvard Business School provides a unique environment for case research. Dean John McArthur encourages case-based course development, and provides for the long lead times necessary. The Division of Research, under Professors Ray Corey and Jay Lorsch, provide funding for travel, for research assistance, and for editorial and graphics support. Polly Glasser, Kathryn May, Joanne Seagal, and Judy Uhl are always as helpful as possible.

I am very grateful to Carmen Abber for keeping my case files organized, and for typing, revising, and checking the finished manuscript. Her efforts have been invaluable.

Richard Vietor

Strategic Management in the Regulatory Environment

Chapter One

Introduction: The Scope of Regulation

Boston Edison: Overload is a case designed to introduce the broad range of problems encountered by a regulated firm. The situation is set intentionally in 1974, a time of extraordinary upheaval in the electric power business and the American economy at large. For Boston Edison, 1974 represents a watershed in the recent history of regulation. Yet, without a framework for analysis, Edison's management has no way to assess and determine an appropriate course of action.

This case contains virtually all the elements of the framework for analysis and decision making in the essay that follows. It defines a concept of business/government relations, describes the economic justifications for regulation, develops a seven-part framework for analyzing the regulatory environment, and applies that analysis to make strategic decisions. Each part of the framework is illustrated in depth in the cases and industry notes that follow.

Boston Edison: Overload

In hindsight, Boston Edison's experience prior to the 1970s reflects a somewhat peaceful landscape. Company power plants hummed quietly to meet steadily growing demand for electricity. In snug, electrically heated and air-conditioned homes, consumers tried out new appliances, comforted that their electric rates were declining. Stockholders looked on with confidence as ever larger dividend checks arrived regularly.

Hurricane conditions more aptly describe the first five years of the 1970s. Gale force winds rushed in from all sides on Boston Edison's management— consumers howled over soaring electric bills, environmentalists raged about air pollution, opponents of nuclear power dealt damaging blows, politicians roared, and the financial markets sent chilling breezes. Public attention, and to a lesser extent Edison's management, tended to focus on only one issue at a time. The result was a pattern of disruptive shifts in what the polity and the company saw as their central concerns.

By late 1974, these separate winds had come together in a vortex of uncertainty that forced management to face issues for which there were no precedents. When Boston Edison filed for an immense rate increase in November, the public outcry was deafening. Thomas Galligan, Jr., president of the company, wondered if this were not merely another crisis, but a sign of some fundamental change in the nature of his industry.

BOSTON EDISON'S BUSINESS

Boston Edison was the principal supplier of electricity to the Boston metropolitan area, serving 550,000 residential, commercial, and industrial customers. Its service area embraced the city and thirty-nine other municipalities and suburbs. In some towns, customers purchased electricity at retail from Edison; in others, municipal electric departments purchased power wholesale and resold it to residents.

Wholesale rates were subject to the approval of the Federal Power Commission, while retail rates were reviewed by the Massachusetts Department of

---

This case, prepared by Professor Richard H.K. Vietor, is a revision and condensation of Boston Edison (B) (9-376-250), originally prepared by Walter Kiechel III under the supervision of Louis Banks. It is intended as a basis for class discussion rather than to illustrate either the effective or ineffective handling of an administrative situation.

Public Utilities (DPU). Both agencies determined rates on the basis of the company's assets and operating costs. Changes in the price of fuel, however, were passed on directly to consumers through a "fuel adjustment clause." Revenues in 1974 totaled $460 million, of which $160 million was a fuel adjustment charge—this on an investment in plant and equipment of over $1 billion.

Prior to the 1970s, industry observers deemed the management of Boston Edison to be among the most enlightened of utilities. Expenditures on research and development (R&D) were among the highest in the industry. Nuclear options had been explored as early as 1954, and the company was already active by the mid-1960s in curbing the air and water pollution from its generating facilities. Corporate philosophy was summarized as follows in the 1969 annual report: "There is one basic principle we would wish above all to convey: It is in the public interest and in our corporate interest to act as the public would act if it had complete information about our business."

AIR POLLUTION

Boston Edison had completed its conversion from coal to oil-fired generating equipment in the mid-1960s (at the time, it was more economical to burn imported oil). Although this change had alleviated the problem of particulates (soot), sulfur dioxide continued to pollute Boston's air. In 1969, the company engaged Stone and Webster Engineering to study the situation. It concluded that while Edison may have generated 40% of all sulfur dioxide released into the city air, it was responsible for only 15% of ground-level, breathable concentrations. This was due to the height of Edison's exhaust stacks, the location of its generating plants at tidewater, and prevailing westerly winds.

On the basis of this report, Boston Edison adopted fuel-switching as its primary sulfur dioxide control strategy. It would normally burn No. 6 residual oil, with 2.6% sulfur content. When air quality monitoring stations indicated a buildup in ambient pollution, the company would switch (in consultation with public health authorities) to low-sulfur (1%) oil. Fuel-switching was cheaper, of course, than burning low-sulfur oil year round, and it was uncertain whether enough low-sulfur oil were available to do so.

In the public debate about air pollution control during 1969–1970, neither citizen groups nor government agencies found this approach to be acceptable. Most interested parties besides Edison not only advocated year-round burning of low-sulfur oil, but demanded stricter air quality standards than Boston Edison offered. In April 1970, the state Department of Public Health approved rules proposed by the Boston Air Pollution Control Commission that would require uninterrupted burning of low-sulfur oil after October; a year later, the maximum sulfur content of Edison's fuel would have to be reduced to 0.5%. In May, the federal Department of Health, Education and Welfare (under the Air Quality Act of 1967) approved the air quality standards that these fuel regulations were designed to attain.

Boston Edison promptly asked the DPU to reactivate the fuel adjustment clause (which had not been used since the early 1960s) to pass through an extra cost of $22 million a year that the proposed fuel restrictions would entail. In contrast to the hearings on air pollution, the public hearings on Edison's fuel cost pass-through request were sparsely attended. The DPU approved it without hesitation and with little publicity.

Despite this, Boston Edison still objected to the extra costs inherent in the fuel regulations. Accordingly, it petitioned for a one-year delay in implementing them. The Associated Industries of Massachusetts (AIM), whose members were concerned about increases in their own oil and electricity costs, supported and encouraged the company in this effort. As the October 1 deadline drew near, Boston Edison sought variances from both state and city authorities. The company offered a detailed, three-option alternative to full-time burning of cleaner fuel. Each option involved limited degrees of switching (back to high-sulfur fuel), that offered potential savings to consumers as high as $21 million.

At September hearings on the request for a variance, the Public Health Council heard opposition to fuel-switching from a long list of distinguished witnesses, headed by Governor Sargent, a Republican, and Michael Dukakis, the Democratic nominee for Lieutenant Governor. Dr. Alfred Frechette, the commissioner for Public Health, remarked that "we don't care about costs." After deliberating for half an hour, the council denied Boston Edison's request. A local public opinion poll indicated that Massachusetts voters, by a margin of five to one, favored requiring utilities to burn low-sulfur oil at all times, even if it meant a 7% increase in the average consumer's bill.

On October 1, Boston Edison's plants switched to full-time burning of 1% sulfur oil. During the next year, ambient sulfur dioxide levels dropped by half, while electric bills for Edison customers increased 7% for residential use, 8% for commercial, and 14% for industrial. Meanwhile, long-term contracts for oil (at an inexpensive $1.67 per barrel) were voided, as the company went in search for new supplies of clean oil.

Again in 1971, Boston Edison petitioned for a delay of the second-step reduction to 0.5% sulfur oil. Other Massachusetts industries supported Edison's position. At public hearings in September, Maurice Feldmann, an Edison vice president, testified that the fuel adjustment could cost customers as much as $42 million annually. Moreover, very low sulfur oil was in short supply, and could only be expected to become more and more expensive.

Although Edison's request was again denied, less public unanimity on the issues was evidenced. When the Massachusetts Secretary of Commerce complained of environmentalist "overkill," several newspaper editorials and state legislators voiced approval. Some dissension even appeared within the ranks of environmentalists: the Massachusetts Secretary for Environmental Affairs cited the movement as "increasingly inefficient," and called for environmentalists to develop a "clear set of objectives."

In Washington, Congress had enacted the Clean Air Act of 1970, authorizing the Environmental Protection Agency to set nationwide ambient air quality standards. In 1971, the agency promulgated both primary and secondary standards for six pollutants. Primary standards, to protect human health, were to be achieved by 1975; more stringent secondary standards, to protect vegetation and the environment generally, would become effective later. Each state was required to design implementation plans of its own.

Boston's air quality, meanwhile, continued to improve. The average annual parts per million of ambient sulfur dioxide dropped from 0.138 in 1969 to 0.071 in 1970, and again, to 0.039 in 1971. It was expected that in 1972 the trend would take the figure below the primary sulfur dioxide standard of 0.03 parts per million.

But by the end of that year, problems of fuel availability raised questions as to whether even the 1970 rules could still be observed. In fact, by January 1973, supplies of low-sulfur oil were so low that the Public Health Council had to relax the standards for a few weeks. Again in late summer, looming fuel shortages forced Governor Sargent to order a review of the state's regulations, and subsequently urge relaxation. In September, once the EPA's permission was secured, Boston Edison began again to burn 1% sulfur oil; and 2.5% sulfur oil outside the core area of Boston. It appeared that the price of clean air would entail more than higher rates.

NUCLEAR ALTERNATIVE

In 1967, Boston Edison had begun construction of its first nuclear facility—the 650,000 kilowatt Pilgrim Station in Plymouth. Company officials had planned to bring the plant on-stream by the end of 1971. They had worked hard to win local acceptance of the facility. Elaborate environmental studies were conducted. Through company-sponsored meetings and advertisements, Plymouth citizens had been informed of the facts of nuclear power. (They had also been cheered by assurances that local property taxes would drop dramatically when Boston Edison began operating—and paying municipal taxes on—its new facility.) Until 1971, these efforts had appeared successful; there had been no significant opposition to the Pilgrim Station.

In April 1971, Commissioner William Cowin of the Department of Public Utilities noted publicly that Massachusetts residents were beginning to be concerned about the safety of nuclear power. In an interview, Cowin expressed his own view that thoughtful people realized that the Atomic Energy Commission, in its enthusiasm for promoting nuclear power, may not have given the public all the facts. Three months after Cowin made this statement, a federal court in Baltimore ruled in the Calvert Cliffs case that the AEC must require a detailed environmental impact study of all nuclear power plants it licensed. Both these events represented an incipient environmentalist attack on nuclear power.

The effect of these developments on Boston Edison was immediate. In May 1971, the Sierra Club and the Union of Concerned Scientists petitioned the AEC for a hearing on the safety of Pilgrim, before granting its request for an operating license. A group of Plymouth citizens now joined in this petition. In October, after the Calvert Cliffs decision, the AEC agreed to begin full-scale public hearings in December.

This delay, together with similar actions involving five other nuclear generating stations in New England, could have caused regional power shortages leading to brownouts. In view of rising oil prices, it could also have affected generating costs adversely. In a November press conference, Thomas Galligan called on Congress to pass legislation allowing nuclear plants nearing completion to operate under temporary permits.

Licensing hearings on Pilgrim continued for six months, during which time the AEC was also reviewing its own standards for reactor safety. Massachusetts environmentalists opposed any action on Pilgrim until the AEC's internal review was finished. Although this view received widespread publicity, the AEC decided in June to allow Edison to start up the Pilgrim reactor—to 20% of its capacity—pending issuance of a final license.

No sooner had this decision been announced than President Nixon signed into law a bill empowering the AEC to issue final licenses prior to completing its environmental review. Although Governor Sargent asked the commission to delay approving Pilgrim "as long as significant questions about the plant remain unanswered," the AEC granted Edison a full operating license in September.

By early 1973, the Pilgrim nuclear plant was operating at full capacity, and the company announced plans to spend $500 million on a second Plymouth reactor. It also announced an option to build still a third nuclear plant at the Plymouth site.

Operations at Pilgrim Station continued relatively smoothly for several months, notwithstanding a fish kill late in April. Ten thousand menhaden—a fish with little commercial value—perished when they swam into the plant's cooling water discharge canal. At the behest of the state's Division of Marine Fisheries, Edison agreed to cut back power to 50% while the incident was investigated. Edison announced that the cost of this cutback was at least $125,000 to the utility and its customers. State Senator William M. Bulger announced a legislative probe of the situation, commenting that Boston Edison had been "too cavalier" in its promotion of nuclear power.

More serious problems developed in August. The AEC ordered Pilgrim and nine similarly designed plants to reduce power as much as 25% pending investigation of possible engineering problems. The story received front page coverage in the *Boston Globe*, although when the order was lifted two days later, the newspaper reported it in the inside pages.

In October, General Electric advised Boston Edison that it had discovered design problems in the fuel system of two plants it had built that were similar to Pilgrim. The utility cut power to 50% while the problem was examined; environmentalists demanded a complete shutdown. In December, it became evident that elements of the reactor core needed replacement. The plant was shut down for eighty days, to be repaired and refueled at the same time.

The shutdown could hardly have come at a worse time. The oil shortages that had been developing for nearly three years were just then severely exacerbated by the Arab oil embargo imposed two months earlier during the Yom Kippur War.

"BROWNOUTS" AND BROWN MOODS

At least until the Pilgrim nuclear plant went on-stream, Boston Edison's margin of spare generating capacity had been growing dangerously thin. Since electricity is produced and consumed almost simultaneously (no practical storage), a utility's generating capacity must exceed "peak load" demand, even though the peak is far above average load. Peak demand occurs on a daily basis, at the hottest, coldest, and busiest times. Covering peak demand with generating capacity that must sit idle most of the time is an expensive proposition. But if this margin is cut too thin, and available purchases from neighbors are exhausted, voltage reduction—or "brownout"—is a last resort to avoid power failure.

Going into 1970, Boston Edison believed it had sufficient generating capacity. On the basis of predictable trends in the growth rate of demand, it expected to have 15% to 18% reserve above peak. Moreover, beginning in June 1970, Boston Edison had been tied into the New England Power Pool (NEPOOL), a grid system that united more than 90% of the generating capacity of regional utilities. Boston Edison had been a moving force behind the organization of NEPOOL, replacing the previous, less effective power pool. In NEPOOL, member companies were committed to helping one another through periods of crisis.

The first brownout in the Northeast began in New York City in June 1970. Boston Edison confidently reassured its own public, but was itself hit in July. Ironically, that brownout was caused in part by demands upon NEPOOL by New York's troubled Consolidated Edison, together with extraordinary air-conditioning demands. This situation eventually caused a total of eight Boston area brownouts that year. On each occasion, Boston Edison officials assured the public that the 5% voltage reductions did no harm to appliances.

These episodes unfortunately coincided with a series of well-publicized hearings on power industry reliability, conducted in Massachusetts by Senator Edward Kennedy, who was up for reelection that year. The senator's criticism of investor-owned utilities centered on their alleged lack of planning, poor service to customers, and unduly high prices.

In public, industry spokesmen attributed the brownouts to uncontrollable construction delays, slow regulatory procedures, and difficulties in obtaining local approval for new transmission lines. Some expressed the view that the single most important factor behind the summer brownouts was more rapid than expected growth in the use of air-conditioning. In private, some utility officials conceded that electric utilities may have been unduly preoccupied theretofore with lowering the cost of electricity, possibly failing to foresee the apparently sudden increase in demand for power.

An even worse brownout occurred during a cold snap in January 1971. As temperatures dropped to zero, heavy demand and mechanical trouble caused seven generators belonging to Boston Edison and other NEPOOL members to fail. For the first time in company history, Edison spokesmen publicly asked customers to cut back on their consumption of electricity. Customers responded, and the crisis passed, but lights had been dimmed at the State House.

Boston Edison's response to temporary power shortages was complicated by regional aspects of the problem. Construction delays of new power plants elsewhere in New England were beyond Boston Edison's control. Even without delays, lead times were long. In 1970, Edison began a 600,000 kilowatt oil-burning addition to its Mystic Station plant that would not be operational until 1975. Meanwhile, the company had to rely on stopgap measures: stepped-up maintenance, expedited deliveries of supplementary generating equipment, discontinued advertising for air-conditioning, and efforts to strengthen NEPOOL operations.

Had the Pilgrim nuclear plant not been delayed and then plagued by operational and regulatory shutdowns, Boston Edison's capacity situation would certainly have eased by 1973. In August, however, a combination of record heat and equipment failure caused an extensive brownout. For the second time in two years, the company asked the public to cut back on power consumption.

THE SPECTER OF PUBLIC OWNERSHIP

Throughout the 1960s, the public power/private power debate seemed a dead issue in New England. Investor-owned companies controlled over 90% of the region's generating capacity. In the state capitals and in Washington, representatives of private utilities spoke with a powerful, if quiet, voice. Boston Edison reputedly had more lobbyists on Beacon Hill than any other interest in the state. Local newspaper columnists occasionally alleged that Boston Edison's major stockholder, the First Boston Corporation, exercised considerable political influence.

When the public power issue did rear its head, it invariably took the form of the Dickey-Lincoln Project. Every year, Congressman Hathaway of Maine would propose a federal hydroelectric project on the St. John's River in northern Maine. Such a project, he argued, would furnish a "yardstick" with which to compare the cost and reliability of investor-owned utilities in New England. Boston Edison repeatedly led the fight against the proposal. Supporters of the project claimed that the company had spent over $150,000 between 1964 and 1968 to defeat the enabling legislation.

In 1971, proposals for public ownership struck closer to home. In a report to the New England Regional Commission, H. Zinder and Associates, a Washington-based consulting firm, recommended a new, public "regional generation and transmission agency" to meet the Northeast's soaring power needs. The agency, which was viewed as an alternative to NEPOOL, would take over all generating facilities, leaving private utilities with only the distribution function.

While this idea had no chance in the short run, public hearings on the suggestion did provide a platform for critics of privately owned utilities. The Northeast Public Power Association, which supported the idea, claimed that

NEPOOL was a "cartel" of private companies. Consumer representatives pointed to the possibility of cheaper power from a public agency that paid neither taxes nor dividends.

In responding to these charges, the private utilities argued that NEPOOL could do as well as any government agency in negotiating power interchanges with other regions. Boston Edison's President Galligan testified that the Zinder report evinced a bias that "only government-owned operations are considered to be effectively equipped for problem solving" at a time when, increasingly, "people are questioning the desirability of big government." On the cost issue, private utility representatives rhetorically asked how the tax revenues they paid would be replaced. Boston Edison, for example, was the number one taxpayer in most of the communities it served. And finally, the utility representatives noted that government-run utilities, like the MBTA, were scarcely models of efficiency or financial responsibility.

In 1972, Congressman Michael Harrington (D-MA) proposed legislation to create a public power authority for New England. State Attorney General Robert Quinn, engaged at the time in baiting Boston Edison for rate increases, heartily supported the bill. On Beacon Hill, legislation was introduced to permit publicly owned municipal utilities to more freely buy and sell power.

Neither of these proposals made much progress, in part because the private utilities lobbied hard to defeat them. Still, they represented an under-current of serious dissatisfaction with the performance of electric utilities that could escalate at any time. Indeed, nothing was more likely to trigger such an escalation than the kinds of rate hikes that Boston Edison and other companies were requesting more and more frequently.

RISING COSTS AND RATE HIKES

Nothing was more worrisome than the implications of rising operating costs. When requirements for 0.5% sulfur oil took effect in 1971, Edison began paying $4.81 per barrel of fuel. This represented a 270% increase over the $1.67 per barrel that it had paid two years earlier. Although these increases were passed through by using the fuel adjustment clause, doing so made it far more difficult to request a general rate hike to cover other rising costs, including wages, taxes (which had tripled in a decade), construction costs, and capital costs.

Boston Edison needed $100 million to finance capital spending in 1972. This represented a 25% increase over the previous year for expansion of gen-erating and transmission facilities to meet the growth of demand. With interest rates quite high, management needed to strengthen its appeal to potential inves-tors. Accordingly, it filed in February with the Massachusetts DPU for a $42 million base rate increase—the first such request in fourteen years (after two rate decreases in the late 1960s).

The DPU immediately postponed the effective date of the increase for ten months, pending public hearings. Opposition to the proposal came from consumers and politicians. Because of the fuel adjustment clause and Edison's dependence on imported low-sulfur oil, the cost of electricity in Massachusetts was already rising faster than almost anywhere in the country.

The state District Attorney, Robert Quinn, joined forces with consumers. Widely regarded as the front runner for the Democratic gubernatorial nomination, Quinn intervened on behalf of his own office and the state Consumer's Council. In statements to the press that received front page attention, Quinn lumped his opposition to Edison's proposal together with an attack upon New England Telephone's pending request for a $122 million rate hike.

The DPU's rate hearings continued throughout 1972. While the hearings delved into technically complicated problems such as properly calculating Boston Edison's rate base, cost of service, and rate of return, two issues captured the most media attention. First, company advertising was labeled an improper use of ratepayer's money. Why should a natural monopoly, in the midst of a worsening energy crisis, engage in either promotional advertising or image building? Boston Edison countered these criticisms by citing court decisions that allowed utilities to pass through reasonable advertising expenses. It noted further that although it did have a monopoly on electricity, it competed with alternate fuels (for example, natural gas and oil) for potential customers. The company also operated twenty-six retail outlets for electric appliances that benefited from its advertising budget of slightly more than $1 million.

The second area of criticism, Edison's "promotional" rate structure, was of far greater importance. Under this structure, large-volume users of electricity paid less per kilowatt-hour (KWH) than residential customers. Moreover, via a system of declining block rates, the more power a customer used, the less the customer paid per unit of electricity. Critics alleged that such a rate structure encouraged expanded and wasteful energy consumption during a period of shortage, and that big customers should pay their "fair share." But Edison's representatives argued that without such a rate structure, large-volume users might turn to alternative power sources or develop their own generating facilities; this would increase electricity costs to everyone else.

In March 1973, thirteen months after the request, the DPU granted a rate increase, but only for $18 million. Attorney General Quinn protested even this amount, first to the DPU and then in the state supreme court. In April, Standard and Poor's reduced Boston Edison's first mortgage bonds by one credit level to a single-A classification. Representatives of the rating service attributed the downgrading to a deterioration in fixed charge coverage due to construction delays and the absence of "timely and adequate" rate relief.

More bad news followed one week later. At Edison's annual meeting, President Galligan told stockholders that in view of the DPU's decision, per share net would be seventy-five cents lower than the $3.55 earned in 1972. This would be the first drop in a decade. While the company appealed the adverse rate decision, it filed in September for another rate increase of $43 million.

YEAR OF CRISIS

On January 1, 1974, the Organization of Petroleum Exporting Countries raised the posted price of crude oil to $12.65 per barrel—nearly four times its level three months earlier. A few days later, as part of a federal scheme to allocate fuel nationally (Emergency Petroleum Allocation Act), a fuel broker asked Boston Edison to pay $27.50 a barrel for 300,000 barrels of residual oil.

Although Edison officials publicly protested this price, the Federal Energy Agency responded unsympathetically. As one official of the agency put it, "It's a question of pay the price or sit around in the dark and the cold. You decided to depend on foreign oil when it was much cheaper than domestic, dirt cheap in fact, and now it's going to cost you a lot for that decision."

Amid newspaper stories of possible "rolling blackouts"—scheduled outages in one area after another to conserve fuel—Edison officials warned customers to expect 40% increases in electric bills due to fuel adjustment. With its previous request for a rate increase still pending, the company asked for an immediate $36 million emergency increase, in part because electricity demand had fallen off by 12%, with a proportional loss of revenue. This "use less/pay more" paradox was caused, said company spokesmen, by continuing high fixed costs.

By early spring, consumer protests had ballooned into statewide opposition to the fuel adjustment charge as well. Organized groups sprang up, gathering signatures on a petition to the DPU for the utility to absorb its higher fuel costs. Although Boston Edison officials met with representatives of these groups, as well as with legislators and state regulators, their conversations were not particularly productive.

"It is time for the government to step in," announced Attorney General Quinn, "to take over electric utilities in Massachusetts and give the consumer an even break." Lieutenant Governor Donald Dwight asked if the consumer's "forbearance and sacrifice" were to become "a function of some immutable rate of return ordained for the utilities? I say no. Let Boston Edison tighten its belt the way the customer had to tighten his."

In Plymouth, the nuclear plant that could relieve some cost pressure was ready to be put back in operation by mid-March. At the last minute, however, the move was blocked by an MIT graduate student in economics, affiliated with the Union of Concerned Scientists. As an individual intervenor, the student petitioned the AEC to hold hearings on plant safety issues associated with the recent changes to the fuel core. The AEC agreed to listen, and the plant remained closed until July. To replace the lost capacity, the company had to burn $305,000 worth of extra oil daily.

At the 1974 annual meeting, President Galligan announced declining profits on rising revenues, despite the fact that Edison's legal case had recovered the entire $42 million denied from its 1972 rate request. He lashed out against "political opportunism" and "incredible" regulatory procedures. He also attacked the state Public Health Council for "summarily" rejecting the concept of fuel switching, which he claimed could have saved hard-pressed consumers $45 million annually.

Late in April, the investment and utility communities were shocked when New York's Consolidated Edison suspended its quarterly dividend for the first time since 1885. The press immediately scrutinized the financial health of other utilities. On May 9, for example, the *Christian Science Monitor* reported that Boston Edison was "on dangerously shaky financial footing." The price of Boston Edison's common stock had dropped 32% since April 1. The company reacted as quickly as possible, trimming expenditures 23% and closing its retail appliance outlets. It was too late; on May 28, Standard and Poor's downgraded Boston Edison's first mortgage bonds and cumulative preferred shares to a triple-B rating.

Consumer activists, meanwhile, had gathered 200,000 signatures on their anti-fuel-adjustment petition. On Beacon Hill, the state legislature passed and sent the governor a bill regulating fuel adjustment. A DPU hearing would be required in any month when bills were to be increased through fuel adjustment, instead of the present, automatic procedure. Governor Sargent signed it in July, during a series of brownouts.

Later that month Merrill Lynch downgraded its ratings on forty selected utility companies, including Boston Edison. The brokerage company asserted that the electric utility industry was "no longer a haven for conservative investors." This scarcely helped Boston Edison with its desperate mortgage bond issue for $75 million. The company was forced to offer a 12.5% rate, and even then, sales were slow enough to force a reduction to $60 million.

Congressman Harrington chose this opportune moment to launch an initiative petition for the creation of a public power authority. If utility lobbyists blocked it in the legislature, the congressman promised to make it a ballot issue in the 1976 election. At this same time, another initiative drive was being organized to create a flat rate structure, and there was talk of an antinuclear campaign.

Boston Edison's request for a $70 million rate increase in November of 1974 precipitated a consumer rebellion. Consumer organizations immediately called press conferences, denouncing the request. Consumer's Organization for Fair Energy Equality, or COFFEE, opposed the rate hikes, while Massachusetts Fair Share opposed the rate structure.

Toward the end of November, Thomas Galligan reviewed this string of events, trying to make sense out of the apparent unraveling of his industry. Political developments, as disturbing as they were, concerned him little more than the new direction of unit costs and the growth rate of demand.

Galligan wondered if Boston Edison had reached a strategic juncture of some sort, and if so, what that meant for a regulated utility.

Exhibit 1 Income Statement for Boston Edison

YEARS ENDED DECEMBER 31	1974	1973	1972	1971	1970
Operating Revenues:					
Electric	$279,002	$266,292	$218,182	$214,302	$207,021
Steam	14,244	10,432	9,337	9,015	8,287
Fuel and purchased power adjustment	164,101	38,868	40,020	34,385	3,094
Other	3,396	3,075	2,257	1,082	1,349
Total	460,743	318,667	269,796	258,784	219,751
Operating Expenses:					
Operation:					
Fuel	160,817	76,458	68,595	62,146	34,423
Purchased power	34,605	1,088	10,836	14,446	10,407
Other	67,051	63,287	56,778	52,109	49,084
Maintenance	23,012	18,997	18,849	17,029	19,896
Depreciation	34,522	33,303	22,928	21,978	21,066
Taxes other than income taxes	57,567	58,187	49,311	44,319	38,252
Provision for current income taxes	2,935	3,103	(4,364)	4,693	6,656(b)
Provision for deferred income taxes	11,655	5,841	10,559	3,406	5,118
Investment tax credit—net	(312)	(312)	(226)	908	518
Total	391,852	259,952	233,266	221,034	185,420
Net operating income	68,891	58,715	36,530	37,750	34,331
Other Income:					
Allowance for funds used during construction	14,333	8,949	22,186	16,403	10,644
Other	606	401	910	750	1,009
	83,830	68,065	59,626	54,903	45,984
Miscellaneous Income Deductions	391	349	287	308	320
	83,439	67,716	59,339	54,595	45,664
Tax Benefits Applicable to Interest Allocable to Nonoperating Property	2,652	2,524	5,943	5,106	2,785
Income before interest charges	86,091	70,240	65,282	59,701	48,449
Interest Charges:					
Interest on long-term debt	41,955	29,296	26,847	24,526	18,936
Other	13,788	10,405	4,870	3,484	2,569
Total	55,743	39,701	31,717	28,010	21,505
Income Before Extraordinary Credit	30,348	30,539	33,565	31,691	26,944
Extraordinary credit	—	—	2,288(a)	—	—
Net Income	30,348	30,539	35,853	31,691	26,944(b)
Preferred dividends provided	5,512	5,512	5,512	5,512	2,256
Balance Available for Common Stock	$ 24,836	$ 25,027	$ 30,341	$ 26,179	$ 24,688
Common Shares Outstanding (weighted average)	9,535	8,701	7,912	7,468	7,468
Earnings per Share of Common Stock:					
Before extraordinary credit	$2.60	$2.88	$3.55	$3.51	$3.31
After extraordinary credit	$2.60	$2.88	$3.84	$3.51	$3.31

(a) Represents Federal income tax refund of $2,288,000 ($0.29 per share) for the years 1968 and 1969 primarily due to changes in the tax depreciation rates.

(b) Reflects tax reductions of $1,050,000 ($0.14 per share) resulting from increased tax depreciation rates on certain facilities.

Source: Boston Edison, *Annual Report*, 1974.

Exhibit 2 Balance Sheet for Boston Edison

	DECEMBER 31, 1974		DECEMBER 31, 1973	
Assets				
Property, Plant and Equipment, at original cost				
Utility plant in service:				
Electric plant	$1,110,616		$1,078,570	
Steam heating service plant	31,452		30,932	
	1,142,068		1,109,502	
Less: Accumulated depreciation	304,119	$ 837,949	278,847	$ 830,655
Nuclear fuel	41,554		39,545	
Less: Accumulated amortization	16,249	25,305	11,852	27,693
Nonutility property	2,558		3,350	
Less: Accumulated depreciation	1,511	1,047	1,444	1,906
Construction work in progress		202,076		132,920
		1,066,377		993,174
Investments in Nuclear Electric Companies		6,498		6,460
Current Assets:				
Cash	20,670		14,382	
Accounts receivable:				
Customers	64,123		41,693	
Other	517		303	
Materials and supplies, at average cost	24,072		19,783	
Merchandise for resale, at average cost	21		320	
Prepaid expenses and other current assets	784	110,187	808	77,289
Deferred Debits		45,429		26,770
		$1,228,491		$1,103,693

	DECEMBER 31, 1974		DECEMBER 31, 1973	
Liabilities and Capital				
Common Stock, par value $10 per share, authorized, issued and outstanding, 9,534,500 shares	$ 95,345		$ 95,345	
Premium on Common Stock	98,252		98,252	
Retained Earnings	110,414		108,842	
Surplus Invested in Plant	405		405	
Capital Stock Expense—Net	(548)	$ 303,868	(572)	$ 303,272
Cumulative Preferred Stock, par value $100 per share, authorized, issued and outstanding:				
4.25% Series—180,000 shares	18,000		18,000	
4.78% Series—250,000 shares	25,000		25,000	
8.88% Series—400,000 shares	40,000		40,000	
Capital Stock Expense—Net	(86)	82,914	(101)	82,899
Long-Term Debt				
First Mortgage Bonds	447,400		387,571	
Notes Payable to Banks	135,000	582,400	135,000	522,571
Total Capitalization		969,182		907,742
Current Liabilities:				
Long-term debt due within one year	171		—	
Notes payable				
Banks	119,500		65,680	
Other	—		12,850	
Accounts payable	26,243		27,580	
Customer deposits	2,857		2,571	
Taxes accrued	11,344		6,543	
Interest accrued	7,898		5,045	
Dividends declared	7,192		7,192	
Other current liabilities	1,100	176,305	606	128,067
Deferred Credits:				
Accumulated deferred income taxes	70,822		58,018	
Accumulated deferred investment tax credit	7,549		7,861	
Unamortized premium on debt, less expense	533		765	
Other	4,100	83,004	1,240	67,884
		$1,228,491		$1,103,693

Source: Boston Edison, *Annual Report*, 1974.

Exhibit 3 Sources of Construction Funds

YEARS ENDED DECEMBER 31	1974	1973	1972	1971	1970
Statements of Sources of Construction Funds					
Funds Generated Internally:					
Net Income	$ 30,348	$ 30,539	$ 35,853(a)	$ 31,691	$ 26,944
Add—Amounts charged not requiring funds currently:					
Depreciation	34,702	33,332	22,965	22,007	21,095
Deferred income taxes	11,655	5,825	10,543	3,390	5,102
Amortization of nuclear fuel	4,396	9,866	604	—	—
Investment tax credit—net	(312)	(312)	(226)	908	518
Allowance for funds used during construction	(14,333)	(8,949)	(22,186)	(16,403)	(10,644)
Total from operations	66,456	70,301	47,553	41,593	43,015
Less—Preferred dividends declared	5,512	5,512	5,512	5,512	2,552
—Common dividends declared	23,264	21,434	19,523	17,623	16,728
Funds generated internally	37,680	43,355	22,518	18,458	23,735
Funds Obtained from Outside Sources:					
Sale of Securities:					
Common Stock	—	29,850	34,405	—	—
Preferred Stock	—	—	—	—	40,000
First Mortgage Bonds	60,000	—	—	75,000	60,000
Less—Sinking fund & other retirements	—	(12,875)	(355)	(230)	(40,532)
Increase in notes payable to banks	—	60,000	75,000	—	—
Increase (decrease) in other loans	40,970	12,750	(29,220)	6,000	57,700
Sale of utility property	7,940	—	—	—	—
Funds obtained from outside sources	108,910	89,725	79,830	80,770	117,168

YEARS ENDED DECEMBER 31	1974	1973	1972	1971	1970
Statements of Sources of Construction Funds					
Other Funds Provided (Used):					
Deferred fuel costs	(12,818)	(10,551)	1,640	(2,241)	(4,973)
Working capital and other changes	(30,089)	7,103	(6,439)	(4,205)	(6,007)
	(42,907)	(3,448)	(4,799)	(6,446)	(10,980)
Total funds provided	$103,683	$129,632	$ 97,549	$ 92,782	$129,923
Construction Expenditures:					
Plant	102,088	124,823	96,175	91,577	105,084
Nuclear Fuel	1,595	4,809	1,374	1,205	24,839
Total construction expenditures	$103,683	$129,632	$ 97,549	$ 92,782	$129,923
Statements of Retained Earnings					
Balance at beginning of year	$108,842	$103,984	$ 93,166	$ 84,610	$ 76,946
Net income	30,348	30,539	35,853(a)	31,691	26,944
Adjustment of undistributed earnings of nuclear electric companies	—	1,265	—	—	—
	139,190	135,788	129,019	116,301	103,890
Cash Dividends Declared:					
Preferred	5,512	5,512	5,512	5,512	2,552
Common	23,264	21,434	19,523	17,623	16,728
	28,776	26,946	25,035	23,135	19,280
Balance at end of year	$110,414	$108,842	$103,984	$ 93,166	$ 84,610

(a) Includes extraordinary credit of $2,288,000 in 1972 which resulted from Federal income tax refund for the year 1968 and 1969, primarily due to changes in tax depreciation rates.

Source: Boston Edison, *Annual Report*, 1974.

Exhibit 4   Operating Data 1963–1974

YEARS ENDED DECEMBER 31	1974	1973	1972	1971	1970
Peak Capability—KW					
(in thousands):					
New-Boston Station	760	760	760	760	760
Pilgrim Station	670	670	664	—	—
Mystic Station	633	633	633	633	633
Edgar Station	294	291	294	294	386
L Street Station	46	46	136	136	136
Gas Turbines	232	232	225	225	165
Contract Purchases from Canal Elec. Co.	143	143	143	143	140
Other Contracts	176	114	117	121	108
Total	2,954	2,889	2,972	2,312	2,328
Edison Territory Hourly Peak—KW (in thousands)	1,891	2,030	1,912	1,877	1,744
Edison Territory Load Factor	59.7%	59.0%	62.6%	59.9%	60.9%
Generating Station Economy—BTU per Net KWH				10,602	10,707
Generated	10,363	10,309	10,472		
Average Cost of Fossil Fuel—Cents					
per Million BTU	196.15¢	80.50¢	65.09¢	62.55¢	36.21¢
Electric Plant in Service per Edison Territory Hourly					
Peak—KW	$587	$532	$537	$394	$406
Electric Energy:					
Net system output (in thousands):					
Kilowatthours generated	9,316,510	12,373,004	9,589,014	8,749,630	9,233,453
Kilowatthours purchased	1,853,575	(203,292)	1,318,987	1,871,845	1,385,034
Total	11,170,085	12,169,712	10,908,001	10,621,475	10,618,487
Miscellaneous usage:					
Company	13,880	19,570	20,551	17,377	19,616
Transmission	350,535	345,158	354,538	292,984	264,047
Distribution	463,560	453,359	445,848	433,874	436,244
Other	44,349	48,679	181,353(a)	25,357	29,557
Kilomatthours sold	10,297,761	11,302,946	9,905,711	9,851,883	9,869,023
Kilowatthours Sold (in thousands):					
Commercial	3,691,526	3,755,949	3,345,906	3,136,030	2,894,417
Residential	2,404,665	2,524,436	2,389,512	2,278,194	2,149,165
Industrial	1,778,969	2,051,011	1,960,556	1,884,470	1,832,532
Street Lighting	100,074	97,743	91,102	86,625	84,275
Other Utilities:					
Purchasing total requirements	1,053,168	1,205,250	1,733,100	1,697,402	1,591,664
Edison Territory Total	9,028,402	9,634,389	9,520,176	9,082,721	8,552,053
Purchasing partial requirements	1,269,359	1,668,557	385,535	769,162	1,316,970
Total—Edison System	10,297,761	11,302,946	9,905,711	9,851,883	9,869,023
Kilowatthours Sold—Annual Growth Percent:					
Commercial	(1.7)	12.3	6.7	8.3	9.5
Residential	(4.7)	5.7	4.9	6.0	8.5
Industrial	(13.3)	4.6	4.0	2.8	1.4
Street Lighting	2.4	7.3	5.2	2.8	2.5
Other Utilities:					
Purchasing total requirements	(12.6)	(30.5)	2.1	6.6	9.9
Edison Territory Total	(6.3)	1.2	4.8	6.2	7.4
Purchasing partial requirements	(23.9)	332.8	(49.9)	(41.6)	(2.3)
Total—Edison System	(8.9)	14.1	0.5	(0.2)	6.0
Sales Statistics:					
Residential Averages:					
Annual Kwh Use	5,024	5,318	5,105	4,954	4,662
Revenue per Kwh	5.06¢	3.57¢	3.47¢	3.45¢	3.20¢
Annual Bill	$253.96	$190.01	$177.08	$170.67	$149.42
Customer:					
Meters at Year-End	593,752	592,415	587,420	585,129	585,160
Average Number	541,126	537,270	530,753	522,534	523,485
Number of Employees at Year-End	4,042	4,183	4,217	4,219	4,294

(a) Includes 124,365 Mwh of precommercial sales from Pilgrim Station Unit #1.

Source: Boston Edison, *Annual Report*, 1972, 1974.

Exhibit 4, continued

1969	1968	1967	1966	1965	1964	1963
760	800	800	400	388	—	—
—	—	—	—	—	—	—
638	653	653	653	649	631	631
443	445	445	445	453	449	449
162	182	182	227	231	231	231
34	—	—	—	—	—	—
140	140	—	—	—	—	—
72	73	57	81	57	57	57
2,249	2,293	2,137	1,806	1,778	1,368	1,368
1,654	1,636	1,472	1,442	1,363	1,242	1,160
60.1%	58.8%	60.9%	57.2%	56.3%	57.0%	58.0%
10,483	10,309	10,706	10,786	10,962	11,229	10,962
27.45¢	28.23¢	29.44¢	32.04¢	33.18¢	33.67¢	34.21¢
$409	$394	$430	$397	$403	$406	$421
8,917,845	9,081,744	8,794,549	7,935,429	6,490,517	5,692,761	5,608,361
1,134,980	727,381	301,860	180,543	495,484	422,655	123,368
10,052,825	9,809,125	9,096,409	8,115,972	6,986,001	6,115,416	5,731,729
18,906	18,137	18,095	17,796	18,208	17,659	17,321
241,127	219,642	215,750	191,269	149,732	165,900	286,280
438,830	363,850	347,655	352,810	354,825	306,343	166,182
44,264	51,093	37,443	45,790	32,777	58,580	44,122
9,309,698	9,156,403	8,477,466	7,508,307	6,430,459	5,566,934	5,217,824
2,643,200	2,388,731	2,197,215	1,996,659	1,824,497	1,658,899	1,563,417
1,980,787	1,830,919	1,708,111	1,541,808	1,448,401	1,343,993	1,279,727
1,807,113	1,705,628	1,557,342	1,442,046	1,361,008	1,271,174	1,206,057
82,240	79,299	77,024	75,092	73,457	69,444	67,899
1,448,122	1,331,671	1,244,078	1,137,653	1,054,648	958,008	899,874
7,961,462	7,336,248	6,783,770	6,193,258	5,762,011	5,301,518	5,016,974
1,348,236	1,820,155	1,693,696	1,315,049	668,448	265,416	200,850
9,309,698	9,156,403	8,477,466	7,508,307	6,430,459	5,566,934	5,217,824
10.7	8.7	10.0	9.4	10.0	6.1	6.2
8.2	7.2	10.8	6.4	7.8	5.0	6.4
6.0	9.5	8.0	6.0	7.1	5.4	8.3
3.7	3.0	2.6	2.2	5.8	2.3	3.7
8.7	7.0	9.4	7.9	10.1	6.5	4.0
8.5	8.1	9.5	7.5	8.7	5.7	6.3
(25.9)	7.5	28.8	96.7	151.8	32.1	(53.5)
1.7	8.0	12.9	16.8	15.5	6.7	1.3
4,363	4,072	3,837	3,487	3,297	3,080	2,957
3.23¢	3.29¢	3.34¢	3.47¢	3.55¢	3.70¢	3.76¢
$140.75	$133.84	$128.11	$121.14	$117.04	$113.84	$111.27
584,643	583,290	583,223	580,535	572,399	564,584	560,088
516,797	512,054	507,120	504,237	501,122	497,839	494,451
4,100	4,033	3,994	3,968	3,948	4,027	4,047

Exhibit 5   Growth of Boston Edison's Residential Service

	NUMBER OF CUSTOMERS			AVERAGE ANNUAL KWH			AVERAGE ANNUAL BILL		
	1974	*1973*	*% Inc.*	*1974*	*1973*	*% Inc.*	*1974*	*1973*	*% Inc.*
Zone 1 (0–5 Miles)	225,934	226,097	(.1)	3,508	3,646	(3.8)	$191.96	$114.00	33.3
Zone 2 (5–10 Miles)	98,448	97,663	.8	5,324	5,744	(7.3)	$270.14	$205.16	31.7
Zone 3 (10–15 Miles)	75,404	73,968	1.9	6,749	7,238	(6.8)	$323.20	$241.85	33.6
Zone 4 (15–20 Miles)	35,124	34,400	2.1	7,811	8,399	(7.0)	$366.40	$272.81	34.3
Zone 5 (Over 20 Miles)	43,754	42,603	2.7	6,963	7,391	(5.8)	$328.13	$242.58	35.3
Total	478,664	474,731	.8	5,024	5,318	(5.5)	$253.96	$190.01	33.7

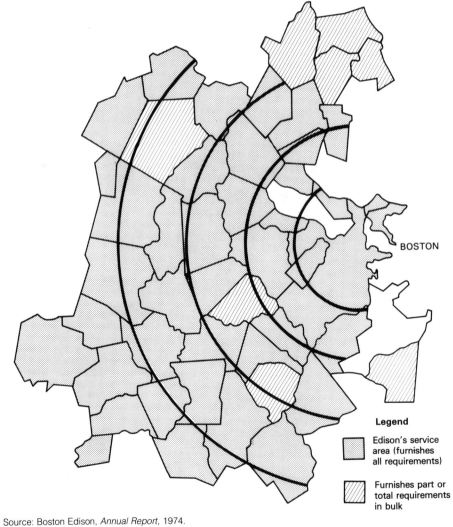

BOSTON

Legend

Edison's service area (furnishes all requirements)

Furnishes part or total requirements in bulk

Source: Boston Edison, *Annual Report*, 1974.

Exhibit 6 Performance Factors in the Electric Utility Industry, 1963–1974

YEAR	GENERAL RATE REVIEWS	AVERAGE COST CENTS/KWH	AVERAGE REVENUE CENTS/KWH	YIELD UTILITY DEBT	RATE OF RETURN ON EQUITY
1963	3	1.33	1.77	4.40	11.4
1964	4	1.30	1.73	4.55	11.8
1965	2	1.27	1.70	4.61	12.2
1966	5	1.24	1.67	5.53	12.4
1967	3	1.24	1.66	6.07	12.4
1968	8	1.24	1.64	6.80	11.9
1969	19	1.22	1.63	7.98	11.8
1970	45	1.25	1.68	8.79	11.2
1971	51	1.34	1.78	7.72	11.0
1972	94	1.40	1.86	7.50	11.1
1973	64	1.49	1.97	7.91	10.8
1974	78	1.96	2.50	9.59	10.2

Source: Compiled from Douglas D. Anderson, *Regulatory Politics and Electric Utilities* (Boston: Auburn House, 1981), pp. 70, 72.

Exhibit 7 Boston Edison Common Stock—Market Price Range*

	HIGH	LOW	DIVIDENDS PAID
1973			
First Quarter	39.12	35	$.61 per share
Second Quarter	36.37	31.37	$.61 per share
Third Quarter	33	29.87	$.61 per share
Fourth Quarter	32.37	24.25	$.61 per share
1974			
First Quarter	29.25	26	$.61 per share
Second Quarter	27.87	14	$.61 per share
Third Quarter	18.25	14	$.61 per share
Fourth Quarter	17.50	14	$.61 per share

*Book Value, $31.70 (1973), $31.87 (1974)

Source: Boston Edison, *Annual Report*, 1974.

Exhibit 8 Interest Rates

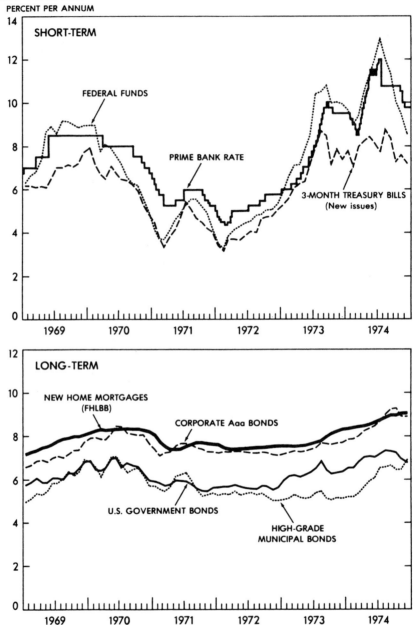

Sources: Department of the Treasury, Board of Governors of the Federal Reserve System, Federal Home Loan Bank Board, Moody's Investors Service, and Standard & Poor's Corporation.

Strategy and Regulation:
A Framework for Management

Too often, business/government relations are taken to mean either the venal interaction of business managers and politicians, through lobbying, campaign contributions, and revolving doors, or the complicated workings of bureaucratic government. Market structure and competition are ignored, and complex organizations are treated as black boxes. But for great corporations doing business in regulated environments, or for regulators committed to the public interest, anecdotage is of little value. Regulation is dynamic and adds layers of economic and political complexity to all the other demands of managing a modern corporation.

This is a central theme in the Boston Edison case. In the early 1970s, managers of Boston Edison faced fundamental changes in the energy economy and in political ideology. Competitive analysis, a long-term grasp of stakeholders, and strategic vision would be essential if shareholders and ratepayers alike were to be well served. But the process of economic, nuclear, and environmental regulation often obscured the issues and complicated the problems of adjustment.

A broader concept of business/government relations embraces the entire field of political stakeholders that shape regulatory policy, and the market structure that regulation shapes. Relations between business and government, in other words, consists of the measures and means by which a firm affects public policy, and more importantly, the effects of government policy on market structure, industry organization, and competition.

Institutional relations and bureaucratic processes are not excluded from this concept, nor are they central. Rather, they play an important role, similar to the role of personnel and operations in the implementation of strategy.

This concept of business/government relations, as a framework for analysis, eschews normative judgments. It shows no preference for either cooperative or adversarial relations. It does not criticize government intervention in the economy, nor political activism by business. The concept accepts these interactions between public and private institutions, and between administrators and entrepreneurs, as established aspects of American political economy.

This perspective also offers a dynamic view of business/government relations. Regulation is rarely static. The market structuring process is continually at work, imposing barriers, defining boundaries, guiding investment, and setting prices. Even in its broadest dimensions, government regulation is surprisingly unstable. Consider natural gas, a mundane commodity, as an example. From the start, there has been an extraordinary instability of regulatory scope and procedure: development of pipeline regulation (1938–46), the wellhead pricing debate (1947–54), individual-producer pricing (1954–60), gas basin pricing

(1960–1968), experimentation (1969–1972), nationwide two-tier pricing (1972–1977), multi-tier pricing and phased deregulation (1978–1985), and Order 436 unbundling (1985–present).

In fact, if we look comparatively at several of the major infrastructural industries that have been regulated over the past half century, we see an impressive pattern of long-term change in business/government relations. Chart 1 illustrates this. Prior to the 1930s, the *federal* government's intervention in most of these industries was limited to chartering, safety, and soundness. Only in the oldest industries—railroads and banking—did the federal government regulate competition. But during the mid-1930s, in the aftermath of abject economic collapse, the federal government intervened across the board, with immense powers, to stabilize and curtail competition.

From the late 1930s to the late 1960s, these industries grew and prospered under increasingly elaborate regulatory regimes. During this period of exceptional economic growth and technological innovation, these industries were developed into integrated national systems—the infrastructural backbone of the American economy.

Beginning in the late 1960s, however, major problems began developing in most of these sectors. Regulation—its procedures, institutions, and people—seemed unable to deal effectively with changing economic and political conditions. Increasingly into the mid-1970s, the regulated companies and their customers seemed ill-served by the *status quo*.

A wave of legislative and administrative reform swept through these regulatory regimes during the second half of the 1970s. Rescissions of authority, new goals, and dramatic innovations in administrative procedure encouraged competition where monopoly had prevailed. Throughout the 1980s, managers and regulators alike struggled to adjust, implementing a peculiar mixed regime of regulation and competition.

JUSTIFICATIONS FOR REGULATION

In the United States, regulation is imposed by government when markets fail to serve the "public interest." (Competition is restored when regulation fails.) Of course, the public interest is defined by an elaborate political process, in which economic considerations are often confused or ignored. These considerations are nonetheless real in the structural characteristics of each industry, at each point in time. Because this text treats regulations as a market structuring process, it is useful to begin by considering the economic justifications for regulation.

Natural monopoly has been the touchstone for rate-base, rate-of-return regulation, practiced by state utility commissions and federal agencies since the late nineteenth century. In some industries, the "economies of scale are sufficiently great so that the unit costs of service would rise significantly if more than one firm supplied service" in the relevant market.[1] At various times, electric

Chart 1 Half a Century of Regulation

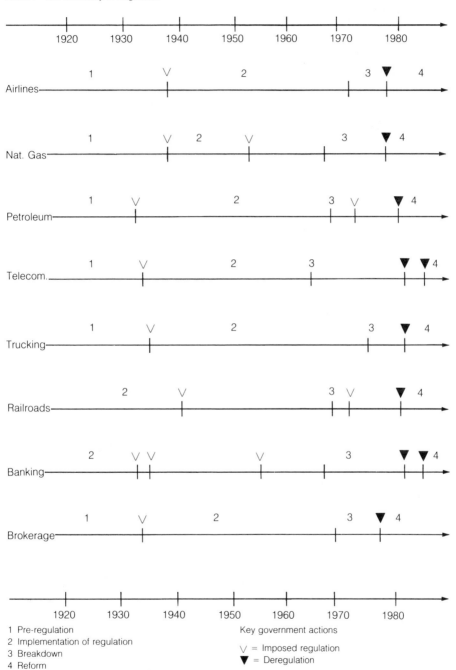

1 Pre-regulation
2 Implementation of regulation
3 Breakdown
4 Reform

Key government actions

∨ = Imposed regulation
▼ = Deregulation

power, natural gas pipelines, railroads, and telephones have been considered natural monopolies.

Because of its efficiency, a natural monopoly is economically desirable, but needs to be regulated by government to prevent abuse of its monopoly power. Historically, regulators set prices to provide a "fair" rate of return, after the cost of operations, on used and useful assets.

Externalities are certain costs to society of producing a good that are not fully paid (or internalized) by consumers. This structural flaw, which creates economic waste, is the justification for regulating environmental pollution, nuclear power, and occupational health and safety. Broadly speaking, there are two ways for government to deal with externalities: either force their mitigation or make users pay. Government can, for example, force a polluter to pay an effluent tax, the revenues from which can be used to clean the water for other users. Or, government can set effluent standards, forcing the polluter to clean or eliminate the effluent stream before it enters the environment. Although the federal government's involvement with externalities has roots in the nineteenth century, most of its authority was established in the late 1960s or 1970s.

Public goods are benefits created by the production of some good or service which spill over onto the public at large (a sort of positive externality). Government usually considers such goods too important to leave to market forces. Monetary stability and the availability of credit, for example, have traditionally warranted various forms of bank chartering and regulation. Likewise, the economic-development benefits associated with transportation and communications networks originally justified government involvement in the telegraph, telephone, and railroad businesses.

Excess competition describes a tendency towards instability, resulting from unprofitably low profits. Low barriers to entry and exit, or supply fluctuations in commodities, can be the cause. Where stability is deemed to be in the public interest, excess competition can justify regulation. The best examples in the American experience are airlines and trucking, where capital is mobile, scale economies may be lacking, and entry costs are nominal.

Economic rent, another justification for regulation, is the extra return on a scarce resource. The talent of an athletic superstar, scarce housing in urban areas, or a depleting mineral resource are examples of where economic rent can occur. Thus, the purpose of regulating the wellhead price of natural gas after 1954, and domestic petroleum after 1973, was to reallocate rents from producers to consumers, or to the federal government.

Mixed rationales. In practice, many regulatory systems have been justified by a combination of market failures, including *inadequate information* and *competitive failure*. Perhaps the best example is banking. Prior to the Depression, banking was regulated primarily as a public good. But the Great Crash in 1929 and the failures that followed were generally blamed on the deceptive and injudicious practices of bankers and brokers, and the public's lack of information regarding the credit worthiness of depository banks and securities issuers. A consensus emerged, at least in Congress, that competition had not served the public interest.

BASIC CONDITIONS

ECONOMIC

demand
supply
industry structure

POLITICAL

ideology
institutions
organized groups

The starting point for any analysis of the regulated environment is the prevailing context of basic economic and political conditions that frame business/government relations. On the economic side, these include macroeconomic conditions, such as GNP growth, inflation, and unemployment, as well as microeconomic demand factors, supply factors (capacity and cost structure, labor relations, availability of resources, and technology), and structural conditions within the relevant industries. In the *Boston Edison* case, for example, high demand growth and declining costs for electricity underwrote a successful regulatory system prior to the 1970s. But the demand effects of stagflation and the supply shock from OPEC combined to produce an entirely new economic context after 1973.

On the political side, prevailing ideology is the baseline for thinking about regulatory change. When public ownership, for example, falls completely outside the purview of prevailing ideology, that obviously affects the public policy options. The prevailing structure of government and of organized interest groups is also relevant, since it is the interaction of these groups that will affect policy. Again, in the Edison case, the absence of organized consumer and environmental groups during the 1960s left the regulatory process rather closed and nonadversarial. But later, with multiple, conflicting regulatory agencies and a host of organized intervenors, the managerial skills needed to implement strategy changed.

Since basic conditions are more or less ubiquitous, they are illustrated by virtually every chapter of this text. But in the three industry notes on transportation, telecommunications, and banking, and in the Boston Edison case, changes in basic conditions are central themes for the analysis.

SOURCES OF REGULATORY CHANGE

Understanding, and possibly anticipating, the sources of regulatory change is a critical responsibility for managers in the regulatory environment. Of course, any specific change is to some extent idiosyncratic, or random; political, bureaucratic, and judicial processes are sufficiently illogical to guarantee this, and the process of historical change is obviously complex. But there are several factors that stand out as particularly important in the process of regulatory change, especially as it affects the strategy of the firm.

Change in the basic macroeconomic and political context is, by definition, the most general source of regulatory change. That this sort of change is general, and often gradual, can make it the most easily overlooked by business managers engrossed in day-to-day operations. These changes can be short-term, such as the business cycle, or more permanent, such as the advent of environmentalism. They can be abrupt, such as the Oil Shock of 1973, or gradual, such as the onset of inflation.

The best and starkest example is the Great Depression. Between 1929 and 1933, aggregate demand fell by 33%; 9,000 banks failed, rail tonnage dropped by 50%, and telephone subscribership fell by 25%. The American economy virtually collapsed, and with it, Americans' faith in unrestricted competition. Unhampered enterprise had failed to serve the public interest; stability and equity assumed a higher priority in the political arena, partially displacing efficiency and free choice. As the economic effects of lost demand forced thousands of firms to the brink of bankruptcy, government regulation was imposed to stabilize prices, rationalize excess capacity, and halt competition.

A more recent example of new basic conditions, which gave rise to deregulation, was the slowdown of economic growth and the rise in inflation that developed after 1968. By the early 1970s, America was in the grip of a stagflation that dramatically undermined rate-base, rate-of-return regulation, and inflated interest rates, that undermined banking. The government's inability to alleviate these problems, together with the bitter experiences of Vietnam and Watergate, thoroughly shook the prevailing faith in government.

New ideas are a second source of regulatory change, clearly related to the first. "Practical men," said John Maynard Keynes, "who believe themselves to be quite exempt from any intellectual influences, are usually the slaves of some defunct economist." Acknowledging the power of interest groups, Keynes had nonetheless concluded that "soon or late, it is ideas, not vested interests, which are dangerous for good or evil."

The onset of economic regulation in the 1930s, while no doubt driven by market failure and a real sense of crisis, owed much to various intellectuals —FDR's so-called "Brain Trust": men like Tugwell, Baruch, Frankfurter, Landis, and Cohen.[2] Similarly, the erosion of intellectual support for regulation that developed during the 1970s had its roots in the theoretical and empirical work of microeconomists such as Meyer, Averch and Johnson, Caves, Joskow, MacAvoy, and Kahn.[3] These academics challenged both the efficiency and social effectiveness of conventional regulation in the transport and energy sectors, and proposed new tools and principles for regulation. Many of them took their work to Washington, to the legislative staffs, the regulatory staffs, and the bureaucracies of the executive branch.

Gradually, this new perspective permeated the political norms of America during the administrations of Nixon, Ford, and Carter. It increasingly commingled with a budding neoconservatism in the Republican Party and the market-oriented, "Chicago School" approach to macroeconomic policy. When regulation finally attracted political interest, the ideas necessary for reform were ready.

Technological innovation is a third source of regulatory change. Important developments in technology either made competition seem inappropriate, or later, changed the prevailing industry economics on which regulatory policy was superimposed.

After World War I, tractor trailers, commercial aircraft, large diameter high-pressure pipelines, and long-distance telephone service were all new technologies. In less than a decade, these technologies reshaped competitive relationships in ways that seemed to warrant regulation. Unrestricted trucking competition threatened the railroads; ease of entry threatened network building in airlines; and natural gas pipelines and long-distance networks appeared to be "natural monopolies."

After World War II, another generation of innovations destabilized regulatory pricing policies, segmentation, and barriers to entry. In airlines, for example, the development of jet aircraft and eventually of widebodies dramatically increased capacity per scheduled flight. Regulatory policies, however, failed to encourage capacity utilization. In banking, the advent of data processing technology created economies of a scale that had not previously existed. In back-office transactions processing, interoffice electronic funds transfer, and front office distribution channels (for example, automatic teller machines), this technology afforded cost and competitive advantages to big bank systems.

In telecommunications, technological innovation dramatically affected regulation. The development of microelectronics and digital computing created a demand for new services in transmission and switching. On the supply side, electronics lowered entry barriers to the terminal equipment market, and microwave did the same for the private-line, long-distance market. Once these technologies were available to entrepreneurs, it became virtually impossible for the Federal Communications Commission (FCC) to maintain its existing tariffs, cross subsidies, and long-standing prohibitions on interconnection.

Entrepreneurship, in both the business and political marketplace, is another factor in regulatory change. For business entrepreneurs, new regulation can pose immense opportunities. Regulation of hazardous wastes, for example, gave the IT Corporation an opportunity to diversify out of industrial cleaning services into a high-growth, high-tech market for hazardous waste management.

The mismatch between new economic or technological conditions and existing regulation can also pose opportunities: disintermediation and non-bank entry in financial services, bypass in telecommunications, and supplemental sources in natural gas. Although examples abound, Bill McGowen of MCI is perhaps the best. Microwave Communications, Inc. started in the private-line resale niche of the long-distance telephone market, where it could cream-skim under AT&T's umbrella of average pricing. From there, it gained interconnection to Bell System local exchanges by effective litigation, and eventually offered switched long-distance service by not paying the huge subsidies required of AT&T.

Political entrepreneurs also play a critical role in regulatory change. Some regulators, bureaucrats, and legislators have a facility for seizing the need for new regulation, or for deregulation, as a political opportunity. Alfred Kahn, committed as he was to marginal-cost pricing, skillfully introduced time of-day electric pricing in New York. Later, he went on to the Civil Aeronautics Board, where he demonstrated the benefits of airline competition. William Ruckelshaus (EPA) and Todd Connover (Comptroller of the Currency) were other entrepreneurs for regulatory change whose strategies are discussed in this text.

The fifth important source of change is regulatory failure. Just as competition seemed not to be serving the public interest in the 1930s, regulation seemed to be failing by the early 1970s. Airline regulation appeared to be causing a spiral of rising costs, declining capacity utilization, and low growth. Bank regulation, especially interest rate ceilings and product restrictions, did not respond quickly enough to changes in financial markets. Disintermediation caused yield problems and eventually a rash of failures among commercial banks and savings and loans. Natural gas offers the most extreme example of regulatory failure; federal regulation during the 1960s actually caused the crisis of gas shortages during the 1970s. And even when regulators tried to change after 1968, the weight of the original Act and adjudicatory precedent defeated their best efforts.

REGULATORY CHANGE

substance
process
institutions

Strategic management in regulated industries requires an accurate and usable understanding of regulation and the institutions that implement regulatory change. Too often, this area is isolated and relegated to specialists in governmental affairs, or lobbyists in a corporation's Washington office. As a result, marketeers, financial executives, and operations managers often fail to understand the dynamics of regulatory change as it constrains their choices and defines opportunities.

Several forms of regulation, and the various processes by which they are implemented, are treated in the chapters of this text: command-and-control regulation of operating standards, performance criteria and rule making, price controls and entry restrictions, and rate structure (especially rate-base, rate-of return regulation). The cases concerning El Paso Natural Gas, Marginalism in New York, and Commonwealth Edison, examine several of these regulatory forms, in both theory and practice. The industry notes document the evolution of regulation through legislation, litigation, and adjudication, as it unfolds over longer stretches of time.

In a number of the cases and industry notes, the institutions of regulation are carefully described. Competition among regulatory agencies is evident in the note on banking regulation, while Ruckelshaus and the EPA focuses on the organizational structure and strategy of an independent regulatory agency.

The chapters focusing on the regulatory process bring two important perspectives to this analytical framework. First, they help students of management to assess regulatory issues from the perspective of regulators themselves —looking at their personal and professional objectives, the political pressures they experience, and their problems of defining "the public interest." Second, they try to open up the black box of a regulatory agency, revealing an administrative institution with all sorts of organizational problems, resource and informational constraints, and above all, potential for strategy.

MARKET STRUCTURE
boundaries
conditions of entry and exit
market segmentation
pricing mechanisms
distribution channels
cost structure
vertical/horizontal integration
number of sellers/buyers

For a business manager, the fundamentally interesting aspect of government intervention is its impact on market structure. Regulations, large or small, shape product and service markets in ways that would otherwise not be. Indeed, that is the goal of regulation: to correct some failure or to redirect operations or competition towards some social (not economic) purpose.

The term "market," as used here, is the interaction of buyers and sellers in the commercial exchange of a particular product or group of related products. Market structure embraces the various characteristics of a market, especially those listed in the preceding box. These markets are dynamic; their boundaries, competitive attributes, and organizational structure change and evolve continuously. And above all, they are shaped by regulation and regulatory change.

Regulation inherently defines market boundaries by establishing jurisdiction. Of course, economic characteristics, such as geography, distribution, price, design, and substitutes, also contribute to the definition of markets, and often clash with regulation. In the energy sector, for example, the Natural Gas Act (1938) defined interstate pipeline transportation of gas as the relevant market for federal regulation. Implementation of this law effectively separated the interstate market from the intrastate market. In telecommunications, a 1913 antitrust decree separated the telephone (voice) from telegraph (data) markets, and confirmed AT&T's integration of the market from end to end (for example, customer premises equipment, local exchange, and long distance). The Glass-Steagall Act (1933) separated the financial services market into two industries—commercial banking and investment banking—which thereafter evolved as separate markets.

Over time, however, technological changes and entrepreneurial pressures can force changes in regulated boundaries. In natural gas, an extreme supply imbalance between interstate and intrastate markets finally forced Congress to reunify the markets in 1978. In the face of record interest rates, investment banks offered money funds while commercial banks began brokering securities. In telecommunications, perhaps the best example was a series of rulings in the FCC's Computer Inquiries, with which the Commission sought to define a sharp line between telephone service (regulated) and enhanced information services (competitive). These decisions, in 1971, 1980, and 1986, were overrun by technological change almost before the ink was dry.

The regulatory definition of market boundaries relates closely to the conditions of entry and exit. Almost any economic regulation by government requires restriction of entry and exit. The absence of equilibrium, for whatever purpose, creates incentives for new firms to enter markets with surplus profits, and for incumbents to exit unprofitable markets. Certificates of public convenience, charters, tariffs, licenses, and other forms of regulatory authorization, are immense barriers to entry and exit. Prior to 1968, for example, any interconnection of non-Bell equipment to the Bell System was unlawful. At the same time, AT&T was expected to provide universal service, even to the most unprofitable markets.

Regulatory barriers to entry and exit, although sustained by the force of law, can not indefinitely withstand extreme political pressures driven by market opportunities. When the cross subsidies from long-distance to local telephone service reached epic proportions, the attraction for new entrants under AT&T's price umbrella became overwhelming—so much so, that it appeared to some to serve the public interest. When railroad rates exceeded trucking costs, restriction of entry became impossible to maintain. And when electric rates exceeded the cost of cogeneration, even the most committed monopolists could not prevent entry.

Segmentation of the market by regulation is critical to the formulation of competitive strategy. It is especially important that managers recognize the artificiality of regulatory segmentation, compared to segmentation that derives from customer or product characteristics. Regulatory segmentation, through tariffs, chartering, or pricing, can be just as important as an economic segmentation, and can endure for a time. Nonetheless, a regulation-defined segment is not only susceptible to technological change and entrepreneurial pressure, but also to political pressure. Thus, MCI's conversion of private-line service into public switched toll was accomplished by effectively lobbying the Federal Communications Commission. Mutual banks in Massachusetts breached their customary segment restrictions on checking accounts by gaining regulatory approval for a NOW account.

In most forms of economic regulation, pricing is directly controlled by government. Not only the level, but also the structure of pricing is usually regulated. As such, price becomes a formulaic vehicle to cost recovery, or a designated means of achieving social policy. The declining block rate structure for electric utilities, rolled-in pricing for natural gas, and the overpricing of long-distance telephone usage, are all good examples.

Competition of any sort entails competitive pricing mechanisms. Thus, with the deregulatory reforms of the 1970s, all sorts of new pricing mechanisms were developed. In airline markets, a staggering array of discount fares and special deals largely replaced standard coach fares. In telephone and natural gas markets, pricing elements (along with service) have recently been unbundled, while still regulated, so that customers will have more accurate signals regarding cost and efficient use. Marketing managers in this environment are rapidly learning how to use less-bundled pricing to segment the market, increase yield, and encourage demand.

Distribution channels, under traditional forms of economic regulation, become highly routinized. In gas, electric, and telephone utilities, distribution channels are usually monopolized—the downstream end of a vertically inte-grated company. In the transport industries commission brokers operated, but usually under cartelized pricing and service terms.

Regulatory changes, particularly with increased competition, can have a tremendous impact on the character and strategic importance of distribution channels. In telecommunications, the deregulation and detariffing of customer equipment created opportunities for phone stores. In natural gas, federal reg-ulations in 1984 and 1985 gave rise to spot markets and brokers. And with airline deregulation, the computerized reservation systems of American and United suddenly provided strategic control of customer access.

This relationship can also work in the opposite way; changes in distri-bution channels can affect regulation. In banking, for example, automatic teller machines and other forms of electronic banking have helped undermine re-strictions on branching, especially across state lines.

Regulation has been notorious for its effects on the cost structure of business. Compliance with red tape, regulatory adjudication and litigation, dis-incentives to cost control, orientation to high-quality service, excessive capital intensity, and in most industries, inefficient industry structure, all raise the costs of regulated business.

When regulation changes, costs change, in both absolute and relative terms. A new air pollution regulation, for example, can raise the operating costs of all forges, but less per unit of output for the largest forges, thereby bestowing a competitive advantage. The reverse can also occur. When technology alters cost characteristics, such as the economies of scale or scope, the resulting com-mercial pressures can force change in regulation. Electronic banking is generally thought to create such economies where none existed before. Thus, it becomes more difficult (and perhaps impossible) for regulators to prevent vertical and horizontal integration.

Generally speaking, deregulation and increased competition force dramatic cost reductions across all aspects of a business: plant, operations, labor force, wages, overhead, and capital. To date, airlines and railroads are stellar examples. Nearly a decade after initial deregulation, firms in these industries still struggle to cut costs from previous levels.

Industry structure is another facet of the market structure that is shaped by regulatory change. Regulation can determine the number of firms, their size and diversity, and the degree of vertical integration. The results range from fragmentation to monopoly. In banking, state and federal authorities restricted charters and mergers to create an immense number of small institutions. In airlines, regulation by the Civil Aeronautics Board maintained an oligopoly of sixteen firms for nearly forty years. And in telecommunications, a combination of antitrust and FCC policies fostered AT&T's vertical monopoly, at least until the late 1960s.

Deregulation, since the 1960s, has stimulated restructuring in virtually every industry. As regulatory barriers to entry are removed, as prevailing segmentation erodes, and as operating conditions are modified, it is not at all surprising that firms divest operations, acquire new ones, and reorganize internally and externally. In railroading, seven giant rail systems have replaced several dozen large and medium railroads that were created in the nineteenth century. In airlines, a score of mergers have led to increased concentration. Telecommunications has been forcibly restructured by an antitrust divestiture, while huge natural gas pipeline networks and regional banks consortia replace familiar and historic names.

These and other changes in a market's structural characteristics, when taken together, attest to the extraordinary dynamism of business markets and the degree to which they are affected by regulatory change. Managers who cannot see or absorb this relationship between government controls and the economic and competitive forces of their business run several risks. First, they miss immense opportunities to improve their competitiveness or, if monopolies, to provide more efficient service and maximize their shareholders' value. Worse still, they fall into a sort of "regulated mentality," in which the status quo becomes the norm, minimizing political "squawk" becomes a strategic objective, and regulation-defined market structure is accepted as natural.

What is needed to grow and compete successfully in this environment is a managerial perspective that views regulation as a continuing source of change in market relationships. Indeed, even when regulation remains stable for a time, management must remain conscious of the relationship between the regulatory framework and other, even more dynamic market factors. And beyond this sensitivity to marketplace effects, the regulated manager must also track the feedback of economic effects into the political arena. It is there that all sorts of stakeholders will contend to reshape regulation in their own interest.

**POLITICAL INTEREST
STRUCTURE**

interest group/stakeholder
[competitors, entrants, substitutes, users, labor]
jurisdictional [federal, state,
local, international]
bureaucratic [political and
professional]
legislative [partisan, regional,
functional specific]

For managers of regulated businesses, the political arena is a second, and almost equally important, environment in which the firm must compete and operate. In this arena, the political counterparts and representatives of all the market participants vie to affect regulatory policy and implementation.

There are several ways to think about the political arena. One can focus on the interaction of stakeholder groups, on institutional relationships, on the interplay of overlapping jurisdictions, or on bureaucratic and legislative processes of decision making. In this text, the cases relate mostly to the first two approaches, while the three industry notes illustrate the latter two.

The starting point for this part of the environmental analysis is an assessment of the economic stakes of all participants in the market, as well as any related interests. For an existing regulatory arrangement, or for some pending or proposed regulatory change, management needs to understand several factors:

1. Who are the affected parties?
2. How are each party's interests affected?
3. How important is the issue to each interested party?
4. How able is each party to exercise political leverage?
5. What coalitions are likely to develop?

Several cases in this book, including Marginalism in New York, AT&T and the Access Charge, and the Comptroller and Non-bank Banks, provide an opportunity for this kind of "stakeholder analysis." Especially in the AT&T case, such an analysis is a central theme.

Having made such an assessment, a regulated firm can formulate a strategy for managing stakeholders, or at least develop an approach for participating in the political process. At this point, however, institutional factors come into play. Management needs to determine the institutional sphere in which the issue will (or should) be settled. If it is the narrow political sphere of the regulatory bureaucracy, then technical, legal, and professional considerations will be more important. If the issue escalates into a wider political environment, involving legislative or executive politics, then public relations, lobbying, and coalition building take on relatively greater importance.

As in the marketplace, long-term and short-term needs are not always consistent. For any large company that must operate indefinitely in a political arena, the costs of any short-term action need to be measured against longer-term objectives and continuing relationships with regulators and all sorts of other stakeholders. Washington, or the state capital, needs to be understood as one of the operating environments in which the interests of customers, shareholders, and employees can be served, and where rivalries must be fought.

STRATEGY OF THE FIRM

Goals
    performance objectives
    structural objectives
    social objectives

Policies
    business:
        [structural/cultural, finance,
        marketing, operations]
    political:
        [regulatory, administrative,
        legislative, stakeholders]

All of this analysis brings us to the strategy of the firm. Given an assessment of basic conditions, a dynamic view of regulatory change, and an understanding of its effects on market structure and political stakeholders, management should be better able to formulate effective corporate strategy.

To be effective in the regulated environment, strategy should have both an economic and a political dimension, and these must be consistent and operationally integrated.

The choice of corporate goals, especially for the firm's long-term direction as an institution, must balance the objectives of public policy with responsibility to the shareholders. In a noncompetitive environment this entails the establishment and maintenance of a regulatory bargain, wherein the firm commits to the public service and the regulator guarantees a fair return to shareholders. In a competitive environment it means choosing quantitative or qualitative performance objectives designed to satisfy financial markets, and still be acceptable to regulators. And in this mixed environment, management usually needs social objectives that are responsive to the underlying political concerns associated with the government's involvement. The shortest route to punitive regulation, or reregulation, is to disregard public sentiment.

To implement these goals, the regulated firm needs to adopt business and political policies that are complementary and reinforcing. An electric utility, for example, that decides to diversify or make a related acquisition, obviously must prepare a coalition of support among user interests, related political interests, and regulators, together with an explanation of how such a move will enhance the firm's ability to serve the public interest. Acceptable solutions to issues of cost allocation, financial effects, and structural arrangements must be provided for regulators in a form that their bureaucratic process can accept. In the converse situation, a decision to pursue reduced regulation of product restrictions by a commercial bank should obviously be matched by an appropriate marketing strategy, and probably a defense against retaliatory entry.

Organizational structure, together with cultural norms and incentive systems, generally need adjustment, or perhaps overhaul, to be responsive to regulatory change. Too often, however, these internal aspects of strategy are the slowest to respond to new market or political conditions. In the recent experience with airline deregulation, for example, efforts to change work rules and attitudes towards costs and customers were slow to begin at most major firms, and even slower to achieve. In railroading and in banking, organizational adaptation to new regulatory environments was exceedingly slow, but in some instances, dramatically effective.

Among the cases that best illustrate strategy formulation in the face of regulatory change are IT Corporation, Commonwealth Edison, American Airlines, CSX, AT&T, and General Telephone of the Northwest. In several of these cases, strategic planning can almost be viewed as a menu of options for cost reduction and revenue enhancement, either through business or political action. Posing the options in this manner underscores the importance of coordination, reinforcement, and an organizational structure that links strategic planning to external affairs from the outset.

PERFORMANCE

Industry   Firm   Society

To complete this framework for managing in a regulated environment, it is necessary to assess the effects of regulation, or of regulatory change, on industry performance, on the individual firm, and on the interests of the broader society.

For the manager, understanding outcomes is important for several reasons. Especially in the regulated environment, performance of individual firms is measured relative to others in the same industry. This is true not only in financial markets and rating agencies, but with regulators. Thus, an airline with a consistently inferior maintenance record attracts the attention and possibly

Chart 2 Framework for Managing in a Regulated Environment

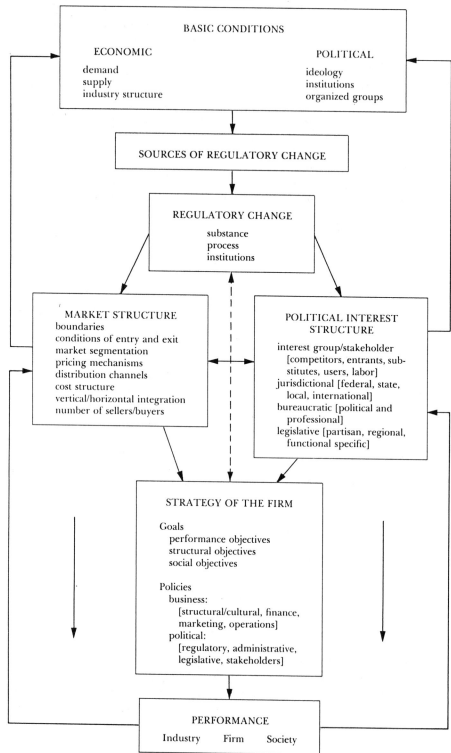

BASIC CONDITIONS

ECONOMIC

demand
supply
industry structure

POLITICAL

ideology
institutions
organized groups

SOURCES OF REGULATORY CHANGE

REGULATORY CHANGE

substance
process
institutions

MARKET STRUCTURE
boundaries
conditions of entry and exit
market segmentation
pricing mechanisms
distribution channels
cost structure
vertical/horizontal integration
number of sellers/buyers

POLITICAL INTEREST
STRUCTURE

interest group/stakeholder
[competitors, entrants, substitutes, users, labor]
jurisdictional [federal, state,
local, international]
bureaucratic [political and
professional]
legislative [partisan, regional,
functional specific]

STRATEGY OF THE FIRM

Goals
performance objectives
structural objectives
social objectives

Policies
business:
[structural/cultural, finance,
marketing, operations]
political:
[regulatory, administrative,
legislative, stakeholders]

PERFORMANCE

Industry   Firm   Society

punitive action of federal authorities. A nuclear power plant that costs more to build, or more to operate, than others is frequently subject to more punitive treatment from its public utility commission. And a Bell Operating Company that charges more for basic service, or earns more on its rate base, than other Bell Operating Companies can expect criticism from its regulators.

To anticipate the future direction of public policy, and the kinds of regulatory issues likely to develop, it is necessary to have a clear perspective of the industry's economic performance as a whole. As noted, industry performance is one key source of regulatory change. Even for a firm outperforming its industry, serious problems in the industry can precipitate major changes in regulatory policy which may undermine a strong firm's competitive advantage. And even more gradual changes, in industry and market structure, eventually change the public policy values that support regulation. The achievement of universal telephone service by the mid-1970s, for example, undermined political commitment to the tradeoffs that had been necessary to achieve that objective.

The final performance consideration for any firm operating in a regulated environment is societal. If the social objectives of public policy are ill-served, or even perceived to be ill-served, the political interest structure will surely realign to change policy eventually. Managers in regulated industries, experienced in their own work and committed to their firms, sometimes have the worst perspective on broad changes in societal objectives. Responding to these changes is often their most difficult, and important, strategic challenge.

A FRAMEWORK FOR MANAGEMENT

This chapter has sought to provide a broader, richer perspective on business/government relations, and an organized framework for strategic decision making in regulated environments. The separate parts of that framework, described in the foregoing pages, are summarized in Chart 2.

At this point, however, the framework is merely a skeleton, with little sense of the immense complexity of regulated businesses or the managerial skills required for success in this environment. The remainder of the text will present real situations that illustrate each element of the framework and require integrated analysis for effective decision making, and will introduce an exceptional group of managers whose professional success afforded them the responsibility of decision making.

NOTES

1. Stephen Breyer, *Regulation and Its Reform* (Cambridge: Harvard University Press, 1982), p.15. Breyer's book is one of the best scholarly studies of regulation. Also, see Alfred Kahn, *The Economics of Regulation: Principles and Institutions* (New York: Wiley, 1970), and James Q. Wilson, *The Politics of Regulation* (New York: Basic Books, 1980).

2. Thomas K. McCraw, *Prophets of Regulation* (Cambridge: Harvard University Press, 1984).

3. Martha Derthick and Paul J. Quirk, *The Politics of Deregulation* (Washington, D.C.: The Brookings Institution, 1985).

Chapter Two

Externalities

This second chapter contains three cases on environmental regulation designed to mitigate the "externalities," or social costs, of some businesses. This is an area in which regulation has generally intensified since the early 1970s. Thus, it provides opportunities to study the bureaucratic and political process of establishing new regulations, the effects of new regulations on the operations and strategy of the regulated firm, and the opportunities created by regulation for a firm in the business of environmental mitigation.

In the first case, William Ruckelshaus is appointed by Richard Nixon to head the newly created Environmental Protection Agency. Ruckelshaus, an experienced business manager, takes over in a superheated political environment apparently undergoing a secular change. For Ruckelshaus, whose boss feels some ambivalence towards the environmental issues, the situation demands difficult organizational and strategic decisions. To get his new agency started on a firm political and financial footing may require some tradeoffs between short-term and longer-term objectives.

The case on Allied Chemical is a landmark in environmental pollution and regulation. It describes the Kepone incident—the first widely publicized environmental disaster involving toxic substances. In the aftermath of the disaster, the company's management deliberates over whether or not to adopt its own program of Total Product Responsibility, or to endorse the Toxic Substances Control Act, a bill then pending in Congress that would impose strict federal regulations.

More generally, Allied must reconsider its corporate policy toward environmental problems, and its organizational adequacy to implement such a policy. Implicit in these choices are issues of social responsibility and potential impacts on competitiveness.

The case concerning IT Corporation carries forward the evolution of environmental regulation from 1970 to 1987. In seventeen years, federal and state regulation of toxic substances and hazardous wastes had made tremendous strides. Tough federal laws, enacted in 1976 and 1980, and then amended in the mid-1980s, had created a substantial new industry—the cleanup, treatment, and management of hazardous wastes.

The IT case provides the information necessary to analyze the broad parameters of the market for hazardous wastes, the direction of its development, and the salient competitive characteristics for the industry. The rest of the case focuses on the strategy and structure of IT, one of the fastest growing firms in the business. By the end of 1986, IT reached a point where its strategy and organizational structure required careful reassessment, especially in light of recent regulatory changes.

William D. Ruckelshaus
and the Environmental Protection Agency

On December 2, 1970, William D. Ruckelshaus took on a new job as Administrator of the Environmental Protection Agency. The EPA was merely an idea embodied in words on a piece of paper; the task of turning that idea into a reality lay ahead. The existing facilities, programs, and people had to be brought together, both physically and organizationally. Their efforts had to be realigned into some kind of coordinated program that reflected the interdisciplinary nature of environmental pollution. Ruckelshaus, then Assistant Attorney General in charge of the Civil Division of the Justice Department, was chosen by President Richard Nixon to be the first EPA administrator on October 31. Others within the Nixon Administration had been offered the job, but had turned it down. Day one for the EPA was less than five weeks away—December 2, 1970.

The EPA, the first new line agency formed by the Nixon administration, was established under a Presidential Reorganization Plan that took effect in October 1970. Creation of the agency had been recommended by the President's Advisory Council on Executive Organization (PACEO), chaired by Roy Ash, to provide a coordinated attack on pollution.

THE SITUATION BEFORE 1970

The state of the environment as an issue of popular concern was gaining momentum in 1970. Membership in both traditional conservation groups, such as the Sierra Club, and in younger, more militant groups like the Friends of the Earth, was increasing. In response to mounting public concern, Congress established the Council on Environmental Quality in 1969, lodging it in the executive office of the President. The CEQ set forth an extensive environmental agenda for the administration by early 1970, and in February, President Nixon delivered a message on the environment which delineated thirty-seven separate goals he wanted to achieve that year.

This case was prepared by Ms. Peggy Wiehl under the supervision of Professor Joseph L. Bower, as a basis for class discussion rather than to illustrate either the effective or ineffective handling of an administrative situation. It is based on a case study prepared by Mr. Gregory B. Mills. Funds for the development of this case were supplied by the Alfred P. Sloan Foundation.

Senator Edmund Muskie, the leading contender for the 1970 Democratic presidential nomination, was also trying to capitalize on the environmental groundswell. He was the major congressional spokesperson for the environment and chairman of the Senate Public Works Subcommittee on Air and Water Pollution. Muskie sponsored some of the early pollution bills, as well as the Resources Recovery Act and the Clean Air Act amendments of 1970. He was an outspoken proponent of Earth Day, held on April 22, 1970, with great public relations success. Widespread media coverage created the impression that millions of Americans were very concerned about environmental degradation.

The creation of EPA brought together in one agency a variety of research, monitoring, standard-setting, grant allocation, technical assistance, and enforcement activities formerly scattered through several departments and agencies. The EPA's designers sought to provide a governmental structure for approaching pollution control problems that treated the total environment as a single, interrelated system.

The EPA inherited 5,743 employees from fifteen agencies. (Table 1 shows the division of the employees and the budget.) These resources were to be used for dealing with six basic types of pollution under a variety of legislative mandates. A description of some of the programs and problems inherited by the agency follows. They constituted the new material for Ruckelshaus' agenda.

Water Pollution

The Federal Water Quality Administration had been moved from HEW to the Interior Department, and then to the EPA. Charged with the control of pollutants which impair water quality, FWQA was broadly concerned with the impact of degraded water quality. It performed a wide variety of functions, including research, standard setting and enforcement, and provided construction grants and technical assistance. Progress against water pollution had been slow, however, in spite of large expenditures of cash. Federal enforcement was limited under the 1965 Water Quality Act to interstate cases, and there had been only intermittent attempts at enforcement. Even as known pollutants were controlled, more were discovered; the mercury scare of early 1970 is an example.

The Bureau of Water Hygiene also joined the EPA from HEW. The BWH's responsibility was to monitor drinking water quality, but it had no enforcement powers.

Air Pollution

The National Air Pollution Control Administration was transferred intact from HEW. NAPCA was responsible for motor vehicle and stationary pollution control and had concentrated research on pollution control methods, without much luck; its regulatory functions were similar to the FWQA's. The 1963 Clean Air Act provided limited enforcement powers, but NAPCA had not been an active enforcement agency, having taken only one polluter to court. Yet

Table 1   Major Units Inherited by the EPA

MAJOR UNITS	PREVIOUS AGENCY	NUMBER OF PERSONNEL	FY1971 BUDGET ($ MILLIONS)	ADMINISTRATOR
Federal Water Quality Administration	Interior	2,670	1,000.	David D. Dominick
Bureau of Water Hygiene	HEW	160	2.3	James McDermott
National Air Pollution Control Administration	HEW	1,100	110.	John T. Middleton
Bureau of Solid Waste Management	HEW	180	15.	Richard D. Vaughan
Pesticides Regulation Division	Agriculture (Agriculture Research Service)	425	5.1	G. G. Rohwer
Office of Pesticides Research	HEW (Food and Drug Administration)	275	10.7	
Research on effects of pesticides on wildlife and fish	Interior	9	0.216	Raymond E. Johnson
Bureau of Radiological Health (Environmental Exposure Division)	HEW	350	9.	John C. Villforth
Federal Radiation Council	Interagency	4	0.144	
Division of Radiation Protection Standards	Atomic Energy Commission	3	0.075	

air pollution was an area of strong public and governmental concern because of periodic occurrences of heavy smog and scientific warnings about health hazards. Lobbyists for the automotive and manufacturing interests charged environmentalists with advocating unreasonable, costly, and technically impossible measures.

Solid Waste

HEW's Bureau of Solid Waste Management moved intact to the EPA. Since it concentrated its efforts on R&D projects, the bureau would be able to expand its activities under the 1970 Resource Recovery Act sponsored by Muskie. This act authorized $460 million over three years for construction of local disposal facilities, federal research on waste recycling, and expanded personnel.

Pesticides

The EPA inherited three pesticide units. One of these units, the Pesticides Regulation Division, with responsibility for registering and labeling all commercially used pesticides, was transferred intact from the Agriculture Department. The transfer was opposed by farm interests, who feared that chemicals would be considered pollutants rather than aids to production. According to Ralph Nader's *Water Wasteland*, the division traditionally had a close working relationship with pesticide companies.

The EPA received 275 of the 475 employees in the Food and Drug Administration's Office of Pesticide Research, which set and enforced standards limiting pesticide residues in food. The FDA, however, retained its authority to remove food with excess residues from the market.

The Interior Department's research projects on the effects of pesticides on fish and wildlife were also moved to the EPA, but this involved only one laboratory.

Radiation

Controversy over the adequacy of federal radiation standards had been growing, and in 1970 scientists and environmentalists called for an immediate stiffening of those standards. The Atomic Energy Commission's authority to set standards and emission limits for radioactivity was transferred to the EPA, although the AEC retained responsibility for their implementation and enforcement.

The EPA received over half of another HEW agency, the Bureau of Radiological Health, whose functions were to monitor the radiation in the air and precipitation and to conduct research into the biological effects of radiation.

Noise

The Reorganization Plan established the Office of Noise Abatement and Control within the EPA; this office was commissioned to undertake a one-year study of the noise problem.

THE NEW ADMINISTRATOR'S VIEW OF THE JOB

Faced with a wide range of publicly visible problems and a confusion of agencies, organizations, and laboratories, Ruckelshaus commented on why he took a job others had rejected:

> What can you expect to accomplish? I think the chance of accomplishing something with a brand-new agency like this, where you have a problem that has a lot of legitimacy to it and high public visibility, and therefore the political support that you need to move forward very fast—the chances of succeeding are enormous.
> I felt there was a chance here, in this area, to try to turn that situation around. To try to start because, number one, there was a lot of public support to do something about it, and there was a real chance to take this process and use it

as effectively as possible, and thereby convince people that government was willing to do something about the problem.

I was convinced then that in spite of all of the faddism that was associated with the problem, there is enormous legitimacy to the issue itself.

Also, the fact that a new agency like this comes along once every fifteen years in the federal government, and a chance to be in on the formation of such an agency was something you just don't get very often.

RUCKELSHAUS

William Ruckelshaus, a native of Indiana, received his law degree from Harvard in 1960, whereupon he joined his father's law firm. Shortly thereafter a family friend appointed him deputy attorney general for Indiana; in that position he drafted the state's air pollution control law and in 1963 represented the state board of health in water pollution abatement actions. In 1966, Ruckelshaus was elected to the state legislature and one year later was named majority leader. He opposed Birch Bayh in the 1968 U.S. senatorial election, but lost. Recruited to the Justice Department, Ruckelshaus was the liaison to college campuses. Although the tough assignment involved responsibilities such as quelling student demonstrations in Washington over the U.S. bombing of Cambodia, he became known as one of the more outgoing and accessible members of the Nixon administration. In spite of his good reputation at Justice, Ruckelshaus' appointment to the EPA drew criticism. Environmentalists were apprehensive about having a confidant of Attorney General John Mitchell heading EPA, especially one who lacked outstanding environmental credentials.

After Ruckelshaus was presented at a White House news conference in November 1970, the national news teams, including Walter Cronkite, came rolling in the door at 20th Street, where Ruckelshaus and company had made a home. Even though the EPA did not yet legally exist, everyone expected full-blown competence, articulate EPA spokespeople, and the ability to do things as if the agency had been in operation for five years.

THE EARLY MOVES

Although coordinating the various agencies the EPA had acquired would be difficult, an EPA task force[1] had been established in July to prepare the groundwork for the agency's start-up. The group examined the structure most appropriate for allowing for a strong top management, which they felt the EPA would need; they also selected key immediate tasks with which the administrator would have to deal.

A special Office of Management and Budget team was assigned to prepare the EPA's budget for Fiscal Year 1972. During its first seven months, the agency would operate on the allocations left in the inherited budgets for Fiscal Year 1971 (see Table 1). So it was important for the administrator to get involved in upcoming legislation and the budgeting process. Acquisition of a permanent headquarters in Washington was essential to establish the EPA's image; the agency had been given half a floor in one building, but administrative control would be facilitated in a location that could house all of the 2,000 EPA employees. Ruckelshaus also had to select his top and middle managers, though constraints on the number of top civil service positions (such as heads of divisions) allocated to the EPA complicated the task.

While the task force aided Ruckelshaus with start-up problems, the administrator was confronted with two major issues: He had to keep the various agencies the EPA had inherited running smoothly while a new organizational structure was being developed, and he had to generate sufficient activity to convince the general public and specific interest groups that the EPA was serious about cleaning up the environment. These problems were intertwined and potentially conflicting. On the one hand, Ruckelshaus needed to minimize disruption during the transition period so that he would have time to create a new organizational structure. The urgency of the attack on pollution demanded that vital ongoing programs not be disturbed or delayed by the realignment. Certain statutory deadlines had been set that the new EPA would have to meet. The concomitant directive to "keep doing things the way you always have," however, meant in some cases to continue to do nothing, or to keep doing things the wrong way. On the other hand, Ruckelshaus recognized that he had to act quickly and dramatically to capture the constituency he needed to make the EPA successful. But if the subordinate agencies continued to do things the way they always had, dramatic action would be impossible. If Ruckelshaus seized the initiative from these agencies, he would only contribute to the disruption and dissatisfaction he was struggling to avoid. To make matters more complicated, Ruckelshaus simultaneously had to consider how to deal with the fragmented policies and people now in his charge, while he pondered what the goals of EPA should be. Ruckelshaus commented:

> I realized very rapidly that I was going to have to grit my teeth for a while with this structure we had chosen in the beginning so that I could absorb enough of this information, sort of through the pores, to get a feel for what we ought to do. I had to go around to all of these regions and to the major laboratories that we had; sit down and listen to these people and just get a feel myself, personally, for what was going on.
>
> There was need to establish for the agency some clear goals that everybody could identify with. I went around and talked to a lot of them in the agency. There were all kinds of different opinions as to what those goals ought to be, including a strong recommendation that there wasn't enough authority. I looked at the two most recent examples of agencies like EPA: OEO and NASA. I looked at them in terms of what their statutory goals were. NASA's had been very narrowly defined, in terms of "let's go to the moon in ten years," and they achieved it—in the process, almost did themselves out of business. OEO, on the other hand, had a very amorphous goal: "let's do something about poverty." Some would say that is what they were doing: *something* about poverty. This was the kind of progress that is very difficult to measure.
>
> I felt that *we* had to be very careful that EPA did not go to either of those

extremes. So, we defined our initial goal as pollution abatement. This was fairly narrow, in the environmental sense, but nevertheless, it was identifiable enough, understandable enough, to let us know what we were doing, so that we could move towards the goal. To the extent that we were successful in achieving that goal, a relatively narrow goal, I felt that the larger responsibilities in the environment would much more naturally gravitate toward that agency than they would if we tried to fight for them at the outset.

INTERNAL DIFFICULTIES

The physical separation of facilities created identity and communication problems. The initial move of agencies into EPA was done largely on paper, and left most of the employees involved sitting at their old desks. In some cases even personnel within the same division were physically separated. Employees complained that they did not feel a part of the EPA. The first pesticide headquarters office, a small room in a shabby office building, was moved three times within five months. The director, Raymond E. Johnson, spent most of his time on the phone trying to keep in touch with employees located in three other buildings while fending off industry representatives anxious to register their concerns. Johnson logged some 600 phone calls in the first six weeks. Said Ruckelshaus:

> I tried to establish initially, with all the key people that we had inherited in the agency, a feeling of mutual trust. I didn't believe that because people had been coming in here telling me what a bum they were, that that was necessarily true. If I didn't trust them and believe in them, there was no way for them to do the same for me. I found that by and large, that works. Human beings respond to that. It is clear to me that you are not going to get loyalty just because you demand it. You have to earn it.
>
> [The key officials] reported directly to me, and I would have Dominick and Middleton ([Commissioners of the Office of Water Programs and the Office of Air Programs, respectively] come in at least once a week for a major reporting session. I tried to call them every chance I got to keep them involved in what I was doing and what was going on. I wasn't so interested about the Pesticide Office and the Solid Waste Office. You could kind of put them aside because there wasn't the same kind of pressure in that area to do something as there was in Water and Air.

Further problems stemmed from the uncertainty—which persisted months after the agency was in operation—about what actually belonged to the EPA. This confusion resulted from the unwillingness of some "donor" departments to give up valuable facilities and personnel. In a number of places the Reorganization Plan had failed to specify precisely what was to be transferred to the EPA. Consequently, high EPA officials had to spend time negotiating with the various departments which were supposed to provide the EPA with its structural components. Perhaps the worst case in this bureaucratic power struggle was the decision made concerning HEW's Twinbrook Research Laboratory in Rockville, Maryland. The first settlement provided for joint ownership of the laboratory with a result that research teams were split down the middle, half belonging to EPA and half to HEW. Both agencies were dissatisfied.

ORGANIZING THE STRUCTURE

The existing bureaucracies were structured by categorical programs.[2] Both the EPA task force and the PACEO felt that a functional organization, in which the agency subunits were responsible for such areas as research, standard-setting, and enforcement, was the most appropriate structure. They devised an evolutionary strategy in which the agency would maintain its programmatic orientation under a Commissioner System. On day one only research and management would be fully functionalized, and the rest of the functionalization would occur in stages.

The Nixon administration's "New Federalism" called for decentralized federal administration and strong regional authority. Moving quickly to delegate responsibility to the regional EPA offices was problematic for several reasons: (1) the need for immediate enforcement action required early centralized control; (2) there was little knowledge of the capabilities of regional personnel; (3) the delegation of authority to the regions was strongly resisted by the bureaucracy at EPA headquarters; (4) the selection of regional administrators required time. Consequently, Ruckelshaus delayed action on the regions. He left the field offices intact and, in an order dated December 4, 1970, assigned an interim coordinator for each of the ten regions.

EARLY STAFFING DECISION

At Ruckelshaus' request, four members of the task force stayed on to help the EPA through the early months. While reorganization was occurring at the top, Ruckelshaus was highly dependent on the existing leadership of the inherited units since neither he nor his assistant administrators were capable of stepping in and running them. To fill the deputy and assistant administrator positions, Ruckelshaus worked with a White House executive search team. Although this could have resulted in clashes over whose nominees would get the jobs, the joint effort proved successful. An early selection was the Assistant Administrator for Enforcement, John Quarles. A member of Interior Secretary Walter Hickel's staff, Quarles was highly recommended and in office on day one.

As noted earlier, Ruckelshaus wanted to "hit the ground running," to show his willingness to "take polluters to the mat." It was Quarles who would orchestrate the enforcement actions. He recalled that Ruckelshaus ". . . was concerned with *establishing the credibility of the agency*. I remember that he mentioned this to me—he emphasized it at about the first meeting we had in November, in advance of his being confirmed. We were talking about what the agency would do at the beginning, and he was very anxious to identify some strong enforcement actions that we could take right at the start."

PAST ENFORCEMENT

To hit the ground at anything beyond a crawl was extremely difficult for Ruck-elshaus and Quarles. Federal agencies had made little headway in combatting pollution. In part this was because of ineffective federal and state laws and unwieldy enforcement provisions, such as the "conference" procedure. This process began with the convening of federal and state officials to discuss the problem. If no action was taken in six months, the hearings could be held. After another six months' waiting period, the case could be taken to court. Before the creation of the EPA, only one polluter (of water) had been taken to court.[3] The difficulty—aside from the time involved—was that the procedure required ac-cusing a state of failing to act, before the federal government could go to court.

WATER

The Water Quality Act of 1965 was passed to strengthen water pollution en-forcement, but it applied only to interstate waterways. (The technical difficulties were similar to the conference restraints—the government had to prove that the welfare of specific individuals was endangered, and also show how much the water quality was affected. Then the polluters were allowed six months to take corrective action.) According to a Nader report, these regulations ignored the most effective standard: effluent controls. FWQA showed little willingness to move against industries and municipalities which were not complying. By De-cember 1970 only thirty states possessed fully approved standards and compli-ance schedules, although the national deadline had been June 30, 1967.

The rediscovery early in 1970 of the Refuse Act of 1899 finally gave water pollution enforcement its broadest mandate. Originally passed to keep navigable waters free of shipping obstructions, it forbade discharges into navi-gable waters and their tributaries without a permit from the Army Corps of Engineers. The penalty was a maximum fine of $2,500 per day and up to one year in jail for the responsible executive. Polluters could be prosecuted in criminal suits to enjoin further pollution, and industries could be compelled to treat dumpings into streams. Civil suits were another enforcement tool. In March 1970 the Justice Department moved against Florida Power and Light, and in July it filed ten civil suits over the mercury discharges.

AIR

As with water, little enforcement action had been taken in the area of air pol-lution. The Clean Air Act of 1967 established a federal policy for stationary polluters. It required NAPCA to designate air quality control regions and establish air quality criteria and emission control techniques. States were then to establish their own ambient air standards and propose implementation plans. By October 1969, however, only twenty-five of the expected ninety-plus regions were designated by NAPCA. By March 15, 1970, fifty-seven regions were designated, five criteria reports completed, and two control technique documents prepared, but by December 1970, none of the plans had been adopted.

Although HEW was authorized to issue maximum levels for auto emissions for 1968 model cars, these were not effective. The certification procedure was suspect, since prototype vehicles submitted to HEW laboratories by auto manufacturers were often pampered. To impose the $1,000 fine specified for violation of federal standards, NAPCA had to show that *each* car was in violation—hardly practical for attaining nationwide compliance.

The pending Clean Air Act amendments of 1970 brought to a halt what little enforcement existed. If passed, they would require NAPCA to set national ambient air quality standards—instead of approving the regional standards—and they would also change federal policy on auto emissions. NAPCA could do little more until the fate of the amendments was decided.

ENFORCEMENT UNDER THE EPA: ACTION

Thus, while the major organizational changes were occurring, Ruckelshaus had to begin to formulate a strategy for dealing with enforcement. Enforcing the pollution laws involved a wide spectrum of groups and issues with which the EPA and Ruckelshaus would have to deal. The administrator had to decide how fast he should act, and against which polluters. Any EPA action had to consider the reactions of the main interest groups: the environmentalists, the press, the White House, and Congress. Ruckelshaus did not want to undermine the EPA's image by making large, costly mistakes in the beginning.

Since the past enforcement of pollution laws had been sporadic at best, and the policy and legislative goals set by the White House were weak, it was unclear what the EPA could actually accomplish. Ruckelshaus stated that he was concerned about the actual White House commitment to the environmental issue, as distinct from the political value of the success of the agency:

> I think this was pretty clearly perceived in the White House as the President's agency. It was his plan that had gone up there, and they saw fairly strong vested interest in seeing the thing succeed. I do not think that perception was nearly as accurate among many as it should have been. Because while there was some pressure in the White House against strict enforcement of these standards, that didn't necessarily mean that they didn't want this *agency* to succeed. They really did.

Ruckelshaus decided that the first major consideration was how to deal with enforcement action. This was important for two reasons: (1) to generate public interest and support for the EPA, and (2) to put other polluters on notice that EPA was serious about enforcement. As a way to build a constituency out of the few materials he had, Ruckelshaus decided to act *immediately*. To meet the need for immediate, visible action, he instituted a series of lawsuits against major polluters.

During EPA's first week, Ruckelshaus brought suit against three cities —Atlanta, Detroit, and Cleveland—for violating the Federal Water Pollution Control Act. Recognizing the need for maximum media coverage, Ruckelshaus took advantage of a December 10 speech invitation from the Mayor of Atlanta to announce these suits. As Ruckelshaus recalled: "I called him up just before I made the speech and told him just exactly what I was going to say, and did he still want me to come, and he said he'd already been elected for the present, so he had no problem."

Then, on December 17 the EPA asked the Justice Department (under the Refuse Act) to prosecute both Jones and Laughlin Steel for discharging pollutants into the Cuyahoga River, and US Plywood Champion Papers for polluting the Great Ohio River. The EPA revoked the conditional certification for two types of heavy duty trucks manufactured by Ford that did not meet the emissions standards. (Ford was required to stop sales of the engines and modify those still on hand before they could be sold.) The agency also sought prosecution against ITT-Rayonier for its pulp mill operations on Puget Sound. The Lake Superior enforcement conference dealing with Reserve Mining's taconite wastes was reconvened. Other companies singled out for enforcement actions were Armco Steel, U.S. Steel, Union Carbide, Du Pont, and General Motors. In its first two months the EPA brought five times as many enforcement actions as all of its inherited agencies combined had initiated in any previous two-month period. Media coverage was heavy, and the agency quickly acquired the activist image Ruckelshaus sought.

Although Ruckelshaus saw these early actions as vital to the agency's credibility, they also bore some risk. They made the EPA vulnerable to attack from conservative members of Congress and the White House. A number of the affected industries publicly called the agency irresponsible. While such general broadsides were unlikely to do damage, the danger existed that the EPA might not be able to back up particular claims.

The pressure of adverse publicity generated by EPA enforcement actions could conceivably force large industries to comply voluntarily with antipollution regulations; but there were many variables associated with compliance. The laws on pollution were changing, making it difficult for the companies to set up a permanent strategy. And publicity would have to extend for a long time to have any real effect; but the case-by-case approach (citing one company's violations) would generate headlines for a few months, then fade into the background.

While these prosecutions were getting under way, other environmental issues appeared. The removal of phosphates and NTA from detergents had long been a source of battle among public health officials, environmentalists, and the manufacturers. On December 19, 1970, the Surgeon General and Ruckelshaus announced that major soap manufacturers had agreed to remove NTA from their detergent products because of the alleged potential hazards. On another front, a Shell Oil platform in the Gulf of Mexico caught fire in the beginning of December, while in mid-December, after a two-year ban instituted following the Santa Barbara disaster, the Interior Department again instituted and approved offshore leasing. Ruckelshaus was bombarded with protesting telegrams, for by that time the still-blazing Shell fire had produced an oil slick three miles long and one mile wide. He announced that the EPA was concerned with the safety of offshore operations, and on December 23 the Justice Department filed charges against four oil companies for their failure to maintain safety devices on oil rigs in the Gulf of Mexico.

NEW LEGISLATIVE TOOLS AND RESPONSIBILITIES

The EPA's enforcement tools were altered by the enactment of new legislation. On December 23, 1970, President Nixon signed the Refuse Act Permit Program into law. This was to be a joint effort by the EPA and the Army Corps of Engineers "to regulate the discharge of pollutants or other refuse matters into the navigable waters of the U.S." The Corps would have administrative responsibility for the permits; the EPA would submit opinions on matters of water quality. Each industrial polluter had to apply for a permit by July 1, 1971, by which time the EPA had to be prepared to advise the Corps on permit requests with which it would be deluged.

Concerning pesticides, a Federal Court in January 1971 ordered the EPA to decide whether production of DDT should be suspended and its interstate transport prohibited. The agency decided to give itself a sixty-day deadline to decide the issue and to request comments from the public on DDT's hazards.

The Clean Air Act Amendments, passed on December 31, 1970, required the EPA to promulgate national primary and secondary ambient air quality standards by January 31, 1971, to provide the basis on which emission standards would later be established. Ruckelshaus had to evaluate whether meeting the deadline was more important than taking extra time for careful judgment. He recognized this as a crucial area of decision, since those amendments changed the entire approach to air pollution:

> The ability we had to review and analyze the standards at that time was almost nonexistent. We inherited almost no analytic capacity. We just didn't have a very good assessment of what the options were; no analysis of what the real choice was as far as the statute was concerned, any secondary or tertiary effects. We had no real analysis of this.

Basing his decision on the EPA's need for public support, Ruckelshaus decided to meet the air standards deadlines. The problem was not so much of creating public interest as it was harnessing existing concerns to support the EPA. He thought that once public support started to diminish slightly, members of Congress and the Administration would receive a lot of complaints about the

EPA's actions. And the commitment of many legislators was only as strong as public opinion. Ruckelshaus noted that:

> For purposes of agency credibility it was important to meet those deadlines [of the Clean Air Act] at the beginning of the agency. I think that in achieving some of them we may have made some mistakes by doing things faster than we were ready to move wisely, but that *had* to be weighed against the fallout of not meeting the deadline, which could have been deadlier to the agency. Once we got established and had to implement the Water Bill [in 1972], I felt we were strong enough as an agency to be able to slip those deadlines if it was unreasonable to meet them and we weren't ready to act.

SECURING AN INDEPENDENT CONSTITUENCY: SOURCES OF PRESSURE

Through the early months of 1971, Ruckelshaus was riding the crest of a wave of public concern over environmental degradation. Ruckelshaus perceived public concern as enabling him to resist pressures from Congress, the White House, industry, or others who might seek to interfere in EPA's activities. The stronger the environmentalist pressure, as long as it did not lead to unreasonable demands, the more autonomy Ruckelshaus would have in his leadership of EPA.

One problem Ruckelshaus faced was the tendency of environmentalists to view public officials as either friends or enemies of the environment; one was either tough or soft on polluters. Media coverage of environmental news reinforced this polarity. Environmentalists had easy access to the press and had the ability to call the public tune on what was tough, and therefore good. As Ruckelshaus put it: "We couldn't afford even the *appearance* of being soft."

The key to Ruckelshaus' ability to maintain public support would thus be his direct relations with the national environmental groups and his dealings with the national media. Ruckelshaus had to consider the best way to communicate with these two groups—how to approach them and how frequently to meet with them. There were numerous requests for speaking engagements; Ruckelshaus had to decide where he could get the most exposure, what issues should be dealt with first, through which medium, and to which groups.

Farmers

There were several special interest groups whose opposition might prove disastrous to the EPA. The farmers were one such group, especially powerful because of their ties to Mississippi Representative Jamie Whitten and other influential members of Congress from rural districts. Ruckelshaus had to assuage their fears that the EPA would underplay agricultural concerns. He noted:

> One of the things that occurred to me very quickly was that farmers were going to be scared to death, [and so were] the agricultural organizations, because we

inherited the pesticides from Agriculture and Interior and HEW. One of the agencies we inherited was created to regulate what another was created to promote. They were both all of a sudden under the same roof. The agriculture organizations were just terrified. There were these environmentalists who were fooling around with their pesticides. Those guys could have an impact on Congress, going in there and screaming about this nutty organization that is going to dry up all the pesticides in the country. We had to make sure that they didn't perceive this agency's role as putting them out of business.

To combat this possibility Ruckelshaus hired a friend with strong ties to the agricultural industry as a consultant; his assignment was to fly around the country reassuring farmers that the EPA recognized their position.

Congress

Despite Ruckelshaus' pleas, the responsibility for the EPA's authorizing legislation remained fragmented among several committees, of which Muskie's and Whitten's were the most important. As Ruckelshaus desired, appropriations were consolidated to treat the EPA's budget as a whole. In February 1971 House Appropriations chairman George Mahon (D., Texas) assigned the EPA to the newly created Appropriations Subcommittee on Agriculture, Environment, and Consumer Protection, chaired by Whitten. Ralph Nader's staff, in their *Water Wasteland* report, called Whitten "the virtual czar of the federal farm bureaucracy."

The urgency of the environmental issue in the public eye and Senator Muskie's personal stakes in the matter meant that Ruckelshaus enjoyed no "honeymoon with Congress."

Whitten and Muskie presented different problems for Ruckelshaus. Whitten could be effectively neutralized by a high level of constituent pressure for strong environmental policy; Whitten's fear of defeat on the House floor of any appropriations bill served to check his power. The danger of cultivating environmental concern was that Ruckelshaus might simply enable Muskie to seize the issue, while criticizing the EPA for its inactivity. This conflict created the need for both grass roots support and "public sanity."

To avoid antagonizing either Whitten or Muskie, the EPA's decisions and actions had to be above the table and defensible. According to Ruckelshaus,

It was just that wherever you got some charge that some industry was in there fiddling around the Administration, trying to get a standard lifted or something, this is the kind of thing that Muskie would land on, and in my opinion, it would destroy that agency if they ever showed it.

Given the whole tenor of the way the press viewed this Administration as favoring big business, we had to just be constantly careful. Not only about whether we were doing the right thing or not, but did we give them the appearance, did we give them something to hold onto to make us look awful—and you didn't need much!

In trying to get the EPA budget through Congress, Ruckelshaus dealt with relatively liberal authorizations committees and a conservative appropriations committee. He stated:

> We had a political problem in that the authorization committees authorized enormous sums of money for all of these programs with no way in the world for us to spend all of it. Any suggestion that the Administration came up with below that authorizing figure would be attacked as inadequate. We had to defend that budget from both sides. We would go in to Whitten, and he would say it was too much; then we would go to the authorizing committee and they would say: "Why didn't you spend all the money we gave you?"

The White House

The pressures exerted on the EPA from the White House were determined to a great extent by President Nixon's personal view toward environmental protection and his calculations of political support. While Nixon had no strong personal interest in environmental policy, he saw the political need for at least the appearance of governmental response to pollution problems. The opposition of environmental groups was a potential thorn in his side, particularly if Senator Muskie could marshal them effectively in his presidential bid. Nixon wanted the EPA to succeed as an effective regulatory agency because it was "his baby," but he also saw the need for "balance"—ecological concern should not endanger the health of the domestic economy. Thus, in February 1971 Nixon assured industrialists that they would not become scapegoats of the drive for cleaner air and water.

The attitude of the White House toward the EPA's policy of cultivating its own independent constituency was not clear. Ruckelshaus noted that "[John] Ehrlichman [Assistant to the President] understood the dilemmas we were facing and the problems that we had. As long as I was in communication with him it was all right."

During early 1971 Nixon's popularity, as measured by the Gallup Poll, was declining. In November 1970 the "Nixon approval index" stood at 57%, the 1970 average. By April 1971 it dipped for the first time below 50%, to 49%. The Cambodian invasion, among other things, contributed to this trend. As public antagonism to the Nixon presidency intensified, the EPA was able to garner some public support simply by placing itself in opposition to the administration. Ruckelshaus saw advantages and disadvantages to provoking White House disapproval:

> I felt that to a certain extent the desires of the White House and my feelings that we needed public support were antagonistic. From time to time to get whacked by the White House probably wasn't a bad thing—in order to gain more public support to do something about the issue. I didn't consciously go out and try to antagonize them into slamming at me. But when it did happen, as it did occasionally, I didn't feel that it had hurt the ability of the agency to move forward.

Every time I was pitted against the White House [on the other hand] it was, in my opinion, a very bad thing. I know that from the point of view of some environmental organizations, if they believe that, it might enhance me somewhat in their eyes. In fact, what happens is that it makes the White House mad. So when you go over there and you are talking about budget items or which direction we ought to go in, the really important policies we are dealing with, they are *already* mad at you. They think you are out there stimulating the publicity.

THE PROBLEM FOR THE FUTURE

In the first six months, Ruckelshaus had created the public activist image he desired for himself and for the EPA. The obvious executive and legislative pressures had been carefully calculated and dealt with. Now that the hectic start-up demands had subsided somewhat, Ruckelshaus had to consider EPA's future course in enforcing pollution control. In spite of the initial flurry of suits and actions against polluters, EPA's effectiveness was being challenged.

The Justice Department and conservationists were criticizing the EPA's approach, accusing the agency of failing to move vigorously against polluters. They charged that since the enforcement procedure was so cumbersome, the EPA depended on negotiation and the conference with publicity as the primary abatement tools. Quarles responded that the EPA had changed the federal policy to a more balanced approach; that previously the emphasis had been totally on voluntary compliance. Now "we stand ready to go to court if necessary . . . and are developing the technical capability to do so. . . . What counts is being *willing* to go to court if that is required . . . and we *have* gone to court."

Ruckelshaus was facing problems concerning legislated deadlines as well. How he chose to deal with them would have precedent-setting importance. He had pledged vigorous use of the Refuse Permit Program, for example, but the Program's legality was being questioned, and it was also unclear whether it was in fact possible for companies to comply with the regulations.

Another key decision coming up involved the automobile emission standards set out in the Clean Air Act Amendments. Auto manufacturers had to file applications on January 1, 1972 for a suspension of the 1975 emission standards for hydrocarbons and carbon monoxide. Such an extension could be granted by the administrator only if "all good faith efforts have been made to meet the standards." It was generally accepted that the auto companies would request such suspensions, after which the administrator had sixty days to act on the requests.

Ruckelshaus commented on the importance of his action on automobile exhaust standards:

The automobile emission problem is *obviously* something we are going to have to deal with. There is going to come a time in '71 and they [the auto companies] are going to come ask me for some more time [to comply with the emission standards]. I am going to have to decide whether or not they have made a "good faith" effort. If this whole situation isn't going to be completely farcical, the first thing I have to do is to convince the automobile industry that we are serious about enforcement. That has been completely clear to me. Otherwise, there will be no way two years hence, or whenever they ask for an extension of time, I could conceivably make a judgment that they have made this good faith effort. So, we have to figure out how we are going to convince them that we are serious.

NOTES

1. The team consisted of about fifteen members from such agencies as NASA, Department of HEW, Department of Transportation, and CEQ. Its work was primarily directed by Howard Messner, an OMB management analyst on special assignment.
2. For a full discussion of this issue see Design for Environmental Protection (C16-74-026, Kennedy School of Government).

3. This involved sewage discharges from St. Joseph, Missouri, into the Missouri River. The conference was convened June 11, 1957, and a court order issued October 31, 1961. For the next six years no attempt was made to monitor the discharges. By the end of 1970, one-fourth of the city's sewage was still being discharged raw into the river.

Allied Chemical Corporation (A)

In June 1976 Richard Wagner, president of the Specialty Chemicals Division at Allied Chemical, faced two difficult decisions. He had to recommend whether Allied should support passage of the Toxic Substances Control Act, then pending before Congress. He also had to decide whether to implement a proposed new program, called Total Product Responsibility, in his division.

Wagner found these decisions especially difficult because of the variety of factors he had to consider, including Allied's business prospects, recent developments in the chemical industry, and the increasing public and governmental concern about the health, safety, and the environmental effects of chemical production. Another important factor was the set of problems related to Kepone, a pesticide produced until 1974 by Allied, and afterward by an outside contractor.

ALLIED CHEMICAL

Allied Chemical was a major producer of chemicals, fibers and fabricated products, and energy. With headquarters in Morristown, New Jersey, the company operated over 150 plants, research labs, quarries, and other facilities in the United States and overseas. In 1975 Allied earned $116 million on sales of $2.3 billion. (See Figure 1 and Tables 1 and 2 for Allied's organization and recent financial performance.)

During the late 1960s and early 1970s, Allied had changed dramatically. One company official said Allied was run as "a loose feudal barony" in the 1960s. *Forbes* called the company "a slow-moving, low-growth, low-profit producer of basic inorganic chemicals, fertilizers, and dyestuffs."[1] Changes began in 1967 when John T. Connor resigned as Secretary of Commerce and became chairman of Allied. Over the course of several years, Connor brought in 250 new executives, pruned failing businesses, established systematic planning and tight cost control, and increased corporate supervision of the divisions. At the same time, he stressed decentralized decision making, and said that innovation and flexibility were crucial to Allied's future.

This case was prepared by Joseph L. Badaracco, Research Assistant, under the supervision of Professor George C. Lodge, as a basis for class discussion rather than to illustrate either the effective or ineffective handling of an administrative situation.

Copyright © 1979 by the President and Fellows of Harvard College. Harvard Business School case 9-379-137, rev. 12/83.

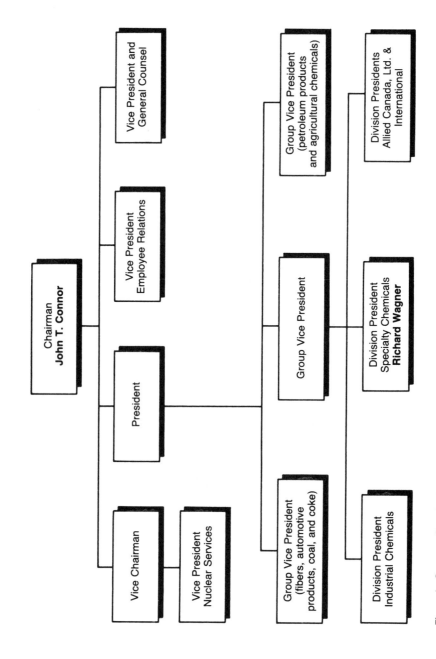

Figure 1 Company Organizational Chart

Table 1 Financial Performance, 1972-1975 ($ in millions except per share data and ratios)

	1975	1974	1973	1972
Sales	$2,333	$2,216	$1,665	$1,501
After-tax income	116	144	90	64
EPS	4.17	5.19	3.27	2.30
Debt/Equity	0.59	0.45	0.49	0.54
Gross margin/Sales	22%	23.3%	24.6%	24.3%
R&D/Sales	1.51%	1.39%	1.73%	1.89%
Pollution control facilities cost	$34.4	$29.0	$28.0	$25.0

Connor's most important step was an $800 million commitment to find and develop oil and gas supplies throughout the world. According to Connor, this strategy would be financed with new capital and with funds "from existing businesses that were losing, had poor prospects, or had severe environmental risks."[2] The largest investments were in Indonesian gas fields and North Sea oil fields. In Indonesia, Allied had a 35% interest in a joint venture with Pertamina, the Indonesian government petroleum agency. The British government had announced its intention to obtain a voluntary 51% participation in the North Sea oil fields, but the form that participation might take had not been determined then.

This energy investment was very risky. Finding and developing new reserves was highly competitive, technically difficult, and very costly. Changes in government regulations or tax laws, either domestic or foreign, could cut profits. And problems with weather, technology, or politics in host countries could delay the start of production. These risks seemed justified as shortages of energy and chemical feedstocks occurred during the 1970s and as the potential payoff from the investment grew. Connor stated that energy could provide as much as half of Allied's profits by the early 1980s.

Table 2 Line of Business Performance, 1974-1975 ($ millions)

	1975		1974	
Line of Business	Income from Sales	Operations	Income from Sales	Operations
Energy (petroleum, nuclear, coal, and coke)	$581	$28	$511	$32
Fibers and fabricated products	504	46	484	81
Chemicals (inorganic, plastics, organic, and agricultural)	1,248	144	1,221	135
Totals	$2,333	$218	$2,216	$248

In mid-1976, however, the return on the energy investment was still small. In fact, it appeared that Allied's energy businesses, taken together, would just about break even in 1976. Allied's U.S. natural gas pipelines lost money because of federal price controls on interstate gas shipments. Its coal and coke business had chronic operating problems and, following a plea of no contest, the company had been fined approximately $100,000 for allegedly failing to meet the Environmental Protection Agency air pollution requirements. Finally, obtaining government approval to operate Allied's nuclear fuel reprocessing plant could prove difficult. Company officials then hoped that 1977 would bring the first profits from North Sea oil, and they expected profits from Indonesian gas sales in 1978.

While Allied had invested heavily in energy, chemicals provided the foundation of company earnings. In 1976, for example, chemicals produced 75% of company profits, even though they represented only 50% of total company sales. Allied produced approximately 1,500 chemicals and sold them to all major industries. These sales were primarily to other chemical manufacturers for use in making their products. Other sales were to dealers, who sometimes resold them under their own names, and ultimately to consumers. The two best years in the history of Allied's chemical business were 1974 and 1975. Sales were expected to weaken later in 1976, however, as a result of the recession that began in 1975.

Allied's fiber and fabricated products had been a steady contributor to company profits. On average, this business accounted for one-fifth of total sales and profits during the early 1970s. Allied made fibers for clothing, carpeting, and auto tires. The company was also the world's largest manufacturer of auto seat belts and shoulder harnesses.

Overall, Allied's record in the early 1970s did not compare favorably with chemical industry standards. Between 1971 and 1975, Allied's return on equity, sales growth, and total assets were the second lowest among the thirteen major diversified U.S. chemical companies. Earnings-per-share growth was exactly the average of the thirteen companies. On the positive side, Allied improved its relative performance in 1974 and 1975, and its energy investment offered the prospect of major improvements in the future.

THE CHEMICAL INDUSTRY

In 1976 chemicals was one of the largest U.S. industries, with annual sales of more than $100 billion. In the twenty years after World War II, chemicals became a high-profit, glamour industry that often grew twice as fast as the GNP. From the mid-1960s to the mid-1970s, however, industry growth had slowed and financial performance dimmed. Among the reasons were higher raw material costs, increased government regulation, the slowdown in U.S. economic growth, and what many considered the maturity of major segments of the industry.

Nevertheless, the industry continued to contribute $3 billion to $5 billion annually to the U.S. balance of payments.

Roughly 80,000 chemical compounds are sold in the U.S. and 500 to 1,000 new ones are added each year. More than 12,000 companies manufacture these chemicals, and most of these companies have sales of less than $5 million per year. The major customer for chemical products is the chemical industry itself. A typical chemical company will buy the product of one chemical company, process it, and sell its product to yet another chemical company. In most cases, a long chain of intermediate processors connects a chemical raw material with its ultimate consumer.

The industry is highly competitive. Many chemicals are commodities and compete on price. Competition comes from both natural products (such as cotton fabric) and synthetic substitutes. Chemical firms also face competition from suppliers—especially oil companies—that integrate forward, and from customers integrating backward. For a highly capital-intensive industry, chemicals have a low degree of concentration. The ten largest chemical companies account for roughly 35% of industry shipments. Low concentration encourages competition by limiting oligopolistic pricing. The industry is also highly cyclical, lagging behind the business cycle by a few months, and vigorous price cutting usually occurs during recessions.

In the past, successful chemical companies tended to follow a basic pattern of growth. They made large investments in research and development, resulting in new products or better processes. These innovations lowered prices and took markets from other chemicals and from natural products. In turn, new markets permitted larger-scale operations, further economies, and further R&D. The R&D investments were the key to successful performance. Half of all chemical products sold in 1970 were not produced commercially in the 1940s. Ammonia fertilizers, sulfa drugs, Dacron, and nylon are some of the results of chemical industry R&D.

Industry prospects were especially uncertain in 1976. The industry earned record profits in 1974 and 1975, an abrupt change from its sagging performance from 1967 to 1973. In response to these profits and to shortages in 1974, a $25 billion capital spending boom took place. This new capacity raised the specter of industrywide overcapacity and renewed price cutting. In fact, the new capacity came on line just as the economic slowdown affected chemical sales in 1976.

At the same time, costs were rising. Environmental laws and high construction costs raised the price of new plants and equipment. Companies were testing more of their products and raw materials for harmful effects, and testing costs were escalating. It was not unusual for tests on just one substance to take several years and cost $500,000. Most importantly, the days of cheap and plentiful oil and natural gas had ended. Chemical companies are disproportionate users of fossil fuels because they need energy to run plants and to use as feedstock for their products. Higher energy costs meant that chemical products in general lost some of their price competitiveness against nonchemical products.

Industry executives were also concerned about an "innovation shrinkage." R&D spending in 1976 would be roughly $1.4 billion, up from $800 million ten years before. But a higher percentage of this spending was going to modify products already on the market or into government-required health and safety research. Reduced R&D seemed to threaten future industry growth.

KEPONE

Wagner had to make his decision at a time when Allied was in the middle of the Kepone affair. Problems related to Kepone had preoccupied Allied executives for nearly a year and seemed to be growing rather than subsiding. Kepone was a DDT-like pesticide used in ant and roach bait in the U.S., and as a banana pest killer abroad. It looked like fine, white dust and was toxic. Between 1966 and 1973, Allied made Kepone at its Hopewell, Virginia, plant or had Kepone made by outside contractors. Profits were under $600,000 a year, and Allied had no health or safety problems with its Kepone production.

In early 1973 Allied needed more capacity at Hopewell for other products, so it sought bids from companies willing to produce Kepone for Allied. This was not unusual: twice before, outside contractors had made Kepone for resale by Allied. The lowest bid by far was submitted by Life Science Products (LSP), a new company owned by two former Allied employees, both of whom had been involved in the development and manufacture of Kepone. LSP leased a former gas station near the Hopewell plant, converted it, and began making Kepone in March 1974.

For sixteen months, LSP produced Kepone under conditions that might have shocked Charles Dickens, according to most accounts. Brian Kelly, a reporter for the *Washington Post*, described the plant as "an incredible mess. Dust flying through the air . . . saturating the workers' clothing, getting into their hair, even into sandwiches they munched in production areas. . . . The Kepone dust sometimes blew . . . in clouds. A gas station operator across the street said it obscured his view of the Life Science plant. . . . Two firemen in a station behind Life Science say there were times when they wondered if they could see well enough to wheel their engines out in response to a fire alarm."[3]

Two months after LSP started operations, Hopewell's sewage treatment plant broke down because Kepone allegedly killed the bacteria that digested sewage. LSP employees soon developed the "Kepone shakes." Some saw doctors provided by "informal agreement"[4] with LSP, but they were diagnosed as hypertensive. This continued until July 1975, when one worker saw a Taiwanese doctor, who sent blood and urine samples to the Center for Disease Control (CDC) in Atlanta. The Kepone levels in the samples were so high that the CDC toxicologists wondered whether they had been contaminated in transit. The CDC notified the Virginia State epidemiologist.

Five days later, the epidemiologist examined several workers at LSP. He later said, "The first man I saw was a 23-year-old who was so sick, he was unable to stand due to unsteadiness, was suffering severe chest pains . . . had severe tremor, abnormal eye movements, was disoriented. . . ."[5] The next day LSP was closed by the Virginia State health authorities.

In early 1976 a federal grand jury in Richmond, Virginia, was called to consider the Kepone events. In May it indicted Allied, LSP, the two owners of LSP, four supervisors at Allied, and the City of Hopewell on a total of 1,104 counts. Most of the counts are misdemeanor charges. Hopewell was indicted for failing to report the massive Kepone discharges and for aiding and abetting LSP. Allied was also indicted for aiding and abetting LSP, for violating federal water pollution laws by dumping Kepone and non-Kepone wastes into the James River before 1974, and for conspiring to conceal the dumping. These cases would then be prosecuted by William B. Cummings, U.S. attorney for Virginia. Allied faced penalties of more than $17 million if convicted.

By the end of June there had been several more legal developments. Allied had publicly denied any wrongdoing. The city of Hopewell had pleaded no contest to the charges against it. Allied's attorneys favored a no contest plea on the pre-1974 dumping charges, but they were confident the company would be found innocent of the other charges. The case would not come to trial until the early fall. Allied also expected suits from the LSP workers, local fishermen, and seafood companies, as well as a large class action suit. These suits would claim damages of astronomical proportions—more than $8 billion.

The Kepone toll had been mounting week by week. The LSP workers were now out of the hospital, but more than sixty of them still reported symptoms of Kepone poisoning. (Mice fed high levels of Kepone had developed tumors that were characterized as cancerous.) The James River was closed to fishing because Kepone tends to accumulate in many species caught for seafood. The James had tens of thousands of pounds of Kepone in its bed, and sales of seafood from the Chesapeake Bay (into which the James flows) were hurt badly. A "60 Minutes" TV report on Kepone damaged Allied's image and reinforced a growing public view that chemicals equaled cancer. Finally, publicity about the Kepone incident increased the likelihood that the Toxic Substances Act would become law.

The impact of Kepone on Allied was traumatic. The company's reputation for environmental safety and responsibility seemed shattered. Settling the court cases could have a significant effect on earnings, and uncertainty about this cost would result in a qualified auditors' statement. Morale was low and hiring had become difficult. Problems also developed in Allied's dealings with federal regulatory agencies, such as the EPA and Occupational Safety and Health Administration (OSHA). These relations depended on good faith bargaining, and Allied met with increasing skepticism and even suspicion. Costly delays in getting permits for new construction resulted. Officials feared the cost of new oxime production facilities at Hopewell would rise more than $10 million because of these delays. (Oximes are organic chemicals used to produce biologically degradable pesticides.)

Allied management felt a strong sense of moral responsibility to the LSP workers, their families, and the Hopewell community. The company funded research aimed at finding a way to eliminate Kepone from the bodies of the LSP workers, and planned to establish a multimillion-dollar foundation to help with the Kepone cleanup and make grants for other environmental improvements.

Wagner found it hard to understand how the Kepone affair happened in the first place. Allied had made Kepone without any health or safety problems, and the LSP owners should have been able to do the same. Hopewell officials knew about the discharges when the sewage facility began having trouble, yet they took no action. The Virginia Air Quality Resources Board had an air-monitoring filter within a quarter mile of LSP, but it was not checking Kepone emissions. Virginia's Water Quality Control Board knew there was a serious problem in October 1974. The board did not use its authority to shut down the LSP plant, but tried to use persuasion to effect changes.

Federal agencies were also involved. In autumn 1974 the Occupational Safety and Health Administration received a letter from a former LSP employee, who claimed he was fired for refusing to work under unsafe conditions. OSHA responded by writing to the LSP owners. They, in turn, wrote back that there was no problem, and OSHA accepted their assurances. The Environmental Protection Agency had sent an inspector to LSP in March 1975. The inspector was uncertain whether the EPA had jurisdiction over pesticides. His letter of inquiry to the EPA regional office in Philadelphia was unanswered in July when LSP was closed.

TOXIC SUBSTANCES CONTROL ACT

In less than a week, Wagner would report to Allied's executive committee on the Toxic Substances Control Act (TSCA). He had to recommend company support for the Act, opposition, or continued neutrality. A neutral stand meant Allied would keep a low profile and issue public statements saying the company supported some features of the Act and opposed others.

TSCA was a new approach to government regulation of harmful chemicals. Previous legislation focused on remedial action, while TSCA aimed at prevention. Senator James B. Pearson (R., Kansas) made this distinction:

> Existing legislation simply does not provide the means by which adverse effects on human health and the environment can be ascertained and appropriate action taken before chemical substances are first manufactured and introduced into the marketplace. At present, the only remedy available under such Federal statutes as the Clean Air Act, the Federal Water Pollution Control Act, the Occupational Safety and Health Act, and the Consumer Product Safety Act, is to impose restrictions on toxic substances after they have first been manufactured.[6]

TSCA was intended to *prevent* unreasonable risks to health and the environment. It gave the Environmental Protection Agency two new powers. The

EPA could compel companies to provide information on the production, composition, uses, and health effects of the chemicals they made or processed. Using this data, the EPA could then regulate the manufacture, processing commercial distribution, use, and disposal of the chemicals.

TSCA had three key provisions. Section four (testing) authorized the EPA to require testing of a chemical for any of several reasons, including clarification of health effects, toxicity, and carcinogenicity. Before requiring tests, the EPA had to show that (1) the chemical could pose an unreasonable risk to health or the environment, or that human or environmental exposure to the chemical would be substantial; (2) there was insufficient data for determining the health and environmental effects of the chemical; and (3) the only way to develop this data would be by testing the chemical. The manufacturer would pay for the testing.

The most controversial provision of TSCA was section five—premarket notification. This required a manufacturer to report its intent to produce any new chemical to the EPA ninety days before doing so. A manufacturer had to make similar notice of plans to produce a chemical for a "significant new use." These reports had to disclose the chemical's name, chemical identity and molecular structure, its proposed categories of use, the amount to be made, its manufacturing by-products, and its disposal. The manufacturer was also required to submit available data on health and environmental effects.

If the EPA found that there was not enough information to judge the health or environmental effects, it could prohibit or limit the manufacture, distribution, or use of the chemical until adequate information was provided. This was the third key provision of TSCA. It gave the EPA broad new powers to regulate the operations of more than 115,000 establishments that made or processed chemicals. TSCA also directed the EPA to weigh the costs and benefits of the testing and regulations that it required under these new powers.

Wagner had to sort out a number of complicated issues to make his decision. He had to ask whether, as a citizen, he thought TSCA was in the public interest. As an Allied executive, he had to consider how support for TSCA would affect Allied's image and how the Act itself would affect Allied's chemical business. This last question was especially difficult, since TSCA could help business in some ways and hurt it in others. For example, TSCA might cut the chances of another Kepone incident. The costs of testing and reporting might give large chemical companies, like Allied, a competitive edge over smaller firms. But these costs would also hurt Allied's bottom line and make chemical products, particularly new ones, less competitive with natural products. Wagner had his assistant, a recent graduate of a leading eastern business school, summarize the major arguments for and against TSCA. The assistant's report is presented in the following two sections.

FOR TSCA

1. TSCA closes gaps in current laws. The Act will require testing *before* exposure, so workers and communities will not be used as guinea pigs.
2. TSCA's cost will be low. The EPA and the General Services Administration estimate total costs to industry of $100-200 million a year. Industry sales exceed $100 billion a year.
3. TSCA will reduce national health care costs by preventing some of the health effects of harmful chemicals. Care for cancer patients alone now costs more than $18 billion per year.
4. Under current laws, the incidence of cancer has been rising and many chemical disasters and near-disasters have occurred.
5. The Act offers protection for the interests of chemical companies. When companies disagree with EPA regulations, they can file a timely law suit and seek a court injunction.
6. TSCA may reduce the risks of doing business in chemicals. The Act may, in effect, put a "government seal of approval" on hazardous chemicals. It could also cut the risk of a company being sued because a customer used its products in a dangerous way.
7. Public support for the Act will help restore Allied's image as a responsible community-minded company.
8. The Act is likely to pass this year, so Allied might as well get on the bandwagon. The Senate has already passed the Act and the current version lacks several features that caused House opposition in past years. Public pressure for passage is building, especially in the wake of the Kepone headlines. The membership of the Manufacturing Chemists Association, the major industry trade group, is split over the Act.

AGAINST TSCA

1. The industry is already sufficiently regulated. Twenty-seven major federal laws now cover almost every aspect of company operations. Large chemical companies like Allied already deal with more than seventy government agencies.
2. Companies already do extensive testing of chemicals before marketing them. The tests sometimes cost several hundred thousand dollars and take several years. They are performed by highly trained scientists working in the most modern labs. Furthermore, companies have a strong incentive to do sufficient testing: They want to avoid the many heavy costs imposed by incidents like Kepone.
3. TSCA will be extremely costly. Dow puts the cost at $2 billion annually; the Manufacturing Chemists Association estimates $800 million to $1.3 billion. There will be less innovation because of excessive testing burdens on new chemicals. U.S. chemical exports will become more costly and less competitive, U.S. jobs will move overseas, and the testing and reporting requirements will hurt or even close many small companies. This will also affect large companies like Allied. We rely on small companies as suppliers, and Allied itself is basically a composite of sixty or seventy small specialty chemical companies.
4. The Act is dangerously vague. The EPA gets very broad powers with few restrictions.

5. Reporting to the EPA under TSCA will require us to disclose trade secrets and other confidential data.

6. Supporting the Act to aid our image or get on a bandwagon will not fool many people. It will be taken as a public relations move and could raise even more suspicions about Allied's motives.

7. It's not even clear there is a bandwagon. The Senate passed the Act in 1972 and 1973, and the House killed it both times. Even though the EPA is lobbying hard for TSCA, the Commerce Department and the Office of Management and Budget oppose it. There is as yet no indication whether President Ford will sign or veto the Act.

8. Many of the reports of chemical "disasters" have been exaggerated by the media and by environmental groups. We should not give in to pressures based on this sort of misinformation.

TOTAL PRODUCT RESPONSIBILITY

Wagner also had to decide whether to implement a new program called Total Product Responsibility (TPR). This program had been developed in 1975 by the engineering and operations services unit, the Specialty Chemicals Division. This seventeen-person staff unit developed policies and procedures related to health, safety, maintenance, and quality control (see Figure 2). TPR would use "tools of policy, procedure, control, and review" to help Allied "properly discharge its legal and moral responsibility to protect its employees, customers, the public, and the environment from harm."

TPR was first proposed in 1975 by R.L. Merrill, vice president of engineering and operations services. Merrill had come to Allied after several years with Dow Chemical and was impressed by Dow's Product Stewardship Program. According to *Business Week*, product stewardship meant Dow would assume "total responsibility for how its products affect people" and Dow's products would carry "a virtual guarantee of harmlessness."[7] Dow had 600 people involved in setting up product stewardship in 1972. They prepared environmental and safety profiles for all 1,100 of Dow's products, and film cassettes for presentations to Dow employees, customers, and distributors. In its first year, product stewardship cost $1 million.

Merrill's original proposal was not for a program as extensive as Dow's. Merrill had suggested a survey of information currently available to Allied on the health and environmental effects of its products. This survey would be followed by whatever tests were needed to supplement existing information. But during 1975 and early 1976, an expanded TPR took shape around this original suggestion. It became important to get complete health and safety information on raw materials, processes, and customer uses of Allied products. And, in turn, it seemed important to make sure all this information was reflected in Allied's everyday operating procedures.

The first step in implementing TPR would be for Wagner to issue a twenty-five-page memorandum on TPR to all management personnel in his

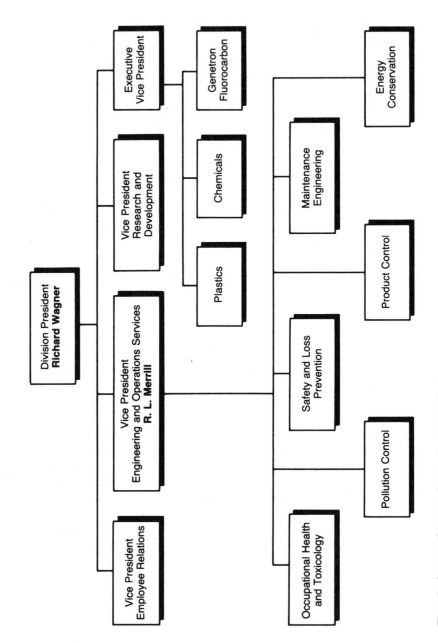

Figure 2 Specialty Chemicals Division Organization Chart

division. The memo would delineate standards of operating and business practice that covered virtually every aspect of division operations. Line management would then have to make sure that operating procedures conformed to these standards. The following excerpts are from the TPR memorandum.

Specifications

Specifications should exist for every raw material . . . and every finished product. . . . No specifications may be changed without the approval of the director of operations/general manager after review with operations services.

Testing

All of the division's products will be reviewed on a priority basis, as determined by our toxicology specialists, to determine the known or suspected undesirable toxic effects which those products may have on our employees, customers, the public, and the environment.

Plant SOPs

Standard operating procedures will be developed by plants for each product area. Procedures will be designed by engineering, technical, and operations groups to provide capability of producing uniform product quality and to insure process continuity. Use of approved procedures will be mandatory and revisions to accepted methods will require approval of preestablished authority levels.

Equipment Testing

Testing procedures and frequencies are to be developed to insure reliability of equipment at the 95% confidence level to minimize the possibility of unforeseen problems arising.

Change Procedure

Changes in R&D, product development, manufacturing, distribution, and marketing that may adversely affect the process, employees, product, customer, the public, or the environment should not be made without the approval of the director of operations, director of marketing, or research laboratory director, as appropriate, and after review of the operations services.

Technical Bulletins

Technical literature and bulletins should include all safety and environmental statements necessary to protect employees, customers, the public, and the environment. Operations services is to receive, edit, and approve all literature and bulletins to assure that all such proper statements are included.

Advertising

Advertising copy should reflect true and accurate statements about our products. Advertising copy should be reviewed by operations services to prevent misleading statements concerning claims in the areas of environmental products' safety, health, and quality assurance.

Product End Use

Marketing departments should make every effort to determine the end use application of each product sold. Consideration should be given to the desirability of using the product in that application and the customer's understanding of the effect of such use on the operation. . . . A product should not be sold to a customer where it is known that the end use application is not proper.

Capability of Existing Customers

Marketing departments have the responsibility to establish the capability of our customers concerning their competency to handle our products in a manner that protects the customers' process, employees, the public, and the environment. Hazardous products should not be sold to customers whose capability is deemed inadequate. If it is determined that an application or end use of the product is improper . . . the sales of this product to that customer should be discontinued immediately.

New Customers

Hazardous products should not be sold to new customers until the capability of that customer is deemed adequate.

Outside Contractors

When outside contractors are to be used to process, reprocess, repackage, or manufacture materials for us, the review should include a determination of the toxicity and hazards of the materials to be handled, and an in-depth study of the contractor's capability to perform the work such as not to endanger the contractor's employees, the public, or the environment. . . . When a contractor is retained, it is the responsibility of the appropriate business area to arrange for periodic inspections and reviews of that contractor's operations by the operations services department.

Wagner had distributed the draft memo within the Specialty Chemicals Division and discussed the program with a variety of line and staff personnel. Reaction was mixed. Leonard Warren, director of marketing services, said:

> I don't know where I come down on this. I know that chemical companies are getting burned in the newspapers and in court, and the result is more and more government people telling us how to do business. We've got to stop this, but we've also got to make money. As I read TPR, it says we're going to say "no" to some people who want to buy from us. We'll also be harassing our current customers and prospects by asking them how they use our products, who they sell to, and what their customers do with their products. Some of them are going to tell us to keep our noses out of their businesses. A lot of our products are virtually commodities and they're already hard enough to sell without the burdens of TPR paperwork, TPR costs, and the mixed signals we'll be giving to our reps.
>
> Now I'm not completely opposed to TPR in some form. After Kepone, it will make Allied's reputation a little better. There are probably some customers that we shouldn't sell to, because they're too risky, and this program will help us get rid of them. In some cases, it might even help sales because it would be a reason for our reps to have even further contacts with customers, and more information about uses of our products could be a useful kind of market research for us.

Another hesitant view came from Joe DeStefano, a production manager at the Hopewell complex:

> My first reaction is that we already do a lot of the things in the TPR memo. The difference is that our current procedures are not formalized and we don't have to get as much clearance before making changes. I can't help wondering whether TPR isn't going to make business a lot more bureaucratic. It seems to me that the government already does enough of that. Under TPR, we would have to go through operations services to do almost anything. We could end up with more paperwork, buck-passing, and bureaucracy. Sometimes I'm not sure what's more important: getting a good product out the door at a profit or complying with a thousand rules and restrictions.

Janet Baker, an associate corporate counsel who handled environmental cases, supported TPR:

> Allied has to do something like TPR. Kepone costs are skyrocketing and we can't afford to let another Kepone happen. TPR sends a clear message throughout the division that health and safety are top priority. We've sent the message before, but it needs vigorous emphasis. If we don't take steps to run our business as safely as possible, the government will do it for us.
>
> But there are problems. Customers and suppliers could well resent our sanctimonious attitudes when we poke our noses into their businesses. Refusals to deal have to be handled unilaterally and without publicity or else we may be liable for conspiracy allegations, antitrust, trade disparagement, or libel suits.

Despite these objections and misgivings, Merrill remained enthusiastic about TPR, arguing:

> Of course TPR won't be free of problems, but it does much more good than harm. It will help our image and cut our risk of environmental and safety problems. Besides, the government is likely to require most of what's in TPR in just a few years. By starting now, Allied can learn to do business under these inevitable new conditions.
>
> It's also absolutely essential that the attitude of Allied managers and workers toward the government start to change. The government is going to be a major factor in the chemical industry for the indefinite future. We can either take an adversary approach and comply with regulations in a minimal, grudging way, or we can recognize that the government is here to stay, learn to cooperate with federal agencies and, as a result, get better results in regulatory proceedings and lower our risks of future Kepones.

In making his decision, Wagner also had to consider the views of Allied's chairman and the executive committee. There was strong support among these executives for "some concrete steps" that would prevent another Kepone and change company attitudes toward government health and environmental rules. At the same time, Wagner could not ignore his division's earnings and performance. In the summer of 1976, sales were weakening as a result of the recession that began in 1975. Wagner wondered if this was the right time to divert managerial time and attention from the chemical business. He was concerned about the possible impact of TPR on the flexibility, decentralized decision making and innovation he had been trying to encourage in his division. In addition, he wondered whether TPR would have kept the Kepone problem from happening in the first place.

FURTHER DEVELOPMENTS

Since 1976 was an election year, Wagner had been paying some attention to the positions candidates took on regulation in general and the chemical industry in particular. Senator Vance Hartke (D., Indiana), who then faced a serious re-election challenge, campaigned hard for greater regulation of chemicals. One of his speeches included the following remarks:

> The hazards associated with chemicals like PCB's, vinyl chloride, BCME, and asbestos have all dramatically illustrated how important it is to get early warning with respect to new chemical substances. . . .
>
> During this (last) five-year period, there have been in excess of one million deaths in this country from cancer. Over a million infants have been born with physical or mental damage. . . . While many of the grave health risks to human beings have declined in recent years, cancer statistics have done just the opposite. In fact, the incidence of cancer was estimated in 1975 to be some 2.5% above the previous year. . . .
>
> It is no accident that the hot spots for cancer in this country are in close

proximity to those locations where the chemical industry is most highly concentrated.

It is tragic that those who rely upon the industry for jobs have essentially become guinea pigs for discovering the adverse effects of chemical substances. It is also tragic that much of the information which has shown the cancer-producing potential of many chemicals has come from death records of employees. For example, of one million current and former American asbestos workers who still survive, fully 300,000 have been projected to die of cancer. This death rate is 50% higher than of the U.S. population at large.[8]

At the same time, Wagner was also aware of growing opposition to government regulation. The leading presidential contenders—Ford, Carter, and Reagan—all sounded the theme of "too much government interference." Academic studies had documented the large indirect costs of regulation, and even reformers like Ralph Nader were very critical of agencies such as the FTC, which Nader said was basically a captive of the industries it regulated. Industry also joined this movement against regulation. Dow Chemical, for example, announced completion of its own "catalogue of regulatory horrors" and claimed it had spent $50 million in 1975 to meet regulations it considered excessive.[9]

NOTES

1. "Risk Rewarded," *Forbes*, March 15, 1977, p. 101.
2. Ibid.
3. Christopher D. Stone, "A Slap on the Wrist for the Kepone Mob," *Business and Society Review* (Summer 1977), p. 4.
4. Ibid., p. 5.
5. Ibid., p. 6.
6. Library of Congress, *Legislative History of the Toxic Substances Control Act* (Washington, D.C.: Government Printing Office, 1976), p. 215.
7. "Dow's Big Push for Product Safety," *Business Week*, April 21, 1973, p. 82.
8. Library of Congress, *Legislative History of the Toxic Substances Act* (Washington, D.C.: Government Printing Office), p. 216.
9. "Dow Chemical's Catalogue of Regulatory Horrors," *Business Week*, April 4, 1977, p. 50.

IT Corporation (B)

On October 22, 1986, a major New York investment bank was holding its annual conference on Hazardous Waste Management at the Parker Meridien. The all-day conference was attended by numerous Wall Street analysts and portfolio managers interested in hazardous waste investment opportunities. Until mid-afternoon, the expansive room had remained nearly half full as six of the largest publicly traded companies competing in the hazardous waste industry gave thirty-minute presentations, followed by numerous questions. Shortly before 3:30 P.M., in anticipation of the presentation by International Technology Corporation (IT), empty seats began to fill and a higher level of energy ran through the attendees. Promptly at 3:30 P.M., the three senior officers of IT began their presentation.

IT's chief executive officer, Murray Hutchison, clicked through the slides with precision and discussed the company's mission:

> International Technology is in a very simple business: the business of solving environmental problems. We have a very straightforward mission, which we see as guiding the company to more than a billion dollars in revenue over the next few years. Simply stated, our mission is to preserve and protect the environment by helping our clients make positive, lasting, substantial improvements in their environmental management practices, in the most economical and sound manner, and to build IT as a great institution.
>
> We are a service business company. If asked the three most important parts of our business, I would reply, "people, people, and people." We are completing our sixtieth year in business this year, and we have just added our 3,000th employee. Of those 3,000, more than 1,500 are technical people, the majority holding advanced degrees.[1]

Bill King, IT's president, discussed the company's business and capabilities:

> I want to emphasize our turnkey capabilities. We assess health and environmental risks and, if they exist, determine their magnitude. We gather waste samples, bring those samples in-house for analysis, and engineer solutions to the problem based on our analytical results. We then implement solutions to waste problems. IT is the only company in the country that has this total capability.

This case was prepared by William B. Bunting and Carl J. Rickertsen (MBA '87), under the supervision of Professor Richard H.K. Vietor, as the basis for class discussion rather than to illustrate either the effective or ineffective handling of an administrative situation.

We are a growth company in a growth industry. Not many billion-dollar industries in our country can truly be characterized as growth industries. Within the industry, our emphasis has been, is, and will continue to be in the private sector. Our customers are primarily the *Fortune* 200 and certainly within the *Fortune* 500.[2]

Finally, IT's chief financial officer, Buzz Mendel, touched on IT's financials, which spoke for themselves (see Exhibit 1). Fiscal 1986 revenues had reached $207 million, up from just over $50 million four years earlier. Profit after tax had grown more than sevenfold, and IT's stock price followed suit. Since the initial public offering (IPO) in December 1983, investors had continued to earn returns far in excess of the S&P 500 index. The stock's performance during 1985 had earned IT a position in the *Wall Street Journal* as one of the "Big Board's 10 Best Performers" (see Exhibit 2).

When the presentation was concluded, the three men took a few questions and left the room to a round of applause. Their presentation had left no uncertainty among the seminar's attendees: This was the leader in the large and quickly growing hazardous waste management industry. As they walked out, so did some twenty others in the room, hoping to catch Murray, Bill, and Buzz for a few private questions about IT's future.

It was exactly this topic that Bill King reflected upon as he walked out of the hotel and onto 56th Street that evening. The presentation had gone very well, and he was proud of IT's successes, the team that IT had built, and the outstanding returns management had created for IT shareholders. On the other hand, King was concerned about a variety of issues that would affect IT and the hazardous waste industry over the coming years.

The regulatory environment had changed very rapidly in the last two years, particularly with the sweeping amendment to the Resource Recovery and Conservation Act in 1984 and the recent reauthorization of the Superfund bill by President Reagan, creating another $9.5 billion to be spent on hazardous waste cleanup.

These regulatory changes had created quickly-changing market dynamics in a market that was approximately $3 billion in size, growing at close to 30% per annum, and highly complex. IT had chosen to focus its efforts on solving a client's problems on-site, but many industry experts did not agree that this was where short- or long-term gains would be made. Finally, what would these changes mean for IT's aggressive acquisition program, which had closed eight more acquisitions in fiscal 1987 alone?

Issues external to IT were not the only thoughts on King's mind as he walked toward the midtown restaurant where he would dine with Murray and Buzz. To respond to the regulatory and market changes taking place around them, IT must have an organizational structure to attack external developments effectively. Of major importance was the success of the planned corporate reorganization, which would significantly alter IT's management structure and chain of command, and would create several new business lines. In addition, IT was installing a large new control system tailored specifically to IT's current and future needs. Finally, King always returned to growth and people. Where would he find the people needed to help IT maintain its growth rate and its quality reputation?

REGULATORY ENVIRONMENT

Prior to the mid-1960s, the handling and disposal of waste was not subject to federal or state regulation. As the tonnage and chemical complexity of the nation's waste grew, it became increasingly apparent that the unrestricted disposal of such wastes posed a serious threat to the environment. Congress responded to the problem by enacting the Solid Waste Disposal Act of 1965 to fund research and technical assistance for state and local planners. In 1970, the scope of the legislation was redirected with the passage of the Resource Recovery Act, which called for sanitary landfills and encouraged conservation efforts, such as recycling, instead of mere disposal.

By the mid-1970s, a significant body of scientific research had begun to emerge, indicating that waste generated by chemical and other industrial processes could be hazardous. As a result, Congress moved to strengthen existing legislation by passing the Resource Conservation and Recovery Act (RCRA) in 1976. This law required the Environmental Protection Agency to set standards for generators and transporters of hazardous wastes and for owners and operators of hazardous treatment, storage, and disposal facilities. Four years later, Congress tried to address the problems of abandoned disposal sites by passing the Comprehensive Environmental Response, Compensation, and Liability Act (CERCLA), or Superfund. CERCLA established a $1.6 billion Hazardous Response Fund to begin the monumental task of identifying abandoned sites, assessing the liabilities of responsible parties, and monitoring the cleanup efforts of the sites over the following five years. By establishing guidelines for handling various forms of hazardous waste, these two acts provided the foundations for a hazardous waste management and treatment industry.

1984 AMENDMENTS TO RCRA

When Congress passed RCRA in 1976, it included provisions for tracking the transportation of hazardous wastes, and it mandated the permitting and the setting of standards for hazardous waste treatment, storage, and disposal facilities. But during the following years, it became increasingly apparent that RCRA would not be adequate to control the nation's hazardous waste. Among the panoply of deficiencies under RCRA, several of the most significant were as follows:

· More waste, generators, and facilities were exempt from RCRA control than were subject to it;

· Many wastes, including dioxins, were not listed as hazardous;
· Recycling was so broadly defined as to exempt virtually any refuse as hazardous waste; and
· There were no restrictions on what substances, regardless of their hazardous nature, could be disposed of in landfills.

Following the passage of RCRA, concerns grew regarding the negative effect of hazardous waste disposal on the groundwater and air, giving rise to the demand for additional legislative protection. The 1984 Amendments to RCRA reflected this movement and represented a clear shift in national policy away from land disposal and toward waste reduction and the use of new treatment technologies. Among the many provisions of these Amendments, several themes emerged that demonstrated this transition, including waste listing and identification, land disposal restrictions, and the expanding scope of RCRA.

WASTE IDENTIFICATION AND LISTING

Prior to the 1984 Amendments, there was considerable ambiguity regarding identification of hazardous wastes. The Amendment moved to clarify this subject by identifying hazardous wastes on two fronts. "Characteristic Wastes" were those substances which were either ignitable, reactive, corrosive, or toxic. "Listed Wastes" were those the EPA identified as being produced by a specific manufacturing process, regardless of their concentration levels. By identifying these substances that were considered to be hazardous, the new law served to close one of the prevailing loopholes. According to Richard Fortuna, executive director for the Hazardous Waste Treatment Council:

> One of the most fundamental deficiencies of the RCRA regulatory system prior to the 1984 Amendments was the fact that many materials that were listed as hazardous wastes under state law were not part of the federal regulatory program. Even such items as dioxin and ethylene-dibromide at the time were not listed or identified as hazardous wastes under RCRA. The 1984 Amendments contain strong directives for the EPA to expand the scope of its waste listing *and* waste identification activities.[3]

LAND DISPOSAL BAN

The RCRA Amendments moved to reduce the disposal of hazardous waste in landfills, deep well injection, pits, ponds, or lagoons by establishing a series of deadlines or "hammers" which prohibited the land disposal of various waste above specific pretreatment standards. The hammers scheduled by the Amendments were as follows:

November 6, 1986

· Dioxins containing waste and spent or discarded solvents.

July 8, 1987

· "California List"—wastes listed as hazardous under RCRA, including liquid hazardous wastes containing certain metals (arsenic, cadmium, chromium, lead, mercury, nickel, selenium and thallium), free cyanides, PCBs, and acids with a pH rating lower than 2.0.
· Liquid or solid hazardous waste containing halogenated organic compounds in excess of 1,000 milligrams per liter.

August 8, 1988

· Contaminated soil and debris from Superfund sites.
· EPA will ban from landfills at least one-third of all listed wastes not on the California List, unless properly pretreated.[4]

June 8, 1989

· Second one-third of all listed wastes will be banned from landfills unless properly pretreated.

May 8, 1990

· Final one-third of all listed wastes will be banned.

Proponents of strict environmental protection applauded this aspect of the reauthorization including its clear implication for requiring a reduction in the volume and toxicity of disposed hazardous wastes. Opponents, on the other hand, pointed to the severe lack of treatment capacity to handle the projected increase in volume of hazardous waste, and to the long delays of eighteen months to five years required to obtain the RCRA Part B permit required to treat hazardous substances.

EXPANDING SCOPE OF RCRA

In addition to a clear definition of a broad range of substances brought under the auspices of RCRA as hazardous waste, the Amendment moved to include additional territory on two fronts. First, the new law specified that generators of more than 100 kilograms (220 pounds) per month were subject to the regulation, whereas the old law only regulated generators of more than 1,000 kilograms (2,200 pounds) per month. In absolute terms, this increased the number of federally regulated generators from approximately 15,000 to about 175,000. Second, the Amendments reached for the first time to cover the estimated five million underground storage tanks containing hazardous substances or petroleum. Also, the Departments of Energy and Defense came under the jurisdiction of RCRA for the first time.[5]

CERCLA

On October 17, 1986, the Congress reauthorized CERCLA, mandating that $9.5 billion be spent over the next five years for the cleanup of abandoned sites. The original act expired on September 30, 1985 and the delay in reauthorization reflected the controversial and politicized environment surrounding the act. While the offices of the EPA dedicated to CERCLA administration and enforcement were carried through this delay by several interim authorizations, the effect of the delay was the virtual shutdown of all forward-oriented CERCLA projects.

In addition, the act outlines the following schedule:

CERCLA Reauthorization Schedule

	NUMBER OF SITES		
	1988	1989	1991
Remedial Investigation and Feasibility Studies (initiated by)		275	200
Remedial Action (initiated by)		175	200
Preliminary Assessment	24,269[a]		
Additional Sites Evaluated by the EPA and Placed on the National Priority List			1,600–2,000[b]

[a]A nonbinding goal, which represented the entire inventory of sites as of October 17, 1986.
[b]EPA estimate.

As was the case with the 1984 RCRA amendments, the reauthorization recognized the need to seek permanent remedies for hazardous waste problems through the use of on-site treatment technologies. First, the new legislation outlined that, to the maximum extent possible, permanent treatment methods other than land disposal and resource recovery methods be employed. Additionally, all off-site transfers of hazardous waste had to go to facilities operating in full compliance with RCRA standards. Second, the Act established a $100 million program to encourage the development of innovative treatment methods. From 1987 through 1990, these funds were to be utilized to start at least ten field demonstrations per year. Up to $10 million annually was allocated to provide financial assistance to companies developing new technologies, and $25 million was directed toward endowing at least five hazardous waste research centers at universities.

The Superfund authorized $500 million to fund the cleanup of contamination from leaking underground storage tanks. Of the five million tanks, it was estimated that over one-third were currently leaking and up to 50% would begin to leak within the next decade.

Finally, to qualify for federal funds at any site, a state must guarantee by 1988 the availability of disposal or treatment capacity for all waste reasonably expected to be generated within the state during the coming twenty years.

THE HAZARDOUS WASTE MANAGEMENT INDUSTRY

The hazardous waste business in the United States began growing in the early 1980s. Development of a market was following two paths.

First, the authorization of Superfund gave the EPA a pool of funds with which to stimulate the private sector's interest in attacking hazardous waste problems. Many companies won contracts and began work on site evaluations and cleanup. Second, RCRA scrutiny of hazardous waste generators stimulated compliance and therefore the need for hazardous waste companies' services to help generators solve their problems. In addition, RCRA prompted many generators to examine their manufacturing processes in an effort to reduce wastes via process control.

Though the market size in absolute dollar terms was already large, the hazardous waste industry was still in a state of infancy and disarray. Numerous problems existed. Although some large waste generators had dramatically reduced their toxic waste streams, the volume remaining for treatment was still quite large. The number of disposal sites, meanwhile, had declined dramatically due to RCRA, and siting of new treatment facilities had come to a standstill as a result of the NIMBY (not-in-my-backyard) syndrome. Furthermore, prior to 1984, RCRA's numerous loopholes, such as the exclusion of small-quantity generators and ill-defined toxicity standards, let many generators ship wastes without full RCRA compliance.

By 1983 another enormous problem came to the fore regarding Superfund. The five-year, $1.6 billion Superfund had apparently accomplished little by way of effective remediation. In fact, mismanagement of the fund by EPA officials had caused a political scandal and forced the resignation of Anne Burford as EPA administrator in 1983. Industry sources in late 1983 estimated that the original Superfund had done little more than create a great deal of paperwork and a lot of cleanup targets; in the five years only two abandoned disposal sites had been remediated.

By 1984, the industry had grown to $2 billion and was in need of regulatory reform, due to many of RCRA's original shortcomings. The 1984 Amendments clarified various issues and redirected the industry, making matters much tougher for large generators and bringing RCRA scrutiny to small waste generators.

In 1985 the Bhopal disaster brought the threat of hazardous substances to the forefront of the news, giving further intensity to the NIMBY syndrome. The hazardous waste industry in the U.S. had continued to grow rapidly, and as the Superfund expired in September 1985, Congress was still deadlocked over reauthorization proposals that ranged from $5 billion to $12.5 billion. Calendar 1985 ended without Superfund resolution and created a lame duck EPA; 1986 would be a critical time for regulators and industry players alike.

By 1986, the hazardous waste management industry had, in the words of one industry spokesperson, "arrived." Though the industry was already large and growing in public importance, several recent regulatory developments had caused it to receive widespread public attention. Among these was the Superfund reauthorization over President Reagan's threatened pocket veto, New York State's approval of a $1.4 billion bond to clean up intrastate hazardous wastes, and the approval in California of Proposition 65, a tough and controversial law concerning the pollution of drinking water sources.

A second source of national interest was the well-publicized "Woburn Trial," in which W.R. Grace and Beatrice were charged with contaminating drinking water that had caused an abnormally high leukemia rate among children in the Woburn, Massachusetts area. Though the two companies were proven to have contaminated drinking sources, the suit was settled out of court for $16.3 million before any leukemia link was traced back to the companies.

The sheer size and growth rate of the hazardous waste management industry had also attracted attention. The total market for primary hazardous waste services had grown in size from nearly $1 billion in 1981 to close to $3 billion in 1986. In addition, the market was forecast to grow at 25% to 30% per annum through at least 1990. The structure of the hazardous waste industry's markets and segments was highly complex, changing rapidly, and marked by a lack of information.

WASTE STREAM SEGMENTATION

Hazardous waste in the U.S. can be categorized broadly as old wastes and new wastes. Old wastes are those which have been generated during the past century, since the beginning of America's industrial revolution. Of the total amount of hazardous waste ever created in the U.S., 93% still exists in landfills, deep injection wells, pits, ponds, and lagoons around the nation. Old wastes were to be mitigated by both Superfund dollars and privately financed cleanup programs. The backlog of waste cleanup is enormous. The EPA has considered over 24,000 disposal sites for inclusion on the National Priority List to be addressed by the Superfund. The EPA further estimates that to clean up these sites alone (which do *not* include private sites on manufacturing grounds), given current low-end cost of treatment which nears $250 per ton, would require expenditures of almost $300 billion.

New wastes are those produced today and in the future by hazardous waste generators in the U.S. In 1984, a survey of hazardous waste generators by the Chemical Manufacturer's Association estimated that producers generate 265 million metric tons of new waste per year, a figure which many experts believe to be on the low side.

Of the total new wastes generated in the United States, 96% were treated or disposed of on-site; 4% were transported off-site and disposed of or treated. Of the nearly eleven million tons of material taken off-site each year, the breakdown of treatment or disposal is as follows:

Landfills	49%
Deep Well Injection	8
Incineration	5
Land Treatment/Solar Evaporation	14
Nonincinerated Treatment	24

The dollar volume spent on new waste treatment and disposal each year can only be estimated. The EPA has calculated that it costs $90 per ton to achieve full RCRA compliance; this implies expenditures of nearly $25 billion per year on new wastes alone. But this estimate was certainly high, since wastewater treatment, the most common on-site method for wastes, was much cheaper than the $90 per ton disposal cost. Recasting the numbers of wastewater treatment costs still implies an annual market of $8.4 billion if all generators act in full RCRA compliance. As RCRA scrutiny intensifies, however, more companies will comply fully, presumably increasing market size.

INDUSTRY SEGMENTATION

The complexities of the hazardous waste industry make strict business segmentation difficult; still, seven areas can be discerned (see Exhibit 3).

Engineering and Consulting

Hazardous waste engineering problems, such as the construction of a large incinerator, are complex and expensive projects; this segment is dominated by several large engineering firms such as Bechtel and Camp, Dresser & McKee. Numerous hazardous waste firms also offer engineering services, including IT and Environmental Systems Company. Firms in this role act as designers, advisors, and general contractors for large projects. Segment size estimates show a 1986 market of $600 million, perhaps reaching $2 billion by 1990.

Analytical Services

Analytical services are comprised of laboratories that analyze waste samples, both old and new. Labs determine the chemical composition of the waste streams and may propose feasible treatment techniques. Lab equipment and staff vary from highly complex and skilled to mundane; gross margins for analysis vary accordingly. Lab services are critical at most stages of waste stream handling. Large competitors include IT, Enseco, and Environmental Treatment Corp. The market for lab services was $250 million in 1986 and should grow to $750 million by 1990.

Transportation, Storage, and Disposal

These three functions are grouped together because they are generally performed in the same service, and priced as one product. Transportation of hazardous waste is self-explanatory and companies require EPA permits to participate. Storage of wastes typically takes place before transportation from the generation site or at the disposal facility. The critical component of this segment is disposal.

Hazardous wastes are disposed of in landfills, ponds, and deep well injection facilities. Disposal sites are studied carefully by the EPA under RCRA and by state agencies; very few, if any new sites will be permitted in the future. Even after treatment, most hazardous wastes contain a residue that must be stored in RCRA regulated facilities. Competitors include Chem-Waste Management, Rollins Environmental, U.S. Pollution Control Inc., Environmental Systems Company, and IT. The market for transportation, storage, and disposal of hazardous waste is likely to grow from $1.2 billion in 1986 to nearly $3 billion in 1990.

Site Remediation

Site-remediation projects are large, engineering-intensive projects which generally occur at abandoned or unpermitted disposal sites, such as Superfund sites. These projects include capping disposal pits to permanently enclose wastes, or constructing retaining walls to stop wastes from leaching through soils. Large competitors in this market include IT and U.S. Pollution Control. This market is likely to grow from $250 million in 1986 to nearly $750 million in 1990.

Processing and Treatment

The processing and treatment of hazardous waste streams is a highly complex and broad area. Each differing waste stream requires a different treatment technique, and hundreds of compounds and treatment techniques exist today. The two broad categories of treatment are incineration-based techniques (burning with oxygen present) and nonincineration-based techniques.

Incineration of hazardous wastes is done on-site, off-site, and by transportable units. Many organic waste streams can be detoxified fully by incineration, while inorganic waste compositions leave a hazardous, inorganic residue. Competitors in incineration include Rollins Environmental, Chem-Waste Management, Environmental Systems Company, and IT. It is estimated that the incineration segment of the treatment market will grow from over $250 million in 1986 to $1.2 billion in 1990.

Nonincineration-based treatment techniques are ubiquitous and generally less proven than incineration. They also tend to focus on a more narrow band of waste streams. Methods include pyrolysis, chemical treatment, and biodegradation. Competitors include many small, entrepreneurial organizations, such as U.S. Pollution Control Inc. and IT. It is estimated that this segment of the treatment market will grow from nearly $400 million in 1986 to nearly $1.5 billion in 1990.

Emergency Response

Emergency response, a critical component of hazardous waste services, involves such events as fuel truck accidents on the freeway and train derailments.

IT has been a leader in emergency response since the early 1980s, when it won a large EPA contract to educate U.S. emergency responders such as fire and police departments. The size of this market is expected to grow from $100 million in 1986 to $300 million in 1990.

Specialized Services

The specialized services segment of the industry includes many firms dedicated to serving highly focused, and sometimes very large, industry niches. For example, Groundwater Technology focuses on leaking underground storage tanks at gas stations; Safety-Kleen, Inc. specializes in the disposal of dry cleaners' used solvents. Decontamination of structures, including those contaminated by asbestos and chemicals, is another emerging market niche with several competitors. This area is expected to grow from over $60 million in 1986 to some $800 million in 1990.

ON-SITE VS. OFF-SITE DEBATE

An overriding issue which affects all of these business segments is the balance between the short- and long-term profits available to those servicing hazardous waste generators on an on-site or an off-site basis. On-site service occurs at the point of hazardous waste creation, typically the grounds of a manufacturing facility. Off-site service requires transportation of the wastes from the point of generation to a remote location.

The argument for the off-site market, excluding any effect of waste minimization, is summarized in the following 1985 report by the Congressional Budget Office:

> The new law [RCRA] should cause a shift toward off-site management. The CBO estimates that some 96% of all waste was managed on-site in 1983. Under the 1984 amendments, however, many more small producers of hazardous waste that find it economic to use off-site facilities will be included under the regulations, and many waste generators previously using substandard on-site land disposal facilities will ship their newly banned wastes to off-site treatment plants. Consequently, the percentage of waste managed off-site should increase from 4% in 1983 to 10% in 1990. This could raise the total volume of waste managed off-site from 10.3 million metric tons (MMT) in 1983 to between 17.6MMT (assuming waste reduction occurs) or 25.3MMT (assuming waste reduction does not occur) in 1990. If no new off-site facilities are built by 1990, the increased demand for off-site services—together with additional demands for off-site treatment and disposal engendered by an expanded Superfund cleanup program—could easily overwhelm current capacity in the commercial treatment industry, particularly for incineration and chemical oxidation services. (Although excess capacity now exists, the difficulty in siting and obtaining permits could constrain development of new, advanced treatment facilities in time to meet new demand.)[6]

Others, including IT's management, argue that servicing clients on-site, where the wastes are generated, is the key to future success in the industry. Proponents of this view point to "joint and several liability" as a key issue, and use IBM as an example.[7] IBM has stated that by 1990, *no* hazardous waste will leave any IBM manufacturing site; all waste will be treated or disposed of on-site. IBM, and other large hazardous waste generators, simply do not wish to entrust outside contractors with the transportation and disposal of wastes off-site because of the huge potential liability risks if anything goes wrong, today *or* in the distant future.

A further reason, beyond liability, is that these firms believe that the pricing of off-site services will, in the future, increase dramatically. This belief is based on two factors. The first is that due to the difficulty of obtaining new treatment or disposal permits from the EPA, price will increase as the supply/demand imbalance worsens. Second, federal and state authorities may levy taxes on existing treatment or disposal facilities, resulting in further price pressure.

INFORMATION GAP

No reliable nationwide estimate of waste management needs can be obtained from existing published data.

Arthur D. Little, Inc.

There is no accurate market data.

Balis & Zorn, Inc.

A major issue that managers of hazardous waste firms must wrestle with is that of the information gap. This problem plagues managers on two critical fronts: waste composition and market size/segmentation data.

The information gap vis-à-vis waste composition causes difficulties for both old and new waste segments. Because records were either never kept, were poorly kept, or have been destroyed, it is not clear exactly what the waste composition is in the 24,000 + sites left abandoned around the United States. This affects not only remediation efforts at those sites, but also the issue of safety risks due to potential and unpredictable adverse chemical reactions between waste streams. The information gap is not nearly as prevalent with regard to new wastes, but is still an issue. There is no publication, by the EPA or any other body, that accurately assesses the volume or composition of hazardous waste streams generated today. Each single generator is aware of the waste streams its process creates, but no accurate compilation exists. This is particularly troublesome as RCRA now covers small-quantity generators, which adds enormous complexity to the new-waste measurement issue.

Market size/segmentation data are equally elusive. Many analysts attempt to generate market size data and subsequent forecasts, but there is little industry agreement with respect to overall size or segment size, except for the conclusion that the market is "big" and "growing quickly."

These two information gaps combine to make planning for treatment technologies, market segment spending, and strategic planning very difficult.

COMPETITION

A variety of competitive forces energized the hazardous waste industry in 1986. The size of the market had created numerous large players, and the forecasted growth combined with the ubiquitous national press coverage was attracting hundreds of new entrants.

The original competitors in the hazardous waste industry as regulation developed through the early and late 1970s were the large trash companies, for which hazardous waste was a simple business extension. These companies include Waste Management of Chicago (whose hazardous waste group is called Chem-Waste Management) and Browning-Ferris (see Exhibit 4). Through the early 1980s, the hazardous waste segments of these firms have grown very quickly and have become increasingly important to firm profitability. To take advantage of the large public-market valuations being placed on hazardous waste companies, in mid-1986 Waste Management sold a 20% interest in Chem-Waste Management to the public for over $200 million, thereby raising cash and distributing the corporate liability associated with hazardous wastes.

Arthur D. Little estimated that there were over 1,500 participants in the hazardous waste industry at the end of 1985, and this number was expected to grow by over 200 companies per year.

Capital was readily available for these fledgling companies. The public markets were generally ascribing price/earnings multiples in excess of forty times earnings to hazardous waste players, making public equity very cheap. In addition, many venture capital firms were joining the fray, with one group of hazardous waste experts out of Chicago raising $50 million fund to invest strictly in hazardous waste start-ups.

Due to different state regulatory jurisdictions, competition tended to take place on a regional basis. This was certainly the case as competition related to new entrants, but was less clear with the large industry players. IT and others argued that because many of their corporate clients were national and international firms, they too need national capabilities and scope. The highly varied state regulatory environments made this effort difficult, but IT and others were aggressively entering new geographic markets via acquisition and other means.

IT: 1981-1986

By 1981, Bill King had been running IT for two years and had already seen immense changes, most importantly the 1980 authorization of Superfund. IT was then a $50 million (sales) company, nearly double its size since King arrived in 1979. As King put it, "We've had to change a great deal to react to quickly changing market and regulatory dynamics. We can never stand still; this business is moving too quickly."

Evolution of a Strategy

In 1981 IT was primarily a California company, whose management believed that having disposal capacity was the strategic key to becoming full-service managers of hazardous wastes. By this time, the EPA had begun curtailing new permits for disposal facilities, and IT had the largest disposal capacity in California, a state with a rigorous regulatory posture toward hazardous wastes. For this reason, IT had significant pricing flexibility at its disposal sites, and was able to generate a great deal of cash. With this source of funds, IT strove to extend its business base beyond California. The first step in this direction was to develop a positive brand image for IT vis-à-vis hazardous wastes throughout the United States.

IT's vehicle for brand establishment was an EPA contract for a national emergency response training program. IT bid for the contract and won, and over the next year trained police and fire departments around the U.S., thereby establishing positive, national, name recognition.

From 1981 through 1983, IT continued to look for expansion opportunities and made the strategic decision to enhance their very strong California disposal presence with regional treatment facilities strategically positioned throughout the country. In this way, IT, which already had engineering, transportation, technical, and analytical capabilities, could offer the entire gamut of services to its clients on a national basis; the new regional treatment centers would complete its full-service scope.

The first of these facilities was a major treatment facility in Louisiana, a state with a vast chemical industry and enormous hazardous waste problems. IT, which was invited into Louisiana by the state government, acquired land and filed permits for a $120 million facility that would offer detoxification, incineration, recycling, and reclamation capabilities in 1981.

Shortly after the start of the Louisiana project, IT began studying the feasibility of two other treatment facilities located in areas with broad hazardous waste problems—Massachusetts and Texas. Again, at the invitation of both state governments, IT agreed to construct treatment facilities.

By late 1982 IT had invested over $20 million in the three projects, mostly in Louisiana. Although the Massachusetts and Texas facilities were still in the early planning stages, local manifestations of the NIMBY syndrome grew fierce. Opposition to the facilities by local constituents, who filed numerous lawsuits, eventually caused IT to delay construction in Louisiana, withdraw its plans in Massachusetts, and put Texas on hold.

On-Site Focus

In December 1983, IT went public at $15.50 per share, valuing the company at over $80 million. The 1983 fiscal year had shown after-tax earnings of $1.74 million, implying a historic price earnings multiple of more than 45. The company went public on the strength of its management team, wide range of services, hazardous waste focus, strong client base, and numerous disposal sites.

For fiscal 1984, IT's first public annual report showed revenues up 44% over the prior year at $93.5 million. Net income was up 160%, at $4.5 million. In February of 1984, IT had acquired a company with extensive engineering and geotechnical experience, including specific expertise in hydrology and groundwater treatment. The annual report highlighted IT's strategic development:

> In recent years, by both acquisition and internal expansion, the company has developed a "turnkey" problem-solving capability that includes environmental problem identification and assessment, solution development, and implementation. The solution to environmental problems frequently requires application of the whole spectrum of the company's capabilities.

This report also noted that "legal actions were filed by a special interest group . . . challenging the issuance of certain permits to the company" regarding the Louisiana treatment facility; "This remand will cause further delay in the development of the proposed complex."

Fiscal 1985 showed revenues up 54% to $144 million, with net income up 41.2% to $6.3 million. In 1985 IT continued to build on its turnkey capability; as King explained, "We expect to continue to concentrate on serving private industry which currently comprises some 90% of our business." During 1985 IT made two more acquisitions, one of a New Jersey environmental services company, and the other a Silicon Valley analytical services firm.

Revenues jumped 34% in fiscal 1986, to $208 million; net income doubled to $15.4 million. Five acquisitions were made in 1986, including a large disposal facility in Bakersfield, California (see Exhibit 5). The 1986 annual report offered IT's first mission statement (see Murray Hutchison's statement at the beginning of this case study). It also emphasized IT's strategy to be a full-line environmental services company solving the clients' problems on-site, the point where wastes were generated. IT had recently bolstered its financial position via a $40 million stock offering at $22 per share (after a 3-2 split in May 1985). By January 1986, IT's stock traded over $40 per share; shareholders were very pleased.

The 1986 annual report also noted that the Louisiana facility was still inoperative due to ongoing local legal difficulties. A consulting firm had been hired to reassess the facility's potential.

OPERATIONS

At the end of IT's fiscal year (March 31, 1986), operations at IT focused around four major groups and one new area, formed during 1985. The new area was Risk Control Services, and the four other areas were Analytical Services, Engineering Services, Decontamination and Remedial Services, and Transportation, Treatment, and Disposal (see Exhibit 6).

Risk Control Services

This newly established group served both the hazardous chemical and nuclear industries with a broad range of consulting and operating services. Dr. Anthony R. Buhl, IT's director of this group, explained its function:

> Liability is inherent in the business world today, but it's not necessarily inevitable. The whole premise of risk control is that, indeed, there are very tangible steps which can and should be taken to limit the potential for risk. Prevention is more cost effective than cure.

Functions of this new group included environmental and compliance audits, industrial health and safety services, health and engineering risk assessments, emergency planning, and emergency response (an ongoing business for IT). Important assignments for 1986 included a study at Three Mile Island to contain core degradation, and a risk assessment study for the 700-mile Alyeska pipeline in Alaska.

Analytical Services

IT has the largest commercial analytical capability in the U.S., with nine operating facilities, generating $20.7 million in revenues, with analytical skills capable of handling chemical, nuclear, and mixed wastes. IT has labs in California, Kentucky, New Jersey, Tennessee, and Texas. The labs performed over 84,000 analyses in 1986 and used advanced measurement equipment including mass spectrometers, high resolution gas chromatographs, and extensive data management equipment.[8]

Engineering Services

IT specialized in geotechnical and chemical engineering, providing services to solve hazardous chemical and nuclear problems. Sales for this group were $37 million in 1986, based on the completion of over 150 computerized air and ground water models and fifteen incineration projects.[9] Working from twelve regional offices and closely coordinating with analytical services, IT's strategy in this area has been to offer technically superior service, reducing site investigation to the minimum. IT licensed a state-of-the-art incinerator design from Von Roll Company of Switzerland for use in this group.

Decontamination and Remedial Services

During 1986, IT managed twenty remedial and decontamination projects in excess of $1 million each, an increase of 122% over the prior year. Staffing in this group has been expanded significantly to handle site remediation of such areas as Dioxin analysis and destruction, PCB (polychlorinated biphenyls) decontamination (which generally results from PCB transformer fires), and asbestos abatement to meet asbestos removal standards and radiochemical remediation.

Transportation, Treatment, and Disposal

IT served the western U.S. with a treatment and disposal service operating at eight facilities in California. The facilities handled a variety of wastes, including solids disposal at the Panoche, California site and petroleum and refinery wastes at the Bakersfield, California site. Revenues from this group were at $93 million in 1986, up from $59 million in 1985. Future emphasis will be placed on providing mobile treatment capabilities to treat waste generation at the source.

Technology Development

In addition to these revenue-generating groups, IT maintained a Technology Development group which operated out of IT's Environmental Research Center in Knoxville, Tennessee. This group carried out a development program which focused on the innovative application of proven technology, and has spent a great deal of time with the introduction of technology in a mobile or transportable form, including transportable PCB decontamination systems and mobile inorganic treatment units.

ORGANIZATION AND CONTROL

Fiscal 1987 at IT began on April 1, 1986, and was certainly King's busiest year to date. He had a record of financial performance that would be difficult for any firm to replicate, an increasingly competitive environment to face, vast regulatory changes to anticipate, and very high shareholder expectations to meet.

King spoke about the customers he was facing:

The customer is very complex in this marketplace. Our primary target is the large, national corporation with a multiple-site hazardous waste generation problem. We can solve their problem from initial risk assessment to transportation, treatment, lab services, and disposal. These big projects are premium price, have long time spans, and are high margin business; we have all the skills to handle these projects in a quality way.

But today there's another customer that has a need in more mature markets. These are local markets we helped create, made some money in, and now everybody's jumped in. Margins are razor thin here, and we've got to be ready to price aggressively. In the past IT has been the high-cost, premium quality player in all markets; today, we are ready to price for quality on large projects and be tough on price in mature, nonproject businesses. That's a lot of what has driven the reorganization.

In the summer of 1986 IT began planning internally to respond to changes that were occurring in the marketplace. This planning effort had two parts: a significant corporate reorganization and a new control system.

The old and new organization charts are shown in Exhibits 7 and 8, respectively. The reorganization was designed to address market changes. From an essentially centralized, functional organization, IT had reorganized into five new, decentralized groups.

Murray Hutchison commented on the reorganization:

A fundamental strategic review of our markets and competitive position has been completed by senior management. This review was undertaken in response to significant changes in markets, competitors, and regulations. The basic question to be answered by the review was how do we organize to better position ourselves in those markets in which we choose to compete.

The primary issue is how to manage our company and approach our clients. What are our services and products the client wants to buy? In summary our clients are buying "problem-solving capability."

Environmental Services

The Environmental Services group was created to handle the highly competitive, price-sensitive segments of IT's product line. Included in this group was emergency response, an area in which IT had extensive historic experience. Clients were local entities, and the objective of this group was to become the low cost provider.

Environmental Projects

The Projects group within IT handled the large assignments from corporate clients. This included engineering projects, analytical laboratories, site remediation, and on-site construction. Emphasis in this group was on premium service and attractive profit margins. This was the core of IT's strategic focus.

Transportation, Treatment, and Disposal

This group, which operated only in the West, had remained intact after the reorganization and essentially handled all hazardous materials as they moved off-site to IT's disposal and treatment facilities. In terms of both revenues and profits, IT's disposal facilities would continue to be essential.

Risk Control Services

Risk Control Services included a new business for IT, risk assessment. Due to disasters like Bhopal and general insurance failures in the U.S., top-level executives at industrial corporations have become very sensitive to their level of environmental risk. This new group at IT functions as a consulting firm to board-level officers to closely examine their company's exposure to potential liability. This high-level contact will fit well with the other components of IT's business.

Corporate Development Group

This group was essentially unchanged by the reorganization and had a very broad mandate, which included numerous staff functions such as corporate communications, investor relations, and corporate image. Strategic planning was also part of this group, with such critical functions as technology planning and acquisition development.

In addition to the creation of the new groups, chairman Murray Hutchison increased his operating responsibility, emphasizing increased involvement with the California disposal facilities.

Meanwhile, IT hired Arthur Young to develop a comprehensive control and job-tracking system to enhance IT billing and payables processing, leading in the future to enhanced MIS reporting availability. One of the goals of the system was to streamline the current job-tracking operations, which were essentially paper-based and handled by several hundred accounting clerks and invoicers. The system, which was completed in the summer of 1986, cost IT over $2 million and was very complex. Buzz Mendel, chief financial officer at the time of the system's finalization, saw the system as critical:

> We needed to manage complicated projects, and their control, in a more automatic way. This is a finance, accounting, and cost control system for internal and external invoices. The system forced key policies on issues such as transfer pricing. This system is working.

Some IT managers, however, viewed the system as too complicated and ahead of its time. King knew that the system was necessary, but concluded that he "would never build a system like this from scratch again."

THE FUTURE FOR IT

Success, King realized, did not make managing a growing business much easier. IT had just gone through a huge reorganization oriented toward enhancing its profitability and focus in both new and old markets. His organization was having difficulty digesting a new cost system, and NIMBY problems had kept the Louisiana facility closed. New entrants were attacking many profitable markets and King was never sure what would happen next in federal or state regulation.

On the other hand, IT was now valued at over $600 million in trading on the New York Stock Exchange, and IT shareholders were thrilled. The hazardous waste industry was large and growing very quickly, and its inherent complexities would be an advantage to a company with IT's broad skills. The fundamentals of IT's industry could hardly be any stronger, and IT had an experienced team to execute in this environment.

As King reached the restaurant, he thought about the presentation, and then the future. IT had been on a roll since its inception; what did they need to do to keep it going?

Exhibit 1 IT Corporation (B): Consolidated Statements of Income ($000)

	FISCAL YEAR END (MARCH 31)			
	1983	1984	1985	1986
Sales	$65,094	$93,515	$143,728	$207,607
Cost of Sales	47,685	68,678	108,524	143,133
Gross Margin	$17,409	$24,837	$ 35,204	$ 64,474
SG&A	12,186	14,871	21,338	32,740
Operating Income	$ 5,223	$ 9,966	$ 13,866	$ 31,734
Interest Expense	3,399	2,228	2,930	1,888
Other Income/Expense	418	282	483	(377)
Gain on Sales of Property	184	115	64	
Income Before Taxes	$ 2,426	$ 8,135	$ 11,483	$ 29,469
Taxes	683	3,610	5,167	14,041
Net Income	$ 1,743	$ 4,525	$ 6,316	$ 15,428
Net Income per Share	$ .32	$ .67	$ .64	$ 1.16
Weighted Average Shares	5,439	7,845	9,829	13,310
Cash Dividends/Share	$ .025	None	None	None
Return on Equity	16.1%	22.3%	15.8%	18.8%

Continued

Exhibit 1 (continued) Consolidated Balance Sheet ($000)

	FISCAL YEAR END (MARCH 31)			
	1983	1984	1985	1986
Assets				
Current Assets				
Cash	$ 736	$ 1,861	$ 2,900	$ 5,952
Accounts Receivable	13,109	19,030	39,093	55,350
Prepaid Expenses	1,386	2,168	2,399	3,374
Deferred Income Taxes	183	441	379	
Total Current Assets	$15,414	$23,500	$ 44,771	$ 64,676
Property, Plant and Equipment	42,274	53,594	69,148	122,307
Less: Accumulated Depreciation	13,838	17,052	21,085	27,658
Net Property, Plant and Equipment	$28,436	$36,542	$ 48,063	$ 94,649
Construction in Progress	19,311	23,585	29,864	31,982
Investments in Affiliates	891	1,146	1,571	
Cost in Excess of Acquired Businesses		3,100	2,968	5,379
Other Assets	633	1,898	3,197	6,647
	$64,685	$89,771	$130,434	$203,333
Liabilities and Stockholders' Equity				
Current Liabilities				
Accounts Payable	$ 4,160	$ 7,629	$ 13,130	$ 15,451
Accrued Wages	2,757	4,541	5,649	12,123
Other Accrued Liabilities	894	2,632	3,378	5,121
Long-Term Debt Due Within One Year	3,237	1,870	825	2,892
Total Current Liabilities	$11,048	$16,672	$ 22,982	$ 35,587
Long-Term Debt	25,501	12,052	38,849	30,652
Convertible Subordinate Debentures	18,000			
Deferred Income Taxes	3,041	5,999	7,578	17,875
Other Long-Term Liabilities	444	286	451	847
Total Liabilities	$53,034	$35,009	$ 69,860	$ 84,961
Convertible 6% Preferred		18,000	18,000	
Common Stock at Par	3,515	5,227	7,938	13,209
Additional Paid-in Capital	45	19,234	17,119	70,734
Retained Earnings	8,091	12,301	17,537	34,429
Treasury Stock			(20)	
Total Common Stockholders' Equity	$11,651	$36,762	$ 45,574	$118,372
	$64,685	$89,771	$130,434	$203,333

Exhibit 1 (continued)   Condensed Consolidated Statement of Quarterly Income[a] ($000)

	3QFY1986	4QFY1986	1QFY1987	2QFY1987
Sales	$ 52,064	$ 52,414	$ 54,749	$ 55,589
Costs and Expenses	42,598	46,736	44,185	44,372
Operating Income	$ 9,466	$ 5,678	$ 10,564	$ 11,217
Interest Expense and Income	539	367	664	860
Income Before Taxes	$ 8,927	5,311	$ 9,900	$ 10,357
Taxes	4,403	2,203	4,604	4,816
Net Income	$ 4,524	$ 3,108	$ 5,296	$ 5,541
Net Income Per Share	$ .33	$ .22	$ .38	$ .20

Condensed Consolidated Balance Sheet ($000)

	3QFY1986	4QFY1986	1QFY1987	2QFY1987
Assets				
Cash	$ 4,807	$ 5,952	$ 2,374	$ 23,091
Accounts Receivable	45,505	55,350	58,428	52,531
Other	3,541	3,374	7,761	6,242
Total Current Assets	$ 53,853	$ 64,676	$ 68,563	$ 81,864
Net Property, Plant and Equipment	63,732	94,649	98,373	108,039
Construction in Progress	30,991	31,982	38,948	45,281
Other Assets	15,347	12,026	17,825	23,897
Total	$163,923	$203,333	$223,709	$259,081
Liabilities and Stockholders' Equity				
Accounts Payable	$ 10,146	$ 15,451	$ 11,576	$ 13,921
Accrued Liabilities	10,841	17,244	16,989	13,794
Current Portion of Long-Term Debt	1,623	2,892	863	2,334
Total Current Liabilities	$ 22,610	$ 35,587	$ 29,428	$ 30,049
Long-Term Debt	21,774	30,652	50,176	76,995
Deferred Taxes and Liabilities	10,841	18,722	20,413	22,405
Common Stockholders' Equity	108,698	118,372	123,692	129,632
Total	$163,923	$203,333	$223,709	$259,081

[a]Fiscal year end: March 31.

Exhibit 2 IT Corporation (B): "Big Board's 10 Best Performers"

COMMON STOCK	CLOSING PRICE	NET GAIN	PERCENT CHANGE	COMMENTS
Texas Instruments	5¾	4⅝	+411.1%	Oil and gas producer had big oil find in Egypt.
Downey Savings & Loan	41⅞	32½	+346.7	Fast-growing thrift rang up 46% nine-month earnings gain.
Triangle Industries	33½	25⅜	+312.3	Wire and cable company acquired National Can.
Tosco	3⅞	2⅞	+287.5	Benefited from turnaround in gasoline refining business.
The Gap	62¾	42⅛	+204.2	Retailer upgraded clothing lines; sales took off.
Americus, AT&T Score Series A	22	14⅝	+198.3	Unit trust for capital gains scores big with investors.
Jewelcor	18⅜	11¾	+177.4	Jewelry concern pulled off strong turnaround in earnings.
Columbia Savings & Loan Association	20	12¾	+175.9	Aggressive California thrift posted 80% nine-month profit gain.
Tonka	27½	17¼	+168.3	Benefited from strong sales of GoBots and Pound Puppies.
International Technology	28¾	17¾	+161.4	Profited from growing need for hazardous waste disposal.

Source: *The Wall Street Journal*, January 2, 1986, p. 3b.

Exhibit 3 IT Corporation (B): Market Segments and Segment Size

Segment	SEGMENT SIZE ($MM)	
	1986(A)	1990(E)
Engineering and Consulting	$ 600	$ 2,000
Analytical Services	150	750
Transportation, Storage and Disposal	1,200	3,000
Site Remediation	250	750
Processing and Treatment		
Incineration	250	1,200
Nonincineration	400	1,500
Emergency Response	100	300
Specialized Services	60	800
Total	$3,010	$10,300

(A) Actual.

(E) Estimated.

Source: IT Corporation.

Exhibit 4 IT Corporation (B): Summary Financials for Major Competitors (Fiscal 1986) ($ millions, except per share data)

INCOME	WASTE MANAGEMENT	BROWNING-FERRIS	ROLLINS ENVIRONMENTAL	U.S. POLLUTION	ENVIRONMENTAL SYSTEMS	ENVIRONMENTAL TREATMENT
Revenues	$2,017.8	$1,327.5	$136.9	$ 57.0	$ 66.5	$101.5
% Revenues		6.5%	100.0%	100.0%	100.0%	100.0%
Hazardous Waste	21.5%					
Gross Margin	$ 478.4	$ 271.4	$ 52.9	$ 30.0	$ 22.7	$ 34.7
%	23.7%	20.4%	38.6%	52.7%	34.1%	34.2%
Pretax Income	$ 431.6	$ 240.8	$ 33.4	$ 12.9	$ 12.0	$ 8.7
%	21.4%	18.1%	24.4%	22.7%	18.1%	8.6%
Net Income	$ 222.3	$ 136.9	$ 18.7	$ 6.9	$ 8.3	$ 4.8
%	11.0%	10.3%	13.7%	12.1%	12.5%	4.7%
E.P.S.	$ 2.11	$ 1.90	$ 0.60	$ 0.81	$ 0.65	$ 0.40
CAPITALIZATION						
Cash	$ 208.7	$ 44.5	$ 10.2	$ 5.9	$ 25.6	$ 47.1
Debt	431.7	111.7	3.5	8.0	46.3	53.6
Equity	1,544.9	748.8	72.1	39.4	38.1	35.5
Net Debt/Equity	14.4%	9.0%	9.3%	5.4%	54.3%	18.4%
Return on Equity	16.6%	21.1%	29.6%	19.2%	24.7%	20.8%

Source: Wertheim Schroder & Co., Incorporated.
195

Exhibit 5 IT Corporation (B): Major Acquisition Time Line

1. June 1982	Analytical Laboratory	California	Cash $300,000; note payable $350,000
2. November 1982	Waste Oil Treatment	Tennessee	Note payable $59,000
3. February 1984	Geoscience, Engineering	Pittsburgh	Cash $1,758,000; short-term installment $1,000,000; assumed liabilities $2,921,000
4. January 1985	Environmental Emergency Response	New Jersey	Cash $590,000
5. January 1985	Analytical Laboratory	No. California	Cash $350,000; note payable $700,000
6. May 1985	Chemical and Nuclear Purification and Recovery	Tennessee	Cash $91,000; royalty at 10% up to $900,000
7. September 1985	Analytical Laboratory	Tennessee	
8. October 1985	Environmental Consulting and Engineering	New Jersey	Cash $6,322,000
9. October 1985	Chemical and Nuclear Risk Control	Tennessee	
10. February 1986	Disposal	California	1,525,000 shares of IT common stock.
11. May 1986	Consulting and Engineering Analytical Laboratory	Texas	
12. May 1986	Incineration Treatment		License agreement with Von Roll Limited of Zurich, Switzerland

Source: IT Corporation.

Exhibit 6 IT Corporation (B): Sales by Business Group, Before Reorganization ($ millions)

	1986 AMOUNT	PERCENTAGE OF TOTAL SALES	PERCENTAGE INCREASE 1985 TO 1986	1985 AMOUNT	PERCENTAGE OF TOTAL SALES	PERCENTAGE INCREASE 1984 TO 1985	1984 AMOUNT	PERCENTAGE OF TOTAL SALES	PERCENTAGE INCREASE 1983 TO 1984
Analytical	$ 20,700	10.0%	66.1%	$ 12,463	8.1%	94.3%	$ 6,413	6.5%	10.2%
Engineering	37,218	17.9	1.4	36,713	23.7	279.2	9,681	9.8	10.7
Decontamination and Mitigation	56,906	27.4	21.8	46,714	30.2	36.3	34,279	34.8	158.3
Transportation, Treatment and Disposal	92,783	44.7	57.9	58,780	38.0	22.2	48,118	48.9	24.9
Total	$207,607	100.0%	34.2%	$154,670	100.0%	57.0%	$98,491	100.0%	48.4%

Source: IT 1986 Annual Report; fiscal year ended March 31.
241

Exhibit 7   IT Corporation (B): Organizational Chart International Technology Corporation (June 1986)

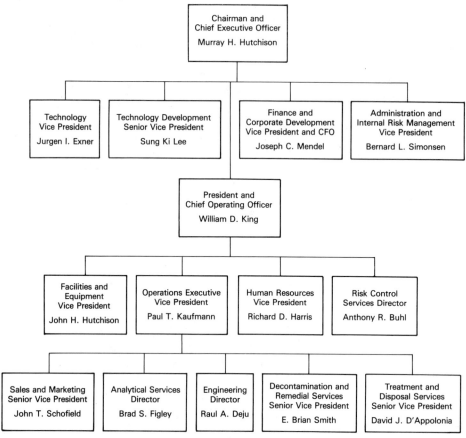

Source: IT Corporation.

Exhibit 8 IT Corporation (B): Organizational Chart International Technology Corporation (December 1986)

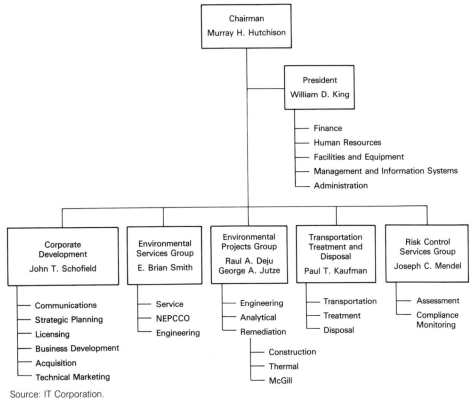

Source: IT Corporation.

NOTES

1. E.F. Hutton Conference on Hazardous Waste Management, New York, October 22, 1986.
2. Ibid.
3. Ibid.
4. As of October 1986, pretreatment standards had not yet been prescribed.
5. Analysts estimated that these two departments had hazardous waste cleanup needs in excess of $10 billion.
6. Excerpted from U.S. Congressional Budget Office, *Hazardous Waste Management: Recent Changes and Policy Alternatives*, May 1985.
7. Joint and several liability, as it applies to hazardous waste treatment and disposal, means that where liability for damage exists, *all* liable parties jointly, *several* of the responsible parties in aggregate, or even *one* potentially responsible party may be held fully accountable for all resulting damages at any treatment or disposal site.
8. IT 1986 Annual Report.
9. Ibid.

Chapter Three

Natural Monopolies

Chapter Three consists of cases on regulation in the electric and gas utility sector, for which "natural monopoly" was the historical rationale. The three case situations, set in 1959, 1975, and 1980, document the procedural problems that eventually developed with rate-base, rate-of-return regulation. Here you will see industries still fully regulated, but where the regulation is obviously not working.

Utility regulation dates from the late nineteenth century, when power generation and distribution exhibited economies of scale that seemed to warrant local monopoly franchises. To avoid abuse of monopoly power, not to mention the corruption of local politics, regulation by independent commission was developed in the more "progressive" states. Nearly half a century later, interstate transmission of natural gas, which had similar characteristics, was brought under the control of the Federal Power Commission by the Natural Gas Act of 1938.

The case on El Paso Natural Gas introduces the principles of cost-based, utility rate regulation. Howard Boyd, who would eventually steer the company through the first energy crisis and into the second, is faced with a decision to appeal a partially adverse rate order by the FPC. The company, intent on expanding its gas exploration and development activities, has sought a higher than usual rate of return by retaining certain tax benefits intended for oil and gas producers.

In order to address the specific technical issues, you must first explore the definitional problems and economic implications of the rate base, the cost of operations, and the intensely political rate of return. In the end, you must decide if the "just and reasonable" rate is financially viable for El Paso's strategic plans.

After almost two more decades, at the very time that Boston Edison experienced an earnings and political crisis, Alfred Kahn took over as chairman of the New York Public Service Commission and introduced a new rate structure (the other side of utility rate making) based on the theory of marginal cost pricing. The case discussing this event draws the connection between regulation and economics, but still in a political environment. To implement his innovation, Kahn must manage an array of stakeholders to win the necessary support.

The case on Commonwealth Edison brings the story of utility rate regulation full circle, to the breakdown of the regulatory contract. Under the leadership of James O'Connor, this huge Chicago utility must decide how to respond to an increasingly adverse regulatory environment. Among the issues at hand are (1) a rate increase that provides sufficient cash flow to cover financial obligations, (2) appropriate accounting treatment of inflation and construction work in progress, and (3) whether or not to delay or cancel construction of three nuclear power plants, in the face of lagging demand.

James O'Connor, a savvy native of Chicago's Southside, must put together a corporate strategy that adequately addresses key changes in both the political and market environment. Among the dilemmas posed by this case is a potential conflict in corporate goals: Commonwealth Edison's ability to serve the best interests of ratepayers and shareholders alike.

El Paso Natural Gas Company
and the FPC

In October 1959, it seemed to Howard Boyd that the Federal Power Commission was frequently incapable of responding to private initiative with creativity or foresight. In August, after five years of delay and deliberation, the Commission had issued its decision on an unusual rate increase for which the El Paso Natural Gas Company had filed in October of 1954. Although El Paso and several intervenors had petitioned for a rehearing, the FPC had just denied it.

Mr. Boyd was all too familiar with the case (referred to as FPC Docket No. G-4769). He had joined El Paso as assistant general counsel just two years before the company had first filed for the rate increase. Boyd had come to the company from Washington D.C., where he had spent five years in the Justice Department and thirteen years with the law firm of Hogan & Hartson. In his first contact with El Paso, Boyd had provided legal counsel for an eminent domain problem that El Paso was having with the secretary of interior. His abilities in that case attracted the attention of Paul Kayser, El Paso's founder. The two shared a dynamic vision of the future of the gas industry, and as Kayser's protege, Boyd had risen swiftly to executive vice president by the time the FPC rendered its decision on G-4769.

The logic of El Paso's request for a rate increase seemed eminently clear to both Kayser and Boyd. El Paso was not questioning the rate of return that the FPC allowed on its pipeline operations. That return was relatively standard, based on the FPC's determination of El Paso's cost of service for delivering natural gas to its customers. Recently, however, El Paso had begun to diversify into the exploration and production of natural gas—a far more risky enterprise than its regular transmission business. Faced with rapidly growing markets for a depleting resource, El Paso's management had determined that it was necessary to expand their own, secure source of supply. In Docket No. G-4769, the company had asked the FPC to grant a separate and higher rate of return on its investments in gas exploration and production. El Paso had asked for the same 6% that the Commission had granted for its transmission business plus the benefits allowed to other oil and gas producers under the Internal Revenue

---

This case was prepared by Professor Richard H.K. Vietor as the basis for class discussion rather than to illustrate either the effective or ineffective handling of an administrative situation.

Service provisions for percentage depletion allowance and intangible drilling expenses.

The Commission, however, had granted only the tax benefits, in lieu of return, which amounted to little more than 8%.[1] To El Paso's management, it appeared as though the Commission had accepted the taxation principle, but erroneously applied it.[2] The FPC had granted only an incomplete package, which under the circumstances was inadequate. At stake was El Paso's plan to commit $200 million to $300 million to exploration and development. For El Paso Natural, with assets of $614 million, that plan amounted to a major diversification and expansion from pipelining into production. But such a move would scarcely be worthwhile if the FPC refused to allow more than 8% return on such an investment. Mr. Boyd pondered the wisdom of appealing the FPC's decision to the Circuit Court of Appeals. He thought it likely that the court would agree with El Paso's position and overturn the Commission's ruling.

THE GAS INDUSTRY

The long-distance transmission and utilization of natural gas first became a business during the 1920s. After World War II, it enjoyed very rapid growth, evolving into a truly national energy industry. In 1946, 3.9 trillion cubic feet (Tcf) of gas were used in the United States, accounting for 13% of total national energy consumption. By 1959, those figures had risen to 11.8 Tcf and 23.5% respectively.[3] On a national basis, the supply of natural gas appeared to be more than ample for the near future. During the 1950s, proved reserves of gas grew at an annual rate of 3.9%, amounting to 261 Tcf by 1959. This made for a reserve to production ratio of 22.5:1, which in common parlance meant enough gas to last for twenty-two years at current consumption rates.

Prior to the mid-1950s, the industry's three sectors—production, transmission, and distribution—had remained distinctive and separate from each other commercially. Most natural gas was produced by oil companies incidental to the exploration and production of petroleum. Gas discovered in concurrence with petroleum was called "residue" or "associated" gas. Where no oil was present, the gas was referred to as "dry" or "non-associated." In either situation, its utilization was made possible by independent gas pipeline companies, which bought the gas in the field after it had been treated to remove impurities and transmitted it through trunk pipelines to industrial users and utility distributors. During the 1950s, the proportion of associated gas in the total natural gas commerce declined steadily.

The pipeline companies had grown very quickly as new technologies made long-distance, interstate delivery of gas competitive with other energy fuels. Large urban markets were ideal for this fuel since the high concentration of commercial and residential users could provide the high load factors necessary to amortize the costly pipelines. Between 1946 and 1959, the assets of the more than 100 pipeline companies grew from $2.105 billion to $11.422 billion for an annual average growth rate of 13.9%. Operating revenues grew at 15.6% percent per year, from $615 million in 1946 to over $4 billion in 1959. Aggregate net income more than doubled to $292 million, providing an average rate of return on common equity of 11.4% in 1959.[4] Most of this immense growth was accomplished by the eight largest firms, which together moved 93% of the gas going into interstate shipments. In this rapid growth period, the average field (or "wellhead") price in natural gas doubled, from $.065 per thousand cubic feet (Mcf) to $.13 Mcf 1959.

REGULATION

By 1959, all three sectors of the natural gas business had come under public regulation. Distributors were regulated by state utility or public service commissions. Interstate pipelines were regulated by the Federal Power Commission under the authority of the Natural Gas Act of 1938. And just recently, the Supreme Court, in *Phillips Petroleum Co. v. Wisconsin* (1954), had ordered the FPC to take regulatory control of the field price of natural gas being sold by independent producers in the interstate market. Although it had not wanted that responsibility, the FPC nonetheless struggled to implement some method of producer price regulation that was logical, legal, and practical. First, it tried setting a "fair field price," based on the weighted average of contract prices already negotiated between producers and pipelines within each gas field. However, in 1955, the Court overturned that method in *City of Detroit v. the FPC*. Since then, the Commission had tried to set prices on a case-by-case basis according to production costs. By 1959, a consensus had emerged among all concerned that this method was a total failure.

The Federal Power Commission was composed of five persons, appointed by the president for staggered terms of five years, assisted by a staff of 866 with an operating budget of $7.2 million. Its authority over interstate pipelines was comprehensive. First, it was responsible for certifying all construction, acquisitions, extensions, and abandonments by pipeline companies doing business in interstate commerce. Second, the Commission dictated accounting standards and requirements for financial reporting. Third, and most important, the FPC determined rates by an exceedingly complex method that penetrated every facet of a firm's activity: capitalization, investment, purchase and sales contracts, operating expenses, depreciation, and taxation. The regulatory process itself was one of Commission adjudication among contending parties, including the petitioner, its customers, competitors, the FPC's own staff, and other interested parties such as state regulatory commissions.

The Natural Gas Act charged the FPC with setting rates for natural gas in interstate commerce that were "just and reasonable." To do so, the Act authorized the FPC to ascertain the cost of service and "the actual legitimate cost of the property of every natural-gas company. . . ."[5] By 1959, a large body of Commission and court precedent had translated this charge into a procedure for cost of service rate regulation based on three concepts: cost of operations, rate base, and rate of return.

Cost of Operations   In approving or fixing a rate for the sale of natural gas by an interstate pipeline company, the Commission first needed to calculate the firm's cost of operation. That had three components: total operating expenses, taxes (including federal income taxes), and depreciation charges. Obviously, this determination involved dozens of controversial judgments as to the appropriateness and allocation of indirect costs.

Rate Base   The second calculation necessary to this process was the valuation of the regulated firm's properties—the rate base—and this step was the most technically complex of the Commission's determinations. Since market forces were absent, value had to be assigned by the FPC to the various forms of property, both tangible and intangible. To do so, the Commission used various criteria, but with the focus on original costs as indicated in the company's books. Whether or not a particular property item was judged "productive" with respect to the rates at issue was invariably a major bone of contention. For a regulated firm like a gas transmission company, this figure was critical, for it was the base against which the regulatory authority applied a percentage of allowed profit.

Rate of Return   The rate of return was the allowed percentage of earnings on the rate base deemed sufficient to cover debt service, dividend obligations on preferred stock, and a return to common equity. Given any particular rate of return, the return to equity was a function of the regulated firm's capital structure. As Alfred Kahn has put it, determination of this rate "has inevitably reflected a complex mixture of political and economic considerations . . . [a]n acceptable compromise between the interests of investors on the one hand and consumers on the other."[6] During the latter part of the 1950s, the rates of return allowed by the FPC ranged from 5.5% to 6.0%.

Calculation of Rates   The actual calculation of rates or rate increases thus stood on the three legs of cost of operations, rate base, and rate of return. The Commission determined the overall revenue requirement for the pipeline company by multiplying the desired rate of return and the rate base and then adding the product to the cost of operations. That sum was divided by the estimated volume of gas to be delivered during the relevant rate period, yielding the average price per unit of gas. The Commission's final, contentious chore was the allocation of those rates among the different categories of users.

Basic Formula for Cost-based Rate Determination

(Rate Base) × (Rate of Return) + (Cost of Operations) = (Revenue Requirement)
(Revenue Requirement) / Units of Gas Sold = Average Rate to Customers

Simplified Hypothetical Example

($549.6 million) × (0.06) + ($160.7 million) = $193.6 million
($193.6 mil.)/625 Billion Cubic Feet = $.31/Mcf average wholesale rate

THE EL PASO NATURAL GAS COMPANY

The company was founded in 1928 when Paul Kayser, a young Houston lawyer, convinced the mayor of El Paso, Texas, that he could build a pipeline to deliver natural gas of higher quality and lower cost than the manufactured coal-gas the city was presently using. After signing up the city's key industrial plants and the existing residential distributor, Kayser contracted the supply of three gas wells in Jal, New Mexico, 204 miles away in the rich Permian Basin oil field. A sixteen-inch pipeline, financed by White, Weld & Company, was completed in six months over a terrain that was "a hellish mixture of solid rock mountains, deep powdery sand, rattlesnakes, and salt flats."[7] On the night of June 18, 1929, the municipal band played while Mayor R.E. Thomson fired a roman candle, igniting a gas jet into a giant flare which signaled the start of natural gas service and the El Paso Natural Gas Company's business.

The Great Depression slowed down the El Paso company—but not much. Between 1931 and 1934, El Paso's pipelines spread across southeastern New Mexico into Arizona, bringing gas service to Bisbee, Tombstone, and finally Phoenix. At Jal, the company expanded its network of gathering lines and wells under contract, constructed treatment facilities to strip the gas liquids and sulfur out of the "sour" Permian gas, and added a gasoline refinery. World War II vastly expanded the demand for natural gas in the Southwest, and by 1943, the El Paso company was supplying fuel for military installations, steel mills, copper smelters, and sixty-two communities.

The truly giant step, however, was still to come. The phenomenal growth of Southern California had far outstripped locally available energy supplies. Paul Kayser had spotted this market's potential before the war ended and had discussed it with Frank Wade, the president of Southern California Gas Company. Wade had asked Kayser for 300 million cubic feet per day (MMcf/d), more than twice El Paso's total daily sales. In August 1945, Paul Kayser flew to Washington to file an application with the FPC to construct a twenty-six-inch pipeline to California. The Commission granted the certificate.[8]

By 1954, the El Paso Natural Gas Company was one of the nation's largest gas pipeline companies, serving more than 10% of the interstate market. Thanks to the Korean War and continuing westward migration, the growth of energy demand in Southern California continued its upward spiral. As Exhibit 1 indicates, the El Paso company grew very rapidly. Between 1945 and 1959, gas deliveries had increased by 33% a year. Gross assets had grown at an annual rate of 38%, operating revenues at 36%, and net income at 21%. By 1959, its pipeline network spanned more than 6,000 miles, and the treatment plants were producing butane, propane, and natural gasoline amounting to one million gallons daily. In 1955, the company had organized a subsidiary, El Paso Natural Gas Products Company, to diversify into petroleum refining, petrochemicals, and retail gasoline marketing under the "Red Flame" brand.

Because of this explosive growth, and because the gas transmission business was a regulated utility of relatively low risk, El Paso's capitalization was rather highly leveraged, even for a pipeline company. Given slightly higher interest rates, shorter maturities, and assurances regarding adequacy of gas supply, insurance companies had been willing to allow capitalization ratios in the neighborhood of 75% debt and 25% equity (electric utilities usually had 40% equity). El Paso had financed most of its growth by mortgage bonds with sinking fund provisions, sinking fund debentures, and preferred stock, leaving only 18.6% for common equity. The El Paso management argued that higher leveraging helped its customers, since the larger interest charges reduced income taxes that would otherwise have been recovered as part of cost of operations, and because the cost of equity was recognized by the FPC in determining the rate of return. On the other hand, it felt that the higher risk justified a somewhat higher rate of return.[9]

Aside from these heavy debt requirements, El Paso's rapid expansion created intense pressure to develop adequate and assured supplies of natural gas. In its early years, El Paso had relied primarily on dry gas from the giant Permian Basin field. But as uncommitted supplies began to dwindle, El Paso increasingly turned to developing residue gas. The development of residue gas was hailed as a great accomplishment in conservation, since most of it had previously been "flared" (burned off as an effluent). El Paso had come to rely on such residue gas for nearly two-thirds of its supply. By 1953, its only other source was the San Juan field in northwest New Mexico which El Paso had begun developing for its huge commitments in California.

Reliance on too much residue gas created several problems, the principal one being that its availability was governed entirely by the market demand for petroleum. Thus, El Paso incurred an undesirable inflexibility of being unable to increase or decrease its liftings of residue gas according to its own load requirements. Moreover, oil production in each field was controlled by the Texas Railroad Commission (and similar agencies in other states) by "prorationing," a system of matching supply with demand. Due to market penetration by oil imports from the Middle East in the mid-1950s, the Railroad Commission was sharply reducing allowable monthly oil production in order to bolster domestic prices. Noting El Paso's dependency on residue gas, the FPC had urged the company in 1953 to do something to improve the situation.

At the time, there were only two feasible ways for El Paso to expand its supply of dry gas: either sign long-term purchase agreements with producers (primarily major oil companies), or undertake to explore and develop its own reserves. To a large extent, the former option would be necessary anyway, since the oil companies controlled immense oil and gas properties and because El Paso's market obligations far exceeded any prospect for eventual self-sufficiency.

But, by developing some of its own supply, El Paso could benefit in several ways. First, its own reserves would be perfectly secure. Second, such reserves might eventually be cheaper than buying, giving El Paso an advantage over other pipeline companies competing for new markets. And third, given the *Phillips* decision, Paul Kayser and Howard Boyd worried about a time when oil companies might avoid the newly regulated, interstate market in pursuit of possibly higher prices in the unregulated intrastate market (gas produced and sold within the same state). Underlying all these considerations was Paul Kayser's personal conviction that gas was a depleting resource that would eventually run out. As early as 1952, Kayser foretold that Boyd would live to see natural gas in serious short supply. That precept became deeply rooted in the psyches of Boyd and most of El Paso's senior managers more than a decade before natural gas *surpluses* even stopped growing.[10]

To meet these needs, El Paso embarked on a program of exploration, lease acquisition, and production development in the early 1950s. It acquired prospective gas acreage in Texas, New Mexico, Colorado, Wyoming, and Arizona. In 1954, it added more property in Oregon, Nevada, and offshore Louisiana. By the end of that year, El Paso held gas rights on nearly two million acres, had brought in one major wildcat discovery in Wyoming, and was laying plans to drill three more wells.[11] Although this program would cost millions over the next decade, Howard Boyd thought it certainly worthwhile if the Federal Power Commission would allow a reasonable return that would justify the higher risks involved. This is why El Paso had applied for a separate and higher rate of return on its exploration and production properties, and why Mr. Boyd now felt compelled to appeal the Commission's recent ruling.

BRIEF FOR EL PASO

Although Docket No. G-4769 commenced in 1954 when El Paso filed for a rate increase of $18 million, the Commission did not open proceedings until 1957, at which time El Paso submitted its brief stating its goals and arguments. Although technically complex, its request had a clear, single purpose. El Paso wanted to receive a higher-than-normal rate of return on that portion of its investments committed to exploration and production. El Paso requested the normal, 6% rate of return on its overall rate base ($549,563,775 for the base year of 1955), but on that portion of assets committed to "well-mouth properties," which amounted to $74,436,273, El Paso claimed that a greater incentive was needed. Paul Kayser explained his views in this regard:

> The incentive to go into the pipeline business is a six percent return . . . [you] have got to have an incentive to the producer to keep him in business . . . and all I am asking for is that the El Paso Company, as a pipeline company, be accorded the same treatment in respect to their production that the producer is accorded, and be given the same incentive.[12]

Since the Commission had yet to figure out how to fix a rate of return for gas producers, El Paso proposed that it be allowed the regular 6% that pipeline activities were accorded, and be permitted to retain the special tax benefits that oil and gas producers were allowed.

Two such tax benefits were involved: the percentage depletion allowance and the right to expense "intangible" drilling costs. In the Revenue Act of 1926, Congress had authorized a tax deduction—the percentage depletion allowance—of 27.5% of gross income (up to a maximum of 50% net income) from oil and gas producing properties. Congress had justified the special deduction on the grounds that oil and gas were wasting assets, and exploration and development were highly risky businesses. The Supreme Court had recently upheld the depletion allowance. The other special tax benefit provided by the Internal Revenue Code allowed two methods for treating intangible drilling costs. Intangible drilling costs "are those costs which are incurred in connection with the drilling of oil or gas wells which will have no salvage value and consist generally of labor, fuel, supplies, surveys, and other like costs . . ."[13] An operator could either amortize such costs in the normal fashion over the life of the well, or could expense them altogether in the year in which they were incurred. El Paso had chosen the latter method.

Under the normal rate-setting procedure, these special tax savings would be included in the FPC's computation of El Paso's cost of operations. As such, those special benefits would be passed through to the ratepayer and El Paso would not itself gain from the incentive as Congress had intended. To get around this problem, El Paso suggested an innovative procedure for computing its cost of operations. El Paso proposed that the Commission include the federal income taxes the company would have paid were it not for the special tax allowances provided by the IRS for depletion and expensing intangible drilling costs. In this way, the benefits of those two allowances would accrue to El Paso the taxpayer, rather than merely being passed through as a savings for its customers. This incentive, if added to the nominal 6% rate of return on its well-mouth properties, would yield El Paso a return more in line with that of other oil and gas producers.

El Paso's management cited several precedents in support of this position. In its recent case with Panhandle Eastern, the FPC had granted the "fair field price" precisely because of the problem raised by pass-through of tax benefits. To quote the Commission:

> Finally, under the rate-base approach, allowances for taxes on the production property are made in accordance with the actual payments made, thus transferring to the ratepayer all the savings of federal income taxes permitted by statute to be enjoyed by gas producers through the allowances made for depletion and intangible well-drilling expenses. . . . To follow this course would, as we see it, clearly contravene the Congressional policy and intent.[14]

However, in *City of Detroit v. FPC*, the Supreme Court had overturned the Commission's decision to adopt fair field pricing in that case, so El Paso had to go with the rate-base method of determining its return on gas production investments.

Taken together, El Paso's deductions from the depletion allowance and expensing of intangible drilling costs amounted to $12,524,384 for 1955. At the corporate income tax rate of 52%, this gave El Paso a tax savings of $6,410,760. If El Paso could retain this amount, together with a 6% rate of return on its well-mouth investment of $74 million, it felt that the "incentive" to continue exploration and production activities (a return of 14.6%) would be sufficient. El Paso concluded its brief as follows:

> El Paso does not seek to retain the tax benefits for selfish purposes, and the Commission is fully aware of the fact that El Paso is diligently engaged in its efforts to find and develop additional gas reserves for its customers. . . . Even the California PUC [the California Public Utilities Commission, an intervenor that opposed El Paso's rate requests] . . . did not go to the extreme of claiming that El Paso would not utilize every dollar of such tax benefits in the exploration, development, and production of natural gas. . . .[15]

BRIEF FOR THE FPC STAFF

Except for some minor differences regarding miscellaneous items, the staff of the Federal Power Commission accepted El Paso's innovative rate brief. The staff noted that El Paso's actual tax liability for 1955 was $5,841,490, after giving effect to the statutory deductions for percentage depletion and intangible drilling expenses amounting to $12,328,384. However, "in accordance with our under-standing of the Commission's views," the staff agreed that the cost of operations be calculated by including an allowance for federal income taxes of $18,169,874.[16]

THE INTERVENORS

Intervening in the proceedings of Docket No. G-4769 were the New Mexico Public Service Commission, the California Public Utilities Commission, Nevada Natural Gas Pipe Line Company, Pacific Gas and Electric Company (PG&E), Southern California Gas Company, Southern Counties Gas Company of California, Southern Union Gas Company, San Diego Gas and Electric Company, the city of Los Angeles, and the attorney general of California. Most of these were El Paso's customers, either opposing the proposed rate increase or concerned with the FPC's allocation of those increases. The California PUC objected in principle to El Paso's proposed retention of special tax benefits, and was backed by the attorney general of California. Edmund (Pat) Brown, then California's attorney general, thought that fighting a rate increase and possibly getting a big refund from El Paso "would be a great plus in my campaign."[17] He was antici-pating a run for the governorship. While all these intervenors filed briefs and participated in the rate hearings, the California PUC and Pacific Gas and Electric presented the broadest and most comprehensive challenges.

BRIEF FOR CALIFORNIA

The California PUC vigorously opposed the tax treatment for which El Paso was seeking approval. It saw El Paso's proposal as a guise for attaining a higher effective rate of return by loading up the cost of service with nonexistent federal income taxes. The PUC contended that all of the parties involved in the case, including itself, had acquiesced in a 6% rate of return on the entire investment of El Paso, including the well-mouth properties. Accordingly, it was only fair that all tax savings be given effect in arriving at the actual cost of service. Moreover, witnesses for the PUC asserted that expensing intangible drilling costs resulted in a tax "savings," rather than a deferral as El Paso claimed. Accordingly, the PUC computed El Paso's income tax obligations as a minus amount of nearly $8 million for the purpose of determining cost of service.

BRIEF FOR PACIFIC GAS AND ELECTRIC

PG&E was California's largest investor-owned utility and among the largest in the country. Its gas purchases constituted 44% of El Paso's sales in 1955, and the proposed rate increase would cost PG&E an additional $8 million. In its tone, at least, the brief of PG&E was more judicious than that of the California PUC. Nevertheless, it provided carefully constructed criticism of El Paso's procedural logic.

PG&E noted that average field prices for natural gas were about $.095/ Mcf in the Permian Basin and $.11/Mcf in the San Juan Basin. By going to a cost method for determining the contribution of its own gas production to its overall cost of service, El Paso stood to gain considerably, according to PG&E:

> The cost of service studies introduced by El Paso and the staff at the hearing in this proceeding both show a cost for El Paso's own production in the Permian Basin of 70.6 cents per Mcf and for El Paso's own San Juan Basin production of 21.2 cents per Mcf.
> With recorded costs of production vastly in excess of the prices at which other producers sell their gas in these areas, El Paso is faced with the dilemma that it is either a very high cost producer or has included costs which are not properly related to the volumes of its production.[18]

From this, PG&E concluded that El Paso had included "a substantial portion of exploration and development costs" and "federal income tax not paid, but claimed . . . ." in its cost of service.[19] PG&E urged the Commission to scrutinize most carefully these unusual assignments of costs.

PG&E also cited two previous cases in which the FPC had indicated that tax treatment such as El Paso was now seeking might be allowed (including the Panhandle Eastern case which El Paso itself had cited). "However," argued PG&E, "since the Commission in each of those opinions adopted the field price method, its dicta with respect to income taxes did not affect the result. . . ." Thus, PG&E was suggesting that El Paso was trying to have its cake (a cost-based return on its production) and eat it too (retention of the tax benefits which the Commission had favored with fair field pricing).[20] Along this same line, the PG&E also cited the Court's dictum in the recently decided *Detroit* case:

> [I]f the Commission gives the companies their option, the traditional rate-base system would naturally be chosen whenever costs of production exceeded the field price. In that event, no risks of exploration, development, or production would fall upon the companies, and it would appear that a small margin of profit should suffice to encourage such activities. It is doubtful that the same margin of profit would be required as might be received by producers who bear their own risks.[21]

Concluding its argument against El Paso's position, Pacific Gas & Electric offered the following comment:

> El Paso has carried on what is probably the most intensive exploration and development program in its entire history during a period when it was asking the Commission to allow it no more than the field price—even though the field price was not high enough to cover costs on the basis of disregarding the benefits of the intangible cost deduction and percentage depletion. The need for additional revenue equivalent in amount to these two tax benefits has not been shown.[22]

EL PASO'S REPLY

In its reply brief, El Paso addressed not only the two central issues—its rate-base method for determining production costs and its tax treatment—but also a dozen or so other significant claims made by one or another of the intervenors. With regard to PG&E's criticisms, El Paso argued that any comparison of costs to field prices was irrelevant since the Court had rejected regulation by "fair field price" in *City of Detroit v. FPC* and, at any rate, the field prices used were ridiculously low.[23] On the appropriateness and necessity of its retaining the two tax benefits, El Paso replied as follows:

> All of the companies in the oil and gas industry account for intangible drilling costs in the same manner as El Paso, i.e. they expense such charges for income tax purposes and capitalize them on their books. Such practice has been followed for approximately forty years. . . . El Paso is only seeking in this case, in respect to intangible well drilling costs, the same treatment accorded those with whom it must compete in its exploration for and development of natural gas reserves to meet its market requirements.[24]

El Paso devoted its sharpest rebuttal to the California PUC, editorializing on the philosophy and regulatory theory motivating that agency:

> Those who purport to represent the consumers served from the El Paso system, and particularly the consumers in California, where the future gas requirements

are greatest, should appreciate the aid granted by Congress, instead of proposing to deprive gas producers of such tax benefits and also seeking to interfere with the exploration for, and the production of, natural gas. . . .

The theories of the California PUC staff . . . are of no advantage whatever to the California gas consumers. . . . What the California PUC staff is actually proposing is a vicious and inescapable escalation spiral in rates.[25]

FEDERAL POWER COMMISSION, OPINION NO. 326

In August 1959, the FPC had issued its opinion on Docket No. G-4769. The Commission approved El Paso's use of a rate-base method for computing the cost of its own gas for inclusion in the overall cost of service. It had also agreed that the tax benefits of percentage depletion and intangible drilling expenses should accrue to El Paso. However, the Commission concluded that the additional return, resulting from El Paso's retention of the two tax benefits amounting to $6,410,790, by itself represented a rate of return on well-mouth properties of 8.61% that was sufficient. Following are excerpts from Opinion No. 326 that express the Commission's rationale:

Plainly the intention of Congress was to grant the advantage of percentage of income depletion to the producers. . . . Congress could not have meant that the benefits be automatically taken from the producers and passed along to the consumers in the case of those companies in the gas industry which happened to be subject to regulation. . . .

$6,410,760 is in effect an additional return to El Paso resulting from the two tax incentives. . . . When it is applied to that portion of El Paso's rate base represented by the well-mouth properties in the amount of $74,436,273, we find that it results in a rate return of 8.61 percent. Using a 6 percent rate of return on its other property, El Paso would earn an overall rate of return of 6.35 percent on its entire rate base of $549,563,775.

The record supports a finding that 6 percent is a fair overall rate of return for El Paso . . . so that we have no difficulty finding that its return will be adequate and its financial integrity maintained. On the other hand, it is not too great because the excess over 6 percent represents an initiative by the law.[26]

The Commission summarized its cost of service computation as follows, supporting data for which appears in Exhibit 2:

Total operating expense	$105,737,546
Depreciation and amortization	20,590,774
Depletion	1,942,773
Federal income taxes	6,980,373
Provision for deferred taxes	5,728,280
Return at 6% on properties other than well-mouth	28,507,650
Return on well-mouth properties through tax incentives relating to intangibles and percentage of income depletion	6,410,760
Revenues from extracted products	(12,067,079)
Other gas revenues	(4,431,166)
El Paso's cost of service for test year 1955	$160,693,628

DISSENT OF COMMISSIONER HUSSEY

Only one commissioner dissented from the majority's opinion, registering the following complaint:

> El Paso's incentive for investment of funds in exploration for and development of natural gas reserves is provided principally from its being permitted to charge to expense, for tax purposes, intangible drilling costs. . . . The majority opinion would grant El Paso a return on producing properties measured by, or roughly equivalent to, the tax savings. . . . No one goes into business merely to accomplish a tax savings . . . the tax incentives designed to compensate for this inordinate risk in the gas producing business are intended as additional return, and the investor expects to obtain a normal return on his investment in addition to the compensation for the inordinate risk of losing his capital.[27]

PETITION FOR REHEARING

Various intervenors had promptly petitioned the FPC to reconsider its decision to let El Paso retain the tax benefits by including "phantom taxes" in its cost of service. The Commission denied their petition. El Paso also sought a reconsideration, again asking for "an allowance of the tax benefits producing an 8.61 percent return on well-mouth properties in addition to the 6 percent return on well-mouth properties. . . ." The Commission likewise rejected this claim, as follows:

> There was no showing in the record that financially El Paso needed a return of 14.61 percent on well-mouth properties, and such a return, unless supported, would impose a wholly unjustified burden on the distributing companies and the consumers.[28]

BEYOND THE COMMISSION

With the Commission's denial for rehearing, the ball was again back in El Paso's court. The company could settle for the incremental benefits the commission had granted, or take its case to the Circuit Court of Appeals. From Howard Boyd's perspective, there were several considerations involved besides the likelihood of a favorable court decision. El Paso sorely needed its reserves of dry gas, and yet, because of the *Phillips* decision of 1954, it remained to be seen how regulation would affect independent oil and gas producers—El Paso's only other source of gas besides itself. To some extent, El Paso's management felt compelled to go ahead with some gas development, regardless of the FPC's decision, just to supply itself and sustain its pipeline business. In this light, the Commission's approval of an 8.61% return on well-mouth properties was better than the usual 6%. Also given the prescience of Kayser and Boyd regarding the inevitable depletion of natural gas, expenditures on leases and exploration appeared eminently sound over the long run.

On the other hand, El Paso was planning a major diversification into retail marketing of petroleum products as well as into exploration and production. To some extent, the former depended on the latter. Could El Paso justify the expenditure of as much as $300 million on further exploration and development of gas reserves for a return of 8.61%? Could it justify the risks involved to its prospective investors? El Paso's responsibility to both its investors and customers seemed to lie with assuring itself of a secure and adequate gas supply. It seemed completely unreasonable that the major oil companies and other independent gas producers should benefit from the special tax incentives in addition to their normal and quite healthy earnings—but not El Paso.

Among gas transmission companies, El Paso had always stayed out front in its growth and initiative. Following Kayser's initiatives, Howard Boyd intended that it would continue doing so. But it seemed like governmental policies, from regulatory, judicial, and possibly other sources, were becoming more significant considerations in formulating and implementing corporate strategy. No doubt this would not be the last time El Paso faced this problem.

Exhibit 1 El Paso Natural Gas Company and the FPC: El Paso Natural Gas Company: Statistics on Growth

	1930	1940	1945	1950	1954	1955	1957	1959
Financial Statistics								
Income Account								
Total Operating Revenues	$1,197,795	$ 6,801,239	$ 8,934,808	$ 41,302,457	$143,842,445	$179,451,092	$ 301,090,537	$ 452,050,189
Net Income before Income Taxes	239,260	3,142,951	3,286,111	8,655,956	15,457,411	28,291,465	41,048,323	49,221,391
Income Taxes	6,760	782,413	1,105,248	2,333,859	3,140,001	8,202,882	6,015,524	12,292,861
Net Income after Income Taxes	282,500	2,360,538	2,180,863	6,322,097	12,317,410	18,858,853	34,506,238	36,928,530
Preferred Dividend Requirement	42,771	103,579	103,579	851,984	3,151,887	3,858,271	6,337,621	8,645,526
Net Available in Common Stock	239,729	2,256,959	2,077,284	5,470,113	9,177,847	15,000,582	28,168,617	28,283,004
Balance Sheet— At December 31								
Gross Investment in System Facilities	5,342,348	22,329,536	33,025,042	241,639,200	614,787,953	663,222,247	1,304,619,479	1,577,583,823
Depreciation and Depletion Reserves	240,725	3,661,827	9,563,375	23,701,328	75,576,261	100,889,903	165,970,789	261,860,981
Net Plant	5,101,623	18,667,709	23,461,667	217,937,872	539,211,692	562,332,344	1,138,648,690	1,315,722,842

Capitalization								
Long-Term Debt, Excluding Current Maturities	4,632,000	10,825,000	12,350,000	184,553,000	365,138,440	765,966,470	863,018,236	
Preferred Stock	963,000	1,479,700	1,479,700	22,286,600	N.A.	76,454,400	141,816,400	138,602,400
Common Stock and Surplus	1,219,743	9,496,033	11,483,178	30,862,257	N.A.	126,452,081	225,292,442	229,999,963
Operating Statistics								
Gas Sold in MCF	5,406,672	31,565,528	44,167,792	264,219,229	645,355,545	710,797,930	1,005,823,792	1,158,441,484
Main Line Peak Day Sales in MCF	18,495	112,006	152,410	978,059	2,038,179	2,055,682	3,016,651	3,622,066
Miles of Main and Branch Transmission Pipe Lines	217	1,503	1,957	4,445	6,374	6,419	9,309	9,974
Number of Compressor Stations	0	7	10	32	67	67	98	110
Treating Plant Capacity (MCF per Day)	20,000	125,000	135,500	703,100	1,341,750	1,344,280	2,171,357	2,638,944
Number of Regular Operating Employees	45	413	624	1,499	3,479	3,857	6,637	7,366

Source: El Paso Natural Gas Company, *Annual Reports*, 1954, 1959.

52

Exhibit 2 El Paso Natural Gas Company and the FPC: FPC Docket No. G-4769: El Paso Natural Gas Company's Cost of Produced and Purchased Gas

COMMODITY		COMMODITY	
Purchased gas	$61,919,013	Administrative and general	
Other gas supply expenses	103,950	expenses	$ 5,505,066
Company used gas	(5,586,481)	Depreciation and amortization	8,319,510
Gas to and from storage	(138,693)	Depletion	1,942,773
Exchange gas	6,051	Taxes:	
Gas well operation and		Other than federal income	1,848,090
maintenance	177,114	Federal income (inc.	
Gas well royalties	4,493,640	deferred)	3,033,530
		Return at 6% for production	
		and gathering (non-	
		well-mouth)	10,451,692
Other production and gathering		Additional return from depletion	
expenses	11,270,905	intangibles	6,410,760
Products extraction expenses	7,316,560	Other gas revenues—credit	(14,411,499)
Exploration and development	4,861,912	Total Cost of Production	$107,523,953
Total Above	$84,424,031		

Source: FPC, Opinion No. 326, August 10, 1959, p. 286.

Exhibit 3 El Paso Natural Gas Company and the FPC: Natural Gas Production Data: El Paso Natural Gas Co., 1953–1959

YEAR	GAS PRODUCED (Bcf)	GAS PURCHASED (Bcf)	GAS RESERVES IN PRODUCING LANDS (Tcf)	CONTRACTS (Tcf)	EXP. & DEV. EXPENSE (IN MILLIONS)
1953	55.6	553	3.1	2.4	$2.010
1954	79.3	617	3.4	15.2	3.163
1955	82.5	682	4.0	18.9	4.860
1956	100.9	755	6.0	22.3	6.595
1957	147.0	837	6.9	21.7	6.809
1958	150.3	813	8.0	23.1	8.055
1959	163.5	933	8.0	21.0	7.36

Source: FPC, *Statistics of Natural Gas Companies*, 1953–1959.

Exhibit 4 El Paso Natural Gas Company and the FPC
El Paso Natural Gas Co.: Sources of Gas

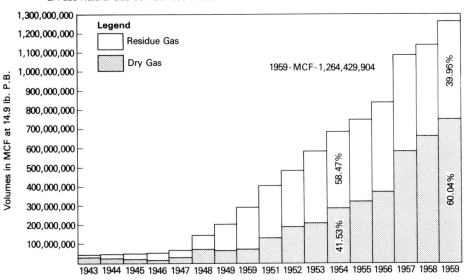

Exhibit 5 El Paso Natural Gas Company and the FPC
El Paso Natural Gas Co.: Sales in MCF, Revenues and Net Income

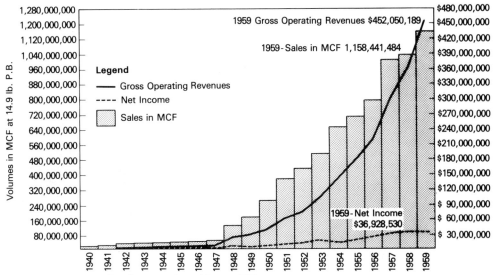

Source: El Paso Natural Gas Company, *Annual Report*, 1959.

Exhibit 6 Composite Natural Gas Operating Expenses, 1949–59

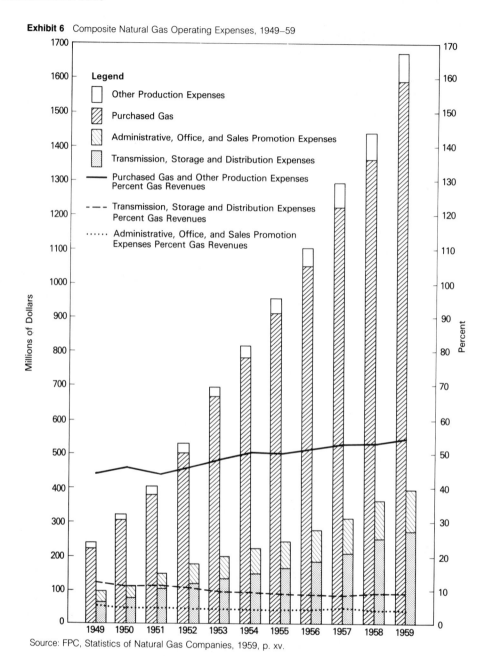

Source: FPC, Statistics of Natural Gas Companies, 1959, p. xv.

Exhibit 7 Balance Sheet Relationships—All Interstate Natural Gas Pipeline Companies, 1950–59

RELATIONSHIP	1959	1958	1957	1956	1955	1954	1950
Gross gas utility plant per dollar of gas operating revenues	2.90	2.97	3.02	2.97	3.00	3.24	3.93
Net gas utility plant per dollar of gas operating revenues	2.26	2.34	2.41	2.36	2.41	2.64	3.23
Current assets times current liabilities	1.26	1.21	1.22	1.10	1.20	1.58	1.21
Percent of total capitalization and surplus							
Common stock	21.1%	19.8%	19.8%	21.0%	21.3%	20.8%	24.2%
Surplus	9.8	9.8	9.9	11.0	10.7	9.9	11.0
Preferred stock	8.9	9.5	8.7	8.4	7.8	7.7	4.8
Long-term debt	60.2	60.9	61.6	59.6	60.2	61.6	60.0
Long term debt							
Percent of gross utility plant	52.5	53.8	54.5	50.5	51.6	54.7	52.4
Percent of net gas utility plant	67.2	68.3	68.2	63.5	64.3	67.1	63.7
Reserve for depreciation of gas plant percent of gross gas plant	22.0	21.0	20.3	20.5	19.8	18.5	17.8

Source: FPC, *Statistics of Natural Gas Companies*, 1959, p. ix.

Exhibit 8 Gas Operating Expense Relationships—All Interstate Natural Gas Pipeline Companies

RELATIONSHIP	1959	1958	1957	1956	1955	1954	1950
Total operating expenses percent of operating revenues	67.2%	66.7%	66.2%	64.6%	63.4%	64.5%	61.7%
Total maintenance charges:							
Percent of total operating expenses	3.3	3.5	3.6	3.8	3.9	4.2	5.0
Percent of operating revenues	2.2	2.3	2.4	2.4	2.5	2.7	3.1
Total Maintenance and depreciation charges percent of operating revenues	11.0	11.2	11.2	11.2	11.6	12.4	12.4
Production Expense							
Percent of operating revenues	54.2	53.1	52.2	50.6	49.4	50.3	45.7
Per mcf sold, cents	18.0	16.9	15.6	14.5	13.9	13.0	8.3
Transmission and storage expenses:							
Percent of operating revenues	8.5	9.0	9.1	9.1	9.2	9.1	10.6
Per mcf sold, cents	2.8	2.8	2.7	2.6	2.6	2.4	2.0
Distribution expenses percent of operating revenues	.5	.5	.5	.5	.5	.6	.6
Customers' accounting and collecting expenses percent of operating revenues	.2	.2	.2	.2	.2	.2	.3
Sales promotion expenses percent of operating revenues	.1	.1	.1	.1	.1	.1	.1
Administrative and general expenses percent of operating revenues	3.7	3.8	4.1	4.0	3.9	4.1	4.4

Source: FPC, Statistics of Natural Gas Companies, 1959, p. xvii.

NOTES

1. Federal Power Commission, Opinion No. 326, August 10, 1959, pp. 260-90.
2. El Paso Natural Gas Company, Annual Report 1959, p. 10.
3. National Coal Association, *Coal Facts, 1978-79,* pp. 58-59.
4. Federal Power Commission, *Statistics of Natural Gas Companies,* 1946, 1954, 1959.
5. *Public Law 75-688,* Sec. 5(a)-Sec. 6(a).
6. Alfred E. Kahn, *The Economics of Regulation: Principles and Institutions* (New York: Wiley, 1970), vol I, p. 42.
7. Frank Mangan, *The Pipeliners: The Story of El Paso Natural Gas* (El Paso: Guynes Press, 1977), p. 46.
8. Ibid., pp. 128-29.
9. Federal Power Commission, Docket Nos. G-4769, G-12948, G-17929, RP60-3; "Brief for El Paso Natural Gas Co. in Response to Commission's Order of December 27, 1961" (April 3, 1962). p. 52-55.

10. Howard Boyd, interview with the author; Houston, Texas, November, 1980.
11. El Paso Natural Gas Company, Annual Report 1954, pp. 15-16.
12. Federal Power Commission, Docket No. G-4769, "Hearing Transcript," pp. 911-13.
13. Federal Power Commission, Docket No. G.4769, "Brief of El Paso Natural Gas Company," February 26, 1957, p. 48.
14. Federal Power Commission, Opinion No. 268, p. 408.
15. El Paso Brief, p. 48.
16. Federal Power Commission, Docket No. G-4769, "Brief of the FPC Staff," March 1, 1957, p. 11.
17. U.S. Congress, House Committee on Interstate and Foreign Commerce Subcommittee on Communications and Power, *El Paso Merger Legislation* (92nd Cong., 2nd sess.), June, September, 1972, pp. 46-47.
18. Federal Power Commission, Docket No. G-4769, "Brief on Behalf of Intervenor Pacific Gas and Electric Company," 1957, p. 6.
19. PG&E Brief, p. 6.
20. Ibid., p. 7.
21. Ibid., p. 12.
22. Ibid., pp. 14, 18.
23. El Paso Brief, p. 34.
24. El Paso Reply Brief, pp. 8, 10.
25. El Paso Brief, pp. 56-57.
26. Federal Power Commission, Opinion No. 326, pp. 267-69, 272-73.
27. Ibid., pp. 289-90.
28. Federal Power Commission, Opinion No. 36-A, "Opinion and Order Denying Rehearing," October 8, 1959, p. 662.

Marginalism in the State
of New York

The only economic function of price is to influence behavior, to elicit supply, and to regulate demand. This is a notion that traditional regulators have great difficulty accepting.

Alfred E. Kahn

On January 29, 1975, the New York State Public Service Commission (NYPSC) issued orders instituting a "generic" rate investigation "to inquire into the merits of, and to develop principles and methodology for, the revision of electric rate schedules." In the preamble to its order, the Commission stated, "Rapidly increasing costs of new generating facilities and the rising cost of fuel make it urgent, in the interest of energy conservation and the efficient use of resources, that the structure of energy prices reflect, to the greatest extent feasible, the variations in the incremental costs of service because of differences in the time of consumption as well as in all other cost-influencing factors."

A year and a half later, after reviewing the record compiled in thirty-five days of hearings and the briefs of twenty-two parties, the members of the commission unanimously concluded that "marginal costs . . . provide a reasonable basis for electric rate structures."

Credit for this extraordinary new consensus belonged largely to Alfred E. Kahn, the fifty-eight-year old chairman of the NYPSC. Yet Kahn remained cautious, knowing that his efforts would all be for naught if he failed to neutralize opposition by politically influential large power users.

A SCHOLAR'S ODYSSEY

That Alfred Kahn, a liberal Democrat, should become the nation's best known evangelist for marginal cost principles—a set of ideas seldom associated with Kahn's liberal noneconomist friends—may seem ironic. Yet an explanation can be found in the long intellectual journey that marked his life.

This case is composed primarily of excerpts from two books by Harvard Business School professors: Douglas D. Anderson, *Regulatory Politics and Electric Utilities* (Boston: Auburn House, 1981) and Thomas K. McCraw, *Prophets of Regulation* (Cambridge, MA: Harvard University Press, 1984). All footnotes have been omitted. The case was prepared, with the authors' permission, as the basis for class discussion rather than to illustrate either the effective or ineffective handling of an administrative situation.

At eighteen Kahn graduated summa cum laude and first in his class from New York University, and before he turned twenty took a master's degree at NYU. He pursued further graduate work at the University of Missouri, then moved on to Yale for his doctorate. During the same years, he also worked at a series of research jobs in Washington, for the Brookings Institution, the Department of Commerce, and the Antitrust Division of the Justice Department.

Between 1940 and 1974, when he took his seat as chairman of the New York Public Service Commission, Kahn wrote two books and coauthored two others. All four proved to be major works. In addition, he managed to publish some two dozen articles and comments, most of them in the *American Economic Review*, the leading journal of the discipline. Nearly all of this writing reflected, in one way or another, the influence of his two principal advisers, Myron Watkins and Joseph Schumpeter. It also evidenced deep intellectual debts to the pioneering institutional economists, Thorstein Veblen and John Maurice Clark.

During this period, classical microeconomics had experienced a slump in popularity from which it was recovering very slowly. Common topics of that subdiscipline included the theories of prices and markets pioneered by Adam Smith, John Stuart Mill, and Alfred Marshall. These giants of an earlier era had long dominated the field of economics. Over the first half of the twentieth century, however, the classical approach suffered three severe blows. The first came from institutionalism. Veblen, among others, savagely attacked Adam Smith's proposition that an invisible hand moved the free market automatically to serve the public interests, with no need for government intervention. The institutionalists asserted that here classicism was simplistic and merely deductive; it sacrificed both common sense and empirical observation to an alleged theoretical rigor that on close inspection turned out to be chimerical. As a case in point, argued the institutionalists, Smith and Mill offered no help for the human costs of industrialization. More than anything else, classicism's implicit assumption that whatever is, is right, angered the institutionalists, who pointed to the Great Depression as a confirmation of their views. Clearly, the invisible hand—if there was one—had guided the world of the 1930s to disaster.

As if the institutionalist attack were not bad enough, classicism, like institutionalism itself, now began to suffer from Keynesian macroeconomics. Thirty years after the depression, many of the best advanced students were attracted to the new Keynesian theories. The remarkable performance of national economies offered a series of practical experiments for the benefit of those scholars and planners who thought in terms of aggregates. National economies were growing very rapidly, and only the "new economics" of Keynes seemed to offer clear explanations. Keynesian economists in many countries became the honored prophets of society.

In fact, almost the entire intellectual history of twentieth-century economics played a part in Kahn's professional career. He entered graduate school during the late 1930s, at the ebb tide of institutionalism but before the flood of Keynesianism. Kahn understood microeconomics, yet felt a greater fascination with the macroeconomic side of his discipline. Even so, he emerged from his training as a disciple of neither school but as a broadly informed empiricist, equipped with an eclectic mixture of research tools, special interests, and what Keynes liked to call "propensities."

In the early 1950s, Kahn's interests began to shift toward regulation and marginal cost pricing. The evidence appears in a book and several articles on antitrust. Within the profession of economics, antitrust forms part of a larger field called industrial organization, which tends to combine some of the old policy concerns of the institutionalists with a more rigorous and theoretical analysis of market structures. The topic is microeconomic and heavily freighted with the ideological overtones that surround every discussion of the role of big business in a democratic society. If the central value implicit in classical micro-theory was allocative and productive efficiency, the central value of antitrust—at least as the practical basis for enforcement of antitrust laws—seemed broader and fuzzier. For Kahn this new concern posed a dilemma he could not easily resolve. As a liberal Democrat writing in a time of national prosperity, he now found himself preoccupied less with the improvement of efficiency than with the promotion of social justice. His book (co-authored with Joel Dirlam) entitled *Fair Competition: The Law and Economics of Antitrust Policy* (1954) may be seen as a struggle between the sentimental feelings of the liberal activist and the reasoned arguments of the analytical economist. In this case, for one of the few times in Kahn's professional life, sentiment routed reason.

By the mid-1950s, shortly after the publication of his book on antitrust, Kahn had begun to interest himself in the related area of regulation, particularly of the oil and gas industries. Again the evidence may be found in a book, which he coauthored and published in 1959, as *Integration and Competition in the Petroleum Industry*. Spinoffs from Kahn's research included articles on the control of crude oil production, an examination of the oil depletion allowance, and—most important for his future interests—a critical analysis of the Federal Power Commission and its role in the regulation of natural gas. Here he faced one of the most controversial and convoluted subjects in the entire history of regulation in America. The stakes at issue in oil and gas regulation were very high; by the late 1950s, the issues had developed such complexity that institutionalist economic methods could no longer be used to study them adequately.

At this point in his career, Kahn began the final stage of his intellectual odyssey. He now became directly involved in the difficult problem of pricing natural gas. In testimony before the Federal Power Commission during the early 1960s, he introduced a set of ideas that later became institutionalized as the "two-tier pricing system." Under FPC regulation, "old" gas, drawn from fields already discovered and producing, would be priced more cheaply than "new" gas, from fields brought into production more recently. Although at the time this seemed to Kahn a worthwhile idea (since it would prevent big companies from reaping unearned benefits from rising gas prices), in fact the two-tier arrangement raised a host of problems.

But Kahn was learning fast now. Public declaration of his transition came in 1970, with the appearance of his *Economics of Regulation*, one of the most important books ever written on the subject. Here Kahn managed brilliantly to fuse the economics of institutionalism and classicism. That achievement, in its turn, led to a new phase of his career: in 1974, he entered public office as a regulator.

THE NEW YORK STATE COMMISSION

During the 1960s the New York State Public Service Commission, like most utility commissions, was a sleepy outpost for political patronage. As one influential commission source observed:

> I think that if you look closely at the composition of the commissions in the sixties and the fifties—which I have—it's not too difficult to see that they weren't very good. The commissioners were almost all political appointees—either defeated candidates or retiring politicians who were basically in need of a job. And it's evident in the performance of the companies. First of all there were very few rate cases—with Con Ed being about the only exception—and they were small. . . . Companies were earning well in excess of (a reasonable) amount and there seems to be evidence that they were expanding capacity at a greater than optimal rate.

In New York this lazy ambience was rudely interrupted in 1969 by a series of rate increases, service failures, and legislative investigations:

> Con Ed came in with a major rate case in 1969 and New York City began experiencing some brownouts. Then there were some real telephone service problems in New York City in 1969—all of which led to greater public attention to the PSC. The legislature (that year) began holding hearings on the PSC, and in the course of the hearings it became clear that the then-chairman of the PSC didn't really know what was going on in his own department and that proved to be a real embarrassment for the governor.

In response to the shortcomings of the NYPSC, Governor Nelson Rockefeller took steps in early 1970 to strengthen the position of chairman by finding a national figure to fill the office. His choice was Joseph C. Swidler, the respected former chairman of the Federal Power Commission (FPC). Swidler had served the FPC from 1961 to 1966, and before that had been general counsel to the Tennessee Valley Authority.

Swidler soon became a commanding figure at the commission and at the Department of Public Utilities, which was reorganized to come under the administrative direction of the NYPSC chairman. Almost immediately after he arrived, Swidler made a number of organizational and programmatic changes. Systems planning was introduced for the first time in the commission's communications, power, and gas divisions. The former head of the Department of Public Utilities, a man staff members described as very authoritarian, was eased into retirement and the interchange between staff and commissioners greatly opened up at regular weekly meetings. Swidler's authorization of an extensive

Chart 1   New York State Public Service Commission

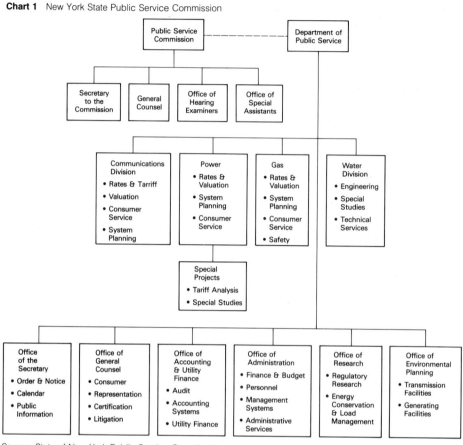

Source: State of New York Public Service Commission, Annual Report, 1975.

"fully allocated cost study" by the staff was the first step the commission took in the direction of designing electric rate structures. Innovative as it was, the fully allocated cost study was not based on principles of marginal cost. Indeed, Swidler was an outspoken critic of marginal cost based rates after leaving the commission; in 1974, he was replaced as chairman by Alfred Kahn.

The New York commission in 1974 regulated more than forty industries, including telephones, buses, water supply systems, docks and wharves, and warehouses. The degree of authority actually exercised, of course, varied widely according to the industry, both in New York and elsewhere. It also varied according to the vigor and resources of the state commissions.

The New York Public Service Commission was second in size only to California's. As chairman, Kahn headed an agency of some 650 persons, with an annual budget in 1974 exceeding $12 million. Kahn received the highest salary of any regulator in the United States—about $51,000—and in addition

Professional Staff		Division of Labor	
Inspectors and investigators	103	Chairman's office	17
Engineers	57	Energy Division	231
Auditors	54	Accounting and utility finance	97
Accountants	28	Communications division	92
Attorneys	21	Office of administration	79
Administrative staff	14	Office of general counsel	46
Rate analysts	13	Office of environmental planning	41
Hearing examiners (admin.		Water division	34
law judges, mostly lawyers)	13	Office of hearing examiners	20
Economists	8	Office of economic research	12

enjoyed a chauffeur-driven limousine and many other benefits. A listing of his professional staff, together with their individual specialties, provides us with a useful index of the nature of the agency at the time Kahn took charge. Notice the dominance of engineers, accountants, and lawyers, and the minor role played by professional economists.

THE REGULATORY ENVIRONMENT

National economic growth, which had averaged more than 4% a year for thirty years, dropped to 2.6% in 1969 and then further, to a negative 0.3% for 1970. (The average for the 1970s stood at 2.87%, nearly a third lower than the rate of the preceding three decades.) And the national inflation rate, which had averaged 2.5% a year in the 1950s and 1960s, climbed to 5.3% in 1971 and averaged 6.7% for the decade of the 1970s. These national trends meant that the economics of the utility business were about to be turned upside down.

Stagflation represented bad news for utilities, and three additional developments made things even worse. First, the environmental movement: Again the watershed year was 1970, when the celebration of Earth Day ushered in the creation of a new federal Environmental Protection Agency. The sudden popularity of environmental concerns hit utilities hard. Power plants pollute the environment in almost every conceivable way—indirectly through the strip mining of the coal they burn, and directly through smoke stack emissions, thermal pollution of cooling water, and leakage of radioactive materials. To prevent pollution, even to control its sources, soon became extremely costly. A utility must pay for nuclear-waste facilities, scrubbers for high-sulfur coal, and towering stacks (some more than 1,000 feet high), and all are expensive. A national consensus, however, required that environmental quality be improved, just when economic growth slowed and inflation and interest rates rose.

A second problem emerged from the sudden slowing of technological progress in the design and fabrication of generating equipment. For almost a century after the construction of Thomas Edison's first electric power plant, technological progress brought steady gains in productivity. Engineers and utility managers had come to take such gains for granted, thinking they would continue indefinitely. Beginning in the 1960s, however, a technological plateau was reached in the industry, as yearly gains came to an unexpected halt, particularly in those large-scale electric generating plants on which most power companies relied. Between 1967 and 1976, utility executives discovered that the most technologically advanced plants, which used steam at very high temperatures to turn gigantic turbines, went out of service almost three times as often as smaller-scale plants. Bigger came to mean not necessarily better, only less reliable.

Then late in 1973 the price of imported crude oil shot up to four times the summer 1973 figure. Utilities were stunned, especially those located in the northeastern United States, where the companies had earlier converted to oil as a fuel less polluting than coal.

The impact of these multiple revolutions transformed the entire economic picture. The overall effect on power companies can be gauged by the rapid rise combined requests for new rate increases.

Because of accelerating inflation, utilities that based their rates on historical costs, as most did, had difficulty in meeting current expenses. Even when a regulatory agency did grant the requested rate increase in full, the time lag between petition and decision guaranteed that the companies would keep running faster and faster in pursuit of outdated targets. By 1974, the length of procedural delays averaged eleven months; and when inflation approached double digits, "regulatory lag" soon became a serious problem.

The combined impact on New York's electric utilities of inflation, higher fuel costs, technological stasis, and other forces may be gauged in the history of rates charged by the Consolidated Edison Company, the state's largest utility. Con Edison served Greater New York City, and there residential customers saw the average monthly electric bill double quickly during the early 1970s (from $10.65 in 1970 to $22.08 in 1974). In 1974, even with these higher rates, Con Edison still found itself in the worst financial shape in its history, so it naturally expected to request from the Public Service Commission still another large increase in rates during 1975.

Kahn knew about the utilities' mushrooming revenue requirements, but he was even more concerned about the structure of their rates. Here, as he wrote in *Economics of Regulation*, he could point to an area in which the professional economist might make a distinctive contribution by starting from a foundation of marginal cost pricing. The existing rate structures contained an implicit

QUARTER ENDING	CASES FILED NATIONALLY DURING QUARTER	TOTAL INCREASES REQUESTED
3/31/70	12	$89 million
3/31/72	22	$171 million
3/31/74	45	$638 million

assumption that the costs of production would always be declining, as indeed they had done until the late 1960s. During those happier years, utility companies had experimented with declining-block rates, under which the price of a kilowatt-hour would be reduced with every increase in the total consumed, much like a volume discount for large purchases in retail stores.

A pioneer in this field, the publicly owned Tennessee Valley Authority, introduced as early as 1933 its radical declining-block rate structure:

First 50 kwh per mo.	3.00 cents per kwh
Next 150 kwh	2.00 cents per kwh
Next 200 kwh	1.00 cents per kwh
Next 1000 kwh	0.40 cents per kwh

The central mission of the TVA was to encourage the widest possible usage of electricity, thereby improving the standard of living in the depressed Tennessee Valley region. This 3¢-2¢-1¢ rate schedule, based on a commercial jingle of the period that touted 3-2-1 Shoe Polish, directly promoted the goal.

Electricity, unlike most other goods and services, cannot be stored efficiently. It must be generated, transmitted, and consumed in almost the same instant. This means that the companies must have enough generating capacity to meet not only the usual demands of their customers (average load) but also the highest demands (peak load). The extra generating capacity needed to meet these peaks, which occur on a daily (and seasonal) basis, was more expensive than base-load capacity. But users had no motive to behave accordingly, since the rate structure was not differentiated by time of day.

Since the companies are often required by law to serve all customers, whatever their demands, utility managers and regulatory commissioners have tended to assume that they themselves have little discretion in raising or lowering either the supply of electricity or the demand for it. Instead, company managers planned for the future by forecasting the total demand their customers would impose, then scheduling the construction of new generating plants to meet the pace of added demand.

Utility managers acted in this way for several reasons. First, they felt the normal urge of business executives to encourage the consumption of whatever they sell. Second, and less obvious, they could factor the full cost of capital expenditures into their company's rate base and thus augment the potential revenues requested from the regulatory agency. Finally, they could take advantage of the rapid rate of innovation in the technology of electric generation, particularly innovation within extremely large plants.

The results of these innovations and scale economies could be read in a steady decline of the consumer's real costs. As Kahn later said, the real price of energy (not electricity alone) had dropped by 43% between 1951 and 1971, a period in which consumer prices as a whole rose by 56%. Electricity seemed uniquely to be a bigger bargain every year.

Then, at the close of the 1960s, this felicitous situation abruptly changed, and the real costs moved steadily higher during the 1970s. Inflation, stagnation, the environmental movement, rising interest rates, technological stasis, and the skyrocketing cost of fuel struck the industry simultaneously. Utilities' marginal cost curves, which had shifted downward since the first Edison stations had opened nearly a century before, now moved ominously upward. Construction of new plants became almost prohibitively expensive. This meant that, for the first time in the industry's history, electricity coming from new plants would cost more than equivalent amounts from existing sources. Thus the declining-block rate structures in effect throughout the United States now gave exactly the wrong signals to consumers.

WORKING WITH CONSTITUENTS

Now the question became not what to do but rather how to do it. How could Kahn convince his fellow commissioners, his 650-member staff, the utilities themselves, and eight or ten different classes of consumers that the old practices of the companies and the commission were inappropriate to current reality?

To begin, he did almost no hiring or firing but instead worked with a few carefully chosen pupils, then a few more, spreading his message in widening circles. Even those who disagreed with a marginal cost philosophy had to respect Kahn's learning, and nearly all staff members appreciated his informal manner. A visitor from the *New York Times* found him padding around the office in his socks. He talked endlessly with his staff about the principles of marginal cost pricing. He delighted in teaching them at every opportunity: over lunch, in meetings, even at the daily swims he initiated. Immersed in the water, visible only from the neck up, Kahn lectured on the technicalities of cross-substitution, elasticities of demand, and marginalism.

Kahn's friendly manner proved especially important in his effort to convert the commission's rate engineers. Because of the technological history of electric utilities—improved technology as a basis for the steady growth of scale economies and declining rates—engineers became enamored of the usual system of volume discounts for businesses and declining-block rates for home consumers. In the engineers' view, large users of electricity deserved to pay less per unit consumed.

Jack Treiber, one of the engineers who became convinced of the importance of marginal cost analysis, made the following summary observation:

> Fred started holding meetings on rate design for anyone interested. I was doing rate design work, so I went. He was the professor and we were the students. We didn't immediately go with it. "What is this marginal cost?" we asked. Finally, it became clear that this was just what we needed to deal with the revenue erosion problem. We were basically there—we just didn't have the buzz words. We needed an economist to give us the buzz words.
>
> Fred's personality, his professionalism, certainly moved things along. But it would have come anyway. What he gave us was a set of principles to deal with a problem we were having. It just seemed so logical—the way to get from A to B. One could easily argue in favor of marginal cost. It was less easy to argue against—you'd have to bring up side issues that weren't that important.

The regulatory process in the United States has been desultory in character. State and federal commissions, somewhat like courts, have seldom initiated action on their own, but instead have responded to petitions or complaints. As a consequence of this reactive role, they find it difficult to change policies quickly, especially when such changes are opposed by powerful interest groups. These groups are often ready to prevent loss of advantage by falling back on litigation calculated to delay any change.

Kahn knew that, in New York, he could not allow for these normal delays, despite the high level of controversy that surrounded his ideas. The commission must move quickly, rather than wait for utility companies to initiate proceedings, especially since nothing could be expected of the companies except additional requests for rate increases.

Kahn found his answer in the device of holding not individual rate cases, but a "generic hearing" instead. His hearing would amount to an intensive study of the rate question, conducted outside the heated atmosphere typical of the usual rate case. Not one company but all companies would be involved, and testimony would include evidence from environmental experts and other specialists interested in the proceedings.

The generic proceeding itself had an informal dimension. Shortly before the commission ordered the proceeding to begin, both the Environmental Defense Fund (EDF) and the state's seven largest privately owned utilities petitioned the commission—within a week of each other—to undertake a general investigation of various proposals for reforming rate structures. The motivations of these groups merit description.

The Environmental Defense Fund

The Environmental Defense Fund's interest in rate reform as an alternative to electric power industry growth dated from its intervention in 1973 in a Wisconsin case. Five months before the New York commission ordered the generic hearing, the Wisconsin Public Service Commission, acting largely on a record developed by the EDF, became the first commission to adopt the principles of long-run incremental cost as a basis for designing electric rate structures. New York was the EDF's next target after Wisconsin. The organization had tried intervening in a Niagara-Mohawk case in early 1974 with only partial success. Kahn's subsequent appointment as chairman encouraged them to seek a generic hearing.

The Utilities

Like the EDF, New York's seven major investor-owned utilities petitioned for a generic hearing, but did so for quite different reasons. Actually, the utilities were divided among themselves over the merits of marginal cost pricing. Some, such as Long Island Lighting Company (LILCO), and Con Edison, faced with huge capital needs and deteriorating load factors, were interested in the concept.

Others like Niagara-Mohawk, which still wanted to expand, were decidedly against abandoning the declining-block rate.

For some of the utilities, the generic proceeding represented a means of slowing down the progress of rate structure reform rather than speeding it up. The generic hearing safeguarded utilities opposed to marginal cost pricing from having to deal with the issue in the context of their own rate cases or from having to follow the precedent of a marginal cost-based rate established in the rate case of a utility more favorably inclined to the concept.

The Governor's Office

When Hugh Carey was elected governor of New York in 1974, he did not attempt to modify Kahn's preexisting views on marginal cost or on marginal cost application to electric rate structures.

The Legislature

There was never any serious legislative attempt to thwart time-of-day rates while Kahn was chairman of the New York State Public Service Commission, but some bills were introduced which would have strengthened the commission's movement in that direction. Rate structure reform appealed to the many legislators who were anxious to demonstrate concern about rising electricity prices. For similar reasons a number of bills were introduced to mandate lifeline rates of various sorts. None passed—in part because Kahn refused to push for the lifeline concept; in part because industrial and commercial users that could not stop time-of-day rates were adamant in their opposition to lifeline; and in part because consumer representatives failed to construct an effective coalition in support of lifeline.

The New York State Consumer Protection Board

Not everyone in New York state government was as favorably disposed toward the NYPSC and its chairman as were the governor's staff and legislative leaders. In particular, Rosemary Pooler, the chairwoman and executive director of the New York Consumer Protection Board (CPB), carried on a running battle with Kahn. This personal animosity would be uninteresting if it had not affected the regulation of electric utilities.

Large Power Users

The only unified opposition to marginal cost-based rates came from large electric users, who feared the proposed rates would cause them to pay more for their electricity. To block the adoption of marginal cost pricing, the large users acted through both the formal and the informal regulatory process.

Large industrial and commercial users' formal opposition to marginal cost pricing was centered in the generic hearing, where they challenged the theoretical justification of marginal cost concept and attempted to cast doubt on evidence presented in support of it from Great Britain and France. Large users hoped second-best considerations would force the commission to abandon its effort, but such was not the case. The commission effectively closed discussion on the marginal cost issue by placing the burden of proof on its opponents. In defense of that action, Alfred Kahn wrote, "What (opponents) neglect to observe is that this consideration applies equally to leaving the price of electricity where it is: The principle of 'second best' raises questions about the validity of basing electricity rates on accounting costs, too."

The industrial consumers' angry response to Kahn's action was to file motions with the commission asserting that Kahn had determined in advance of the generic hearing his own answers to the issues that were to be raised in the hearing. The attorney for one industrial group berated the final decision on marginal cost, "At times I felt Kahn should have just issued copies of his text (*The Economics of Regulation*) as the decision—perhaps with the hard cover replaced by the soft one. The hearings produced nothing. They were simply an expensive seminar designed to give us Fred Kahn's view."

As expected, the commission ruled against the motion to disqualify Kahn.

THE GENERIC HEARING

A number of difficult issues needed to be addressed in the generic hearing and in specific cases before a new rate structure based upon marginal costs could be designed. Some of these issues were primarily technical; others had important political implications. Chief among these issues were the following: (1) the question of whom to meter for time-of-day usage; (2) the problem of "second best"; (3) the problem of "shifting peak"; (4) the related problem of "needle peaks"; (5) the definition of marginal costs; (6) lifeline rate proposals; (7) the disposition of excess revenues; and (8) the electric industry's charge of discrimination and its threat to relocate in response to new rates.

Whom to Meter?

Because time-differentiated rates would require new meters for all customers to whom the new rates would apply, one of the issues the commission needed to address was whom to meter. Alfred Kahn observed:

> The only economic function of price is to influence behavior. This is a notion that traditional regulators have great difficulty accepting. . . . But of course price can have this effect on the buyer's side only if buyer's bills do indeed vary depending on the amount of their purchases. For this reason, economists in (the) public utility field are avid meterers; and if they were costless, we would like to have meters just as complicated as necessary to measure every dimension of consumption that has an independent marginal cost—numbers of telephone

messages, the time each one is placed, the number of minutes each one consumes, the number of miles it traverses, the number of kilowatts and the instant at which each is taken, the number of feet of distribution system required to serve each customer; and so on.

For large customers, even rough cost-benefit analysis suggested the advantage of metering, but for small customers the answer was less clear. New time-of-day residential meters cost nearly $150 whereas standard meters cost only $23.

The Problem of "Second Best"

A familiar theoretical objection to applying marginal cost principles in designing rate structure is the problem of "second best." In brief, antimarginalists argue that in a world in which other prices deviate from marginal cost it is impossible to conclude as a general proposition that setting prices equal to marginal costs in any single sector will be desirable. Antimarginalists maintain that without knowledge of the extent to which all other prices in the economy (besides that of electricity) deviate from marginal costs, there can be no certainty that the use of marginal costs in designing electric rates alone will improve the allocation of resources, since it is the relative prices of various goods and services which are pertinent in influencing the behavior of buyers. Facing the commission, then, were the two related questions: "Is the problem of second best sufficiently important to render any change in rate structures harmful? If not, what deviations from marginal cost should be made in light of second-best considerations?"

The Shifting Peak

If electricity taken on-peak is priced higher than that which is taken off-peak, a possible consumer response is to defer some consumption to off-peak periods. Indeed, for environmentalists and others, this response is the chief advantage of peak-load pricing, inasmuch as it improves load factors and diminishes the need for additional plant capacity. One practical problem, however, is that customers may shift so much of their consumption off-peak that a new peak is created, necessitating a further revision in the rate structures.

Needle Peaks

If seasonal and time-differentiated rates succeed in discouraging some peak consumption, they may still create "needle peaks" that could destroy any improvement in utility load factors. A possible needle-peak-creating scenario is the following:

> Con Ed institutes a seasonal and time-related rate of its New York City and Westchester County customers. The utility has a summer peak, so rates from noon until 6:00 P.M. in July and August are especially high. The high rates

discourage customers from using their air conditioners on all but the three or four hottest days of the summer, but on those days they are turned on full force, creating a huge surge in demand. Since Con Ed has no way of knowing in advance precisely which days in the summer will be the hottest, its rates cannot fully discriminate between those who are responsible for the needle peak and those who take power on other summer days.

The result of this lack of discrimination is that rates on the hottest days are too low to cover the incremental cost of service, thereby encouraging excessive demand. Meanwhile, rates on other summer days are too high, which discourages some consumption that would improve the utility's load factor.

An optimal rate structure would differentiate by temperature at time of use. Even if this differentiation did not improve load factors, it would at least assign the burden of the marginal costs to those who were responsible for them. In the absence of a temperature-sensitive rate, the commission needed an alternative strategy for dealing with needle-peak problems.

The Definition of Marginal Costs

Defining marginal cost in an effort to price electricity can be both complex and confusing. The familiar proposition from elementary economics that "sunk costs are sunk"—and therefore irrelevant to incremental price and output decisions—focuses attention on the variable costs of production in plants already in existence. Short-run marginal cost is the addition to total variable cost associated with the production of the next incremental unit of output. The customers who should be charged the marginal cost are those who are responsible for the increase in variable costs. If they are charged the full marginal cost, such customers can determine for themselves whether the extra cost they impose on society is worth the benefit they derive from the last unit of output they consume.

These principles are simple in the abstract, and they give a clear pricing rule: Prices should be set to equal short-run marginal costs on the smallest increment of output possible. However, the principle implies that price must include all of the variable costs, regardless of when they are realized. If additional production today will cause capital equipment to be utilized more intensely and therefore to wear out faster, the costs of replacing that capacity should be included in the variable costs. For this reason, in practical application marginal cost pricing may consist of setting rates equal to long-run incremental cost (LRIC). LRIC measures the change in total costs when output is increased or decreased by an increment of a block of output for an extended period of time, during which system capacity can be altered. How long this period should be—that is to say, how many costs should be considered variable—will depend upon the planning perspective utilities and regulators employ, something that obviously will vary from one instance to another and may be a matter of dispute.

Consider, for example, the assignment of responsibility for the cost of additional plant capacity. In the short run, when plant capacity is considered fixed, marginal cost pricing would ignore capacity charges; but if it is determined that a longer planning period is justified, a method must be devised to assign these costs among various users. The economic principle to be applied is clear: If the same capacity serves all users, capacity cost should be levied only on those whose use requires the expansion of capacity, the peak users.

In the production of electricity, however, the same capacity does not necessarily serve all customers. Generally, utilities cope with diurnal and seasonal variations in the demand for electricity by employing several types of generators, some of which are constantly in use—baseload plants—and some of which are used for shorter periods of time—cycling and peaking units. Companies do this to minimize the total cost of providing service at a specified level of reliability. Baseload generators (nuclear and coal generators) have high capital costs but relatively low operating costs, whereas peaking units (gas-fire turbines) have low capital costs and high operating costs. A typical daily load curve and the generation dispatched to meet a cyclical load is shown in Chart 2.

Since utilities construct gas turbines to meet a small increment in demand, it is the capacity charges for the turbines which should be passed on to peak users. Suppose, however, that a utility has a suboptimal mix of generating plants—that is, it has too much peaking or cycling capacity and not enough of the more efficient baseload capacity. Marginal costs comprehend only current and future costs. Should an optimal rate structure include any capacity costs under conditions of excess peaking capacity but insufficient baseload capacity?

The previous example of the utility with too little baseload capacity is not merely hypothetical. As a result of the enormous increases in the price of oil which followed the OPEC embargo of 1973, New York's downstate utilities felt they had too much oil-fired capacity and not enough coal or nuclear capacity to minimize total costs. Their short-term construction plans consisted only of substituting baseload capacity; no net additions to plant capacity to meet peak requirements were planned.

If the issue of defining marginal costs is troubling for regulators, it is at least a familiar issue. Any ratesetting rule encounters the problem of whether costs may be recovered if incurred inefficiently.

Lifeline Rate Proposals

Lifeline rates have been described as having a low-cost initial block for residential users on grounds of "need." Everyone, the argument goes, needs a certain amount of electricity and proponents of the lifeline concept contend that society should provide for such needs through differential pricing, imposing larger burdens on other presumably more affluent users of electricity. Such rates are clearly not intended to serve the goal of economic efficiency, but electric rates have never been designed exclusively to foster the goal of efficiency. The issue before the commission was that of determining the extent to which rates based on marginal cost should be modified to include other social goals, such as those advocated by the lifeline proponents.

Chart 2 Dispatching Generation to Meet a Cyclical Load

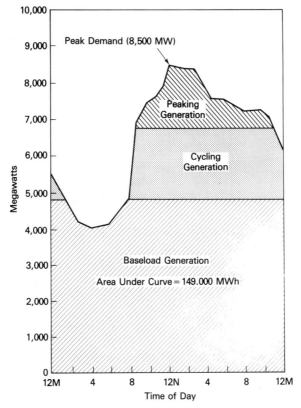

$$\text{Daily Load Factor} = \frac{\text{daily energy}}{24 \text{ hr.} \times \text{peak load}} = \frac{149{,}000 \text{ MWh}}{24 \text{ hr.} \times 8{,}500 \text{ MW}} = 0.73 = 73\%.$$

Source: Robert G. Uhler, *Rate Design and Load Control* (Palo Alto, CA: Electric Utility Rate Design Study, November 1977), p. 15.

The Disposition of Excess Revenues

Rate structures based on marginal costs are designed independently of the process that sets a utility's overall revenue requirement. Only by chance will marginal cost-based rates return to the utility precisely the amount of revenue deemed reasonable for it to earn. It is much more likely in an inflationary world that marginal cost-based rates will generate revenues in excess of those the utility is allowed to earn by traditional ratemaking rules. (Regulators in most states value a utility's rate base at "original cost"—the price paid by the utility to purchase the assets in the first place—or at their "fair value"—a cost typically higher than original cost, but less than the cost of replacing the assets.) Thus the question arises, "What is to be done with the excess revenues if the utility is not allowed to keep them?" Some means must be found to reduce electric rates without distorting the price signals that are the *raison d'être* of marginal cost.

The economic principle that could guide the disposition of such revenues is the so-called "Ramsey rule" (or "inverse elasticity rule"), which suggests simply that the extra revenues should be rebated to consumers in inverse relations to their elasticity of demand. The less responsive to price changes customers are, the greater their reduction in rates should be, and vice versa.

While the inverse elasticity rule is, again, a simple and noncontroversial proposition in the abstract, its application is both difficult and controversial. First, the rule requires a large amount of information about customer responsiveness to price changes. Second, despite the primitive quality of demand elasticity estimates, industrial and commercial users fear that regulators will operate on a hunch that the demand of residential consumers is more inelastic than their own, and use the inverse elasticity rule to shift to them greater responsibility for utility revenue requirements. Lifeline proponents are quick to make this assessment as well, and so have been wholehearted advocates of the inverse elasticity concept. They argue that their proposals are compatible with economically efficient rates—even though economic efficiency is not their primary goal—because residential demand for the first block of electricity is almost undoubtedly most inelastic.

Industry's Charges of Discrimination and Threats to Relocate

Finally, the application of any new methodology to the setting of electric rates is certain to be criticized as discriminatory if it is not to be applied universally. The commission needed to address the issue of discrimination and also had to face industry's threat that it would leave the state if electric rates proved to be too unfavorable, taking jobs with it.

The generic hearing succeeded in convincing some, but not all, of the interested parties about the benefits of marginal cost pricing. The Environmental Defense Fund, the City of New York, and the Long Island Lighting Company were the strongest supporters. Several other utilities, including Consolidated Edison, the Public Service Commission staff, and the State Consumer Protection Board approved, although less vigorously. Niagara-Mohawk (a large utility), the Industrial Power Consumers Conference, the Rockland County Industrial Energy Users Association, Airco, and a variety of other industrial users, were adamantly opposed.

THE MEETING OF JULY 8, 1976

A month before the commission issued its decision in the generic hearing, a group of industrial users were to meet with Kahn to protest the move toward time-of-day rates. The meeting was arranged by John Dyson, commissioner of the state's commerce department, to whom the large electric consumers had turned for help when it became evident that they were not winning the battle against marginal cost pricing in the formal regulatory process. Dyson had a reputation as an outspoken advocate of economic recovery and industrial development in New York, and he reportedly enjoyed a close association with Governor Carey. Dyson was known to have attacked the Department of Environmental Conservation and the Department of Education for imposing undue burdens on business, and for inefficiency, and had received a great deal of press attention and business support as a result.

In anticipation of this meeting, Kahn called yet another meeting of his staff. There had to be a way to alleviate this remaining block of concentrated opposition, if marginalism were to succeed. The Commission's final order in the generic rate proceedings had to be something that everyone could at least live with.

Commonwealth Edison (A)

On March 1, 1980, James J. O'Connor was elected chairman and chief executive officer of the Commonwealth Edison Company—the nation's third largest investor-owned electricity utility. O'Connor, a forty-two-year-old Harvard MBA and a native Chicagoan, had been president of the company for three years, during a time of difficulties for electric utilities generally, and Commonwealth Edison (CWE), in particular.

In 1979, the 100th anniversary of Thomas Edison's invention of the incandescent light bulb, CWE suffered one of its least profitable years in recent memory. Its interest-coverage ratio reached an all-time low, and its credit standing was reduced twice in eleven months. The Illinois Commerce Commission, under new leadership, handed down a rate decision so adverse as to precipitate a cash-flow crisis that halted construction at CWE's Braidwood nuclear power plant, south of Chicago.

An accident earlier in the year at the Three Mile Island plant in Pennsylvania had caused a crisis for the U.S. nuclear industry. The aftershocks of TMI were of no small consequence to Commonwealth Edison, since it operated six nuclear power plants and had six more under construction. Even before TMI, the Illinois Commerce Commission (ICC) had begun an investigation of CWE's ambitious nuclear construction program.

Late in April 1980, with the construction case still pending before the ICC, Jim O'Connor faced the difficult decision of whether or not to delay completion of the nuclear power plants. This decision, O'Connor felt, had to be made by summer, when the company would apply for the largest rate hike in its history.

THE COMMONWEALTH EDISON COMPANY

Samuel Insull, an emigrant from England to the United States who served for a time as secretary to Thomas Edison, moved to Chicago in 1892 to take control of Chicago Edison, one of the city's thirty electric companies. Five years later, Insull outsmarted Chicago's corrupt city council and took control of Common-

---

This case was prepared by Professor Richard H.K. Vietor as the basis for class discussion, rather than to illustrate either the effective or ineffective handling of an administrative situation.

wealth Electric—a dummy franchise they had created to extort him. In 1907, the forty-six-year-old Insull merged the two companies to form Commonwealth Edison.

By 1980, CWE was a vertically integrated electric power company, the sole supplier of electricity to eight million people in Chicago and northern Illinois. It maintained coal reserves, produced its own uranium, built and operated its own power plants and transmission network, and sold electricity, mostly at retail, to residential, commercial, and industrial customers.

CWE's service area of 11,525 square miles in northern Illinois included 400 municipalities besides the city of Chicago, and a diverse mix of commerce, industry, and agriculture. Among the company's 2.9 million customers were seven wholesale distributors, two electric railroads, 11,000 public authorities, and 230,000 businesses. Nine hundred large industrial customers purchased one-third of CWE's output, contributing 24% of its revenue. Smaller businesses accounted for an additional 32% of sales. Although residential customers contributed only 34% of Edison's revenues, they were by far its most important clientele, with regard to the company's social responsibilities and its customers' political influence (see Exhibit 1).

GENERATING CAPACITY AND THE CONSTRUCTION PROGRAM

Power generation was the heart of CWE's business, and of late the most politically salient of its activities. On August 7, 1979, the company provided 13,804 megawatts of electric power and still maintained a gross reserve margin of 31.5% (see Table 1).

Thirty-five generating units at thirteen plants provided baseload and cycling capacity of 16,000 megawatts. Oil and gas turbines for emergency peaking, and a pumped storage facility in nearby Michigan, provided the balance of the system's capacity (see Exhibit 2).

Table 1   System Capability and Peak Load

YEAR	TOTAL SYSTEM CAPABILITY (mw)	SYSTEM PEAK LOAD (mw)	TOTAL RESERVE PERCENTAGE	ANNUAL LOAD FACTOR
1979	18,148	13,804	31.5%	55.9%
1978	17,480	13,720	27.4	56.5
1977	17,169	13,932	23.2	53.3
1976	15,484	12,907	20.0	55.2
1975	16,333	12,305	32.7	56.0
1974	15,698	12,270	27.9	55.1
1973	14,713	12,462	18.1	55.0
1969	10,875	9,295	17.4	57.9

Source: Commonwealth Edison Company, *1979 Financial Review*, p. 15.

Table 2   Generation by Fuel Source (billions of kilowatthours)

YEAR	COAL	NUCLEAR	OIL	GAS	TOTAL	FUEL COSTS MILLS PER KILOWATTHOUR
1979	28.3	25.2	7.2	1.9	62.6	15.35
1973	36.0	17.5	4.1	1.9	59.5	4.63
1969	38.2	.8	.3	6.0	45.3	3.03

Source: Commonwealth Edison Company, *1979 Financial Review*, p. 14.

In 1969, a year before passage of the Clean Air Act and four years before the first oil shock, Commonwealth Edison relied on coal to generate 85% of its power; oil and natural gas were its other principal fuels, except for the first unit of its Dresden nuclear facility. Nuclear power, however, accounted for 30% of CWE's generating capacity by the time oil prices quadrupled and coal prices were doubling (see Tables 2 and 3).

With the start-up of its Dresden #1 reactor in 1960, Commonwealth Edison became one of the first utilities in America to generate electricity commercially by nuclear fission. It had built six more nuclear plants in the late 1960s. Its experience with construction and operating costs was so favorable that it planned six more units in the early 1970s, to meet the demand it forecast for the eighties.

Based on load-growth projections in the range of 6% annually, the company ordered two 1,100 MW units (LaSalle Station) in 1970, two more (Byron Station) in 1972, and two more (Braidwood Station) in 1973. After thoroughly investigating each case, the Illinois Commerce Commission found the projects warranted, and readily issued Certificates of Public Convenience and Necessity.

MANAGEMENT AND ORGANIZATION

The Commonwealth Edison Company was organized in seven operating divisions, employing 16,000 people. Nearly one-third of these employees were in management. The company's senior management, located in modest quarters

Table 3   Cost of Fuel Consumed (cents per million BTU)

YEAR	COAL	NUCLEAR	OIL (#6)	OIL (PEAKER)	GAS	AVERAGE
1974	58.7	16.5	102.6	223.4	81.5	55.5
1977	104.8	19.9	251.1	284.1	209.9	83.4
1979	168.7	28.6	355.8	364.8	279.7	138.6
12 mo. 3/31/80	177.6	29.3	407.0	429.3	292.4	145.3

Source: Commonwealth Edison Company, *Data Book*, March 1980, p. 14.

on an upper floor of the First National Bank of Chicago building, worked in a surprisingly informal environment. Lack of an organizational chart, a long tradition of job switching among senior executives, and the CEO's personality appeared to account for this.

Responsibility for operations was divided among the three line executives who reported directly to Jim O'Connor. Wallace Behnke, Jr., the vice chairman, headed up financial and accounting activities and fuel purchasing. Bide Thomas, one of two executive vice presidents, was responsible for industrial relations, load management, and conservation, marketing, purchasing, and division operations. Byron Lee, Jr., the other executive vice president, headed engineering, generation and transmission activities, nuclear licensing, and environmental compliance. Also reporting directly to O'Connor were the vice president for legal affairs, the directors of community relations and nuclear safety, and the manager of nuclear plant construction.

Horizontal job switching was an important aspect of CWE's management policy. Functional managers, vice presidents, and even executive vice presidents were expected to exchange jobs periodically. With relatively little trepidation, engineers assumed responsibility for personnel, auditors took over power production, and marketing managers became financiers. In addition to developing experienced general managers, this practice was thought to create extremely fluid channels of communication and a high degree of organizational coherence.

Jim O'Connor himself was the third ingredient that distinguished CWE's management. The *Chicago Daily News* described O'Connor as "Edison's Mr. Energy," with reference to his propensity for working twelve-hour days six days a week. Others knew him as the company's "Mr. Outside"—the man responsible for maintaining a constructive regulatory climate.

O'Connor went to work for Commonwealth Edison in 1963, after receiving degrees from St. Ignatius High School in Chicago, Holy Cross College, Harvard Business School, and Georgetown Law. Although his first assignment at CWE was digging pole holes, O'Connor was made administrative assistant to the chairman of the executive committee after two years. That position was uniquely suited to provide an apprenticeship in the political and regulatory aspects of utility management. By the time O'Connor became president, there supposedly was no one in Chicago politics, or scarcely in Illinois, that he didn't know and get along with. Even after his appointment as chairman, O'Connor remained one of CWE's two registered lobbyists.

O'Connor had long been as devoted to community activities as he was to nuclear power—something he urged of all CWE's senior executives: "Our fortunes will rise or fall with the fortunes of Chicago, so we have to help make Chicago a better place."[1] He was, in fact, outspokenly critical of business leaders who were ineffective in civic affairs. O'Connor himself served actively as director or trustee for four corporations and twenty-one other organizations, including the Field Museum of Natural History, the Chicago Urban League (past chairman), the Lyric Opera, the Chicago Unit of the American Cancer Society, Associates of Harvard Business School, Holy Cross College and Northwestern University, the Catholic Charities Board of Advisors, Michael Reese Medical

Center, the Children's Home and Aid Society of Illinois, Boy Scouts of America, the Chicago Area Council, and the Board of Citizenship Council of Metropolitan Chicago.

O'Connor's primary goal for Commonwealth Edison was to provide reliable electric service at the lowest possible long-term cost. This, he believed, was something more than a strategic objective. Rather, it was a guiding principle, not subject to change, that distinguished utility management from that of other firms. And yet it was consistent with management's secondary objective of providing fair and attractive earnings to investors.

O'Connor was committed to nuclear power as the best means for achieving these goals. Yet in the spring of 1980, the issue of delaying construction appeared to some observers to pose an inconsistency between these two purposes.

THE REGULATORY CLIMATE

The regulatory climate, according to Jim O'Connor, "is the paramount factor" that determined the outcome of the company's rate requests. By climate, O'Connor meant the mood of, and surrounding economic and political influences on, the commissioners of the Illinois Commerce Commission. Second in importance was the U.S. Nuclear Regulatory Commission, which licensed and set construction and operating standards for all of CWE's nuclear power plants.

Like most other electric companies, Commonwealth Edison suffered from a badly tarnished public image. Power shortages early in the 1970s, difficulties with air and water pollution, and involvement with nuclear power contributed. But it was the large annual rate hikes, spelled out for consumers on a monthly basis, that had aggravated all these problems of customer and public relations with which utilities normally coped (see Exhibit 3).

THE ILLINOIS COMMERCE COMMISSION

These circumstances had caused the regulatory activities of the Illinois Commerce Commission, and selection of its five commissioners, to become highly publicized, if not politicized. In fact, bills were pending in the state legislature to make the office of commissioner elective instead of appointive. As things stood, the governor appointed commissioners, with consent of the state senate, for overlapping five-year terms (with minority party representation required).

The Illinois Commerce Commission had a staff of 283, and an operating budget of $7.5 million. The commission had jurisdiction over 218 utilities in Illinois; besides gas and electric utilities, there were telephones, intrastate trucks, radio stations, buses, railroads, and sewer and water companies. Hearing examiners generally conducted proceedings, although commissioners themselves would hear oral arguments in important cases. Proceedings in major rate cases could last as long as eleven months. Indeed, as rate requests had gotten larger, the commission tended to wait the maximum time allowed, in order to delay the rate increases. The ICC's professional staff participated actively by introducing evidence and cross-examining witnesses.

In March 1979, Governor James Thompson, a Republican, appointed Michael Hasten, his thirty-four-year-old special assistant, as chairman of the commission. Hasten's previous experience was in private law practice and as assistant director of the Illinois Department of Insurance. Hasten took office vocally, determined to make a record as a hard-nosed protector of the public interest. He hired some talented young staff members, used the press freely and effectively to publicize his stance, and tended to rely on common sense to make decisions on very complex technical issues.[2]

THREE MILE ISLAND

If drama was on Hasten's agenda, then his timing was perfect. Two weeks after he became chairman of the ICC, an emergency reactor cooling system failed at the Three Mile Island nuclear plant in Harrisburg, Pennsylvania, resulting in the worst accident in the history of commercial nuclear power. The TMI accident affected political and regulatory conditions in Illinois in several ways.

The Nuclear Regulatory Commission announced a six-month freeze on nuclear licensing, while its staff concentrated on studying the TMI accident. These developments would certainly delay completion of nuclear plants still under construction. Later in 1979, the Kemeny Commission, appointed by the president to study the situation, recommended improvements in nuclear-plant safety that required costly and time-consuming modifications to operating plants as well as those under construction. Moreover, the commission's concern for human safety focused on two existing plants that were near large urban areas. One of these was Commonwealth Edison's Zion Station, about forty miles north of Chicago. For several months, the NRC deliberated over whether or not Zion should be shut down, or at least ordered to operate well below capacity.

For a time, these events on the national scene revitalized the lethargic antinuclear movement in Illinois. Activist groups conducted a few rallies, wrote letters to the editors of local newspapers, and took what legal action they could to challenge construction and licensing of the six nuclear plants that CWE had under construction. In an effort to prevent the licensing of Byron Station, the second of Edison's three nuclear plants under construction, the Rockford League of Women Voters had hired Myron Cherry, who according to Ralph Nader, was "the only lawyer in the country who has stopped the construction of a nuclear power plant."[3]

Antinuclear pressures in other states also had an impact on Commonwealth Edison. In the fall of 1979, the governors of South Carolina, Nevada, and Washington, the only three states with nuclear waste storage facilities, banned shipments from Commonwealth Edison, the largest nongovernment source of nuclear waste. Allegedly due to carelessness, CWE had more violations of packaging and shipping regulations than any other shipper.[4] This situation posed a difficult political problem for Governor Thompson, who supported CWE's nuclear program but certainly didn't want the onus of proposing a storage facility for Illinois.

THE SECOND OIL SHOCK

Nuclear fuel was not CWE's only problem in 1979. Triggered by the Iranian Revolution, a second round of oil-price hikes by OPEC commenced in August. By early 1980, the price of crude oil had risen from about $14 a barrel to $32. The price of natural gas was also rising, according to provisions in the Natural Gas Policy Act of 1978. Low-sulfur coal prices were following suit, in part due to the federal strip mining control act that took effect in 1977. Economic growth had begun to slow.

CWE'S RECENT PERFORMANCE AND THE 1979 RATE CASE

In April 1979, Commonwealth Edison had filed for a rate hike of 18.3%, just after a year of exceptional earnings performance. In 1978, revenues had risen 16%, net income 32%, and earnings per common share, 15%—and this with a rate increase of only 3.1% (see Exhibit 4).

But inflation, high interest rates, and the immense capital requirements of CWE's nuclear-plant construction program were taking their toll. Commonwealth Edison, in the words of its financial vice president, was "facing a financial crisis."[5] Moody's Investor Service had evidently recognized this in January 1979, when it derated Edison's first mortgage bonds to AA.[6]

At the time, CWE's five-year construction budget was $4.4 billion, not including an additional $581 million for nuclear fuel investments during that period (1979 to 1983). With only $440 million likely to be available from internal cash generation, it appeared that CWE would need to borrow $1.4 billion to meet its cash requirements for 1979 alone.[7]

INTEREST COVERAGE RATIO

By April, when it made its request for a $452 million rate hike, CWE had already arranged four security issues, providing about half ($681 million) of its 1979 financing. Little more could be done with equity, since Edison's common stock was already selling for fifteen percent below book value. Moreover, after the company sold $200 million of first mortgage bonds in June, it could issue no more senior debt, since its interest coverage ratio would fall below the level (2.50) required by the indentures in its mortgage bonds.

Interest coverage refers to the ratio of earnings available for meeting

Table 4 Interest Coverages Before Income Taxes, 1973–1979 Commonwealth Edison Company

YEAR	MORTGAGE INDENTURE (EMBEDDED BOND INTEREST COST ONLY)	SEC METHOD (TOTAL INTEREST)*
1973	3.38	3.37
1974	3.11	3.06
1975	3.13	3.27
1976	3.57	3.31
1977	2.72	2.69
1978	2.86	2.77
1979	2.22	1.99

*Interest charged during construction is included in earnings available for coverage under SEC method, whereas it is excluded from earnings available for purposes of CWE's indenture.

Source: Commonwealth Edison Company, "Testimony of Robert J. Schultz," in Illinois Commerce Commission, Case No. 83-, Exhibit 1, Schedule 1.2.

interest on debt, to that interest. It can be computed either before or after taxes, and either including or excluding the credit for interest charged to construction (allowance for funds used during construction, or AFUDC).[8] Table 4 shows CWE's interest coverage ratios, which in an earlier era had been as high as 7.0. Since utilities were so highly leveraged, interest coverage was the single most important determinant of credit ratings and, therefore, an important factor in the cost of debt.

Commonwealth Edison could not complete its 1979 financings without raising its interest coverage ratio, and that would only be possible if a substantial interim rate hike were granted in a few months. Here, in fact, was the crucial link between rates and revenues on the one hand, and capital budgets and external financing on the other. It was not that the rate hike would have significantly reduced borrowing requirements; rather, it would have raised the level of the company's financial measures, especially the interest coverage ratio.

THE INTERIM RATE ORDER

CWE petitioned for an immediate, interim rate increase of $225 million—enough to raise its coverage ratio to 2.87 by year's end. To facilitate matters, the company agreed not to contest the normal substantive issues until after the interim decision, as part of the proceedings for the final order.

For a variety of reasons, the case went poorly for Commonwealth Edison. Most important, the ICC staff made an arithmetic error in computing what it believed was the minimum necessary rate hike to assure an indenture coverage ratio of 2.5. It recommended a $45 million increase, *on an annualized basis*, which unfortunately amounted to just $9 million for the ten weeks to which it applied. CWE had actually needed $45 million just for that period.

The commission delivered its decision by a 4 to 1 margin in September 1979, allowing this rate increase of only 1.65%. And even that was too generous for Chairman Hasten, who voted against any rate increase whatsoever, commenting that the company has "a great, long way to go to get any ultimate relief."[9]

Later on the same day as the ICC's decision, James O'Connor announced that a decision had been made to halt construction at the Braidwood nuclear power plant, to slow down work at the Byron facility, and to immediately implement other cost-cutting measures to avert a potential cash-flow crisis. The commission's decision, and Hasten's position in particular, indicated a lack of support for Commonwealth Edison's nuclear construction program.

THE FINAL RATE ORDER

The final phase of CWE's 1979 rate case was completed in an atmosphere of recrimination and editorial rhetoric. Consumer groups in Northern Illinois generally commended Chairman Hasten and the commission, encouraging them not to "cave in" to pressure from Commonwealth Edison.

A prominent Chicago investment banker, however, released a letter to the governor in which he said that "the ICC has lost credibility among members of the investment community."[10] CWE's year-end performance figures for 1979 did appear dismal—especially its interest coverage ratio, which fell below 2.0, and the percentage of its net earnings that was cash (rather than allowance for funds used during construction). Of the 100 largest electric utilities, only nine were worse off by the first measure, and five by the second. The median coverage ratio for utilities with AA bonds was 2.8 (excluding AFUDC).[11] This condition prompted Moody's to derate CWE's bonds for a second time, from AA to A (and its debentures to Baa). "We hope the ICC will take note of our action," said a spokesperson for Moody's. "It's up to them to improve the situation."[12]

CWE itself began an advocacy advertising campaign, quite unlike the moderate image advertising in which utilities traditionally engaged. The first ad dealt with nuclear waste storage, and the second, with rates. "We're working for you," it declared, "and we need a raise" (see Exhibit 5).

In the rate proceeding, Commonwealth Edison presented new arguments in support of a rate base that would justify a rate hike of $450 million (see Exhibit 6). This time the ICC generally agreed, although two innovative and controversial mechanisms were employed.

Construction Work in Progress (CWIP) was one of these mechanisms. This referred to inclusion in the rate base of all or part of the capital expenditures on nonproducing plants still under construction. The point of including it was to generate cash income (as part of the rate of return), rather than noncash earnings from AFUDC, the interest on construction expenditures that would be capitalized when the plant entered service.

CWIP had become a regulatory controversy throughout the United States, since construction projects by utilities tied up so much capital for so long. Earlier in 1979, the ICC allowed a small amount of CWIP for the first time, in a case involving Illinois Power. Consumerists objected, on the grounds that CWIP entailed an intergenerational transfer (from current consumers to future ones), and that investors, not rate payers, should bear the carrying costs of asset creation. Antinuclear activists supported this position, since it served their objectives.

Commonwealth Edison asked to include 10% ($343 million) of its construction investment in its rate base. By replacing some AFUDC with this CWIP, said Edison's financial expert, "the book cost of completed projects is lower, so rates are lower in the future. The amount of the utility's reported earnings are not significantly affected, but their quality improves."[13] Citizens for a Better Environment, an intervenor in the case, argued unsuccessfully that no CWIP should be included, since the need for it was a result of the nuclear construction program, reflecting poor planning and management by Edison.[14]

An inflation adjustment to the CWE's rate base was the other significant issue. CWE argued that to be fair and reasonable, rates had to give consideration to inflation. To accomplish this, Edison proposed adjusting the original cost valuation of plant in service by a weighted deflator. By accepting a modified version of this technique, the commission authorized a 21% ($1 billion) increase in the rate base.

With CWE's rate base set at $6.024 billion, expected 1979 operating expenses at $2.327 billion, and revenues at $2.645 billion, and with inflation and load growth for 1980 estimated to be 7.7% and 3.8%, respectively, the commission concluded that Commonwealth Edison should raise its rates by $389 million, to attain a rate of return of 8.37%.

When the ICC announced this increase in February 1980, reactions were mixed. According to an analyst for Goldman, Sachs, it meant that Edison was "out of the swamp, but not out of the woods."[15] Jim O'Connor hoped it indicated an improving regulatory climate. But sign-carrying protestors greeted the decision with outrage, accusing Michael Hasten of providing a "bailout" for CWE's nuclear-plant construction program.[16]

THE NUCLEAR-PLANT CONSTRUCTION CASE

Now that the rate case was completed, the ICC reopened the construction case. After the 1979 rate case had begun, the Illinois Commerce Commission suspended its investigation (begun five months earlier) of Commonwealth Edison's nuclear-plant construction program. In view of the excess reserve margins forecast by the company, the commission had felt it "should examine the economic reasonableness from the utility's and ratepayer's viewpoints of continuing or delaying the construction schedule of the Byron and/or Braidwood stations."[17]

Load Growth

Technically, Commonwealth Edison's original decisions to build six more nuclear power plants were not at issue. Nor were its management's methods of forecasting load growth, which subsequently had proven so optimistic. But since many intervenors raised these points, Edison's management felt obliged to defend itself.

By 1978, when the construction case began, CWE had lowered its ten-year forecast of load growth to 5.05% per year. Given its construction schedule (and planned retirements) at that time, the company expected its total reserve margin to reach 29% in 1983, when the last two nuclear plants entered service, and to decline thereafter. A reserve margin of 14% over peak load was deemed adequate by Edison, although most utilities set the required level higher.

In 1979, the company reduced its estimated load growth to 4.5%, and announced a one-year delay in completion of all six nuclear generating units. In January 1980, Commonwealth Edison further reduced its rolling estimate of load growth, this time to 4.2%, and added another year to its schedule for Braidwood, pushing back the service dates for its two units to 10/83 and 10/84 (see Exhibit 7). This delay would help maintain CWE's five-year capital budget, and was necessary, since time had been lost by the work stoppage at Braidwood and by several modifications recently ordered by the Nuclear Regulatory Commission.

Delay, however, was the last thing James O'Connor wanted. CWE's position in the construction case was to adamantly oppose any delays whatsoever, on the grounds that they would be exceedingly costly to ratepayers.

The Econometric Brief

Commonwealth Edison bolstered its argument against delay with an array of econometric studies that showed these costs over the projected lifetime of the nuclear plants. Late in February, in informal discussions with ICC staff and some of the intervenors, CWE agreed to adopt two sets of parameters for its studies: (1) load-growth rates of 4%, 2%, and 0%, and (2) delays of two and four years for the two units at Braidwood, since they were the furthest behind. The discounted present value of revenue requirements over the life of the plant was calculated using a discount rate of 10.3%, CWE's average cost of capital. The results, shown in Exhibits 8 and 9, are summarized in Table 5.

By any measure, the cost of delaying construction was substantial, even if load growth were assumed to be 0%. The most important factors were inflation, the cost of substitute fuels, and carrying charges. Delaying Braidwood's 2,200 megawatts of nuclear capacity would necessitate the use of far more expensive coal and oil. Per kilowatthour, No. 6 cycling oil was six times as expensive as

Table 5   The Present Value Revenue Requirement Penalties of Delaying Construction at CWE's Braidwood Plant

	LOAD GROWTH		
	4%	2%	0%
Two-Year Delay			
PV revenue requirement			
(10/83) penalty ($mil.)	698	469	311
Breakeven discount rate	77%	33%	21%
Four-Year Delay			
PV revenue requirement			
(10/83) penalty ($mil.)	1,363	906	567
Breakeven discount rate	72%	31%	19%

Source: Commonwealth Edison Company, "Studies Analyzing Various Construction and Operating Schedules for the Braidwood Station, Presented by John C. Bukovski," 1980, in Illinois Commerce Commission, Case No. 78-0646, p. 3.

nuclear fuel. Carrying charges, although reduced in the early years by a delay, would be higher in later years—more than offsetting the temporary savings.

Using many of the same parameters, the ICC's staff performed its own econometric studies. Its higher discount rate and shorter plant life reduced the costs of delay by a few million dollars, but not enough to prevent it from appearing very unattractive.

Although none of the intervenors, which included several consumer and environmental groups, had any credible econometric projections, they persisted in attacking CWE's construction program in disregard of its elaborate studies. Since Edison was projecting a surplus reserve margin for most of the 1980s, common sense seemed to indicate either delay or cancellation. "Engineering economics," according to a spokesman for the Community Thrift Clubs, "is merely an aid to judgment, not a substitute for it."[18]

Intervenors also complained that Edison's management had ignored other options besides timely completion of the nuclear plants. For example, why couldn't CWE sell the Braidwood plant, or at least some ownership participation, to another electric utility?

In fact, shortly after the construction case had begun, Jim O'Connor did send out invitations to twenty-four neighboring utilities, offering to undertake such discussions. But so far, none had responded positively, despite the fact that CWE's new nuclear plants were among the least expensive of any being built in the United States (see Exhibit 10). Moreover, since most other utilities had their own surplus capacity, Commonwealth Edison was also largely unsuccessful at arranging wholesale contracts for its surplus electricity.

Considering Delay

Despite the significant cost of delay, there were some reasons for considering it as a serious option in the spring of 1980. Among these were the following:

1. Major redesign and rework of piping and structure at LaSalle Station, resulting from findings at reactors with similar containments in Europe
2. Other increases in engineering work load caused by new requirements of the Nuclear Regulatory Commission based on "lessons learned" at Three Mile Island
3. Better projections of materials and manpower required at the Byron and Braidwood Stations
4. Cash constraints limiting the rate of work at Byron and Braidwood in 1979 and 1980, and which appear to be continuing for several years
5. Continuing evidence that the load-growth forecast was too optimistic

At a meeting of the senior staff budget group on March 31, 1980, the engineering department indicated that in consideration of the preceding factors, it appeared that the existing construction schedule could not be maintained; certainly without exceeding the current five-year capital budget, approved by the board of directors just two months earlier, by about $400 million—$115 million in 1985 alone (see Exhibits 11 and 12). At this point, the finance side of the house reiterated its concern about CWE's ability to raise any additional capital whatsoever, beyond the ambitious target of $1.1 billion already scheduled for 1980.

As a result of this meeting, Jim O'Connor instructed all responsibility centers to review the costs and timing of hundreds of planned projects in addition to the big three nuclear plants. This review, which turned up further cost escalations, indicated that even if all expenditures were rigidly constrained, capital expenditures for 1980 would exceed the budget by $100 million, even if the nuclear plants *were* delayed. The staff prepared a series of budget options (Exhibit 13).

Jim O'Connor had been chairman for two months, and introduced his new management team at the annual meeting of the stockholders in mid-April. No mention had been made at that meeting either of changing the construction schedule or the capital budget. Significant mid-year adjustments were uncommon.

O'Connor certainly wanted to maintain both the nuclear-plant construction schedule and the capital budget. To delay the nuclear-plant construction program, even just the Braidwood units, would be costly to ratepayers. Increasing the capital budget, however, would stretch even further the company's financial resources, to the detriment of stockholders.

A change at this juncture would alarm the capital markets, where analysts were already wary of Commonwealth Edison. Ratepayers, too, would not understand a delay, since CWE had just received such a large rate hike. And with the construction case approaching its conclusion, the costs of delay were receiving publicity prepared by Edison itself.

Waiting, however, would do little good. The regulatory climate was exceedingly important. The Illinois Commerce Commission, and for that matter, the public, should be kept informed. In mid-summer, Commonwealth Edison would again have to apply for a rate hike—and this time for something more than $600 million.

The sooner this matter of the capital budget/nuclear construction schedule was settled, thought O'Connor, the better.

Exhibit 1 Electric Revenues, Kilowatthours and Customers: Commonwealth Edison Company

	1979[1]	1978	1977	1976
Electric Operating Revenues (in millions)				
Residential	$ 912.8	$ 816.9	$ 708.7	$ 652.3
Small commercial and industrial	895.4	815.5	705.2	656.1
Large commercial and industrial	646.0	560.1	456.6	408.6
Public authorities	194.5	175.7	150.6	141.1
Electric railroads	11.1	9.7	8.2	7.6
Total revenues from ultimate consumers	$ 2,659.8	$ 2,377.9	$ 2,029.3	$ 1,865.7
Sales for resale	43.7	47.5	49.5	27.7
Other revenues	17.4	17.4	16.2	14.8
Total	$ 2,720.9	$ 2,442.8	$ 2,095.0	$ 1,908.2
Percent outside Chicago (ultimate consumers)	66.2%	65.4%	64.4%	63.8%
Kilowatthours (in millions)				
Generated (net)	62,133	66,879	63,093	60,717
Purchased and interchanged (net)	5,824	1,892	2,974	2,557
Total electric output	67,957	68,771	66,067	63,274
Deduct—losses and company use	3,899	4,730	4,618	4,937
Total available for sale	64,058	64,041	61,449	58,337
Sales:				
Residential	17,753	17,541	17,015	16,114
Small commercial and industrial	18,877	18,864	18,142	17,433
Large commercial and industrial	20,361	19,982	18,765	17,655
Public authorities	5,513	5,572	5,443	5,345
Electric railroads	348	348	336	334
Total sales to ultimate consumers	62,852	62,307	59,701	56,881
Sales for resale	1,206	1,734	1,748	1,456
Total sales	64,058	64,041	61,449	58,337
Percent outside Chicago (ultimate consumers)	67.3%	66.6%	65.7%	65.2%
Number of Electric Customers (at end of year)				
Residential	2,678,137	2,636,181	2,593,172	2,557,466
Small commercial and industrial	229,289	227,563	224,322	222,001
Large commercial and industrial	885	827	817	798
Public authorities	11,035	10,872	10,895	10,753
Electric railroads	2	2	2	2
Resale	7	8	9	8
Total	2,919,355	2,875,453	2,829,217	2,791,028
Increase over previous year	43,902	46,236	38,189	31,077
Average Revenue Per Kilowatthour				
Residential (excluding light bulb service)	5.11¢	4.63¢	4.14¢	4.03¢
Small commercial and industrial	4.74	4.32	3.89	3.76
Large commercial and industrial	3.17	2.80	2.43	2.31

[1]Includes approximately $33.7 million additional electric operating revenues and about 625 million kilowatthours, principally residential, resulting from the change to monthly from bi-monthly billing in late March 1979.

[2]Reflects a reduction of 22,000 customers resulting from the sale of noncontiguous electric properties in 1974.

Source: Commonwealth Edison Company, *1979 Financial Review*, pp. 4–5.

Exhibit 1 (cont.)

	1975	1974	1973	1972	1971	1970	1969
	$ 609.2	$ 519.8	$ 474.3	$ 431.7	$ 378.7	$ 340.4	$ 304.0
	585.2	487.8	425.8	389.1	344.9	313.7	286.2
	357.6	306.7	246.8	219.1	177.8	155.3	139.4
	124.5	98.7	82.8	72.9	63.5	54.4	48.6
	6.9	6.3	5.7	6.2	5.9	5.5	5.4
	$ 1,683.4	$ 1,419.3	$ 1,235.4	$ 1,119.0	$ 970.8	$ 869.3	$ 783.6
	24.7	27.4	19.2	11.3	10.0	9.4	9.8
	14.2	12.9	11.6	9.9	8.8	8.3	7.7
	$ 1,722.3	$ 1,459.6	$ 1,266.2	$ 1,140.2	$ 989.6	$ 887.0	$ 801.1
	63.1%	62.6%	62.7%	62.1%	60.8%	59.9%	59.0%
	58,265	58,449	59,388	53,870	48,264	47,613	45,382
	2,817	2,226	2,091	3,134	4,771	3,147	2,903
	61,082	60,675	61,479	57,004	53,035	50,760	48,285
	4,386	4,409	4,379	4,674	4,270	3,919	3,898
	56,696	56,266	57,100	52,330	48,765	46,841	44,387
	16,166	15,086	15,451	14,491	13,740	12,999	11,826
	16,721	16,236	16,626	15,453	14,820	14,243	13,378
	16,912	17,967	18,126	16,512	14,652	14,241	13,781
	5,113	4,786	4,852	4,274	4,032	3,774	3,563
	330	320	335	391	390	400	385
	55,242	54,395	55,390	51,121	47,634	45,657	42,933
	1,454	1,871	1,710	1,209	1,131	1,184	1,454
	56,696	56,266	57,100	52,330	48,765	46,841	44,387
	64.4%	63.7%	63.2%	62.4%	61.3%	60.4%	59.7%
	2,527,728	2,497,271	2,484,951	2,434,198	2,379,535	2,345,231	2,308,041
	220,771	220,227	223,042	221,494	220,311	220,000	221,149
	794	780	769	735	672	658	665
	10,648	10,256	10,175	9,893	9,664	9,385	9,099
	2	2	2	2	2	2	2
	8	9	8	8	8	6	6
	2,759,951	2,728,545[2]	2,718,947	2,666,330	2,610,192	2,575,282	2,538,962
	31,406	9,598	52,617	56,138	34,910	36,320	54,917
	3.75¢	3.42¢	3.04¢	2.95¢	2.72¢	2.58¢	2.53¢
	3.50	3.00	2.56	2.52	2.33	2.20	2.14
	2.11	1.71	1.36	1.33	1.21	1.09	1.01

Exhibit 2 Generating Stations, Capability and Output: Commonwealth Edison Company

NAME OF STATION	LOCATION	NUMBER OF UNITS	WEIGHTED AVERAGE AGE OF CAPACITY AT DECEMBER 31, 1979 (YEARS)	NET CAPABILITY AT DECEMBER 31, 1979 (mw)	TOTAL OUTPUT FOR 1979 (millions of kwh)
Nuclear					
Dresden	Near Morris	3	11	1,795	8,402
Quad-Cities	Near Cordova	2	8	1,183[1]	6,563
Zion	Zion	2	6	2,080	10,279
				5,058	25,244
Coal[2]					
Powerton	Near Pekin	2	6	1,700	5,665
Joliet	Near Joliet	3	16	1,414	6,027
Kincaid	Near Taylorville	2	12	1,212	4,056
Will County	Near Lockport	4	21	1,093	4,547
State Line	Hammond, Indiana	2	21	508	2,415
Waukegan	Waukegan	3	21	774	3,289
Crawford	Chicago	2	20	548	1,953
Fisk	Chicago	1	21	341	1,327
				7,590	29,279
Oil and Gas					
Ridgeland	Stickney	4	28	606	2,411
Collins	Near Morris	5	2	2,698	4,674
Emergency peaking units and hydro	(Various)	96	11	1,872	1,061
				5,176	8,146

Net generating capability owned at December 31, 1979 and net generation in 1979	$\underline{\underline{12}}$	62,669
Pumped storage (Near Ludington, Mich.)[4]	17,824[3]	1,172
Deduct—Energy delivered for pumping	624	(1,708)
Output provided by purchases and diversity exchanges (net)	_____	5,824
Net system capability at December 31, 1979 and system output for 1979	18,448[5]	67,957
Deduct—Oil and gas fired emergency peaking capacity owned at December 31, 1979	1,872[5]	
Net system capability at December 31, 1979 excluding oil and gas fired emergency peaking capacity	16,576	

[1]Based upon the Company's 75% ownership.

[2]Ignition gas and limited amounts of boiler gas are used at some coal-fired stations.

[3]Before deducting summer limitations of 300 mw at date of summer peak.

[4]Represents the Company's entitlement to one-third (624 mw) of the capability of the Ludington pumped storage plant owned by Consumers Power Company and Detroit Edison Company. Excludes sales for resale to seven municipal utility systems.

[5]Before deducting summer limitations estimated at 172 mw for owned steam-electric generating capacity and 362 mw for oil and gas fired emergency peaking capacity.

Source: Commonwealth Edison Company, *1979 Financial Review*, p. 16.

Exhibit 3   The History of Electric Rate Increases and Decreases: Commonwealth Edison Company

DATE OF FILING/DECISION	COMPANY REQUEST DOLLARS	PERCENT	ICC ACTION DOLLARS	PERCENT
June 25, 1953 (F)	$ 17,500,000	6.5		
Feb. 1, 1954 (D)			$ 17,500,000	6.5[1]
July 23, 1957 (F)	$ 26,434,000	7.3		
June 19, 1958 (D)			$ 26,434,000	7.3
Feb. 2, 1962 (F)	($ 4,222,000)	(0.9)		
March 5, 1962 (D)			($ 4,222,000)	(0.9)
Apr. 17, 1964 (F)	($ 12,490,000)	(2.4)		
June 1, 1964 (D)			($ 12,490,000)	(2.4)
Nov. 8, 1965 (F)	($ 5,200,000)	(0.9)		
Dec. 15, 1965 (D)			($ 5,200,000)	(0.9)
Aug. 15, 1969 (F)	$ 45,800,000	6.1		
July 3, 1970 (D)			$ 36,000,000	4.8
Jan. 14, 1971 (F)	$ 95,200,000	10.4		
Dec. 13, 1971 (D)			$ 65,900,000	7.1
Feb. 16, 1973 (D)	(second part)		$ 32,500,000	2.9
May 15, 1973 (F)	$154,000,000	12,65		
Apr. 11, 1974 (D)			$134,700,000	10.7
Oct. 4, 1974 (F)	$241,000,000	15.6		
Feb. 18, 1975 (D)			$ 90,000,000	5.8[2] (interim)
Sept. 2, 1975 (D)			$116,155,000	6.8
Nov. 19, 1976 (F)	$279,600,000	14.5		
Oct. 14, 1977 (D)			$152,663,000	7.65
Jan. 20, 1978 (F)	$125,000,000	5.6		
Dec. 14, 1978 (D)			$ 74,880,000	3.1
Apr. 6, 1979 (F)	$452,000,000	18.3		
Interim	$225,000,000	9.2		
Oct. 15, 1979 (D)			$ 45,200,000	1.65[3] (interim)
Feb. 7, 1980 (D)			$344,400,000	12.77

[1]This was the first Edison rate increase in a 66-year period that had been marked by 26 rate reductions.
[2]Total rate increase equals $206,155,000, 12.6%.
[3]Total rate increase equals $389,600,000, 14.42%.
Source: Commonwealth Edison Company.

Exhibit 4 Statement of Consolidated Income (in millions): Commonwealth Edison Company

	1979[1]	1978	1977	1976
Electric Operating Revenues	$2,720.9	$2,442.8	$2,095.0	$1,908.2
Electric Operating Expenses and Taxes:				
Fuel	$ 962.8	$ 753.8	$ 592.3	$ 489.1
Purchased and interchanged power—net	163.2	50.9	71.3	46.9
Operation	406.2	354.2	307.8	286.4
Maintenance	179.1	164.5	142.9	121.2
Depreciation	250.1	228.9	212.4	196.9
Taxes (except income)	305.7	320.9	280.4	250.7
Income taxes				
Current—Federal	61.6	70.1	11.3	33.4
—State	8.7	9.4	6.5	7.3
Deferred—Federal—net	46.1	76.1	78.9	92.6
—State—net	6.1	6.7	6.9	8.2
Investment tax credits deferred—net	(4.0)	32.5	57.3	45.2
	$2,385.8	$2,068.0	$1,768.0	$1,577.9
Electric Operating Income	$ 335.1	$ 374.8	$ 327.0	$ 330.3
Other Income and (Deductions):				
Interest on long-term debt	$ (298.4)	$ (240.9)	$ (204.1)	$ (167.8)
Interest on notes payable	(36.4)	(16.2)	(10.2)	(5.0)
Allowance for funds used during construction				
Borrowed funds, net of income taxes	68.9	44.6	29.4	16.3
Equity funds	153.3	114.7	75.5	50.4
Current income tax credits applicable to non-operating activities	77.3	51.3	35.9	21.2
Gain on sale of noncontiguous electric properties (net of income taxes)	—	—	—	—
Miscellaneous—net	(3.1)	(7.3)	(6.7)	(3.6)
	$ (38.4)	$ (53.8)	$ (80.2)	$ (88.5)
Net Income	$ 296.7	$ 321.0	$ 246.8	$ 241.8
Provision for Dividends on Preferred and Preference Stocks	81.7	66.9	54.1	48.5
Net Income on Common Stock	$ 215.0	$ 254.1	$ 192.7	$ 193.3
Average Number of Common and Common Equivalent Shares Outstanding	85.8	76.9	67.4	60.5
Earnings per Common and Common Equivalent Share	$ 2.51	$ 3.30	$ 2.86	$ 3.20
Cash Dividends Declared per Common Share	$ 2.60	$ 2.45	$ 2.40	$ 2.40

The Notes to Financial Statements in the Company's Annual Reports to Stockholders are an integral part of the above statements.

[1]During 1979 the Company changed from bi-monthly to monthly billing for residential and certain commercial customers. For the year 1979, this change resulted in additional operating revenues of approximately $33.7 million and additional net income of approximately $10.4 million or about 12¢ per common share.

Source: Commonwealth Edison Company, *1979 Financial Review*, p. 8.

Exhibit 5

WE'RE WORKING FOR YOU. AND WE NEED A RAISE.

About eight months ago, we asked the Illinois Commerce Commission for an emergency rate increase. Several weeks ago we got a very small portion of it.

Now, we can't blame you if you're not broken up about that. It seems like every time you turn around these days, prices are going up. So it must be nice to see somebody hold the line for a change.

But this isn't the right time.

We're getting hit by inflation the same as you. It's costing us more and more to generate the electricity you use. And the plain truth is, we can't keep up.

Transformers that were $600 five years ago cost us $950 now. Fifty-eight percent more.

The poles that we need to hold our power lines. Fifty-three percent more.

The crossarms on those poles. One hundred and thirty-three percent more.

And that's just for instance. It's the same story with every piece of equipment we need.

If that's not enough, wages have gone up, and just about everything else as well. Even our state and local taxes are sixty-five percent higher than they were back then. Three hundred and thirty-seven million dollars in 1978 alone, the biggest tax bill in the state.

So the money's been going out faster than it's been coming in. Earnings are down. And our stock has sunk to less than half its 1967 value.

If we can't turn that around, if we can't keep attracting investors, if we can't borrow the money we need at reasonable rates, we simply won't be able to keep going. Not only won't we be able to cover the rising cost of day-to-day operations, we won't even be able to

maintain the kind of reliable service you're getting now. Because reliable service takes new plants and equipment to handle the increasing demand for electricity.

But say the impossible actually happened. No one ever bought another appliance or built another home; no new office buildings went up and factories never expanded an inch; northern Illinois quit growing tomorrow. Even then we'd still need new plants and equipment. Virtually everything we own, from wires and poles to our generating stations themselves, is going to wear out. Sooner or later, one by one, they'll have to be replaced.

The trouble is, that's an awfully expensive proposition. More than one billion six hundred million dollars for a single generating station, like the one we're finishing up right now at LaSalle. And what our customers pay for electricity doesn't begin to provide enough money.

The difference has to come from investors. Only, investors aren't likely to put up the money without a fair rate of return, which they won't get as long as our rates stay where they are. And whether you realize it or not, where our rates are is cheap compared to most places our size.

Roughly half of what they pay in New York City. Over twenty-five percent less than in Boston or Newark. Even substantially less than in lots of smaller cities close to home, like Terre Haute and Des Moines; and their costs—for wages, land, construction, and much more—aren't anywhere near what ours are.

There's just one solution. Adequate rate relief. A realistic increase, and soon. Before it's too late.

Since we're all in the same boat, we thought you ought to know.

Commonwealth Edison

This ad is paid for by the company and not published at our customers' expense.

Exhibit 6 Commonwealth Edison (A): Commonwealth Edison's Rate Base for 1979 Rate Case (in millions)

	ACTUAL 1978	FORECAST 1979 (CWE)		ADJUSTED 1979 (ICC)
Electric plant at original cost				
Plant in service	$6,687	$7,185		$7,185
Deduct:				
Accuml. depreciation	1,808	2,022		2,022
Accuml. deferred income taxes	774	847		866
Other	93	86		86
Net plant at original cost	$4,012	$4,230		$4,211
Weighted value of net plant				
Original cost (75%)			$3,158	
Current value (25%)			2,070	
		Total	$5,228	
Other rate base items				
Nuclear fuel stock account	$ 176	$ 190		$ 190
Plant held for future use	74	138		67
Working capital requirements				
Fossil fuel inventories	117	303		197
Other	64	72		60
Construction work in progress on which				
AFUDC is not capitalized	16	19		19
Construction work in progress		343		343
Deduct operating reserves	13	14		14
Total	$ 434	$1,051		$ 862
Original cost rate base			$5,073	
Less resales to municipalities			55	
		Total	$5,018	
Fair value rate base			$6,090	
Less resales to municipalities			66	
		Total	$6,024	

Source: Illinois Commerce Commission, Order No. 79-0214, pp. 4, 12.

Exhibit 7 Commonwealth Edison (A): Commonwealth Edison Company, Load and Capacity Statement, January 18, 1980 (in megawatts)

CAPABILITY	1980	1981	1982	1983
Total capability	17,914	18,962	19,710	20,818
Less: owned oil-fired combustion turbine peaking capacity	1,510	1,510	1,510	1,510
Net capability (excluding oil-fired combustion turbine peaking capacity)	16,404	17,452	18,200	19,308
Peak load	15,090	15,780	16,550	17,290
Total reserve margin	2,824	3,182	3,160	3,528
% total reserve*	18.7%	20.2%	19.1%	20.4%
Net additions & retirements since previous peak	0	1,078	1,078	1,120
Capacity addition program		LAS1	LAS2	BY1

*Percent reserve is reserve margin expressed as a percent of peak load.

LAS = LaSalle Nuclear Plant
BY = Byron Nuclear Plant
BR = Braidwood Nuclear Plant
FOS = (not authorized)

Source: Commonwealth Edison Company.

Exhibit 7 (cont.)

1984	1985	1986	1987	1988	1989
23,028	24,118	23,893	24,119	23,806	24,906
1,510	1,510	1,510	1,510	1,510	1,510
21,518	22,608	22,383	22,609	22,296	23,396
17,980	18,700	19,450	20,230	21,020	21,840
5,048	5,418	4,443	3,888	2,786	3,066
28.1%	29.0%	22.8%	19.2%	13.3%	14.0%
2,240	1,120	0	0	0	1,100
BY2	BR2				FOS
BR1					FOS

Exhibit 8 One Plant-Delay Cost Scenario

				DIFFERENTIAL REVENUE REQUIREMENTS ($1000's)				
Year	(1) Operation and Maint.	(2) Insurance	(3) Real Estate Taxes	(4) System Increm. Prod. Cost	(5) Carrying Charges	(6) Revenue Requirements	(7) PVRR to 10/83	(8) Cum. PVRR to 10/83
1980	0	0	0	0	37	37	48	48
1981	0	0	0	0	189	189	224	273
1982	−6708	0	0	0	−4156	−10864	−11694	−11421
1983	−9081	−653	−3954	23000	−27601	−18289	−17846	−29267
1984	−11639	−4398	−7629	86000	−211549	−149215	−131993	−161260
1985	−13689	−6107	−3074	85000	−281942	−219812	−176272	−337531
1986	−8378	−2098	798	54000	−28790	15532	11291	−326240
1987	−657	337	800	36000	119780	156260	102982	−223258
1988	−898	153	800	7000	114882	121937	72852	−150406
1989	−760	153	800	1000	110221	111414	60344	−90061
1990	−1038	153	800	0	105648	105563	51832	−38229
1991	−401	153	800	0	101171	101723	45279	7050
1992	593	153	800	0	96785	98331	39679	46729
1993	637	153	800	0	92493	94083	34417	81147
1994	684	153	800	0	88293	89930	29824	110970
1995	736	153	800	0	84185	85874	25817	136787
1996	792	153	800	0	80169	81914	22325	159113
1997	851	153	800	0	76245	78049	19284	178397
1998	915	153	800	0	72416	74284	16639	195035
1999	983	153	800	0	68679	70615	14339	209374
2000	1057	153	800	0	65142	67152	12361	221735
2001	1136	153	800	0	62183	64272	10726	232461
2002	1221	153	800	0	60053	62227	9414	241875
2003	1313	153	800	0	19089	21355	2929	244803
2004	1411	153	800	0	−5317	−2953	−367	244436
2005	1518	153	800	0	43175	45646	5145	249581
2006	1631	153	800	0	73598	76182	7784	257365
2007	1754	153	800	0	71540	74247	6877	264242
2008	1886	153	800	0	69478	72317	6073	270315
2009	2027	153	800	0	67413	70393	5359	275674
2010	2178	153	800	0	65349	68480	4726	280400
2011	2342	153	800	0	63283	66578	4165	284565
2012	2517	153	800	0	61219	64689	3669	288234
2013	2707	153	800	0	59155	62815	3230	291464
2014	2910	153	800	0	57091	60954	2841	294305
2015	3127	153	800	0	55027	59107	2498	296802
2016	3362	153	800	0	52964	57279	2194	298996
2017	3615	153	800	0	50900	55468	1926	300923
2018	3885	153	800	0	64824	69662	2193	303116
2019	0	0	0	0	118333	118333	3377	306493
2020	0	0	0	0	121059	121059	3132	309625
2021	0	0	0	0	41545	41545	974	310599
2022	0	0	0	0	4	4	0	310599
2023	0	0	0	0	0	0	0	310599
2024	0	0	0	0	0	0	0	310599
Total	−5461	−8176	11741	292000	1994262	2284366		

Source: Commonwealth Edison Company, "Studies Analyzing Various Construction and Operating Schedules for the Braidwood Station, Presented by John C. Bukovski," in Illinois Commerce Commission, Case No. 78-0646, appendix, p. 34.

Exhibit 9 Summary by Major Cost Category of Incremental Revenue Requirements of Delaying, with Different Load Growths, Commonwealth Edison's Braidwood Nuclear Plant ($1,000s)

	(1) OPERATION AND MAINT.	(2) INSURANCE	(3) REAL ESTATE TAXES	(4) SYSTEM INCREM. PROD. COST	(5) CARRYING CHARGES	(6) REVENUE REQUIREMENTS	
TOTAL −5461		−8176	11741	794000	1994262	2786366	
PVRR TO 10/1/1983							
10.3% −40803		−9797	−7094	621347	133906	697560	4% load growth,
6.0% −37076		−9899	−3702	685058	476440	1110821	2 year delay
77.3% −29073		−4676	−7716	233756	−192288	2	
TOTAL −5461		−8176	11741	497000	1994262	2489366	
PVRR TO 10/1/1983							
10.3% −40803		−9797	−7094	393215	133906	469428	2% load growth,
6.0% −37076		−9899	−3702	431646	476440	857408	2 year delay
32.7% −35986		−7522	−9373	263359	−210481	−4	
TOTAL −5461		−8176	11741	292000	1994262	2284366	
PVRR TO 10/1/1983							
10.3% −40803		−9797	−7094	234387	133906	310599	0% load growth,
6.0% −37076		−9899	−3702	255819	476440	681581	2 year delay
20.6% −39446		−8770	−9282	194458	−136962	−3	
TOTAL − 16734		−16012	22128	1745000	4356634	6091016	
PVRR TO 10/1/1983							
10.3% −82441		−17879	−14994	1230269	247801	1362757	4% load growth,
6.0% −77824		−18655	−8939	1413276	963408	2271266	4 year delay
71.8% −45846		−6620	−11393	346604	−282754	−8	
TOTAL − 16734		−16012	22128	1092000	4356634	5438016	
PVRR TO 10/1/1983							
10.3% −82441		−17879	−14994	773595	247801	906083	2% load growth,
6.0% −77824		−18655	−8939	886972	963408	1744961	2 year delay
30.9% −64920		−12268	−16506	451812	−358121	−4	
TOTAL − 16734		−16012	22128	597000	4356634	4943016	
PVRR TO 10/1/1983							
10.3% −82441		−17879	−14994	434302	247801	566789	0% load growth,
6.0% −77824		−18655	−8939	492724	963408	1350714	4 year delay
19.3% −75585		−15254	−17504	343035	−234611	0	

Source: Commonwealth Edison Company, "Studies Analyzing Various Construction and Operating Schedules for the Braidwood Station, Presented by John C. Bukovski," in Illinois Commerce Commission, Case No. 78-0646, appendix, p. 41.

Exhibit 10   Estimated Nuclear Construction Costs (dollars/kw^2)

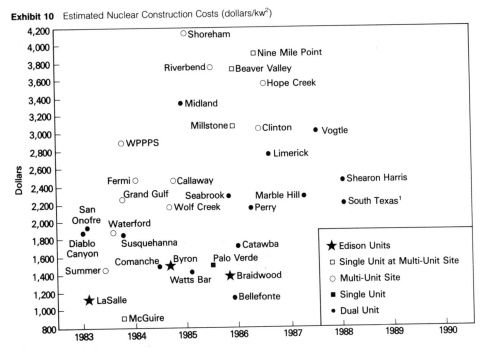

[1]No AFUDC included.

[2]For single units, the symbols shown on this chart represent the utilities' estimated date for commercial service. For multi-unit stations, this represents the average of the utilities' estimate of the commercial service dates of each unit under construction.

Source: Commonwealth Edison Company.

Exhibit 11 Commonwealth Edison (A): Commonwealth Edison Company Five-Year Capital Budget January 31, 1980 (in millions of dollars)

	1980	1981	1982	1983	1984	5-YEAR TOTAL
Production	900	980	695	500	395	3,470
Transmission	60	70	60	60	55	305
Distribution	120	125	130	130	135	640
General plant	20	25	15	10	15	85
Total	$1,100	$1,200	$900	$700	$600	$4,500

Source: Commonwealth Edison Company.

Exhibit 12 Commonwealth Edison (A): Commonwealth Edison Company Estimated Cash Flows of "Big Three" Nuclear Plants —Direct Costs (in millions of dollars)

PROJECTS	SERVICE DATE	EXPENDITURE PRIOR TO 1980	CURRENT BUDGET		ADDITIONAL MONEY TO HOLD SCHEDULE	
			1980	5-YEAR TOTAL	1980	5-YEAR TOTAL
Braidwood	10-83/10-84	1,370.7	174.7	1,108.3	18.7	176.2
Byron	10-82/10-83	1,369.7	257.8	893.9	47.3	190.7
LaSalle	12-80/12-81	1,299.6	241.7	451.2	49.6	68.7
Total		4,040.0	674.2	2,453.4	115.6	435.6

Source: Commonwealth Edison Company.

Exhibit 13 Commonwealth Edison (A): Possible 5-Year Budgets for Various Combinations of Service Dates for Byron, Braidwood & LaSalle (includes other project reductions and additions) All $ Include Indirects—8.0% Esc. & 8.0% AFUDC ($ in billions)

PRESENT AUTHORIZED BUDGET			1980	1981	1982	1983	1984	5-YEAR TOTAL	
			$1.10	$1.20	$0.90	$0.70	$0.60	$4.50	*Cost to Complete "Big 3"
Budget Plan	Service Dates	Years Delay							
I	BY 82, 83	0							
	BR 83, 84	0	$1.25	$1.25	$1.05	$0.85	$0.50	$4.90	$0.44
	LS 80, 81	0							
II	BY 82, 83	0							
	BR 4/86, 4/87	2.5	1.20	1.20	1.00	0.80	0.70	4.90	1.08
	LS 80, 81	0							
III	BY 82, 83	0	1.20	1.20	1.10	0.80	0.70	5.00	1.15
	BR 4/86, 4/87	2.5							
	LS 80, 6/82	0.5 U2							
IV	BY 82, 83	0							
	BR 88, 89	5	1.20	1.15	0.90	0.70	0.65	4.60	1.74
	LS 80, 81	0							
V	BY 83, 84	1							
	BR 85, 86	2	1.20	1.20	1.05	1.00	0.80	5.25	1.19
	LS 80, 81	0							
VI	BY 83, 84	1							
	BR 4/86, 4/87	2.5	1.20	1.20	1.00	1.00	0.80	5.20	1.30
	LS 80, 81	0							
VII	BY 83, 84	1							
	BR 86, 87	3	1.20	1.20	1.05	1.00	0.80	5.25	1.48
	LS 80, 81	0							
VIII	BY 83, 84	1							
	BR 88, 89	5	1.20	1.10	0.95	0.90	0.75	4.90	1.96
	LS 80, 81	0							
IX	BY 83, 84	1							
	BR 88, 89	5	1.20	1.15	1.00	0.90	0.75	5.00	2.04
	LS 80, 6/82	0.5 U2							

*These are the costs required to complete the "Big 3" projects by the service dates shown. They are in addition to costs included in the present authorized budget.

Source: Commonwealth Edison Company.

NOTES

1. Quoted in *Chicago Daily News*, May 9, 1977, p. 30.
2. *Chicago Sun Times*, February 17, 1980.
3. Quoted in the *Rockford Register Star*, January 18, 1980.
4. *Chicago Sun Times*, October 18, 1979, and *Waukegan News-Sun*, November 1, 1979.
5. Commonwealth Edison Company, "Exhibits Including Testimony Submitted by Robert J. Schultz," May 1979, in Illinois Commerce Commission, Case No. 79-0214, p. 2.
6. Illinois Commerce Commission, "Order on Petition for Interim Rate Increase," September 12, 1979, in Case No. 79-0214, p. 2.
7. Schultz Testimony, Case No. 79-0214, p. 2 and Exhibit 3.2.
8. Ibid., p. 6.
9. Quoted in *Chicago Sun-Times*, September 13, 1979.
10. Quoted in *Chicago Tribune*, October 4, 1979.
11. Testimony of Neill Dimmick, Chief Accountant, Illinois Commerce Commission, Docket No. 78-0646, "Investigation of the Plant Construction Program of Commonwealth Edison," August 30, 1980, staff Exhibit 11.1.
12. *Chicago Tribune*, November 3, 1979.
13. Commonwealth Edison Company, "Appendix: Excerpts from the Record," December 20, 1979, in Illinois Commerce Commission, Case No. 79-0214, p. A7.
14. Cited in CWE, Brief in ICC 79-0214, p. 95.
15. *Chicago Sun-Times*, February 7, 1980.
16. *Chicago Tribune*, February 7, 1980.
17. Illinois Commerce Commission, Order No. 78-0646, p. 3.
18. "Suggestions of Community Thrift Clubs, Inc.," in Illinois Commerce Commission, Case No. 78-0646, p. 5.

Chapter Four

Excess
Competition

After exploring environments of increasing regulation and failing regulation, you will probably enjoy turning to an environment of deregulation. The airlines business, where economic regulation originally seemed warranted by "excess competition," was probably the most appropriate place for deregulation to begin.

Chapter Four begins with a case on American Airlines, eighteen months after Congress passed the Airline Deregulation Act of 1978. The senior management of American faces the full thrust of deregulation—several years ahead of Congress' phased-in schedule. Robert Crandall takes over as president and chief operating officer, with his company losing $120 million in the first six months of 1980. Price wars are raging, the economy is slowing, and American's routes are being attacked from all sides, by new entrants, expanding regionals, and other major carriers.

This case explores every aspect of airline management and operation: route structure and fleet composition, personnel and training, labor relations, organization, marketing, and finance. Careful analysis is necessary to understand the effects of regulation and the impact of deregulation, and to consider the strategic options and develop a full-blown business plan for adjusting to a radically new environment.

Next, we turn from the airlines to surface freight transportation, with the first of three industry notes in this text. This note documents a century of regulatory and industry history in the railroad business, and half-century in trucking. Here, in two very different competing industries, you can see the importance of structural characteristics, how they precipitate regulation in the first place, and how they are subsequently shaped by regulation. This note, more than any other part of the book, is designed to show the dynamism of markets and of regulation. Law-by-law, amendment-by-amendment, the ground transportation industry evolves along with transport technology and the American economy. The linkages between market failure, the public interest, public policy, regulatory institutions, market structure, industry structure, and politics, are laid out end to end, and then reversed, after they begin to fail in the 1960s. The concept of business-government relations is graphically illustrated in this note.

The CSX case is the focal point for the evolution described in the preceding note. Its central themes are the organization issues associated with regulatory change, and efficient asset deployment. CSX was organized in 1980 as the holding company for a merger of the C&O/B&O and Seaboard railroads. Since the merger, the two huge railroads had remained separate operating entities, and CSX had acquired a major gas transmission company and an affiliated barge line. By 1985, CSX had made significant progress adjusting to the railroad and trucking deregulation that had occurred since Congress passed the Staggers Act and the Motor Carrier Act in 1980. Still, as the industrial economy stagnated, as competition intensified, and as cost-cutting continued mercilessly, the company's chairman, Hays Watkins, realized that more needed to be done if his railroads were ever to earn their cost of capital.

American Airlines (A)

The first year of airline deregulation was "one of the most difficult and tumultuous years in our history," commented Bob Crandall, president of American Airlines. "As an industry, we seemed bent on giving away the store."

But 1979 paled in comparison to the first half of 1980; American Airlines ran an operating loss of $121 million—the worst, by far, in its history. Passenger traffic had slumped industrywide. The price of jet fuel doubled. Intense competition on American's key routes and wild discounting of fares squeezed yields and forced load factor below the breakeven point, turning the bottom line red (see Tables 1 and 2).

In July, Bob Crandall, AA's forty-five-year-old senior vice president of marketing, was appointed president and chief operating officer. Al Casey, the chairman of American Airlines, charged Crandall with returning the company to profitability and making the shift from regulation to the competitive struggle that lay ahead. "We should view 1980 as the beginning of a decade of continuing change and challenge," said Crandall. "Our task is to find a strategy for responding to that challenge."[1]

THE TRADITION OF AMERICAN AIRLINES

In the stable environment of federal regulation, American Airlines had grown steadily and, until the 1970s, prospered. From its first scheduled mail flight by Charles Lindbergh in 1926, American grew to become the second-largest domestic carrier, with a reputation for quality service.

American Airways, the immediate forerunner of today's company, was a consolidation of eighty-five small airline companies in 1929 and 1930. Flight attendants made their first appearance in 1933, when American began flying the eighteen-passenger Curtiss Condor. The DC-3 soon became the company's workhorse, providing passenger service until the late 1940s. C.R. Smith, elected president when the company was reorganized as American Airlines in 1934, continued as CEO until 1968. Under his management, American Airlines pioneered a number of firsts: airfreight service (1944), family fares (1948), Magnetronic Reservisor—an electronic reservations system (1952), nonstop

Table 1 Trunk Airlines: Operating Profits/(Loss) First Half, 1980 ($ millions)

	REVENUES	EXPENSES	PROFIT/LOSS	MARGIN
American	$1,746	$1,867	$(120)	(7.0)%
Braniff	741	801	(60)	(8.1)
Continental	497	522	(25)	(6.6)
Delta	1,582	1,508	74	4.6
Eastern	1,704	1,700	4	0.3
Northwest	740	791	(51)	(6.9)
Pan Am	1,672	1,781	(109)	(6.3)
TWA	1,581	1,633	(52)	(4.0)
United	2,108	2,222	(113)	(5.4)
Western	470	513	(42)	(9.2)
All Trunks	$12,845	$13,340	$(495)	(4.0)%

transcontinental service (1953), transcontinental jet service with the Boeing 707 (1959), and SABRE—a computerized reservations system (1964).

During the 1970s, American introduced widebody jets (the DC-10 and Boeing 747), added Caribbean routes to its network, and invented Super Saver fares (1977) to stimulate discretionary travel. Besides its air passenger and freight services, American operated a major airport catering service (Sky Chefs), a flight training program (AA Training Corporation), and a small oil development subsidiary.

By 1980, American's fleet consisted of 240 aircraft, providing service to more than 120 cities. Its 41,000 employees helped fly thirty million passengers over thirty-three billion passenger miles in 1979. One-third of that traffic was produced on American's nine key routes, between New York, Dallas/Fort Worth, Chicago, Los Angeles, and San Francisco. By providing more and better services than most of its competitors, American had succeeded in building an image as the "businessman's airline." Its cost structure reflected as much.

Table 2 Load Factor of Trunk Airlines (12 months ending 6/30/80)

	ACTUAL	BREAKEVEN	SPREAD
American	62.5%	66.8%	(4.3)
Braniff	55.0	61.4	(6.4)
Continental	56.6	61.5	(4.9)
Delta	60.6	58.6	2.0
Eastern	65.3	65.2	0.1
Pan American	60.8	64.2	(3.4)
Northwest	53.1	56.4	(3.3)
TWA	60.8	64.7	(4.2)
United	61.8	65.9	(4.1)
Western	56.6	61.3	(2.9)
All Trunks	60.4%	63.3%	(2.9)

Regulation, as well as technological progress, had contributed to this era of growth. Under the Air Commerce Act of 1926 and the Civil Aeronautics Act of 1938, the airlines industry was closely regulated. While the Federal Aviation Administration dictated safety standards and air-traffic operating procedures, the Civil Aeronautics Board (CAB) controlled entry, exit, and price. Airlines were granted a protected franchise in each market, or city pair, with a limited number of competitors. In return for profitable, high density routes, each carrier was obligated to provide service to dozens of smaller communities with scarcely enough traffic to warrant a terminal. The CAB set fares sufficiently high to pass through rising costs, and structured them to cross-subsidize the national air transport network.

Prior to 1978, the CAB had never certified a new trunk airline. The sixteen original trunk carriers, of which American was one, had since been reduced to ten by merger. Besides these ten, regulation had sustained a dozen regional and local airlines, 258 commuter lines, four intrastate carriers, and a couple of charter companies.

During the last few years of this regulatory regime, American's financial performance had failed to match either its image or the average for the industry. Its average operating margin of 0.75% was well below the average of 3.5% for domestic trunk carriers. As growth slowed and energy prices rose, American Airlines found itself saddled with relatively inefficient aircraft, a high-cost route structure (long, nonstop trips), and relatively costly labor contracts.

A management crisis early in the decade had not helped. American's trouble began in 1972, when two senior executives were indicted on bribery and kickback charges. Less than a year later, George Spater, American's chairman, admitted to making an illegal campaign contribution of $55,000 to Richard Nixon—this while running a $33 million operating loss. In an atmosphere of crisis and deteriorating morale, the Board called C.R. Smith out of retirement, at least long enough to arrange for new management.

Smith promptly recruited Al Casey, formerly president of The Times Mirror Company, for replacement as President and CEO. It would be Casey's job to restore confidence in American by repairing its financial structure and reorganizing its senior management. During the next five years, Casey did just that. With the help of Bob Crandall, who had just joined American as senior vice-president of finance, Casey set up a centralized system of budgeting. The field work this entailed gave Crandall a uniquely detailed knowledge of American's operations. Casey also initiated efforts to centralize maintenance and training operations and to dispose of the company's Americana Hotel properties. In 1978, he announced a dramatic decision to relocate corporate headquarters from New York to the Dallas/Fort Worth Regional Airport.

Perhaps of greater importance was Casey's painstaking development of a new, young management team and a simplified organization. First, he moved Crandall to marketing, as a senior vice president. In 1975, Crandall was elected to the Board, where he joined Donald Lloyd-Jones, the senior vice president of operations who was already a director. During the next four years, four other employees were also tapped for key positions. Tom Plaskett replaced Crandall as vice president of finance; Jack Pope became treasurer in 1978; Don Carty was moved from information systems to the controller's office; and Wes Kaldahl, after stints in planning at two other airlines, returned to American as the senior planning officer (see Exhibit 2).

The first-half losses in 1980 seemed to provide the impetus necessary to make dramatic organizational changes. Crandall, with his tough-minded ideas about competitiveness, and his dogged preoccupation with the bottom line, had earned a reputation as an unconventional manager for the airlines industry. In July 1980, Casey appointed Crandall president and chief operating officer. With a solid management team in place, this appointment gave Crandall the authority to make real changes in the company's strategy, in the face of deregulation.

SOURCES OF CHANGE

President Jimmy Carter signed the Airline Deregulation Act into law in October, 1978. The Act set a timetable for phasing out restrictions on entry, exit, and pricing—and the CAB itself—by 1985. The Act's major provisions were to take effect gradually, to allow for a smooth adjustment: a limited degree of automatic entry, a procedure for acquiring dormant route authority, a zone of reasonableness for fares, and a procedure for airlines wishing to terminate service to a community. The Board would continue indefinitely to exercise control of joint fares, customer rights (in the case of lost baggage, smoking, or bumping), and antitrust matters (such as mergers, discriminatory pricing, and carrier agreements).

Despite the Act's intent, the process of deregulation proved chaotic from the outset. Wes Kaldahl described the first order of business:

> The law stipulate(d) that (dormant) routes should be awarded on a first come, first served basis. Unfortunately, no one knew what this meant until the CAB posted a sign on its front in Washington. The sign instructed the airlines to form a single, orderly line outside the building until the President had actually signed the legislation. . . . United was first in line because one of its people happened to be walking past CAB headquarters as the sign was being posted . . . and by the end of the day, a total of 19 airlines were camped outside the Board's doors. The problem then became one of holding your place in line. One airline person left her ninth place in line to use the bathroom. When she returned, those behind her refused to let her back in. The ensuing controversy led some carriers to post guards with the representatives. Finally, the CAB ruled—in an ironic regulatory twist—that those standing in line could take restroom leaves without losing their places—but only if they first got permission from the people immediately in front of and in back of them.[2]

Fare flexibility came sooner than expected, at the discretion of the Board. Initially, it just lifted ceilings in markets of less than 200 miles, and granted 50% and 30% upward fare flexibility in the markets of between 201 miles and 400 miles, and greater than 400 miles. But these constraints were short-lived, so that "by the spring of 1980, carriers were essentially free to determine the routes they served and the prices they charged."[3]

Deregulation had scarcely begun when the Iranian Revolution precipitated a second oil crisis. Between January 1979 and July 1980, the price of crude oil jumped from $12.70 to $30.00 per barrel; the price of jet fuel increased from forty to ninety cents per gallon. Together, the domestic trunk airlines spent $5.9 billion on fuel in 1979—25% of total operating costs. Since fuel costs were the second largest part of airline operating costs (next to wages), these sharp increases continuing through the first half of 1980 had immediate implications for route structure, fleet mix, and price competitiveness.

Economic slowdown during the first half of 1980, together with record-high inflation, was another source of trouble—but apparently a temporary one. Earl Ditmars, American's chief economist, based his pessimistic forecast on the expectation of a mild recession (-0.7% GNP growth) and a negative price elasticity of demand resulting from huge airline fare hikes. He thought that industrywide traffic could decline 6%, and American's somewhat more. (Its Caribbean traffic would be hurt by the recession, and its 1979 performance had been artificially inflated by the strike that shut down United for two months.) This grim outlook—compounded by a 19% prime rate and the competitive entry by four new carriers—was "certainly the most depressing" in Ditmars' twenty-seven years of experience.

COMPETITIVE IMPACT ON AMERICAN

Although American's revenues were up 13% in the first half of 1980, expenses increased more than 24%. Its operating loss of $120 million reduced earnings per share by 200%, to $$-2.88$. Besides these common measures, performance in the airline business is measured and interpreted by several more technical indicators. Among these are revenue passenger miles (RPM), available seat miles (ASM), load factor (RPM/ASM), productivity (ASM per employee), yield (revenue/RPM), and share gap (RPM market share minus ASM market share) (see Exhibit 1).

In 1980, revenue passenger miles for American Airlines were down 15.1%—three times as severe a drop as the industry average. Wild fare discounting and competitive entry in many of American's key routes was a major cause. Although fares had increased substantially since 1978, the traffic traveling on discount fares was up from 45% to 53%. Due in part to this revenue dilution, yield increased only 34% (see Exhibit 3).

The "Transcon Wars" broke out in May, 1979. "The top two transcontinental markets (New York to Los Angeles and San Francisco) represent about $750 million in revenues for the industry," explained Tom Plaskett "—the highest stakes game in the ongoing deregulation saga."[4] American's share of this market was $250 million. World Airways started passenger service between New

York and California with a one-way fare of $108. Then Capital Airways (previously a charter company) entered the market, and TWA expanded the war to the "semi-transcon" market, announcing a $119 fare for Chicago to San Francisco. When American matched this in March 1980, TWA cut its price again to $99.

Pricing "madness" went from bad to worse in May, when Eastern tried breaking into the transcon market with a one-way unrestricted price of $99. All of the major carriers—American, United, and TWA—matched, but World reduced its fares to $88. Tentative efforts by American to firm up prices or reapply market-segmenting restrictions were rebuffed, as cut-rate fares spread to the "peripheral transcon" markets of Boston, Washington, and Philadelphia. American hoped to cancel its lowest fares when the tourist season ended in September, but recognized that it could only do so if United and TWA would follow suit.

Besides World and Capital on the transcontinental routes, American had four other new entrants to contend with:

1. Midway Airlines, serving five cities from Chicago's Midway Airport, competed with American to and from Detroit and Washington, and had announced new service to New York for November;
2. Southwest Airlines was expanding out of Texas to several sunbelt cities;
3. New York Air had announced plans for extensive operations in the Northeast;
4. People Express, another start-up, announced plans for cut-rate service in the Northeast.

In addition to these "low-cost" entrants, several established carriers had attacked American's key Dallas/Fort Worth routes, to New York, Los Angeles, Phoenix, and Tucson. The results, so far, were excess capacity, yield deterioration, and reduced connecting support for other American flights.

Despite these severe competitive pressures, American Airlines had thus far managed to protect its premium market share. It maintained a positive gap between its share of traffic and its share of seating capacity (see Exhibit 4). With regard to service, scheduling, and pricing, American was apparently competitive—just not profitable. Although American maintained a higher-than-average load factor, its breakeven level was higher still.

AMERICAN AIRLINES OPERATIONS

In July 1980, as Bob Crandall formally took control of American's operations, he knew that these new competitive conditions posed strategic implications for every facet of the business: fuel, fleet, route structure, labor productivity and corporate culture, marketing, and finance. These problems, after percolating for months, were now clear. It remained for Crandall to choose and implement solutions.

Fuel

"The biggest and most serious of our cost problems," said Crandall, "is fuel."[5] At $1.2 billion, fuel cost was 30% of total costs and 59% of direct aircraft operating expenses. But since the airlines had no control over absolute price, the "real key is comparative price and comparative use," vis-à-vis the competition.

In the short term, American Airlines was stuck with disadvantageous purchase contracts (until 1981). Its suppliers were charging a market price of eighty-eight cents per gallon, while most of its competitors had access to price-regulated sources (eighty-one to eighty-six cents). Unfortunately, it was United, American's toughest competitor, that had the biggest cost advantage of eight cents per gallon. This differential so restricted American's ability to match prices, that it could not begin its planned service to Hawaii until it obtained a competitively-priced source of fuel.

Comparative use, or fuel efficiency, was a longer-term aspect of the problem. Fuel efficiency depended on (1) flying conditions, (2) aircraft weight, and (3) aircraft type. The first of these was difficult to control, although a small savings could be realized by improved pilot procedures. American had already initiated conservation-oriented flight training and computerized flight planning; fuel efficiency was designated a priority of aircraft maintenance.

Weight reduction had a greater potential for conservation, but would require complicated procedural changes or costly remodeling. Fuel loads, for example, could be more carefully calibrated, but with some reduction of flexibility. Existing seats could be replaced by lightweight slimline seats. It was estimated that an investment of $16.2 million would yield fuel savings of $2.1 million annually. And similar, although smaller, gains could be made by reducing baggage space, carpeting, and magazines. But this might pose a trade-off with service.

Fleet

Size and composition of aircraft fleet was the largest factor of comparative fuel efficiency. It was also the heart of any airline's strategy, much as route structure was the soul. "On a comparative basis," Bob Crandall bluntly put it, "American's fleet is less fuel efficient than the fleet of almost any other carrier."

Older engine technology, too many engines per aircraft, and inappropriate route assignments all contributed to the problem. Particularly troublesome for American were its large number of 707s and 727-100s. The 707's four engines, designed in the late 1950s, were simply too fuel-inefficient for the number of passengers it could carry. And even with only three engines, the 727-100 was inefficient on short flights, where two-engine aircraft were preferable. Yet on longer flights, as Exhibit 5 indicates, it cost more to operate per ASM than the newer, 727-200 stretch version. Even the relatively new, wide-body jets—Boeing 747s and DC-10s—could be inefficient in the face of low load factors or use in shorter-than-transcontinental routes.[6]

In the short-term, options for adjusting aircraft mix were limited not only by operations (pilot training, maintenance, and route structure), but by the aircraft market as well. In 1980, for example, the market for widebody aircraft was very weak, since everyone was suffering from excess seating capacity. On the other hand, the demand for twin engine jets—the DC-9 and B737—was so great that asking prices were extremely high. The only reasonable opportunity at the time involved fifteen 727-200s that Braniff was trying to sell for $8 million apiece.

Another, albeit limited, option in the medium-term was reconfiguration of aircraft seating. As Exhibit 6 indicates, seating density had generally been rising in the airline industry. Yet American lagged this trend, in part due to the negative impact of greater seating density on customer satisfaction. Although the availability of slimline seats somewhat mitigated this tradeoff, and offered the additional benefit of weight reduction, higher density was still perceived as a degradation of quality of service, especially among business travelers.

As for the longer-term, American's management had recognized problems with its fleet, including fuel efficiency, noise pollution, and the overhead entailed by a multiplicity of models, since before the second oil shock. Thus, in those halcyon days of 1978, American Airlines placed an order for thirty Boeing 767s (with options for twenty more), for about $25 million apiece. State-of-the-art avionics would allow the 767 to be flown by two pilots, rather than the usual three. With 199 seats, this twin-engined jet would quietly deliver 33% greater fuel efficiency per ASM than the 707. The planes would be delivered at a rate of one per month, beginning in September 1982.

In November 1979, American's board of directors approved these commitments as part of the fleet plan summarized in Table 3. It tentatively included some medium-range aircraft, labeled N170; this referred to the Boeing 757. Early in 1980, American announced it would buy fifteen 757s (with an option for fifteen more), pending financing of $717 million, to replace its 727-100s beginning late in 1983.

This plan, of course, was based on assumptions about traffic growth, profitability, and route structure that no longer appeared realistic in view of American's unsatisfactory performance during the first half of 1980.

Route Structure

American Airlines' route structure could scarcely be less suited to deregulation. The average length of American's flights was the longest among domestic carriers (excluding Pan Am). Its system, providing service to seventy-four cities, was exceedingly fragmented. In fact, it appeared more like five separate systems: transcontinental markets, mid-continent connecting markets (Dallas/Fort Worth, Chicago, and St. Louis), the Northeast business market, the Caribbean tourist market, and miscellaneous routes (see Exhibit 7). All of this

Table 3   1980–1985 Fleet Plan (Presented to Board of Directors in November 1979)

| Aircraft | AUGUST FLEET COUNT | | | | | | 1980–85 Change |
	1980	1981	1982	1983	1984	1985	
B-747	8	8	8	8	8	8	—
DC-10	34	34	34	34	34	34	—
B767	—	—	—	11	30	44	+44
B707	53	46	46	30	18	—	(53)
N170	—	—	—	15	28	38	+38
B727-223	88	104	110	110	110	110	+22
B727-023	57	57	54	45	29	27	(30)
TOTAL	240	249	252	253	257	261	+21

entailed considerable costs, such as complicated scheduling of flight crews and aircraft, underutilized ground crews and customer service personnel, and extensive investments in ground facilities.

Thirty-five percent of American's traffic was concentrated in ten of the nation's busiest markets. Ironically, these high-density, point-to-point (nonstop) markets provided ideal opportunities for entry by new low-cost carriers, or expansion by established regionals.

American's route structure had already undergone considerable change since deregulation (see Exhibits 8 and 9). In the first rush of new opportunity, during 1979, American had inaugurated service to fifty new city-pairs. Only thirty-four were discontinued, including five of the new transcontinental routes. Most of the expansion occurred at the three mid-continent connecting hubs—Dallas/Fort Worth, Chicago, and St. Louis. At the huge Dallas/Fort Worth airport, American operated 142 departures daily—57% of its system total—using nineteen gates for its largest "complex" (a nearly simultaneous arrival and departure of multiple aircraft). Shrinkage, meanwhile, was concentrated in the Northeast, miscellaneous, and Mexican markets. By mid-1980, however, these ambitious moves had been scaled back considerably; discontinuations (29) and planned discontinuations (29) far outstripped inaugurations (13).

Although size and configuration of American's route structure was most closely tied to the nature of its fleet (and vice versa), another important consideration was a growing pattern of airport dominance. Delta, for example, was widely viewed as having nearly monopolized connecting traffic at its home base in Atlanta. Similar patterns of dominance were becoming apparent at O'Hare, in Chicago (United and American), Dallas/Fort Worth (American and Braniff), St. Louis (TWA), Denver (Continental), and Pittsburgh (U.S. Air). Notwithstand- ing strong customer preference for nonstop flights, these connecting hubs seemed to offer new economies of scale (concentrated ground facilities) and scope (a geometric relationship between number of flights and city-pairs indirectly served); they helped facilitate traffic control and protect against competitive pricing or promotional action on individual (origin and destination) routes.

Other considerations, besides composition of fleet and hub operations, included traffic potential, competition, marketing strategy, availability of gate space, and financial capacity. Route structure could be altered within these general parameters to increase or decrease the number of cities served, the number of markets, reliance on transcon markets, reliance on connecting complexes, tourist routes, business routes, domestic versus international routes, or shorter versus longer routes.

Crystalization of any such changes into some sort of more coherent system would be a function of whatever broad strategy Bob Crandall and his management team chose to adopt.

Labor Productivity and Corporate Culture

Labor productivity, and related aspects of corporate culture, probably concerned Bob Crandall more than any other single issue. There were several reasons for this.

Labor costs constituted 37% of American Airlines' operating expenses. It was the biggest variable cost, and the one with the greatest potential for differences between carriers. Wage and benefits expenses (which had increased 207% and 336% respectively since 1970) were a problem vis-à-vis low-cost new entrants with young, nonunion employees. According to CAB Chairman Marvin Cohen, the average cost of a flight crew (B737) for trunk carriers was $418 per hour in 1979; for local carriers it was $260, and for Southwest, just $163. "If the incumbents want to remain competitive in these [point-to-point] markets," concluded Cohen, "they must find ways to reduce costs."[7]

American Airlines' labor productivity, in terms of ASMs, had grown only 1.5% annually throughout the 1970s; the industry's average growth was 2.8%; United's was 3.3%. In absolute terms, Southwest Airlines, a new low-cost competitor, delivered 41% more ASMs per employee than American in 1980; United, 9% more.

American's problem with productivity was no doubt complicated—but rapid growth in headcount and the restrictive work rules of its unions were crucial. In 1978, American had 37,821 employees; as of July 1980, it had 41,326, an increase of 9% that compared unfavorably with ASM growth of just 2.6%.

Approximately 59% of American's employees were represented by labor unions. The Transport Workers Union (TWU), an AFL-CIO affiliate, was the largest; it represented about 11,000 people in maintenance, stores, flight instruction, and dispatch. Nearly 4,000 pilots were organized in a company union (Allied Pilots Association); Flight Engineers had a separate union (Flight Engineers International Association, AFL-CIO), as did American's 5,600 flight attendants (Association of Professional Flight Attendants). These unions were proud of both the compensation levels and work rules they had won during the '60s and '70s.

There were a few aspects of these contracts that bothered Crandall even more than compensation levels. For flight crews, work rules and seniority limited "stick time"—the time pilots actually worked at flying airplanes—to about forty-four hours a month, and circumscribed management's flexibility in crew scheduling. Similarly, hard hours for flight attendants had declined to about fifty-three hours monthly. Among the worst problems with the TWU contract were its prohibition of part-time workers and extremely narrow job definitions with prohibition on any crossover. These restrictions prevented American from efficiently manning for peak-load traffic, and induced widespread redundancy in ground operations. Thus, a tractor driver, occupied three hours a day, could not assist with baggage, refueling, or aircraft cabin preparation.

Since the TWU's contract had just been renegotiated, and the pilots' and flight attendants' had more than a year to run, Crandall was not contemplating immediate solutions. Yet he was certain that something needed to be done, other than direct confrontation. Given the high fixed costs and importance of market share in what was basically a commodity business, the strike weapon was devastatingly effective. The most recent example was the two month strike of United in 1979, resulting in a $263 million operating loss for the year. Confrontation, moreover, would not be conducive to the sort of team-oriented atmosphere on which American depended for its exceptional service performance.

From long experience, Crandall understood just how entrenched these attitudes and practices had become. It was scarcely surprising that these unions had fought deregulation more vehemently even than management. It was much the same for unorganized employees in customer service, administration, and management. Although "deregulation" was frequently an object of conversation, analysis, and handwringing, the pervasiveness of its implications had yet to be internalized. Crandall was absolutely determined to change this situation soon, but without a sledgehammer. To this extent, Crandall's problem with union work rules and corporate culture had something in common.

Marketing and Customer Service

American Airlines had a reputation for effective marketing and top quality customer service. Its introduction of the Super Saver fare in 1977 was considered highly innovative. Its jingle, "We're American Airlines, doing what we do best," was widely recognized and typical of its promotional effectiveness. And SABRE, American's computerized reservation system, was by far the biggest in the industry. SABRE not only provided American with a shelf-space advantage (a schedule-display bias) among independent travel agents, but with an immense customer data base.

Customer service was the heart of American's marketing strategy. In the past, American had generally sought to maintain its positive share gap by cultivating an image as the number one carrier in terms of service. According to a *Time* magazine survey, airline passengers cared most about the following aspects of service: efficient check-in, baggage handling, on-time performance, seat comfort, performance of flight attendants, performance of reservation agents, and carry-on baggage facilities.[8] Although American had maintained the best on-time performance record since 1978, its rank in overall service, as measured quarterly by surveys of passengers, had slipped sharply in 1979 to second, after

United. In the first quarter of 1980, however, American regained the top slot, after hastily implementing a service enhancement program. But despite this recovery, it remained several percentage points below the ratings it achieved in January 1978.

Producing this sort of premium service, without premium wages, was a tribute to good training (American maintained the largest, and reputedly the best, flight training academy), personnel management, and high morale. Although pleased by this record, Bob Crandall felt that it must be better still: "We simply cannot provide any passenger with an excuse to fly another airline." But he also realized that it would be difficult to maintain, let alone improve, these ratings if labor-management relations deteriorated, or if cost cutting impinged directly on quality of service.

In the face of continuing and serious pressures on yield, product distribution and pricing were both important to the revenue side of American's problem.

Over the past few years, the volume of airline traffic booked by travel agencies had grown rapidly, to 63% of airline business by 1980; automated agencies alone accounted for 16% of American's passengers. Since 1976, American had spent $85 billion on SABRE (and related automation), and the number of agencies in SABRE continued to grow at a rate of nearly 400 a month (the next two largest systems were United's and TWA's). Despite immense success in this channel, Bob Crandall was concerned that deregulation might interfere. Agent fees had been standardized under CAB regulation, but it now looked as if the Board would deregulate those rates too. If so, it would certainly have a significant competitive impact on the travel agency business.

Effective pricing policy was even more critical to yield. This was the area of greatest innovation and chaos since deregulation. Thus far, American had taken a cautious approach to pricing innovation, especially since market share was not its problem. "The ideal discount fare," Crandall felt, "will be one which combines substantial generation with modest dilution."[9] Advance-purchase and minimum-stay restrictions helped segment the market, between peak and off-peak travel, and prevented full-fare travelers from taking advantage of discounts. SABRE also allowed American to impose capacity limits on five categories of travelers for each route. Thus it could, for example, dedicate 30% of a flight's seats to various discounted fares, while reserving the rest for its full-fare, business customers. In the past, these frequent business travelers had been absolutely vital to American. If other airlines could attract them with uneconomic fares, then the fruits of even the most careful yield management would be limited.

Finance

With its current fleet plan, American Airlines needed $5.7 billion, over the next five years, to finance the purchase of new aircraft (and investment in ground facilities). This was nearly triple its capital spending during the last five years, yet its operating margin was now inadequate to support the necessary borrowing. It had, therefore, a "financing gap." This gap was the heart of Crandall's strategic dilemma.

Jack Pope, American's financial vice president, explained how the company's financial situation had changed in the eight months since the Board approved the last fleet plan:

> The fleet plan [was] recommended on the basis that it meets both operating and financing requirements. . . . In estimating those sources of funds that are generated internally, a 1980-1985 scenario was used which incorporated an 11% revenue growth and an operating profit margin that increased from 3.1% in 1980 to 6.3% in 1985 for an average of 4.7%. This financing requirement, when added to existing debt, resulting in required debt level which fit comfortably into our debt capacity as defined by our senior loan agreements.[10] So everything was fine last year since we had an affordable fleet plan which provided a modest 5% growth in capacity per year in addition to providing the scheduled retirement of older aircraft. [See Exhibit 10.]
>
> Well, what happened? The combined effect of the 1979 earnings shortfall, an increase in projected capital expenditures, and the discouraging forecast for 1980 operating results has created a projected financing gap. By 1983, external financing requirements will simply outstrip our ability to support these borrowings, and, as a result, the financing gap reaches two billion by the end of 1985. And this assumes that we achieve an average operating profit margin of 5% through 1985. [See Exhibit 11.]
>
> It is obvious that we face a serious financing dilemma. We must replace our existing inefficient fleet and we also want to grow. There are only three solutions to the problem—improve our profitability, reduce capital spending, or open new sources of capital for American.[11]

Each of these potential solutions, however, was fraught with problems. Although each 1% improvement in operating profit margin would reduce the gap by $170 million, even a 5% operating margin meant revenue must grow 24% annually. If capital spending were reduced, either plans for growth or fleet modernization would have to be sacrificed. Neither was attractive in the prevailing competitive environment. And finally, the development of new sources of capital was easier said than done. Before deregulation, when route franchises guaranteed cash flow, insurance companies had been the prime source of airline financing. With deregulation, that source dried up overnight. Now, with the extraordinary instability that prevailed in the airline industry, Pope and Casey —the team responsible for American's financing—faced a real challenge.

DEREGULATION STRATEGY

Late in July of 1980, Bob Crandall had the experience, the facts, the management team, and the authority he needed. He and Al Casey had been outspoken in their opposition to deregulation. Neither man thought it was in the best interest of consumers, the airlines, or the nation. It was, nonetheless, a reality, and American Airlines was a victim. Crandall recognized and understood the company's problems, as well as its distinctive strengths. He was determined that American Airlines should survive, and with the right strategy, prosper.

Exhibit 1 American Airlines (A): Traffic and Employment Analysis

AMERICAN AIRLINES

	1972	1973	1974	1975	1976	1977	1978	1979	1980
Scheduled Service (Mil.)									
Rev. Pass. Miles	19,366.3	20,654.3	20,487.9	20,870.6	23,072.3	24,634.0	28,987.1	33,363.9	28,178.1
Percent Change	10.4	6.7	−0.8	1.9	10.5	6.8	17.7	15.1	−15.5
Avail. Seat Miles	36,289.4	39,005.8	35,271.6	36,682.3	39,441.1	41,850.7	45,487.5	49,484.6	46,633.7
Percent Change	3.1	7.5	−9.6	4.0	7.5	6.1	8.7	8.8	−5.8
Load Factor	53.4	53.0	58.1	56.9	58.5	58.9	63.7	67.4	60.4
Breakeven Load Factor	51.5	54.4	56.4	58.0	56.1	57.0	61.0	67.5	62.6
Employees	35,484.5	37,111.0	35,642.5	35,118.3	35,565.8	36,929.0	37,821.9	40,098.0	40,392.5
Percent Change	−2.0	4.6	−4.0	−1.5	1.3	3.8	2.4	6.0	0.7
Pay Per Employee($)	14,457.4	15,385.9	16,198.9	18,086.9	19,865.6	21,633.4	23,926.6	25,720.1	27,907.6
Percent Change	9.5	6.4	5.3	11.7	9.8	8.9	10.6	7.5	8.5
ATM's Per Employee	178,483.9	175,017.2	162,796.6	172,969.5	172,358.5	175,830.3	181,261.4	182,941.2	170,561.3
Percent Change	4.6	−1.9	−7.0	6.2	−0.4	2.0	3.1	0.9	−6.8
RTM's Per Employee	77,012.6	76,436.9	77,685.3	79,743.7	87,173.7	89,938.3	98,172.8	103,517.4	87,523.6
Percent Change	9.7	−0.7	1.6	2.6	9.3	3.2	9.2	5.4	−15.5
Other Ratios									
Avg. Flight Stage	754	743	783	784	787	789	804	888	929
Percent Change	3.2	−1.5	5.4	0.1	0.4	0.3	1.8	10.4	4.7
Avg. Trip Length	1,000	1,009	1,027	1,046	1,057	1,051	1,043	1,084	1,096
Percent Change	3.2	0.9	1.9	1.8	1.0	−0.6	−0.7	3.9	1.1
Utilization in Hours	9.02	9.07	8.54	8.72	8.98	8.91	8.98	9.55	8.63
Percent Change	0.8	0.5	−5.8	2.1	3.1	−0.8	0.8	6.3	−9.7
Avg. Seats/Aircraft	129.4	135.9	132.7	136.1	139.8	142.4	147.1	146.6	147.4
Percent Change	4.6	5.0	−2.4	2.5	2.7	1.9	3.3	−0.4	0.6

Total Industry

Scheduled Service (Mil.)	1972	1973	1974	1975	1976	1977	1978	1979	1980
Rev. Pass. Miles	149,813.5	160,786.0	161,610.6	161,211.2	177,268.8	191,427.5	224,732.0	256,938.6	246,837.5
Percent Change	13.2	7.3	0.5	−0.2	10.0	8.0	17.4	14.3	−3.9
Avail. Seat Miles	282,408.9	308,411.6	294,636.9	300,260.2	320,019.8	342,644.8	365,520.3	408,151.1	418,707.3
Percent Change	3.6	9.2	−4.5	1.9	6.6	7.1	6.7	11.7	2.6
Load Factor	53.0	52.1	54.9	53.7	55.4	55.9	61.5	63.0	59.0
Breakeven Load Factor	49.8	49.3	51.5	53.2	52.6	52.8	57.2	62.4	59.4
Employees	283,020.0	299,438.0	292,586.0	285,202.5	289,945.3	293,574.0	308,373.5	336,002.5	336,207.9
Percent Change	1.3	5.8	−2.3	−2.5	1.7	1.3	5.0	9.0	0.1
Pay Per Employee($)	13,568.5	14,295.9	15,676.9	17,037.9	18,437.7	20,699.9	22,422.1	23,920.9	26,690.8
Percent Change	9.0	5.4	9.7	8.7	8.2	12.3	8.3	6.7	11.6
ATM's Per Employee	160,549.1	162,464.5	157,719.7	162,666.5	168,138.4	176,105.8	172,659.3	172,941.9	176,083.3
Percent Change	2.0	1.2	−2.9	3.1	3.4	4.7	−2.0	0.2	1.8
RTM's Per Employee	73,405.0	73,802.0	75,455.7	76,108.4	82,202.0	86,985.5	92,900.3	94,172.9	89,848.0
Percent Change	8.5	0.5	2.2	0.9	8.0	5.8	6.8	1.4	−4.6
Other Ratios									
Avg. Flight Stage	503	504	505	507	511	520	530	565	586
Percent Change	−2.0	0.2	0.2	0.5	0.7	1.8	1.8	6.7	3.8
Avg. Trip Length	857	863	840	847	859	858	867	874	895
Percent Change	0.6	0.8	−2.7	0.8	1.4	−0.2	1.1	0.8	2.3
Utilization in Hours	8.59	8.94	8.34	8.28	8.45	8.78	9.07	9.53	8.94
Percent Change	1.5	4.1	−6.6	−0.7	1.9	3.9	3.3	5.2	−6.2
Avg. Seats/Aircraft	124.1	130.8	135.6	139.6	143.6	146.9	150.4	154.7	159.1
Percent Change	2.9	5.4	3.6	3.0	2.8	2.3	2.4	2.8	2.9

Source: Merrill Lynch, Airline Industry Annual Financial Statistics, December 1982.

Exhibit 2 American Airlines Organization Chart

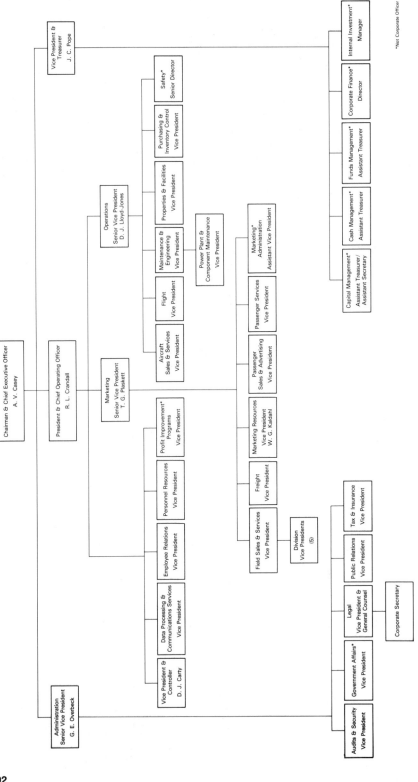

Exhibit 3   American Airlines (A): Actual and Effective Yields for Major Airlines[a]
(in cents per passenger mile)

	1978	1979	1980
American Airlines			
Passenger Yield	07.96¢	08.17¢	11.11¢
Effective Yield*	06.93	07.05	09.57
Braniff International			
Passenger Yield	08.80	08.94	10.97
Effective Yield	07.68	07.77	09.31
Continental Airlines/Texas International			
Passenger Yield	08.17	08.74	11.06
Effective Yield	07.12	07.48	09.53
Delta Air Lines			
Passenger Yield	08.70	09.31	11.71
Effective Yield	07.53	08.00	10.10
Eastern Air Lines			
Passenger Yield	08.54	09.08	11.15
Effective Yield	07.36	07.84	09.64
Northwest Airlines			
Passenger Yield	07.94	08.03	09.76
Effective Yield	06.51	06.75	08.10
Pan American (including National Airlines)			
Passenger Yield	07.67	08.00	09.48
Effective Yield	06.25	06.51	07.77
Republic Airlines/Hughes Airwest			
Passenger Yield	12.32	12.96	16.07
Effective Yield	10.79	11.17	14.03
Trans World Airlines			
Passenger	07.65	08.12	10.13
Effective Yield	06.47	06.90	08.58
United Airlines			
Passenger Yield	07.58	07.47	09.88
Effective Yield	06.66	06.38	08.53
USAir			
Passenger Yield	12.29	12.88	16.26
Effective Yield	10.90	11.29	14.31
Western Airlines			
Passenger Yield	07.20	08.07	10.10
Effective Yield	06.20	06.89	08.59

[a]Effective yield = actual yield minus sales and commission expenses.

Source: Salomon Brothers, *Industry Analysis*, May 31, 1983.

Exhibit 4a American Airlines Degree of Competition, Proportion of Traffic Obtained from Routes also Served by Other Carriers

	1977	1978	1979	1980
Braniff	12.3%	11.3%	20.8%	21.3%
Continental	6.5	7.4	6.0	5.7
Delta	12.3	12.3	11.3	13.2
Eastern	2.1	2.0	1.8	15.6
Frontier	42.4	0.3	0.1	0.0
Hughes Airwest	1.1	0.9	1.1	0.4
National	2.0	1.8	1.1	1.2
North Central	0.4	0.4	0.9[a]	—
Northwest	7.4	2.3	7.8	8.2
Ozark	1.3	1.1	1.3	1.7
Pan Am	0.3	0.3	13.8	15.2
Piedmont	0.5	0.1	0.0	0.0
Republic	—	—	1.2[b]	3.0
Southern	0.4	0.3	0.2[a]	—
Texas International	0.3	0.4	6.5	8.3
Trans World	47.5	48.2	46.6	45.8
United	43.0	45.8	45.2	41.5
USAir	3.6	3.2	3.4	2.8
Western	0.5	0.5	0.5	0.4

[a]January 1–June 30.

[b]July 1–December 31.

Source: Salomon Brothers, *Industry Analysis*, May 16, 1983, p. 6.

Exhibit 4b   American Airlines Share Gap on Five Key Routes, 1980

		AA	UNITED	TWA	OTHER
Los Angeles—New York	RPM	31.1	25.1	26.7	8.6
	ASM	28.5	28.3	23.9	8.8
	Share Gap	2.6	−3.2	2.8	−.2
Chicago—Los Angeles	RPM	36.1	42.9	11.5	8.6
	ASM	34.9	44.6	8.5	12.1
	Share Gap	1.2	−1.7	3.0	−2.5
Balt/Wash—Los Angeles	RPM	42.4	35.5	22.1	—
	ASM	38.3	41.4	20.4	—
	Share Gap	4.1	−5.9	1.7	—

		AA	DELTA	BRANIFF	TEX. INTL
Dallas/FW—Los Angeles	RPM	43.8	39.7	14.2	2.3
	ASM	39.1	43.8	14.6	2.4
	Share Gap	4.7	−4.1	−.4	−.1
Dallas/FW—Chicago	RPM	57.3	—	42.7	—
	ASM	50.5	—	49.5	—
	Share Gap	6.8	—	−6.8	—

Source: American Airlines, monthly traffic reports.

Exhibit 5a American Airlines Aircraft Operating Costs[a]

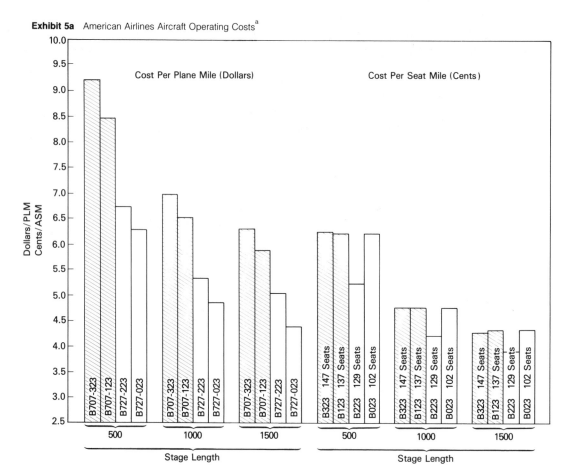

Exhibit 5b   American Airlines Aircraft Operating Margins[a]

	PASSENGER SERVICE		
Aircraft	Percent of System Seat Miles	Load Factor	Operating Profit/(Loss) (Millions)
B747	6.7%	54.4%	$ (7.4)
DC-10	25.1	55.1	(24.7)
B707	22.9	60.0	(74.7)
B727-223	30.2	62.5	14.5
B727-023	15.1	62.7	(21.4)
Total	100.0%	59.9%	$(113.7)

[a]Data from first half, 1980.

Source: American Airlines.

Exhibit 6a   American Airlines (A): Average Aircraft Seating Densities

	1976	1980	INCREASE
B747	338 Seats	366 Seats	+28 Seats
DC-10	240	264	+24
B707-323	144	148	+ 4
B707-123	133	137	+ 4
B707-223	125	129	+ 4
B727-023	91	102	+11

Exhibit 6b   American Airlines (A): B727-223 Seating Configurations of Major Carriers

Carrier	SEATS F	Y	T	PITCH F	Y	COB'S	CLOSETS
American	12	117	129	38"	35"	1+	1+
United	14	118	132	38	34	1	1
TWA	16	118	134	38	34	0	1
Delta	14	123	137	37	34/33	1	0
Braniff	20	109	129	38	34	0	2
Eastern	12	124	136	37	34	0	2

Source: American Airlines.

Exhibit 7 American Airlines (A): Route System

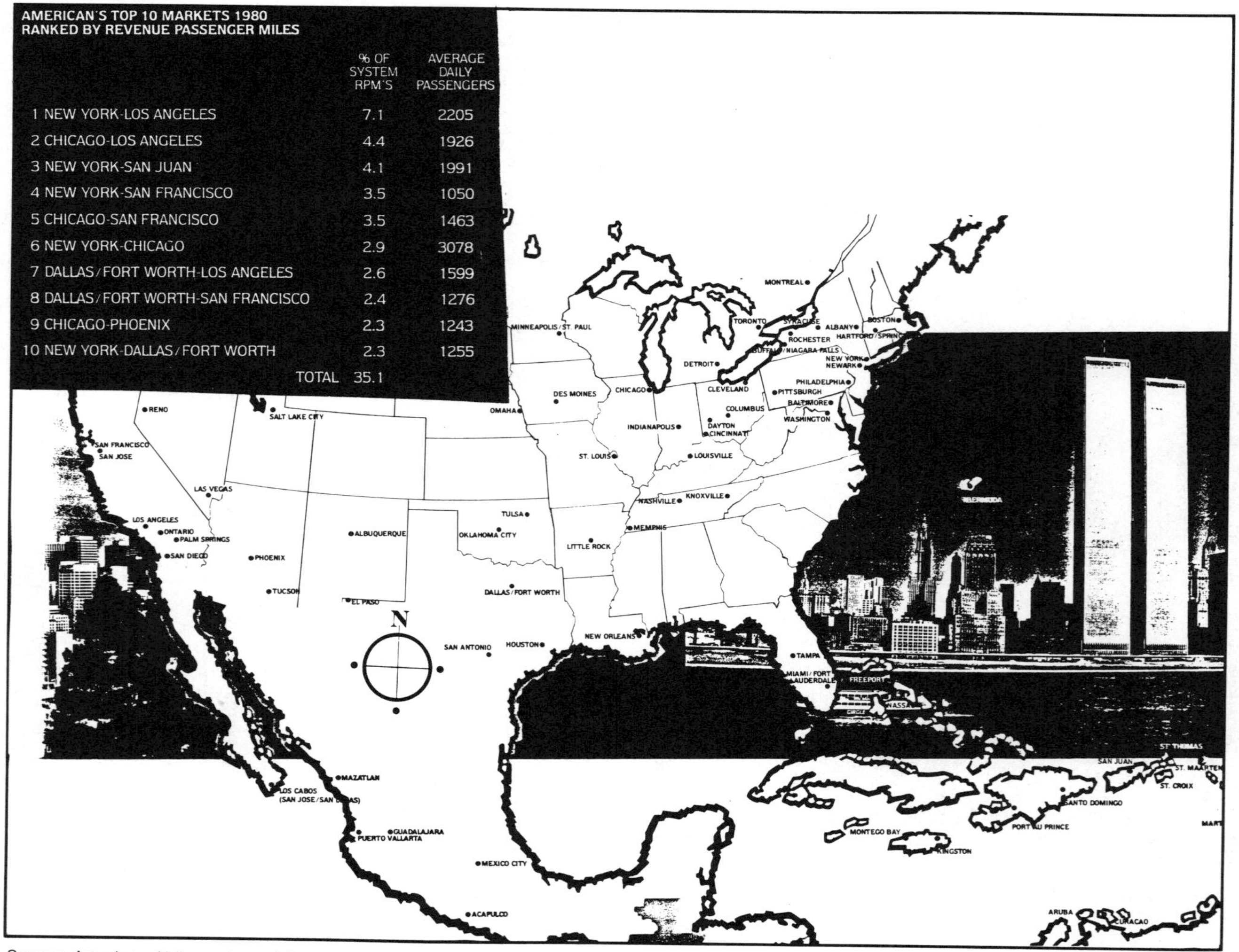

AMERICAN'S TOP 10 MARKETS 1980
RANKED BY REVENUE PASSENGER MILES

	% OF SYSTEM RPM'S	AVERAGE DAILY PASSENGERS
1 NEW YORK-LOS ANGELES	7.1	2205
2 CHICAGO-LOS ANGELES	4.4	1926
3 NEW YORK-SAN JUAN	4.1	1991
4 NEW YORK-SAN FRANCISCO	3.5	1050
5 CHICAGO-SAN FRANCISCO	3.5	1463
6 NEW YORK-CHICAGO	2.9	3078
7 DALLAS/FORT WORTH-LOS ANGELES	2.6	1599
8 DALLAS/FORT WORTH-SAN FRANCISCO	2.4	1276
9 CHICAGO PHOENIX	2.3	1243
10 NEW YORK-DALLAS/FORT WORTH	2.3	1255
TOTAL	35.1	

Source: American Airlines, *Annual Report, 1980.*

198

Exhibit 8 American Airlines (A): Route Changes

1979 MARKET ACTIVITY

Transcontinental Markets

Markets	Inaugurated	Discontinued
LAX— BWI		9/5
YUL	4/29	9/5
SAN— CLE	6/7	11/1
DTW	6/7	10/1
SFO— IAD	6/7	8/1
MIA	1/20	6/25

Semi-Transcontinental Markets

Markets	Inaugurated	Discontinued
IAH— PHL	1/20	
LAS— CLE	1/20	
DTW	1/20	
LAX— BNA	6/7	
NYC— DSM		6/7
SFO— MEM	6/7	

Chicago Markets

Markets	Inaugurated	Discontinued
DFW— LAS	6/7	
SLC	1/20	
ORD— IAH	6/7	
MSP	1/20	
RNO	4/29	

St. Louis Markets

Markets	Inaugurated	Discontinued
STL— ALB	6/7	
CMH	6/7	
WAS	11/1	
SDF	6/7	
SYR	6/7	
SFO	6/7	
SLC	1/20	

Markets	Inaugurated	Discontinued
CLE— CVG		6/7
SDF		6/7
CVG— CMH		6/7
CRW		5/22
DAY		6/7
IND		6/7
MEM		6/7
PIT		6/7
SDF		6/7
ELP— TUS		6/7
IAH— BNA		11/1
MEM	6/7	
LAS— RNO	6/7	
LAX— ONT		6/7
PSP		11/1
SFO	1/20	

Exhibit 8 Continued

1979 MARKET ACTIVITY

Markets	Inaugurated	Discontinued	Markets	Inaugurated	Discontinued	Markets	Inaugurated	Discontinued
Northeast Business Markets			Hawaii Markets			PHX— LAS	6/7	
BUF— DTW		6/7				LAX		8/1
ROC		6/7	Mexico Markets			SLC— RNO	1/20	
NYC— BDL		4/29	DFW— GDL	4/29		SAN	1/20	10/1
PVD		2/24	LAP	4/29		TUS— SAN		11/1
SYR— DTW		12/13	MZT	4/29		SFO		10/1
ROC		6/7	SJD	4/29		YYZ— YUL	9/5	
WAS— IND	6/7		GDL— MZT	8/1				
			PVR	4/29				
			MZT— LAP	4/29		Caribbean Markets		
Dallas/Ft. Worth Markets			SJD	4/29		SJU— MIA	1/20	
DFW— BDL	6/7					PHL	1/20	
MIA	1/20		Miscellaneous Markets			BDA— PHL	4/29	11/1
MSY	1/20		ABQ— SFO	1/20	6/7	NYC— FPO	12/13	
TPA	1/20		BNA— CVG		6/7	MAS	2/15	
ABQ	1/20		PIT		6/7	SXM	1/20	

200

1980 MARKET ACTIVITY (* planned)

Transcontinental Markets

Markets	Inaugurated	Discontinued
LAX—EWR		3/2
PHL		1/15
SFO—CLE		9/3*
DTW		9/3*
TUS—JFK		4/15

Semi-Transcontinental Markets

Markets	Inaugurated	Discontinued
LAX—BNA		12/17*
OMA		8/1
SFO—MEM		9/3*
OKC		9/3*
SAT		10/26*

Northeast Business Markets

Markets	Inaugurated	Discontinued
BOS—CLE		9/3*
BUF—CLE		12/17*
NYC—CMH		10/1*
PHL		1/15
WAS—IND		9/3*

Chicago Markets

Markets	Inaugurated	Discontinued
ORD—ABQ	6/12	
DSM		12/13*
LAS	1/15	
OMA		12/13*
RNO		9/3*
SEA	6/12	

St. Louis Markets

Markets	Inaugurated	Discontinued
STL—CMH		12/17*
IND	6/12	
SYR		12/17*
LAS	6/12	
LIT	6/12	
SLC		10/26*

Miscellaneous Markets

Markets	Inaugurated	Discontinued
BNA—LIT		6/12
SDF		1/15
TYS		12/17*
DSM—OMA		8/1*
DTW—IND		6/12
ELP—LAX		12/17*
SAT		6/12
IAH—CVG		9/3*
MEM		4/27
LAS—RNO		9/3*
MEM—LIT		6/12
SDF		9/3*
OKC—TUL		9/3*
PHX—IAH		3/2
LAS		10/26*
OKC		9/3*
ONT		9/3*
SFO		6/12
SJC		3/2
SJC—OAK		2/15

Exhibit 8 Continued

1980 MARKET ACTIVITY (* planned)

Markets	Inaugurated	Discontinued	Markets	Inaugurated	Discontinued	Markets	Inaugurated	Discontinued
PHL		4/27		Hawaii Markets		SLC—RNO		2/1
			RNL—LAX	12/17*		TUS—PSP		4/15
						YYZ—YUL		9/3*
Dallas/Ft. Worth Markets				Mexico Markets			Caribbean Markets	
DFW—IAH	6/12		ACA—MEX		4/27	SJU—IAD		4/27
OAK		2/15	DFW—LAP		1/15	PHL		4/15
RNO	1/15		MZT		9/3*	STX—EWR		7/20
SEA	6/12		SJD		6/22	IAD		4/27
SMF	6/12		GDL—MZT		9/3*	MIA—AUA	7/18	
			PVR		12/17	PAP	6/12	
			MEX—SAT		1/15	SDQ	6/12	
			MZT—LAP		1/15			
			SJD		6/22			

Source: American Airlines.

Exhibit 9   American Airlines Route Structure, 1979–1980

Market Clusters	NUMBER OF CITY PAIRS*		NUMBER OF FLIGHTS/DAY #	
	1979	1980	1979	1980
Transcontinental	19	12	36	22
Semi-transcontinental	20	23	49	49
Northeast Business	21	26	115	107
[New York-Chicago]			[23]	[15]
[New York-Detroit]			[15]	[11]
Chicago Business	16	17	67	59
Dallas/Fort Worth	34	39	117	125
Southwest	32	27	65	57
St. Louis	**	13	**	24
Mexico	12	9	11	8
Caribbean	20	26	36	25
Miscellaneous	39	16	67	22
Total	213	208	563	498

*These are June data for both years.

#These are approximate, since the original data include complications, such as less than 7 flights weekly or changes within the month.

**The St. Louis market cluster was not so segmented in the 1979 data.

Source: American Airlines, schedule planning, monthly reports, 1979 and 1980.

Exhibit 10   American Airlines (A): Financial Requirements of American Airlines Capital
Budget, November 1979

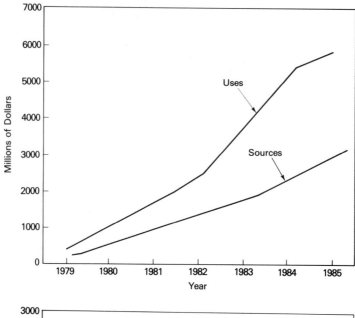

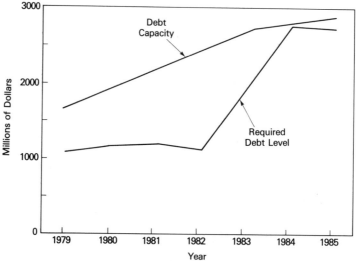

Source: American Airlines.

Exhibit 11 American Airlines (A): Financial Situation as of June 1980

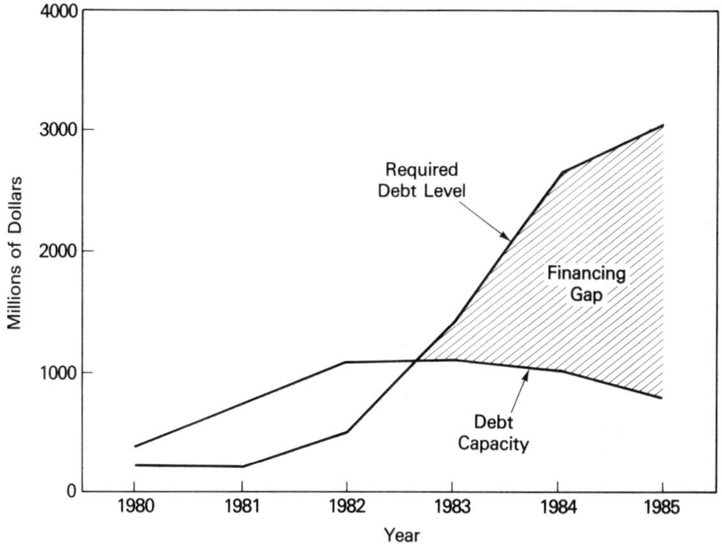

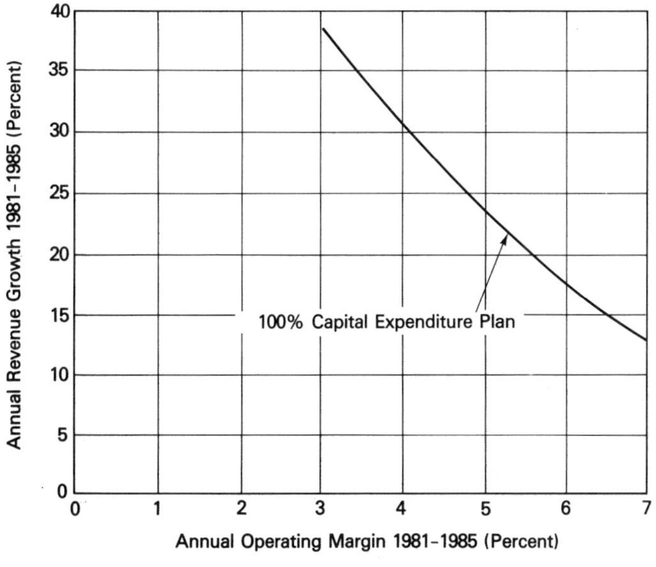

Source: American Airlines.

Exhibit 12 American Airlines (A): Consolidated Balance Sheet

ASSETS (in thousands)	DECEMBER 31, 1979	DECEMBER 31, 1978
Current Assets		
Cash and short-term investments (Note 2)	$ 452,143	$ 537,230
Receivables, less allowances for uncollectible accounts (1979–$16,639; 1978–$11,927)	495,077	395,471
Inventories, less allowances for obsolescence (1979–$26,708; 1978–$21,697)	142,335	95,987
Prepayments and other current assets	14,405	8,834
Total current assets	1,103,960	1,037,522
Equipment and Property (Notes 3 and 5)		
Flight equipment, at cost	1,967,776	1,742,594
Less: accumulated depreciation	953,072	860,531
	1,014,704	882,063
Purchase deposits with manufacturers of flight equipment	111,179	99,529
	1,125,883	981,592
Land, buildings and other equipment, at cost	545,571	459,063
Less: accumulated depreciation	258,430	216,403
	287,141	242,660
Total equipment and property—net	1,413,024	1,224,252
Equipment and Property Under Capital Leases (Note 4)		
Flight equipment	656,803	675,689
Land, buildings and other equipment	152,002	34,014
	808,805	709,703
Less: accumulated amortization	365,857	344,669
Total equipment and property under capital leases—net	442,948	365,034
Investments and Other Assets		
Investment in and advances to unconsolidated subsidiaries (Note 11)	83,528	83,573
Non-current receivables, less allowances and deferred income (1979–$4,309; 1978–$6,006)	28,617	6,097
Route acquisition costs—net	42,608	43,700
Other	67,810	7,540
Total Investments and other assets	222,563	140,910
Total Assets	$3,182,495	$2,767,718

Exhibit 12 Continued

LIABILITIES, REDEEMABLE PREFERRED STOCK AND COMMON STOCKHOLDERS' EQUITY (in thousands)	DECEMBER 31, 1979	1978
Current Liabilities		
Accounts payable	$ 362,763	$ 268,197
Accrued salaries and wages	134,924	106,319
Other accrued liabilities	135,032	133,794
Air traffic liability and customers' deposits	260,531	202,600
Current maturities of long-term debt	48,818	35,174
Current obligations under capital leases	41,074	40,303
Total current liabilities	963,142	786,387
Long-Term Debt, less current maturities (Note 5)		
Senior debt	530,260	419,358
Subordinated convertible debentures	138,398	158,628
Total long-term debt	668,658	577,986
Obligations Under Capital Leases, less current maturities (Note 4)	501,689	410,272
Other Liabilities		
Deferred federal income tax (Note 6)	124,018	155,988
Other liabilities and deferred credits	11,928	9,188
Total other liabilities	135,946	165,176
Commitments, Leases and Contigencies (Notes 3 and 4)		
Redeemable Preferred Stock (Note 8)		
Cumulative—without par value, aggregate redemption value—$125,000,000; 10,000,000 shares authorized; 5,000,000 shares issued and outstanding	107,314	106,218
Common Stockholders' Equity (Notes 5, 7 and 9)		
Common stock—$1 par value; 60,000,000 shares authorized; shares issued and outstanding: 1979—28,696,000; 1978—28,681,000	28,696	28,681
Additional paid-in capital	332,511	332,395
Retained earnings	424,539	360,603
Total common stockholders' equity	785,746	721,679
Total Liabilities, Redeemable Preferred Stock and Common Stockholders' Equity	$3,182,495	$2,767,718

Source: American Airlines, *Annual Report, 1979.*

NOTES

1. Robert L. Crandall, "Opening Remarks, System Marketing Management Meeting," April 2, 1980.
2. W.G. Kaldahl, "Remarks Before the International Association of Convention and Visitors Bureaus Midyear Seminar," Chicago, February 2, 1979.
3. Office of Economic Analysis, Civil Aeronautics Board, *Competition and the Airlines: An Evaluation of Deregulation*, December 1982, pp. 22-23.
4. Tom Plaskett, in "American Airlines Marketing Meeting," Spring 1981, p. 31.
5. *Supra*, Note 1, p. 18.
6. The estimated useful lives and residential values of American's fleet, as used for asset classification, are as follows: Boeing 747s, 14 years—15%; Boeing 707s: (acquired 1959), fully depreciated—$100,000; (acquired 1963-68), 15 years—$100,000; Boeing 727, 16 years—10%; DC-10s, 16 years—10%.
7. Quoted in Robert Joedicke, "The Goose That Laid Golden Eggs," in Lehman Brothers Kuhn Loeb Research, *Industry Comment*, February 18, 1981, p. 12.
8. Cited in American Airlines, "System Marketing Management Meeting—Service Quality Progress," April 2, 1980.
9. Robert Crandall, "Special Report to Employees," *Flagship News*, August 11, 1980, p. 4.
10. Covenants in some long-term insurance company loans at low fixed interest rates required that the ratio of funded indebtedness to stockholders' equity, plus subordinated debt less intangible assets, could not exceed 2.08.
11. J.C. Pope, "The Financing Challenge," American Airlines Finance Management Meeting, July 8-9, 1980.

Note on Freight Transportation and Regulation

INTRODUCTION

This note describes the evolution of surface-transport markets, the railroad and the motor carrier industries, and their regulatory environment.

The Interstate Commerce Act of 1887 initiated federal regulation of railroads, an industry that by then had already experienced fifty-five years of development. That legislation established the Interstate Commerce Commission, the prototype of future federal regulatory agencies. Trucks were first used for transport during World War I after the railroad industry had already flourished for eighty-five years. By the 1930s, trucking companies had invaded the freight carriage market, but then the Depression savaged both the rail and trucking industries. Regulation enveloped the motor carrier industry with the passage of the Motor Carrier Act in 1935. Thereafter, two large industries, competitors in overlapping markets but structurally very different, were regulated by the same federal agency according to similar legal principles and administrative procedures.[1]

In 1980, all this was reversed. Congress reacted to accumulated political and economic pressures by enacting two laws: the Staggers Rail Act and the Motor Carrier Act of 1980. The economic forces unleashed by these reforms induced extraordinary changes in the railroad and the motor carrier businesses, changes that are still unfolding today.

THE EVOLUTION OF FREIGHT REGULATION

Railroads: 1830–1887, Early Growth to Regulation

During its growth period, the railroad industry was by far the largest industry in America. The feasibility of the steam locomotive was first demonstrated in England in 1829. Americans responded with enthusiasm; by 1840,

---

This note was prepared by Research Associate Helen Soussou, under the supervision of Professor Richard H.K. Vietor, as a basis for class discussion rather than to illustrate either the effective or ineffective handling of an administrative situation.

Chart 1 Growth of Rail and Truck Transport

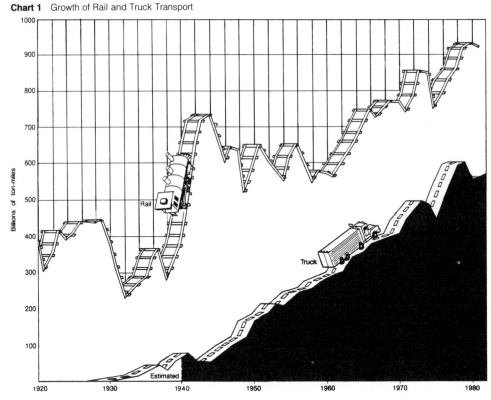

Source: Transportation Association of America

American railroad mileage equalled canal mileage. During "the miraculous decade" of the 1850s, routes between Chicago and the East Coast were built. As
railroad development integrated the Midwest into the nation, the basic patterns
of interregional trade were realigned, reinforcing western links with the Northeast and decreasing the importance of the South.[2] In 1869, the transcontinental
link was completed, and by the mid-1870s, 90% of commerce between the East
and the West was carried by rail. Expansion during the 1880s was extraordinary.

Although railroads often brought prosperity, bankruptcies were nonetheless common. Fed by financial speculation, the industry overbuilt during its
intense growth period. Some systems retained a monopoly status, while other
routes had multiple parallel lines. Capacity utilization remained low, even on
the more densely travelled routes.

Public Entity? Railroads appeared different from canals and roads, in
that it was not feasible for multiple railroad companies to use the same trackage.
The nature of the equipment and the difficulty of meeting and passing other
trains prohibited it. Thus, the facilities and the carrier were owned by the same

Chart 2 Miles of Railway in the United States by Decades

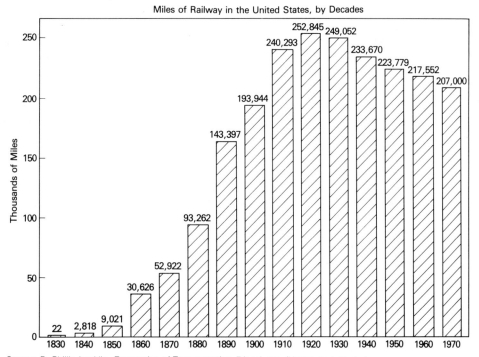

Source: D. Phillip Locklin, *Economics of Transportation*, 7th ed. rev. (Homewood, Ill.: Irwin, 1972), p. 111.

company.[3] This complicated the question of public versus private interests in the law.

From the beginning, railroads had the power of eminent domain—the power to obtain property for a *public purpose*. In 1837, the courts reaffirmed that a railroad was *public* in nature and use even though it was privately owned.[4]

Pricing Conflicts and Antecedents to Federal Regulation

Pricing was a complex issue for railroads, and it became a major source of political controversy among consumer and shipper groups. It was difficult to itemize the cost of transporting a specific item because so many factors were involved. In addition, marginal costs seemed to be much lower than total costs in the railroad industry. Pricing was not just a competitive weapon, but a means to monopoly power. When conditions permitted, high prices subsidized artificially low ones. Generally speaking, the value-added concept was used in railroad pricing; that is, higher value products were charged higher rates.

Price wars were common and could be disastrous for a railroad company.

To alleviate these problems, Albert Fink, President of the Louisville and Nashville Railroad, organized one of the first pooling associations in 1875. Its purpose was to set rates in order to prevent price wars and to parcel out traffic so that each railroad that belonged would survive. Although similar pools were formed elsewhere, pooling did not succeed in the long run because some members of the pool were always ready to undercut others.[5]

Freight rates were proportionally higher for short hauls than for long ones because of higher costs per mile; indeed, the rate for a specific long haul was often less than the rate for a fraction of that same route (where there was no competitive alternative). The grain-producing areas of the Midwest, during the 1880s, especially suffered in this regard. One railroad executive testified to the Senate's Cullom Committee in 1885 that local freight rates, based on cost, subsidized long-haul rates based on demand, which often involved competition between commercial centers.[6] Captive shippers, victims of this system, protested, but the shippers in the West whose goods were carried on the long haul, and the New Englanders who received them, supported the status quo.

Railroads, meanwhile, played a central role in early growth of some of the nation's largest corporations by selectively and secretly offering rebates. Some giant firms like Standard Oil demanded such favors. Conversely, the Pennsylvania Railroad had a monopoly in Pittsburgh, which it used to demand higher freight rates from Carnegie's steel company than from its competitors. Similarly, many coal mines in the eastern anthracite regions had access to only one rail line and, therefore, had no choice in rate matters. In other situations, as described by railroad managers to the Cullom Committee, railroads faced with impending competition were approached by affected shippers seeking lower prices.[7]

In 1877 a group of independent oil producers pushed for the first interstate commerce bill in an effort to halt Standard Oil's practice of using rebates to undermine its competition. They supported a measure which prohibited rate discrimination and rebates, required the posting of tariffs, and relied on the courts for enforcement. Similar bills were reintroduced each year until 1887, when Congress enacted the Interstate Commerce Act.

Railroad management was increasingly frustrated by the industry's volatility. Senator Shelby M. Cullom of Illinois devised a pro-railroad bill that passed the Senate in 1885. It too prohibited rebates and discrimination, and advocated publication of reasonable rates. But it did not outlaw pooling; it had a more flexible long-haul–short-haul clause, and it proposed a federal commission rather than the courts to enforce pool rates.[8]

State Commissions Congressional legislation was modelled after two different types of state regulatory commissions that had evolved to regulate railroads as "common carriers." In Massachusetts, Charles Francis Adams led in the creation of a "weak" commission in 1869. This form relied on effective leadership and the limelight effects of adverse publicity as regulatory tools.[9] As the first railroad commissioner in Massachusetts, Adams succeeded in establishing this indirect approach; it was subsequently adopted by fourteen states. Illinois, declaring that railways were "public highways," instituted a more aggressive, "strong" commission form in the 1870s; many Midwestern and southern states followed its example. To deal with the short-haul–long-haul problem, the Illinois Commission developed new ratemaking rules that set maximum rates and established mileage units which increased in size as trip distance increased.

In its 1886 *Wabash* v. *Illinois* decision, the Supreme Court objected to Illinois's attempt to set interstate rates between Illinois and New York; regulation of interstate commerce was a federal responsibility. The court's decision forced congressional action.[10] The Interstate Commerce Act prohibited pooling and all forms of rate discrimination; appeals of short-haul–long-haul rate inversions were allowed in special circumstances. Railroads would have to set "reasonable and just" rates and report them to a new, five-member Interstate Commerce Commission (ICC). The ICC could investigate and make rate decisions, but had to rely on the courts for enforcement.

Railroads: 1887–1930, Growth Peaks and Regulation Varies

Soon after the Interstate Commerce Act was passed, the Supreme Court pulled its teeth. In an 1889 decision, the Court ruled that no ICC action would be final until after a court review; in 1897, the Supreme Court nullified the ICC's power to set maximum rates; and in 1898, the Court crippled the short-haul–long-haul clause. From 1887 to 1905, the Supreme Court heard sixteen appeals involving the ICC and decided fifteen of them in favor of the railroads. Rate wars and discrimination prevailed.

The depression of 1893 brought cutthroat competition and a wave of mergers. In the South, three major systems emerged: the Southern, the Seaboard, and the Atlantic Coast Line. In the West, the Union Pacific, the Southern Pacific, and the Illinois Central joined together. In the Northwest, the Great Northern merged with the Northern Pacific.[11] The large eastern railroads, meanwhile, used interlocking directorates and stock control instead of mergers to combat rate wars.

The Progressive Era Abuses in railroad practice during the depression of the 1890s and growing resentment toward big business fueled hostility toward railroads and led to a series of amendments. The Elkins Act of 1903 prohibited rebates. The Hepburn Act of 1906 restored the ICC's authority to set maximum rates. The Mann-Elkins Act of 1910 reinforced the short-haul–long-haul clause and it permitted the ICC to suspend a new rate while evaluating its fairness. With these new powers, the ICC reduced rates by nearly 50%.

As the volume of rail traffic increased, major capital improvements were required: double tracks, electric signals, heavier locomotives and cars, and improved grading. Capital investment from 1897 to 1907 was greater than that during the great construction boom of the 1880s. However, by 1910 the tide had begun to ebb; traffic volume continued to increase, but investment declined.

The Mann-Elkins Act and rate reductions at the ICC had reduced railroad control over routes and pricing. Consolidation had been discouraged by the Supreme Court's Northern Securities decision in 1904, and by an ICC report in 1907 that opposed any combination which might reduce competition.[12] J.P. Morgan's unsuccessful attempt to use the New Haven railroad to create a monopoly in New England only exacerbated the downturn. Spectacular train wrecks on the rundown New Haven line made national headlines and fed antimonopoly sentiment.

War and Public Management   When the United States entered World War I in 1917, the railroads first attempted to work together to handle traffic, but the cooperation necessary to clear bottlenecks simply failed. On December 29, 1917, President Wilson took over railroad operations. Under federal administration, locomotive and car design were standardized, some circuitous routes were eliminated, and the statistical database was refined. A Board of Railroad Wages and Working Conditions, created in 1918 with membership equally divided between management and labor, represented the first attempt to regulate railroad wages. The aim was to prevent wartime strikes. Collective bargaining occurred for the first time in the railroad industry.

After the war ended in 1918, Congress debated privatization. Britain, France, Germany, and Canada set up centralized, government-controlled rail systems at this time. Americans had experienced wartime nationalization and could now choose their regulatory path from a broad range of experience. Debate was intense, involving principles which had gained popularity during the war, including the value of managerial efficiency and the concept of a fair rate of return. In the end, nationalization was rejected. Congress passed the Transportation Act of 1920, attempting to set policy through planning as well as by broadening ICC power in ratemaking, industry structure, and financial oversight.

The Transportation Act directed the ICC to recommend a plan for consolidating the nation's rail systems, combining weak roads with strong ones. (Even before the war, 8.8% of U.S. track was in receivership.) Professor William Ripley of Harvard drafted a plan that would divide the nation into six territories and nineteen major rail systems. In the East, Ripley suggested five trunk lines of which the New York Central and the Pennsylvania were the strongest. But the railroad industry adamantly opposed the ICC's plan. As the ICC commented in 1925,

> The differences of opinion which have developed both within and without the Commission, in regard to the form which such a complete plan of consolidation should take are so numerous and so difficult to reconcile . . . that a majority of the Commission have been impelled to the belief that results as good . . . are likely to be accomplished . . . in a more normal way.[13]

The "normal way" was for the railroads to take the initiative and for the Commission to passively review. Without enforcement power, the Commission appeared helpless in the face of corporate interests whose power was established over generations. The holding company was used effectively by railroads during the 1920s to circumvent ICC review. Rail revenues rose 40% from 1920 to 1928.[14] Under the 1920 Act, the ICC was supposed to determine the aggregate value of railroad properties, to provide for a fair rate of return of 6%. Yet, with rate increases during the 1920s based on industry accounts, returns rose from 2.96% to 5.15%.[15] To further aid weak railroads, the 1920 Act had directed the Commission to favor them when it set joint rates. For the first time, the ICC was allowed to set minimum rates. Congress wanted no more rate wars with their destabilizing consequences for the losers.

Railway Labor

The Brotherhood of Locomotive Engineers was founded in 1863 to organize railroad labor. Several other unions developed before 1900. During World War I, labor made significant gains in collective bargaining, in the standardization of practices and policies, and in the development of union organization.

In 1926, during a period of favorable economic conditions, the Railway Labor Act (RLA) was written jointly by labor and management and passed by Congress. This law, as amended in 1934, remained the railroad industry's primary labor relations policy nearly sixty years later, in 1985.

The RLA created the National Railroad Adjustment Board (NRAB) with thirty-six members divided evenly between labor and management. The NRAB had final authority to settle grievances arising from interpretation of labor contracts. Elaborate procedures were established to reach those agreements:

1. Old agreements remained in effect until new ones were signed.
2. New negotiations could be sought by either side after three years of the previous agreement.
3. Collective bargaining was the first step; if that was unresolved . . .
4. Mediation would be tried by a National Mediation Board (NMB), appointed by the President and approved by Congress.
5. If no gains were made by the NMB, binding arbitration would be offered; if accepted, the arbitrator's decision would be binding.
6. If arbitration was refused, the NMB had thirty days to ask the President to act, if it thought interstate commerce was seriously threatened.
7. If notified, the President could appoint an Emergency Board, which had thirty days to investigate the conflict and report back. (On several occasions, the Emergency Board received time extensions.)
8. Either side could accept or reject the Emergency Board's recommendations.
9. If they were rejected and no one settled within thirty days, then labor could strike. (As it turned out in practice, Congress, on occasion, intervened to prevent a strike and compel more negotiations.)[16]

A multitude of work rules had developed in the rail industry over the preceding half century. Most of those rules remain in effect today. As conditions have changed, many of them appear archaic and rigid, but they originated when the nature of railroad management demanded an authoritarian approach—a semimilitaristic chain of command, because trains had to keep moving constantly on single tracks, to meet schedules, with safety a paramount concern. Employees' hours were irregular, and travel patterns kept them away from home. Thus, work rules specified two bases of pay—time worked or distance traveled; they rigidly defined numbers of employees required to run equipment ("crew consists"), and specified the tasks that each employee should perform. The rules multiplied over time.

Railroads and the Depression

From 1929 to 1932, railroad tonnage and revenue fell 50%. The industry reduced operating expenses by nearly half and dividends by three quarters, but net income of $977 million in 1929 turned to a $122 million loss in 1932. Almost 75% of Class I railroads failed to earn enough to cover fixed charges.

The Reconstruction Finance Corporation, created by Congress in 1932, lent $512.5 million to eighty-one railroads. A National Transportation Committee, composed of prominent business leaders, was organized to study regulation. The Committee recommended regional consolidation into a national system, authority for railroads to purchase nonrail transportation companies, a halt to government subsidy of competing modes, and ICC regulation of all transportation. Franklin Roosevelt took office one month later.[17]

The National Recovery Act of 1933 encouraged formation of industry associations with the goal of fostering cooperation. The American Association of Railroads, created in 1934, allowed the railroads to cooperate more formally and become active, influential players in legislative issues.

The Emergency Railroad Transportation Act of 1933 temporarily created a Coordinator of Transportation. Joseph Eastman, whom the President appointed as Coordinator, assessed the problems caused by intermodal freight competition, as between rail, motor (truck), and water transport. Railroad interests, he found, objected to federal subsidy of both highway and waterway construction, and to the fact that only railroads were regulated. Truckers, meanwhile, viewed regulation as a means of controlling price wars and cutthroat competition. Eventually, Eastman concluded that all transportation regulation should either be left to the antitrust division or should be regulated by the ICC in a similar manner. He preferred the latter, suggesting the extension of the railroad regulatory structure to motor carriage and barges.

COMPETITION AND REGULATION BECOME INTERMODAL: 1930-1980

Trucking was radically different from railroads. Railroads were large, capital-intensive businesses with a high proportion of fixed assets. Truckers often started out as "one-man shows" and many remained small, unsophisticated businesses.

Little capital was needed to start a trucking company. Initial investment for a truck was small. Terminals came later and even then, were inexpensive when compared to the fixed plant of a railroad.

The truck was first developed for World War I needs. Trailers were invented in the 1920s and Fruehauf, the nation's largest trailer builder, entered the market in the late 1920s. By 1930, high pressure pneumatic tires had been introduced, trucks had cabs, and tractors with trailers were used. The trucking industry became a formidable competitor for carriage of freight in the early 1930s.[18]

Thirty-three states already regulated motor carriers, but not very effectively. Legislation for interstate regulation was first introduced in Congress in 1925; thirty-seven unsuccessful bills followed. Until the Depression, shippers, most motor carriers, and truck equipment manufacturers opposed regulation; only the ICC and the railroads had favored it.

The Motor Carrier Act of 1935

This important legislation dealt comprehensively with the regulation of entry and rates in trucking. It remained largely unchanged until 1980. The 1935 Act divided the motor carriage industry into three segments: common carriage, contract carriage, and exempt carriers. Exempt carriers, including carriers of agricultural commodites and shippers providing their own transport, were not regulated.

A common carrier is one which makes itself available to carry the freight of any person or company. To obtain a certificate from the ICC, common carriers must prove their ability to provide service and the need for the service. The authorizing certificate stated the specific commodities or class of commodities that a trucker could carry, as well a regular route. Although irregular route carriers were permitted to carry goods between specified points within a territory, they could not pick up or drop off goods along their route unless stops had been specified on the certificate. Rates were treated similarly to railroad rates. The ICC could set minimum or maximum rates or actual rates. In 1936, the ICC raised motor carrier rates to tie them to rail rates.

The Transportation Act of 1940

This legislation expressed the trends in transportation policy of the previous decade. Aside from adding regulation of water carriage, this Act was noteworthy for its preamble, defining a National Transportation Policy. The statement called for regulation to preserve the inherent advantages of each type of transportation and to prevent destructive competition among carriers. The ICC interpreted Congress's intent to mean that one transport mode should not be permitted to undercut the rates of another even if, in doing so, the competitor covered all its costs. Industry was supportive.

With the tacit approval of the ICC, regional rate bureaus became more

Chart 3 Motor Carrier Industry Structure

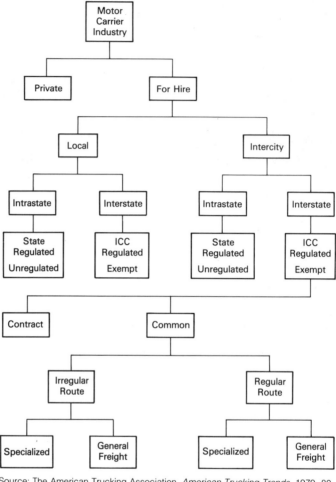

Source: The American Trucking Association, *American Trucking Trends*, 1979–80.

formalized. Railroads used the bureaus to interchange traffic and to set tariffs jointly. Although a railroad could set an unauthorized rate on its own tracks, the collegial atmosphere of bureaus discouraged independent action. The procedures for charging a rate became very complex over time. The motor carrier industry also created rate bureaus, beginning in the late 1930s. Since many motor carriers were small, unsophisticated operations, rate bureaus functioned almost as a regional trade organization—advising on accounting and operational practices as well as handling the setting and publication of a myriad of detailed tariffs, which all had to be classified according to commodity, weight, perishability, value, distance travelled, etc.[19]

In 1945, the Supreme Court ruled that regulated industries were not immune to the antitrust laws. The Railroad and Trucking Associations mounted a massive lobbying campaign that led to the passage of the Reed-Bulwinkle Act in 1948 (over President Truman's veto). That Act gave railroads and motor carriers authority to operate rate agencies if they received ICC approval in advance.

War brought economic recovery to the rail industry. Between 1939 and 1944, railroad operating revenues rose from $4 billion to $9.5 billion. All but one of the thirty-nine Class I railroads in receivership during the depression were able to reorganize. The war on two fronts helped balance the rail system's increased load. The railroads were nationalized only once, for three weeks, when labor problems threatened shipments. With higher earnings, the railroads were able to reduce their long-term debt by about $2 billion, or (20%).[20]

The motor carrier industry also thrived during World War II. Tonnage increased strongly through 1943 (see Exhibit 1), and there was a new awareness of the need for a strong highway system. The Federal Aid Highway Act of 1944 extended the system of interstate highways created in 1921 to 40,000 miles, connecting all major cities and important international routes.

The years following World War II were a period of prosperity, of rebuilding and of technological advances for the nation as a whole. Both railroads and motor carriers shared in this prosperity. Railroads committed a large share of their postwar capital to the changeover from steam to diesel engines. Dieselization permitted the retirement of equipment that dated back to the Depression and that had seen heavy use during World War II. Technological improvements led to more intense intermodal and intramodal competition. In 1956, construction began on the interstate highway system, the largest public works program in the nation's history. The technology of trucks continued to improve, enabling motor carriers to haul heavier products for longer distances.

Rail passenger traffic, a historically significant and warmly remembered part of American history, began declining after 1951. The "blue chip" railroads of the East also suffered from structural changes in the postwar economy. Eastern railroads served old industrial areas, many of which declined as postwar growth moved south and west. Lighter weight, higher value products that became more important to the northeast were more easily transported by truck. Eastern railroads built to carry anthracite coal lost business when oil and gas became popular alternative fuels.[21]

For railroads, the recession that struck in 1957 lasted until 1961; latent problems became overwhelming. In 1957, rail revenues dropped 40% and earnings, 17%. Both the New York Central (NYC) and the Pennsylvania Railroad (PRR) earned less than 0.6% on invested capital. The Jersey Central, Lehigh Valley, Erie, Lackawanna, New Haven, and Boston and Maine railroads registered net losses. Some railroads sought route abandonments. The Pennsylvania Railroad and the New York Central announced their intention to study a merger. But a tie-up of the PRR and NYC threatened to upset the competitive balance among eastern railroads, causing alarm among the smaller roads that feared for their survival.

Robert Young, the flamboyant president of the NYC, committed suicide early in 1958. All concerned wondered if his successor, Al Perlman, would pursue the merger idea. In November 1958, presidents of the "outer seven" railroads held a summit conference in Cleveland. The Erie, the Lackawanna, the Delaware and Hudson, the Baltimore and Ohio, the Chesapeake and Ohio, the Nickel Plate and the Reading railroads were represented. New England railroads held their own meeting in Maine. In 1959, Perlman announced that he thought a merger was unwise at that time and that coordination might be more appropriate.

Merger Fever

During this volatile period, the Erie and the Lackawanna, two weak, largely parallel, railroads merged, but continued to decline. The Chesapeake and Ohio (C&O), a financially healthy road, acquired the ailing Baltimore and Ohio (B&O). The Norfolk and Western, a strong road controlled by the PRR through stock ownership and board membership, sought control of the Nickel Plate, another healthy road, and the Wabash, a connector between the two. The atmosphere was tumultuous. The ICC could not handle all of the complex merger issues swiftly. The Justice Department opened its own investigation. In January 1962, the PRR did an about-face and signed a merger agreement with the NYC.

Congress, meanwhile, took note of all this merger activity. Senator Estes Kefauver submitted a bill for a moratorium on mergers through 1963. At the hearings, John Meyer, an economist from Harvard, testified that mergers were a symptom, not a cause. The problem was declining traffic volume. Meyer found that with increasing size, railroads had problems managing unwieldy organizations. Kent Healy of Yale also testified that there were no economies of scale for railroads with more than 10,000 employees, and that diseconomies occurred with more than 19,000 employees.[22]

The PRR and NYC merger proceedings lasted six years, until approval by the Supreme Court in 1968. Stuart Saunders, PRR's president since 1963, pursued the merger single-mindedly. He negotiated the Luna-Saunders Attrition Agreement, which guaranteed a job after merger to all those employed by either railroad as of 1964. This duel quelled labor, but meant that those employees laid off between 1964 and 1968 were rehired in 1968.

When the Justice Department opposed the merger, Saunders responded by opening negotiations to include the ailing New Haven. The Justice Department agreed to withdraw its opposition if the New Haven were included and if the ICC approved the merger. The ICC did approve, providing that the New Haven retain some of its commuter lines.

When Penn Central was reorganized in February 1968, operations were merged immediately. Everything went wrong. Premerger planning proved ineffectual; the two computer systems were incompatible; the merged company opened unfinished classification yards and closed others that had no replacement. Two very different management cultures clashed bitterly. Shippers lost their products for weeks, customers left in droves, and connecting business fell apart.

In 1970, with first quarter losses at $102 million, Penn Central filed under section 77 of the Bankruptcy Act. The holding company's real estate assets were preserved separately. Trustees sought numerous solutions to no avail. The bankruptcy court planned to liquidate the company in July, 1973.

Congress, the ICC, and the Department of Transportation (DOT) all held hearings on the northeast rail crisis. Congress had already created the National Railroad Passenger Corporation (Amtrak) in 1970 to relieve private railroads of responsibility for passenger service. Neither Congress nor the railroads seemed to know what to do.[23]

A partial solution, however, did materialize; the Regional Rail Reorganization Act of 1973 (the "3R Act") established the United States Railway Association to plan a restructured system. Union Pacific wrote the bill, First National City Bank supplied its financial data, and the United Transportation Union contributed the labor provisions. The Act passed with little debate.[24] It provided up to $1.5 billion in loan guarantees, to acquire and rehabilitate the assets of bankrupt companies. The legislation also created the Consolidated Rail Corporation (Conrail) to operate the new system. It guaranteed lifetime standard-of-living maintenance to employees with five years seniority.

Conrail commenced operations on April 1, 1976. The new system included the Central Railroad of New Jersey, the Erie Lackawanna, the Lehigh and Hudson River, the Lehigh Valley, the Penn Central, and the Reading. Despite reorganization, Conrail continued to run large deficits for the next several years, as the oil shock dragged the entire economy into recession.

Congress tried again in 1976, with the Railroad Revitalization and Reform Act (the "4R Act"). This law provided $2.1 billion in additional funds for Conrail and other railroad subsidies. The 4R Act aimed to "rehabilitate and maintain . . . and restore the financial stability of the rail system of the United States." It took several steps to loosen rate regulation. The ICC could only intervene in rate-level controversies when market dominance existed; seasonal flexibility in rates was permitted to encourage better equipment utilization, and separate pricing was allowed for some services which were previously bundled in a single tariff. Merger and abandonment procedures were streamlined.[25]

The Motor Carrier Industry

The development of the motor carrier industry, meanwhile, was just about opposite of the railroads; it was growing rapidly and its roadways were expanding through federal funding. Improved truck technology facilitated invasion of the railroad market as lighter weight, higher value products favored trucking, while heavy industry, the railroads' traditional customer, declined.

Trucking was an industry of small businesses in the early 1950s. By 1967, fifty companies traded stock publicly, and many had transcontinental operating authority or operating rights in several regions. By 1977, truck transport earned 71% of total freight revenue.[26]

Regulated trucking service was segmented by truckload (TL) and less-than-truckload (LTL) hauls. LTL required more capital because terminals were needed to break and reassemble loads. And since union labor (Teamsters) prevailed in LTL firms, costs were higher than for truckload carriage.

The industry was also segmented by type of carrier: common carriers, contract carriers, exempt carriers, and private carriers. Regulation affected each group in different ways. Contract carriers' certificates limited the number of firms a carrier could serve at one time (eight) as well as the products it could carry. All types of carriers were highly restricted in backhauling. Operating certificates became tangible assets that were bought and sold. Acquisition was the easiest way to grow. Application to the ICC drew protests from competitors already in the territory, even though they might not be using their territorial rights at the time.

The American Trucking Association (ATA), grew into a federation of thirteen trucking conferences, each representing haulers of specific kinds of freight. Affiliated associates from each state also belonged to the ATA. This was a powerful lobby. Regionally, rate bureaus were also supportive groups to truckers, offering consultation in financial matters to an inexperienced businessman.

PRESSURES FOR REGULATORY REFORM

Intermodal Competition

Intermodal rate conflict was a major issue at the ICC. Minimum rate decisions during the 1950s and 1960s showed inconsistency, but leaned more often toward motor carriers and barges. Appropriate means for allocating costs was a perennial problem.[27]

In the 1959 Sealand case, for example, the ICC decided that proposed railroad piggyback rates would destroy coastwise water carriers, whether or not they covered fully distributed costs. The Commission ruled that railroad rates must remain higher than barge rates. The federal district court reversed that decision. In 1963, the Supreme Court concurred with the district court and returned the case to the ICC for reconsideration.[28]

The famous "Big John" case involved Big John aluminum hopper cars: larger, lighter, and more efficient grain carriers. The Southern Railroad spent $14 million on this new technology to compete intermodally. With lowered costs, Southern sought a rate reduction of up to 60%. The ICC tentatively granted the request in 1963, but when truckers, barge companies, the Tennessee Valley Authority, and southern grain processors protested, the Commission reversed its decision. A district court overruled the Commission; in 1965 the Supreme Court upheld the district court. When forced to reconsider, the ICC reasoned that Southern's competition was unregulated and, therefore, not under ICC responsibility.[29]

The "Ingot Molds" case of 1965 involved the transport of ingot molds from Pittsburgh to Steelton, Kentucky.[30] The Pennsylvania and the Louisville and Nashville railroads sought a joint rate equal to the rate of their competitor, a barge-truck service which had held this market since 1953. The rates of both competitors were less than fully distributed costs, but the barge service came closer to meeting full costs. The Commission disapproved the lower costs, citing the need to use fully allocated costs, and to protect the barge-truck service. Railroads argued for variable costs, but this time the Supreme Court supported the Commission's reasoning.

During the 1960s, meanwhile, economists turned their attention to economic regulation, developing a body of analytical literature. The Ford Foundation gave a grant to the Brookings Institute to study economic regulation, funding conferences as well as books, and helping to build excitement. The American Enterprise Policy Institute followed suit. Ralph Nader's consumers organization published a widely read critique of the ICC, *The Interstate Commerce Omission*. In 1971, Alfred Kahn published his landmark work, *The Economics of Regulation: Principles and Institutions*, the first application of marginal cost theory to regulatory institutions.

George Stafford, chairman of the ICC, began to see some need for change. In 1975, for example, the ICC prohibited both rail and truck rate bureaus from protesting rate filings by members. In 1976, the ICC extended commercial zones (regulation free zones) around major cities, thereby expanding exemptions.

In 1977, President Carter appointed Commissioner Dan O'Neal, an advocate of deregulation, as ICC chairman. O'Neal, with a narrow majority at the Commission, appointed a task force to study ways to ease entry. The report, which recommended twenty-nine changes, produced a wave of protests from industry groups. The Commission, meanwhile, increased its rate of approval of entry applications by allowing private carriers to engage in for-hire carriage. O'Neal even suggested that the ICC grant licenses for truckload carriage to anyone who met the fitness standard, and that rates be deregulated within a zone of reasonableness.

The Department of Transportation (DOT) pushed even further, complaining that the ICC was still interpreting the 4R Act too stringently. The AAR pushed for relaxed rates and the use of long-term contracts. In May 1979, the ICC deregulated railroad carriage of fresh produce. In June, President Carter and Senator Kennedy jointly submitted a bill to deregulate motor carriage. Carter appointed three new ICC commissioners, of whom two were economists and all three favored deregulation.[31]

But the trucking industry was furious; so was Senator Howard Cannon, Chairman of the Senate Commerce Committee. Cannon opened a conference on motor carrier regulation in October 1979, by telling O'Neal to stop deregulating by rule-making. Yet he promised that Congress would pass new legislation. And indeed, the Motor Carrier Act of 1980 took effect on July 1, 1980.[32]

The passage of the Motor Carrier Act, meanwhile, gave impetus to the passage of the Staggers Rail Act in October 1980. And the chairmanship of the ICC passed in January 1980 to economist Darius Gaskins, a protégé of Alfred Kahn.

The Motor Carrier Act liberalized entry by stipulating that the burden of proof against a new applicant lay with protesting incumbents. It cut down gateway and circuitous route limitations, ended operating certificate restrictions, and permitted broader categories of freight, service to intermediate points, round-trip authority, and other efficiencies. Contract carriers were allowed to serve an unlimited number of shippers, and private carriers could charge for carrying freight for their subsidiaries. In pricing, the Act created a 10% zone of rate flexibility. Only carriers doing business on a route could vote on the rate for the route, and any carrier could charge a rate different from the collectively set rate. The Act set up a commission to study the question of continued antitrust immunity for collective ratemaking.

The Staggers Rail Act opened with the goal of providing for the restoration, maintenance and improvement of the physical facilities and financial stability of the rail system. It added a section to the National Transportation Policy, listing fifteen new policies in support of these goals.

The Staggers Act permitted a railroad to set any rate where there was competition (that is, when the railroads did not have "market dominance" over a shipper). It created a zone of rate flexibility for market dominance cases tied to quarterly increases for inflation. It encouraged the use of contracts. Railroads could cancel routes that did not earn 110% of variable costs, or add surcharges to those routes. Roads with inadequate revenues could charge fees to cover total operating costs (on lines with less than three million gross ton miles). The ICC would determine annually which railroads were "revenue adequate." Joint discussion of single-line rates in rate bureaus was forbidden, and only participating carriers could discuss joint-line rates.

The Competitive Environment: Motor Carriers

Applications for operating authority increased abruptly, and existing carriers sought territorial extensions. Most applicants were truckload (TL) carriers. Price discounting began at once, startling companies accustomed to regularly rising prices. Exhibit 2 shows posted and real rate changes over the 1975 to 1982 period. Only in 1984 did pricing pressure begin to ease in some segments, although discounting continued among LTL carriers. Customized contracts reflected tradeoffs between price and service features, and the growth of private fleets slowed as truckload carriers became more cost effective.

Teamster membership (in trucking) dropped from 300,000 in 1980 to 200,000 in 1984. Some of the large unionized motor carriers set up nonunion subsidiaries. Nonunion wages averaged about 25% less than union rates. In the 1985 national contract negotiations, the Teamsters were forced to accept a two-tier wage structure. Meanwhile, owner-operators, the cheapest labor source, became increasingly important to nonunion companies. As business conditions improved in 1983 to 1984, and demand for high quality owner-operators increased, companies that competed on cost risked unionization and competition for the best drivers.

The first wave of consolidation occurred soon after deregulation (see Exhibit 3). A second wave occurred during the more prosperous years of 1983 to 1985 when the used-truck market tightened and banks were more ready to call bad loans.[33] Market share shifted to financially strong LTL carriers with geographic networks and marketing initiative; some nationals acquired local companies to balance a threat from railroads to their long-haul business. Others developed links with railroads to offer intermodal services in a combined truck-rail package. The number of Class II ($1-5 million revenue) carriers decreased substantially from 1978 to 1984. Regional carriers that opted to stay local generally fared better.

The number of freight brokers increased from about 60 in 1980 to more than 4,500 in 1985.[34] Brokers offered custom services to large shippers; they helped private fleets find backhauls; they served shippers and carriers that could not afford a marketing or sales department. Some brokers offered other services such as freight-bill auditing, shipment tracing, and claims handling. Large truckers like Ryder/PIE opened their own brokerage subsidiaries.

The Competitive Environment: Railroads

In 1985, the twenty-six Class I Railroads shipped 98% of rail freight and employed 92% of rail personnel. Several hundred smaller railroads served as feeders. At 350,000 in 1984, railroad employment had decreased by 150,000 since 1979 (see Exhibits 4 and 5 for data on decrease in railroad employment). Idle rolling stock was reduced by more than 100,000 cars.

Railroads had a competitive advantage in the shipment of low-value bulk commodities over long distances. (Coal, for example, accounted for 39% of all rail traffic). Electric utilities were the principal buyers of steam coal, and the steel industry for metallurgical coal. Railroads faced relatively little intermodal competition in medium and long hauls of ores and certain agricultural commodities. Barges competed with rails where track ran close to the waterways. In 1984, barges carried 15% to 20% of all coal, 25% of domestic grain, and 50% of export grain. Railroads also competed closely with trucks in the carriage of new motor vehicles, in fresh produce, and in full truckloads of freight moving 500 miles or more (through piggyback services). Trucks appeared to have inherent advantages for less-than-carload, high-value freight and for freight that traveled less than 500 miles.[35]

Freight-shipment contracts facilitated planning for equipment needs and permitted customization of service. Confidentiality in contracts, permitted by the ICC in 1982, led to additional growth in their use.

As railroads struggled to improve marketing, the question of market dominance remained an issue, particularly with coal shippers and their customers, the electric utilities. Between 1981 and 1983, the ICC came to accept the railroad view that indirect product and geographic competition should be considered in market-dominance cases. Product competition is the idea that a consumer could substitute another product from another supplier; for example,

Table 1 Trends in Rail Contracts—1980–83†

BY COMMODITY	NO. OF CONTRACTS	BY RAIL	NO. OF CONTRACTS
Chemicals & minerals	3,021	Chicago & North Western	2,030
Forest products, lumber & paper	2,220	Southern Pacific	1,741
Grain & grain products	1,792	Union Pacific Sys.	1,485
Food products	1,586	CSX System	1,175
Iron, steel, metals & scrap	1,376	Burlington Northern	849
Coal	541	Conrail	779
Autos & parts, machinery, etc.	394	Chicago Milwaukee	672
Other	1,371	Santa Fe	485
Total contracts	12,301	Norfolk Southern	436
		Missouri-Kansas Texas	388
		Soo Line	375

†Excludes intermodal contracts.

Source: Interstate Commerce Commission.

Source: "Railroads Prosper in Post-Staggers' Era," *Standard and Poor's Industry Surveys*, December 20, 1984, p. R26.

an electric utility could substitute oil or natural gas for coal. The ICC leaned toward the Staggers Act's call for railroad revenue adequacy in deciding market-dominance cases.

The electric utilities and the coal industry joined to seek legislative remedies for market-dominance decisions and also to change from the use of return-on-investment (ROI) criteria for evaluation of railroad revenue adequacy to return on equity (ROE). These shippers argue that railroads were financially healthier than ROI measures showed. But railroads countered that their coal rates had increased less than allowed because of competition (especially for export coal), and that the cost of electricity had increased by a much larger percentage than the transportation part of that cost.

Employment had been declining gradually in railroads for many years due to decreased volume and increased productivity. Yet during the first post-Staggers labor pact, signed in 1981, direct pay increased by 25.6% and total compensation increased by 32.9% over three years. New labor negotiations started again in 1984. Issues included work rules and pay rates. Railroads sought to eliminate the fireman position, but the union demanded that the 5,000 firemen still in the industry be let go only through attrition. Old work rules gave on-board rail employees a full day's pay for every 100 miles travelled. In 1985, a tentative agreement reached with the United Transportation Union, stipulated that firemen could be eliminated by attrition and that the full day's pay rule could be extended two miles a year to a maximum of 108 miles. In turn, labor won another cumulative wage increase of 10.9% over thirty-two months, plus a $565 cash bonus.[36]

By 1985, the nation had six very large railroads, three in the East and three in the West; they comprised 76% of the nation's rail mileage, 82% of total rail revenues and 85% of railroad ton miles. The six were Burlington Northern, CSX, Conrail, Norfolk Southern, Santa Fe–Southern Pacific (in the process of merger hearings during 1985), and Union Pacific. Most of these giants were the product of mergers that have occurred since 1980:

Merger	*Completed*
Burlington Northern–St. Louis San Francisco (Burlington Northern)	November 1980
Chessie System–Seaboard Coast Line Ind. (CSX Corporation)	November 1980
Norfolk & Western–Southern Railway (Norfolk Southern)	June 1982
Union Pacific–Missouri Pacific (Union Pacific)	December 1982
Guilford Transportation–Boston & Maine	June 1983
Delaware & Hudson (Guilford Transportation)	January 1985

Most of the largest railroads have become diversified holding companies. CSX became the first railroad to purchase a barge company in 1984 when it acquired American Commercial Lines, a subsidiary of Texas Gas Resources which it had bought in 1983. In 1984, Norfolk Southern purchased North American Van Lines, a nationwide household goods and general freight trucking company. Regulatory changes paved the way for these nonrail transport acquisitions. In earlier years, railroads were forbidden from owning other transport modes.

Another trend was the divestment of shortline branch railroads. Before deregulation, railroads were reluctant to sell to another railroad because of the complexities of joint ratesetting. But about fifty new shortlines appeared between 1980 and 1985, amounting to a total of about 300 operating shortlines.

All of the major railroads earned profits during the 1982 recession. The financial picture of railroads was helped by the Economic Recovery Tax Act of 1981. It allowed railroads to write off previously nondepreciable assets over a five-to-fifty year period, and speed up depreciation on rolling stock and betterments. Between 1980 and 1985, railroads invested heavily in modernization and maintenance of plant and equipment. They also consolidated facilities and continued to abandon underused tracks. In 1983, Class I railroads earned a 7.3% return on equity (the average for all manufacturing industries was 10.5%). Price/earnings multiples of rail stocks were much improved from the 1970s.

The well-being of railroads is, as always, tied to the economy, heavy manufacturing, and competition with other transport modes. The United States Industrial Outlook of 1985 predicted an average annual increase of 2.8% in tons of freight hauled from 1985 to 1989.

President Reagan wanted to celebrate the ICC's 100th birthday by abolishing it. In 1986, he submitted legislation to complete deregulation of motor carriage and to transfer oversight of railroads to the Justice and Transportation departments.

Chart 4 Class I Railroad Route Structures

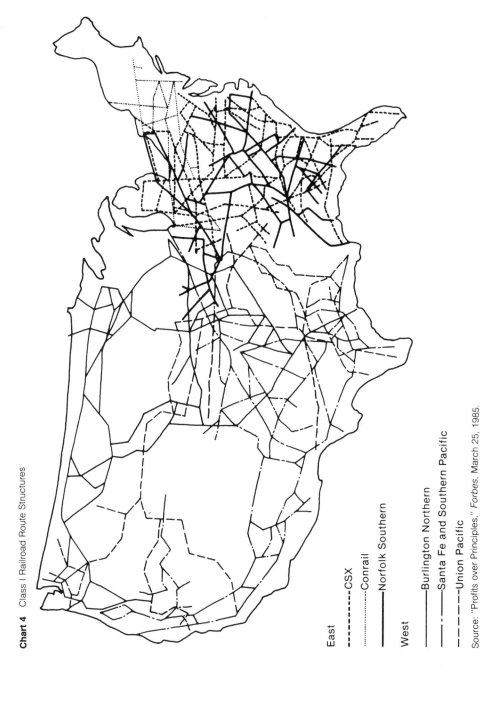

East

- - - - - CSX

.... Conrail

———— Norfolk Southern

West

———— Burlington Northern

—·—·— Santa Fe and Southern Pacific

— — — Union Pacific

Source: "Profits over Principles," *Forbes*, March 25, 1985.

228

Exhibit 1 Domestic Intercity Ton-Miles by Modes (billions of ton-miles)

Year	RAIL Amount	%	TRUCK Amount	%	RIVERS AND CANALS Amount		%
1939	339	62.3%	53	9.7%	20		3.7%
1940	379	61.3	62	10.0	22		3.6
1945	691	67.2	67	6.5	30		2.9
1950	597	56.2	173	16.3	52		4.9
1955	631	49.5	223	17.5	98	#	7.7
1960	579	44.1	285	21.8	121^e	(81)	9.2
1965	709	43.3	359	21.9	152	(110)	9.3
1970	771	39.7	412	21.3	205	(156)	10.6
1975	759	36.7	454	22.0	243	(180)	11.8
1980	932	37.5	555	22.3	311	(227)	12.5
1981	924	38.1	527	21.7	312	(231)	12.8
1982	810	36.0	520	23.1	288	(217)	12.8
1983	841	36.4	548	23.7	289	(218)	12.5
1984	936	37.5	602	24.1	306^e	(239)	12.3

^{e} = Estimated.

* = Includes both for-hire and private carriers and also mail and express.

= Figures in parentheses include only domestic traffic originating and terminating within each respective segment.

Most of remaining percentage = oil pipelines.

Source: "Transportation in America," Transportation Policy Associates, Washington, D.C., 1985, p. 6.

Exhibit 2 Indexes of Real Freight Rates and Average Compensation

SAMPLE SIZE	1975	1976	1977	1978	1979	1980	1981	1982
Rates Paid by Shippers								
TL 35	100	100	100	99	95	88	81	75
LTL 30	100	103	105	104	101	98	91	89
Rail 23	100	102	96	102	101	100	90	93
LA-Denver Posted Rates (Class 100)								
TL	100	102	101	na	93	90	89	102
LTL	100	105	107	na	103	103	110	117
Average Compensation								
All employees	100	94	103	96	94	93	87	89
Drivers and helpers								
Mileage basis	100	117	124	109	105	105	106	100
Hourly basis	100	88	114	92	92	92	92	90

Source: Thomas Gale Moore, "Rail and Trucking Deregulation," in Leonard W. Weiss and Michael W. Klass, eds., *Regulatory Reform: What Actually Happened.* Copyright © 1986 by Thomas Gale Moore. Reprinted by permission of Little, Brown and Company, p. 32.

Exhibit 3 Number of For-Hire Carriers: 1978–1984

YEAR	CLASS I (OVER $5 MILLION)	CLASS II ($1–$5 MILLION)	CLASS III (UNDER $1 MILLION)	TOTAL
1984	1,088	1,554	27,370	30,481
1983	1,139	1,631	24,411	27,517
1982	1,144	2,139	22,059	25,722
1981	1,031	2,293	18,563	22,270
1980	947	2,164	14,610	18,045
1979	992	2,754	13,337	17,083
1978	1,045	2,929	12,900	16,874

Source: *Commercial Carrier Journal*, July 1985, p. 108.

Exhibit 4 Employment in Transportation and Related Industries (Number of Persons in Thousands)

Transportation Service	1950	1955	1960	1965	1970	1975	1980	1981	1982	1983
Air Transport	86	128	191	229	351	362	453	453	442	450
Bus—Intercity & Rural	47	43	41	42	43	39	38	38	37	32
Local Transport	157	127	101	83	77	69	79	83	84	86
Railroads	1,391	1,205	885	735	627	538	532	503	432	377
Oil Pipeline	29	27	23	20	18	17	21	22	22	22
Taxi	121	124	121	110	107	83	53	52	45	40
Trucking & Trucking Terminals	557	688	770	882	998	996	1,189	1,149	1,121	1,133
Water	237	237	232	230	215	190	213	202	194	189
Totals	2,625	2,579	2,364	2,331	2,436	2,294	2,578	2,502	2,377	2,329

Source: "Transportation in America" (Washington, D.C.: Transportation Policy Associates, 1985), p. 18.

Exhibit 5   Railroad Industry Performance in Recent Years

	1969	1975	1978	1979	1980	1981	1982	1983
Net operating income (millions)[a]	1,724	629	632	1,111	1,566	1,444	742	1,781
Revenue ton-miles (billions)	768	754	858	914	919	910	798	828
Employees (class 1 rails) (thousands)	578	488	472	483	459	436	379	322
Miles of class 1 railroad lines owned (thousands)	197	192	176	170	165	162	159	na
Average hourly earnings[a]	9.98	11.46	12.47	12.26	11.96	11.82	12.26	12.87
Average annual earnings (100 of dollars)[a]	244	274	304	300	288	283	291	311
Revenue per ton-mile[a]	3.55	3.66	3.49	3.46	3.34	3.37	3.21	3.02

[a]All monetary figures are in 1982 dollars.

Source: From Thomas Gale Moore, "Rail and Trucking Deregulation," in Leonard W. Weiss and Michael W. Klass, eds., *Regulatory Reform: What Actually Happened*. Copyright © 1986 by Thomas Gale Moore. Reprinted by permission of Little, Brown and Company, p. 25.

Exhibit 6 National Economic vs. Transport Trends 1939–1984

Year	GROSS NATIONAL PRODUCT* (Billions of Dollars) Amount	(a)	INDUSTRIAL PRODUCTION (1967 = 100) Index	(a)	INTERCITY TON-MILES# (Billions) Amount	(a)	INTERCITY PASSENGER-MILES@ (Billions) Amount	(a)
1939	320	27	22	18	544	26	310	24
1940	344	29	25	21	618	30	329	25
1945	560	47	41	34	1,028	50	346	27
1950	535	45	45	38	1,063	51	504	39
1955	658	55	59	49	1,274	61	711	55
1960	737	62	66	55	1,314	63	781	60
1965	929	78	69	74	1,638	79	917	71
1970	1,086	92	108	90	1,936	93	1,181	91
1971	1,122	95	110	92	1,954	94	1,225	95
1972	1,186	100	120	100	2,072	100	1,296	100
1973	1,254	106	130	108	2,232	108	1,342	104
1974	1,246	105	129	108	2,212	107	1,307	101
1975	1,232	104	118	98	2,066	100	1,355	105
1976	1,298	109	131	109	2,202	106	1,460	113
1977	1,370	116	138	115	2,307	111	1,529	118
1978	1,439	121	146	122	2,466	119	1,601	124
1979	1,479	124	153	128	2,573	124	1,590	123
1980	1,475	124	147	123	2,487	120	1,558	120
1981	1,512r	127	151	126	2,430	117	1,574	121
1982	1,480r	124	139	116	2,252	109	1,609	124
1983	1,535	129	148	123	2,311	115	1,675r	129
1984	1,639	138	164	137	2,554	123	1,765e	136

(a) Index with 1972 = 100

*Total output of goods and services in constant 1972 dollars.

e Estimated

#Includes both regulated and unregulated carriers, but excludes coastwise traffic.

@ Includes both for-hire and private carriers, including auto travel.

Source: "Transportation in America" (a compilation of statistics), Transportation Policy Associates, Washington, D.C., 1985, p. 3.

Exhibit 7 Nation's Freight Bill[a] (millions of dollars)

	1960	1965	1970	1975	1980	1981	1982	1983	1984p
Highway									
Truck-Intercity									
ICC-Regulated	7,214	10,068	14,585	22,000	43,000	47,900	44,100	46,500	52,100
Non-ICC-Regulated	10,744	13,560	18,968	25,400	51,645	52,338	57,682	62,333	68,565
Truck-Local[x]	13,498	20,120	28,819	37,287	60,545	72,784	75,010	80,946	87,678
Bus	42	70	122	156	235	260	249	246	242
	31,498	43,818	62,494	84,843	155,425	173,282	177,041	190,025	208,586
Rail									
Railroads	9,028	9,923	11,869	16,509	27,702	30,502	27,134	27,318	30,128
Water									
International	1,765	2,081	3,187	4,928	8,279	8,603	8,097	8,545	10,186
Coastal, Intercoastal	747	692	834	1,136	3,155	3,493	3,545	3,791	3,584
Inland Waterways	312	381	473	950	1,725	1,871	1,823	1,763	1,763[e]
Great Lakes	227	213	239	348	513	570	335	660	456
Locks, Channels, etc.	287	391	376	526	1,156	1,203	1,219	1,158	1,167
	3,338	3,758	5,109	7,888	14,816	15,740	15,019	15,917	17,156
GROSS NATIONAL PRODUCT (billions of dollars)	506.5	691.1	992.7	1,549.2	2,631.7	2,957.8	3,069.3	3,304.8	3,662.8
GRAND TOTAL % OF GNP	9.25%	8.84%	8.44%	7.46%	8.09%	7.93%	7.65%	7.56%	7.49%

[a]Includes mail and express.

[x]Excludes use of small trucks for personal travel.

[e]Estimate.

[p]Preliminary.

Oil pipeline accounts for most not included under highway, rail and water.

Source: "Transportation in America," Transportation Policy Associates, Washington, D.C., 1985, p. 4.

Exhibit 8 Transportation Revenue vs. General Price Trends (revenues in cents per ton-mile or passenger-mile)

	Average Revenue per Ton-Mile vs. Producer Prices					
	RAIL (CLASS 1)		TRUCK (CLASS 1)[a]		Producer Price	
Year	Revenue per TM	Index 1947 = 100	Revenue per TM	Index 1947 = 100	1967 = 100	1947 = 100
1947	1.08	100	4.77	100	74	100
1950	1.33	123	4.98	104	79	107
1955	1.37	127	6.20	130	86	116
1960	1.40	130	6.60	138	94	127
1965	1.27	118	7.30	153	96	130
1970	1.43	132	8.50	178	110	149
1975	2.04	189	11.60	243	163	220
1980	2.85	264	18.00	377	247	334
1981	3.18	294	20.00	419	270	365
1982	3.21	297	20.77	435	281	380
1983	3.12	289	22.01	461	285	385
1984	3.09	286	22.16	465	291	393

[a]Represents LTL carriers. Specialized carriers (TL): 1980—8.64; 1981—9.12; 1982—9.32; 1983—9.06.

Source: "Transportation in America," Transportation Policy Associates, Washington, D.C., 1985, p. 11.

Exhibit 9 Expenditures for New Plant and Equipment by Transport and Related Industries (Billions of Dollars)

	1950	1960	1970	1980*	1980#	1981	1982	1983	1984	1985^e
Non-Manufacturing Industries:										
Air Transport	.10	.66	3.03	3.66	4.01	3.81	3.93	3.77	3.02	3.23
Railroad Transport+	1.18	1.16	1.78	4.24	4.25	4.24	4.38	3.92	5.32	5.74
Other Transport	1.09	1.30	1.23	2.84	3.82	4.00	3.64	3.51	4.57	4.55
Total Transport	2.37	3.12	6.04	10.74	12.08	12.05	11.95	11.20	12.91	13.52
Total Non-manufacturing	12.82	21.66	47.76	104.31	179.81	194.70	196.75	190.97	213.86	226.69
% Transport	18.5%	14.4%	12.6%	10.3%	6.7%	6.2%	6.1%	5.9%	6.0%	6.0%
TOTAL ALL INDUSTRIES	20.21	36.75	79.71	192.51	295.63	321.49	316.43	302.50	343.57	372.94

@See source data for activities covered in both old and new series.   * Old series ends.   # New series begins.

^{e}Estimated by source.

+ These figures compare with AAR data for capital expenditures by Class 1 railroads only, in billions of dollars, as follows: 1.07 in 1950; .92 in 1960; 1.35 in 1970; 3.62 in 1980; 2.85 in 1981; 1.98 in 1982; 1.81 in 1983

Basic Source: "Survey of Current Business," Bureau of Economic Analysis, U.S. Department of Commerce, published monthly.

Source: "Transportation in America" Transportation Policy Associates, Washington, D.C., 1985, p. 23.

Exhibit 10 Piggyback Loadings

| Year | REVENUE CARS | | | | TRAILERS AND CONTAINERS |
	United States	Eastern District	Southern District	Western District	
1957	249,065	130,211	6,155	112,699	—
1958	278,071	139,070	8,903	130,098	—
1959	416,508	204,010	10,687	201,811	—
1960	554,115	263,817	21,128	269,170	—
1961	591,246	299,605	37,749	253,892	902,260
1962	706,441	369,840	64,783	271,818	1,139,220
1963	815,773	394,898	105,511	315,364	1,294,090
1964	920,827	446,311	129,417	345,099	1,455,523
1965	1,076,820	508,189	173,762	394,869	1,664,929
1966	1,224,337	564,348	207,163	452,826	1,912,419
1967	1,277,410	568,089	225,053	484,268	1,983,793
1968	1,509,843	659,471	276,373	573,999	2,419,217
1969	1,539,797	632,433	303,236	604,128	2,497,586
1970	1,449,519	565,518	311,225	572,776	2,363,200
1971	1,356,394	511,877	319,422	525,095	2,203,530
1972	1,448,075	599,177	354,184	494,714	2,407,034
1973	1,630,795	610,874	403,929	615,992	2,758,044
1974	1,609,876	594,208	405,404	610,264	2,752,825
1975	1,307,520	463,779	337,005	506,736	2,238,117
1976	1,505,945	456,670	422,272	627,003	2,538,318
1977	1,688,806	471,965	483,050	733,791	2,850,231
1978	1,840,588	469,436	524,014	847,138	3,177,291
1979	1,857,705	479,662	508,903	869,140	3,278,163
1980	1,687,121	456,404	445,460	785,257	3,059,402
1981	1,752,479	449,634	471,020	831,825	3,150,522
1982	1,920,377	474,275	538,149	907,953	3,396,973
1983	2,347,530	556,343	645,702	1,145,485	4,090,078
1984	2,688,949	645,949	678,003	1,364,997	4,565,743

Note: Mail and express traffic moving in piggyback service is included in above data beginning with 1963.

Exhibit 11 Average Length of Haul (miles)

| Year | RAILROAD | | Truck[c] | Rivers |
	System[a]	Carrier[b]		
1947	408	216	200	NA
1950	416	218	235	NA
1955	430	228	296	256
1960	442	239	341	282
1965	447	257	337	297
1970	490	276	365	330
1975	516	309	446	358
1980	590	378	503	425
1981	600	381	516	444
1982	604	403	532	438
1983	613	428	527	463
1984	617	436	538	464e

[a]System = joint railroad movement.

[b]Carrier = shipment originates and terminates with same railroad.

[c]Class I common carriers of general freight only.

Source: "Transportation in America," Transportation Policy Associates, Washington, D.C., 1985, p. 24.

Exhibit 12 Price Indexes for Total Railroad Freight and Selected Groups With Year-To-Year Percent Changes (1969 = 100)

	DEC. 1981	DEC. 1982	DEC. 1983	DEC. 1984	12/83– 12/84
Total Railroad Freight*	337.8	351.9	357.2	374.8	+4.9%
Farm Products	322.8	338.9	345.3	364.2	+5.4
Metallic Ores	366.8	389.5	396.6	413.6	+4.3
Coal	365.3	387.5	391.8	406.2	+4.0
Non-metallic Minerals	379.3	399.3	404.0	427.6	+5.8
Food Products	340.0	352.8	357.2	376.1	+5.3
Wood and Lumber Products	335.8	349.9	365.6	382.7	+4.6
Pulp, Paper and Allied Products	314.1	327.5	331.6	346.3	+4.4
Chemicals and Allied Products	325.6	339.2	343.2	363.3	+5.9
Clay, Concrete, Glass and Stone Products	362.7	379.3	383.8	405.5	+5.7
Primary Metal Products	333.2	344.8	348.9	365.1	+4.6
Transportation Equipment	325.8	325.8	329.7	344.5	+4.5

*The price index for total railroad freight includes groups not shown separately.

Source: The above chart is reprinted from: "Railroad Industry: A Merrill Lynch Quarterly Update and Review" by permission of Merrill Lynch, Pierce, Fenner & Smith Incorporated.

Copyright 1985, Merrill Lynch, Pierce, Fenner & Smith Incorporated.

Exhibit 13 Labor Costs as a Percentage of Operating Revenues in 1984 and 1983

	WAGES		PAYROLL TAXES		EMPLOYEE BENEFITS		TOTAL	
	1984	1983	1984	1983	1984	1983	1984	1983
Burlington Northern	32.3%	34.4%	6.3%	6.4%	4.5%	4.6%	43.1%	45.4%
Chicago & North Western	42.4	42.8	8.5	7.7	4.4	4.1	55.3	54.6
CSX Corporation	35.0	39.5	9.1	8.2	4.5	4.0	48.6	51.7
Norfolk Southern	33.8	35.8	7.0	6.6	4.3	4.4	45.1	46.8
Santa Fe Industries (a)	35.4	37.3	6.9	7.0	4.7	5.0	47.0	49.3
Southern Pacific (a)	34.4	37.4	7.1	7.1	3.9	3.9	45.4	48.4
Union Pacific	30.8	31.9	6.8	6.3	7.7	7.1	45.3	45.3
Conrail (b)	32.1	32.7	6.4	6.1	3.6	3.7	42.1	42.5

Note—The percentages, with the exception of Chicago & North Western in 1983, reflect the change to depreciation accounting.

(a) On December 23, 1983, Santa Fe Industries and Southern Pacific merged to form Santa Fe Southern Pacific, but the rail operations remain separate.

(b) Conrail's 1984 financial results include a provision for restoration of wages to industry standards for the full second half of 1984. Wages in 1983 and the first half of 1984 were 12% below industry standards.

Source: The above chart is reprinted from: "Railroad Industry: A Merrill Lynch Quarterly Update and Review" by permission of Merrill Lynch, Pierce, Fenner & Smith Incorporated.

Copyright 1985, Merrill Lynch, Pierce, Fenner & Smith Incorporated.

Exhibit 14 Price-Earnings Ratios—Selected Railroad Stocks

	YEAR END PX. 1977 + 1978 EARNS.	YEAR END PX. 1978 + 1979 EARNS.	YEAR END PX. 1979 + 1980 EARNS.	YEAR END PX. 1980 + 1981 EARNS.	YEAR END PX. 1981 + 1982 EARNS.	YEAR END PX. 1982 + 1983 EARNS.	YEAR END PX. 1983 + 1984 EARNS.	YEAR END PX. 1984 + EST. 85 EARNS.	PX. 5/15/85 + EST. 86 EARNS.
Burlington Northern	4.8	2.7	3.7	9.2	11.8	4.9	6.9	6.3	7.4
Chicago and North Western*	3.1	33.6	1.7	6.4	NM	10.5	20.5	17.7	11.5
CSX Corporation (a)	9.0	4.4	4.3	5.4	7.2	8.2	7.9	6.9	7.2
Norfolk Southern (b)	7.9	3.4	3.7	4.6	7.9	9.7	8.2	7.5	8.3
Santa Fe So. Pac. (c)	6.5	3.5	5.0	9.2	10.1	8.6	10.1	9.5	10.0
Union Pacific	8.8	6.4	8.6	18.4	15.4	13.2	12.7	8.9	11.0
Average of Stocks*	7.4	4.1	5.1	9.4	10.5	8.9	9.2	7.8	8.8
S&P 500	7.7	6.5	7.3	8.8	9.7	10.0	9.9	9.2	10.2

Note: 1983, 1984, and 1985 figures include benefits from a change to ratable depreciation accounting from the retirement-replacement-betterment method.

*Chicago and North Western not included in the Average of Stocks.

(a) Prices and earnings prior to 1980 are for Chessie System.

(b) Prices and earnings prior to 1982 are for Norfolk & Western.

(c) Prices prior to the year-end 1983 are the average of Santa Fe Industries and Southern Pacific adjusted for merger. Earnings are pro forma.

NM—Not meaningful.

Source: The above chart is reprinted from: "Railroad Industry: A Merrill Lynch Quarterly Update and Review" by permission of Merrill Lynch, Pierce, Fenner & Smith Incorporated.

Copyright 1985, Merrill Lynch, Pierce, Fenner & Smith Incorporated.

Exhibit 15 Statistical Analysis of the Truck Industry—Private and For-Hire Carriers—1984

FLEET SIZE	TOTAL FLEETS	TOTAL VEHICLES[a]	# of STRAIGHT TRUCKS OPERATED	# of TRACTORS OPERATED	# of TRAILERS OPERATED	# of BUSES OPERATED	# OF OFF-HIGHWAY VEHICLES OPERATED
500 and Over	4,125	5,789,064	2,050,475	821,640	2,359,457	231,285	326,207
100–499	14,142	2,073,167	695,856	361,775	699,368	130,581	185,587
50–99	14,151	729,498	247,361	127,837	223,955	51,666	78,679
25–49	20,217	526,493	205,903	83,241	138,928	40,557	57,864
10–24	20,692	256,574	118,069	39,200	58,458	17,562	23,258
TOTAL	73,327	9,374,769	3,317,664	1,433,693	3,480,166	471,651	671,595

[a]Does not include passenger cars.

Source: *Commercial Carrier Journal*, July 1985, p. 107.

Exhibit 16a Financial Data on Major Trucking Firms

YEAR	NUMBER OF FIRMS IN GROUP	RETURN ON TRANSPORTATION INVESTMENT (%)	PAYROLL TO REVENUE (%)	REVENUE PER TON-MILE[a] (¢)	INDUSTRY BANKRUPTCIES
1973	1144	25.7	na	na	na
1974	972	25.5	na	na	231
1975	803	19.5	43.4	21.5	240
1976	748	19.7	43.2	22.0	276
1977	963	22.8	41.7	21.7	193
1978	857	24.0	41.7	20.1	162
1979	721	14.5	40.2	19.7	186
1980	704	15.1	39.4	19.9	382
1981	704	11.1	38.7	19.4	610

[a]1982 dollars.

Source: Thomas Gale Moore, "Rail and Trucking Deregulation," in Leonard W. Weiss and Michael W. Klass, eds., *Regulatory Reform: What Actually Happened.* Copyright © 1986 by Thomas Gale Moore. Reprinted by permission of Little, Brown and Company, p. 33.

Exhibit 16b Regulated Common Carriers: Revenue and Profit, Percent Change in 1984 from 1983

ANNUAL REVENUE CATEGORY	GROSS OPERATING REVENUE	NET PROFIT AFTER TAXES
Top 50 ($97.7 million–$4.5 billion in gross operating revenues)...................	9.6	−2.6
Top 100 ($57.1 million–$4.5 billion)	9.0	2.3
Second 100 ($30.5–$56.3 million)..................	7.1	−25.0

Source: *U.S. Industrial Outlook 1985*, p. 52–54.

NOTES

1. Dudley F. Pegrum, *Transportation Economics and Public Policy*, 2nd ed., rev. (Homewood, Ill.: Irwin, 1973), pp. 16, 244-49, 268.
2. Much of this historical material was drawn from Alfred Chandler and Richard Tedlow, *The Coming of Managerial Capitalism: A Casebook on the History of American Economic Institutions* (Homewood, Ill.: Irwin, 1985), Chapters 7, 9, 10, 11.
3. D. Phillip Locklin, *Economics of Transportation*, 7th ed., rev., (Homewood, Ill.: Irwin, 1972), p. 119.
4. Ibid., p. 125.
5. Chandler and Tedlow, *The Coming of Managerial Capitalism*, p. 291.
6. Thomas Manning and David Potter, *Government and the American Economy 1870—Present* (New York: Holt, 1952), pp. 61-62. Testimony by George Parker, Vice President, Cairo Short Line Railroad, taken from Report of the Senate Select Committee on Interstate Commerce, 49 Cong., 1st sess., Senate Report 46, pp. 906-8.
7. Ibid., p. 60. Testimony of C.M. Wicker to the Cullom Committee, taken from report cited in note 6, pp. 777-78.
8. Ari and Olive Hoogenboom, *A History of the ICC* (New York: Norton, 1976), p. 7.
9. Thomas McCraw, *Prophets of Regulation* (Cambridge: Harvard University Press, 1984), pp. 19-25.
10. Hoogenboom and Hoogenboom, *A History of the ICC*, p. 12.
11. Chandler and Tedlow, *The Coming of Managerial Capitalism*, p. 278.
12. Richard Saunders, *The Railroad Mergers and the Coming of Conrail* (Westport, Conn.: Greenwood Press, 1978), p. 35.
13. Robert B. Carson, *Main Line to Oblivion* (Port Washington, N.Y.: Kennikat Press, 1971), p. 80.
14. Ibid., p. 91.
15. Hoogenboom and Hoogenboom, *A History of the ICC*, pp. 104-5.
16. Merrill Lynch, *Railroad, Industry: A Merrill Lynch Quarterly Update and Review*, May 1985, p. 14.
17. Hoogenboom and Hoogenboom, *A History of the ICC*, pp. 119-25.
18. For an overview of trucking regulation, see Paul MacAvoy and John Snow, *Regulation of Entry and Pricing in Truck Transportation* (Washington, D.C.: American Enterprise Institute, 1977); also, John F. Spencer, "Trucking: A Retrospective," *Handling and Shipping Management* (October 1982) (a reprint).
19. Leonard Duggin, General Manager, New England Motor Rate Bureau, interview held October 15, 1985.
20. Carson, *Main Line to Oblivion*, pp. 134-39.
21. Some material about the railroads in the 1950s and the 1960s was drawn from Carson, *Main Line to Oblivion* and Saunders, *The Railroad Mergers and the Coming of Conrail*.
22. Saunders, *The Railroad Mergers and the Coming of Conrail*, pp. 172-74.
23. Hearings before the Special Subcommittee on Freight Car Shortages of the Committee on Commerce, 93rd Congress, 1st session, S. 1149 Serial 93-14, March 13 and 16, 1973, p. 61.
24. Saunders, *The Railroad Mergers and the Coming of Conrail*, pp. 307-9 and George Hilton, *The Northeast Railroad Problem* (Washington, D.C.: American Enterprise Institute, 1975), p. 34.
25. Public Law 94-210, 90 Stat. 31.
26. Daniel Overbey, *Railroads: The Free Enterprise Alternative* (Westport, Conn.: Quorum Books, 1982), 38-39.
27. Alfred Kahn discusses these issues in *The Economics of Regulation: Principles and Institutions* (New York: Wiley, 1970), Vol. II, pp. 21-24. He cites, also, other authors who have looked closely at ICC responses to rail efforts to reduce rates during this period.
28. 372 U.S. 744 (1963)—ICC v. NY, NH, and Hartford RR Company.
29. 321 ICC 582 (1963); 325 ICC 725 (1965).
30. 323 ICC 758 (1965); 326 ICC 77 (1965).
31. Martha Derthick and Paul Quirk, *The Politics of Deregulation* (Washington, D.C.: The Brookings Institution, 1985), pp. 36-37.
32. Thomas Gale Moore, "Rail and Trucking Deregulation," in Leonard Weiss and Michael Klass, eds., *Regulatory Reform—What Actually Happened* (Boston: Little Brown, 1986), pp. 14-39.
33. "The Trucking Industry" (a roundtable), *Wall Street Transcript* (June 4, 1984), p. 74090.
34. Parry Desmond, "Broker Boom Attracts Big Boys," *Commercial Carrier Journal* (May 1985), p. 87.
35. "Railroads Prosper in Post-Staggers Era," *Standard and Poor's Industry Surveys* (December 20, 1984), R20-R21.
36. "A Pact That Could Break the Railroads' Labor Logjam," *Business Week* (October 21, 1985), p. 41.

CSX

"There is a gap between our current five-year forecast and where we need to be financially in five years," Hays Watkins told his Board of Directors in May of 1985. Watkins, a lifelong railroader and a central figure in the recent deregulation, was chairman of CSX, a holding company that owned two of the nation's largest railroads—the Chessie System Railroads and the Seaboard System Railroad.

The Board had recently adopted as its goal a 15% return on invested capital (ROIC) by 1990. This only confirmed a change in focus, one that emphasized shareholder value, that had evolved over recent months. Yet neither CSX nor most other railroads had earned their cost of capital for more than a decade. And since 1980, with the simultaneous passage of the Motor Carrier Act and the Staggers Rail Act, the industry had been thrust into a less regulated environment, forced to compete aggressively for investors' capital and a share of a declining market. Alex Mandl, senior vice president of corporate development (responsible for strategic planning) posed the problem this way:

> The railroad business is a shrinking business and there is no way around that. It's not because we do anything wrong; it's not because we do a poor job; it's because things are shifting in our economy and people do business differently, in terms of how they manage their inventory, in terms of how they handle their size of shipments, etc. Some characteristics of the rail mode do not fit shippers' criteria. On the bulk side, it fits very nicely; we will achieve decent returns. On the merchandise side, it's going to continue to decline as we go on. The rail business is roughly two thirds of our company.
>
> Over the last few years, cash generated from the rails has been substantially reinvested in the rails without improving returns. Since CSX was formed, over $2.7 billion has been reinvested in the rail business that has not been a profitable, capital deployment.
>
> Let's think about where we should go, given our rail base, given our transportation base. Where do we have the confidence, skills, experience, and understanding, to take that base and build upon it?

This case was prepared by Research Associate Helen Soussou, under the supervision of Professor Richard H.K. Vietor, as a basis for class discussion rather than to illustrate either the effective or ineffective handling of an administrative situation.

THE CREATION OF CSX

On November 1, 1980, CSX was organized to accomplish a merger of Chessie System, Inc. and Seaboard Coastline Industries, Inc. Chessie was a Cleveland-based holding company; its primary components were the Chesapeake and Ohio (C&O) and the Baltimore and Ohio (B&O) Railroads, but it owned many small lines as well. Among these was the Western Maryland, controlled by the B&O. The C&O, which relied heavily on the coal business in West Virginia, had acquired the B&O in 1963, in serious financial straits. Seaboard, in turn, was the product of a 1967 merger of two southern railroads: the Seaboard Air Line Company and Atlantic Coast Line. In 1980, it was in the process of acquiring the Louisville and Nashville Railroad. Seaboard, which also owned a number of smaller lines, collectively called itself the Family Lines Rail System. Prior to 1980, these tie-ups were mostly "parallel," offering economies through reduction of competing lines.

Three-way merger discussions between Southern Pacific, Seaboard, and Chessie developed sporadically throughout 1977, but collapsed after Southern Pacific attempted a partial takeover. In May 1978, Hays Watkins of Chessie and Tom Rice of Seaboard started a new round of talks, bilaterally. "We started talking," recalled Watkins, "and the more we talked, the more we realized that by putting two regional railroads together, there was very little overlap, but we could certainly cover a lot of territory." There were only thirteen miles of overlapping routes, out of 27,000 route miles. But this sort of "end-to-end" merger could provide a competitive advantage over both railroads' competitors (Conrail, Norfolk and Western, and Southern Railroad).

"By putting them together," explained Watkins, "we were able to give many more customers one system service covering with both origin and the destination; shippers would rather deal with one entity than two." Where the two systems touched, in Richmond, Cincinnati, and St. Louis, consolidations of shop facilities and coordination of traffic would be possible. "One thing led to another," said Watkins:

> We found that the two roads had roughly the same profit level; Seaboard was bigger in mileage, but not as dense as Chessie. We negotiated. We had director meetings and there was a good feeling; it was a good mental fit, and finally we said, "let's split everything right down the middle." That broke the logjam. From then on, all our plans were on the basis of a corporate partnership.

By the time the Interstate Commerce Commission (ICC) approved the merger in 1980, Prime Osborn III had become chairman of Seaboard. He and Watkins implemented a careful strategy of combining equals. The Penn Central merger experience, where clashing cultures produced disastrous results, loomed large in these fragile measures. Hays Watkins recalls:

> CSX from the very beginning was designed as a merger of equals. We had two chief executive officers: Osborn, head of Seaboard, and me, head of Chessie.

We had four senior officers, two from Chessie, two from Seaboard. The board was made up of 12 people with Chessie backgrounds, and 12 people with Seaboard backgrounds, and the headquarters was only selected after an exhaustive search—Richmond was neutral ground. Everything we did was designed to send signals that neither group had taken over the other. We went through lot of ceremonial hat-dancing around here.

Following the merger, a four-member policy board, with a headquarters staff of thirty-nine, provided loose coordination for the CSX holding company, following the three P's: policy, planning, and policing. Its members were the joint chairmen, Hays Watkins and Prime Osborn, and the two chief operating officers, Paul Funkhouser (Seaboard) and John Collinson (Chessie). Later, the chief financial officer, Robert Hintz, and the senior vice president of law and public affairs, John Snow, were added to this group. Each railroad, meanwhile, would remain a separate system, in style and operating substance. As Hays Watkins put it, "each railroad has gross revenues of $2 to $3 billion, and that's big enough—rather than create a super railroad." But each was expected to coordinate decisions and actions with the other, and to adopt a "CSX perspective."

The Chessie System served the Northeast and the Midwest with many branch lines and relatively short distances between major metropolitan centers. It was primarily a high-volume hauler of coal, with iron, steel, and motor vehicles among its other important products. Chessie's operations were thus geared to high-volume, bulk traffic. Its financially aggressive management preferred high leverage and minimum liquidity (see Chart 1).

Seaboard hauled relatively less coal, and no export coal, yet was well connected to major southeastern seaports. It was a strong carrier of general merchandise, including manufactured products, phosphate, chemicals, food and farm products, paper and forest products, industrial materials, and construction materials. Seaboard's legacy from the post-Civil War building lag included fewer branch lines and longer distances between metropolitan centers. And since the South's industrial renaissance had coincided with the trucking industry's rapid growth, Seaboard had to be aggressive in developing business. Seaboard conducted a large volume of lower-margin, piggyback traffic, based on extensive relationships with brokers (of piggyback freight). At the point of merger, Seaboard's aggressiveness in marketing seemed to mirror Chessie's strengths in finance.

Besides the two railroads, which contributed about 90% of the company's revenues, CSX controlled several other assets. CSX Resources managed holdings in real estate, oil, gas and timber. It was a joint-venture partner in major real estate projects that included hotels, office buildings, shopping centers, and a large residential development. The Greenbrier Hotel, a luxury resort in White Sulphur Springs, West Virginia, was one of Chessie's prized possessions. In the Southwest, CSX Resources was a partner in lease acquisitions, seismic studies, and well-drilling. It had partial interests in 200 wells and held properties with potential reserves in the Appalachian Overthrust. CSX Minerals managed cor-

Chart 1   Composition of CSX Railroad's Freight

Principal Rail Commodities by Carloads (Thousands)

Commodity	1982	1983	1984
Automotive	257	308	346
Chemicals	295	321	335
Construction Materials	348	403	438
Food	175	158	147
General Commodities	206	260	281
Grain	283	252	258
Intermodal	622	763	845
Metals	217	269	306
Paper	726	723	714
Phosphates & Fertilizers	527	590	594
Coal	2,090	1,804	2,282
Total	**5,746**	**5,851**	**6,546**

Principal Rail Revenue Producing Commodities (Millions of Dollars)

Commodity	1982	1983	1984
Other	—	—	$176
Automotive	$208	$185	$358
Chemicals	$256	$325	$446
Construction Materials	$367	$407	$329
Food	$252	$292	$152
General Commodities	$151	$174	$240
Grain	$213	$212	$251
Intermodal	$266	$224	$376
Metals	$207	$302	$247
Paper	$231	$214	$482
Phosphates & Fertilizers	$465	$461	$314
Coal	$1,668	$1,445	$1,687
Total	**$4,554**	**$4,554**	**$5,058**

Source: *CSX Annual Report,* 1984.

porate coal-land development and worked with other coal producers in its rail territory. In West Virginia, Kentucky and Maryland, CSX Minerals held mineral rights to 673,000 acres, containing an estimated 1.3 billion tons of recoverable coal reserves, half of which was low in sulfur.

CSX owned several other businesses, including Beckett Aviation, which managed a fleet of executive aircraft for corporate clients and provided related aviation services; Cybernetics and Systems, Inc., created to develop management information services for the Seaboard Railroad; and a newspaper publishing company and cable TV interests.

COMPETITION AND DEREGULATION, 1980–1984

John Snow, who served in the Ford Administration's Department of Transportation and had since joined the Chessie System and then CSX as head of government affairs, recalled that early on, "very few people from the railroads had any appreciation that it was the regulatory system that was doing them in." As substitutes had developed, "the rail system hadn't been able to adjust. You couldn't disinvest, and you couldn't price the plant to reflect its new capital values. We were stuck there with the regulated price structure."

A century of regulation had engendered a sort of common-carrier mentality that permeated the business. Railroaders, in other words, focused on guaranteed capacity. Marketing staffs regularly forecast too optimistically; operating departments embraced costs that fit the optimistic forecasts; and equipment managers (considered support staff) were penalized if they did not have, at all times, enough equipment available to meet potential demand. Within the industry, the idea of deregulation took getting used to. In 1977, as Watkins explained,

> We had our first meeting on the subject of deregulation and we took an informal poll among the top officers. There were two people in favor of complete deregulation. Everyone else, the other ten or eleven, had reservations in varying degrees. We would laugh and say everything in our shop was equal and so our policy of deregulation was passed by a vote of 2 to 12. The two that voted for it, incidentally, were John Snow and me.

"Once every other week" since then, according to an article in *Industry Week*,

> Hays T. Watkins eases his gray 1979 Oldsmobile Toronado out of his condominium driveway in Richmond, VA., threads his way through suburban streets to Interstate 95, drops a dime in the toll booth basket, and heads for Washington, D.C.
>
> In an era when many CEOs find themselves enmeshed, however reluctantly, in government relations, Mr. Watkins meets the task with unusual élan. By his own estimate, he spends one-fourth of his worktime on government related activities. And he's adept at it; he is widely credited for playing a pivotal, behind-the-scenes role in spearheading the landmark railroad deregulation legislation of 1980.
>
> He does considerably more than merely testify or make speeches on issues. . . . Mr. Watkins has taken it upon himself to personally visit senators from each of the 22 states—as well as representatives from each legislative district—in which CSX has operations. . . . In addition, he's an habitué of the Dept. of Transportation (DOT), the Interstate Commerce Commission (ICC), the Federal Trade Commission, and other federal agencies whose decision affect his company. . . . Indeed, asserts John W. Snow (who accompanies Mr. Watkins on his Washington trips and shares the driving): "Hays has sensitized this entire corporation to government relations—right down to the engineer on a train. He has institutionalized it."*

The purpose of the Staggers Rail Act of 1980 was "to provide for the restoration, maintenance, and improvement of the physical facilities and financial stability of the rail system of the United States." From Watkins' perspective, "Staggers was the most dramatic and most drastic piece of action that the railroad industry had had in the last 100 years." Railroads were freed to raise and lower

Industry Week, October 18, 1982, p. 40.

rates wherever they met competition from other railroads, from trucks, or from barges.

The ICC had moved fairly quickly to implement the new law. In 1981, the Commission deregulated piggyback freight, including all rail or trucking services offered by a railroad under a single bill of lading. In January 1983, the ICC allowed railroads to create their own motor-freight services; a year later it allowed railroads to acquire existing motor carriers.

The Commission imposed new accounting rules, substituting "rateable depreciation" of track-and-structure repairs for the historic method of "retirement-replacement-betterment." The Economic Recovery Tax Act of 1981, meanwhile, permitted five-year depreciation of the "frozen asset base" of rolling stock and facilities; cash taxes were replaced by deferred taxes, and the industry's cash-flow position was further enhanced by the use of tax-benefit leases.

Rules remained in cases of market dominance (that is, when no other supply was available to the customer, or no other transportation was available to the shipper) and for joint-rate setting (rates involving moves on multiple carriers) in certain circumstances. Since trucks could reach most shippers, market dominance was mostly confined to bulk commodities such as coal, that could not efficiently be shipped by truck. These new rules were designed to help railroads attain "revenue adequacy." Variable costs set the floor on such rates, while upward adjustments were guided by an inflation index published quarterly by the ICC. By 1984, railroads could charge 180% of variable costs, while roads with "inadequate revenue" were granted an extra 4% zone of flexibility. Importantly, the ICC decided to recognize alternative products and geographic sources as providing elements of competition.

Some shippers objected to the terms of Staggers and its implementation, while others benefited immensely. Continuing issues included the standards and accounting methods used to measure railroads' financial well-being; the administration of joint rates, through rates, and switching agreements; and the standards for determining market dominance. Yet some of these differences, under the ICC's auspices, were resolved through negotiations between shippers and the Association of American Railroads.

Concurrent with these developments were the effects of the Motor Carrier Act of 1980. With this legislation, Congress eliminated entry and pricing restrictions in the motor carrier industry. Since the economic barriers to entry were low in this business, entrepreneurs flocked to enter inefficient markets. Incumbent truckers responded by reducing labor costs wherever possible, and discounting prices by more than 20%. With the recessionary slump in traffic during 1981 and 1982, cutthroat competition intensified the pressure on railroads.

Labor Practices

The United Transportation Union (UTU), the Brotherhood of Railway and Airline Clerks (BRAC), and the Brotherhood of Maintenance-and-Way Employees (BMWE) were the three largest unions in the railroad industry. Together they represented over 60% of rail employees. Fifteen other unions represented other staff and railroad crafts. Wage rates and benefits were negotiated nationally, while work rules were sometimes handled locally. Under the National Railway Labor Act (which also applies to airlines), railway labor agreements generally remained in effect until superseded by a new one. Each agreement specified a moratorium during which issues could not be raised; only after it expired could either party request amendments. Negotiations usually entailed a lengthy process, that occasionally involved intervention by the President and Congress of the United States.

The three-year contract negotiated in 1981 had provided increases in total compensation of 32.9%, gradual elimination of cabooses (in certain areas), and creation of a commission to study long-standing disagreements over work rules. John Collinson attributed the huge increases to a mistaken attitude that the Staggers Act was a source of "freedom" to "automatically pass through labor costs." Some railroaders were saying, "Gosh, we can't take a strike. We have to settle this thing and boy, we have this new-won freedom!" At that time, explained Collinson, "people who had been around the industry really didn't recognize what new competitive forces were being created by trucking deregulation at the same time that we were getting deregulation."

When national negotiations were reopened at the end of June 1984, the unions sought 30% wage increases over the next three years, a continuation of cost-of-living adjustments, and reinstatement of some work rules. This time, however, management sought a two-tiered wage system, with new employees starting at 70% of existing wage levels; elimination of special work payments and COLAs; and an end to the system of a day's pay for 100 miles traveled. Paul Funkhouser explained this last item as follows:

> Traditionally, a man is paid on a hundred miles or eight hours. This comes from years ago, when the average speed of a railroad was 12.5 miles an hour. The average speed now is up, so that you can go a hundred miles in two or three hours, but we are still stuck with the hundred-mile rule.

Worse still, noted Watkins, rules of this sort had differential effects on the various railroads which tended to undermine their solidarity in the national negotiations: "What is important to us running up and down mountains has no relevance to the Union Pacific running 80 miles an hour across Nebraska."

Truck and Rail Competition

Railroads continued, in the 1980s, to lose market share to truck carriage under difficult competitive circumstances (see Exhibit 1). Deregulation of trucking in 1980 forced a reduction of labor rates and prices. After federal legislation extended size and weight limits in 1982, truck unit capacity increased up to 25%. Although rail (and barge) was a more economical mode for commodities such as coal, ores, and grain, many other products were competitive intermodally, or better suited to truck carriage. Choice of mode was affected by price, accessibility to the shipper, reliability in handling the product without damaging it, and speed. Railroads could have an advantage when shipments were large, distance carried was great, and final destinations were not numerous, but trucking competition existed even in these cases.

The railroads struggled to increase productivity and efficiency, to meet truckers' costs. They developed several methods for handling local distribution. Some acquired trucking companies and warehouse facilities, while others started their own. Still others worked out cooperative arrangements with local trucking firms while concentrating on the rail portion of the trip. Because of intense competition with trucking, railroads earned relatively thin profits on piggyback traffic (trailer on flat car/container on flat car), but nonetheless continued investment in this segment because it offered the best possibilities for growth.

Major Rail Systems

Since 1979, mergers by large railroads had produced an industry dominated by six major regional railroads—three in the East and three in the West.

Merger		Completed
Consolidated Rail Corporation (federal)	[Conrail]	1976
Chessie System–Seaboard Coast Line	[CSX]	11/80
Burlington Northern–St. Louis/San Francisco	[BNI]	11/80
Norfolk & Western–Southern Railway	[NS]	6/82
Union Pacific–Missouri Pacific	[UP]	12/82
Santa Fe–Southern Pacific	[SFSP]	12/83
	(ICC deadline)	10/86

These six roads carried 76% of the nation's rail freight in 1984. Guided by their historical strengths and constraints, each system sought to adapt to merger, deregulated markets, and intense nonrail competition. BNI, UP, SFSP, and CSX became diversified holding companies; Norfolk Southern and Conrail remained transportation companies.

CSX's rail competition was primarily with eastern railroads. As yet, the large western roads, although coping with similar challenges, did not compete directly with CSX. Exhibit 2 shows revenues, earnings, and assets for all six railroads.

These larger rail systems had generally prospered since 1980. So far, deregulation appears to have helped, although Robert Claytor, chairman of NS, had commented in 1985 that "if you remove the ITC and accelerated depreciation, an 18 percent return on investment drops to between 6 and 7 percent." Even during the 1982 recession, all Class I railroads maintained profitability, and 1984 was absolutely bountiful.

The *Burlington Northern*, located primarily in the Northwest, was the nation's largest railroad in mileage; it stretched from Seattle to Pensacola, Florida. BNI was trying hard to streamline operations. In 1984, about 95% of its total ton-miles traveled on BNI main lines; it originated about 90% of its tonnage; 40% of its revenues were derived from coal, primarily from the Powder River Basin in Wyoming. Nearly 200 unit trains (trains dedicated to single-product, long-term contractual service) moved 98% of BNI's coal tonnage. BNI's railroad workforce had shrunk by 29% since 1981. Its 1984 operating ratio of 78.6% was the lowest among the major carriers. BNI's nontransportation operating income jumped to 30% after it acquired El Paso Natural Gas in 1983. Among BNI's other operating units were oil and gas exploration, coal properties, and forest products.

The *Union Pacific*, also heavily invested in oil and gas, earned half of its 1984 revenue and 39% of its income from nontransportation sources. UP reduced its debt in 1984 by $143 million and continued a stock repurchase plan begun the year before.

The merger late in 1982 with Missouri Pacific and Western Pacific extended UP's system from the West and Gulf coasts to the Mississippi River and Chicago. Marketing and sales were joined immediately after merger. Rail operations of the two companies, one a western long-hauler and the other a relatively dense midwestern network of shorter hauls, remained separate. MP's contribution to the merger included its Transportation Computer System— perhaps the industry's most sophisticated system for billing, accounting, dispatching, and monitoring rolling stock. UP adapted it for all its own operations.

With 18% of its traffic in coal, UP's business was relatively well-balanced. Its capital program in 1984 focused on modernization of road and yard facilities. Together with the Chicago and Northwestern Railroad, UP completed a 107-mile route into the Powder River Basin—a direct competitive challenge to BNI. It also coordinated with the Chessie System a rapid intermodal service into the East. It already had a similar arrangement with Conrail for the Northeast.

The *Santa Fe–Southern Pacific* merged its nonrail assets early in 1984, but continued to operate the two railroads separately, pending completion of the ICC merger evaluation. This parallel merger, the largest yet, was intended to achieve efficiencies by eliminating duplicate track and facilities. But other western railroads had sought contingencies that, if accepted by the ICC, would effectively negate some of the potential benefits.

Like the others, SFSP had several nonrail subsidiaries with assets in pipeline transport, oil and gas production, coal properties, forest products, and real estate. These produced more than 80% of its income in 1984.

Conrail, the government-owned system, had made a remarkable comeback since its creation in 1976 out of Penn Central and other bankrupt roads in the Northeast. With $7 billion in federal funds, Conrail had invested heavily to rehabilitate deteriorated physical plant. Likewise, federal funds were used to reduce its workforce from 100,000 to 37,000. Other factors helping Conrail were favorable abandonment rules and the transfer of passenger service to local authorities.

By 1981, with the basic rebuilding completed, Conrail's management under Stanley Crane focused on technology and innovation to become competitive. By 1984, computer systems and automated controls had enhanced productivity in every facet of operations. Conrail offered new or lost customers their money back if delivery was not on time. It began warehousing to help customers reduce inventories. It cooperated with truck and barge companies while maintaining control of the account. It offered rate concessions when negotiating industrial-development deals. And it developed sophisticated programs for labor-management participation, promoting the sort of employee motivation needed for quality service. In eight years, Conrail had reduced its breakeven volume by 60%, raising profits to impressive levels.

Despite these efforts and its monopoly position throughout much of the Northeast, Conrail's markets were problematic. Of all six major systems, Conrail had the lowest percentage of originated traffic, and much of that consisted of high-value merchandise carried for relatively short distances, thus very sensitive to truck competition. Some of its major customers, such as steel and automobile manufacturers, had been shrinking for some time; nor did Conrail have much of the rail-dependent, bulk commodity traffic.

Congress, meanwhile, had ordered the sale of Conrail once it became profitable. In congressional hearings early in 1985, Elizabeth Dole, the Secretary of Transportation, had emphasized the Administration's desire to sell Conrail to a buyer that would guarantee its long-term viability. After evaluating fifteen bids, the Secretary recommended in February that the government accept Norfolk Southern's bid of $1.2 billion. She rejected a proposal from Conrail's management, received just a month earlier, for a public offering by Morgan Stanley of $1.2 billion.

Among the parties to that proposal was CSX, which offered to take a 10% share. Even earlier, CSX had sought a division of Conrail between itself and Norfolk Southern, arguing that sole acquisition by either of the two large eastern competitors would run afoul of antitrust policy. CSX adamantly opposed an acquisition of Conrail by Norfolk Southern. Hays Watkins explained his views as follows:

> Conrail is a fierce competitor now. I don't mind competing against them, but I'm not going to compete and risk our money with a company that has 75% of the rail business. Therefore, if Conrail and Norfolk Southern get together we will abandon the entire B&O, and withdraw and put our resources in other areas.

Worse still, Hays Watkins felt that to reduce competition might threatened a shipper backlash:

> We now have three systems in the East; we compete. The customer benefits and we benefit and we have a chance. But if two of the three get together (and it would be the same if Conrail and CSX got together), if you have such a monopoly in the Northeast, the Staggers Act will be repealed—under these circumstances, we are inviting re-regulation.

Congress would be deliberating on the issue for at least another year.

When the Southern Railroad and Norfolk & Western merged in 1982 to form *Norfolk Southern*, the two companies had among the lowest operating ratios among Class I railroads (see Exhibit 3). N&W served large coal mines, an advantage that permitted lower costs. (In 1984, NS served 150 mines; CSX served 385 relatively smaller ones.) And Southern had a history of leadership in labor productivity and plant modernization.

Immediately after the merger, Norfolk Southern combined sales departments; other departments followed, including mechanical and engineering functions. Only operations remained separate in 1984. NS originated about 70% of its traffic (compared to 73% for CSX), and had the longest average haul length in the East. Thus far, Norfolk Southern has chosen to remain a transport company. Besides bidding for Conrail, NS purchased North American Van Lines in 1984. This large trucking company ($654 million in revenues) carried high-value freight, with owner-operator drivers and an extensive network of agents. NS had recently maintained the highest cash flow in the industry; from 1981 to 1984, it was the only big railroad whose funds from operations exceeded capital investment and dividend requirements.

Competition for rail traffic between the three eastern roads continued to intensify as revenue-ton-miles declined. The Staggers Act permitted new leeway in interchange of traffic, pricing, and service. That, together with the end-to-end mergers, led to more single-line service and more closed gateways. NS, for example, had lost its Chicago-Philadelphia-Baltimore intermodal business when the Chessie terminated joint route service. Acquisition of Conrail would solve that problem for Norfolk Southern, and indeed, permit it to control northeast gateways upon which CSX relied. It would also give NS the volume necessary to decrease its operating ratio still further.

THE CSX RESPONSE

Two weeks after Congress passed the Staggers Act, the ICC approved the CSX merger. As the first major merger since the Penn Central fiasco, and the first large "end-to-end" merger, the joining of Chessie and Seaboard had no good precedent. For CSX management, these were uncharted waters, in the midst of a storm.

They moved quickly, nonetheless, to secure contracts with new customers, taking some market share from Norfolk & Western. "We got out ahead of the N&W," explained John Snow, "with initial contracts on coal and lower rates," taking "a big share of the market." Similarly with iron ore from the Great Lakes region, CSX went from thirty or forty to "roughly 80 percent or more of the business." This end-to-end service gave CSX a "competitive advantage," according Hays Watkins, "and it is why the Norfolk & Western and Southern had to merge." So when those contracts come up for renewal in 1986-87, John Snow cautioned, "N&W is not just going to sit by."

Chessie's export coal business (like N&W's) had boomed from 1979 through 1982, largely due to Poland's political crises. The ports at Baltimore and Hampton Roads jammed with vessels waiting to be loaded. Chessie tried everything, including war piers and floating cranes, to increase capacity. Finally, it made a deal providing land and concessionary rates for a major coal shipper to build a $75 million terminal that gave Chessie the dumping capacity it needed.

In March 1981, meanwhile, when the ICC deregulated piggyback traffic, CSX responded by organizing CMX, a nonunion trucking subsidiary. And to meet customers' desire for reduced inventories, it also entered warehousing. In 1982, CSX introduced the Orange Blossom Special, a unit train that combined rail and truck service to speed fresh produce from Florida to metropolitan markets in the Northeast in as little as twenty-four hours. To make this cost-effective, CSX had negotiated crew assignments of 200 miles, as opposed to the usual 100. "With the Orange Blossom Special," said Watkins, "we can undercut the truckers in price and in time and in equipment." For this innovative project, CSX received the "Golden Freight Car" award, a coveted industry prize for marketing.

Shortly after the merger, CSX had initiated consolidation projects where it was possible to share train yards, terminals, shops, piggyback facilities, and car manufacturing. Next came joint purchasing of supplies and joint development of a car-monitoring system. Management bonuses were tied to coordination objectives. Since the merger had caused anxiety among employees, emphasis during 1981 and 1982 was placed on building friendly ties between personnel of the two railroads.

Table 1 CSX Railroad Plant, 1981–1985

	TOTAL TRACK MILES				
	1981	*1982*	*1983*	*1984*	*1985*
Seaboard	25,221	25.223	24,785	23,894	23,112
Chessie	21,296	20,843	21,138	19,549	19,173
Total	46,517	46,066	45,923	43,443	42,285
	LOCOMOTIVES (OWNED AND LEASED)				
Seaboard	2,633	2,452	2,214	2,157	2,164
Chessie	1,725	2,090	2,017	1,933	1,876
Total	4,358	4,542	4,231	4,090	4,040
	CARS (OWNED AND LEASED)				
Seaboard	125,086	116,621	112,123	108,847	95,823
Chessie	119,133	110,896	106,955	104,641	96,553
Total	244,219	227,517	219,078	213,488	192,376

Source: CSX Corporation.

As to reinvestment, Conrail set an influential example for the entire industry, especially CSX. As Bill Sparrow, CSX vice president and treasurer explained,

> Early Conrail management (1976-80) poured buckets of government money into fixing up lines, cars, and locomotives that were in bad shape. Then when Stan Crane showed up, Conrail exited a lot of high-cost markets, cut out non-profitable lines and yards, and became very service competitive. Crane was excellent at recognizing reality.

CSX pursued a similar course with the help of the Economic Recovery and Tax Act. In 1981, Chessie completed a $71 million, ultramodern classification yard at Cincinnati. In Toledo, it developed a $30 million iron ore pellet terminal to speed transfers from rail to ship. Other capital improvements included new car and locomotive repair facilities, piggyback terminals, automobile loading facilities, phosphate-loading berths, and bridges. In 1982, CSX added five new transloading facilities (warehouses) for commodities to the twenty-five it already operated.

Diversification

In 1983, CSX sold its newspaper publishing and cable TV interests. At the same time, it signed an agreement with MCI granting a nonexclusive right of occupancy to 4,000 miles of rail right-of-way for the purpose of installing fiber optic cable. The agreement also included provisions which granted CSX access, at no cost, to MCI's circuits. Then, in 1983, CSX entered a joint venture with Southern New England Telephone to build and market a 5,000 mile fiber optic system of its own. Named LIGHTNET, the system began undergoing construction in 1984.

Also in 1983, the opportunity arose to acquire Texas Gas Resources (TXG), an integrated natural gas pipeline with gas exploration and production operations. Realizing that the rail business faced a long-term decline, and that the end-to-end merger had not provided enough growth to counteract it, Hays Watkins started looking for acquisition prospects:

> We looked at financial services, we looked at insurance, we looked at the brokerage businesses of various kinds, things that would not be in direct conflict with transportation. Then Texas Gas came along.
>
> Texas Gas also owned American Commercial Lines (a major barge company on the Mississippi and Ohio) and as we went to this concept of one stop shipping or total transportation, our lawyers felt it was within the law (even though it had never been done) and would certainly be an advantage if we could offer water transportation in addition to rail and highway. Another attraction was the fact that Texas Gas was a very well-managed, financially strong, conservative company, and we felt it would fit in.

CSX bought Texas Gas for $1.06 billion. ACL, the barge subsidiary, remained in trust until 1984, when the ICC approved CSX control of the company.

Objectives and Incentives

CSX and its predecessor railroads had traditionally used earnings per share to evaluate management (without considering *per se* the return earned on the investment that went into achieving it). But as the transport business became more competitive, Watkins and other senior managers at CSX were increasingly concerned by the fact that CSX stock consistently sold below book value. From discussions with securities analysts, Watkins recalled,

> We came to realize that companies that did not customarily earn their cost of capital sold at a lower P/E ratio than companies that did. We had studies made internally and realized that if we could earn our cost of capital, which we calculated at roughly 15%, then our stock should be selling substantially above book value. We then decided we had to earn at least our cost of capital. In 1984, ROIC was at 9% to 10% overall. Texas Gas Transmission and Exploration were already above 15%. We said, let's set our goal at a 15% rate of return by 1990 with the target that every unit, including the railroads, would earn at least 15%. We established targets for each year, for each unit, and then we keyed our entire bonus plan to that.

A new executive bonus plan, called the "Management Incentive Compensation Plan," was developed. It replaced an earlier focus on pretax earnings, using one-year time horizons, with the new focus on ROIC (using earnings and capital employed by each business unit and six-year target).

The new MICP and the 15% ROIC goal were first introduced to the Board of Directors at its December 1984 meeting. As a part of its strategy of achieving 15% ROIC by 1990, CSX aimed to become the lowest cost and most efficient transportation company (trucking or rail) within its service area by 1990. "In the past," said Watkins, "we had gone on earnings per share, but at the February 1985 meeting, the board formally said okay, 'asset management, return on invested capital is the name of the game.'"

Strategic Planning

Before coming to CSX (corporate), Alex Mandl and his staff at Seaboard had instituted a strategic planning process in 1982 and 1983. A parallel process was instituted at Chessie. Their presentation in April 1984 had included analysis that pointed to the following trends:

1. Macroeconomic trends included a dramatic increase in foreign trade with increased container traffic, a shift from heavy manufacturing to a service and high-technology economy, and an evolution towards a world economy;
2. growth in the economy and in other transportation modes had outpaced railroad growth; rail had lost, and was continuing to lose, market share (revenue);
3. bulk commodities accounted for more than two-thirds of rail revenues, but bulk traffic would remain almost flat;
4. the major growth potential in freight rested with general merchandise, but rail general merchandise traffic had declined;

5. anticipated moderate gains in trailer on flat car (TOFC) traffic would be more than offset by losses in boxcar and TOFC would remain a small portion of total freight traffic (see Exhibits 1 and 4).

Mandl's group recommended that bulk transport be treated as a mature business and that cash derived from it either be returned to the holding company for investment or be applied toward long-term growth in the general merchandise area, building on Watkins' concept of an integrated transportation company which would provide a shipper with a total transportation package. This was perhaps the turning point for recognition within CSX of an inevitable decline of the railroad industry, particularly with the concomitant question of what CSX should do about it.

Organizational Problems

Although most aspects of the effort to coordinate the two railroads had made considerable progress, problems still existed in marketing and sales. As Paul Funkhouser explained,

> Seaboard was the second largest handler of piggyback in the United States with a substantial plurality of its traffic based on dealing with third party wholesalers. The shippers' agents and consolidators were almost a second sales force, closely identified with the bulk of their businesses in that area.
>
> Chessie, on the other hand, had been in a highly competitive situation and had always had some question about the profitability of piggyback traffic. They didn't have the identity with the third party group and their business wasn't built up along those lines. They thought that the way to go was in the retail market, eliminating the middle party broker. You could get more money, you could get the margin. Brokers mainly consolidate. They would have a relationship with a lot of customers. They would give volume and we would give a volume discount.
>
> Seaboard attempted to move to retail and it resulted in a tremendous amount of lost business and the antipathy of the brokers. There were shippers who complained that they had people from two (CSX) sales forces calling on them.

John Collinson, president of Chessie, had been in railroading for forty years and had come up through the ranks with Watkins. Troubled by the roadblocks in marketing and sensing a need to integrate further, he talked to Watkins about these issues and said, "Maybe this is an opportune time for you to do something."

Watkins, who had also sensed a need for change, talked to a number of his key people to solicit ideas about direction and organization. He worked out a plan and announced several changes in February, 1985.

Organizational Changes

1. Collinson was appointed chairman of the CSX Railroads and chairman of a new committee to study the alternatives for railroad reorganization;

2. Richard Leatherwood, from Texas Gas, became vice chairman of the two railroads and joined Collinson as vice chairman of the rail reorganization committee;

3. Alex Mandl was brought in from Seaboard to corporate headquarters to head up corporate development and strategic planning and to join Collinson's committee;

4. Corporate vice president, John Snow (government affairs) received a new assignment, as president and CEO of the Chessie System Railroads.

5. Both Snow and Richard Sanborn, Seaboard's president and CEO, joined Collinson's reorganization committee.

These management changes coincided with the Board's formal adoption of asset management and the 15% ROIC target. Watkins also changed the name of the CSX Policy Committee to "Management Committee," emphasizing the shift in focus from coordination towards strategic direction. The Management Committee included Watkins, Funkhouser, Collinson, Snow, Leatherwood, Sanborn, Hintz, Mandl, Jim Ermer (senior vice president, finance), and Joe Bobzien (president and CEO of American Commercial Lines).

Just as these changes were being announced, CSX was also recruiting James Hagen, the senior vice president of marketing and sales at Conrail, to come and combine the sales and marketing departments of Chessie and Seaboard.

Board of Directors Meeting, May 1985

The Management Committee realized by April that performance for the year would not meet financial projections. Watkins explained to the Board of Directors in May that CSX would attack the problem on two fronts: the Collinson committee's study of rail reorganization, and the Management Committee's focus on strategic planning for each CSX business unit. He predicted that a clear and coherent strategy would be in place by May 1986, and implementation would be underway.

Watkins concluded the meeeting with the following statement: "Our vision of CSX is profoundly different from five years ago. Our challenge is to realize that vision five years hence. Today we will begin to understand how we will effect these changes in between."

Exhibit 1 Freight Projections

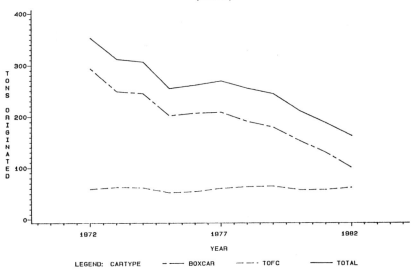

U.S. RAILROADS ORIGINATED TONNAGE
(MILLIONS)

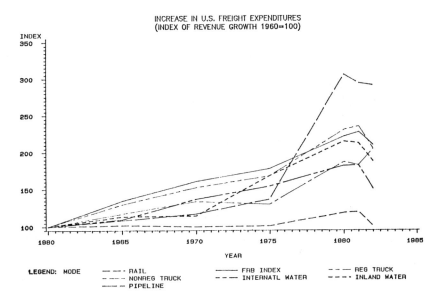

INCREASE IN U.S. FREIGHT EXPENDITURES
(INDEX OF REVENUE GROWTH 1960=100)

Exhibit 1 Continued

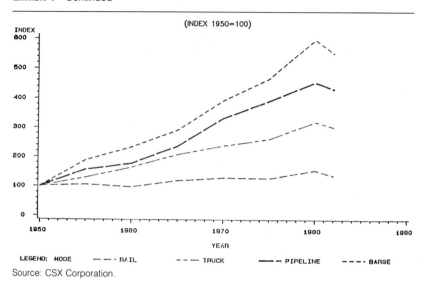

Source: CSX Corporation.

Exhibit 2 Financial Comparisons—Six Major Railroads (millions of dollars)

	1984	1983	1982	1981	1980
CSX					
Transportation Revenue	$5,427	$4,749	$4,644	$5,180	$4,646
Other Revenue	2,507	1,142	265	252	195
Net Income	465	272	414	461	343
P/E Ratio (High-Low)	8–6	13–7	7–4	7–5	7–6
Assets	11,636	11,004	9,199	9,013	8,256
Percent Operating Income = Transport	69%	72%	77%	82%	82%
Rail Capital Investment	748	427	511	509	535
Norfolk Southern					
Transportation Revenue	3,525	3,148	3,359	3,592	3,214
Other Revenue (Net Other Income)	173	139	202	166	117
Net Income	482	357	462	569	478
P/E Ratio (High-Low)	8–6	12–9	10–6	a	a
Assets	8,667	8,208	7,890	7,586	6,888
Percent Operating Income = Transport	100%	100%	100%	100%	100%
Rail Capital Investment	474	307	513	648	658
Conrail					
Transportation Revenue	3,379	3,076	2,999	3,557	3,368
Net Income (Loss)	500	313	174	39	(244)
Assets	6,236	5,703	5,505	5,705	5,628
Percent Operating Income = Transport	100%	100%	100%	100%	100%
Rail Capital Investment	555	455	361	385	474
Burlington Northern					
Transportation Revenue	4,490	4,058	3,802	4,521	3,317
Other Revenue	4,666	450	391	315	310
Net Income	608	413	395	350	334
P/E Ratio (High-Low)	7–5	10–5	14–8	10–5	10–3
Assets	11,424	10,901	7,061	6,742	6,082
Percent Operating Income = Transport	68%	97%	97%	81%	70%
Rail Capital Investment	611	522	539	524	569
Santa Fe Southern Pacific					
Transportation Revenue	5,037	4,551	4,589	5,237	4,812
Other Revenue	1,625	1,466	1,397	1,260	1,109
Net Income	491	334	356	492	538
P/E Ratio (High-Low)	10–8	15–14	b	b	b
Assets	11,649	11,388	10,947	10,775	10,067
Percent Operating Income = Transport	33%	27%	22%	51%	55%
Rail Capital Investment	711	489	444	782	959
Union Pacific					
Transportation Revenue	3,942	3,701	1,831	2,160	2,061
Other Revenue	3,974	4,819	4,094	4,215	2,811
Net Income	494	297	332	429	423
P/E Ratio (High-Low)	13–9	17–12	15–9	19–10	23–8
Assets	10,392	10,218	10,278	7,366	6,430
Percent Operating Income = Transport	61%	57%	37%	41%	41%
Rail Capital Investment	607	341	179	134	385

[a]Norfolk and Western = 1981: 6–4; 1980: 6–3. Southern = 1981: 7–5; 1980: 7–4.

[b]Santa Fe = 1982: 12–6; 1981: 13–7; 1980: 10–4. SoPac = 1982: 10–6; 1981: 9–5; 1980: 8–5.

Sources: Annual reports, Standard & Poor's stock reports, Value Line reports.

Exhibit 3 Statistical Comparisons—Six Major Railroads

	FREIGHT EMPLOYEES (thousands)		OPERATING EXPENSE PERCENT OF FREIGHT REVENUE				COAL CARRIED (millions of tons)				TOFC/COFC LOADED FLAT CARS (in thousands)			
	1983	1979	1983	1982	1981	1980	1983	1982	1981	1980	1983	1982	1981	1980
CSX														
B&O	12.7	16.6	101.9	100.9	93.4	93.6	38.4	41.7	49.3	45.4	57	51	53	54
C&O	15.3	20.2	92.4	90.5	88.9	87.8	65.2	70.0	70.9	71.7	4	2	6	8
Seaboard	28.8	35.1	94.0	97.0	91.4	91.7	73.5	81.6	85.8	79.7	242	198	174	170
Norfolk Southern														
M&W	17.6	23.4	86.9	81.8	74.6	77.9	72.3	83.9	88.5	86.5	72	56	56	66
Southern	17.5	21.4	84.8	86.1	81.0	82.1	43.3	47.0	45.3	48.5	211	195	155	123
Conrail	39.4	76.3	95.7	104.2	102.2	110.6	62.8	66.8	72.0	78.4	357	303	286	283
Burlington Northern	40.5	51.0	86.5	93.7	91.9	91.8	129.2	123.9	114.4	108.9	187	156	172	166
Santa Fe Southern Pacific														
Santa Fe/AT[a]	25.8	33.7	93.8	96.1	93.6	89.7	25.6	24.3	26.8	21.3	349	281	262	228
Southern Pacific/SSW[b]	30.4	39.8	106.0	102.2	97.3	96.2	6.7	7.4	7.6	6.4	225	161	102	107
Union Pacific														
Union Pacific	21.5	20.7	88.5	90.5	86.1	86.5	25.0	26.6	32.6	28.0	103	84	66	61
Missouri Pacific	17.2	28.0	91.2	89.9	88.0	87.5	40.4	37.4	31.7	32.3	59	56	75	67

[a] AT = Atchison Topeka

[b] = St. Louis Southwestern Railway Company.

Source: *Statistical Appendix Class I Railroads, 1979–83,* United States Railway Association, March 1955.

Exhibit 4 Truck-Rail Projections

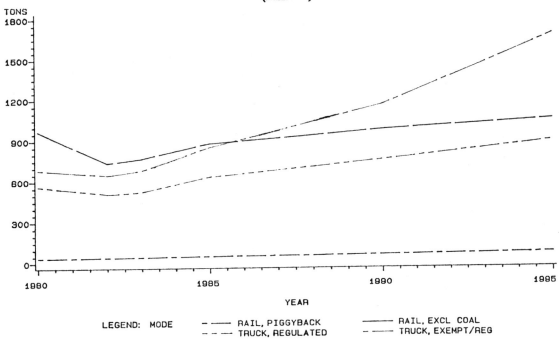

DRI FORECAST: TRUCK/RAIL TONNAGE (MILLIONS)

LEGEND: MODE
- — RAIL, PIGGYBACK
- - — TRUCK, REGULATED
—— RAIL, EXCL COAL
- —— TRUCK, EXEMPT/REG

TOFC versus Truck

| | INTERCITY TRAFFIC (MILLIONS OF TONS) | | |
	1983	*1995*	*Avg. % Growth*
All Intermodal	46	78	4.4
All Truck	2091	3120	3.4

Total Domestic Shipments (Annual Percent Growth)

	1983–85	1985–95
Manufactured Goods	5.2	3.0
Bulk Commodities	2.1	1.2

Source: CSX Corporation.

Exhibit 5   Consolidated Balance Sheet CSX Corporation and Subsidiaries (Millions of Dollars)

	1984	1983	1982	1981	1980
Assets					
Current Assets					
Cash and short-term investments	$ 377	$ 314	$ 528	$ 457	$ 346
Accounts receivable	1,178	1,175	728	863	861
Inventories	458	424	251	271	250
Other current assets	142	153	111	115	91
Total	2,155	2,066	1,618	1,706	1,548
Investments					
Properties	9,143	8,589	7,257	6,989	5,612
Affiliates and other companies	137	115	96	124	127
Other assets	201	234	228	193	236
Total	9,481	8,938	7,581	7,306	5,975
Total Assets	$11,636	$11,004	$9,199	$9,012	$7,523
Liabilities and Shareholders' Equity					
Current Liabilities					
Accounts payable and other current liabilities	$ 1,663	$ 1,542	$1,229	$1,278	$1,134
Current maturities of long-term debt	261	282	167	173	180
Total	1,924	1,824	1,396	1,451	1,314
Claims and other long-term liabilities	343	343	355	439	439
Deferred Income Taxes	1,828	1,511	1,321	1,203	550
Long-Term Debt	2,302	2,466	1,866	2,005	2,068
Redeemable Preferred Stock and Minority Interest	330	334	316	291	279
Total	4,803	4,654	3,858	3,938	3,336
Common Shareholders' Equity					
Common stock	150	146	42	42	41
Other capital	1,639	1,571	1,233	1,205	1,184
Retained earnings	3,120	2,809	2,670	2,376	1,648
Total	4,909	4,526	3,945	3,623	2,873
Total Liabilities and Shareholders' Equity	$11,636	$11,004	$9,199	$9,012	$7,523

Source: CSX Annual Reports: 1984, 1983, 1982.

Exhibit 6 Chessie and Seaboard Earnings Statements[1] (Thousands of Dollars)

	1984	1983	1982	1981	1980
	Chessie System Railroads				
Rail Revenue	$2,214,556	$1,981,578	2,095,963	$2,269,011	$2,036,000
Merchandise	1,013,769	910,552	874,276	1,069,058	995,555
Coal, coke, iron ore	1,090,250	966,565	1,109,605	1,084,986	921,481
Other	110,537	104,461	112,082	114,967	118,964
Rail Expenses	$1,982,551	$1,841,603	$1,910,409	$1,960,257	$1,762,001
Labor, fringe benefits	1,258,543	1,201,115	1,119,184	1,076,761	933,933
Materials/supplies/other	453,780	388,696	494,841	552,431	538,154
Locomotive fuel	143,307	129,009	165,701	203,037	169,868
Depreciation	126,921	122,783	130,683	128,028	120,046
Operating Income	232,005	139,975	185,554	308,754	273,999
Realty Income	28,272	32,886	36,994	22,128	33,999
Other Income	35,345	19,371	58,612	113,276[2]	28,752
Interest Expense	63,519	62,963	61,789	64,120	66,952
Income Taxes	87,619	39,254	60,926	153,847	102,835
Net Earnings	$144,484	$90,015	$158,445	$226,191	$166,963
Fixed Charge Coverage	4.65X	3.05X	4.55X	6.93X	5.03X
Wage Ratio	39.1%	44.1%	41.5%	37.5%	36.6%
	Seaboard System Railroads				
Rail Revenues	$2,785,804	2,518,056	2,407,200	2,736,346	2,411,446
Merchandise	2,052,021	1,911,157	1,743,336	2,024,601	1,846,066
Coal, Coke, iron ore	670,723	553,769	605,209	646,434	495,324
Other	63,060	53,130	58,655	65,311	70,056
Rail Expense	2,387,148	2,233,051	2,245,296	2,360,613	2,116,453
Labor, fringe benefits	1,169,575	1,126,833	1,088,814	1,091,124	977,749
Materials/supplies/other	818,458	738,878	731,244	769,833	712,882
Locomotive fuel	261,123	245,620	276,395	347,207	288,310
Depreciation	137,992	121,720	148,843	152,449	137,512
Operating Income	398,656	285,005	161,904	375,733	294,993
Realty Income	62,743	28,213	29,120	27,312	30,003
Other Income	30,986	26,884	244,728[3]	128,070[4]	48,898
Interest Expense	103,426	106,023	104,441	114,435	100,886
Income Taxes	142,644	81,321	68,107	179,308	77,745
Net Earnings	$246,315	$152,758	$263,204	$237,372	$195,263
Fixed Charge Coverage	3.52X	2.48X	3.05X	3.46X	2.82X
Wage Ratio	31.7%	34.6%	35.1%	31.5%	32.8%

[1]Richmond Fredricksburg and Potomac Railroad Company not included. RFP 1984 revenues = $57.5 million, net earnings = $19.4 million.

[2]Includes $36 million in tax leases.

[3]Includes sale of publishing and cable TV interests and MCI agreement.

[4]Includes $65 million in tax leases.

Source: Financial Supplements to Annual Reports (1984, 1983, 1982).

Exhibit 7 Eleven-Year Summary of Financial Statistical Data CSX Corporation

(MILLIONS OF DOLLARS, EXCEPT PER SHARE AMOUNTS)	1984	1983	1982	1981	1980	1979	1978	1977	1976	1975	1974
Summary of Operations											
Operating Revenue											
Transportation[1]	$5,427	$4,749	$4,644	$5,180	$4,646	$4,184	$3,555	$3,291	$2,995	$2,669	$2,769
Natural Resources[2]	2,507[3]	1,142	265	252	195	170	138	139	130	107	102
Other Income	33	16	246[4]	70	38	47	18	29	25	35	37
Operating Expense											
Transportation	4,726	4,290	4,275	4,465	4,058	3,666	3,321	2,909	2,618	2,393	2,382
Natural Resources	2,190	965	157	151	111	104	87	90	89	73	68
Interest Expense	242	215	171	182	176	186	182	165	158	144	141
Earnings Before Income Taxes	809	437	552	704	534	445	211	295	285	201	317
Income Taxes	344	165	138	243	191	119	30	48	65	32	106
Earnings for the Year	$ 465	$ 272	$ 414	$ 461	$ 343	$ 326	$ 181	$ 247	$ 220	$ 169	$ 211
Dividends	154	133	120	111	87	77	77	NA	NA	NA	NA
Retained Earnings (12/31)	3,120	2,809	2,670	1,905	1,648	1,453	1,293	NA	NA	NA	NA
Earnings Per Share	$ 3.15	$ 2.07	$ 3.30	$ 3.73	$ 2.90	$ 2.81	$ 1.55	$ 2.11	$ 1.90	$ 1.48	$ 1.88

[1]*Transportation.* In 1984, segments included: rail (Chessie, Seaboard, RF&P railroads); barge (ACL; other related transportation (CSX Becket Aviation, CSX Communications, Inc., Cybernetics and Systems, Inc., and Fruit Growers Express).

[2]*Natural Resources.* In 1984, segments included: energy (Texas Gas Transmission, Texas Gas Exportation, CSX Minerals, and the New River Company); others (CSX Hotels, Inc., CSX Resources, Inc., other real estate operations, and the holding company).

[3]The substantial 1984 increase reflects the purchase of Texas Gas Resources in August 1983.

[4]Includes sale of cable TV and publishing subsidiaries ($110 million) and grant to MCI of non-exclusive right of occupancy ($23 million).

Source: CSX Annual Report, 1984, 1980.

Exhibit 8 Consolidated Operating Statistics Chessie System Railroads

	1984	1983	1982	1981	1980
Traffic					
Freight Revenue ($000)	$2,104,019	$1,877,177	$1,983,881	$2,154,044	$1,917,036
Revenue ton miles (millions)	59,180	50,617	50,588	53,606	54,937
Average revenue per ton mile					
Coal	.0293	.0322	.0345	.0336	.0288
Merchandise freight	.0462	.0440	.0467	.0484	.0423
All freight	.0356	.0371	.0392	.0401	.0349
Average revenue per ton					
Coal	8.81	8.87	8.51	7.63	6.73
Merchandise freight	12.41	12.54	13.10	13.10	11.47
All freight	10.24	10.01	10.16	9.82	8.71
Tons of coal exported (millions)	19.0	18.3	29.1	28.4	30.4
Export coal as a % of total US exports	23.6%	23.9%	27.7%	30.7%	41.8%
Originated traffic (millions of tons)					
Coal	98.1	82.7	93.4	90.0	90.6
Freight	42.4	38.8	33.9	43.3	43.4
Railway Operating Expenses ($000)	$1,982,551	$1,841,603	$1,910,409	$1,960,257	$1,762,001
Way and Structure	338,856	360,759	371,979	334,219	291,533
Equipment	487,104	436,393	459,780	494,753	423,700
of which:					
Locomotive	106,322	96,121	103,385	101,507	92,522
Freight cars	247,780	233,218	237,143	294,216	244,595

Exhibit 8 Continued

Traffic	1984	1983	1982	1981	1980
Transportation	977,482	876,658	931,227	944,884	880,451
of which:					
Train operations					
Train and engine men	387,012	350,259	396,528	409,048	374,083
Train fuel	182,236	159,184	170,319	162,194	149,495
Yard operations					
Switch crews	118,808	106,586	137,343	167,653	151,213
Yard and terminal clerical	193,199	175,818	201,495	210,518	196,929
Other operations	107,372	96,344	114,999	115,391	111,010
TOFC/COFC services[1]	56,807	55,031	59,816	57,812	54,249
Clerical, accounting employees	37,255	28,240	36,948	37,374	44,724
Fringe benefits	12,077	8,443	6,261	5,233	6,428
General and Administrative	179,109	167,793	147,423	186,401	166,317
Officers: general administration	11,255	9,933	9,455	9,954	8,979
Salaries/expenses/clerks/attendants	66,353	77,778	69,338	72,998	65,851
Legal, secretarial	12,645	11,416	11,263	8,077	7,938
Sales and marketing	23,226	24,949	12,359	10,818	9,700
Taxes (excluding income and payroll)	20,966	21,659	19,586	19,273	19,851
Fringe benefits	22,754	20,524	21,812	17,969	15,313
Other	21,910	1,534	3,610	47,312	38,685
Operating Statistics					
Operating Ratios					
Maintenance ratio	37.3%	40.2%	39.7%	36.5%	38.8%
Transportation ratio	44.1%	44.2%	44.4%	41.6%	43.2%
Operating ratio	89.5%	92.9%	91.1%	86.4%	90.2%
Average Freight Haul (miles)					
Per revenue ton	288.0	269.9	259.1	244.8	249.7
Gross ton miles per gallon of fuel	716	705	626	586	539
Average number railway employees	29,219	30,805	33,539	36,080	37,712

[1]TOFC/COFC: Trailer on flat car/container on flat car.

Source: Financial Supplements to Annual Reports (1984, 1983, 1982).

Exhibit 9 Consolidated Operating Statistics Seaboard System Railroad

	1984	1983	1982	1981	1980
Traffic					
Freight Revenue (000)	$2,722,744	$2,464,926	$2,348,545	$2,671,035	$2,341,390
Revenue ton miles (millions)	80,243	73,928	69,416	82,238	81,742
Average revenue per ton mile					
Coal	.0238	.0222	.0248	.0213	.0212
Merchandise freight	.0394	.0390	.0384	.0390	.0316
All freight	.0339	.0333	.0338	.0325	.0286
Average revenue per ton					
Coal	7.63	7.53	7.85	7.71	6.44
Merchandise freight	12.52	12.31	12.10	11.39	9.59
All freight	10.81	10.77	10.61	10.20	8.69
Tons of coal exported (millions)	2.8	1.4	1.6	7.2	4.9
Export coal as % of total US exports	3.5%	1.8%	1.5%	7.3%	5.9%
Originated traffic (millions of tons)					
Coal	74.9	62.2	65.5	75.8	69.6
Freight	124.4	121.6	110.7	135.0	146.1
Railway Operating Expenses ($000)	2,387,148	2,233,051	2,245,296	2,360,613	2,116,453
Way and Structure	345,205	325,479	371,876	356,892	316,911
Equipment	679,928	619,042	589,935	603,807	540,884
of which:					
Locomotives	175,259	137,706	140,977	155,987	141,122
Freight cars	380,407	349,065	322,778	349,477	305,907

Exhibit 9 Continued

Traffic	1984	1983	1982	1981	1980
Transportation	1,145,079	1,092,582	1,096,933	1,198,758	1,079,960
of which:					
Train operations	592,063	558,105	567,269	646,353	557,464
Train and engine men	262,959	240,845	226,579	237,384	211,912
Train fuel	251,647	231,479	254,603	319,378	262,364
Yard operations	181,718	178,446	185,828	201,168	195,056
Switch crews	115,311	112,437	113,527	120,072	114,202
Yard and terminal clerical	43,926	42,940	41,918	43,019	48,169
Other operations	24,136	24,685	17,973	16,485	18,715
TOFC/COFC services[1]	20,033	21,176	14,802	14,039	15,871
Clerical, accounting employees	34,816	39,096	38,368	39,542	37,044
Fringe benefits	150,739	131,085	136,614	132,063	107,791
General and Administrative	216,936	195,948	186,552	201,156	178,698
Officers: general administration	32,311	27,158	27,943	37,442	34,233
Clerks/attendants	69,999	64,836	61,242	55,999	43,740
Legal, secretarial	14,538	13,171	13,577	13,794	10,464
Sales and marketing	3,430	3,576	3,764	5,717	11,796
Taxes (excluding income/payroll)	35,629	31,923	34,440	40,920	30,770
Fringe benefits	27,445	25,832	26,273	26,907	25,077
Other	33,584	29,452	19,313	20,377	22,618
Operating Statistics					
Operating Ratios					
Maintenance ratio	36.8%	37.5%	40.0%	35.1%	39.4%
Transportation ratio	41.1%	43.4%	45.6%	43.8%	44.8%
Operating ratio	85.7%	88.7%	93.3%	86.3%	91.5%
Average Freight Haul (miles)					
Per revenue ton	318.7	323.5	313.8	314.3	303.4
Gross ton miles per gallon of fuel	541	535	518	510	480
Average number railway employees	28,285	29,597	30,231	35,368	36,493

[1]TOFC/COFC: Trailer on flat car/container on flat car.

Source: Financial Supplements to CSX Annual Reports (1984, 1983, 1982).

Exhibit 10 CSX Officers

Hays T. Watkins, Chairman & Chief Executive Officer, CSX. D.o.b. Jan. 26, 1926. Educ.—Western Kentucky Univ., B.S. in Acct., 1947; Northwestern Univ., MBA, 1948. Date Employed by CSX (or predecessor)—1949. 1964–71, VP—Finance, C&O-B&O; 1971–73—Pres. and CEO, C&O-B&O.; 1973–75—Chair. and CEO, Chessie Syst. Inc.; 1975–80—Chair. and Pres., Chessie Syst., Inc.; 1980–82—Pres. and Co-CEO, CSX; May 1982 to present—Chairman and Chief Exec. Officer, CSX. *Business and Professional Affiliations*—Dir., Atmospheric Fluidized Bed Devel. Corp.; Black & Decker Mfg. Co.; Kentucky Eco. Devel. Corp.; Westinghouse Electric Corp.; Richmond, Fredericksburg and Potomac Railroad; Bank of Virginia Co.; Member, Nat'l Coal Council; Board of Visitors, College of William & Mary; Virginia Bus. Council; Bus. Advisory Council, Trans. Center, Northwestern Univ.; Chair., Center for Innovative Technology—Commonwealth of VA; Member of Board, Wash. Dulles Task Force; Member, The Conference Board; Business Roundtable; American Inst. of CPA's; Trustee—The John Hopkins Univ., Balt., MD. *Awards:* 1982 Excellence in Mgt. Award—Industry Week Magazine; 1984 Man of the Year Award—Modern Railroads Magazine; 1984 Silver Award—Financial World CEO of the Year.

A. Paul Funkhouser, President, CSX. D.o.b. Mar. 8, 1923. Educ.—Woodberry Forest School, Orange, VA; Princeton Univ., B.A.—1945; Univ. of Virginia Law School, L.L.B.—1950. Employment before CSX—Hunton, Williams, Anderson, Gay & Moore, Richmond, VA (1950–52); Norfolk & Western Railway, Law Dept., Roanoke, VA (1952–63); Penn. Railroad (Penn Central) (1963–75). Date Employed by CSX (or predecessor) Apr. 1, 1975. 1975 to 1975—Senior VP—Exec. Dept., Seaboard Coastal Lines; 1975–78—Exec. VP, SCL Industries, SCL & L&N; 1978–80—Pres. & Dir., SCL Industries, SCL, Vice-Chairman & Dir., L&N; 1980–82—Pres. & Chief Exec., FLRS, SCL & L&N; Dir., CSX; 1980 to present—Dir., CSX; May 1982 to present—Pres., CSX; *Business and Professional Affiliations*—Dir.—Universal Leaf Tobacco Co.; Dir.—Chemical Bank; Chair., Board of Trustees, Hollins College; Trustee: Virginia Foundation for Independent Colleges, Colgate Darden Graduate Business School Sponsors, Inc. (Univ. of Va.); *Award:* Modern Railroads—Man of the Year 1982.

John T. Collinson, Vice Chairman, CSX. D.o.b. July 29, 1926. Educ.—Cornell Univ., B.S.—Civil Eng. Date Employed by CSX (or predecessor)—1946. 1946–64 Various positions Eng. Dept., B&O; 1964–66—Chief Eng., C&O and B&O; 1966–71—Chief Eng.—Maint., C&O, B&O; 1971–73—General Manager Chief Engineer, Chessie; 1973–76—VP for Operations and Maintenance, Chessie; 1976–78—Exec. VP—Operations, Chessie; 1978–80 President—C&O-B&O; 1980–85—CEO, Chessie System Railroads; 1985 Vice Chair., CSX; Chair., Chessie Syst. Railroads, Seaboard Syst. Railroads. *Business and Professional Affiliations*—Dir. of CSX, RF&P, Monumental Corp.; Nat'l Mine Service and the Nat'l City Corp.

Richard L. Leatherwood, Vice Chairman Chessie Syst. and Seaboard System RR. D.o.b. April 22, 1939. Educ.—Univ. of Tenn., B.S. (1962); Rutgers Univ., M.S. (1964); Georgia Inst. of Technology, Ph.D. in Industrial & Systs. Eng. (1972). Employment before Texas Gas—Transaction Systs., Inc. (1972–76); CSF Ltd, (1976–77). Also, 1st Lieutenant, US Army Transp. Corps (1964–66). Date

Exhibit 10 Continued

Employed by CSX (or predecessor) May 9, 1977. 1977–79—VP, Planning & Systems (American Freight Syst.); 1979–81—VP and Asst. to the Pres. (Texas Gas); 1981–82—Senior VP and Chief Fin. Officer (Texas Gas); 1982–83—Exec. VP (Texas Gas); 1983–85 Pres. and CEO (Texas Gas); 1985—Vice Chair., Chessie Syst. Railroads and Seaboard Syst. Railroads. *Business and Professional Affiliations*—Member of the board of dir. of the Interstate Natural Gas Assoc. of America, the Amer. Petroleum Inst., the Nat'l Ocean Industries Assoc., the Nat'l Assoc. of Manufacturers, and the Kentucky Eco. Dev. Corp.; member, Inst. of Mgmt. Sciences.

Alex J. Mandl, Senior Vice President Corporate Development. D.o.b. Dec. 14, 1943. Educ.—B.A. Eco., Willamette Univ., Salem, OR; M.B.A., Univ. of CA, Berkeley. Employment before CSX—Boise Cascade Corp., Boise, Idaho: 1969–73, various positions in Finance; 1973–80—Asst. Treasurer, Boise Cascade Corp., Boise, Idaho. Date Employed by CSX (or predecessor) Sept. 20, 1980. 1980–82—Senior VP—Finance, Seaboard Coast Line Railroad Co., Jacksonville, FL; 1983–85—Senior VP—Finance & Corp. Planning, Seaboard System Railroad; 1985 Senior VP—Corporate Dev., CSX Corp. *Business and Professional Affiliations*—Financial Exec. Inst.; Society of Int'l Treasurers; Young Presidents' Organization, Inc.; Business Week Corporate Planning 100; Boards: Chessie Motor Express, Inc.; Seaboard System Railroad, Inc.; Chessie System Railroads; Cybernetics & Systems, Inc.; Chair. of Gen. Comm., Treasury Div. of Asso. of American Railroads; Chair. of the Board, Fruit Growers Express, Inc.; Member, Advisory Board of Dir. of Atlantic Nat'l Bank of FL.

John W. Snow, President and Chief Exec. Officer, Chessie System Railroads. D.o.b. Aug. 2, 1939. Educ.—Kenyon Coll., Univ. of Toledo B.A. 1962; Univ. of Virginia—Ph.D. 1965; George Wash. Univ., L.L.B. 1967. Employment before CSX—1965–67—Asst. Prof. of Eco.—Univ. of Maryland; 1967–72—Wheeler & Wheeler (Wash., D.C. Law Firm); 1972–73—Asst. General Counsel, US Dept. of Trans.; 1972–75—Adjunct Prof. of Law, George Wash. Univ. Law School; 1973–74—Deputy Asst. Sec't for Policy, Plans of Int'l Affairs; 1974–75—Asst. Secretary for Gov't Affairs, US Dept. of Trans.; 1975–76—The Deputy Under Sec't, US Dept. of Trans.; 1976–77—Administrator, The Nat'l Highway Traffic Safety Adm.; Spring 1977—Visiting Prof. of Econ.—Univ. of VA; Spring 1977—Visiting Fellow, American Enterprise Inst.; Date Employed by CSX (or predecessor) May 1, 1977. May 1977–80—VP—Gov't Affairs—Chessie Sys. Inc.; Nov. 1980–84—Senior VP Corp. Services—CSX; 1984–85—Exec. VP—CSX; 1985—Pres. and Chief Exec. Officer, Chessie System Railroads. *Business and Professional Affiliations*—American, Federal, District of Columbia and Virginia Bar Association.; Univ. of Maryland (School of Public Affairs), Board; Univ. of VA (Burkett Miller Center) Board; American Enterprise Inst. (Visiting Fellow); Yale Univ. School of Mgt. (Distinguished Fellow); Sovran Finan. Corp.—Board; W. VA Roundtable.

Richard D. Sanborn, President & CEO—Seaboard Syst. Railroad. D.o.b. June 3, 1936. Educ.—Pub. Schools, Sanbornville, NH; Grad. Magna Cum Laude, Univ. of New Hampshire, June 1957; grad. Harvard Law Sch., June 1960. Employment before CSX—G.E. Co. Date Employed by CSX (or predecessor)

Exhibit 10   Continued

Nov. 1, 1961. 1961–71—Atty., Asst. to Gen. Counsel; Asst. to VP—Law, SCL, Jacksonville, FL; Jan. 1972 to May 72—Special Asst. to Pres., SCL; 1972–73—Special Asst. to Pres., L&N, Louisville; 1973–78, VP Exec. Dept. SCLI, SCL, L&N, Jax; 1978–80—VP Exec. Dept. & Asst. to Chair., SCL; Aug. 1980–82—Senior VP Admin., Family Lines Rail Syst; May 1982 to Jan. 1983—Pres. & CEO, Family Lines Rail Syst.; 1983 to present—Pres. & CEO, Seaboard Syst. Railroad. *Business and Professional Affiliations*—Phi Beta Kappa; Mass. and FL Bar Assocs.; Amer. Bar Assoc. Dir. First Kentucky Nat'l Corp.; American Railroad Foundation.

R.L. Hintz, Executive VP, and President and CEO Texas Gas Resources.
D.o.b. May 25, 1930. Educ.—B.S.B.A. Magna Cum Laude Northwestern Univ.; M.B.A. N.W. Univ.; Employment before CSX—Allied Radio, Inc.; Allstate Ins. Date Employed by CSX (or predecessor) Nov. 15, 1963. 1978–80—Senior VP—Finance, Chessie System; 1980–84—Senior VP—Finance, CSX; 1984 to present—Exec. VP; 1985 Pres. and CEO, Texas Gas Resources Corp. *Business and Professional Affiliations*—A.M.A. Finance Council; FEI, Advisory Board; VCU School of Bus., Univ. of Richmond—E. Claiborne Robins School of Bus.—Exec. Advisory Council, VPI Advisory Council; Dir.—Robertshaw Controls; Third Nat'l Corp., St. Joseph's Villa; Nat'l Mine Service Co. and various internal boards of directors.

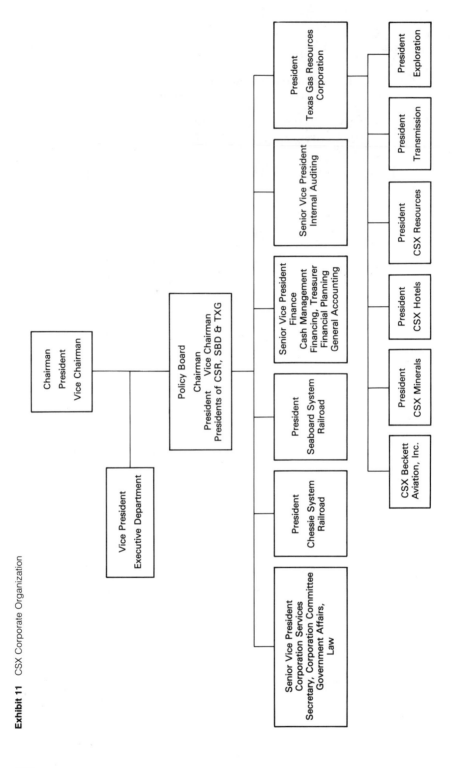

Exhibit 11 CSX Corporate Organization

Exhibit 12 Chessie System Railroads Organization June 1, 1984

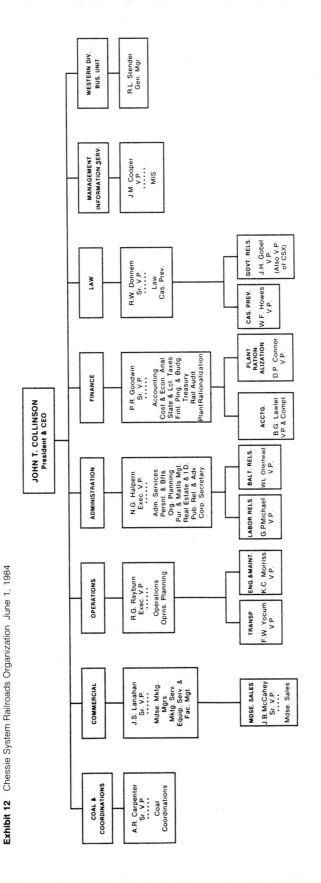

Exhibit 13 Seaboard System Railroad Organization

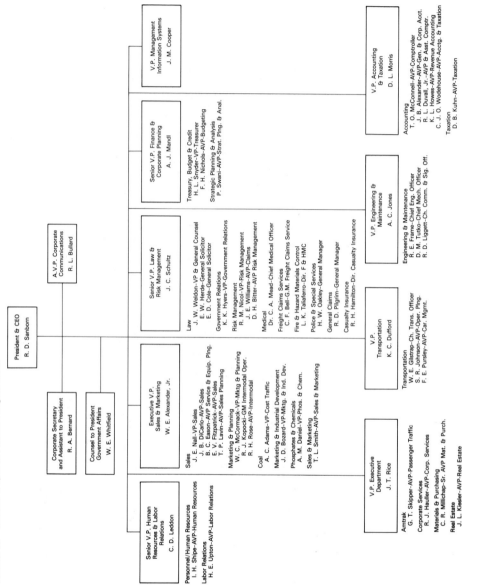

Exhibit 15 CSX Route Structure

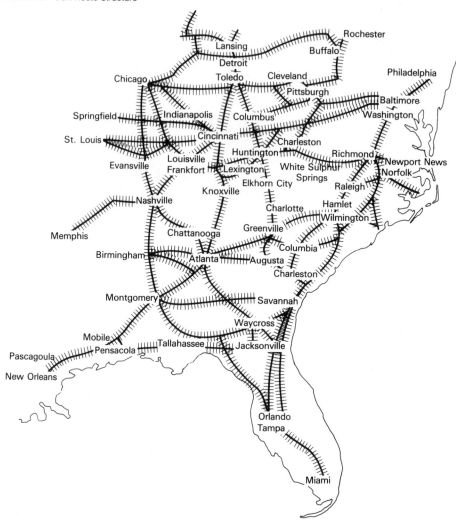

Chapter Five

Public Goods

Chapter Five takes the reader from a deregulated, substantially competitive environment to a mixed environment of regulation and competition. This is the most treacherous of regulated environments, as it simultaneously requires regulatory and competitive strategies that are fundamentally contradictory.

Telephony was originally regulated because it provided a public good of overriding importance—an integrated network for electronic voice communications among people. It also appeared to be a natural monopoly, at least in the local exchange, and probably the interexchange segment as well. But since the late 1960s, this high-tech, high-growth industry has experienced wracking regulatory changes in customer equipment, long-distance, enhanced information services, and in the local exchange. The Bell System, once the world's largest company, has been shattered in eight pieces, with the lines of competition drawn by a federal judge.

Yet despite the introduction of widespread competition in most of the market's segments, telecommunications in the United States, much less the rest of the world, is still far from deregulated. The first case study in this chapter traces the evolution of regulation and deregulation in telecommunications, from 1913 to 1984. Although it reinforces some of the concepts previously discussed, it focuses much more on the sources of regulatory change, and especially relationships between technology, industrial economics, and regulation.

The AT&T case study is probably the most complicated strategic situation in the entire text. The case requires a stakeholder analysis of the FCC's Access Charge Plan. This new system of pricing access to local telephone exchanges would replace cross-subsidies, based on historical cost allocations designed to facilitate universal service. Its development, concurrent with divestiture, precipitates a political controversy of major proportions.

For AT&T, this issue is vitally important. Its successful implementation will dramatically affect financial performance and the company's strategy for entering the Information Age. When the Access Plan suffers a major political setback, it raises the question of how AT&T might have managed the process more successfully. More importantly, the Plan's collapse early in 1984 forces AT&T to reassess its strategy in the market environment of equal-access competition, and in the Washington political arena. The formulation of this strategic plan requires the first full application of the framework.

The case on General Telephone of the Northwest is a companion to the AT&T case for strategy formulation in the mixed environment. This local-exchange company, far smaller than AT&T, is faced with the prospect of an eroding monopoly in its five-state service territory. Kent Foster, a young executive from the parent company, GTE, has recently taken over as CEO. He has had a year to assess the market, the political environment, and the company's human, organizational, and operational resources. He has an idea for a strategy, but needs to choose the appropriate policies to convert it into reality.

Telecommunications in Transition

On the first day of 1984, the Bell System was dissolved and the U.S. telecommunications industry began a new era. Extraordinary changes in technology, in public policy, and in the marketplace had eroded and finally nullified the dominance of the world's largest company.

Although the breakup was a visible event, the process of deregulation, begun in the 1970s, wrought equally important changes in the structure of the telecommunications industry. Telephone equipment was fully competitive, long distance carriers were beginning to compete, and local telephone companies were preparing for competitive entry.

The merging of computer and telecommunications technology, together with deregulation and divestiture, opened new opportunities for entrepreneurs willing to chance what was becoming a high-stakes, competitive free-for-all; the U.S. market for primary telecommunications services, already over $100 billion annually, would likely double in six years.[1]

For residential and business customers, these changes created unprecedented choice and confusion in the marketplace. With the transition from regulated monopoly towards unregulated competition, economics had begun to drive cost and pricing considerations toward a new philosophy that the "cost causer pays" for products and services consumed.[2]

This way of thinking challenged a fifty-year-old legacy of public policy. Never before had telephone rates been an issue. However, by 1984 telecommunications had become an object of intense political debate at both the state and national levels. Implicit in those debates were the future structure and quality of the nation's telecommunications industry.

THE PUBLIC POLICY LEGACY

Since the passage of the Communications Act of 1934, the Federal Communications Commission (FCC) had directed the telecommunications policy of the United States. The FCC's jurisdiction in interstate and international communications included telegraph, radio and television broadcasting, cable television,

Research Associate Dekkers L. Davidson prepared this note under the supervision of Professor Richard H. K. Vietor as the basis for class discussion, rather than to illustrate either the effective or ineffective handling of an administrative situation.

and satellites. In telephony, federal policy had served to integrate local exchange service and foster the development of a national, switched network.

According to its mandate, the FCC was "to make available, so far as possible, to all the people of the United States a rapid, efficient, nationwide, and worldwide wire and radio communications service with adequate facilities at reasonable charges."[3] Implicit in this charter was the idea that widespread (or *universal*) service was socially desirable, and that telecommunications systems were *natural monopolies*. Together, these ideas justified extensive involvement by government in telecommunications.

Universal service entailed three aspects of "the public interest":[4]

1. *Network considerations.* Each additional subscriber increased the value of the telephone system to other subscribers. A larger telephone network provided the opportunity for each subscriber to communicate with a larger number of other individuals.

2. *Contribution to society.* Proponents of universal service claimed that phone service was necessary to bind society together. They drew an analogy to the roadway network, contending that a network was essential whether or not all parts were self-sufficient.

3. *Essentiality to individuals.* Telephone service had sometimes been viewed as a necessity to individuals (rather than to society as a whole). It was argued that no citizen in a humane society should be deprived of the availability of telephone service.

Although the goal of universal service had become widely accepted, explicit reference to it did not appear in the language of the Communications Act of 1934, or in the language of FCC decision making before 1980.

Until recently, federal regulatory policies had ensured relatively stable markets for telecommunications, each based on a single supplier of equipment and service. These markets were viewed as natural monopolies, in which one firm could provide any level of service at lower average cost than two or more firms. Accordingly, they were regulated by rate-base, rate-of-return methods. The Common Carrier Bureau of the FCC did this for interstate telecommunications; within state boundaries, state public utility commissions (PUCs) had this authority.

REGULATORY TRANSITION AND MARKET DEFINITION

Service markets in the telecommunications industry have been segmented interactively by technology and regulation. Since the 1960s, federal and state regulatory authorities have struggled to respond to accelerating technological innovation. The result was a complex structure of fragmented service markets, each designed to achieve a different set of public interest goals. (This structure is depicted in Figure 1, pp. 284–285.)

Most service markets involved the same basic forms of communications service: voice, data, text, graphic, visual, and signal. *Voice* generally refers to vocal conversation between two or more people, or to message and sound broadcasting. *Data* refers to digital-coded communications between machines. *Text* is printed alpha-numeric material, such as telegrams or teletype. *Graphic* refers to pictorial information produced, for example, by a facsimile system. *Visual* refers to such diverse media as a personal visit, television, and video teleconferencing. Paging, alarms, and telemetry are examples of *signaling.*[5]

These forms, usually used in combinations, were readily substitutable for each other. For example, a personal communication could take the form of a visit (voice/visual), letter (text), telegram (text), greeting card (graphic), mailed tape recording (voice), telephone call (voice), and so forth. Consumer choice among these options depended on taste, price, and expected performance. Different forms, moreover, could also be complementary; a visit (voice/visual) might entail prior telegrams (text) and phone calls (voice).

Customers, however, made little distinction between service markets. Their demands in the marketplace tended to continuously break down the regulatory market segmentation, driving toward a single set of objectives for all service markets. It was becoming apparent that objectives mandated for single-supply service markets were gradually giving way to the objectives of competitive suppliers in an integrated market.

Most of these markets for communications services, besides being blurred from the consumer's perspective, required extensive use of the nationwide telecommunications network to be economically feasible. Accordingly, the FCC had ordered interconnection of facilities among firms serving the various markets. Few of the services were provided through entirely independent telecommunications networks, but rather, through interconnected facility combinations. And at the heart of this network was the Bell System.

BREAKUP OF THE BELL SYSTEM

The dissolution of the Bell System had profound implications for the telecommunications and computer industries. Although the antitrust settlement would serve the government's goal of fostering competition in telecommunications, it was still unclear how AT&T's divestiture of the Bell Operating Companies (BOCs) would serve other prevailing public policy goals, such as universal telephone service. There was no precedent for gauging the precise effect of breaking up the Bell System. The last time the government initiated such an action was with Standard Oil in 1911, at which time the oil industry was unregulated. But AT&T, with $150 billion in assets and nearly 100 years of experience in controlling the enormous telecommunications system, was regulated at the federal, state, and international levels.

Figure 1 Regulatory Defined Service Markets

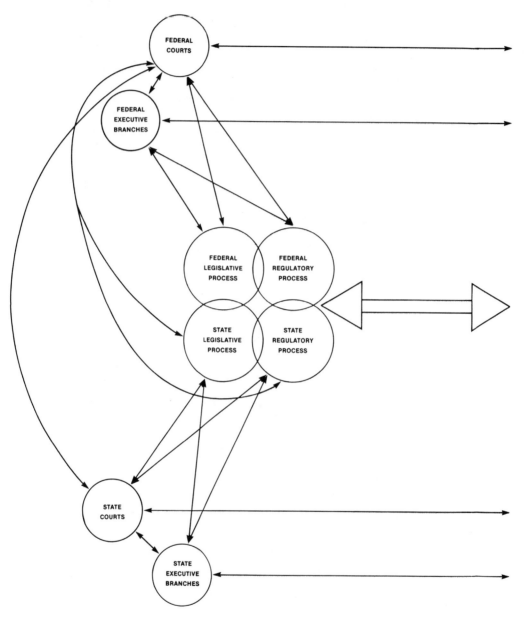

Source: AT&T Telecommunications Policy Task Force, *The Dilemma of Telecommunications Policy: An Inquiry into the State of Domestic Telecommunications by a Telecommunications Industry Task Force,* 1977. Reprinted with permission.

Figure 1 (continued)

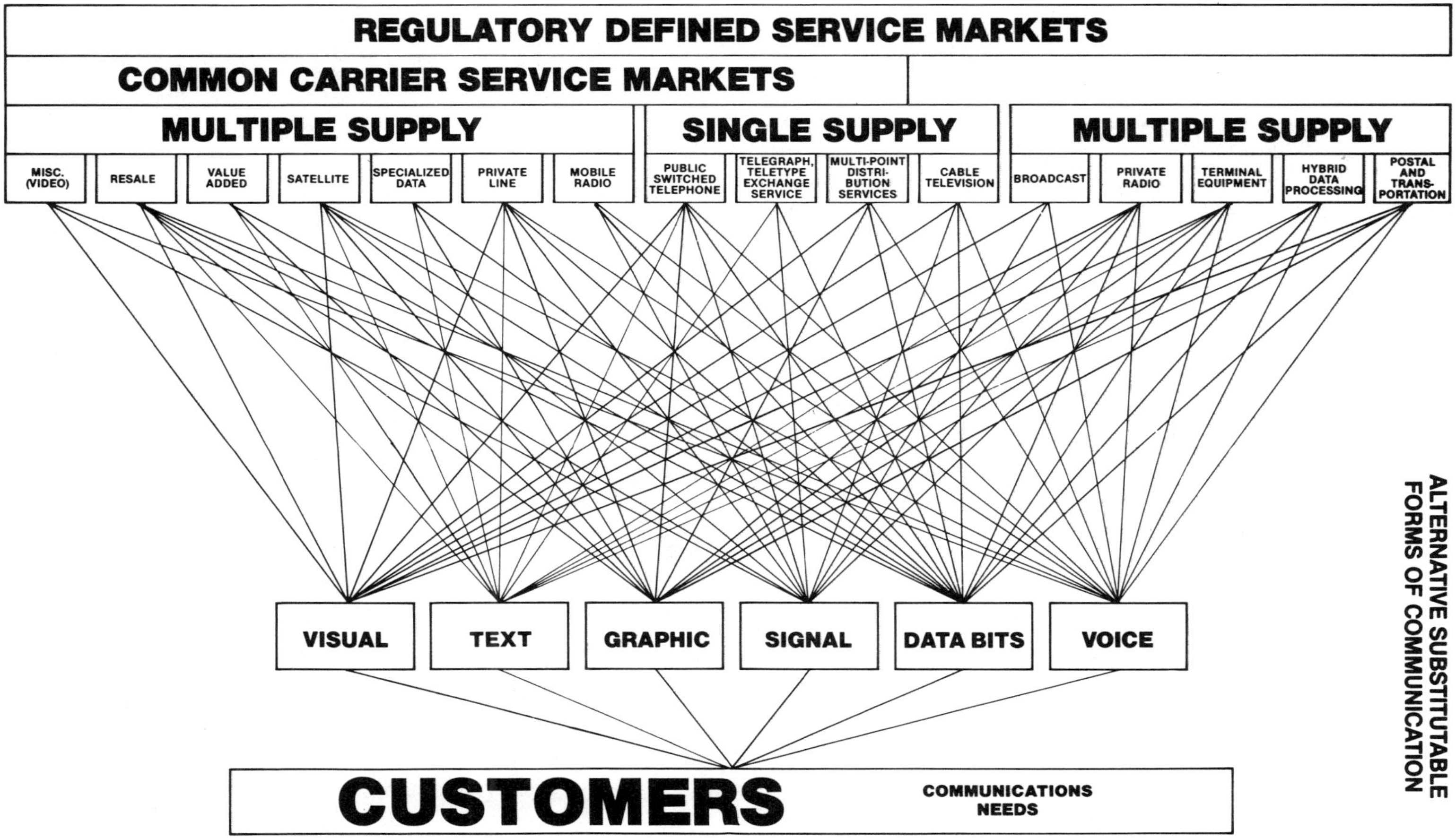

ALTERNATIVE SUBSTITUTABLE
FORMS OF COMMUNICATION

REGULATORY DEFINED SERVICE MARKETS

COMMON CARRIER SERVICE MARKETS

MULTIPLE SUPPLY

SINGLE SUPPLY

MULTIPLE SUPPLY

MISC. (VIDEO) | RESALE | VALUE ADDED | SATELLITE | SPECIALIZED DATA | PRIVATE LINE | MOBILE RADIO | PUBLIC SWITCHED TELEPHONE | TELEGRAPH, TELETYPE EXCHANGE SERVICE | MULTI-POINT DISTRIBUTION SERVICES | CABLE TELEVISION | BROADCAST | PRIVATE RADIO | TERMINAL EQUIPMENT | HYBRID DATA PROCESSING | POSTAL AND TRANSPORTATION

VISUAL | TEXT | GRAPHIC | SIGNAL | DATA BITS | VOICE

CUSTOMERS

COMMUNICATIONS NEEDS

The Government Initiates Action

The Department of Justice brought suit against the Bell System in 1974. In its legal challenge to Bell's monopoly, the government alleged that the company had illegally manipulated its dominant position in all three segments of the telecommunications market—customer premises equipment, local exchange services, and long distance services—in order to monopolize the entire industry. Eighty-two episodes of "monopolizing behavior" were alleged; over sixty of those claims were outstanding when the antitrust suit was finally settled. Most of the government's allegations centered on the markets for customer premises equipment and long distance services. (For its part, AT&T denied any improper behavior and pointed out that all its pricing practices had been closely regulated by the federal government since 1934.)

Anticompetitive behavior was alleged in AT&T's responses to the attachment of foreign (non-Bell) devices to the Bell switched network. When such devices were interconnected with the network, AT&T used the argument of "network harm" to require that customers obtain a shielding device before hooking up their own terminal equipment. Another allegation involved familial bias in procurement (a "buy Western Electric" edict) that prohibited competitors from selling to Bell Operating Companies. Coordinated timing of tariff changes and the introduction of new products and services were used, according to the government, to control migration in equipment use to AT&T's advantage. And finally, the suit charged illegal cross-subsidization between services, allowing AT&T to engage in predatory pricing of its equipment, thus driving out new entrants.

In the long distance arena, AT&T was charged with pricing its services *without regard to cost*, and although it was never shown that prices were below costs, the government contended this was a form of predatory pricing. In addition, AT&T was accused of using its local exchange operations to prevent long distance entrants from gaining a timely and quality network connection. The company had also allegedly used court and regulatory proceedings to delay or thwart attempted entry.

The government's suit came amid growing evidence that new competition from non-Bell companies was already providing wider choices in telecommunications products and services, often at lower prices than those charged by AT&T. The suit charged that this emerging competition, spurred partly by court orders and FCC decisions, had been unfairly restrained by AT&T's efforts to protect its monopoly position. The case against AT&T rested heavily on the premise that control of the telephone network should not be used to dominate the related field of communications equipment, and that control of local telephone networks should not be used as a basis for eliminating potential competition in long-haul transmission. Most observers acknowledged that the suit was not designed to attack local telephone service, a public utility function that nearly everyone regarded as a natural monopoly. And the government's suit did not ignore the fact that the history of the telephone industry was one of declining costs and increased efficiency. Instead, the Justice Department suggested that innovation in telecommunications would move forward at a faster pace in a competitive, rather than in a regulated, environment.

AT&T Fights Back

Throughout the remainder of the decade, AT&T, under the leadership of John DeButts, contested the antitrust suit along with a plethora of regulatory exceptions that were permitting selective entry into the telecommunications industry. Legislative initiatives to resolve some of the issues led by AT&T met with hardly any success. So, when Charles Brown was elevated to the top post at AT&T in 1979, public policy in telecommunications was still largely shaped by a law written nearly a half century earlier.

Agreement Is Reached

In January 1982 William F. Baxter, assistant attorney general, and Charles L. Brown, chairman of the American Telephone and Telegraph Company, settled the long-running government suit. The Baxter-Brown settlement was unique in antitrust history, since no previous consent decree had called for restructuring a major industry. In agreeing to end the antitrust case in an out-of-court settlement, AT&T admitted to no wrongdoing. The company needed to clear the air of uncertainty so it could begin to more fully compete in the telecommunications markets of the future. The changes called for by this agreement, as approved and modified by Federal District Court Judge Harold H. Greene, would radically alter pricing and service offerings in telecommunications, right down to local exchange telephone rates.

The final judgment divested AT&T of its local telephone operations. The former Bell Operating Companies were consolidated into seven regional holding companies, each with assets of $12–21 billion, but were prohibited from entering long distance markets. The new AT&T would provide long distance telephone services and would retain Western Electric, the dominant manufacturer of telephone equipment. It would also keep its international subsidiaries and Bell Laboratories, one of the preeminent research organizations in the world. And the modified judgment affirmed that AT&T could offer data transmission and processing services. The modified final judgment left the new AT&T with total assets of $40 billion, and with a much greater opportunity to participate in the expanding markets for advanced telecommunications services.

Although consumerists and potential competitors initially cheered news of the Bell System's breakup, skepticism was nonetheless widespread. According to two highly regarded economists, the antitrust objective of furthering competition could well serve to undermine some important and long-standing goals of regulation:

> The objectives of regulatory policy will not be furthered by the decree. Telephone rates will be deaveraged, unbundled, and, for local services, increased by as much as eighty percent. This should end the expansion of and reduce the quality of local service. Regulatory standards for common carriers will no longer prevail, as unregulated competition will drive resources away from universal low-cost bulk service for a small fraction of the business community.
>
> Who then stands to gain from the AT&T settlement? Clearly AT&T has won by losing, by having been left with the cream of its old services but with the restrictions on its ability to compete in those services removed. Bell has simultaneously freed itself from both the antitrust laws and regulatory control. As for the public, we seem to have lost by winning.[6]

THE MIXED REGULATORY ENVIRONMENT

The telecommunications system has three major components: customer premises equipment (CPE), local exchange companies (LEC), and interexchange carriers (IXC). These are shown in Figure 2.

Customer premises equipment (CPE) refers to the end points of a telecommunications network—the equipment installed and accessed exclusively in the customer's residence or place of business. The most common varieties of terminal equipment included ordinary telephone sets, key telephone sets (KTS), private branch exchanges (PBXs), and modems. A KTS provided only a few telephone lines, selected by the user by pushing the appropriate key. A PBX, used by larger businesses, was a switching center that connected each telephone on the customer's premise to an appropriate outside line. A modem (modulator-demodulator device) connected a telephone to a computer or computer terminal.

Figure 2 Basic Components of a Telephone System

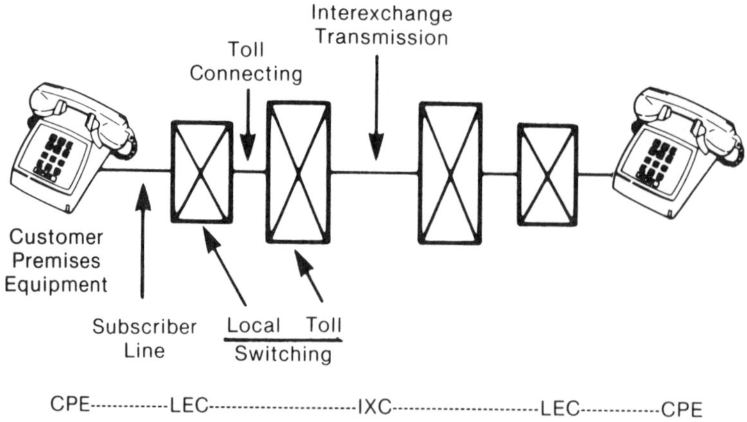

Source: American Telephone & Telegraph Company

Local exchange companies (LECs) transmit voice or data communications from one customer premise to another via a certain local route. The equipment and links at this point in a telecommunications system were generally hard-wired. Local exchange services were provided by the Bell Operating Companies and nearly 1,500 other independent phone companies. Under terms of the AT&T divestiture, LECs were permitted to provide service within 160 newly prescribed LATAs (local access and transport areas), which closely conformed to the U.S. Census Bureau's Standard Metropolitan Statistical Areas. As of 1984, these LATAs supplanted all existing telephone exchanges.

Interexchange carriers (IXCs) handle long distance transmission of voice and data communications over an interstate-inter-LATA network, interstate-intra-LATA network, and an intrastate-inter-LATA network. Only AT&T was subject to rate regulation by the FCC. For intrastate transmission, all common carriers were regulated by state PUCs.

Until the early 1970s, AT&T dominated all three system components. Western Electric produced most telephones and network switching equipment; the twenty-two Bell Operating Companies controlled 82% of the local exchange services; and the Long Lines Department had a virtual monopoly in the inter-exchange service market. But by 1984, after more than a decade of regulatory transition, all three of these telecommunications submarkets were extraordinarily dynamic and complicated.

Customer Premises Equipment (CPE)

Historically, interconnection to the public network of noncarrier-provided equipment had been restricted. Regulators generally accepted the notion that the carriers (local exchange companies) did not merely provide communications facilities, but rather offered "end-to-end" communications service. Carriers were held responsible for maintaining total communications capability, which required control over ownership of all facilities attached to the network. Service to the vast majority of subscribers who did not use a foreign attachment had to be protected; no unauthorized interconnection to the network was permitted.

Since access to the CPE market traditionally required a vendor to be a telephone company, Western Electric had developed a symbiotic relationship with the Bell Operating Companies. The Bell companies' practice of leasing, rather than selling, equipment had the effect of extending product life cycles until fully depreciated. With relatively long regulatory-approved depreciation schedules, it was rare for equipment to be retired prematurely in favor of newer, more modern equipment. This practice served both the Bell System and regulators quite well; with a fully extended product life cycle, CPE prices remained relatively stable.

The propriety of restrictions on foreign attachments was first addressed by the FCC in 1956 in the *Hush-A-Phone* case, involving a foreign attachment which was a rubber cup-like device and which provided more private conversation when attached to the microphone portion of a telephone handset. A U.S. Court of Appeals held that the FCC's restrictions on this device were unlawful interference with the telephone subscriber's right to privacy.

In a separate development in 1956 AT&T signed a consent decree, ending a government antitrust suit that sought the divestiture of Western Electric from the remainder of the Bell System. Under terms of this settlement, AT&T was permitted to retain Western Electric but was barred from retailing data processing products and services, even though many of the most noteworthy Bell Labs patents had spawned the computer age. AT&T, however, could use computer hardware and software for its internal needs, such as central office switching.

Competitive Entry   As customer demand for specialized terminal equipment developed (partly inspired by the computer revolution), there were plenty of suppliers to the telephone industry that were eager to enter the market. Terminal equipment was no longer of itself a natural monopoly. In 1968 the landmark decision (allowing interconnection of non-AT&T equipment to AT&T lines) was handed down in the *Carterfone* case. The legal issue was whether or not the telephone industry's tariffs were reasonably justified by the need to protect the technical integrity of the public switched network or other public interest considerations. The FCC found they were not, and ruled that the entire tariff provision restricting interconnection of equipment was unlawful. This decision was a turning point in public policy.

Henceforth, the telephone industry had to justify any restrictions on the attachment of customer-owned equipment to the network. A new principle was established, giving the customer a choice of equipment, subject only to those restrictions necessary to insure the technical integrity of the telephone system. This escalated the issue to a consideration of how the network's technical integrity could be protected in an environment of competition in the supply of most types of terminal equipment. Coupled with a growing need for more sophisticated electronic terminal equipment, this decision opened up a growing market for a variety of new manufacturers of key telephones and PBX systems.

Many entrants opted to sell to operating telephone companies—including Bell—while others chose to compete head-on by installing and servicing terminal equipment for business customers. The first group generally relied on the electromechanical technology then favored by Bell. The second group of "pure interconnects" was among the first to offer electronic PBX systems.

Competition did not initially make a dent in AT&T's revenues from terminal equipment. Competitors' revenues came mainly from expanding the market with new product features and price reductions. Bell's large share of the installed base gave it considerable leverage over a broad range of products. According to some competitor estimates, Bell had as much as 80% of the CPE business in the early 1970s. With such a large market share, it was alleged, Bell could engage in strategic pricing to fend off competitive threats. Many large customers favored Bell simply because of its long-standing reputation for quality.

Confidence in the Bell System's "end-to-end" responsibility, coupled with the high cost of switching, served to check the market positions of the entrants. Not until the end of the 1970s did equipment based on microprocessors open the door to real competition and renewed growth in PBX sales.

As a practical matter, the conditions necessary for sustained competition in the CPE market were not fully established until the FCC's registration program was put into place during 1977. Until then, AT&T had required the use of protective-connection attachments with any non-Bell equipment that was being interconnected to the network. With registration, most equipment satisfying minimal performance standards could be registered, and then directly connected. Since then, CPE sales have expanded rapidly.

Deregulation In its 1980 decision in *Computer Inquiry II*, the Federal Communications Commission decided to fully deregulate customer premises equipment. The arbitrary boundary between data processing and communications was finally dissolved. This decision reflected the fact that CPE could be freely separated from the underlying utility service to which it had been attached. This ruling also allowed AT&T to get directly involved in computer-related product and service offerings from which it had been barred since 1956. Because of their market position and power, however, both AT&T and GTE (General Telephone) were required to market unregulated customer premises equipment through a separate subsidiary. Such an organizational arrangement—with the subsidiary at arm's length from the parent—was believed necessary to avoid the possibility of unfair cross-subsidization between regulated and unregulated product and service offerings.

The merging of the computer and telecommunications industries was most apparent in the customer premises equipment market—and especially so with PBXs. A PBX provided businesses with local, intrapremise telephone service as well as a connection to the local exchange and interexchange companies. By providing on-site switching for intraoffice communications (thereby avoiding the local exchange companies for such calls), PBXs had proven to be economically sound from the customer's viewpoint. Furthermore, the PBX's multiplexing capability allowed savings from the shared use of trunk lines (those circuits connecting the PBX to the local exchange), since not every telephone within the private branch exchange needed to use a circuit simultaneously.

A PBX's telephonic functions (that is, switching, signaling, queueing, routing) could easily qualify it as a subset of the computer industry. In fact, for a long time these same functions had been performed with computer-driven central office switching equipment, and on a much larger scale by LECs and IXCs. For customers with sophisticated communications needs, the PBX had evolved into a minicomputer. In fact, Rolm (considered a pioneer in PBX manufacturing) first offered equipment that was based on a small Data General minicomputer, with special software for managing telephone switching operations. Telephone appliances incorporating a voice handset and a computer screen and keyboard were rapidly becoming available, creating new opportunities for computer terminal and telecommunications manufacturers to integrate and compete. The newest PBXs not only could handle the usual phone-call traffic but also could be used to tie together computers and word processors, leaving the PBX as the on-site communications hub.

In the minds of most industry observers, the ramifications of the AT&T divestiture went far beyond restructuring the telecommunications industry alone. In an interesting coincidence, the government announced it was dropping its long-standing antitrust suit against IBM (the computer colossus) on the very same day it settled the AT&T antitrust case. With more than 30 years of experience in computers, IBM stood ready to benefit if it could supply state-of-the-art, computer-driven telecommunications systems in the U.S. market. Since IBM already marketed PBXs in Europe and had installed private computer networks, few technical barriers existed that could impede its efforts. The computer company also held a one-third share in Satellite Business Systems (SBS) —a specialized common carrier—and a small interest in Rolm, a leading PBX manufacturer. Many predicted that AT&T and IBM would eventually square off against one another in the fast-growing market for "compunications"—the result of the confluence in computer and telecommunications technologies.

Regulatory decisions and technological developments in the CPE market served mainly to convince customers, both residential and business alike, that there were alternatives to the traditional supply of products and services in telecommunications. With the twin events of divestiture and deregulation, customer demand for new and better performance features was likely to significantly expand the market.

In 1984 the PBX market represented the most competitive part of the customer premises equipment business—a $3.1 billion market, growing at 20% per year. The market was roughly divided among the following major competitors:[7]

AT&T	29%
Rolm	15
Northern Telecom	14
Mitel	12
GTE	5
NEC	4
Others	21
	100%

Local Exchange Companies (LEC)

Over a hundred years ago, the telephone industry began, providing local service to residents. In 1877 the Bell Telephone Company was established and it flourished as a patent monopoly until the turn of the century. Faced with competition from other companies in the early twentieth century, AT&T (the parent of the Bell Operating Companies) grew through acquisition of unclaimed territory and the purchase of rival firms. AT&T faced its first antitrust suit in 1913. Accused of anticompetitive behavior under the Sherman Act, AT&T

promised to dispose of its stock in Western Union, to interconnect with independent local telephone companies, and to cease acquiring competing companies. The agreement, in the form of a letter from AT&T Vice President N. C. Kingsbury, has become known as "the Kingsbury commitment." Since the letter was sent prior to any formal legal proceedings, the settlement was not an actual consent decree. It did, however, endorse AT&T's long-distance monopoly and its dominance in the local-exchange segment of the telephone market.[8]

Under terms of the more recent antitrust settlement, the Bell Operating Companies were separated from AT&T and its long distance, manufacturing, and research departments. The BOCs were reorganized into seven regional holding companies, for financial and marketing reasons, although they continued to provide local exchange service under their older, more familiar names. The BOCs surrendered all imbedded (regulated) terminal equipment to AT&T under terms of the antitrust settlement. They were, however, allowed to retain their Centrex service offerings, which were often an effective substitute for PBX products. BOCs were permitted to reenter the CPE business following divestiture, providing they established a separate subsidiary. Under terms of the modified final judgment, the court transferred the lucrative Yellow Pages business from AT&T to the BOCs. (Figure 3 shows the BOCs' new geographical territories.)

The territory not originally owned or acquired by the Bell companies was generally outlying rural land that was sparsely populated. In time, some 1,500 independent non-Bell telephone companies (telcos) established service to these areas, using a variety of corporate organizations.[9] A few, like GTE, the

Figure 3   Bell Operating Companies' Geographical Territories

US WEST
Mountain Bell
Northwestern Bell
Pacific Northwestern Bell

Pacific Telesis
Nevada Bell
Pacific Telephone

Bell South
Southern Bell
South Central Bell

Southwestern Bell

NYNEX
New England Telephone
New York Telephone

Bell Atlantic
New Jersey Bell
Bell of Pennsylvania
Diamond State Telephone
Chesapeake & Potomac
    Telephone Companies (4)

Ameritech
Ohio Bell
Indiana Bell
Michigan Bell
Illinois Bell
Wisconsin Telephone

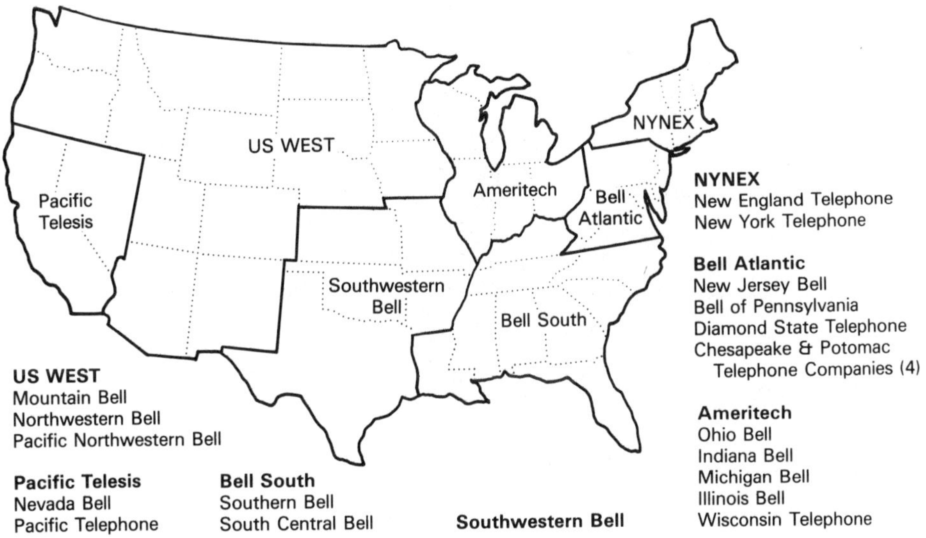

Source: Author's depiction of territories.

largest independent telco, set up multistate companies. Many independents, however, simply encompassed one or two community exchanges. Cooperatives, which were an attractive form of organization for farmers, could benefit from this assistance of the Rural Electrification Administration. (The shaded areas in Figure 4 show independents' geographical territories.)

Universal Service   Residential telephone service had made considerable progress since World War II. The number of households in America had doubled, and penetration of telephone service had increased from 62% to 95% since 1950.[10] Conversion to dial service was completed, direct distance dialing became widely available, and one-party service became the industry standard. More and more subscribers added extension telephones, and the proportion of subscribers with flat rate service increased. While the independent telephone companies tended to lag slightly behind the Bell System, they too had completed the transition to single-party dial service. Advent of universal service occurred during a period of rapidly rising income and of monthly service charges that were constant or falling in real terms (see Figure 5.)

By 1983 the average residential telephone bill for basic local exchange service was $11. The average household paid an additional $6 for telephone equipment, $18 for toll calls (state and interstate long distance), and $3 in taxes; the average total bill was $38. Demand for residential local exchange service was relatively price insensitive (elasticity = −.10); this implies that a 10% increase in price will reduce demand by 1%. Demand for residential long distance service was much more sensitive to price (elasticity = −1.31); this implies that a 10%

Figure 4   Geographical Territories of Independent Telephone Companies

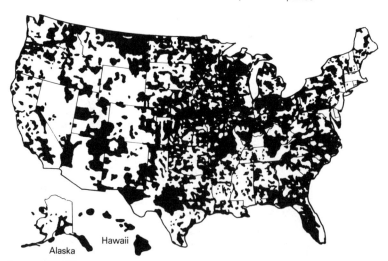

Source: AT&T Telecommunications Policy Task Force, *The Dilemma of Telecommunications Policy: An Inquiry into the State of Domestic Telecommunications by a Telecommunications Industry Task Force,* 1977. Reprinted with permission.

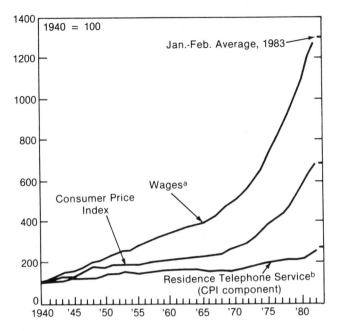

Figure 5 Relative Cost of Telephone Service
Source: Bureau of Labor Statistics.

ªAverage gross hourly earnings in manufacturing.

ᵇIncludes charges for local service (individual and party lines), toll, and excise tax.

decrease in price will increase demand by 13.1%. In general, business users were slightly less price sensitive in their patterns of demand for both local and long distance services.[11]

Rate Regulation   In an earlier era, when only local service was provided, each telephone company recovered its total costs from its own subscribers. State regulation established the obligations of these local exchange companies as public utilities. Since the value of telephone service was determined by the number of persons who could be accessed over the telephone network, statewide ratemaking encouraged the concept of "value of service" pricing. The exchanges served by a telephone company were grouped according to size, with rates set in proportion to the exchange size. The telephone company was allowed to set rates that generated sales equal to its revenue requirements (its total cost of providing service in the state); however, the rates charged in any particular exchange had no direct relationship to the costs of providing service in that exchange. Statewide ratemaking especially benefited rural areas, which were generally more costly to serve, per subscriber, than more densely populated urban areas.

In 1924 the Colorado Public Service Commission issued a landmark decision rejecting the argument of the City of Denver that its telephone rates should be based only on the costs of providing service in that city. The commission's argument was based on the societal value of service:

> The user of toll service is benefited by the establishment of a statewide telephone system, and the residents of Denver derive directly and indirectly sub-

stantial benefits from the operation of the telephone system throughout the state. It follows that the revenue from the telephone service rendered in Denver must be considered in the light of necessities of the system as a whole.[12]

On another dimension, "value of service" allowed charging the business customer more than the residential customer, on the grounds that service was more valuable to the business person. The business community even supported this concept, recognizing that wider telephone subscription would increase its access to customers. Thus, the pattern of telephone ratemaking, from its earliest stage, was based on the premise of making telephone service available to as large a proportion of the public as possible. Implementation of this public policy, through the widespread adoption of "value of service" pricing, was possible only because the telephone company was recognized as a monopoly.

Revenue Separation   With the interconnection of local networks and development of long distance services, it became necessary to share revenues from services that were provided by local and interexchange companies. The interconnection of systems regulated at the local and national levels required that the property, revenues, and expenses of each telephone company be sepaarated in order to determine the cost, and hence charges, for the services provided within each interstate and intrastate jurisdiction. The most difficult and controversial aspect of separations concerned the local exchange network, which was jointly used to provide both local exchange and toll services.

The greatest proportion of the costs of the local network was insensitive to use. These costs were fixed, in the sense that they did not vary with the amount of traffic carried or the number of calls made. Rather, they tended to vary with the number of subscribers served and the costs of connecting each subscriber to the system. They were referred to as *subscriber plant* or *nontraffic sensitive* (NTS) costs.

The nontraffic sensitive subscriber plant had three parts: a circuit (or local loop) to each subscriber, customer premises equipment, and inside wiring. The largest component was the local loop, which included the costs of providing and maintaining a conduit for transmitting messages between a customer's premises and the phone company's local office—usually a copper wire either carried on poles or in underground conduit. Thus, every dollar of the costs of providing these facilities that could be allocated to long distance service meant a dollar reduction in the revenue requirements that needed to be recovered through the rates for basic local exchange telephone service.

Two opposing cost recovery concepts lent controversy to the separations procedures applicable to the local exchange network. The one that prevailed until the 1930s held that all of the costs of providing the local exchange network should be recovered through rates charged for local exchange service. This approach reflected technological distinctions between local and toll service in the earlier days of telephony. Its proponents held that long distance rates should be based on the direct costs of those facilities used exclusively to provide long distance service, for example, toll switching centers and transmission facilities. The opposing view held that the costs of providing toll service included a portion of the costs of local facilities necessary to originate and terminate toll calls.

In 1931 the Supreme Court settled the issue in *Smith* v. *Illinois Bell*. In that case, the Court overturned early separations policy with this decision:

> While the difficulty in making an exact apportionment of the property is apparent and extreme nicety is not required, only reasonable measures being essential, it is quite another matter to ignore altogether the actual uses to which the property is put. It is obvious that, unless an apportionment is made, the intrastate service to which the exchange property is allocated will bear an undue burden. . . .[13]

Since 1943 the telephone industry had developed a system of "separations and settlements" to deal with the problem of assigning costs and allocating revenues. The first part of the process, called "jurisdictional separations," is shown in Figure 6. Each local operating company separated its costs into two categories: interstate and intrastate. Costs identified as interstate were recovered through tariffs filed with the FCC. Costs identified as being intrastate were recovered through a combination of intrastate toll rates and charges for local service approved by state public utility commissions. The local telephone company collected both interstate and intrastate charges from its customers on a monthly basis.

Revenues from interstate toll service were deposited in a nationwide pool, from which AT&T settled with each independent company. Each telephone company withdrew from this pool an amount equal to the costs it allocated to the provision of interstate service, including a return on investment. Internally, the Bell System used a similar settlement process, known as the "Division of Revenue" process. The allocation of costs was based on a measure of relative usage, that is, the portion of time that facilities were in use. Since about 3% of

Figure 6 Separations

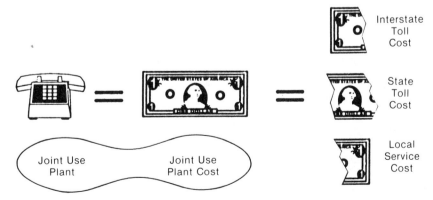

Source: American Telephone & Telegraph Company.

total telephone usage was interstate in 1943, about 3% of subscriber plant costs was allocated to interstate service.

In 1952 the method of apportioning costs between interstate and intrastate services was significantly altered. Measures of relative usage were weighted in order to assign an increased share of costs to the interstate jurisdiction. Subsequently, the method of apportioning costs was changed several times; in each case, a larger share was assigned to interstate service (see Figure 7). By the early 1980s, 7.9% of the total time that subscriber plant was used was devoted to interstate calls. But because this measure of relative use had been weighted, 26% of subscriber plant costs were actually assigned to interstate service and recovered through interstate toll revenues.

Decisions to assign a disproportionate burden of costs to interstate service occurred in a time of declining long distance costs (reflecting the conversion to direct dialing and rapid technological advances) and rising local service costs (reflecting rising input prices and the absence of similar technological advances). State regulatory officials were anxious to maintain low local rates and were hesitant to grant requests for rate increases, in view of the political risks involved. In many states, ratepayers voted for their public utility commissioners. The FCC's Joint Board of federal/state regulators, recognizing that local rate increases did not serve the goal of universal service, agreed to use excess revenues from toll service to support below-cost local rates.

The issue of subscriber plant costs was not a small one. More than half the telephone industry's costs were incurred by local telephone companies for the linkage between each subscriber and the local telephone office, and from there access to the entire telephone network.[14] By the early 1980s the industry-wide revenue requirement necessary to recover total subscriber plant costs was $39 billion, while total industry revenues (local, intrastate, and interstate toll)

Figure 7   History of Nontraffic Sensitive Exchange Plant Allocated to Interstate

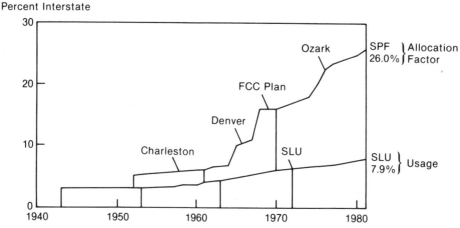

Source: American Telephone & Telegraph Company.

were $80 billion.[15] The large size of subscriber plant costs as a proportion of total costs meant that decisions about how local-loop costs were recovered would have a substantial impact on the industry's future structure. (Figure 8 reflects the relative investment in telephone plant and equipment.)

Rapid progress in computer technologies made possible more efficient electronic telephone switching systems for toll and local switches, as well as for customer switchboards (that is, PBXs). Even more impressive economies were delivered by newer transmission technologies (microwave, satellites, fiber optics), mostly for long distance services, although these facilities were beginning to be installed by local exchange companies as well. The local loop, which was still mostly old-technology copper wire, had undergone relatively few technological enhancements. Multiplexing, which allowed multiple uses of the local loop, had been the most dramatic improvement to date (Figure 9 depicts the relative economies offered by newer technological developments.)

There was a general belief inside the industry that the local loop bottle-neck would be solved in the near future as the conventional telephone industry sought to provide new enhanced services to its subscribers. However, until technological developments comparable to those in switching and transmission occurred on the local loop, the costs of providing local access and distribution would continue to represent an ever-increasing proportion of the total costs of providing telephone service.

By 1984 outright deregulation of the CPE business and the entry of competing interexchange (long-distance) carriers meant that local exchange companies were the only component of the telecommunications system that remained *fully regulated*. Nevertheless, the LECs faced some serious competitive challenges,

Figure 8   Telephone Network Investment by Independent and Bell Companies

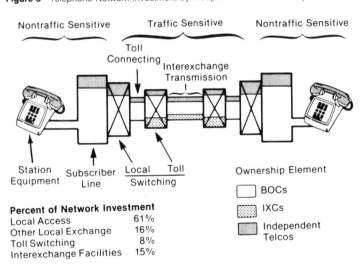

Percent of Network Investment

Local Access	61%
Other Local Exchange	16%
Toll Switching	8%
Interexchange Facilities	15%

Source: Author's estimates.

Note: Size of symbols reflects relative investment, 1980 levels.

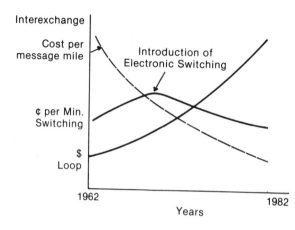

Figure 9 Changing Cost Characteristics
Source: Bell Laboratories. Reprinted with permission.

despite oft-repeated pledges of support from policymakers who upheld their monopoly status.

Eroding Monopoly Traditional practices of averaging phone rates state-wide (the "value of service" concept) were certain to be challenged by some important business customers. In the past, telcos were able to subsidize more costly service in rural areas by averaging it with rates in densely populated cities, where the cost of providing the service was considerably less. If that were to continue, many businesses would begin to bypass the local telephone company and its higher rates. In many telco territories, a few customers—usually large businesses—accounted for a large portion of revenues and earnings.

With sophisticated communications technologies widely available in the marketplace, the threat to bypass the conventional telephone network loomed quite large. In fact, many large users and some small users acting in concert with one another had already erected their own private microwave and satellite systems to bypass the local loop. Bypassing allowed for a number of possibilities: development of an inhouse local network at reduced cost, direct interconnection to a long distance network, thereby avoiding some of the diseconomies of the local telco, and total bypass of both local and long distance networks (end-to-end path). Bypass was usually undertaken to reduce costs, although in some cases it was done to meet highly specialized communications needs that could not be delivered by the conventional system. (See Figure 10.)

Most LECs, in their drive to align prices with costs, were expected to begin pushing usage-sensitive (measured) pricing schemes for local services, much as had been the billing practice for toll calls. Since 88% of residential users were now accustomed to flat (unmeasured) pricing for local calls, such a change would be dramatic and was likely to raise political protests in many state jurisdictions.[16] Moreover, the impact that new rate schemes would have on the long-standing goal of universal telephone service was uncertain. But, if regulators did not allow the new phone companies a reasonable return on investment, some telcos might have to curtail service to unprofitable areas. Cost-based pricing was

Figure 10 Bypass: Some Alternatives to the Conventional Telephone System.

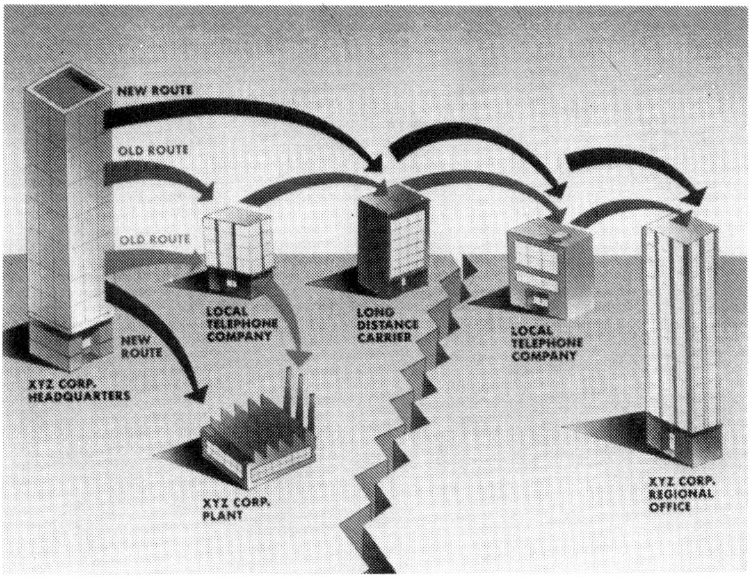

Source: *Fortune*, April 16, 1984. Illustration by Terry Allen. Reprinted with permission.

also essential if telcos were going to profit from the new applications that were being used via their networks. Without measured service, a computer user could tie up a phone for hours, paying no more than a customer making a three-minute call. The telcos' managers' new hard-nosed attitude towards regulators stemmed mostly from their new focus on profitability—a direct impact of divestiture.

One high-growth market which phone companies hoped to capture was the transmission of computer data. Nationally, about 60% of the network was controlled by computer-controlled, electronic switches.[17] A far smaller portion of local equipment could handle the on-off digital pulses used by computers. Before these digital messages could be transmitted through the rest of the network, they would have to be converted to audio tones; this added to the cost of carrying the data. In the past, many telcos had first upgraded their technology at the oldest locations; marketing considerations would probably dictate technology choice in the future. Earlier failure to upgrade network capability had given rise to a host of private local area networks (LANs), whereby a specialized carrier would build a digital termination service employing a variety of electronic switching components and high-speed, high-quality transmission systems (such as fiber optics) to meet selected business customer needs. For residential phone users, CATV operators were beginning to provide an alternative technology to the copper wire, thereby promising some economical opportunities for bypass in the future.

Decisions to apply limited financial resources for upgrading the local network would also affect entry choices by long distance common carriers. Under terms of the divestiture, interexchange carriers such as AT&T Communications, MCI, and GTE Sprint could enter local markets (intra-LATA) with permission from state PUCs. If allowed to file state tariffs, the ability of these carriers to selectively offer advanced local services was certain to have a "cream-skimming" effect on market choice. For their part, the BOCs were enjoined from transmitting services beyond their LATAs, although this legal restraint was likely to be challenged in due course.

Cellular radio, which would bypass much of the local exchange, offered telcos a chance at a huge new market. According to some estimates, cellular radio could make mobile telephone services an annual $2.5 billion business by 1990.[18] In a cellular mobile system, an area was divided into a honeycomb of cells, each having its own transmitter. These low-powered radios were linked by a computer system and, as a caller moved from cell to cell within an area, the computer automatically switched the conversation from one frequency to another. Subscribers to such a system could also transmit and receive data at high speeds over a fixed-station cellular radio.

Perhaps the most challenging new business that telcos would encounter was the PBX market. Consumer telephones were considered by most experts to be low-margin products that were no longer associated primarily with the local phone company. The PBX business, however, was viewed as the door to the office of the future, and all the telcos had a distribution channel with customers already in place. The Bell breakup promised to give new and existing manufacturers a strong chance to link up with BOCs that were no longer tied to AT&T's Western Electric.

In 1984 the top ten telephone companies dominated the local exchange market, as the estimates for that year show:[19]

	REVENUES ($ BILLIONS)
1. NYNEX (BOC)	$10.707
2. Bell South (BOC)	10.513
3. Ameritech (BOC)	8.901
4. Bell Atlantic (BOC)	8.732
5. GTE	8.400
6. Pacific Telesis (BOC)	7.896
7. Southwestern Bell (BOC)	7.880
8. U S WEST (BOC)	7.596
9. United Telecommunications	1.910
10. Continental Telcom	1.905

Interexchange Carriers (IXC)

The achievement of a truly nationwide telecommunications network took decades of regulatory and technological integration. Prior to World War II the industry was still highly fragmented, with some 53,000 telephone systems and lines in the United States.[20] The reluctance of most established telcos to serve high-cost rural areas (while capital was needed to add customers in existing exchanges) was a principal reason for the existence of such a large number of disparate networks.

Long-distance transmission, on the other hand, required that high engineering standards be adopted throughout the nationwide network, including the local exchange facilities which originated and terminated toll calls. By the 1980s, the need was obvious for common technical standards, for extensive coordination and planning among telephone companies, and for a method of systematically incorporating new technologies into the network. Higher-quality long distance (toll) facilities would have been useless without improvements in the quality of local exchange facilities.

Indeed, commitment to the concept of end-to-end service reflected not only the common carrier's responsibility to provide adequate and reliable service, but also the need to integrate new technology into the network in a manner that both improved the overall capability of that network and preserved the ability of every subscriber to communicate with every other subscriber. The planning and coordination of the nationwide network was undertaken largely by the Bell System.

The advent of strong federal regulation coincided with the increasing nationwide scope of the telephone network. State regulators were among the most active proponents of the Communications Act of 1934, reflecting their appreciation of the economic and technological trends in the industry. Only federal regulation could provide the institutional framework and requisite legal authority for the implementation of a national communications policy. Although the FCC's jurisdiction was limited to interstate communications, the manner in which it responded to developments in this segment of the network was of decisive importance for the development of the industry as a whole.

In 1941 the FCC issued a decision requiring a uniform interstate toll rate. In reaching that decision, the FCC carefully differentiated the telephone industry from other common carrier industries (such as railroads) where rate uniformity was not required. The telephone industry, declared the commission, was a monopoly of great and social economic importance; differences in rates for the same service, whatever the reason, was undesirable.

Nationwide geographic averaging of the high-cost areas with the low-cost areas was justified, since it assured availability of the same service to many customers. This allegedly benefited all subscribers, because the value of telephone service in the network was proportionate to the number of other parties with whom contact could be made. It also simplified the calculation of charges, since a uniform mileage rate for interstate toll messages and for private line services applied everywhere.

Another form of rate averaging was technological. Within a given segment or area of communications network, the equipment in use for the same service was typically of varying ages, degrees of technological advancement, and operating costs. Moreover, the technology was changing continually. The primary criterion of technological integration was that different generations of technology had to work together in such a way that a technological breakthrough in one area did not harm service in any other area, but could still be put in use to enhance productivity and service. Thus, uniform rates charged to the user reflected this cost-averaging concept. Under this system, the national telecommunications network developed and flourished, absorbing the latest technological advances. (See Figure 11.)

AT&T was also responsible for network management (facilities planning and call routing), and was obligated to provide standby facilities for use in the event of a national disaster. Through its interconnection to its BOCs and all independent telcos, AT&T's Long Lines Department (later renamed AT&T Communications) virtually controlled the entire market for interexchange long distance communication. Although the use of new technologies (such as microwave, satellite, and fiber optic transmission) drove down the costs of long distance service, all the savings didn't accrue to toll callers, but were used to stabilize local telephone rates. By 1970 the capacity of those long distance economies to lend an ever-increasing subsidy to the local companies had been largely exhausted. Since that time, long distance rates have risen because of increases in NTS subsidy costs. The changes shown in Table 1 reflect the increased interstate revenue requirements with corresponding decreases in intrastate revenue requirements.

Figure 11 National Telecommunications Network

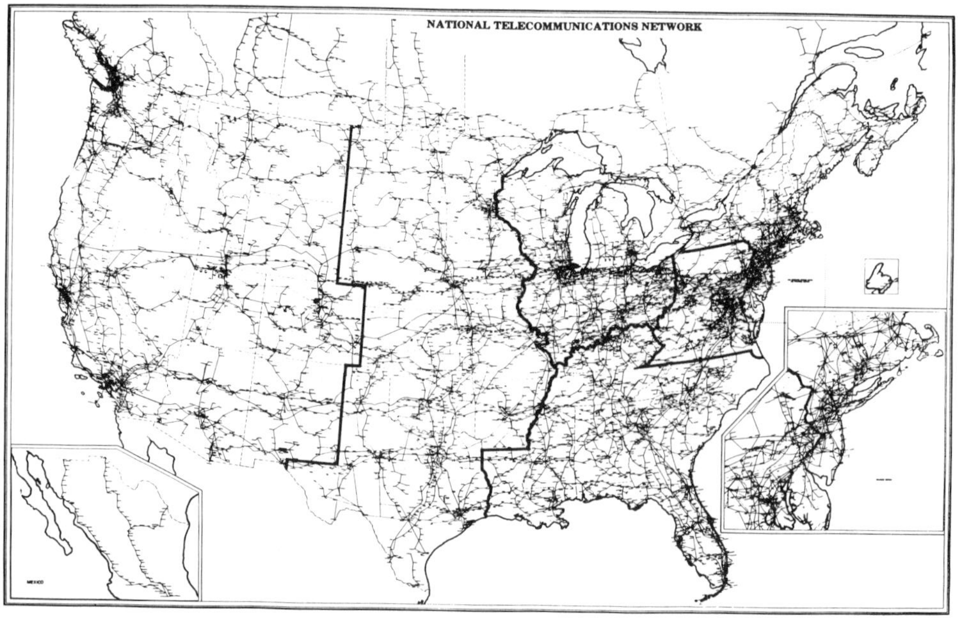

Source: AT&T Telecommunications Policy Task Force, *The Dilemma of Telecommunications Policy: An Inquiry into the State of Domestic Telecommunications by a Telecommunications Industry Task Force*, 1977. Reprinted with permission.

Table 1   Increases in Interstate Support of Local Rates ($ millions)

YEAR	INTERSTATE RATE CHANGES	CHANGES IN NTS COST ALLOCATION TO INTERSTATE	YEAR	INTERSTATE RATE CHANGES	CHANGES IN NTS COST ALLOCATION TO INTERSTATE
1956		40	1969		108
1957			1970	−237	
1958			1971	+175	+131
1959	−47		1972		+270
1960	−3		1973	+135	+320
1961			1974		+360
1962		+465	1975	+328	+460
1963	−30		1976	+209	+620
1964			1977	+73	+670
1965	−98	+134	1978		+840
1966			1979	+499	+1170
1967	−104		1980		+1066
1968	−20				

Source: American Telephone & Telegraph Company.

Despite price increases during the 1970s, the historic economies in long distance remained impressive when viewed over a longer period. (See Table 2.)

Competitive Entry   It was the development of microwave facilities that first began to create openings in AT&T's long distance monopoly. Microwave transmission technology, which was developed for defense purposes during World War II, involved the use of super-high-frequency radio waves. It offered advantages over wire and cable transmission in that it incorporated greater capacity with lower cost over existing land equipment, and it provided good transmission quality and reliability. Microwave transmission required relay towers only every twenty to thirty miles, with a minimum of maintenance. The transmission route could be erected quickly and, since cable and wire were not required all along the route, expensive land and surface rights-of-way for telephone poles and wires were no longer necessary.

In a narrowly defined 1959 ruling, called *Above 890*, the FCC first allowed use of private microwave transmission above 890 megahertz. This ruling paved the way for specialized common carriers (SCCs) to eventually operate outside the national telecommunications network. After ten years of legal wrangling, the FCC approved the first SCC license application, and a small company named Microwave Communications, Inc. (MCI) was allowed to offer intercity trunk circuits for business users on the busy Chicago-St. Louis route.

Similar applications to provide specialized communications services soon arrived at the FCC and forced a rethinking of the concept of monopoly-interexchange service. The FCC's 1971 *Specialized Common Carrier* decision established the feasibility of competitive entry in certain specialized communications mar-

Table 2 Rates for Interstate Message Telephone Service (constant 1984 dollars)

(3-MINUTE CALL)	1934	1984
New York City—Los Angeles	$58.96	$1.61
Boston—Chicago	21.19	1.42
Washington, D.C.—Baltimore	2.05	.97

Source: American Telephone & Telegraph Company.

kets. The FCC presumed that such competition would be limited to the private line service, that it would lead to the development of new and innovative services separate from existng services provided by the telephone industry, and that it would expand the total communications market rather than cut into established markets such as Message Telecommunications Service (MTS).

This decision affected three categories of domestic communications carriers: domestic satellite carriers, value-added carriers, and specialized common carriers.

Domestic Satellite Carriers Domestic satellite carriers (domsats) included American Satellite (Continental and Fairchild Industries), GTE, Hughes Communications, Satellite Business Systems (Aetna, IBM, and Comsat), RCA Communications, and Western Union. These carriers transmitted via satellite, and their major business was television broadcasting (because satellites could efficiently broadcast one signal simultaneously to hundreds of receiving earth stations). A number of domsats, however, had the capability to provide two-way network arrangements, which would appeal to large users of telecommunications systems. Satellite Business Systems (SBS) was the most prominent of the group and could handle the flow of intracompany communications transmitted via satellite to and from stations located near customer premises.

Value-Added Carriers Value-added or resale carriers owned and operated equipment that provided switched-data and recordkeeping services. Value-added carriers included GTE Telenet, Tymnet, and Graphnet. AT&T Information Systems was also expected to offer an enhanced network service in the future. These carriers transmitted data, but did not generally build their own communications systems. They leased circuits from other carriers, added features such as data transmission switches, and then resold the circuits in packages. The major suppliers of the circuits were the telephone companies.

Specialized Common Carriers Specialized common carriers (SCCs) were companies that built and operated their own intercity, microwave transmission facilities, or that leased circuits from other carriers on certain routes. SCCs, later known as other common carriers (OCCs), included MCI Communications, GTE

Sprint, and U.S. Transmission Systems, a subsidiary of ITT. A host of smaller OCCs operated regionally.

Subsequent proceedings identified several services that would be open to competition. Among these were such private line services as CCSA and FX. CCSA (Common Control Switching Arrangement) service was a switched private line service that allowed several locations of a customer to share a private line circuit. FX (Foreign Exchange) was a service whereby a subscriber could lease a private line to a distant exchange office and then directly switch, thus appearing to be a local subscriber line. In effect, FX allowed a customer to subscribe to local exchange telephone service (without incurring a toll charge) in exchange areas other than the one in which the customer was physically located.

Despite the fact that private line service represented a relatively small portion (roughly 10%) of total interstate revenues, the nature of private line (selected point-to-point) service made it ideal for the application of microwave and satellite transmission.[21] Since most private line customers were businesses which had purchased this service to gain an economical bulk rate, it was likely that further cost reductions incumbent in new technologies would draw interest. Even though the FCC prohibited the formation of such networks for general use, the specialized common carriers were able to use the definition of *private line service* to provide services that the telephone companies felt duplicated Message Telecommunications Service (MTS). Although the FCC attempted to more sharply define the services open to competition, it became apparent that no clear distinction could be drawn between the markets for competitive private line service and what was monopoly Message Telecommunications Service (MTS). In economic terms, the two types of services were substitutes for one another, especially for large-volume business users who constituted a significant portion of the MTS market. In technological terms too, the distinction between private line service and message telephone service was rapidly dissipating.

When MCI first tried in 1975 to enter the long-distance MTS market in direct competition with AT&T Long Lines, the FCC refused approval. In its *Execunet I* decision, the FCC reiterated that it had allowed only for "specialized carriers" to compete in private line service offerings. On a plea from MCI, the FCC was overruled by a court of appeals, and the company was allowed to offer MTS-like services. Next, in 1978, AT&T argued that it was not required to interconnect with MCI. Once again, the FCC upheld the status quo in *Execunet II*, only to be overruled by a federal court. In requiring interconnection, the judge cited the lack of clarity in the earlier FCC decisions regarding specialized common carriers.

In 1978 MCI was paying local-business-line rates for the connection between its switches and the offices of the local phone companies. The Bell System companies then filed a new tariff featuring much higher rates for the services used by competitors in originating and terminating long distance messages. MCI protested that the new tariff was unlawful, anticompetitive, and insufficiently supported. Given the FCC's previous inability to determine the lawfulness of tariffs, it was not clear how this matter would be resolved. At the

suggestion of the assistant secretary of commerce, the FCC encouraged negotiations in an attempt to produce an interim method of compensation to be paid
by OCCs to local phone companies. In the meantime, the FCC was to mount a
full inquiry into the matter of competition in the MTS-WATS (Wide Area Telecommunications Service) market and would determine a more permanent arrangement for how the other common carriers would pay for access to the local
exchange. After *Execunet*, the FCC attempted to adapt to the new judicially
imposed reality by further lowering entry barriers. The FCC required AT&T
to permit the resale and sharing of heavy-use, bulk-rate circuits by its competitors,
which allowed a relatively new enterprise—that of the long distance reseller—
to flourish.

Accommodating Competition During the several months of negotiations
in 1978, local companies generally took the position that, if they had to interconnect with other long-distance carriers, they should receive the same contribution towards supporting the local loop that was received from conventional
long-distance traffic. But the OCCs argued that (1) the quality of service they
received was less than equal (OCC circuits were patched through a central office
and transmission quality was not considered to be of the same level as AT&T's;
also, OCCs' customers had to use a pulse-signaling telephone and were required
to dial 22 or 23 digits to gain access to the long distance carrier), (2) they had
never agreed to provide contributions to support the local loop, and (3) they
should pay only the local business rate.

Under private line rates, customers paid 100% of their share of local
loop usage while MTS-WATS rates required a 330% allocation—hence the long
distance subsidy of local rates. Ultimately, AT&T and the OCCs reached an
agreement, known as ENFIA (Exchange Network for Interstate Access) under
which the OCCs would make some contribution to the local loop but would pay
lower rates than AT&T would. The OCCs paid telcos about 5 cents per minute
of local access; AT&T paid 15 cents. Since AT&T's average toll call generated
approximately 30 cents per minute in revenue, the local access charge was obviously a significant portion of cost.

Fostering competition in the long-distance market was further complicated because AT&T, with 90% of the market, also provided local service for
82% of the nation's customers.[22] Hence, before the antitrust settlement both the
FCC and competitors worried that Bell Operating Companies might favor AT&T's
Long Lines Department. For a competitive long-distance market to be workable,
other long-distance carriers had to obtain access to the customers served by the
local telephone companies. Accordingly, the FCC announced that it would develop a system of access charges to compensate local telephone companies for
the use of their facilities to complete long-distance calls.

Regulatory Transition After extensive proceedings, the FCC issued its
initial *Access Charge* decision in December 1982. The traditional system of pooling
and sharing interstate toll revenues was to be replaced with a new system in

which each local telephone company recovered its own costs through a series of access charges. Subscribers would pay access charges, in the form of a *fixed* monthly fee, which would compensate the local phone company for a part of the subscriber plant costs allocated to interstate service. Long-distance carriers would pay *variable* access charges based on the volume of interstate traffic that the local company originated or terminated for the long-distance carrier. The access charges paid by long-distance carriers would compensate the local company both for traffic sensitive costs, such as switching, and for subscriber plant costs not recovered directly from subscribers. Over time, the proportion of fixed costs paid by subscribers would *increase* and the proportion paid by long-distance carriers was to *decrease*. By 1990 local companies would recover most of the fixed costs that were being allocated to interstate service through the use of subscriber access charges.

Under the FCC's access charge rules, charges imposed on long distance carriers would pay for traffic sensitive costs and also generate revenues to finance a "Universal Service Fund," designed to assist local phone companies with un-usually high fixed costs. Thus, over a period of time, the current practice of recovering fixed costs through interstate toll revenues would be largely elimi-nated.

Under the terms of the antitrust settlement, each Bell Operating Com-pany was required to provide equal access to all long-distance carriers. When equal access was finally provided (in most cases by 1986), all long-distance carriers would pay equal rates for using the subscriber loops provided by local telephone companies. Until equal access was provided, the FCC would have to determine the differential between the rates paid by AT&T and those paid by competing carriers who did not receive interconnection of equal quality. In its access charge decision, the FCC ruled that the current differential (known as the ENFIA discount) should be substantially reduced. Competing carriers claimed this re-duction was unwarranted and would be detrimental to them. Yet without a reduction, competitors could continue to undercut AT&T's prices on high-vol-ume, long-distance services. OCCs were currently able to charge 30% to 50% less than AT&T on popular long distance routes. AT&T claimed this was "cream skimming."[23]

By 1984 it was quite clear that new ways of communicating were changing the patterns of competition. For common carriers, the need to shift to cost-based pricing was of paramount importance. For AT&T, saddled with a premium local access charge, the problem was acute. Its elaborate rate structure, replete with geographical and technological averaging, was being fractured by selective com-petitive entry. The OCCs, still benefiting from the ENFIA discount, knew that once equal access was provided, their primary cost advantage would be gone forever. And above all loomed the prospect of bypass.

Bypass represented both an opportunity (if it was economic) and a threat (if its circumvention was attractive to customers, even though uneconomic). All common carriers were equipped with sophisticated technologies which would then offer large customers low-cost bypass systems. Such private networks would allow customers to escape the intrastate subsidy (urban to rural) burdens and work around local bottleneck, low-grade switching devices. In one of the ironies of the Bell breakup, AT&T was seen as a likely bypass of the local networks that were then being managed by AT&T's offspring—the seven regional telephone companies.

Uneconomic bypass presented the greatest threat to common carriers. New technologies and regulations made it difficult to distinguish between communications vendors and their customers. A number of large companies and institutions with national and international network needs were contemplating the possibility of erecting their own private systems, utilizing fiber optics, microwave, and satellite transmission. This would allow them to avoid paying subsidies of statewide rate averaging and the subsidies implicit in the higher toll rates. This would be uneconomic bypass from a societal viewpoint, since most customer-powered networks would not have the scale or scope to undercut the common carrier's direct costs of providing an equivalent service. Should the bypass trend accelerate—which common carriers feared—fewer and fewer large customers would remain on the network to provide a contribution to the non-traffic sensitive local plant.

Even with a new pricing structure, such as the FCC's proposed access charge, basic communications was likely to become a commodity business, with price becoming the distinguishing factor. While voice transmission still dominated 90% of telecommunications revenues, data communications was expected to grow at a much brisker rate of 20% to 30% a year.[24] Consequently, the common carriers were beginning to shift to value-added services in order to differentiate themselves in what was becoming an increasingly competitive market. Such flashy features as automatic economic route selection were used to establish a company's reputation and provide a larger share of market—and profits. The problem facing carriers was to determine which features to add and when to make the offering.

According to one estimate, telecommunications accounted for just over 10% of what Americans spent on their total communications needs.[25] The rest went for such things as postage, preparing written correspondence, and travel expenses. Carriers were beginning to build all-purpose transmission systems to gain the maximum flexibility in providing services that were needed. Older technology had demanded that the networks specialized in one type of information: video, data, or voice. But modern technology in the information age made it possible to use one system for all.

In 1984 the long-distance (interexchange) market was divided thus among the following major competitors:[26]

AT&T Communications	92%
MCI Communications	4%
GTE Sprint	.2%
ITT	.5%
Others	1.5%
	100%

But because long-distance market share was difficult to calculate, it had become a major issue between AT&T and OCCs. While AT&T claimed an aggregate share of 78%, its competitors argued the actual share was much higher, ranging between 92% and 96% of the market. AT&T pointed out that those figures were inflated by premium access charges—those revenues collected and passed back to LECs.

1. "Telecommunications: Everybody's Favorite Growth Business—The Battle for a Piece of the Action," *Business Week*, October 11, 1982. p. 60.
2. Federal Communications Commission, Common Carrier Docket No. 78-72, Phase I; Third Report and Order, December 22, 1982.
3. Pub. L. No. 73-416, 48 Stat. 1046 (1934) (codified at 47 U.S.C. §§151–609 (1976).
4. U.S. Congress, Congressional Budget Office, *Local Telephone Rates: Issues and Alternatives*, January 1984, p. 25.
5. AT&T's Telecommunications Policy Task Force, *The Dilemma of Telecommunications Policy: An Inquiry into the State of Domestic Telecommunications by a Telecommunications Industry Task Force*, Chart 4, Washington, D.C., 1977.
6. Paul W. MacAvoy and Kenneth Robinson, "Winning By Losing: The AT&T Settlement and Its Impact on Telecommunications," *Yale Journal on Regulation* 1 (1983):41.
7. "The Bell Breakup: For Business, A Burst of Competition," *New York Times*, December 29, 1983, p. D18. Also see "Changing Phone Habits," *Business Week*, September 5, 1983, p. 68.
8. U.S. Congress, Congressional Budget Office, *Local Telephone Rates*, p. B-1.
9. Leland L. Johnson, "Why Local Rates Are Rising," *Regulation*, July/August 1983, p. 31.
10. U.S. Congress, Congressional Budget Office, *Local Telephone Rates*, p. B-3.
11. Ibid., p. 27.
12. AT&T Telecommunications Policy Task Force, *The Dilemma of Telecommunications Policy*, p. II-3.
13. *Smith* v. *Illinois Bell Telephone*, 282 U.S. 133 (1930).
14. Federal Communications Commission, Common Carrier Docket No. 78–72, Phase I; Comments of the Bell Operating Companies, August 6, 1982.
15. U.S. Congress, Congressional Budget Office, *Local Telephone Rates*, p. 7.
16. "Telecommunications: Everybody's Favorite Growth Business," *Business Week*, October 11, 1982, p. 61.
17. "What the Spinoff Will Mean to the Customer," *Business Week*, September 5, 1983, p. 76.
18. Ibid., p. 66.
19. Standard & Poor's *NYSE Stock Reports*.
20. Telecommunications Policy Task Force, *The Dilemma of Telecommunications Policy*, p. II-4.
21. Ibid., p. B-1.
22. Telecommunications Policy Task Force, *The Dilemma of Telecommunications Policy*, p. V-4.
23. "Telecommunications: Everybody's Favorite Growth Business," *Business Week*, October 11, 1982. p. 61.
24. "The Bell Breakup," *New York Times*, December 29, 1983, p. D18.
25. "Telecommunications: Everybody's Favorite Growth Business," *Business Week*, October 11, 1982, p. 62.
26. "The Bell Breakup," *New York Times*, December 29, 1983, p. D18.

AT&T and the Access Charge

Walter Kelley was aghast at the Federal Communications Commission's latest order. On February 15, 1984, the FCC so drastically revised its access charge plan that it threatened AT&T Communications' long-term competitiveness.[1] Kelley was the senior vice president who had coordinated AT&T's participation in the development of the plan—a plan designed to rationalize the "crazy quilt" pricing structure of the long-distance telephone market and assure lasting competition.

Access charges were to replace the traditional subsidy that long distance callers contributed—through artificially high rates—to the fixed costs of local telephone service. Telephone users, under the plan, were to begin paying a flat rate monthly fee for access to the long distance network. This method of recovering costs would replace an arcane system of transfer pricing known as *division of revenues* and *settlements* that, in the FCC's view, was not compatible with the new competitive environment. The transfer of access costs to users, in the face of new technological advances, would discourage large users from building private networks to bypass the conventional telephone network. And eventually, the Access Charge Plan would put AT&T and its long distance competitors on an equal footing.

After five years of painstaking study, the plan had been scheduled to take effect January 1, 1984, coincident to the breakup of the Bell System. But this timing, together with other increases in local rates and deregulation of telephone equipment, had confused the public and generated political friction among a host of interested parties. The pressure was so intense, in fact, that the FCC had twice delayed implementation.

Trouble in Washington had intensified the previous October. In a strongly worded letter to the FCC, eight long-distance carriers—AT&T's principal competitors—complained that their "very survival" was threatened by the Access Charge Plan.[2] A week later, state utility regulators challenged the FCC's jurisdiction and authority in court. Surprisingly, the secretary of commerce also rebuffed the FCC, criticizing access charges on grounds that they put the small long distance companies at a disadvantage to AT&T. Then, the House of Representatives passed a bill that would outlaw several key aspects of the plan. The principle behind access charges, that the "cost causer pays," survived

Dekkers L. Davidson, research associate, prepared this case under the supervision of Professor Richard H.K. Vietor as a basis for class discussion rather than to illustrate either the effective or ineffective handling of an administrative situation.

only by a narrow margin when the Senate tabled consideration of companion legislation.[3]

Walter Kelley couldn't help but note the irony of this situation. While over the past fifteen years the FCC had effected many structural changes on the industry, it had been the courts that had ordered most of the major public policy changes in telecommunications: the right of specialized carriers to provide long-distance services, and the divestiture itself. In this instance, where the FCC had taken the initiative, its plan had been politically rebuffed by Congress. And there was a further irony: two years earlier, AT&T's top management had settled a long-standing antitrust suit by agreeing to terms for breaking up the Bell System. Kelley and others at AT&T presumed that the divestiture would finally dissipate antagonism toward the "largest company on earth." But scarcely two years later, the new AT&T—now a third its former size—was again the target of fierce political attack. (See Exhibit 1 for a financial profile of the new AT&T.)

The new AT&T consisted of two basic businesses: (1) AT&T Communications, still regulated by the FCC and state commissions, which would provide long-distance telecommunications services, and (2) AT&T Technologies, newly deregulated, which would manufacture and sell switching, transmission, and terminal equipment, and conduct basic research. Information Systems, a subsidiary of AT&T Technologies, would deliver the corporation into the markets of the computer-based information age. But during the company's transition to a high tech future, AT&T Communications was expected to contribute nearly two-thirds of total revenues, according to industry analysts. (See Exhibit 2 for AT&T's organization chart.)

This latest version of the Access Charge Plan would impose additional local-subsidy costs on all long-distance carriers; yet it would further discount the share of those costs borne by AT&T's nonregulated, interexchange competitors. Local telephone companies could still earn the FCC-authorized rate of return on the interstate portion of their ratebase by imposing on AT&T a disproportionate burden of those local exchange costs. The financial impact, according to AT&T, would be devastating.[4] Return on interstate investment was estimated to drop below 5%, and return on equity to less than 3%. With its market share of profitable customers already eroding, the company could see no opportunity to restore earnings to a reasonable level. Thus, the plan as revised threatened AT&T's near-term profitability and its long-term strategy alike.

In light of recent developments, Walter Kelley knew that AT&T faced some difficult political and business problems. Clearly, this required the company to reexamine all its strategic options. AT&T might immediately petition the FCC to reconsider the order, on the basis of its unfavorable financial impact on the company. Or, it could proceed more cautiously, recognizing that the FCC was still resolving some key elements in the plan as well as other important regulatory matters. The company could also explore ways to marshal wider support for access charges, thereby defusing the still remaining political opposition to the plan. Although it was difficult to ignore the tremendous uncertainty inherent in the transition from regulation to competition, AT&T needed to press ahead with its business strategy, regardless of any handicaps it had been dealt.

THE TELEPHONE NETWORK

When AT&T was still the dominant provider of long-distance service, the operation and regulation of the nationwide telephone network had been relatively straightforward. When a customer made an interstate call, it normally originated with the use of a home telephone or, in a business location, with a telephone that might be connected through private branch exchange (PBX) switching equipment. A phone call traversed the *inside wiring* at the home or office and then the *loop* (usually a pair of copper wires) between the customer's premise and the switch at the telephone company's local exchange.

The phone company ordinarily owned these facilities—including the telephone, inside wiring, loop, and local exchange switch. The local company used them to provide franchised service within an exchange and to originate and terminate calls between exchanges, including interstate calls. These local exchange companies included the Bell Operating Companies and about 1,500 independent telephone companies.

A large portion of local exchange costs was fixed, or *nontraffic sensitive* (NTS)—not varying with the amount or type of calls handled. The systemwide revenue requirement to recover these NTS costs (for wires, poles, and local switching equipment; see Figure 1) amounted to about $38.8 billion for 1982.[5]

The remaining portion of local exchange and interexchange costs for

Figure 1 Telephone Network Facilities

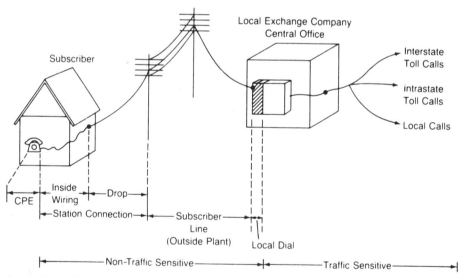

Source: Adapted from John McGarrity, "Implementing Access Charges: Stakeholders and Options." Cambridge: Program on Information Resources Policy. © 1983 by the President and Fellows of Harvard College. Used with permission.

Note: Nontraffic sensitive plant.

switching and transmission facilities varied over the long term with usage. These *traffic sensitive* costs increased as the volume of calls grew.

Once a long-distance call reached the local exchange central office, it was switched and routed to the facilities of the interexchange carrier. Until MCI and other competitors entered the market in 1978, this was the business of AT&T Long Lines (later called AT&T Communications). Once the call was routed through the interexchange carrier's network of switching and transmission facilities, it was switched back to the facilities of the local company serving the destination and then routed by the reverse process to the terminating phone.

The same facilities (that is, the loop) in the local community, which normally carried toll calls (both interstate and intrastate), also carried local calls. Through a *separations* procedure prescribed by the FCC, the cost of both these nontraffic and traffic sensitive, jointly used facilities had historically been divided between the interstate and intrastate jurisdictions. (See Figure 2.)

Since the late 1940s, however, federal and state regulators had been allocating a larger and larger share of these costs to the interstate jurisdiction, for recovery from interstate long distance toll revenues. Technological innovation was significantly reducing the unit cost of long distance telecommunications, especially relative to the costs of local plant. By using cost reductions in long-distance service to offset increases in local service costs, overall telephone rates were effectively stabilized. At a time when the Bell System provided 82% of all local service and virtually all long distance service, this policy was merely a matter of transferring costs—an easy accommodation to political compromise between state and federal regulators. By 1982 the interstate revenue requirement to recover these NTS costs amounted to nearly $9 billion, or more than three times proportionate long distance usage.[6] (Figure 3 traces the evolution of these separations agreements.)

As a result, there was a sizable gap between what local subscribers paid for access and what it cost companies to provide it. The average subscriber-line

Figure 2 Separations

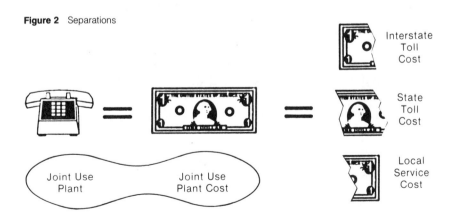

Source: American Telephone & Telegraph Company.

Figure 3   History of Local Exchange, Fixed Costs Allocated to Interstate Service

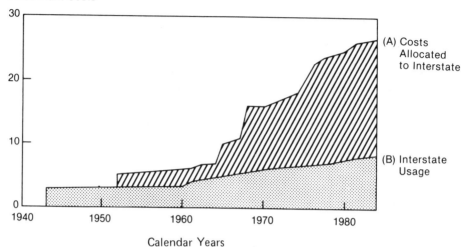

Percent of Local
Fixed Plant Costs

(A) 26.0%—Interstate subscriber plant factor (percentage of subscriber plant costs
allocated to interstate service).
(B) 7.9%—Interstate usage as percent of total calling minutes.

cost for the Bell System was about $26 per month. Residential rates, however, averaged less than $10 a month. Of the $16 difference, about $7 came from *inter*state toll service and $9 from various *intra*state services. These averages varied widely from state to state. In Wyoming, for example, a subscriber line in 1981 cost $45 a month, to which interstate tolls made a $25 contribution. In Pennsylvania, local lines cost only $20 a month and received an interstate contribution of just $4.[7]

This policy of overpricing toll calls to reduce basic monthly charges had created a complicated pattern of cross-subsidies. The largest of these flowed from toll users to nontoll residential users and from urban to rural customers, with some regional differences as well. This practice of cross-subsidy was a national policy of long-standing. Its goal, as stated in the Communications Act of 1934, was "to make available, so far as possible, to all people of the United States a rapid, efficient nationwide and worldwide radio and communications service with adequate facilities at reasonable charges."[8] This reflected the idea that the value of the network increased as subscribers were able to reach more people in more places.

LONG-DISTANCE COMPETITION

In the late 1970s, other common carriers (OCCs) sought to use the facilities owned by local telephone companies to originate and terminate their own long-distance traffic. Initially, some OCCs thought about building their own local networks but abandoned the idea presumably because of the high costs involved. Local distribution of long-distance traffic was obviously necessary for these carriers to compete effectively against AT&T in the long-distance market. When Microwave Communications, Inc. (MCI) first tried to offer public switched service in 1977, about a third of the revenue generated from traditional long-distance traffic was being used to subsidize local loop costs.[9] If, as the Bell System argued, carriers like MCI were permitted to use local facilities without making a similar contribution to the subsidy, AT&T's long-distance business would be unfairly disadvantaged. Any selective entry into major markets, moreover, would interfere with AT&T's practice of averaging access and transmission costs in its rates.

Despite the FCC's concurrence with these complaints, the federal courts ruled that MCI could provide a competitive, public switched service. In 1978 MCI began interconnecting its long distance microwave network to local exchanges.

The advent of competition in long-distance service was complicated by several factors. One was quality of connection. The central switching offices of local phone companies were equipped to interconnect with only one long-distance carrier—AT&T. OCCs could be wired into these offices, but the quality of connection could be inferior to AT&T's. Then too, the customers of OCCs had to dial as many as twenty-three digits to identify their billing accounts and make their calls. MCI and other new OCCs claimed that local Bell Operating Companies could technically provide equal access with software-driven switches, but because of their bias towards AT&T, were obstructing interconnection.

In response, AT&T complained that OCCs were essentially retailing private lines as a public switched service. Private line rates, under separations procedures, were not weighted with any of the subsidy. In other words, while AT&T's rates for public toll service were ladened with three times as much NTS cost as its relative usage of NTS plant, AT&T's new competitors carried no such burden.

The FCC would obviously need new rules to cope with the advent of long-distance competition.

ENFIA: THE DISCOUNT

In late 1978 the carriers reached agreement under the FCC's aegis on the ENFIA (Exchange Network Facilities for Interstate Access) tariff. Under this tariff, new carriers would contribute to nontraffic sensitive costs, but their rate would be less per minute of usage than that of AT&T. This supposedly offered a kind of rough justice for competition until 1984, by which time the FCC promised a more permanent arrangement.[10]

In the negotiations over ENFIA, local companies argued that they should receive the same contribution to NTS costs from competitive long distance carriers as they received from AT&T. But the OCCs effectively countered this claim with the *inferior-connection* argument. After all, why should their subscribers pay the same for lesser service?

The FCC, under court mandate to allow competition, accepted this argument for discounted access. The OCCs were to pay for access to the local exchange at a rate discounted from what AT&T paid. (Originally, ENFIA provided OCCs a negotiated discount of 65% below what AT&T paid per minute for local access. As OCC sales volume grew, the ENFIA discount decreased to 55%, and then again to 45%, which is where the discount stood in late 1983.) More precisely, OCCs were to pay this discounted rate on an estimate of usage of their own facilities (and the private line facilities that they leased from AT&T). This estimate was based on the OCCs' public reports of their average minutes of use.

This ENFIA discount applied to the fixed costs of jointly used plant associated with the interstate MTS-like and WATS-like services offered by the OCCs. MTS (Message Telephone Service), which was AT&T's regular long distance offering, was a publicly switched service which originated and terminated through jointly used local exchange facilities. WATS (Wide Area Telecommunications Service), which was AT&T's bulk-rate offering, was commonly used by business to call from a single location to multipoint locations. Unlike an MTS call, a WATS call originated through dedicated facilities and terminated, like MTS, through jointly used facilities. (See Exhibit 3 for a schematic diagram of basic telecommunications services.)

Private Line Service (PLS) was AT&T's bulkrate, dedicated service that originated and terminated through dedicated local exchange facilities. It was used primarily by businesses with high-volume, specific point-to-point communications needs. Since a PLS subscriber directly paid all local fixed and variable costs associated with the use of that private line, there had been no rationale for adding a subsidy. But when the FCC allowed unrestricted resale and sharing of private line facilities and WATS, a new industry—the long distance reseller—began to flourish. Resellers would lease private line *facilities* and also WATS from AT&T or an OCC and retail them as an MTS-like service for a targeted segment

Table 1 ENFIA Interstate Access Charge Disparities, October 1983

SERVICE CATEGORY	INTERSTATE NTS ASSIGNMENT AS A % OF RELATIVE USE	REVENUE RECOVERY AS A % OF COSTS ALLOCATED TO INTERSTATE	OCC DISCOUNT
AT&T: MTS	330%	100%	—
OCCs: MTS	330%	55%	45%
AT&T: WATS (both ends)	330%	100%	—
OCCs: WATS (open end)	330%	55%	45%
OCCs: WATS (closed end)	100%	50%	50%
AT&T: Private line	100%	100%	—
OCCs: Private line	100%	50%	50%

Source: American Telephone and Telegraph Company (FCC Filing, August 6, 1982).

of the market. (For example, they could lease private line facilities between two locations like New York and Chicago, and then separately buy local access so they could retail this combination of facilities.) As intended by the FCC, this resale function allowed businesses without their own networks to take advantage of the wholesale price structure of PLS and WATS.

The ENFIA tariff, as shown in Table 1, reflected the differences in cost allocation and recovery between these substitutable services.

ENFIA, in effect, became the means of delivering competition in the long-distance market. The OCCs viewed it as just compensation for unequal access; AT&T saw it as a crutch for cream skimming. Although designed as an interim measure, ENFIA had already affected the structure of the market and created vested interests among diverse parties.

THE FCC PLAN: ACCESS CHARGES

In 1978 when the courts upheld MCI's right to offer public long-distance service, the FCC opened a sweeping investigation into the structure of MTS and WATS markets. The FCC had hoped to rationalize the basic economics of the industry and to establish transition rules for fair and open competition. But as the FCC realized five years later, the task turned out to be "the most difficult ever to come before the Commission." It was also "the most important."[11]

The FCC's proceedings, as previously noted, overlapped the antitrust court's final orders for codifying the terms of AT&T's divestiture. Thus, the court had ordered local companies to provide access of equal quality to all long distance carriers over a three-year schedule. And like the FCC, the court had also discarded the old system of settlements, division of revenue, and the ENFIA tariff.

The FCC's decision in December 1982 reflected its efforts to achieve balance among four objectives: efficient use of the network, elimination of unreasonable discrimination among rates for interstate services, prevention of uneconomic bypass, and preservation of universal service.

First, it was inefficient to charge callers solely on the basis of usage, since subscriber plant costs did not vary with usage. Because the marginal cost of using the local loop was zero, reasoned the FCC, the price should also be zero. Charging a higher price per minute to use that loop in order to complete a long-distance call discouraged toll usage and caused a loss to economic efficiency of $1.6 billion annually.[12]

A second problem was the past preference for private line facilities, caused by the exclusive allocation of NTS subsidy costs to MTS and WATS. This was held to be discriminatory in that large users who were able to lease private networks could escape much of the NTS subsidy loaded on MTS and WATS. OCCs and resellers, who could unbundle private line and WATS respectively, were also relieved of much of these subsidies and could effectively charge lower rates for roughly equivalent services.

Bypass was the latest concern. New technology allowed large users to erect their own networks, bypassing local telephone companies *and* long-distance carriers. Regulators were most disturbed by uneconomic bypass that could occur when users developed private networks at a cost above the common carriers' but below the carriers' subsidy-laden rates. Bypass of this nature, in the FCC's view, was an immediate and largely irreversible threat to the public network. If too many large customers were to desert, smaller customers would bear the entire costs of the system, with higher rates and less ubiquity than otherwise.

Finally, there remained a public policy commitment to universal service that the FCC felt could best be achieved by relating prices to actual costs. Toward this end, overcharging toll users in order to promote lower residential rates had become counterproductive.

The Access Charge Plan provided that each local telephone company would recover its costs through a series of access charges, rather than through the subsidy on interstate toll revenues. There were three elements to the plan: (1) a *flat* Customer Access Line Charge (CALC), (2) a *variable* Carriers Common Line Charge (CCLC), and (3) a Universal Service Fund (USF).

Customer Access Line Charge (CALC): Under the Access Charge Plan, every local subscriber would pay access charges in the form of a fixed (per-line) monthly fee to compensate the local phone company for part of the subscriber plant costs that were allocated to interstate service. This flat rate charge, or CALC, would be obligatory for local subscribers—a dramatic departure from past practice of usage-based (per-minute) charges on long-distance calls that were optional. A *special access* surcharge would be levied on private lines.

In the original FCC plan, the charge for residential access would start at $2 a month in 1984, rising to $4 in 1986, and eventually to full cost of $6 to $8 a month by 1989. For business users, access charges would start out at $6 a month in 1984 and likewise rise to full cost. These were maximum amounts that each local phone company could charge subscribers for access; the CALC could be less in lower-cost states.

Carriers Common Line Charge (CCLC): The FCC chose to phase in its plan for cost-based pricing in order to moderate its effects on local rates. Thus, long-distance carriers would continue to pay a variable (per-minute-of-use) access fee. This CCLC would be computed on a cumulative monthly minutes-of-use basis for MTS and WATS service. Initially, it would compensate local companies for fixed costs as well as traffic sensitive costs, such as switching. Over time, the proportion of fixed costs paid by the long-distance carriers through the CCLC would decline—shifting to subscribers—until 1990, when carriers would pay only for traffic sensitive costs.

The FCC's plan would also resolve subsidy differentials among long distance competitors. Since AT&T still enjoyed superior-connection capabilities, it would initially continue to pay more than OCCs for local access. This *premium*, a new surrogate for ENFIA, was still designed to give a discount of 35% (AT&T would pay $2.2 billion more) in the plan's first year. This discount would shrink to 23% in the second year and to 12% in the third year. It would expire in

September 1986, when local companies were obligated to provide equal access to all long distance carriers.

Universal Service Fund (USF): The Access Charge Plan would also require long distance carriers to finance a Universal Service Fund, to assist local phone companies with unusually high fixed costs. The fund would subsidize rates, especially in rural areas, where subscriber line costs were highest. All interexchange carriers would contribute.

Together, these transitional elements of the original access charge plan are illustrated in Figure 4.

In mid-February 1984, after months of intense political debate, the FCC made several major changes in this plan:

· The residential and single-line-business CALC was delayed until 1985 and capped at $4. Instead of recovering $4.0 billion for NTS costs, this CALC and special access surcharge would generate $1.3 billion.
· The OCC's discount would be set at 55% of AT&T's total access costs. (In the original plan, the OCC discount was set at 35% of NTS costs.)
· AT&T's access cost would be increased approximately $2.0 billion to cover shortfalls caused by these revisions.[13]

These elements of the revised plan are illustrated in Figure 5.

The Prize: Lower Long-Distance Rates?

By restructuring long-distance rates, the Access Charge Plan was supposed to induce more innovative service offerings at lower overall rates. The previous October, in fact, AT&T had announced a rate reduction of $1.75 billion—its biggest ever—in conjunction with access charges. Since end users and OCCs were to pay a larger share of the NTS cost burden, AT&T's own cost of access would decline, permitting it to reduce long-distance rates. Even with the significant reductions in MTS and WATS prices that AT&T proposed, its rate of return would increase from 10.1% to 12.75%—the maximum allowed by the FCC.

This immediate rate reduction, scheduled to concur with the implementation of access charges, would help fulfill the FCC's promise. From AT&T's viewpoint, this rate cut would also make AT&T's long-distance rates more competitive with discount carriers, like MCI and Sprint, whose lower prices had attracted large subscriberships. Although access charges would cause an increase in monthly telephone bills, lower long-distance rates would offset all or part of the increase for frequent long-distance callers.

FCC revisions, however, had cast serious doubt on these proposed rate reductions. With the access charges delayed, AT&T suspended its reduction, pending the outcome of the FCC's final decision on the plan. AT&T's prospective earnings are illustrated in Table 2.

Figure 4 Original FCC Access Charge Plan

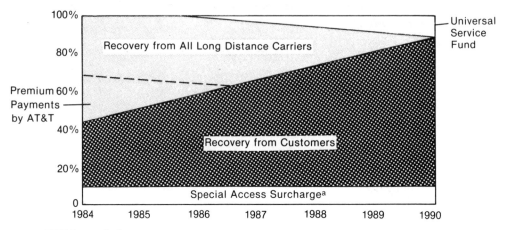

Recovery of Local Fixed Plant Costs
Assigned to Interstate Service

Source: AT&T Communications.

[a]On special long distance service.

Figure 5 Revised FCC Access Charge Plan

Recovery of Local Fixed Plant Costs
Assigned to Interstate Service

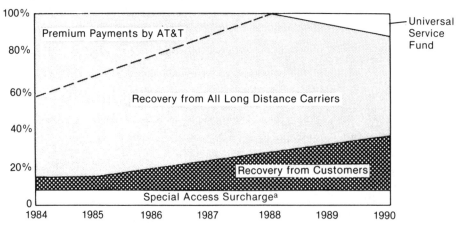

Source: AT&T Communications.

[a]On special long distance service.

STAKEHOLDERS

"There never was in the world two opinions alike." That view, once offered by Montaigne, certainly applied to the debate over access charges. With multibillion-dollar stakes, there was no shortage of opinions on how access charges should be settled. Everyone, it seemed, had a better idea: that someone *else* should pick up the fixed costs of the local exchange plant.

Telephone Companies

Local exchange companies had perhaps the greatest stake. Removal of the NTS subsidy was vital to their long-term financial health. Perpetuation of the status quo, most telcos believed, would surely cause large users to bypass the telephone system altogether. Burdened with old copper wire plant in the local loop, telcos needed to recover their costs. Most believed the FCC's plan was an economically sound method for doing so. Like AT&T Communications, the local companies were scrambling to realign their own pricing practices so that users would pay for the direct cost of services consumed. Some telcos had already proposed usage-sensitive pricing schemes as a replacement for fixed-price, un-limited-calling plans. A few companies had actively supported state access charges to alleviate the intrastate toll subsidy for local service, which was often as large

Table 2 AT&T Communications—Rates and Earnings Comparison ($ in billions)

	10/3/83 RATE FILING	CURRENT VIEW
Access Charge Plan		
CALC/surcharges	$4.0	$1.3
OCC % discount	35.0%	55.0%
AT&T financials		
Access charges	$15.5	$17.4
Earnings ratio	18.9%	4.9%
AT&T rate changes[a]		
MTS	−10.5%	?
WATS	−6.9%	?
800 Service	+1.3%	?
PLS/FX	+15.3%	?
Directory assistance	75 cents	?
Revised earnings ratios	12.75%	?

Source: AT&T Communications (FCC Filings, October 3, 1983, and February 27, 1984).

[a]Prices are established to yield an equivalent 12.75% return in each service category. (See Exhibit 4 for more detailed financial data.)

as the interstate subsidy. Thus, most of the 1,500 local telephone companies generally supported the principles underlying access charges.

Competition, according to NYNEX Chairman Delbert Staley, required that "prices be set based on costs."[14] The threat of bypass, in his view, was very real. Many large business customers in New York City paid as much as $600 or more per month in usage charges to cover a service that cost less than $25 to provide. These customers were finding ways—through cable TV, microwave, and satellite—to bypass the local network to complete long distance calls. Many heavy users, in fact, could choose to bypass the facilities of local companies for technological reasons (that is, transmission bottlenecks) and those of conventional long distance for public policy reasons (that is, regulatory-induced high rates). Two examples in the New York area were (a) the Teleport being built by the N.Y.–N.J. Port Authority, Merrill Lynch, and Western Union, and (2) the use of cable TV to provide access to satellite facilities of other carriers. According to Staley, a whole new industry had arisen, dedicated to finding and exploiting bypass technologies. With existing technology, it was "a simple matter to directly connect a large office building or industrial complex to the facilities of inter-exchange carriers."[15]

The degree to which bypass threatened the revenues of NYNEX was no small matter. Because large banking, financial, and other commercial institutions were so concentrated in the New York area, approximately one-third of 1% of NYNEX's business customers provided one-third of all long-distance revenues, and only 5% of its customers provided approximately 70% of its long-distance revenues. "The loss of just a few of these largest customers," warned Staley, "can seriously affect our future business."[16]

John Hayes, vice president of Southwestern Bell Telephone, also elaborated on the negative impact of bypass:

> Bypass is here and it is likely to grow. As for the potential consequences as bypass grows, the following scenario will unfold. As large business customers deploy their own bypass systems and leave the local network, fewer customers remain to share an increasingly larger portion of the company's plant investment. Those remaining customers will primarily be comprised of residential and small- and medium-sized business customers. Rates must rise to recover the cost of that investment. As rates rise, more customers find it economically beneficial to leave the network in favor of bypass technology. As a result, the telephone company is left serving the high-cost, low-revenue customers. Or, in a strict economic sense, we end up losing the winners and winning the losers.[17]

General Telephone's position regarding access charges was similar to that of the Bell Operating Companies. Its chairman, Theodore Brophy, felt the Access Charge Plan was "sound in principle." He described bypass as "a current and growing reality, [as the] array of technological alternatives is growing in variety and reducing in cost." Still, GTE complained about the "inadequacy" of AT&T's premium access charge, arguing that it jeopardized OCCs, such as GTE's own recently acquired long distance company, Sprint.[18]

Rural telephone companies showed general support for access charges but urged that the provisions of the Universal Service Fund be large enough to sustain reasonable local rates. Some small companies, like the Wyoming Telephone Company, expressed "concern for the impact of access charges on rural exchanges," arguing that "the benefits of competition in these areas will likely redound only to large subscribers, creating upward pressure on basic local rates."[19]

Federal Communications Commission

The current thrust in the FCC's access charges predated the Reagan administration, but the pitch in favor of more competition—and less regulation—took on more zest with the appointment of Mark Fowler as chairman. With a background as a communications (broadcast) lawyer, Fowler came to the FCC in early 1981, convinced that FCC regulation was not serving the public particularly well. He set out, in what others described as an evangelical mission, to bring more competition to telecommunications, radio, and television. According to one journalist, Fowler's anthem was "let the marketplace decide"; the chorus was that "bigness is not necessarily badness."[20] Within two years of his arrival, the FCC staff completed its lengthy inquiry on access charges. The plan, claimed Fowler, would bring immediate long-distance savings, and by fostering competition in the long term, it could yield price cuts as large as 30% to 40%.

Some economists were quick to embrace the principle of economic efficiency that supported the Access Charge Plan. Among the advocates for access charges was Alfred Kahn, a former adviser to President Carter and architect of airline deregulation. Kahn viewed the long-distance toll subsidy of local service as a *tax* that was economically irrational, distorting market mechanisms and limiting consumer choice. Although the Bell System had performed nobly for decades, according to this economist, it was "a welfare state with the power to tax and use the proceeds to do good things."[21]

Kahn's impact on FCC thinking with respect to marginal cost pricing was evident in the actual wording of the Access Charge order. Although critics of access charges, especially those in Congress, argued that pricing should reflect *benefits* derived from calling long-distance (implying an obligation to support the local exchange), Kahn argued that pricing ought to reflect only the *costs* of providing the service. Prices should be equated to marginal costs, which consumers would then equate to marginal benefits. Access charges were based on this logic: since the marginal cost of connecting an interstate call through the local loop was zero, the price (that is, the carrier's access fee) should also be zero.

Within the FCC, there was continuing debate over how best to promote competition and still maintain public policy goals. The ENFIA tariff was at the heart of these discussions. Some felt the OCCs had enjoyed a discount long enough; others adamantly urged its continuance. ENFIA was sometimes referred to as "regulatory paramutual betting," denoting its handicap aspect. But despite these differences, the FCC still felt that access charges were the best remedy for making the transition from a regulated monopoly to competition. Fowler complained of congressional "obstructionists" who sought legislative overrides to access charges; he warned of "a national catastrophe in the making" if access charges were thwarted. Maintenance of government-imposed subsidies would turn the industry into "an economic Beirut" and result in "a crumbling, rapidly deteriorating public phone network."[22]

Despite the FCC's delay and subsequent compromise in its access charge plan, Chairman Fowler still held firmly to his vision of competition. Early in 1983, in a speech before large telecommunications users, Fowler spoke of his blueprint for the future:

> In my mind, we are heading ultimately towards a regulation-free telecommunications marketplace, a world where competitors offer an abundance of facilities and services constrained only by imagination and the capital market. What will be [the] benefits? An abundance of choice, both in equipment and services—new products, lower costs, more jobs, new sophisticated means to transfer information, convenience in society, freedom from drudgery, and higher quality of life.
>
> The consumer needs to replace the bureaucrat on the throne of regulation. As President Reagan has stated, we are moving as a nation from smoke stacks to high tech. We as regulators must not delay that process. How will we get to the haven of no regulation? The journey will be a long one. But we have a compass and a map. Our compass is "unregulation." Our map is to incrementally free up selected markets and participants within those markets until the necessity for regulation's surrogate function is displaced by the primary regulator—the consumer. Keep in mind that our goal throughout this [transition period] must be effective competition, not effective regulation.[23]

State Public Utility Commissions (PUCs)

The telecommunications revolution and the AT&T breakup had swamped many utility regulators. Already struggling with backlogs of electric- and gas-rate cases, they were now confronted with the ramifications of divestiture and a wholesale realignment of telephone rates. Fifteen years earlier, public utility regulation was considered a relatively low-pressure job handed out as a political reward. But when energy prices soared and utilities began to struggle with rising costs, rate regulation became a political nightmare. Following this, AT&T and the changes in telecommunications had put more pressure on regulators, trying to cope with the problems of new technologies, competition, federal intervention in telephone pricing, and a renewed consumer outcry over the largest requests ever for rate increases. (See Exhibit 5 for a survey of rate increase requests.)

Almost every single state commission had filed comments and objections to the FCC's plan. The Michigan Public Service Commission was first to insist that the entire burden of fixed NTS costs be placed on interexchange carriers. Access charges combined with accelerated depreciation, would allegedly hit consumers "like a sledge hammer," driving many off the telephone network.[24] The Michigan appeal, which gained a following among other commissions, also noted that Judge Harold Greene (who presided over the AT&T split) had stated that access charges were contrary to the ends sought by divestiture. Concerns for bypass were also greatly exaggerated, according to the Michigan commission; if bypass became a problem, it could be dealt with when it happened.

The brief filed on behalf of the state of Vermont was representative of rural concerns. Vermont worried about the future of universal service and complained that federal de-averaging of local costs would hurt rural telephone subscribers most. A number of commissions agreed with Vermont's contention that there was little evidence that bypass was induced by artificially high toll rates. Access charges were discriminatory from this perspective because they called for a flat fee for interstate access even if subscribers never made a long-distance call. This would be tantamount to a local subsidy of long distance.

The National Association of Regulatory Utility Commissioners (NARUC) petitioned a federal court to block the imposition of access charges. NARUC was a quasi-governmental, nonprofit organization which represented state officials and proclaimed an obligation to "just and reasonable" rates. A summary of NARUC's argument, filed October 12, 1983, is excerpted following:

> Congress clearly intended, and so provided in the express language of the Communications Act of 1934, that jurisdiction over telecommunications be divided between the federal government and the states. The federal government was granted authority over the interstate and international communications while authority over the intrastate sphere was reserved to the states.
>
> The FCC's flat-rate end-user charge, because it is not tied to use of the interstate network, constitutes a charge for intrastate service. As such, it is violative of the FCC's statutory authority which denies the Commission jurisdiction to impose charges on the intrastate network. It is also violative of [court] mandates that the costs of local exchange must be shared by the interstate and intrastate systems because both use those facilities to provide service.
>
> The FCC asserts that the "threat of uneconomic bypass" justified its imposition of a flat-rate end-user access charge not tied to interstate network usage. The NARUC maintains that there is scant, if any, hard evidence in the record which shows either that uneconomic bypass is a significant problem in the near future. Speculation, conjecture, and a pessimistic forecasting of what *might* happen do not constitute the factual basis necessary to fulfill the requirements of [administrative action].[25]

As of February 1984, the NARUC case had yet to be heard. The FCC, AT&T, and other long-distance companies were expected to contest it vigorously.

Other Common Carriers (OCCs) and Resellers

OCCs and resellers generally showed little sympathy for AT&T's latest dilemma. Many noted that their "giant competitor" had acquiesced to and benefited from past political accommodations between federal and state regulators. These recent long-distance entrants were still irked that they had to pay local costs which they "did not cause" and for which they were "not responsible." In their view, the local telephone companies—particularly Bell's—had not satisfactorily demonstrated a reasonable relationship between actual cost of providing local access and its price. In fact, OCCs felt the telcos were unfairly using access charges as a vehicle to profitability. The fact that local companies filed their access charges with the FCC just ninety days prior to their proposed implementation—the bare minimum for advance notification—infuriated OCCs and resellers alike.

In principle, the OCCs and resellers favored elimination of the long-distance subsidy and supported the idea of flat end-user charges as embodied in the Access Charge Plan. Like AT&T, the OCCs had cause to worry that artificially high long distance rates would drive large users to bypass. But the proposed reduction of the ENFIA differential caused OCCs to oppose the Access Charge Plan. As originally proposed, the nominal discount would immediately be reduced without any immediate change in local interconnection. The discount would then be gradually eliminated as equal access became available in local exchanges.

The "very survival" of the OCC industry was threatened by access charges, according to a letter from eight major OCCs and large resale companies.[26] (Signatories to the "Eight Carrier Letter" included United States Transmission Systems, U.S. Telephone, Satellite Business Systems, EMX TeleCom, MCI Communications, GTE Sprint, The Western Union Telegraph Company, and Lexitel Corporation.) The eight companies, accounting for 85% of all OCC revenues, had asked in October 1983 for a major rethinking of the ENFIA reduction in the Access Charge order.

They warned that the goal of a competitive long-distance market structure would "never be realized with the level of access charges imposed on competing carriers under the Commission's . . . access charge plan." The transitional mechanisms chosen by the Commission would "unduly increase the competitive advantage which AT&T enjoys . . . that is because the current differential in the AT&T/OCC interconnection charges will be reduced dramatically . . . even though the inferior interconnections now provided to AT&T's competitors will remain the same." Under ENFIA, OCCs received a 45% negotiated discount from AT&T's cost of local access. In their October plea to the FCC, however, the OCCs indicated that their actual discount was more in the range of 65%–75%. The disparity was due to a lower reported minute count that "does not represent actual holding [talking] time." With access charges, the nominal discount would in a "flash cut" be reduced to 35%. Changes in minute count basis would further reduce the discount to 25%, according to the OCC's claim.

Their economic analysis, they said, "made one thing clear—the implementation of the Access Charge Plan would preclude the OCCs from becoming meaningful competitors." Projected 1984 income for the eight carriers would be $484 million if ENFIA remained in effect; with access charges, combined losses of $506 million to $721 million would result. In view of AT&T's original intention to lower some rates by 10%, OCCs complained that to maintain their current retail rate differential, a matching price cut would be required, further compounding their financial problems. According to the eight carriers, "If OCCs raised prices to account for the access charge increases, many subscribers will not . . . tolerate the inconveniences and quality differences associated with an OCC's inferior access. Certainly, the ability to attract new subscribers will be largely undermined." (See Exhibit 6 for various OCC pricing and cost scenarios showing the impact of access charges.)

The dramatic impact of access charges on the health of OCCs reverberated in the capital markets. Following the FCC's announcement of its original access charge plan, MCI's stock price plummeted $4\frac{7}{8}$, to $15\frac{1}{4}$. More than 16.5 million shares of MCI were traded that day—an OTC (over the counter) record. (MCI was the only publicly traded OCC that was not part of a larger business.)

U.S. Congress

Lawmakers who recognized the technological drift away from monopoly in telecommunications had been trying for years to amend the Communications Act of 1934. But legislative efforts had failed to gain wide industry approval or congressional consensus. Court decisions (such as *Carterfone* and *Execunet*) along with FCC decisions had meanwhile imposed significant changes on the industry. And although Congress generally approved of the Bell System's divestiture, many members worried about its impact on universal telephone service.

In 1982 Representative Timothy Wirth, a Democrat from Colorado who chaired the House Telecommunications Subcommittee, proposed legislation which, in its sponsors' view, attempted to maintain universal service while also accounting for the structural changes brought to bear by divestiture. This bill recognized that the long-distance subsidy had to be dealt with in light of growing competition in the interexchange market. AT&T, claiming this legislation would be inadequate, successfully blocked the bill in an intensive lobbying campaign which relied heavily on a massive letter-writing effort by employees and stockholders.

As public confusion over the impending breakup of AT&T became widespread, more than a dozen bills were introduced to temper the possibility of local rate increases. A staff report by the House Commerce Committee attributed requests for local rate increases to divestiture and access charges.[27] The various bills would extend FCC jurisdiction to intrastate, inter-LATA (local access and transport area) services previously in the regulatory province of states. To prevent bypass, a few bills would tax bypass systems, or prohibit them altogether.

According to David Aylward, staff director of the House Telecommunications Subcommittee, the prospect that any of these bills would pass had at first appeared remote. Recent congressional efforts to enact new legislation on telecommunications had been so strongly rebuffed that, in Aylward's opinion, there still was no sufficient consensus in Congress. But that changed when Representative John Dingell, chairman of the Commerce Committee, became involved in the telephone debate. Distressed by the prospect of local telephone rate increases, Dingell helped mobilize partisan support for Wirth's newer telephone bill (H.R. 4102). Both Dingell and Wirth welded a coalition of some twenty-five or thirty House Democrats who, although they had received relatively little mail regarding telephone rate hikes, felt something needed to be done to modify the ill-effects of divestiture and access charges.

The Dingell-Wirth Bill would prohibit access charges for residential and small-business subscribers. The traditional method for recovering NTS costs would be maintained, and bypassers would be required to contribute to the costs of their local loop. The bill would provide a larger subsidy to small companies than did the Universal Service Fund. A Universal Service Board would be created to insure widespread availability of telephone service. Lifeline Service (residential service with a limited number of outgoing calls at a nominal rate) would be required in every state. Support for this bill came from state regulators, consumerists, many small businesses, and—to the dismay of AT&T—its union, the Communications Workers of America (CWA).

Local and national consumer organizations were the most vocal in support of legislative alternatives to the Access Charge Plan. The Consumer Federation of America—the largest consumer advocacy organization in the country, claiming membership of thirty million—called the access charge "an unjust proposal that will benefit few at the expense of many." The Consumer Federation in a news release dated December 9, 1983, urged support of the House and Senate alternatives. It decried a "civil war strategy" by AT&T that had cast this as a "state versus state issue." It claimed that "what is at stake is not which state wins or which state loses, but the fact that a massive transfer of wealth from residential consumers to large long-distance users and long-distance carriers will unfairly jeopardize universal telephone service in this country."

Congress Watch, an organization founded by Ralph Nader to monitor legislative action on Capitol Hill, was also critical of access charges and especially of AT&T's rate-reduction filing. AT&T's proposal was to reduce long-distance rates 10.7%, or approximately $1.75 billion. However, consumerists believed that access charges would save AT&T almost $4 billion in access fees to local companies. According to a Congress Watch news release on October 14, 1983, the consumerists felt that AT&T had "lied in an effort to line its corporate coffers." (In actuality, access charges would save *all* interexchange carriers, including AT&T, $4 billion.)

The Missouri Public Interest Group (MoPIRG) said that "AT&T was engaged in a campaign of half-truths, misleading statements, and deliberate distortions of divestiture." MoPIRG also criticized the media for not digging behind AT&T's "snow job on the public, [the worst] since the oil and gas industry came to town in 1978 claiming to represent the public's best interest." A MoPIRG news release dated December 8, 1983, elaborated as follows:

> AT&T has jumped on the FCC bandwagon to stick it to the average consumer. No sooner had the ink dried on the consent decree, AT&T began its efforts to

distort divestiture as an excuse for raising local rates. . . . AT&T continues to make claims that local service is subsidized by long distance. This claim is being used as an excuse by Bell Operating Companies, such as Southwestern Bell in Missouri, to seek a re-pricing of flat rate service which will ultimately double the cost of phone service. . . . The subsidy is not an Alexander Graham Bell-given fact about phone service.

Small businesses also complained loudly about access charges, citing the harm that telephone rate hikes would have on their fledgling enterprises. Congressman Ron Wyden, who was campaigning against Senator Robert Packwood in Oregon, called for an increase in the line exemption for small businesses. This no doubt pleased the National Federation of Independent Businesses, who claimed in an April 9, 1984, news release that "those with two and three lines will have absolutely unbearable charges."

Just prior to the vote on the House bill, the Communications Workers of America jolted AT&T management by publicly supporting congressional alternatives to the FCC Access Charge Plan. The union, which traditionally had been an ally of the company in its government affairs, was still smarting from the effects of the divestiture; unresolved issues included employment security, seniority, and the portability of pension rights. In the most recent collective bargaining agreement, AT&T had disputed a critical union issue of vested pension benefits. Consequently, many saw the union's support for legislation as a result of problematic labor relations. And the CWA's statement did have an impact on the thinking of many in Congress, particularly Democrats in the House of Representatives.

Substantial opposition to legislation came from AT&T, OCCs and resellers, local telephone companies, the FCC, and large telecommunications users. Although the rationales varied considerably according to each group's individual self-interest, most agreed with Charles Brown, AT&T's chairman, that it was "too late for Congress to have second thoughts about . . . competition . . . or the Bell System breakup."[28] Outlawing bypass would not only be impractical but would inhibit the technological leadership by the United States in a key industrial sector.

Heavy users of the national telecommunications system were sympathetic to the abolition of the toll subsidy. To a degree, the largest U.S. corporations could partially avoid the subsidy anyway by using private networks. And many large users just wanted to see telecommunications driven in the same way their own businesses were driven—by economic considerations. However, firms not large enough for a private system found the toll subsidy burden particularly onerous.

A case for access charges was presented by Mobil Oil in October 1983 on the op-ed pages of major newspapers. This piece, entitled "Sorry, Wrong Number" took Congress to task for trying to destroy the promise of competition in telecommunications:

This is the age of deregulation, and, while change is often painful, consumers have been its chief beneficiaries. We've seen how deregulation of oil brought prices down. We saw how deregulation of the banks gave savers big and little a much wider choice of higher-yielding accounts. Congress had its chance, early in the game, to get involved in the deregulation of the telephone industry. Congress sat on its hands. Now that a viable plan is about to take effect, Congress shouldn't change the ground rules just before game time. Both the Senate and House bill represent wrong numbers, at the wrong time. Both deserve immediate disconnection.

The International Communications Association (ICA), representing large telecommunications users, contested legislative alternatives to access charges. According to ICA's lobbyist, these bills would "generate major subsidies which do not focus on needy consumers, perpetuate economic inefficiencies on local exchange service, inhibit technological innovation in telecommunications, and create a new and complex bureaucracy to administer a new entitlement program."[29] While ICA supported the FCC's rationale for access charges, it resented suggestions that large users would bypass the conventional telephone network. AT&T, it was noted, had "artfully swung the bypass discussion from themselves to the users." Indeed, there was widespread conjecture that AT&T and other interexchange carriers would become large bypassers themselves. Furthermore, AT&T's 15% increase of private line rates, filed along with MTS and WATS reductions, had irritated ICA members who questioned whether AT&T's rate of return was excessive in light of a relatively inflation-free economy.

AT&T's action regarding its rate reduction filing caused suspicion among a number of those in Congress. John Dingell believed AT&T was using the FCC plan as a guise to "swell corporate coffers" and dubbed access chargers "the great phone robbery." During committee hearings, an easel chart suggested access charges would lower AT&T's cost by $4 billion; however, only $1.75 billion was being passed on as rate reductions. The other $2.25 billion was allegedly a windfall to AT&T. (AT&T explained that the $4 billion would be divided as follows: $1.75 billion were MTS rate cuts, and $.2 billion were WATS rate cuts to be passed on to users; $1.40 billion would be sent to local companies, allowing them to increase their rate of return on NTS plant to 12.75%. Similarly, AT&T would use $.6 billion to raise its rate of return to the FCC-authorized maximum return of 12.75%.) In November 1983, the Universal Telephone Service Preservation Act (H.R. 4102) passed the House of Representatives easily by voice vote.

Companion legislation introduced by Senator Robert Packwood, chairman of the Commerce Committee, would delay the access charge for two years and require bypassers to contribute to the NTS costs of local companies. Lifeline Service would still be optional on a state-by-state basis, and the Universal Service Fund would be managed by a joint federal-state panel.

The Senate bill was never voted on. A bipartisan group of senators headed by Robert Dole wrote to FCC Chairman Mark Fowler, urging the FCC to rethink its plan and at least delay residential-user charges until 1985. But even though the FCC obliged the very next day, consideration of Packwood's bill was prevented by a vote of only 44 to 40. Clearly, the FCC could not ignore congressional concerns if it was to avoid legislation that might bar access charges permanently.

AT&T'S VIEW: FRUSTRATION

The FCC's postponement and subsequent compromise of its access charge plan came as a blow to AT&T's management. The seige of public and private opposition was not only discouraging, but policy developments since October 1983 were disastrous from AT&T's perspective. With the original plan, the company's earnings would have been 12.75%; with compromised access charges, AT&T might earn less than 5%. If there were no rate reductions for AT&T's customers, its subscriber base would continue to erode from competition. In short, the blessings of access charges—lower prices and higher earnings—had somehow given way to a prospect of continuing high prices (relative to OCCs) and lower earnings.

AT&T's management was particularly annoyed by the stance OCCs had taken, claiming that the OCCs' grim analyses of the FCC plan's financial impact "were faulty and surely exaggerated." Thriving OCCs, such as MCI, were no longer in need of the regulatory advantage provided by the ENFIA tariff. It seemed outrageous that the OCCs had "deliberately undercounted usage on private lines to gain added leverage from the ENFIA tariff." (See Exhibit 7 for historic data on MCI and AT&T.)

In a letter to Mark Fowler, AT&T pointed out how its own subscribers were disadvantaged by the premium access cost:

· AT&T must serve *all* routes, unprofitable as well as profitable. OCCs pick only the high-volume, low-cost routes, that is, the profitable routes.
· AT&T serves *all* customers, unprofitable low volume users as well as heavy users. OCCs target their offerings to appeal only to high-volume, low-cost, profitable users.
· AT&T serves *all* customers twenty-four hours a day. OCCs frequently "balance" their load by limiting residence customers to off-peak hours.
· AT&T provides redundancy, alternate routing, and disaster-hardened facilities. OCCs use these facilities as fallback facilities, without bearing the standby costs.
· OCCs lease facilities from AT&T when the volume of OCC business is less than sufficient to justify putting in their own systems. As soon as their volumes build up, the OCCs abandon AT&T-leased facilities and replace them with their own. AT&T, on the other hand, is obligated to have facilities in place to serve all needs, when needed.
· AT&T designed, engineers, operates, and manages the national long-distance network (determining technical parameters, calling procedures, protocols, and switching hierarchies). OCCs obtain the benefits of this research and design, but

provide zero contribution to the effort. They simply applique their own services on top.

· OCCs have full freedom to enter and exit markets at will, with full discretionary pricing, flexibility, and very limited cost support. AT&T cannot enter or exit markets without regulatory approval, and has limited pricing flexibility with full cost support required. It is understandable that the OCCs would seek to achieve as large a discount as they could possibly get. Access costs are a major part of the cost of doing business. . . . In AT&T's case, access will represent over 60% of our total expenses in 1984. We too would like to pay less—but at whose expense?[30]

AT&T also disputed Congress's contention that universal service was in jeopardy. A report by Wharton Econometric Forecasting, commissioned by AT&T, concluded that residential demand for local service was relatively insensitive to change in price, but long-distance service was highly elastic.[31] This analysis indicated that a 10% *increase* in local service prices would reduce local service demand by 1%. For residential long-distance service, a 10% *decrease* in long-distance prices would result in a 13.1% increase in long-distance service demand. Separately, the FCC had concluded that 1.6% of telephone subscribers, at most, might drop off the network as a result of its access charge order.[32]

The Wharton study also concluded that the average price of telephone services would be reduced; long-distance prices would fall enough to more than offset increases in local-service prices; demand for long distance telecommunications would increase significantly; reductions in local-service demand would be small; and, universal service would be maintained through Lifeline Service and Universal Service Fund initiatives. Moreover, lower rates for telephone service would reduce inflation, increase disposable income and consumption, create new jobs, and stimulate growth of real GNP by $46 billion.

Congress had "played election-year politics," according to AT&T, by proposing to "regulate the telecommunications industry just as the promise of competition is about to be realized."[33] While pressure for legislation had subsided, the FCC was operating under a close rein of Congress. In AT&T's view, much of the "soundness in economic thinking" had given way to polical considerations.

FAIR OR NOT: COMPETITION AHEAD

As Walter Kelley reviewed these events and assessed the positions of various stakeholders, the challenge facing AT&T appeared formidable. It was remarkable that so much had gone wrong in so short a period. The most recent reversals with access charges made it necessary to rethink the company's strategy at all levels and across most management functions. Although AT&T should certainly continue to seek a level playing field on which to engage the competition, it was not all clear how to proceed. Meanwhile, AT&T needed to consider contingencies for competing with a handicap.

In the words of a competitor, AT&T faced the public relations "challenge of the century." If the latest round of public debate accomplished anything, it probably served to generate even more confusion about divestiture and the access charges. In some cases, loose rhetoric had generated consumer suspicion of AT&T's motives. The nomenclature of access charges was partly responsible. "Why," so many were asking, "should telephone users be required to pay for access to a long-distance network that they might not use?" Questions like this one persisted: "Why was the benevolent toll subsidy being washed away at this point in time?" If AT&T was to have any success in mobilizing support for the next round of debate over access charges and telephone rate levels, it would at least need to mitigate these concerns.

What Approach to Legislation?

On the legislative front, AT&T would have to consider how best to deploy its lobbyists. Although active debate over telephone legislation had subsided, there was a recognized need to continue the educational process on Capitol Hill. Yet, in the face of what could be best described as congresssional skepticism of AT&T's position, the company needed a strategy for building a constituency for access charges. AT&T's stockholders had the most to lose if access charges were not fully restored and implemented. Yet, company executives knew that they should proceed cautiously. Massive letter-writing campaigns, while proving the point that the "squeaky wheel gets greased," were the curse of Capitol Hill. Another deluge of AT&T stockholders' letters might be viewed as heavy-handed, and could provoke trouble.

What Approach to FCC?

AT&T's approach to the Federal Communications Commission could perhaps be less subtle. In the words of one AT&T executive, "Courage [by FCC commissioners] had been replaced by compromise, and AT&T's earnings were the chips given away." The company needed immediate relief from the latest version of the FCC's plan. Just as OCCs had projected financial doom to persuade the FCC, AT&T could now point to its own financial forecasts to argue for emergency modification of access charges. The FCC, trying to balance conflicting interests, had thus far failed to satisfy very many of the parties to the access charge affair; and it had yet to deliver the price of lower long-distance rates.

Although access charges were of paramount importance, AT&T had to consider other issues which required the FCC's attention. For instance, AT&T was now the only fully regulated interexchange carrier. It alone was required to file lengthy cost-support data to justify rates, to pre-announce service offerings, and to endure a lengthy investigation process to change prices in response to competitive challenges. In addition, the company was finding FCC restrictions imposed by the *Computer Inquiry II* rulings to be burdensome from a marketing perspective. Separate subsidiary requirements were hurting AT&T in its competition with Rolm, Northern Telecom, Mitel, NEC, and GTE Corporation. Consequently, forbearance of rate regulation and relaxation of *Computer Inquiry II* restrictions were issues that probably could not await the outcome of access charges.

What Approach to Marketing?

For AT&T's marketing organization, the resolution of access charges had immediate and long-term consequences. Given continuing delay and uncertainty, something had to be done to counter the competitive inroads being made by OCCs and resellers. In the preceding few years, the loss of customers to rival carriers had reached 3,000 per day. Most were highly prized residential customers who made more than $25 a month in long distance calls, or business customers who made calls worth more than $50 a month. (See Exhibit 8 for AT&T Communications' market share data.) In these key customer groups, AT&T's market share had slipped to as low as 61% and showed signs of continued erosion. Although its aggregate share of the market was much higher, at 78%, it was obvious to the company's marketing management that market share did not connote market power. In fact, market share for long distance companies was difficult to calculate and had become a major political issue between AT&T, OCCs, and resellers. Although AT&T claimed an aggregate market share of 78%, its competitors argued that the actual share was much higher, ranging between 94% and 96% of the long-distance market. AT&T argued that these higher projections included revenues collected that were really premium access costs passed along to local companies. Therefore, AT&T complained that it was not nearly as dominant as the OCCs and resellers liked to suggest. On the other hand, OCCs and resellers believed local access dollars should be included in AT&T's market share projections, arguing that AT&T's premium cost reflected premium service and therefore a premium position in the marketplace. Other possible methods to calculate market share, such as number of circuits, circuit mileage, and long-distance plant investment, provoked similar quarrels within the industry. Thus, in view of AT&T's losses, the company would need to devise a marketing program that considered issues of pricing and promotion—especially with equal access scheduled to begin shortly in some areas of the country.

In the longer term the provisions to allow equal access for all carriers by mid-1986 presented some unique opportunities as well as threats. As equal access was phased in, every telephone subscriber would be asked to choose a long distance telephone company. Differences in dialing requirements (that is, extra digits) and in quality of transmission would disappear as central offices were programmed to handle multiple carriers. And with equal access, each interexchange carrier would pay equal costs for access to local exchange companies; the OCC discount would no longer exist. All of the major players in the long-distance market were already preparing to address this "once-in-a-lifetime cutover" to equal access. The first equal access trial set for Charleston, West Virginia, was only five months away. (See Exhibit 9 for the first year's equal access schedule.) Once users chose their long distance company, it was presumed most would stay with that service for years to come. MCI and GTE/Sprint had been pushing low-cost service for years, and consumers already associated these companies with long distance. Ironically, AT&T had a more difficult challenge. According to company marketing surveys, only about half the public linked long-distance service with AT&T, having long associated such service with its local Bell Operating Companies. In part, this lack of brand awareness could be attributed to the company's previous utility-like status and strategy which stressed generic telephone usage. While the issue of price competition was an obvious concern, it needed to be considered in light of the company's future market profile vis-à-vis competitors.

AT&T's Financial Considerations

On the financial side, the delay and compromise of access charges posed short- and long-term problems of their own. With a projected interstate earnings rate of 4.93%, AT&T Communciations was certainly not in a positon to help with the corporation's transition to a high tech company (see Exhibit 4). Just as its ability to reduce rates was thrown into question, so too was its dividend policy. Traditionally, Bell System stock had provided stable and secure returns for its owners—so much so that the *old* AT&T was widely held as the investment choice of America's widows and orphans. Similarly, AT&T's debt ratings had always been considered as excellent in the minds of investment bankers. Failure to maintain the projected payouts would tarnish the financial reputation of the new AT&T. It would also come as another blow to small shareholders who were still confused by the disaggregation of their Bell System stock holdings.

The delay of access charges had accelerated the company's thinking pertaining to the difficult financial tradeoffs ahead. One factor considered in those calculations was how the company might reduce costs borne in a monopoly era, but which later became vulnerable in a competitive one. Costly early-retirement schemes had already been offered to reduce salary expense, and sizable layoffs had resulted from consolidation of Western Electric facilities. More cost-cutting procedures seemed necessary and inevitable, as the "largest company on earth" was now divided and competing for business. In a risky, more competitive world, AT&T would have to rethink its financical strategy regarding not only its dividend policy, but its approach to capital formation as well.

Although marketing and financial issues dominated strategic discussions within the company, matters of network engineering and operations surely had long-term importance as well. For in the upcoming year, MCI Communications (AT&T Communications' most prominent rival) had announced plans to spend nearly $1 billion on new plant; AT&T, with revenues more than ten times as large, was planning to spend $1.3 billion. Clearly, old ways of maintaining and upgrading long distance facilities would be reconsidered. In the past, AT&T

Communications modernized its oldest plant first, thereby evenly distributing new technologies across its network. In a more competitive world, interexchange carriers were likely to match modernization more closely to marketing considerations. With AT&T's closest rival spending an equivalent amount on plant investment, those decisions would have more bearing on the company's overall strategic capabilities than ever before.

The Future for AT&T: Complex Issues of Competition

These were complex issues that confronted the management of American Telephone & Telegraph. Less than two months into a postdivestiture environment, the company had learned critical and painful lessons about competition, regulation, and politics. It was time to apply those lessons to reshaping an environment in which AT&T Communications could compete effectively.

Exhibit 1 AT&T Financial Profile: 1983 (Old) *vs.* 1984 (New) ($ in millions, except per share amounts)

	OLD AT&T 1983[a]	NEW AT&T 1984[b]
Total operating revenues	$ 67,599	$ 56,544[c]
Total operating expenses	47,160	51,565
Net operating revenues	20,439	4,976
Net income	7,188	2,110
Annual dividend (per share)	$5.40	$1.20
Per share earnings	$7.88	$2.02
Number of shares (weighted average)	894.1	989.1
Total assets	$153,510	$ 34,277
Shareholders' equity	65,147	13,229
Long-term and intermediate debt	45,320	9,469
Current liabilities	40,700	6,764
Employees	992,000	385,000

Source: *AT&T Information Statement and Prospectus*, November 8, 1983.

[a]For the 12-month period ended June 30, 1983 (unaudited).

[b]Revenue, income, employee, and dividend data are estimates for 1984; assets and liabilities are consolidated on a pro forma basis from June 30, 1983, to reflect divestiture.

[c]Note that this financial forecast is for newly restructured entities with new modes of operation and new tariff structures for which comparable historical results do not exist. The extent of the changes required as a result of divestiture do not permit meaningful comparisons between forecasted results and the results for periods prior to 1984. In addition, the 1984 financial forecast reflects significant changes in accounting policies, including the consolidation of Western Electric and the adoption of accounting policies appropriate for nonregulated enterprises. As an example, "total operating revenues" include revenues collected to pay NTS subsidies of local exchange facilities.

Exhibit 2 AT&T Organization Structure as of January 1, 1984

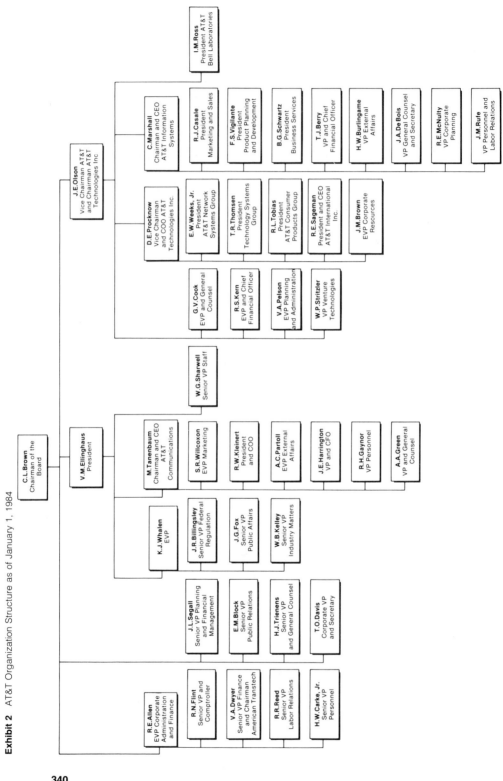

Source: AT&T.

340

Exhibit 3   Basic Telecommunications Services

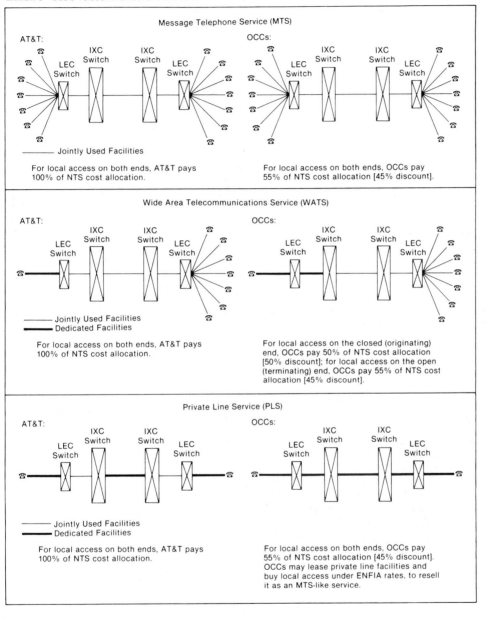

Message Telephone Service (MTS)

AT&T:

OCCs:

———— Jointly Used Facilities

For local access on both ends, AT&T pays 100% of NTS cost allocation.

For local access on both ends, OCCs pay 55% of NTS cost allocation [45% discount].

Wide Area Telecommunications Service (WATS)

AT&T:

OCCs:

———— Jointly Used Facilities
▬▬▬ Dedicated Facilities

For local access on both ends, AT&T pays 100% of NTS cost allocation.

For local access on the closed (originating) end, OCCs pay 50% of NTS cost allocation [50% discount]; for local access on the open (terminating) end, OCCs pay 55% of NTS cost allocation [45% discount].

Private Line Service (PLS)

AT&T:

OCCs:

———— Jointly Used Facilities
▬▬▬ Dedicated Facilities

For local access on both ends, AT&T pays 100% of NTS cost allocation.

For local access on both ends, OCCs pay 55% of NTS cost allocation [45% discount]. OCCs may lease private line facilities and buy local access under ENFIA rates, to resell it as an MTS-like service.

Exhibit 4 AT&T Communications' Financial Scenarios for 1984 ($ in billions)

OCTOBER 1983 (WITH ORIGINAL ACCESS CHARGE PLAN)	MTS AMOUNT	WATS AMOUNT	PLS AMOUNT	TOTAL INTERSTATE
Total revenues	$17.65	$ 6.50	$ 3.43	$27.58
Expenses				
Maintenance	.57	.21	.47	1.25
Depreciation and amortization	.55	.19	.22	.96
Commercial and marketing	1.04	.37	.27	1.68
Traffic and operating rents	1.53	.32	.32	2.17
Relief and pensions	.42	.13	.21	.76
Miscellaneous and other taxes	1.33	.49	.37	2.19
Access charge	9.83	4.20	1.51	15.54
Federal taxes	.98	.23	(.03)	1.18
Total expenses	$16.25	$ 6.14	$ 3.37	$25.76
Net earnings	$ 1.40	$ .36	$ .06	$ 1.82
Average net investment	$ 5.79	$ 1.95	$ 2.48	$10.22
Earnings ratios	24.32%	18.47%	2.75%	17.97%

OCTOBER 1983 (WITH ORIGINAL ACCESS CHARGE PLAN, INCLUDING PROPOSED RATE CHANGES)	MTS AMOUNT	WATS AMOUNT	PLS AMOUNT	TOTAL INTERSTATE
Total revenues	$17.35	$ 6.25	$ 3.84	$27.44
Expenses				
Maintenance	.59	.21	.48	1.28
Depreciation and amortization	.58	.19	.22	.99
Commercial and marketing	1.05	.37	.27	1.69
Traffic and operating rents	1.55	.31	.31	2.17
Relief and pensions	.42	.13	.21	.76
Miscellaneous and other taxes	1.31	.46	.40	2.17
Access charge	10.65	4.19	1.45	16.29
Federal taxes	.43	.14	.18	.75
Total expenses	$16.58	$ 6.00	$ 3.52	$26.10
Net earnings	$ .77	$ .25	$ .32	$ 1.34
Average net investment	$ 6.04	$ 1.94	$ 2.48	$10.46
Earnings ratios	12.72%	12.79%	12.78%	12.75%

Exhibit 4   (continued)

FEBRUARY 1984 (WITH REVISED ACCESS CHARGE PLAN, NO RATE CHANGES)	MTS AMOUNT	WATS AMOUNT	PLS AMOUNT	TOTAL INTERSTATE
Total revenues	$16.52	$ 6.71	$ 3.35	$26.58
Expenses				
Maintenance	.69	.28	.61	1.58
Depreciation and amortization	.49	.19	.19	.87
Commercial and marketing	1.03	.39	.28	1.70
Traffic and operating rents	1.33	.25	.23	1.80
Relief and pensions	.33	.11	.19	.63
Miscellaneous and other taxes	1.16	.48	.38	2.02
Access charge	11.31	4.83	1.28	17.42
Federal taxes	(.01)	.05	.05	.09
Total expenses	$16.33	$ 6.58	$ 3.21	$26.13
Net earnings	$ .18	$ .13	$ .14	$ .45
Average net investment	$ 5.20	$ 1.91	$ 2.03	$ 9.14
Earnings ratios	3.55%	6.77%	6.72%	4.93%

Source: AT&T (FCC Filings, October 3, 1983, & February 27, 1984).

Note: Totals may not add up exactly due to rounding.

Exhibit 5 Survey of Local Telephone Rate Increase Requests

SUMMARY OF LOCAL TELEPHONE RATE INCREASES

State	1982 increase	1983 increase	Stated Rationale							
			Anticipated increases	FCC access charge decision	FCC depreciation decision	Deregulation of CPE	AT&T divestiture	Long distance competition	Loss of long distance subsidy	Normal operating expenses increases
Alabama		[a]$117,000,000	C	C	A	C	C			A
Alaska							C			
Arizona		[b]79,000,000								B
Arkansas		[b]138,000,000		B	B	B		B		
California		[a]1,400,000,000		B	B		B			B
Colorado		[a]38,000,000	C		B		C			
Connecticut	$89,024,000		C				C			A
Delaware		[b]25,900,000		B	B		B			
District of Columbia		[b]82,000,000		B	B		B			
Florida		[a]113,000,000								
Georgia		[b]158,463,000		B	B	B				B
Hawaii	[b]82,368,000			A	A	A				B
Idaho	[b]34,000,000		C	C	C					
Illinois		[a]21,000,000							A	A
Indiana		[b]96,000,000		B	B	B	B			B
Iowa		[b]68,800,000			B	B				
Kansas		[b]213,000,000								
Kentucky			C	C						
Louisiana			C	C	C					
Maine		[a]11,400,000	C				C			
Maryland		[b]218,000,000		B	B	B	B	B		
Massachusetts			C	C						
Michigan	[b]550,000,000		C	A	A	A	B			B

344

State	Amount						
Minnesota	a56,000,000	C					
Mississippi		C		B	B		
Missouri	b254,000,000		B	B	B		B
Montana	b20,710,000		B	B	B		
Nebraska	a8,033,000	C		C	C		B
Nevada	a5,857,000	C		C	C		A
New Hampshire	a8,380,000	C		C			A
New Jersey	b245,000,000	C	A	C			
New Mexico	b86,100,000		B	C			
New York	b86,100,000		B	C	B		B
North Carolina	b143,974,447	C		B	B		
North Dakota		C		B	C		
Ohio	b179,838,000	B			B		
Oklahoma	b301,000,000				B		
Oregon	a36,400,000		B	B	B		B
Pennsylvania	b378,000,000				B		
Rhode Island	b21,139,000				C		
South Carolina		C		C	C		
South Dakota	b21,500,000	B	B	B	B	B	B
Tennessee	b218,000,000	B.	B	B	B		
Texas	b1,000,000,000		B	B	B		
Utah	b43,961,000	C	C	B	C		
Vermont	b16,000,000	C		B	C		
Virginia	a63,826,000	C			C		
Washington	a71,000,000	C	B		B		
West Virginia	a71,000,000	C			C		
Wisconsin	a55,113,000	C					
Wyoming		C	C		C		C

Source: U.S. House of Representatives, Committee on Energy and Commerce.

Note: A—1982 increase, B—1983 increase, C—anticipated increase.

a Granted

b Pending

Exhibit 5 (continued)

BELL OPERATING COMPANIES
SURVEY OF RATE INCREASE REQUESTS AND AWARDS

	Amount Requested ($ in millions)		Amount Awarded ($ in millions)		
	Before	1983	Before	1983	Total
Alabama	—	—	—	—	—
Alaska	—	—	—	—	—
Arizona	—	78.3	—	38.6	38.6
Arkansas	—	—	—	—	—
California	—	—	—	—	—
Colorado	—	—	—	—	—
Connecticut	—	—	—	—	—
Delaware	15.9	—	1.0	6.4	7.4
District of Columbia	—	82.0	—	42.0	42.0
Florida	285.1	—	—	93.6	93.6
Georgia	—	158.5	—	37.7	37.7
Hawaii	—	—	—	—	—
Idaho	28.9	1.0	—	14.1	14.1
Illinois	40.6	247.5	—	112.3	112.3
Indiana	—	—	—	—	—
Iowa	44.7	—	18.7	6.7	25.4
Kansas	63.5	161.8	—	60.7	60.7
Kentucky	—	—	—	—	—
Louisiana	238.6	—	—	0	0
Maine	49.8	—	—	13.1	13.1
Maryland	125.4	139.9	—	131.2	131.2
Massachusetts	—	—	—	—	—
Michigan	451.0	—	—	171.9	171.9

State					
Minnesota	83.6	—	55.0	(2.4)	52.6
Mississippi	—	135.8	—	110.9	110.9
Missouri	—	20.7	—	4.8	4.8
Montana	33.0	—	—	6.2	6.2
Nebraska	3.1	—	—	5.9	5.9
Nevada	—	—	—	—	—
New Hampshire	—	—	—	41.5	41.5
New Jersey	59.3	—	—	63.7	63.7
New Mexico	55.6	86.1	—	229.8	229.8
New York	708.4	—	—	36.7	36.7
North Carolina	—	122.5	—	8.3	8.3
North Dakota	—	19.0	—	—	—
Ohio	—	—	—	88.4	88.4
Oklahoma	—	139.7	—	66.4	66.4
Oregon	—	96.7	—	198.5	198.5
Pennsylvania	—	378.9	—	23.3	23.3
Rhode Island	87.6	37.4	—	(51.8)	20.4
South Carolina	—	—	72.2	(1.6)	(1.6)
South Dakota	—	9.0	—	—	—
Tennessee	—	—	—	(43.6)	221.8
Texas	428.8	—	265.4	18.0	48.7
Utah	72.9	43.2	30.7	8.5	8.5
Vermont	16.5	—	—	8.5	8.5
Virginia	94.1	109.6	66.5	93.5	160.0
Washington	146.7	—	—	56.9	56.9
West Virginia	58.4	—	—	26.9	26.9
Wisconsin	99.0	158.1	—	133.0	133.0
Wyoming	—	16.0	—	1.5	1.5

Source: American Telephone and Telegraph Company.

Note: Data for general rate cases; not included are interim awards for cases still pending at year-end and miscellaneous amounts from appeals. Carrier access charges not included.

Exhibit 6   Financial Effects of Original Access Charge Plan on OCCs and Resellers

	REVENUES (billions)	PRE-TAX INCOME (millions)
Historic View (July 1982–June 1983)		
Actual results (with ENFIA)	$1.93	$327
Revised results (with original access charge plan) Maintain prices	$1.45	($185–278)
Revised results (with original access charge plan) Reduce prices 10%[a]	$1.89	($154–280)
Prospective View (January 1984–December 1984)		
Projected results (with ENFIA)	$4.66	$484
Projected results (with original access charge plan) Maintain prices	$2.56	($506–721)
Projected results (with original access charge plan) Reduce prices 10%[a]	$4.57	($300–595)

[a]Price reduction of 10% would roughly match AT&T's proposed rate reduction.

Source: "Eight Carrier Letter" of OCCs and Resellers, October 4, 1983.

Exhibit 7 Comparative Historical Data: AT&T and MCI

AMERICAN TELEPHONE AND TELEGRAPH COMPANY

Capitalization (12/31/83)	($ millions)	(%)
Current liabilities	$15,868.7	10.6
Deferred credits	26,055.0	17.4
Long & intermediate term debt	44,810.3	30.0
Common equity	60,762.4	40.6
Preferred equity	1,522.5	1.4
	$149,529.8[a]	100.0

[a]Reflects $510.9 million ownership interest of others in consolidated subsidiaries.

Financial Statistics

Year 12/31	Gross Revenue	Net Income	Number of Shares	Market Value per Share	Book Value per Share	Earns. per Share	Div. per Share	Div. Pay %	Avg. P/E
1974	$26,174	$3,169	559.76	$53.000–39.625	$61.21	$5.27	$3.16	60	8.8
1975	28,957	3,147	582.02	52.000–44.750	64.45	5.13	3.40	66	9.4
1976	32,816	3,829	607.41	64.625–50.875	69.80	6.05	3.70	61	8.5
1977	36,495	4,543	657.63	65.375–58.375	75.32	6.97	4.10	58	8.9
1978	40,993	5,272	669.55	64.750–56.875	79.92	7.74	4.50	58	7.9
1979	45,408	5,674	710.37	64.750–51.625	85.39	8.04	4.80	51	7.2
1980	50,791	6,079	754.83	56.500–45.000	65.74	8.19	5.00	61	6.2
1981	58,214	6,888	815.11	61.500–47.500	67.52	8.55	5.30	62	6.4
1982	65,093	6,992	896.43	64.625–49.875	69.07	8.06	5.40	67	7.1
1983	69,403	5,747	965.73	70.250–59.000	62.92	8.40	5.40	69	10.8

Source: Moody's Handbook of Common Stocks, Spring 1984 edition. Reprinted with permission.

Exhibit 7 (continued)

MCI COMMUNICATIONS CORPORATION

Capitalization (3/31/83)	($ millions)	(%)
Current liabilities	$480.7	13.7
Deferred credits	169.4	4.8
Long & intermediate term debt	1,721.5	49.1
Common equity	1,135.7	32.4
Preferred equity	0	0
	$3,507.4	100.0

Financial Statistics

Year 3/31	Gross Revenue	Net Income	Number of Shares	Market Value per Share	Book Value Share	Earns. per Share	Div. per Share	% Div. Pay	Avg. P/E
1977	$ 62.8	$ 1.7	80.53	$ .875– .375	$ .51	$.03	$0.00	0	20.8
1978	74.0	2.5	81.17	.875– .125	.42	.03	0.00	0	16.7
1979	95.2	3.5	84.06	1.375– .625	.37	.03	0.00	0	33.3
1980	144.3	7.1	128.98	2.125–1.000	.54	.01	0.00	0	NM
1981	234.2	18.7	151.27	3.625–1.125	.98	.05	0.00	0	47.5
1982	506.4	86.5	192.24	9.125–2.750	1.26	.46	0.00	0	12.9
1983	1,073.2	170.8	234.14	22.875–6.500	3.27	.85	0.00	0	17.3

Source: Moody's Handbook of OTC Stocks, Spring 1984 edition. Reprinted with permission.

Note: Revenue, income, and share amounts in millions (except per share amounts).

Exhibit 8 Market Share Data for AT&T Communications

BUSINESS MARKET	Revenue Distribution (interstate MTS)[a]		Competitors' Penetration of Market Segments[b] % Business Establishments Using a Competitor's Long Distance Service	
Expenditures on Interstate Long Distance ($ per month)[c]	% Customers	% Revenue	Nationwide	Where at Least One Competitor Available
$ 0–10	69	2	3	5
10–50	17	8		
50–100	6	8	32[e]	46[e]
50–150	d	d		
100–500	6	25		
150–500	d	d		
500–1000	1	14	41	56
1000–4000	0.6	24		
$4000 and over	0.1	20		

RESIDENTIAL MARKET	Revenue Distribution (interstate MTS)[f]		Competitor's Penetration of Market Segments[b] % Subscriber Households Using a Competitor's Long Distance Service	
Expenditures on Interstate Long Distance ($ per month)[c]	% Households	% Revenue	Nationwide	Where at Least One Competitor Available
$ 0–10	74	20	2	3
10–25	17	29		
25–50	7	26	13[e]	19[e]
50–100	2	16		
$100 and over	1	9	25	34

Source: American Telephone and Telegraph Company (FCC Filing, April 2, 1984).

Note: Nationwide data excludes Alaska and Hawaii.

[a]Data derived from customer billing records as of June 1982.

[b]Data obtained through national surveys conducted by an independent market research organization in the fall of 1983.

[c]Expenditures on interstate long distance include AT&T, MTS, and outward WATS and competitors' equivalent services.

[d]Includes some portions from the $100–500 interstate expenditure category.

[e]Average competitors' penetration: for business market, every category above $50; for residence market, every category above $25.

[f]Data derived from market analysis of revenue and customers as of October 1983.

Exhibit 9 Equal Access Schedule, 1984

The following schedule shows the date and place where equal access will first become available. As of these dates, in these places, subscribers may designate the interexchange carrier that will carry all of their long-distance calls; subscribers will be able to reach any interexchange carrier by dialing just four digits. As equal access becomes available, each interexchange carrier will pay equal costs for access to local exchanges. With the phased implementation of the full schedule (July 1984–September 1986), AT&T and its competitors will compete for subscribers on an equal basis.

DATE	PLACE OF FIRST EQUAL ACCESS (CITY—END OFFICE)
July 15, 1984	West Virginia (Charleston, S. Charleston)
August 19, 1984	Minnesota (Minneapolis—Orchard)
August 24, 1984	California (San Francisco—Alameda) Nevada (Virginia City, Silver Spring, Carson City, Butte, Churchill)
August 25, 1984	Colorado (Denver)
August 27, 1984	Georgia (Atlanta—Toco Hills, Courtland St) Alabama (Mobile—Springhill)
August 30, 1984	Indiana (Indianapolis—Trinity, Melrose)
August 31, 1984	Texas (Houston—W. Ellington) Illinois (Chicago—Wabash, Dearborn)
September 1, 1984	Massachusetts (Eastern—Back Bay) New York (Metro New York City) New Jersey (Hackensack, Clifton) Pennsylvania (Philadelphia—Pennypacker, Locust) Delaware (Wilmington) Maryland (Baltimore—Liberty, Columbia) Washington, D.C. (Metro) Virginia (Norfolk) Ohio (Cleveland, Columbus) Michigan (Detroit) Wisconsin (Stevens Point, Milwaukee) Oregon (Portland)
October 1, 1984	Washington (Seattle)
October 22, 1984	Florida (Jacksonville)
October 28, 1984	Kentucky (Louisville—New Albany)
November 17, 1984	Utah (Salt Lake City)
November 26, 1984	Louisiana (Shreveport—Monroe) Tennessee (Memphis)
December 1, 1984	Rhode Island
December 16, 1984	Idaho (Roberts, Moore, Howe, McKay, Island Park, Arco, Idaho Falls)
December 29, 1984	Idaho (Boise)

Source: Federal Communications Commission.

1. Federal Communications Commission, Common Carrier Docket No. 78-72, Emergency Petition for Reconsideration, filed by American Telephone & Telegraph Company in the matter of MTS and WATS Market Structure, February 27, 1984.
2. Federal Communications Commission, Common Carrier Docket No. 78-82, "Eight Carrier Letter to Honorable Mark S. Fowler," October 4, 1983.
3. Federal Communications Commission, Common Carrier Docket No. 78-72, Third Report and Order, December 22, 1982.
4. Federal Communications Commission, Common Carrier Docket No. 78-82, Emergency Petition for Reconsideration by AT&T.
5. U.S. Congress, Congressional Budget Office, *Local Telephone Rates: Issues and Alternatives*, 98th Congress, 2nd sess., January 1984, p. 7.
6. Ibid.
7. Leland L. Johnson, "Toward Competition in Phone Service: Why Local Rates are Rising," *Regulation*, July/August 1983, p. 35.
8. The Communications Act of 1934, 47 U.S.C.
9. John McGarrity, "Implementing Access Charges: Stakeholders and Options," Program on Information Resources Policy, Center for Information Policy Research (Cambridge: Harvard University, 1983).
10. U.S. Congress, Congressional Budget Office, *Local Telephone Rates*, p. A-2.
11. Federal Communications Commission, Common Carrier Docket No. 78-72, Third Report and Order.
12. Federal Communications Commission, Common Carrier Docket No. 80-286, Comments of the National Telecommunications and Information Administration, August 17, 1981.
13. Federal Communication Commission, Common Carrier Docket No. 78-72, Memorandum Opinion and Order, February 15, 1984.
14. U.S. Congress, Senate Committee on Commerce, Science, and Transportation, and House Committee on Energy and Commerce, Joint Hearings, *Relating to the Preservation of Universal Telephone Service*, 98th Cong., 1st sess., May 1983, p. 184.
15. Ibid.
16. Ibid., 213.
17. Ibid.
18. Ibid., 286.
19. Federal Communications Commission, Common Carrier Docket No. 78-72, comments filed by Wyoming Telephone Company, December 22, 1983.
20. Richard Stergel, "Evangelist of the Marketplace," *Time*, November 21, 1983, p. 58.
21. "A Quantum Leap for Communications," *Business Week*, November 28, 1983, p. 96.
22. "Bell Breakup Will Be Painful Before Benefits Start to Appear," *Washington Post*, December 11, 1983, p. A14.
23. Mark S. Fowler, "Address Before the Communications Network Conference," January 31, 1983.
24. U.S. Congress, *Relating to the Preservation of Universal Telephone Service*, p. 123.
25. U.S. Court of Appeals, District of Columbia Circuit, National Association of Regulatory Utility Commissioners, *Brief of Petitioner on Review of Orders of the Federal Communications Commission*, October 12, 1983.
26. Federal Communications Commission, Common Carrier Docket No. 78-72, Eight Carrier Letter, October, 1983.
27. U.S. Congress, *Relating to the Preservation of Universal Telephone Service*, p. 95.
28. Charles Brown, chairman of AT&T, Letter to U.S. Representatives and Senators, October 9, 1983.
29. International Communications Association, "Universal Service Legislative Concerns," December 6, 1983.
30. Federal Communications Commission, Common Carrier Docket No. 78–72, James R. Billingsley to Mark S. Fowler, November 2, 1983.
31. Wharton Econometric Forecasting Associates, "Impact of the FCC Access Charge Plan on the U.S. Economy," November 1983.
32. Federal Communications Commission, Common Carrier Docket No. 78-72, Third Report and Order.
33. AT&T pamphlet, "At Stake for the Nation," 1983.

General Telephone of the Northwest

In April 1984 Kent Foster took stock of his strategic plans in light of developments over the past year—his first as president of General Telephone of the Northwest (GTNW):

> Our strategy calls for us to build on what we know best—our core business. And at the heart of our business is the local communications network. At General Telephone, however, we do not think of this as just plain old telephone service. We are in the business of moving information anywhere and in any form.

This philosophy would set the tone for change at GTNW. The concept of the telephone utility had passed; GTNW was to become a competitor contesting every major segment of the telecommunications market.

During the past few years, the telecommunications industry had been buffeted by changes in technology, regulation, and competition. For traditional players such as General Telephone, it was a tumultuous period. Deregulation and divestiture had transformed a relatively stable environment into one of high risk and uncertainty. Confusion prevailed in both the marketplace and the regulatory arena. Foster was nonetheless determined to guide his company into a leadership position in the industry. Yet the company faced challenges both external and internal to its operation.

GTNW's monopoly franchise had begun to erode as specialized telecommunications companies offered customers sophisticated systems at favorable prices. Large customers could erect their own networks, bypassing the telephone company altogether. A new rate structure was needed; cost causation—not public policy rationales—would have to dictate prices. But such dramatic change was certain to draw public protest and intense political scrutiny.

Adapting to competiton would also require some changes in the management and operation of the company. GTNW would need a marketing focus to take advantage of competitive opportunities. Streamlining organizational structure, increasing productivity, and focusing on profitability would be vital. None of these changes, however, would be achieved quickly or easily; some were certain to be painful for employees distinguished for their service and dedication to GTNW. Time was one thing that Kent Foster had little to spare. At best,

Research Associate Dekkers L. Davidson prepared this case under the supervision of Professor Richard H.K. Vietor as the basis for class discussion, rather than to illustrate either the effective or ineffective handling of an administrative situation.

thought Foster, GTNW had a one-year "window of opportunity" before competitors would start moving into the Northwest.

PROFILE: GENERAL TELEPHONE OF THE NORTHWEST

General Telephone Company of the Northwest (GTNW), headquartered in Everett, Washington, was a subsidiary of GTE Corporation. GTNW provided local telephone service and equipment to parts of five northwestern states; the company was regulated by different public utility commissions (PUCs) in each state jurisdiction. (See Figure 1 for map of GTNW territory.) The largest independent telephone company in the region (and second overall to Pacific Northwest Bell and Mountain Bell in each of their respective territories), GTNW served some 671,000 subscribers. In 1983 the company earned $76 million on revenues of $541 million. Its operations were geographically divided as follows: Washington (57%), Oregon (29%), Idaho (13%), Montana (1%), and California (1%). GTNW employed approximately 6,100 people. (See Exhibit 1 for GTNW financial and operating data.)

The company was organized from an association of small, rural telephone companies, growing through merger and acquisition until its operation encompassed five states. GTE first acquired an interest in the association in 1931; it grew by adding other independent exchanges to its base of operations. Since the Bell System telephone companies had earlier acquired the territories encompassing the major urban areas in the region, General Telephone was left to manage the telephone systems in outlying suburbs and rural areas of the Northwest.

The Northwest Company, as it was affectionately called, was among the smaller telephone companies, wholly owned by GTE (formerly General Telephone and Electronics) Corporation, a $13 billion conglomerate based in Stamford, Connecticut. Taken together, GTE's seven domestic telcos represented the nation's second largest local telephone system, with assets of $24 billion. (See Exhibit 2 for financial data on the parent corporation, GTE.)

Although incorporated into GTE's Telephone Operating Group, GTNW conducted its business with relative autonomy. Officers were appointed by the parent, but managed GTNW as an independent business; the company engaged its own outside directors, most of whom were prominent leaders in the Northwest. While corporate treasury provided equity infusions, the company was responsible for raising its own capital. GTNW generally purchased switching and transmission equipment from GTE's Communications Systems; it also marketed GTE-made customer premises equipment. Corporate staff provided strategic planning assistance and established annual financial targets for each of its telephone companies. It was normal corporate practice to rotate personnel between assignments at different telcos and to move people between field management and corporate staff.

The Telephone Operating Group accounted for the lion's share of cor-

Figure 1   GTNW Operating Territory

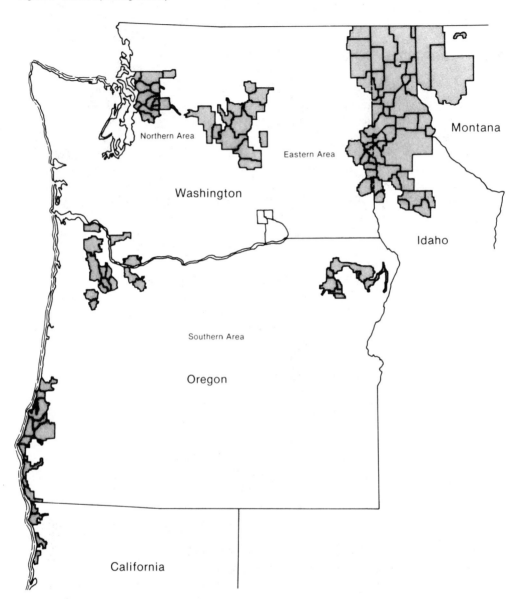

porate revenues and earnings; GTE's track record outside the regulated telephone business was mediocre. In recent years, however, GTE had concentrated resources on developing a wider stake in telecommunications. The 1983 acquisition of Sprint—the nation's third-largest long-distance system—underscored GTE's aspiration to play a major role in every aspect of the evolving telecommunications markets.

By 1983 GTE's portfolio of telecommunications operations was extensive and included local exchange operations, Yellow Pages advertisements, cellular radio, communications equipment and systems, residential and business telephone products, satellite earth stations, a long distance telephone system, and a nationwide data network with high-speed packet switching. (See Exhibit 3 for a profile of GTE's various businesses.)

GTE could not, however, jointly market its telephone equipment with its local exhange and long-distance services. The FCC's rules in *Computer Inquiry II* (1980) required both GTE and AT&T to sell communications equipment at arm's length from regulated operations. In order to acquire Sprint, GTE was bound by an antitrust edict not to jointly offer local and long-distance telephone services. Despite these restrictions, most industry experts believed GTE was well-positioned in the rapidly growing communications markets of the future. It had already beaten AT&T into some markets because the Gulliver-like AT&T had been tied up with Lilliputian-style government controls.

The breakup of the Bell System had signficantly altered GTE's competitive outlook. GTE was now the largest integrated telecommunications company in the United States; it was engaged in basic research, equipment manufacturing, and the provision of telephone service. With divestiture, however, AT&T would be able to move aggressively into GTE exchange areas and construct alternative local distribution systems, such as mobile telephone service. It could also sell its Western Electric equipment and data transmission services directly against GTE.

AT&T, of course, was only one among a host of strong competitors: Rolm, Northern Telecom, Mitel, and NEC were vying for a piece of the lucrative equipment market. MCI Communications and Satellite Business Systems (SBS), along with many long-distance resellers, were vigorously contesting the interexchange business. In addition, IBM, Xerox, RCA, and Wang loomed large on the competitive horizon; each was readying itself to compete in the burgeoning "compunications" industry created by the convergence of computer and telecommunications technology.

REGULATORY TRANSITION: THE PASSING
OF THE TELEPHONE UTILITY

Technology, regulation, and competition had dramatically reshaped the structure of the telecommunications industry. Competition, Foster felt, would inevitably extend to most major markets. Although he welcomed the opportunity to compete in this new telecommunications era, Foster was concerned about GTNW's freedom to participate in these emerging markets. Whether the industry or its state regulators liked it, in his words the "marketplace was voting"—displacing regulation's role in defining optimal market structures. Foster was concerned that "while regulators cannot control the market, they can control the telephone company's participation in it."

Regulatory flexibility would be difficult for General Telephone to attain, and for the state commissions to provide. Under regulation, GTNW had relied on rate relief to maintain healthy financial returns. With competition, however, rate hikes would be counterproductive if rivals offered lower-priced equivalent services. In a free market, customers would determine financial returns, prices, and costs. Foster knew his company could not ask for regulatory change to be delivered on a silver platter. It was critical that the industry not traumatize the transition process.

Foster's foremost concern involved universal telephone service: the concept that telephone service should be available to all at "just and reasonable rates." Although publicly reaffirming his commitment to universal telephone service—something that was cherished in the rural Northwest—he certainly realized that some kind of accommodation to competition would be necessary.

For regulators, deregulation was a complex issue which involved surrendering control of the industry. It also meant a very large investment of resources for state commissions; nearly every PUC had been deluged with requests for rate hikes, questions on depreciation allowances, petitions for competitive entry, and a myriad of other complex problems. With competitors—particularly smaller businesses—seeking to enter particular markets, there surely would be pressure applied to handicap the larger monopoly-like telephone companies.

Four issues were of paramount importance: usage-sensitive pricing, access charges, pricing flexibility, and business with affiliates.

Usage-Sensitive Pricing

For years, GTNW—like most other telcos—had followed a practice of billing its subscribers on a flat rate basis for local calls made in and around their exchange area. In Washington, subscribers who owned their own telephone paid a monthly charge of $13.96 for rotary-dial service, or $14.71 for push-button service. That monthly fee included connection to GTNW's central office and unlimited local calling (generally within a fifteen-mile radius). Consequently, subscribers paid the same amount to GTNW, regardless of the number of local calls that they made during the month. In contrast, GTNW billed state toll calls (made beyond the radius of the caller's local calling area) on a time-of-day, length-of-call, and mileage basis.

Flat rate service was universally popular with telephone subscribers: they generally paid a fixed amount to call freely, without concern for a minute meter.

It was estimated that almost 90% of all subscribers nationwide used the flat rate option. This practice also allowed relatively easy policing of the affordability of telephone service and was thus favored by many state regulators and politicians.

However, the widespread acceptance of the flat rate bill was somewhat startling in the face of evidence suggesting that many subscribers might benefit from measured pricing of local service. Calling patterns were skewed: approximately 7% made no local calls in a given month while just 17% accounted for more than half of all local calls made in that period. Studies in certain states had shown that as many as 65% of subscribers overpaid for local service under a flat rate. (A local phone bill had two parts: a basic *service charge*, which included connection or access to and usage of the local exchange, and a state *toll charge*, which included intra-LATA—intrastate calls made beyond the immediate local exchange area. Some local telephone companies also billed for interstate long-distance calls; this was a service performed for long-distance carriers under contract.)

The concept of *Usage-Sensitive Pricing* (USP), or local measured service, was not new. USP was a pricing mechanism in which customer charges were based on a number of variables related to the cost of providing service. Under USP, the customer could maintain access to the telephone network for a lower price (estimated to be 50%–60% less) than under flat rate pricing. In addition, USP's rate elements were designed to reflect the amount of usage generated by each customer, thereby permitting that customer the opportunity to control his or her telephone bill. Usage elements included number of calls, duration of the call, distance or mileage of the call, and time of day (day, evening, night).

Some forms of USP were used in most states; USP had been under trial ever since 1975 and was usually available at the option of the customer. But despite efforts to market USP, consumer acceptance had been nominal at best. USP was viewed wearily by some subscribers who felt it was just another way for the telephone company to raise its rates.

Kent Foster had been surprised to find such sweeping resistance to an idea that allowed customers to control their own proposition: light users would no longer subsidize heavy callers. Opposition from a chimney-sweep business in Oregon was illustrative of resistance to USP. This small business employed marketers who spent their entire day prospecting customers by telephone; on average, they generated almost 2,000 calls per month on each of the company's three lines. GTNW's receipts per line: a scant $12.

GTNW knew it faced an uphill task. A number of objections would have to be addressed before USP could be successfully introduced. In public hearings, a parade of witnessess including representatives from elderly groups, volunteer organizations, small businesses, and consumer associations had voiced concerns about this pricing proposal. In their view, USP would:

- Confuse consumers already bewildered by deregulation and divestiture;
- Jeopardize universal telephone service: some would drop service;
- Hamper the work of volunteer and charitable organizations;

- Isolate the elderly and handicapped who rely on telephone service for security and social contact;
- Burden the elderly, poor, and unemployed, living on a fixed income;
- Hurt small businesses that rely heavily on local service to reach customers;
- Increase rates, to cover expensive measurement devices;
- Invade subscribers' privacy with call measurement;
- Destabilize local rate base.

In light of this position, GTNW needed to carefully consider its introduction to USP. Such a pricing scheme, in which the "cost causer pays" for services consumed, was essential to the company's long-term strategy. Without USP or some similar arrangement, GTNW's plans to promote network usage and to market new services would be fruitless. And if the company was left to carry plain "vanilla-type" service, its rates would inevitably rise as competitors skimmed off profitable services. Three options for implementing USP were under review:

OPTION	BUSINESS CUSTOMERS	RESIDENCE CUSTOMERS
A	Non-optional USP	Non-optional
B	Non-optional USP	Optional USP
C	Optional USP	Optional USP

Foster knew that GTNW would have to proceed cautiously. The company had to determine how, when, and where to first propose and then implement USP. Ultimately, of course, USP would have to prove itself in the marketplace.

Access Charges

GTNW's single greatest asset—and perhaps the biggest advantage for all local telephone companies—was its local distribution system: the subscriber lines that extended from the central office to each telephone user. Paying for those lines, however, had become a major political issue, just as the industry was trying to deal with the fallout from deregulation and divestiture.

When a customer made a call of any kind—local, state toll, or interstate toll—it normally originated with the use of a home telephone or, in a business location, with a key telephone that might be connected through *private branch exchange* (PBX) switching equipment. The call would traverse the inside wiring and then the local loop between the customer's premise and the switch at the telephone company's local exchange office. The telephone company ordinarily owned these facilities and used them to provide franchised service in their territory.

A large portion of these local exchange costs were fixed, or *nontraffic sensitive* (NTS)—not varying with the amount or type of calls handled. Once a call reached the central office, the costs of switching and sending the call along the network were considered *traffic sensitive*, since the volume of traffic would, in the long term, influence the level of investment plant and hence, costs.

Through court order and federal regulation, the costs of this nontraffic sensitive plant was divided between the interstate and state jurisdictions. It had been effectively argued that since toll callers needed the subscriber line to complete their calls, they should make some contribution to paying for it. Consequently, interstate toll calls were deliberately overpriced (far above any proportion of subscriber line usage), serving to subsidize the subscriber line charge. State commissions encouraged a similar overpricing of intrastate toll calls. These combined subsidies delivered the low line charges thought necessary to guarantee the availability of "just and reasonable rates."

As a result of these practices, there was a sizable gap between what local subscribers paid for access and what it cost companies to provide it. For example, the Bell System's average subscriber line cost was about $26 per month (GTNW's was $20). Residential rates, however, averaged less than $10 a month. Of the $16 difference, about $7 came from intrastate toll service and $9 from interstate services.

With divestiture and the split in AT&T's local and long distance operations, the Federal Communications Commission (FCC) had proposed to replace this *variable* (based on minutes of *use*) interstate subsidy with a *flat* (based on number of subscriber *lines*) interstate access charge. The fixed fee for local access would thereby reflect the manner in which the cost was incurred. The FCC reasoned that a new access charge scheme was necessary to (a) safeguard universal service, (b) promote economic efficiency, (c) prevent bypass, and (d) avoid discrimination between communications services.

Proposals for a state access charge had been simultaneously considered by many PUCs; with one exception, each was flatly denied. That lone exception was allowed by the Washington Utilities and Transportation Commission (WUTC). WUTC implemented a customer access line charge of 99¢ for four months *and* reduced intrastate, intra-LATA[1] toll by 4.5%. In April 1984, WUTC increased intrastate toll 4.7%, and increased GTNW's basic rates 25¢ per line per month, replacing the CALC.

On the eve of divestiture—and the implementation of access charges—the FCC was forced to compromise and delay its plan; the WUTC quickly canceled its trial. Despite the active support of the *traditional* telephone industry, access charges had been derailed. A coalition of stakeholders had mobilized to thwart the FCC's plan: small long distance companies such as MCI and GTE Sprint, Congress, consumerists, and state PUCs all argued about the deleterious effect on telephone subscribers. They complained that universal service might be jeopardized; they contended that bypass fears were unfounded.

Although the principle behind access charges—that the "cost causer pays"—had survived, the future of the plan remained uncertain. Meanwhile, the telephone industry (GTNW included) grew more wary of the threat of bypass. If the makers of public policy did not act quickly, large users would soon begin to erect their own communications sytems.

Pricing Flexibility

Because GTNW was treated as a public utility, its prices had to meet standards set by law. Telephone rates were not typically based on the route-by-route cost to provide that service. Yet, both nationally and within the state, competitors could enter the long-distance business, offering service on specific routes. Not surprisingly, entry occurred where the cost to provide service was lower than the rates charged by the telephone company. More often than not, those markets were *calling corridors* connecting densely populated metropolitan areas which carried a large volume of voice and data communications. Communications-equipment manufacturers were similarly targeting the large, relatively easy-to-serve customer in their marketing programs.

If GTNW chose to meet the competitive challenge in a timely fashion, it would face stiff legal obstacles to the type of direct, effective response which unregulated competiton demanded. For example, in Washington, every rate or charge of the regulated company had to be on file in the tariff. Changes in the rates charged by the telephone company for competitive services could not, without special approval, take effect for thirty days. And if a rate change was filed, the WUTC had the power to suspend the change for a period of ten months after it would have otherwise gone into effect. Should a rate change involve an increase, GTNW would have to prove to the commission that the increase was just and reasonable.

When competitors diverted customers from the regulated services, the possibility existed that GTNW investment would be idled. Costs still remained which had to be recovered by those still using regulated services. Upward pressure on rates was a likely consequence.

Kent Foster knew that regulatory lag could cripple some of the company's future ventures. Regulators had to determine which markets were competitive and and then allow telcos immediate flexibility in matching rivals' inroads. Tariff requirements had to be modified. Acting in concert with other telephone companies, GTNW had tried to win pricing flexibility before the Washington state legislature. That legislation remained pending.

Affiliated Businesses

Another type of restriction which affected telephone companies was the barrier against entering into contracts or arrangements with affiliated companies without regulatory approval. Payments made under such contracts, even if approved by regulators, could still be ignored in rate hearings if proof of the cost to the affiliate was not satisfactory. With vendor relations open to public scrutiny, both the telco and the vendor could be disadvantaged. In one case, a supplier had declined to bid a GTE contract, citing disclosure requirements of telephone regulation.

According to Kent Foster, decisions about where telcos buy their support services and equipment would reflect the emerging competition in telecommunications markets. Concerns about cross-subsidization between regulated and unregulated business could be dealt with on a case-by-case basis. The existing blanket of regulation should not be sustained in the current environment. But, despite this logic, legislation to relax restrictions on business affiliates had thus far stalled.

THE REGULATOR'S VIEW

GTNW's service area sprawled over five states; this called for compliance to the rules and regulations of five different state public utility commissions. Although this complicated implementation of a uniform business strategy, some benefits might be derived. Since each commission had its own unique views about the industry, and since each was organized differently, there was an opportunity to try new regulatory schemes in one area before making modifications or trying to win wide approval. (Exhibit 4 describes the five different state public utility commissions).

Not surprisingly, reaction to cost-causation rate proposals varied between jurisdictions, and views of the ongoing telephone deregulation were also mixed. The contrast in outlook between the commissions of Idaho and Washington was particularly noteworthy.

Idaho Public Utilities Commissioner Perry Swisher, a former journalist, was upset by many of the recent changes in the industry. He spoke about his frustrations with the process:

> Many thought deregulation would be a simple matter of combining the free market with regulated activity; it just isn't that easy! PUCs are being put in a reactive mode; the FCC is making major decisions without consulting the people who have to live with their schemes. MCI started it: they found out how to "crack the safe" [open up competition] in the great American tradition of making money.
>
> And divestiture is just making life even more difficult for the people of Idaho. It's just another example of how the East—especially the academic community between Boston and Washington—tries to dictate public policy. They have no idea how government policy in telephones, highways, railroads, and airlines helped to integrate this region into the rest of the country. Many of these policies are being scrapped in the name of "economic efficiency." Telecommunications is a big mess right now. And it must be just awful for General Telephone.

Dick High, a commissioner with previous experience in the Idaho legislature, recognized that it was no longer possible for regulation to sustain the local telephone monopoly. Even though legislation might be passed that could tax bypass systems, it would do little to stop competition in other areas. He felt that consumers had been dealt too many changes, too quickly, and that things had to slow down:

> In our hearings, we hear it everyplace: "I can't stand anymore [rate changes]." Over the past ten years, our people have had to deal with the quadrupling of oil prices, big jumps in electricity, gas decontrol, and now telephone deregulation.

Nobody wants us to tamper with universal service and I don't blame them a bit. We do, however, recognize the plight of telephone companies; something needs to be worked out on a commonsense basis.

Conley Ward, PUC president and telephone expert, was generally skeptical of the industry's cost-causer-pays arguments. If USP was the consumer bargain that so many claimed it was, why had acceptance been so poor? And with the added cost of call measurement and discrete call billing, Ward questioned the degree of overall societal gain:

> You can just wear yourself out chasing cost causation. I don't really think it is always efficient. For example, on our drive back from a public hearing in Pocatello, we stopped briefly at a state park along the Snake River; a teenage guard stopped us at the gate to collect a $1 admission fee. Now that's not too much to pay, but I really doubt that he collects enough during the week to even pay his minimum wage.
>   Usage pricing might not be a bargain at all. It could cause enormous social dislocation that could be very harmful. The telephone is the lifeline for elderly and disabled people; some need to make long telephone calls as a social outlet. We can't allow that to be changed overnight.

The PUC agreed that targeted subsidies to the needy was not an appropriate answer. Lifeline Service—a budget option—would only add to *welfare Americana*, thereby extending government bureaucracy.

The Washington Utilities and Transportation Commission held a decidedly different view of things. Commissioner Mary Hall (on leave from the University of Washington) believed deregulation and divestiture had been necessary for both the industry—AT&T in particular—and consumers. Hall had drawn controversy as the prime mover behind WUTC's state access charges; she believed it was appropriate public policy, in light of prevailing technology and societal goals. According to Hall, state PUCs needed to become more assertive in planning the telecommunications transition: "We've been conditioned to react." A view of the telephones was needed, in her opinion.

> You can begin with the definition of *universal service*. The Communications Act of 1934 talks about "availability" and "reasonable prices." That has largely been accomplished. Now we have to concentrate on distributing newer, more modern technologies. A new definition of universal service is the order of the day: it should point towards universal use of "intelligent telephones—the personal computer" at home and work. After all, that's where technology is moving.
>   As state regulators, we must help institutions adapt to technological change. There is a general resistance to technology, perhaps because it entails changes in our comfortable ways of doing things. It's unfortunate, because we could stand to benefit from such things as electronic informations sytems, self-help programs in education, and health care. It's doubly tough because institutions adapt to change even slower than individuals.
>   The telephone companies are struggling with technological adaptation at this moment. They must quickly adjust to their cusomers' more sophisticated communications needs. And they must diversify into enhanced system offerings;

they have a solid base to leverage into businesses such as alarm systems, remote medical monitoring, electronic Yellow Pages, and so on.

Cost causation will eventually guide pricing policies. Access charges were an attempt to restructure prices. Usage-sensitive pricing can work, but everyone involved must be keenly aware of the human factor. I am an ardent supporter of economic theory; but, you can never forget that people live with decisions grounded in such theory. It must be applied properly, reasonably, and fairly.

ADAPTATION IN PROGRESS: PREPARING FOR COMPETITIVE REALITIES

As Kent Foster looked back on his first year as president of GTNW, he was awed by "the quantum waves of change" that had so drastically altered the fundamentals of the business. The past twelve months had delivered dizzying changes for the Northwest Company, GTE, and the industry. These included (1) his own appointment—an outsider—as GTNW president, (2) marketing of deregulated telephone equipment, (3) a hot political debate over access charges, (4) changes in depreciation schedules, (5) acquisition of the long distance company Sprint, (6) the sudden resignation of GTE's president, Thomas Vanderslice (a former General Electric executive, widely regarded as an agressive manager who was a driving force behind the Sprint acquisition), and (7) the breakup of the Bell Sytem.

Foster had been elevated to his post on April 1, 1983. (He later recalled it was April Fool's Day, which prepared him to expect the unexpected as the transition in telecommunications confounded interested participants and outside experts alike. He never had to worry about encountering a dull moment.) With thirteen years at GTE, Foster came to the Northwest Company with extensive field experience in engineering and operations. Most recently, he had held high-level corporate staff assignments involving network planning, marketing, and business planning. Foster began his career at GTE with an undergraduate degree in electrical engineering and a master's degree in management; he had progressed rapidly through GTE's management ranks.

According to long-time veterans of the GTNW, Foster's appointment was "symbolic of the overall changes taking place in the industry." He had achieved the presidency of the $500 million telephone operation at the very early age of thirty-eight. One vice president described Foster as "aggressive, articulate, and sincere" in pursuing his goals: "He came on like a winner reassuring employees that they would have a chance to participate in the future of the company." Although Foster was not viewed as a typical "telephone person," he had earned the respect of many service-minded GTNW employees when he reaffirmed his commitment to the basic business. Said Foster, "Despite all the razzle-dazzle technology, our basic priority is right where it has always been: local service will continue to be the bedrock of our business."

At the invitation of the outgoing GTNW president, who was retiring after many long years of service at GTNW, Foster moved to the Northwest three months prior to his formal appointment as president, and spent that time trying to understand the characteristics of the region. He described his early findings and outlook:

> The flow in this country has always been towards the West. It has always been the area of potential in this country, the place where the future unfolds. . . the place where the best expression of the American experiment will be worked out.
>
> Being a newcomer to this part of the country isn't necessarily a disadvantage. I'll be able to see this region with a fresh perspective.
>
> To me, the people and their attitudes are just as impressive as the [large] territory. . . . It seems to me there's a mindset here that says, "We're going to do some things right that other parts of the country did wrong."
>
> There's another Northwest characteristic that's pretty hard to miss. There is an underlying essence of optimism in the people here; regardless of whatever troubles may exist, the feeling seems to be: "We can handle it."

Even so, Foster knew that many people at GTNW still felt uneasy about the shift from regulation toward competition. And some perhaps mistakenly believed that he had been sent by corporate to give GTNW a *fitness test* which meant more layoffs. It would not be easy to assuage those concerns.

A prolonged recession had wracked the Northwest; the effect on GTNW had been severe. In five years the company had reduced its work force by 27%—a loss of some 2,200 jobs. Top managment could not expect talk of streamlining ranks to be quickly embraced. Recent decisions to centralize service functions (billing, customer inquiry, and telephone stores) had done little to quell job security fears. GTNW employees were trained to be service-oriented and were proud of their close links to the communities in which they operated. Customers, particularly those located in outlying rural areas, saw GTNW as their tie to the outside world; it was *their* local telephone company.

The economic fortunes of the Northwest had historically been closely tied to the success of a few key industries—aerospace, aluminum, fishing, and forestry. The emergence of a high tech base of electronics firms in and around Seattle, Washington, and Portland, Oregon, had some effect in moderating the "boom or bust" cycles to which the region was accustomed. Much of the expansion was occurring in the company's territory, as suburbs were favored areas for building new offices, factories, and research centers. Prior to the economic downturn, the Northwest's population had expanded at a brisk pace, business had been robust, and GTNW's growth (in terms of number of customer lines) exceeded that of all other domestic telephone companies. The subsequent turn of events was, therefore, a bitter pill for the region in general and GTNW in particular. As international trade with Asia had grown, the Northwest had gained greater prominence as the "Gateway to the Pacific."

Although the region had just come out of the economic doldrums, it still faced some significant political and economic uncertainties. Cheap energy, the engine for so much business growth, was no longer plentiful; the recent financial collapse of the Washington Public Power Supply System (WPPSS)—a massive nuclear energy project—meant that the cost of electricity was certain to rise significantly.

In order to develop a competitive edge, Foster believed that his organization's culture needed transformation. An orientation to customer needs and greater attention to cost were necessary for GTNW to compete effectively. New job skills and modified employee attitudes about the business of providing telephone service were needed, in Foster's view. The company would have to learn to compete in markets, and its employees would need to develop new relationships for working in cooperation with one another. The infamous *fiefdoms* of the department heads, though effective in the past, no longer served the company well. According to Foster, until everyone—in every department and every job—focused on the needs of the customer, GTNW's bottom line would be in jeopardy.

His first step was to create a *democracy of ideas*, whereby the vice presidents acted as a cabinet, working together to reach a common level of understanding before making decisions. Foster made a concerted effort to delegate as much decision making as possible to this group of functional experts. After a year of managing-by-cabinet, Kent Foster seemed reasonably satisfied that decision making was more effective. (See Exhibit 5 for a profile of GTNW's top officers.)

Next, he tried to meet with as many employees as possible; at the end of his first year, he had personally met nearly 4,000 GTNW employees and had plans to see the remaining 2,100 within the next six months. These sessions had been perhaps the most enjoyable—and at times the most challenging—part of his job. In Foster's words, they also had been "the most important."

He had been struck by the contrast between meetings with middle management and craft employees. He normally spent a few minutes addressing each group and provided plenty of time for questions. Although management sessions had been interesting and productive, they had prompted few hard questions. Foster sensed a reluctance on management's part to challenge the process of adaptation that it was enduring. In contrast, encounters with craft employees were punctuated by lively and aggressive queries.

One meeting in particular made a lasting impression. It was to have been an early morning *tailgate talk* with about a dozen installers prior to daily rounds. These dawn *bull sessions* conducted on the tailgate of their trucks around coffee were a daily ritual. During his pre-dawn flight from Everett to the small, rural Oregon community, however, Foster was informed that the meeting had been moved to the town's library. Fifty people were expected.

As the sun broke through the morning fog, Foster arrived in town to find the library surrounded by some 150 gray GTNW trucks. Inside he found 300 to 400 people awaiting his arrival. A few had driven for over three hours on their own time to make the 7:00 A.M. meeting. Somewhat astonished by the turnout—and a bit overwhelmed—Foster dispensed with prepared remarks and opened the meeting to questions. Nearly everyone in the audience jumped up off their chairs to ask a question. Most simply wanted to know the company's plans and what role they could play. The message was clear: "Tell us what needs to be done and we'll figure out how to do it."

The confusion of the past few years had taken a toll on GTNW's people, leaving them frustrated and anxious about their jobs. In subsequent employee meetings, Foster tried to put the future into focus:

> What's happening here is fundamental. The telecommunications industry is becoming something it never was before—a part of the free market. The free market has been described as a process of *creative destruction* . . . The new, the innovative constantly forcing aside the antique and the obsolete . . . the leading edge of enterprise continually replacing what has gone before.
>
> Deregulation presents all kinds of challenges and opportunities to GTE—a chance, in short, to become a full service telecommunications company. We can move into unregulated or lightly regulated areas such as long distance service, data transmission, electronic mail, satellite communications, cellular radio. . . . These opportunities contain an element of risk, obviously, but they are also high potential areas. We've already decided to take that risk, to become active in virtually every phase of electronic communications.

Now it was time to measure the company's progress, to assess its strengths and weaknesses; any adjustments would need to be made quickly. In less than two months, GTNW's executive officers (Foster's cabinet) would fly east to corporate headquarters for a strategy/operations review. As they prepared for that meeting, each vice president spoke about the major challenges ahead. The company's goal was clear: *to be the carrier of choice* for the customers in their territory.

Regulatory Matters

Bypass was perhaps the greatest concern. With bypass, telephone companies immediately lose revenues, but not cost. Unlike a competitive loss which might later be reclaimed, users who bypassed the telephone company were likely to be lost for many years as they sought to financially justify their communications investment.

In the view of one telephone expert, if business customers in only 125 locations in the state of Washington elected to bypass the public switched network, the state's telephone industry could lose 20% of its long-distance revenue. Should that occur, the contention was that local rates would have to be increased more than $3 per month to cover the revenue shortfall.

According to Bill Stern, vice president-Revenue Requirements, bypass was not an imagined threat:

> Within our operating territory, there are major entities who have already constructed their own facilities; Boeing, Tektronics, and the State of Washington itself are among the organizations who are presently bypassing the network. We are also aware of other entities who are considering establishing their own networks. Technology is driving the costs of bypass down, making it economically attractive for an increasing number of entities. As more and more large users

elect to bypass, the burden . . . is spread over a smaller group of customers, thereby increasing the pressure on local rates even further.

Competition in both the regulated and unregulated arenas meant that GTNW would have to reduce costs and eliminate overhead expenses that had been more easily borne in a regulated regime. The company also needed the ability to set its prices in relation to those costs. Promoting network usage and marketing new services would be pointless if the company could not realize additional revenues. Cross-subsidization between telephone services and flat rate billing for local calls could no longer be sustained. Yet, each of these practices were considered near-sacred elements of public policy in telecommunications.

Marketing and Customer Service

Larry Bricker, vice president-Marketing and Customer Service, outlined his goal: "Our mission is to capitalize on the distribution, service delivery systems, and maintenance capabilities we currently have in positioning this company's operations to profitably participate in future telecommunications business opportunities."

The merging of the telecommunications and computer industries created unprecedented opportunities for telephone companies. GTNW, which had invested heavily in modernizing its network, appeared well-equipped to venture into many of these new information markets. Bricker's plan was to leverage the local network to stimulate usage of existing service while aggressively promoting new products and services. These included:

Dial-It Services: Offer special numbers for information on a variety of subjects: weather, sports, stock transactions, horoscopes, traffic reports, state and federal government actions, and so forth.

Friendship Operators: Provide regular operator contact (that is, a daily call) to the elderly or disabled living alone.

Telemessage Service: Provide custom-calling feature that stores and forwards voice messages, thus ending "telephone tag" between callers.

Alarm Systems: Offer sophisticated telephone equipment that can sense a burglary or fire and automatically summon emergency services.

Medical Diagnostics: Provide *intelligent terminal* that will assist doctors in monitoring patients who live far from a medical facility.

Meter Reading: Furnish enhancements to the local loop that would enable gas and electric utilities to read meters from their own office, thereby avoiding monthly on-site visits.

Agent Services: Furnish communications expertise to businesses that do not have their own communications managers. Act as single point-of-contact, coordinating all telecommunications purchases, selecting most cost-efficient vendors of voice/data systems and long-distance services.

Network Consulting: Design, construct, and manage client's local and long-distance private networks, with on-site personnel responsible for daily operation.

Local Area Networks: Provide a communications system that allows a number of different kinds of electronic devices—computers, remote terminals, facsimile devices, and printers—to communicate with one another. Furnish with existing coaxial cable links or fiber optics.

Equipment/Systems Marketing: Market enhanced voice and data equipment to customers inside and outside territory.

International Sales: Furnish customer premises equipment, switching gear, transmission facilities to foreign countries (with particular attention to developing Asian nations).

Cable Television: Construct local distribution facilities for cable television companies; manage system.

Videotext: Provide capability for electronic funds transfer (EFT), telephone shopping, stock market transactions, electronic mail system, interactive educational programs, video games.

Although these market opportunities excited Bricker, he knew that the company faced some immediate problems. Marketing was highly complicated in an environment where prices were not cost-based. Promoting network usage, although desirable as a means of preventing competitive loss and share erosion, would yield no net revenue gain.

GTNW's status as a public utility had not deterred competitors from providing substitute products and services. Although its distribution system (the local loop) was considered secure—far too costly for anyone else to duplicate— there was concern that unless steps were taken to broaden its use, it would become the carrier of low-profit, low-growth voice messages.

Cable television and microwave communications were the prime competitive threats. CB radio, cellular radio, and satellite were lesser challengers, but deserved close monitoring. Interexchange carriers, such as AT&T, MCI, and GTE's Sprint, also could be considered competitors: each was capable of providing local networks to heavy business users, thereby drawing business from GTNW. And with regulatory permission, these long distance companies could potentially enter the intra-LATA[2] business by targeting selective high-volume traffic corridors. Bypass—competition by GTNW's very own customers—could also be considered a major problem; client interviews revealed that economic bypass could already be justified. Bricker estimated that by 1989 some 17% of GTNW's business could be lost to bypass systems.

Deregulation had already transformed the market for customer premises equipment into a competitive free-for-all. With a fifteen-month supply of telephones overhanging the residential market (a two-month inventory was the norm), profit margins were slim for even the best-positioned manufacturers. Customers were now presented with a bewildering array of product choices and payment options (lease or buy). GTNW's share in the residence telephone market eroded quickly; once holding near-total grip on residence sales, its share had dropped below 70%. Making money in "plastic" (telephones) no longer seemed a sure thing. In a cost-cutting move, GTNW had curtailed the number of Phone Marts where consumers could purchase equipment. The wisdom of that move was hotly debated; telephone stores were a highly visible presence of the telephone company, and closing some down could confuse consumers.

In the business market, the field of competitors selling PBXs was also crowded. GTNW could sell sophisticated equipment, too, but was still considering how best to organize its sales force. Although the company did not need to organize a separate subsidiary (an FCC requirement that applied to AT&T and the Bell Operating Companies), there could be some advantages to such an organizational scheme. If properly staffed, specially trained, and effectively compensated, this group might make impressive gains in the highly competitive PBX market. But there were drawbacks to such an arrangement. Separate subsidiary requirements had confounded AT&T/BOC employees and customers alike. With a dual sales force (one regulated, the other competitive), it was possible for two sales representatives from the same company to visit a customer on the same day, offering virtually the same product at different prices. Besides generating confusion, this arrangement could wreak havoc with cost control efforts.

Prospects in the private network market, however, were brightening. GTNW had organized account teams to individually serve its largest 100 accounts; these customers generated over 15% of total company revenue. And despite some erosion in market share, the number of customer-generated requests for proposals (RFPs) was growing. By mobilizing interdepartmental teams from marketing, operations, and engineering, the company was finding itself in contention for many network construction projects. In fact, the confusion in the just-divested Bell Operating Companies had caused many large users to seek out GTNW.

Bricker faced organizational problems as well. His department was by far the largest, employing nearly 80% of the company's work force. Customer service (order processing, consumer inquiry, repair work, billing) accounted for 5,000 employees; sales and marketing included 200 people. Many service functions had already been consolidated: the billing function, which had been dispersed in sixteen locations, was now performed in one office; order entry, once conducted in ten locations, was now done in three places. Automation and consolidation of these functions had dampened employee morale; a number of workers, unable to move, had simply lost their jobs. In some outlying areas, consumers were instructed to send any nonworking phones in for repair; GTNW would no longer maintain a large, decentralized repair outfit.

Extensive preoccupation with service matters made it difficult to establish a full-fledged sales group. According to Bricker, it was "tough to talk service" with customers when involved in a sales presentation. (GTE's telcos had not enjoyed a particularly good reputation for service quality; an earlier failure to employ sophisticated central office switching gear had been rectified, but negative consumer perceptions still lingered. Thus, not surprisingly, salespeople often found themselves engaged in answering customer-service questions.) Although separating sales groups might solve some problems, many customers would resist the move; they wanted a "single point of contact" with the telephone company —especially in the wake of the Bell System breakup.

As Bricker studied a chart entitled "GTNW: Market Profile, 1984," he searched for a telltale strategic indicator. The statistics provided plenty to think about:

- Major metro areas constitute 70% of population, 80% of multiline revenues, 90% of competitive encounters.
- 100 accounts (0.007%) generate 15% of business revenues.
- 30% of account base tied to "growth" industries.
- Market share in business systems is 82%.
- Market share in residence systems is 69%.

Bricker's strategy was to prevent network erosion, segment competitive prices, and invest wisely. He now had to ask himself which elements of the marketing and service program should be continued, emphasized or eliminated?

Public Affairs

Public Affairs needed to develop a *pull strategy* to encourage acceptance of new regulatory policies, employment practices, and marketing campaigns. Fearless feedback was required; GTNW needed full employee involvement if change was to be effectively adopted. Clare Coxey, vice president-Public Affairs, described the department's mission; "We evaluate public and employee attitudes, examine policies and procedures through their eyes, plan and execute programs to earn their acceptance." Public Affairs would undoubtedly play a major role in fostering the transition from regulation to competition.

GTNW could not expect the public, its regulators, and elected leaders to readily understand or accept its arguments for restructuring. "The management mindset must be correct," noted Coxey. "We must avoid thinking that *they* [politicians, regulators, consumerists] just don't understand *us*. In most cases, it's *us* who don't understand the genuine social and political issues at stake. And we can't cry about politics spoiling our plans. We have to be in there communicating our views, while at the same time recognizing the valid arguments of people who may oppose us."

Coxey's communications program was extensive. On the political front, it included lobbying activities, political action committees, media education programs, and public-issue panel discussions including state and federal legislators. Public Affairs was also active with consumers. GTNW reached its far-flung subscriber base via bill inserts, consumer roundtables (targeted to specific *opinion leaders*), and speakers' bureaus. The company kept its pulse on worker attitudes by maintaining regular contact to top-level executives and by conducting regular employee surveys. Public Affairs had to develop an effective communications program that would be informative and persuasive, with GTNW seeking to undo nearly 100 years of telephone service tradition. This program would have to be directed both externally (to politicians, regulators, and consumers) and internally (to employees and suppliers).

Engineering and Operations

Herman Hu, vice president-Network Engineering and Construction, described the role of his organization: "Our job is to position the network for competition—to feature competitive services—while remaining the lowest-cost provider of basic telephone service." Although the installation of new technologies was important, there was an equally critical need to upgrade the older facilities as well, such as analog carrier and radio systems, copper cable, and electromechanical switching equipment.

According to Hu, the local system's capacity and capability could be selectively expanded. Multiplexing—the conditioning of circuits to make them capable of handling more calls—was only one way that technological innovations could be applied to the company's old copper wires. With the advent of equal access (in which all long distance companies would have similar quality connection to the local network), GTNW stood to benefit handsomely, since it was equipped to provide equal access on 99% of its lines. At the same time, Hu was preparing the network to handle usage-sensitive service options.

Digital switching and fiber optic transmission made it possible for GTNW to offer state-of-the-art communications services to its most demanding and sophisticated customers. Already, Hu's group had outfitted 30% of GTNW's primary market areas with fiber optics; plans were under way to increase fiber to a 90% utilization level. In addition, the development of remote switching units, which allowed the company to build mini-central offices, appeared to be a promising method of serving a diverse and decentralized customer base.

Changes in applying new technologies also had to be considered in light of GTNW's profit and public policy (that is, universal service) objectives. Already the company's primary market areas (major metro locations) accounted for 82% of customer lines, 38% of switching entities, and 73% of the capital budget. A utility with monopoly status could afford—as was GTNW's practice—to evenly distribute newer technologies and enhancements; although urban areas were usually the first to benefit, rural customers eventually derived similar benefits as well. Some network projects would be challenged under a competitive environment. GTNW's practice of maintaining backup facilities (to be deployed only in emergencies) helped fulfill public service obligations. It was, however, a costly investment—one that could not easily be sustained. So, too, was the company's practice of planning and erecting facilities in advance of projected use. Long investment cycles (five to ten years) ensured the availability of adequate communications facilities to meet the regions' growth projections. With the advent of competition, difficult tradeoffs between profit maximization and social obligations would have to be confronted.

Robert Myres, vice president and general manager of the Northern Area, described the role played by Operations: "We maintain the central offices and deliver repair services that support the marketing and customer service side of the company." TEL-CEL (Telephone Customer Expectation Level) was GTNW's key service index. Compiled by an outside consulting firm, the monthly evaluation—based on interviews with customers—provided critical market feedback. In April 1984, eight performance categories were gauged, each measuring the overall level of customer satisfaction. The results were as follows: service order—Phone Mart—contact (received a 96% satisfaction rating), installation service (92%), repair service (92%), directory assistance operator (96%), toll assistance operator (97%), local dial services (95%), long-distance dial services (94%), and billing services (91%). According to Myres, these tabulations, which were provided for each discrete work unit, had strong influence on salary and advancement decisions for most company employees.

Since operations personnel were always in the field, Myres saw no reason why they could not take advantage of their customer contact to act as sales representatives. Operations' challenge was to deliver repair service to a far-flung customer group at the lowest cost possible. GTNW would have to pursue cost reductions "with a vengeance" without hurting the efficiency of what Myres termed its "goodwill ambassadors."

Human Resources

Telephone people were generally regarded as having been "recruited, trained, and rewarded in a utility environment—one that put a premium on universal telephone service." Service was ingrained in GTNW's personnel; they were measured by customer complaints, not revenue generation. They were, concluded Hank Borys, vice president-Human Resources, doing "the job we taught them to do."

Borys described his charter as follows: "We must provide expertise and professional guidance to assist the general management team to effectively plan, acquire, deploy, maintain, develop, motivate, and retain the people resources of GTNW—consistent with the financial, productivity, and market requirements of our business." Changing the climate at the company would be no easy task. GTNW, like most traditional participants in the industry, was experiencing a clash of cultures; differences persisted between management and union, between young and old workers, and between market-oriented and service-oriented employees.

Aside from the deregulatory fallout, the past few years had been difficult for GTNW's work force. The recession had severely curtailed the craft ranks, causing dislocations for everyone—even those who had retained their jobs. Under provisions of the union contract, jobs had to be filled on a seniority basis. This caused multiple job *bumping;* many were thrown into new positions, often unequipped with the relevant job skills. The latest decisions to consolidate customer service functions had generated further uneasiness. Foremost on Borys' mind was to persuade the union to work with a more flexible contract—one that would not trigger multiple bumping and losses in productivity. In light of the recent retrenchment, however, such a plea was likely to meet stiff resistance. Many employees—both craft and management—simply could not believe that their job security was in jeopardy. The telephone business had been known for its cradle-to-grave employment practices; layoffs, according to one long-time manager, "just didn't happen."

"Seniority is when you are old enough to know most of the answers, but not young enough to be asked any of the questions." That quip, sometimes heard among veteran GTNW employees, underscored concern about polarization between the company's senior and junior employees. Many of the company's top managers (several of them engineers) had joined the telephone business just after World War II, when the network was undergoing tremendous growth and modernization. They had spent their lives and devoted their careers to building "the best damn telephone system in the world." The newer management hires, who often could skirt the bygone "up through the craft ranks" promotions practice, arrived to confront competitive challenges and were less appreciative of the company's accomplishments under a regulatory scheme. It was the younger group of employees that would soon inherit the company and shape its destiny in a competitive world. Although change and adaptation were clearly the order of the day, the company would have to take care not to dispense with the ingredients that had made the company so successful in the past. Many would continue to be important elements of future company strategies. It was, therefore, essential that the young and old employees worked together in cooperation and with mutual respect for one another.

Employees devoted to delivering customer service had not readily adopted a marketing orientation. To many, marketing conjured up images of hucksters "peddling the public to buy what they didn't need or want." (This was not an unnatural feeling for service-conscious employees to express.) Borys explained: "For decades, we have roused our people to serve the public, to reach customers stranded by some natural disaster—be it a flood or a raging forest fire—to install service right on schedule, to be courteous, and above all, to be loyal." The employees had done this well. GTNW's service reputation, or—as Borys pointed out—its ability to "market a standardized service to nearly everyone in the territory," had made the company slow to recognize that changed technology and changed customer requirements had created a changed marketplace. Success would depend on discerning and meeting customer needs on an individualized basis, industry by industry, company by company, and individual by individual.

To do this, GTNW would need to retrain much of its work force. Experienced employees who knew the business would have to relearn it; new hires would begin fresh but would have to understand the technical workings of the telephone industry. The company, equipped with its own training center, already devoted considerable resources to the continuing education of employees; employees spent nearly two weeks off-the-job at the training center each year. Borys was confident that GTNW employees could adjust—they just "needed to be better equipped and motivated by success, not fear of failure." Employees, concluded Borys, "just want to perform their work, and do it well." Top management had to figure out how to help them do just that.

Finance and Control

GTNW was now in "a good position to fund its capital spending plans," noted Stuart Schwerin, vice president-Finance. He described his role as one of "ensuring adequate capital recovery, which will permit us to leverage our basic business into new ventures." Equally important in his view was getting some control over the company's cost structure. In a regulated environment, costs were pooled and then *allocated* to services; the result had been one gigantic "averaging machine of costs." It still was not possible to precisely determine how much it cost GTNW to deliver a particular product or service. With competition, however, costs had to be identified and controlled to a greater extent.

Monty Leavitt, vice president of New Service Administration, was responsible for coordinating GTNW's cost control campaign. Nicknamed "BEST," the program was one that relied heavily on employees' suggestions and involvement. Its goal was to achieve high quality at low cost so the company could become the best competitor.

Benchmarking, the process of comparing the cost structure of existing and potential competitors,[3] had been an ongoing activity during the past two years. Financial and operating data on rivals were compiled, analyzed, and compared to GTNW's own cost structure to help identify an appropriate cost structure for competition. Although this had helped to prune some costs, GTNW was still saddled with relatively high costs compared to many other information companies.

Legal

Lee Coulter, vice president and general counsel, executed GTNW's rate filings and coordinated all litigation activity. It was anticipated that the company would define its legal strategy much more broadly. In the past, GTNW usually wound up in court as a defendant, trying to justify a rate hike, a construction project, or an employment practice. According to Coulter, the mentality of those filing suit seemed to have been "they're good guys, let's go after them." In the face of competition, however, the company was ready to shed any such "good guy" image. If it was necessary, the company was prepared to legally contest its right to compete in the Northwest's information markets. A legal offensive, therefore, could be a measure of how aggressive the telephone company would become in facing up to competitive realities.

A "WINDOW OF OPPORTUNITY"

Although pleased by the progress made so far, Kent Foster still felt uneasy about the slow pace of change both inside and outside the company. GTNW simply could not afford to wait for public policy makers to reshape the environment; it had to be creative regardless of any handicaps. Foster's greatest worry was that employees, accustomed to regulation, might behave in a constrained manner—believing they could not shape their own destiny. Accustomed to security, employees would have to learn to take risks. The company, for its part, would have to learn to tolerate some mistakes in order to succeed over the long term.

It was time for Kent Foster and his cabinet to assess the company's position. Less than two months remained before they would present their plans for corporate review. And within one year, competition would begin to arrive on the fertile turf of the Northwest.

As Foster pondered the changes that had taken place and the ones that were still to come, he paused to consider the legacy of the telephone industry and its people. The final words of the Pulitzer Prize-winning book—*The Soul of the New Machine*—which chronicled the remarkable development of the enhanced computer, came to mind:

> It was a different game now. Clearly the machine no longer belonged to its makers.

Exhibit 1 GTNW: Financial and Operating Data

	OPERATING REVENUES '000					OPERATING EXPENSES '000									
Year	Local Service	Access Service	Toll Service	Misc Net of Uncoll	Total	Maint.	Traffic	Commercial	Adv & Mtg	Gen Ofc Sal. & Expense	Other	Controllable Expense	Depreciation	Oper Taxes	Total Exp & Taxes
	1	1.1	2	3	4	5	6	7	8	9	10	11	12	13	14
1974	$ 76,456	$ 0	$ 69,378	$ 3,534	$149,368	$ 24,223	$ 8,580	$ 6,127	$1,789	$ 9,650	$ 5,718	$ 56,087	$ 27,119	$30,742	$113,948
1975	$ 80,831	$ 0	$ 80,212	$ 4,163	$165,206	$ 27,437	$ 8,794	$ 7,086	$1,861	$10,174	$ 6,996	$ 62,348	$ 29,950	$34,411	$126,709
1976	$ 93,258	$ 0	$ 98,580	$ 4,839	$196,677	$ 33,706	$10,135	$ 8,775	$2,419	$12,792	$ 8,097	$ 75,924	$ 33,054	$43,649	$152,627
1977	$105,627	$ 0	$118,255	$ 5,415	$229,297	$ 42,940	$11,534	$11,543	$3,249	$15,969	$12,260	$ 97,495	$ 39,720	$44,443	$181,658
1978	$118,756	$ 0	$148,947	$ 6,543	$273,246	$ 55,447	$13,851	$16,717	$4,376	$17,501	$13,919	$121,811	$ 45,614	$48,881	$216,306
1979	$138,324	$ 0	$189,364	$ 8,404	$336,092	$ 75,117	$16,505	$19,836	$5,415	$22,447	$20,960	$160,280	$ 57,485	$44,167	$261,932
1980	$156,061	$ 0	$225,291	$10,244	$391,596	$ 77,627	$17,069	$22,496	$5,798	$26,916	$25,159	$175,065	$ 69,810	$53,006	$297,881
1981	$169,027	$ 0	$268,422	$ 8,798	$446,247	$ 86,674	$17,464	$23,587	$6,978	$31,192	$29,410	$195,305	$ 78,524	$67,606	$341,435
1982	$199,343	$ 0	$297,474	$ 8,650	$505,467	$103,240	$19,661	$25,135	$6,959	$36,973	$38,133	$230,101	$ 91,329	$75,546	$396,976

First Quarter	$ 51,401	$ 0	$ 74,229	$ 2,787	$128,417	$ 25,325	$ 4,787	$ 6,209	$1,301	$ 8,313	$10,907	$ 56,842	$ 26,514	$20,084	$103,440
Second Quarter	$ 52,599	$ 0	$ 79,851	$ 3,063	$135,513	$ 25,985	$ 4,965	$ 6,608	$1,414	$ 8,231	$10,171	$ 57,374	$ 27,666	$22,465	$107,505
Third Quarter	$ 54,167	$ 0	$ 79,429	$ 3,606	$137,202	$ 25,185	$ 5,653	$ 6,935	$1,627	$ 8,057	$10,276	$ 57,733	$ 27,448	$22,400	$107,581
Fourth Quarter	$ 53,767	$ 0	$ 75,447	$ 3,913	$133,127	$ 26,819	$ 5,056	$ 7,556	$1,864	$ 8,921	$10,741	$ 60,957	$ 27,231	$19,109	$107,297
Year End	$211,934	$ 0	$308,956	$13,369	$534,259	$103,314	$20,461	$27,308	$6,206	$33,522	$42,095	$232,906	$108,859	$84,058	$425,823
First Quarter	$ 52,228	$40,801	$24,014	$14,541	$131,584	$ 26,962	$ 4,571	$ 6,705	$1,463	$ 8,373	$12,113	$ 60,188	$ 27,655	$19,488	$ 107,331

(A) Invested Capital: Income Available for Fixed Charges Divided by Common Stock, Preferred Stock, Funded Debt, Other Notes Payable, and Retained Earnings.

Total Capital: Income Available for Fixed Charges Plus Extraordinary and Delayed Items, Divided by Common Stock, Preferred Stock, Funded Debt, Other Notes Payable, Retained Earnings, and Unamortized Investment Tax Credit.

Common Equity: Net Income Available for Common, Divided by Common Stock Plus Retained Earnings.

The information contained in this report is unaudited and intended for internal management use and does not include certain reclassifications and disclosures necessary to meet standards for external financial reporting.

379

Exhibit 1 (continued)

	INCOME '000'			PER LINE PER MONTH				TWELVE MONTHS CUMULATIVE									
								Return on Average (A)				Operating Ratios					
Net Oper Income	Income Before Fixed Charges	Net Income For Common	Total Oper Rev	Control-lable Exp	Total Exp & Taxes	Net Oper Income		Invested Capital	Total Capital	Common Equity	Earnings Per Avg Share	Cont Exp /O-R	Exp & Taxes/O-R	Interest Coverage	Interest and Prfd Dividend Coverage	Inter-nally Gener. Funds	Year
15	16	17	18	19	20	21		22	23	24	25	26	27	28	29	30	
$ 35,420	$ 36,582	$19,669	$29.34	$11.02	$22.38	$ 6.96		8.84%	8.68%	10.82%	$3.01	37.55	76.29	3.00	3.00	52%	1974
$ 38,497	$ 39,537	$22,278	$30.78	$11.62	$23.61	$ 7.17		9.10%	8.90%	11.70%	$3.35	37.74	76.70	3.27	3.27	72%	1975
$ 44,050	$ 45,298	$27,609	$34.33	$13.25	$26.64	$ 7.69		10.04%	9.73%	13.84%	$4.15	38.60	77.60	4.06	3.54	82%	1976
$ 47,639	$ 49,578	$29,453	$37.45	$15.92	$29.67	$ 7.78		10.08%	9.69%	13.88%	$4.23	42.52	79.22	3.82	3.33	56%	1977
$ 56,940	$ 60,243	$35,785	$41.37	$18.44	$32.75	$ 8.62		10.57%	10.03%	14.31%	$4.55	44.58	79.16	3.66	3.28	44%	1978
$ 74,160	$ 77,518	$42,787	$47.17	$22.50	$36.76	$10.41		10.72%	10.18%	13.96%	$4.32	47.69	77.93	3.08	2.74	33%	1979
$ 93,715	$ 96,976	$46,821	$51.86	$23.18	$39.45	$12.41		10.56%	10.01%	12.40%	$4.24	44.71	76.07	2.66	2.31	50%	1980
$104,812	$116,046	$63,504	$56.85	$24.88	$43.50	$13.35		11.81%	10.98%	14.27%	$5.18	43.77	76.51	3.08	2.70	81%	1981
$108,491	$116,385	$64,866	$64.11	$29.18	$50.35	$13.76		11.57%	10.72%	13.61%	$5.29	45.52	78.54	3.21	2.80	118%	1982

1983

$ 24,977	$ 26,853	$14,808	$64.93	$28.74	$52.30	$12.63	11.41%	10.55%	13.30%	$5.21	44.68	79.12	3.27	2.85	121
$ 28,008	$ 30,423	$18,656	$68.25	$28.90	$54.15	$14.11	11.71%	10.83%	13.98%	$5.52	43.75	79.16	3.49	3.02	140
$ 29,621	$ 32,154	$20,672	$68.98	$29.02	$54.08	$14.89	11.89%	10.90%	14.14%	$5.62	43.74	79.59	3.58	3.10	132
$ 25,830	$ 28,930	$17,482	$66.22	$30.32	$53.38	$12.85	12.12%	11.09%	14.56%	$5.84	43.59	79.70	3.72	3.22	136
$108,436	$118,360	$71,618	$67.10	$29.25	$53.48	$13.62	12.12%	11.09%	14.56%	5.84	43.59	79.70	3.72	3.22	136%

1984

$ 24,253	$ 26,885	$15,724	$65.00	$29.73	$53.02	$11.98	12.20%	11.15%	14.62%	6.25	43.96	79.96	3.79	3.29	131

Exhibit 1 (continued)

	TOTAL TELEPHONE PLANT '000' OMITTED					CAPITALIZATION (C)		CUSTOMER LINES						EMPLOYEES			
		Additions			Plant in Service Per Line				Gain								
Year	Amount (B)	Gross (B)	Net (B)	Depr Res (D)		'000' Omitted	Total Per Line	Total in Service	Quarter	Year To Date	Year to Date %	Res Ext to Res Main %	Party-1 Res Mn. Total Res Mn*	Number	Per 1000 Lines	Wages and Salaries '000'	Year
	31	32	33	34	35	36	37	38	39	40	41	42	43	44	45	46	
1974	$ 551,443	$ 62,647	$ 47,212	$ 95,954	$1,231	$ 428,290	$ 979	437,647	—	23,568	5.7 %	46.5%	60.7%	4,779	10.9	$ 48,945	1974
1975	$ 594,953	$ 56,855	$ 43,509	$114,269	$1,255	$ 443,038	$ 958	462,349	—	24,702	5.6 %	48.4%	64.5%	4,866	10.5	$ 54,729	1975
1976	$ 657,911	$ 80,850	$ 62,958	$131,449	$1,292	$ 466,510	$ 939	496,976	—	34,627	7.5 %	49.9%	67.5%	5,291	10.6	$ 65,843	1976
1977	$ 750,962	$113,010	$ 93,051	$153,437	$1,355	$ 526,629	$ 989	532,312	—	35,336	7.1 %	52.5%	71.5%	6,070	11.4	$ 81,537	1977
1978	$ 910,731	$186,176	$159,769	$173,426	$1,481	$ 637,524	$1,108	572,691	—	40,379	7.6 %	54.8%	74.4%	7,313	12.8	$105,207	1978
1979	$1,145,648	$275,915	$234,917	$191,353	$1,646	$ 833,900	$1,351	617,053	—	44,362	7.7 %	56.3%	77.3%	8,401	13.6	$133,476	1979
1980	$1,314,920	$229,744	$169,272	$211,274	$1,900	$ 956,951	$1,491	641,920	—	24,867	4.3 %	56.7%	79.9%	7,919	12.3	$148,119	1980
1981	$1,438,015	$188,374	$123,095	$229,330	$2,047	$1,005,591	$1,521	660,944	—	19,024	3.0 %	56.8%	81.1%	7,477	11.3	$158,155	1981
1982	$1,513,084	$132,526	$ 75,069	$271,871	$2,168	$1,000,572	$1,520	658,215	—	(2,729)	(0.4)%	55.4%	83.2%	6,676	10.1	$164,885	1982

																1983
First Quarter	$1,525,499	$ 21,185	$ 12,365	$291,258	$2,170	$1,004,404	$1,522	659,885	1,670	1,670	0.3 %	54.6	83.5	6,455	9.8	40,169
Second Quarter	$1,541,689	$ 25,216	$ 16,240	$312,002	$2,181	$ 990,449	$1,498	661,285	1,400	3,070	0.5 %	53.9	83.7	6,323	9.6	40,873
Third Quarter	$1,557,725	$ 21,522	$ 16,036	$335,107	$2,189	$ 990,379	$1,489	665,067	3,782	6,852	1.0 %	52.6	84.2	6,322	9.5	43,057
Fourth Quarter	$1,573,014	$ 35,381	$ 15,289	$342,984	$2,176	$ 981,857	$1,461	671,869	6,802	13,654	2.1 %	51.1	84.7	6,244	9.3	42,403
Year End	$1,573,014	$103,304	$59,930	$342,984	$2,176	$981,857	$1,461	671,869	13,654	13,654	2.1 %	51.1%	84.7%	6,244	9.3	$166,502

																1984
First Quarter	$1,590,732	$ 29,873	$ 17,718	$360,333	$2,181	$ 956,367	$1,412	677,317	5,448	5,448	0.8 %	49.5	84.4	6,173	9.1	42,108

(B) Includes Telephone Plant under Construction, Telephone Plant Acquisition Adjustment, and Property Held for Future Use.

(C) Includes Common Stock, Long Term Debt, Other Notes Payable, Preferred Stock, and Retained Earnings.

*1982 and 1983 %'s have been restated to reflect the impacts of CPE.

The information contained in this report is unaudited and intended for internal management use and does not include certain reclassifications and disclosures necessary to meet standards for external financial reporting.

Exhibit 2 GTE Corporation and Subsidiaries: Financial Data, 1978–1983

	BUSINESS GROUP DATA						
Continuing Operations	1983	1982	1981	1980	1979	1978	Annual Growth Rate (1978–1983)†
				(Millions of Dollars)			
Consolidated Results							
Revenues and sales*	$12,944	$11,767	$10,710	$ 9,680	$ 8,672	$ 7,560	11.2%
Operating income*	2,488	2,320	2,233	1,966	1,836	1,729	7.9
Net income							
(applicable to common stock)	949	814	688	589	637	550	10.9
Return on common equity	16.0%	16.3%	15.6%	14.7%	17.8%	16.9%	—
Return on investment	9.6%	9.4%	9.0%	8.4%	8.9%	8.3%	—
Depreciation	1,767	1,488	1,278	1,130	994	866	15.0
Plant additions	3,591	3,031	3,009	2,755	2,599	2,138	9.3
Identifiable assets	24,223	22,199	20,857	19,286	17,708	15,618	8.8
Average investment	16,986	15,673	14,866	13,771	12,281	11,123	8.7
Research and development	262	257	215	196	140	108	19.9
Employees (in thousands)	185	190	196	194	193	182	—
Foreign Operations (included above)							
Revenues and sales	$ 2,059	$ 2,081	$ 1,963	$ 1,841	$ 1,547	$ 1,399	8.6%
Net income	36	65	86	74	76	35	—
Identifiable assets	3,464	3,341	3,272	3,053	2,742	2,613	6.1

Telephone Operations

Operating revenues—						
Toll	$ 4,639	$ 4,357	$ 3,884	$ 3,295	$ 2,849	$ 2,419	14.4%
Local	3,281	3,066	2,641	2,325	2,101	1,947	11.7
Other	449	389	339	300	261	225	14.7
Total revenues	8,369	7,812	6,864	5,920	5,211	4,591	13.3
Operations and maintenance	3,983	3,815	3,241	2,817	2,458	2,073	14.5
Depreciation	1,614	1,379	1,184	1,046	921	800	14.8
Taxes other than income	498	457	398	348	310	309	11.1
Operating income	2,274	2,161	2,041	1,709	1,522	1,409	10.9
Interest and other—net	728	729	690	621	503	424	11.9
Income taxes	620	589	634	504	460	488	6.4
Net income	$ 926	$ 843	$ 717	$ 584	$ 559	$ 497	13.9%
Plant additions	$ 2,431	$ 2,677	$ 2,680	$ 2,506	$ 2,424	$ 2,029	3.7%
Identifiable assets	$19,286	$18,522	$17,360	$15,837	$14,290	$12,646	8.9
Average investment	$14,923	$14,265	$13,315	$12,203	$11,013	$10,044	8.5
Rate orders received (annualized)**	$ 322	$ 350	$ 458	$ 164	$ 25	$ 9	—
Return on common equity	15.5%	15.4%	14.3%	13.0%	13.9%	13.6%	—
Gross toll messages (in millions)	2,370	2,252	2,156	1,984	1,815	1,645	7.6
Customer lines (in thousands)	11,619	11,352	11,208	10,867	10,461	10,018	2.9
Operating company employees (in thousands)	109.3	116.3	119.3	116.2	114.5	107.3	—
Customer lines per employee	106.3	97.6	93.9	93.5	91.4	93.3	—

†Least-squares method, percentages have been omitted where not meaningful.

*Consolidated revenues and sales reflect eliminations of intergroup sales, except for sales of construction and maintenance equipment and supplies by Communications Products to affiliated telephone companies, as discussed in Note 1 to the financial statements. Operating income is after deduction of general corporate expenses not allocated to individual business groups which totaled $118 million, $113 million, $101 million, $87 million, $61 million and $51 million for the years 1983–1978, respectively.

**Includes intrastate toll and local rate awards.

385

Exhibit 2 (continued)

BUSINESS GROUP DATA

Continuing Operations	1983	1982	1981	1980	1979	1978	Annual Growth Rate (1978–1983)
				(Millions of Dollars)			
Communication Services*							
Sales	$ 578	$ 107	$ 80	$ 45	$ 28	$ 21	83.0%
Operating income (loss)	82	(27)	(24)	(28)	(12)	(1)	—
Net income (loss)	33	(12)	(17)	(18)	(9)	(4)	—
Depreciation	54	19	15	10	8	7	45.9
Plant additions	975	108	35	31	21	8	—
Identifiable assets	1,723	214	137	116	110	48	77.4
Average investment	813	130	86	59	41	36	74.2
Sprint customers (in thousands)	943	535	200	80	47	14	—
Communications Products							
Sales	$2,551	$2,454	$2,199	$2,071	$2,028	$1,759	7.4%
Operating income	144	153	113	130	158	163	(2.4)
Net income	48	41	26	16	50	53	(1.6)
Depreciation	52	45	43	41	34	30	11.0
Plant additions	94	90	104	97	67	47	13.5
Identifiable assets	1,817	1,850	1,730	1,642	1,554	1,296	6.7
Average investment	877	935	1,014	1,036	913	845	.7
GTD-5 EAX lines shipped (in thousands)	1,297	832	96	—	—	—	—
Electrical Products							
Sales	$1,480	1,422	$1,593	$1,680	$1,468	$1,242	2.1%
Operating income	106	146	204	242	229	209	(13.1)
Net income	42	65	90	95	100	78	(12.1)
Depreciation	43	38	36	32	28	26	10.7
Plant additions	47	80	87	73	51	42	6.1
Identifiable assets	1,160	1,173	1,193	1,152	1,035	918	4.6
Average investment	806	833	822	804	707	647	4.7

Parent Company and Other

Net expenses	$ (71)	$ (93)	$ (97)	$ (56)	$ (30)	$ (41)
GTE preferred stock dividends	(29)	(30)	(31)	(32)	(33)	(33)
Total	$ (100)	$ (123)	$ (128)	$ (88)	$ (63)	$ (74)
Plant additions	44	76	103	48	36	12
Identifiable assets	237	440	437	539	719	710

†Least-squares method, percentages have been omitted where not meaningful.
*Reflects Sprint from date of acquisition except for customer data.

Telephone Operations Revenue

TELEPHONE REVENUES BY AREA
(in millions)

1. California — $1,945
2. Midwest — $1,890
3. Southwest — $ 887
4. Florida — $ 863
5. Southeast — $ 587
6. Northwest — $ 541
7. Hawaii — $ 368
International and other — $1,288

Source: GTE Annual Report, 1984.

Telephone Operations Revenues
(In Billions of Dollars)

Legend: Toll, Local, Other

78	79	80	81	82	83
$4.6	$5.2	$5.9	$6.9	$7.8	$8.4

Exhibit 3 Profile of GTE Businesses

GTE at a Glance

Business Group	Products/Services	1983		1982	
		Revenues/ Sales	Net Income	Revenues/ Sales	Net Income
			(in millions)		
GTE Telephone Operating Group		**$8,369**	**$926**	$7,812	$843
Telephone Companies	19 companies provide local telephone service and sell or lease phones and terminals				
GTE Directories	Sells Yellow Pages advertising and publishes 900 telephone directories				
GTE Mobilnet	Provides cellular mobile radio telephone service				

GTE Diversified Products and Services Group

		1983		1982	
Communications Products		**$2,551**	**$ 48**	$2,454	$ 41
GTE Communication Systems	Supplies complete line of communications equipment, systems, and support services, including digital switching and PABX systems, transmission equipment, and residential and business telephone products				
Sylvania Systems Group	Reconnaissance systems, command, control and communications systems, tactical telephone switching networks, laser and electro-optical devices, lithium battery power systems, and satellite earth stations				
Communications Services		**$ 578**	**$ 33**	$ 107	$(12)
GTE Sprint	Operates third largest long-distance telephone system in United States				
GTE Telenet	Operates nationwide data communications network utilizing "packet-switching;" also provides Telemail* service and markets medical and financial information services				
GTE Electrical Products		**$1,480**	**$ 42**	$1,422	$ 65
GTE Lighting Products	Manufactures more than 6,000 types of Sylvania lamps. Also produces photographic lighting products, lamp fixtures and related products				
GTE Precision Materials	Manufactures metal, plastic and ceramic materials, parts and components; specialty and refractory metals; high-purity chemicals and electronic and electrical assemblies				

Source: GTE Annual Report, 1984.

Exhibit 4   State Regulatory Commissions

Washington: The Washington Utilities and Transportation Commission was composed of three commissioners appointed by the governor in staggered six-year terms. WUTC had experimented with a "negotiation process" in order to improve the existing procedural framework for rate making. Legislative confirmation of two commissioners had been pending for two years. Although WUTC had taken initiative on state access charges, recent rate orders had been considered disappointing.

Regulatory Evaluation: Average (Regulatory Research Associates)
Average (Argus Research)

Oregon: The Oregon Public Utility Commission was unique in that this regulatory body was directed and administered by a single commissioner, appointed by the governor for a four-year term. The present commissioner had reorganized the functions and responsibilities of his telecommunications staff, resulting in the formation of specialty groups primarily concerned with the fulfillment of special tasks and assignments. Oregon has been responsive to industry initiatives in the area of direct sale of equipment, deregulation of inside wiring, application of depreciation rate changes.

Regulatory Evaluation: Above Average (Regulatory Research Associates)
Slightly Above Average (Argus Research)

Idaho: The Idaho Public Utilities Commission was composed of three commissioners, appointed by the governor in staggered six-year terms. The staff is undergoing reorganization. Commissioners have expressed some skepticism of telephone industry proposals with regard to access charges and usage-sensitive pricing; universal service concerns predominate regulatory outlook.

Regulatory Evaluation: Average (Regulatory Research Associates)
Average (Argus Research)

Montana: The Montana Public Service Commission consisted of five commissioners, elected by the public in staggered six-year terms. Recent decisions by the PSC requiring telephone companies to sell equipment—both regulated and unregulated—through a separate subsidiary were being contested in court.

Regulatory Evaluation: Below Average (Regulatory Research Associates)
Below Average (Argus Research)

Exhibit 4 (continued)

California: The California Public Utilities Commission was composed of five commissioners appointed by the governor in staggered six-year terms. This PUC has been innovative and active in dealing with a wide range of industry problems. California had not been reluctant to rebuke companies for poor operating performance; it had levied a fine on one GTE company for repeated service failures.

Regulatory Evaluation: Above Average (Regulatory Research Associates)
Above Average (Argus Research)

Source: Regulatory Research Associates released its evaluation in July 1983; Argus Research announced its rating in June 1983.

Note: Regulatory evaluations were performed by utility consultants who regularly monitored rate cases and policy decisions of most state commissions.

Exhibit 5 GTNW Officers

Kent B. Foster, President Elected president in April 1983. He began his telephone career in 1970 with GTE of the Southeast. He held several positions with GTSE including: supervising engineer; cost engineer; plant engineer; vice president–operations staff; vice president–network planning, engineering and construction. Corporate staff assignments included: vice president–planning and analysis, telephone and network services; vice president–marketing; vice president–marketing and business planning. B.S., Engineering, North Carolina State University; M.S., Management, University of Southern California.

Larry R. Bricker, Vice President–Marketing and Customer Service Elected vice president in April 1982. He began his career in 1960 with GTE of Indiana. He held various assignments in the traffic department before being promoted to corporate staff where he held positions as director of residence resource analysis and director of customer services. B.S., St. Francis College; MBA, St. Francis College (Fort Wayne, Indiana).

William E. Stern, Vice President–Revenue Requirements Elected vice president in April 1980. He began his career in 1966 in GTE's financial development program and held assignments as a budget coordinator, financial analyst, and financial administrator in various GTE companies. Held position as director of revenues and earnings for GTE's Michigan Company before returning to corporate staff as director–revenue planning. B.A., Dartmouth College; MBA, Columbia University.

Exhibit 5 (continued)

> *O. M. "Monte" Leavitt, Vice President–New Service Administration*
Elected vice president in 1971. He transferred to GTNW in 1965 after serving in several capacities for GTE of California, which he joined in 1957. Posts included traffic planning supervisor and safety director. B.A., Whittier College, UCLA. Holds active leadership positions in various community organizations.

> *Stuart L. Schwerin, Vice President–Finance* Elected vice president in February 1981. Prior to joining GTE, he served as an audit manager with Arthur Andersen & Company. He began his telephone career in 1974 when he was appointed corporate director of accounting policy. Served as vice president and controller of GTE Michigan and regional vice president of finance for GTE's Western Region Telephone Operating Group. B.S., Business Administration, Lehigh University. Certified Public Accountant, New York State.

> *Ronald R. Koch, Vice President–Controller* Elected vice president in February 1977. He had over twenty-five years service with GTE, eighteen years of which were spent with GTE California. Has held various positions in accounting, budget, treasury, and internal audit before being transferred to GTE corporate staff. B.S., Accounting, UCLA.

> *Clare D. Coxey, Vice President–Public Affairs* Elected vice president in September 1979. He began his telephone career in 1960 with GTE Michigan. Positions included: cost studies engineer; rates and tariffs engineer; construction foreman and executive assistant. Served in GTE's Washington office as assistant to the vice president–revenue requirements. Was director of business relations in GTE Indiana. B.S., Business Administration, Eastern Michigan University.

> *Henry M. Borys, Vice President–Human Resources* Elected vice president in 1971. He began his telephone career in 1953 as director of industrial relations for GTE's Upstate New York Company and later became personnel director at GTE Michigan and GTE Indiana. B.S., Industrial Relations, Cornell.

> *Herman S.L. Hu, Vice President–Network Engineering and Construction*
Elected vice president in August 1982. He began his telephone career in 1952 as an assistant plant engineer with the Hawaiian Telephone Company. Has held a number of positions with GTE, most associated with the engineering department. Served as planning engineer and planning director. B.S., Civil Engineering, University of California at Berkeley. Active in various community organizations.

> *Robert M. Myres, Vice President–General Manager: Northern Area*
Elected vice president in January 1979. He started in the industry in 1946, joining

Exhibit 5   (continued)

a small independent telephone company. Has held several positions in operations and engineering, including plant director and supply director. Attended Everett Junior College and various telephone engineering programs.

C. Lee Coulter, Vice President and General Counsel   Elected vice president in 1968. Most of his career has been spent in private law practice in Washington. Served for three years as an attorney and legal examiner for the Washington Utilities and Transportation Commission. Served for many years as general counsel for the Association of Washington Business and Washington Independent Telephone Association. Currently chairman of the board of directors of the Association of Washington Business. B.A., J.D., Northwestern University.

Source: Supplied by author.

1. A LATA, or Local Access and Transport Area, was the geographical territory within which local telephone companies were permitted to operate.
2. Local telephone companies could offer only intra-LATA calling services; the inter-LATA market was reserved for interexchange companies, such as AT&T, MCI, GTE Sprint, and other OCCs.
3. Existing rivals included companies such as GTE's other domestic telephone companies, Pacific Northwest Bell, Mountain Bell, AT&T Communications, MCI Communications, and Satellite Business Systems. Potential rivals examined included IBM, Cox Communications (a cable TV firm), Dow Jones, and large newspaper conglomerates.

Chapter Six

Mixed Rationales

This last part of the text explores the commercial banking industry in a flux of market-driven change, with regulatory reform lagging far behind.

In this vitally important industry, several different structural failures once justified overlapping and thoroughgoing regulatory control. Banks, it was argued, were intimately linked to the public good through credit formation and economic growth. Banks were "different" because they accepted deposits from individuals who lacked the information to assess their creditworthiness. They could not be too closely affiliated with non-banking businesses, for fear of unwise insider deals, and they needed to be restrained from excessive competition, which could lead to excessive risk.

The first part of this chapter is an industry note on regulation and competition in commercial banking. It describes the origins of banking regulation in the United States, its effects on the structure of financial services markets, and recent regulatory changes driven by new economic conditions, technological developments, and entrepreneurial pressures. This note, like the two before it, provides perspective on the process of change over time.

The Comptroller and Non-Bank Banks is the second section in this chapter. Todd Conover is a Reagan appointee and a determined advocate of deregulation. The issue of non-bank banks is an appropriate place to end, since it was still unresolved and open-ended at the time this text was published. The non-bank bank is a perfect symbol and illustration of the dynamic tension that rules government intervention in the American economy. The non-bank bank is a wedge, or loophole, created by regulatory restriction of competitive forces that would otherwise occur. As such, it becomes a sort of pressure point for economic and political entrepreneurs. In the case presented here, Conover is trying to use non-bank banks to force Congress to undertake legislative reform. But the politics in this industry are more complicated than perhaps anywhere else, and Conover is just one, albeit important, participant.

Regulation and Competition
in Commercial Banking

By 1985, the regulatory framework established for commercial banks during the depth of the Great Depression had crumbled. Over the past few years, the marketplace for financial services had undergone a rapid tranformation from its traditional balkanized structure to one that was far more integrated. The financial system—with banking at its heart—could no longer be characterized by specialized institutions offering distinctive products and services in marginal competition with one another.

Commercial banking, once a tightly regulated and stable operation, was becoming a competitive and turbulent business, undermining many of the historic tenets of banking policy. A bank, protected by regulation, was supposed to be a safe haven for people's savings. Bank regulation, along price, product, and geographic dimensions, had inhibited competition to ensure "safety and soundness" of the financial system. But that approach was now challenged by changes in economic conditions, technology, regulation, and the demand for financial services.

Enterprising competitors, not subject to so tight a web of regulation, had recently captured a significant portion of savings that might otherwise be lodged with commercial banks. To stem those losses, banks were forced to compete fiercely amongst one another and against their unregulated counterparts for business. As a result, the profits of commercial banks had been severely squeezed, and public confidence shaken. With bank failures at a fifty-year high, the industry faced a test of survival.

Despite the revolutionary changes in the financial marketplace, the process of market restructuring was far from complete. Some bank deregulation had occurred, but philosophical differences and uncertainty were blocking further policy changes. Disagreements persisted over the benefits of deregulation, fairness of competition, and soundness of the financial system. And some, noting its unique public responsibilities, argued forcefully for maintaining the separation between banks and other lines of finance and commerce. Implicit in that view was the assumption that banks were "special."

This note was prepared by Research Associate Dekkers L. Davidson, under the supervision of Professor Richard H.K. Vietor, as the basis for class discussion.

PUBLIC POLICY LEGACY

The conflict between rural values and urban reality was etched in the first major political controversy following ratification of the U.S. Constitution in 1789. That controversy involved issues of monetary and fiscal powers for the new federal government; it was eventually resolved with the creation of a central bank governed by twenty private investors and five government officials.

America's "First Bank" operated nationwide and performed basic banking functions of accepting deposits, issuing bank notes, making loans and purchasing securities. Although useful to commerce and to the federal government, the bank—which was not only the largest bank of its time, but the largest corporation—frightened state-chartered banks, farmers, small businesses, and local politicians. Its twenty-year charter was allowed to expire; subsequent efforts to establish a "Second Bank" touched a popular nerve of resistance and met with no lasting success.

State-chartered private banks proliferated, issuing a bewildering variety of bank notes that were sometimes of little value. The federal government, without a central regulating mechanism over banking and credit, lacked a safe repository for its own funds, a reliable mechanism to transfer them from place to place, and adequate means to market its own securities. State regulation did not help. This system was plagued by inadequate bank capital, risky loans, and insufficient reserves against its bank notes and demand deposits. Furthermore, the American economy was increasingly hampered by the uneven pattern of capital formation inherent in a state-chartered banking system.

During the Civil War, Congress passed the National Banking Act of 1863 which returned a greater measure of clarity and security to American banking and finance. The Act provided for the creation of nationally chartered banks and, by taxing the state bank notes out of existence, the legislation provided that only the national banks could issue bank notes—a currency backed by the U.S. government. A newly created Office of the Comptroller of the Currency was given authority to examine national banks' compliance with lending limits and reserve requirements.

To the surprise of many who had supported the national banking legislation, state-chartered banks survived without the power to issue bank notes. In fact, as the use of checks increased, state banks fared well. Demand deposits (checking accounts) and not bank note issues became the most important source of bank funds. State banking commissioners continued their own role in tandem with the comptroller. The existence of this "dual banking system" provided some important regulatory "checks and balances" between federal and state authorities. Centralization and concentration of government power were prevented by the diversity of views regarding critical regulatory needs—including the need for flexibility in the face of changing local markets.

The National Banking Act of 1863 proved inadequate. Banking remained essentially a local function with no mechanism to regulate the flow of money and credit which was necessary to assure the nation's system of finance.

Without a central banking structure, America's financial picture was increasingly characterized by inelastic currency and immobile reserves. The amount of currency in circulation often depended more on the value of bonds held by national banks than on the needs of the economy. Money could not easily be shifted to areas of particular need, a problem that worsened with the emergence of an industrial economy. And the inelasticity in the currency tended to aggravate matters rather than alleviate them, causing the economy to gyrate wildly and uncertainly between booms and busts.

In 1907, Congress initiated a study of the nation's money system. The Pujo Committee hearings persuaded most of the American people that ultimate control over America's banking and financial system rested in the hands of a tiny group on Wall Street—a "money trust." In its report, the Pujo Committee expressed concern that securities underwriting might become dominated by big bankers, who would thereby possess effective control of American industry. The committee generally concluded that purchases and sales of securities were illegal, and expressed "grave doubt" about the power of national banks to buy and sell bonds.[1] President Woodrow Wilson called for a system that would vest control in the government, "so that the banks may be instruments, not the masters, of business and of individual enterprise and initiative."[2]

The Pujo Committee's recommendation that national banks be prohibited from underwriting never received congressional attention. But its work did lead to passage of the Federal Reserve Act of 1913, establishing a "system" of twelve federal reserve banks. National banks were required to join the Federal Reserve System, but remained under regulatory authority of the comptroller; membership was optional for state-chartered banks. As the nation's central bank, the "Fed" was primarily responsible for the conduct of monetary policy; it also regulated state-member banks and bank holding companies. In executing its monetary policy-making functions, the Fed bought and sold government securities ("open market transactions"), supervised the issuance of federal notes and controlled the amount of currency in circulation, fixed the "discount rate" charged on loans to member banks, and determined the level of reserves that had to be kept on deposit with federal reserve banks.

With the outbreak of World War I, national banks became increasingly involved in the securities business; the federal govenment encouraged this new practice by allocating nearly half of its war bonds for distribution through national banks. The banks, which had overcome the traditional skepticism of large masses of people who saved money, found it easy to approach customers a second time with other securities. The recently installed Federal Reserve Board tacitly endorsed the legality of the bank securities affiliate by permitting state banks and trust companies to become members of the Federal Reserve System, without requiring them to divest their securities underwriting affiliates.

National banks, which had pondered the legality of securities affiliates, interpreted this move as a go-ahead signal to enter investment banking. The resulting increase in the number of state-chartered securites affiliates and the rapid growth of securities markets gave rise to a concern about the viability of the national banking system. But the comptroller, fearful of driving banks out of the national banking system, did not enforce existing securities restrictions on national banks; he subsequently became the driving force behind legislation expanding national bank powers.

Passage of the McFadden Act in 1927 reaffirmed the power of national banks to underwrite investment securities. A less prominent provision of the law allowed national banks to establish branches for the first time, but precluded interstate bank branching; intrastate branching continued to be governed by state law. The passage of the McFadden Act, coupled with the rising stock market, stimulated greater participation by commercial banks in investment banking. By the end of the decade, commercial banks, both state and national, had become the dominant force in the investment banking field.

At the same time that this trend toward relaxation of permissible securities activities was taking place, further pressure to relax those restraints arose as the traditional commercial loan business enterprises were able to relieve their debt burden through robust earnings or by issuing new stock. The largest and financially strongest corporations were especially quick to seize upon the opportunity to liquidate their debt in the presence of an active and rising stock market. Bank performance was already showing signs of weakness. Depressed farm conditions, combined with a reduced loan portfolio—that was not conforming to expected performance standards—was leading to an increase in bank insolvencies.

The stock market crash of 1929 undermined the public's confidence in the banking system, causing widespread withdrawals of bank deposits. Within three years of the first "bank run," nearly 9,000 banks had failed, and one-quarter of the nation's private financial assets lay in ruins.[3]

Investigation disclosed that some banks had serious conflicts of interest in connection with securities activities. Some banks had taken over the portfolios of speculative investments from securities affiliates to shore up the affiliate. Many banks had made excessive and imprudent loans that were tied either to their securities affiliates or to their customers who purchased stock on margin. The desire of large metropolitan banks to promote their securities business led them to abuse their relationships with regional correspondent banks which often relied on such city banks for investment advice. And some banks pushed the sale of their own bank stock through affiliates to depositors of the institution.[4]

Congress responded to this unprecedented financial crisis by adopting the Banking Act of 1933. The most significant sections of that legislation, which was commonly referred to as the Glass-Steagall Act, created a wall separating commercial banking from investment banking. Banks were prohibited from purchasing securities for their own account; they could, however, purchase less risky government bonds. Underwriting was similarly restricted. Member banks of the Federal Reserve System, which included the prominent national banks, could not affiliate with nor own an investment bank. Glass-Steagall kept securities firms out of banking by prohibiting the acceptance of deposits by any person or firm engaged in issuing, underwriting, selling, or distributing stocks, bonds, or other securities.

To help restore confidence in the banking system, the Banking Act established federal deposit insurance for individuals' deposits. Many depositors in failed banks had been unable to recover their savings, and those banks that did survive were badly damaged when their customers, fearful of spreading failures, withdrew their funds. The Federal Deposit Insurance Corporation (FDIC) was the third agency created specifically to regulate the banking industry. Because of the government's explicit stake in deposit insurance, the cost of deposits was regulated for the first time at the federal level, with a zero interest ceiling placed on demand deposits. The new system of insurance and interest-rate ceilings was designed to restrain competition, a direct result of the perception that "excessive competition" had helped precipitate the banking crisis.

The nation's banking policy proclaimed an overriding "public interest" in the "stability" of the financial system. Its tenets included the following:

1. *Safety and Soundness.* To ensure health of the financial system, lending limits, capital ratios and debt reserves were required to guarantee that credit risks were diversified, and that the bank had adequate resources to absorb losses that might occur. Liquidity, available as a "safety net" to the bank, prevented an individual bank failure from triggering a wider financial crisis.
2. *Consumer Protection.* To foster public confidence in the banking system, deposit insurance, disclosure requirements, and antifraud preventions were established.
3. *Efficiency.* To promote effective allocation of capital and development of strong links between users and demanders of capital, competition was promoted, but constrained so as not to be "excessive."

The combined elements of banking regulation created a highly fragmented market for financial services. Even so, the capital markets in the United States, encouraged by public policy, soon provided a highly efficient connection between the providers and the users of funds, directing resources into the most productive investments in the nation's economy.

REGULATORY FRAMEWORK

The U.S. financial services market is unique for its size, diversity of products, and range of different institutions involved. Over $6.2 trillion in private financial assets are handled by more than 50,000 different firms, from small credit unions with a few thousand dollars in assets to large money-center banks with over $100 billion in assets. Together, these financial intermediaries, accounting for 15% of the gross national product, serve as the "central nervous system" of the nation's economy.

Banks, savings and loan associations, and credit unions had all prospered from cheap money due to interest rate restrictions, and from the advantage afforded by federal deposit insurance. Nondepository institutions were also subject to regulatory oversight, but financial supervision was generally less stringent. Securities and commodity trading was subject to some federal regulation, but

Table 1 Total Private Financial Assets Percent Held By Different Financial Service Firms (Volume in Billions of Dollars)

	1950		1960		1970		1980		1984	
Depository Institutions	$ VOL	% MKT	$ VOL	% MKT	$ VOL	% MKT	$ VOL	% MKT	$ VOL	% MKT
Commercial Banks	149.6	50.6	228.3	37.4	504.9	36.7	1360.9	35.4	2012.9	32.5
Savings and Loans	16.9	5.7	71.5	11.7	176.2	12.8	629.8	16.4	989.9	15.9
Mutual Savings Banks	22.4	7.6	41.0	6.7	79.7	5.8	173.0	4.5	206.4	3.3
Credit Unions	1.0	0.3	6.3	1.0	18.0	1.3	69.6	1.8	115.8	1.9
Non-Depository Institutions										
Life Insurance Companies	62.6	21.2	115.8	19.0	200.9	14.6	456.1	11.9	692.4	11.1
Private Pension Funds	7.1	2.4	38.2	6.2	110.4	8.0	264.8	6.9	623.4	10.0
State and Local Government Retirement Funds	4.9	1.7	19.7	3.2	60.3	4.4	200.4	5.2	354.9	5.7
Other Insurance Companies	11.7	4.0	26.2	4.3	49.9	3.6	177.4	4.6	240.5	3.9
Finance Companies	9.2	3.1	27.6	4.5	64.0	4.7	180.1	4.7	294.1	4.7
Open-End Investment Companies	3.3	1.1	17.0	2.8	47.6	3.5	47.3	1.2	161.9	2.6
Securities Brokers and Dealers	4.0	1.3	6.7	1.1	16.2	1.2	34.6	0.9	60.5	0.9
REITs	0.0	0.0	0.0	0.0	0.9	0.1	6.8	0.2	4.7	0.1
Money Market Funds	0.0	0.0	0.0	0.0	0.0	0.0	78.4	2.0	209.7	3.4
Federal Agencies and Mortgage Pools	3.2	1.1	11.5	1.9	46.5	3.4	165.1	4.3	249.1	4.0
TOTAL	$295.9	100.0%	$609.7	100.0%	$1375.5	100.0%	$3844.3	100.0%	$6216.2	100.0%

Source: Board of Governors of the Federal Reserve System, *Flow of Funds.*

insurance was supervised exclusively by state authorities. Finance companies operated relatively free of federal or state regulation.

The financial assets of the commercial banking system were by far the largest of any intermediary in the system. In contrast to most other institutions, banks served the financial needs of all the "primary" sectors. Banks not only accepted deposits from all the primary sectors, but also helped meet the credit demands of each sector.

RELATIONSHIP OF COMMERCIAL BANKS TO THE PRIMARY FINANCIAL SECTORS

Commercial banks were the largest source of short-term financing for business corporations, and they extended intermediate-term credit to business as well. Banks held a significant portion of the outstanding debt of the federal government and retained the largest fraction of the outstanding debt of state and local governments. They were also an important source of consumer debt and mortgage financing. Commercial banks were active in lending to foreign corporations and governments, and served as an important source of liquidity for other financial intermediaries, through correspondent and interbank (Fed funds) relationships. Commercial banks alone issued demand deposits, which together with currency, were the primary means of payment for goods, services, and various financial transactions.

With government regulations so pervasive, banks had long operated in a stable environment. Profitability was guaranteed by the "spread" or price margin between regulated interest rates paid to depositors and the market rates charged for loans to bank customers. Banks traditionally turned a profit by pooling risk and by taking advantage of interest rate movements. Quipped one veteran money lender: "American bankers for decades have operated by the 3-6-3 rule—pay depositors 3% interest, lend money at 6%, and tee off at the golf course by 3 p.m."[5] And in the words of a firsthand observer of the Great Depression, bankers were "not supposed to be smart; they were supposed to be safe."[6]

Bank assets—which generate earnings—consisted of cash and bank balances, securities, commercial and industrial loans. Banks always had to maintain an adequate amount of currency on hand to meet operational needs. The Federal Reserve Board required that its member banks keep reserves equal to a stated percentage of deposits to guarantee that the banking system could meet unexpected deposit outflows. These reserves and reserve requirements served as the focal point for executing monetary policy. Loans were the largest class of assets held by commercial banks and the source of most of their profitability. Most were business loans, which were generally short-term, periodically reviewed credit arrangements. The remaining class of assets consisted entirely of U.S. government securities, which served both earnings and liquidity purposes.

Bank liabilities—which generate expenses—consisted of demand deposits, savings and time deposits, short-term borrowings, and capital. The original source of most bank funds was demand deposits. These deposits, payable "upon demand," served the transactions needs of depositors. Since banks could not pay interest on demand deposits, these deposits had been a relatively inexpensive source of funds. Savings and time deposits technically required "notice" before a withdrawal could be made. In return, banks paid depositors a stipulated rate of interest. Many large banks offered a particular form of time deposit, the "certificate of deposit" (CD). These large deposits left with the bank for a short, specified period of time had become an important source of funds in recent years. In addition, banks had the ability to borrow short-term funds from the Fed and its member banks. Lastly, bank capital served as a final source of funds, although capital ratios were carefully supervised to ensure the soundness of the bank.

By 1985, there were nearly 14,500 commercial banks in the United States. Although there had been no significant change in the number of banks during the past fifty years, branching had proliferated. There were also enormous differences in terms of both the class and size of commercial banks. The vast majority of banks were small institutions, with only a few large banks. In fact, over 80% of these institutions had less than $100 million in assets; 40%

Chart 1 Relationship of Commercial Banks to the Primary Financial Sectors

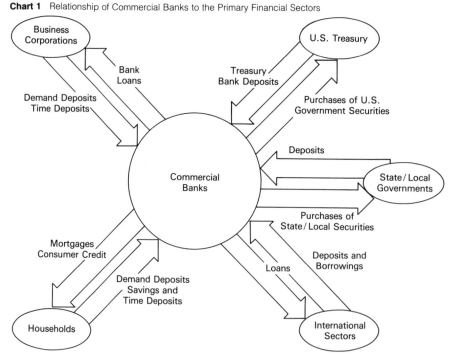

Source: J.O. Light and William L. White, *The Financial System* (Homewood, Ill.: Irwin, 1979), p. 202.

had less than $25 million in assets. By contrast the ten largest banks controlled nearly 40% of total banking assets.[7]

The dual banking system provided for three major regulatory categories of commercial banks: national banks, generally the largest institutions (with 60% of total bank assets) were regulated by the Office of the Comptroller of the Currency; state member banks (with 18% of total bank assets) were regulated by the Federal Reserve Board in tandem with state authorities; state nonmember banks (with 22% of total bank assets) were regulated by the Federal Deposit Insurance Corporation in association with the states. A lawyer viewing these confusing rules and laws observed, "No student of bank regulation can be less than apologetic about the complexity of the regulatory scheme, the voluminous compilation of promulgated permissions and restraints, the overlapping of regulatory authorities, and the intermixture of jealously guarded prerogatives."[8]

Differences in regulatory permissions and prohibitions and in regulatory philosophies from one type of financial institution to another had significantly affected the competitive position of each type of bank.

OFFICE OF THE COMPTROLLER OF THE CURRENCY (OCC)

The comptroller of the currency, under the general supervision of the Treasury Department, regulated and supervised 4,800 national banks under federal statutes that spelled out permissible and prohibited activities in great detail. The comptroller had to approve applications for the formation of new national bank charters, the conversion of state-chartered banks to national charters, the establishment of branch offices by these banks, and mergers and consolidations that produce a national bank. Bank examinations that determine financial soundness, quality of management, and compliance with laws and regulations were regularly conducted.

FEDERAL RESERVE BOARD (FRB)

Aside from its primary monetary policy functions which extended to both national and state "member" banks, the board was directly responsible for the examination of the approximately 1,100 state member banks. There was generally no adopted uniform state banking law; state banks were subject to varying laws and regulations from state to state including those governing their chartering and branching. The FRB had to approve mergers involving a state member bank; it had supervisory authority over the banks with regard to various consumer protection statutes.

Holding companies of both state and federal banks were regulated by the Federal Reserve Board. The bank holding company had become the preferred form of organization for nearly 75% of the nation's commercial banks. Under this corporate charter, bank holding companies could diversify their

Chart 2   Member Bank Income and Expenses

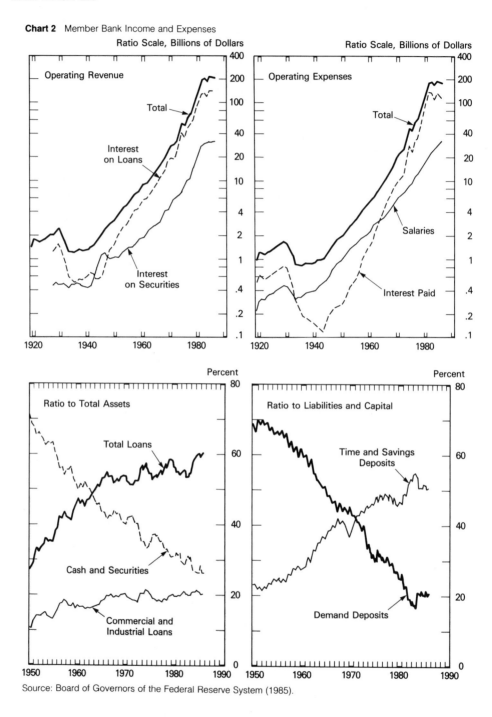

Source: Board of Governors of the Federal Reserve System (1985).

Chart 3 Commercial Banks in the United States

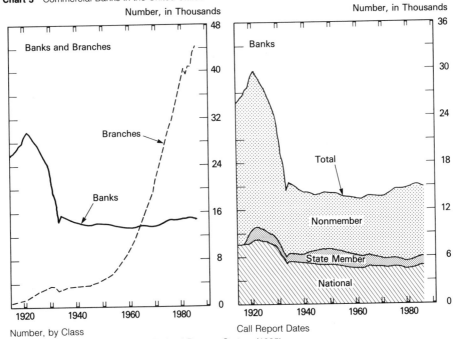

Number, by Class
Source: Board of Governors of the Federal Reserve System (1985).

Chart 4 Existing Regulation of Banks and their Holding Companies

Regulatory Agencies ⟶

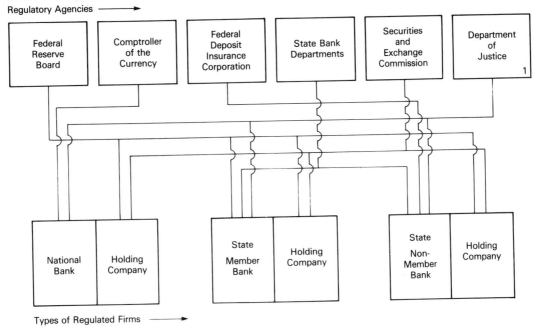

Types of Regulated Firms ⟶

1 Antitrust Enforcement only

Chart 4   (continued)

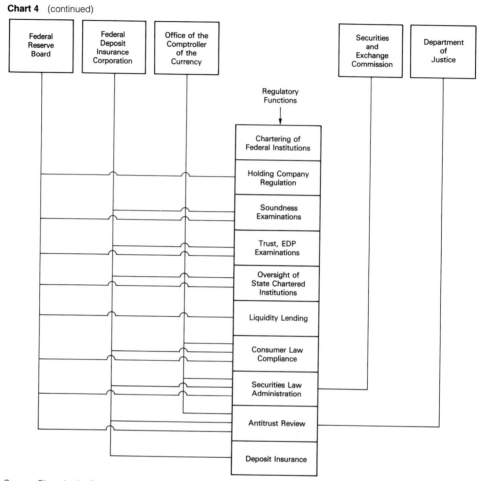

Source: Blueprint for Reform: The Vice President's Report of the Task Group on Regulation of Financial Services (1984).

operations, often circumventing some of the limitations on product and geographic diversification. The Fed determined what activities could be performed in bank holding companies or in its nonbank subsidiaries.

FEDERAL DEPOSIT INSURANCE CORPORATION (FDIC)

The FDIC was primarily responsible for administering the federal deposit insurance program and promoting safe and sound banking practices through its supervision of insured banks. Primary responsibility for the supervision of national banks rested with the OCC, and that for state member banks with the FRB. Thus, the primary thrust of FDIC regulation and supervision is directed at the approximately 8,600 FDIC-insured state banks that are not members of the Federal Reserve System. Because deposit insurance was generally quite important to the financial success of depository institutions, the FDIC, which must approve the applications of nonmember state banks for deposit insurance, had an important voice in the establishment of banks actually chartered by the various states. In addition to the administration of other prudential requirements, the FDIC may approve or disapprove of changes in control of state nonmember banks that are insured by it. It must also approve the establishment and relocation of branch offices.

By the mid-1980s, it had become clear that the regulatory framework for banking and finance was under serious assault. Depository institutions were finding that some government regulatory constraints that once benefited them were now a substantial handicap. They were increasingly competing with one another on the basis of regulatory disparities and with their unregulated competitors by attempting to circumvent government regulations.

Concerns about the significant overlap, duplication and fragmentation of banking supervision had periodically led to proposals for streamlining the regulatory apparatus. A recently released vice presidential task force report had suggested creation of a Federal Banking Authority, which would consolidate all bank regulation into one agency, leaving the Fed and FDIC to concentrate on monetary policy and deposit insurance respectively. Reforms in the federal deposit insurance system were also under review. Many ideas had been advanced to strengthen private incentives to control risk taking by institutions offering insured accounts. These included proposals to tie insurance premiums to some measure of risk; strengthen capital requirements; increase the risk exposure of large depositors; strengthen disclosure requirements; and privatize all or part of the deposit insurance system.

MIXED REGULATORY ENVIRONMENT

By the early 1980s, the structure of the financial system was increasingly being shaped by the forces of competition. Banks faced competition from other depository institutions, nondepository institutions, and large nonfinancial corporations. Regulations that barred entry into "protected" markets were undermined by changes in the financial environment. Competition—along price, product, and geographic dimensions—had sweeping ramifications for public policy in banking. The industry appeared in the early stages of a major regulatory transition. Sharp differences of opinion characterized debates about the future structure of the banking industry; some advocated further deregulation, while others firmly pressed reregulation of certain aspects of banking.

PRICE REGULATION

Price regulation, or ceilings on interest rates, was a central tenet of Depression-era banking legislation. It prohibited the payment of interest by member banks of the Federal Reserve System on demand deposits and authorized the board

Chart 5   Primary Dimensions of Competition

		Price of Input or Output	Scope of Products and Services	Geographic Scope of Activity
Primary Dimensions of Regulation	Federal	Regulation Q	Banking Act of 1933 (Glass-Steagall) Bank Holding Company Act	McFadden Act Douglas Amendment to Bank Holding Company Act
	State	Usury Laws		Branching Limits

Deregulation —————— - — — — — — — — —▶ ....▶

to set maximum rates of interest that member banks could pay on time deposits. Under this authority, the Fed issued its Regulation Q. Eventually, ceilings were applied to all federally insured banks, on the grounds that deposit insurance gave regulators a special responsibility to protect the commercial banking industry from pressures that could strain reserves. Fears about "excess competition" also provided the basis for many state usury laws; but these interest limitations applied only to the cost of *borrowed* money.

Until the 1960s, the legal constraints on interest rates payable on time deposits had no practical effect since market rates were generally below the Regulation Q ceiling. Because banks could not attract depositors with more favorable interest rates, they competed on a less explicit price standard. Deposits were solicited by offering promotional gifts and "free" checking accounts. Most important, banks saturated their markets with offices in order to provide customers with as much convenience as possible; they competed with "bricks and mortar." But erratic behavior by monetary authorities and a rising trend of inflation shattered the stability—and prosperity—of banks.

By 1965, rising market interest rates exceeded the ceiling mandated by Regulation Q. A "regulatory spread" developed between the cost of these deposits and the market-determined rates at which the deposits could be lent. In addition, the long-standing regulatory spread on interest-free demand deposits increased. During this period, the short-term financing demands of business and consumers grew very rapidly. But the traditional sources of most bank funds, "free" demand deposits, were becoming less accessible.

Large depositors were becoming more sophisticated with respect to cash management; they were less willing to hold demand deposits at a time when interest-bearing time deposits could yield significantly higher returns. In response, commercial banks sought to tap non-bank sources of money to fund escalating demands for credit; the large denomination certificate of deposit (CD) was invented and grew quickly to become the largest source of bank funds. To stimulate the economy, the Regulation Q ceiling was deliberately raised by the Fed to encourage the growth of bank time deposits. CDs, which had an initial maturity between one month and one year, were "negotiable" and could be traded in secondary markets.

The evolution toward a national CD market left banks with a liability structure whose costs were closely tied to open-market interest rates. In early 1968, interest rates began to rise again, threatening the Regulation Q-controlled CD market. This time, the Fed refused to raise the interest ceiling and most maturing CDs were not renewed by depositors. Large banks relieved the pressure of the contracting CD market by borrowing from foreign markets; the parent holding companies of these banks helped by bidding for funds in the commercial paper market. In addition, banks relied increasingly on the interbank federal funds market, "overnight funds" from corporate customers, and repurchase agreements (equivalent to a loan or interest-bearing deposit from a non-bank). Thrift institutions, which were heavily punished by inflation and interest rate restrictions, had started to offer NOW ("Negotiable Order Withdrawal") accounts, which combined the interest-bearing features of time deposits with the checking account privileges normally reserved for demand deposits. NOW accounts, which originated in New England, soon spread to other states.

The Fed, unable to prevent circumvention of Regulation Q, suspended interest rate restrictions on time deposits over $100,000 in 1973. While holders of larger deposits generally were able to avoid the restrictions on deposit interest rates, smaller "consumer depositors" remained subject to Regulation Q.

But this disparate treatment of depositors proved untenable. Mutual fund management companies that invested in short-term corporate obligations (CDs and commercial paper) developed rapidly. Because of large yield spreads between large- and small-denomination time deposits, mutual companies intermediated to offer households attractive savings alternatives. Attempts to "tune" the ceiling structure for different categories of deposits resulted in a proliferation of regulated accounts, from two in 1965 to twenty-four by 1978.[9] But as interest rates rose through the 1970s, disintermediation—the diversion of funds into unregulated instruments—accelerated.

Deregulation of consumer time-deposit interest rates began in 1978, when the Fed authorized a six-month, $10,000 certificate of deposit. Even though a large minimum deposit was required, the amount invested in these less regulated certificates grew to $178 billion by 1980. But this attempt to restrain disintermediation did not stop the savings outflow.

The money market fund (MMF), another ceiling-free investment vehicle, was also becoming extremely popular. Even though it was not insured, balances in these accounts jumped from $6.4 billion in 1978 to $78.4 billion by the end of 1980.[10] Technological advances made it possible for investors to hold checkable deposits in nondepository institutions; they could easily write checks on their balances in securities accounts or mutual funds. The securities industry was the most prominent manager of these funds, and helped to accelerate the disintermediation trend.

Faced with this shift away from rate-regulated accounts, depository institutions demanded the authority to compete on equal terms with the new consumer savings vehicles that were not subject to Regulation Q. Congress responded with passage of the Depository Institutions Deregulation and Monetary

Chart 6   Savings Deposit Inflows versus the Interest Rate Gap

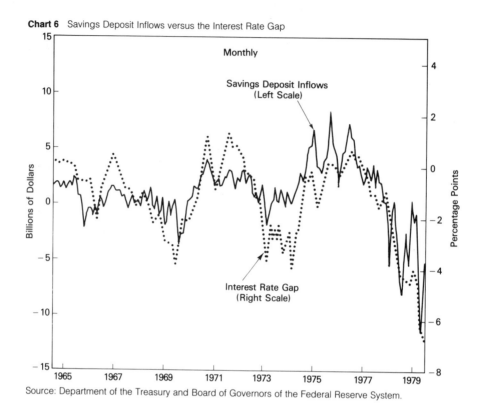

Source: Department of the Treasury and Board of Governors of the Federal Reserve System.

Control Act of 1980. The act mandated gradual removal of all federal interest rate ceilings (Regulation Q) and preempted many state usury laws, the latter of which capped interest earnings on loans. But uniform reserve requirements were imposed to bolster solvency ratios: Depository institutions that had not previously been subject to the Fed's capital standards—and had enjoyed a lending advantage—would now compete on a more equal basis.

By 1982, however, high and volatile interest rates convinced many depositors that the high rates earned on even relatively small balances held with money market funds more than offset their lack of federal insurance. The Garn–St. Germain Depository Institutions Act of 1982 instructed regulators to create and provide insurance for a savings vehicle comparable to the unregulated MMF—the money market deposit account (MMDAs). Congress also expedited the schedule for eliminating interest rate ceilings. In its first year of existence, the MMDA attracted $230 billion; while some depositors converted from rate-regulated accounts, nearly $55 billion was siphoned off the unregulated, uninsured MMFs.

The elimination of most price regulation meant traditional core deposits would cost more than in the past. Banks would have to make their own decisions about interest rates and those determinations would be shaped primarily by competitive pressures. In some local markets, cutthroat competition for deposits had developed, cutting sharply into banks' profit margins. As a result, banks were tending to price each service based upon its cost; "free" checking was vanishing.

In addition to its impact on interest expense, inflation had caused other bank costs to increase. Rising personnel expenses, between 15% to 20% per year for many banks, contributed further to the earnings squeeze. In a competitive era, cost control would be essential. To cut costs, most banks made extensive use of advanced information technology; but applications were confined mostly to the "back office" administrative, transaction processing, and account processing activities. The enormous growth of transactions had swamped manual processing systems, forcing ever-increasing reliance on technology as a cost-control tool. For example, only in recent years had the annual rate of growth in the number of checks slowed, from about 7% to about 5%. Even so, the financial services industry processed nearly fifty billion transactions at a cost of $20 billion in 1980; that volume was projected to double by 1990.[11] Through deployment of automatic teller machines (ATMs), banks were scaling down the costs of their retail branch networks.

Balance sheet management would also require much more attention. With rate deregulation, deposits were extremely liquid and could easily be moved with even the slightest change of interest rates. As a result, yields and maturities on bank assets (loans) would have to be carefully matched to bank liabilities (deposits). Although the "liability side" of balance sheets had been deregulated, banks still remained subject to regulation of their assets.

PRODUCT REGULATION

Federal law, as articulated in the Glass–Steagall sections of the Banking Act of 1933, embodied a long-standing policy of separating banking from other fields of finance and commerce. The functional limitations on bank activities could actually be traced to the English pattern of banking, which was designed to prevent London bankers from competing with merchants in the sale of goods and services. Moreover, this separation was provided to ensure that credit decisions would be made in a fair and impartial manner. The attempt to define "the business of banking," and to bar entry into other activities, had been the norm of functional regulation at both the state and federal level even before passage of the Banking Act.

Glass–Steagall prohibited banks from engaging in nonfinancial businesses outside the scope of traditional banking, either directly or indirectly through its subsidiaries. Banks, owing to their legacy of speculative use of depositor savings during the Great Depression, were also forbidden a role in securities and underwriting placement. The securities industry, likewise, was denied access to banking markets.

During the next two decades, bankers were reconciled to operating in an environment dictated by government management of money. In the trough of the Great Depression, the fundamentals of banking involved converting frozen investments into liquid funds; the New Deal years required bankers to find profitable outlets for idle funds. During World War II, the industry was to support war-loan drives, and to help finance productive enterprises contributing to the war. But in the aftermath of the war victory, there was an immense upward surge in America's standard of living. A radical expansion in consumer credit ensued.

While all this was in motion, commercial bankers were, "in a paradoxical sense, actively passive."[12] Most banks had ample reserves, a strong liquid position based on government securities acquired during wartime financing and low interest rates. Loans were made on the basis of funds available, and bankers rarely had to search beyond demand or time deposits for funding. "The banking accent of the day was on 'assets management'—another name for the 'funds using' side of a bank's balance sheet. 'Liability management'—another name for an active 'funds seeking' or 'funds buying' side of the balance sheet—was not a predominant concern of bankers."[13]

By the beginning of the 1950s, however, this passive approach to banking was under challenge. The demand for credit absorbed nearly all available deposit funds; inflation was on the rise. Competition for deposits was no longer a contest where commercial banks were rivals of one another. "It was now a contest between commercial banks and newly invigorated financial intermediaries—pension funds, mutual investment funds, credit unions, and savings and loans."[14] Between 1945 and 1960, though commercial bank savings increased 116%, mutual funds channeling private savings into equities increased 661%. Pension funds, a form of involuntary savings, increased 826%. Credit unions, starting from a very modest base, increased 1,005%. And deposits in savings and loan associations, which had always led the mortgage field, increased 641%.

A wave of bank mergers began, largely in response to the changed financial landscape. As the merger movement gained momentum, federal legislators and regulators, along with small bankers, tried to curb it by rules, antitrust enforcement, and restrictive legislation. Meanwhile, the fifty or so small bank holding companies then in existence moved quickly to acquire more affiliates while they still had a chance to expand. But Congress, wary of bank diversification, soon fixed its attention on bank holding company legislation. A consensus was impossible to achieve; sharp differences divided small and large bankers, as well as splitting federal and state regulators.

After seven years of debate, Congress finally approved the Bank Holding Company Act of 1956. The new law "was neither a freeze nor a death sentence. Its stated purpose used the word 'control,' not 'prohibit' or 'prevent.' "[15] Bank holding companies were allowed to expand, but could do so only under the regulatory scrutiny of the Federal Reserve Board. A bank holding company was defined as a corporation that controlled 25% or more of the voting shares of at least two banks, or otherwise controlled election of a majority of directors.

The Bank Holding Company Act established standards for the board in considering applications to form bank holding companies and for the acquisition of a bank by a bank holding company. One long-standing objective accomplished by the 1956 Act was the separation of activities unrelated to banking from multistate holding companies. The Act prohibited ownership of shares in non-bank corporations, other than approved bank-related activities, and required bank holding companies to divest themselves of such shares within two years.

Multibank holding companies were allowed to engage in certain activities—owning and managing a bank holding company property, providing services to subsidiary banks, operating a safe deposit company, and liquidating property acquired by subsidiary banks. Beyond these specifically permitted activities, the board was permitted to allow other non-banking activities that were "of a financial, fiduciary, or insurance nature" if they could pass the test of being "so closely related to the business of banking . . . as to be a proper incident thereto."[16] Although the act initially had little impact, it eventually provided for some bank diversification; these included real estate, insurance, management consulting, travellers cheques, securities transactions, data processing, investment advisory services, and courier services.

After 1956, one-bank holding companies—exempted from the Bank Holding Company Act—began to proliferate. These companies had mostly been small banks and their non-banking activity primarily involved local real estate and insurance. But when Congress simplified some of the act's merger standards in 1966, many of the nation's largest banks converted to the one-bank holding company form. This corporate organization allowed banks to use the holding company to circumvent Regulation Q, to capitalize on "back office" economies of scale, to diversify beyond bank-like product offerings, and to cross state boundaries.

Fears about excessive concentration of economic power led Congress to amend the Bank Holding Company Act in 1970. Small banks and state and federal regulators worried that if a bank were allowed to be part of a large conglomerate, American industry would develop along the lines of the Japanese zaibatsu, that combined ownership and control of major banks and industrial firms. As a result, one-bank companies were brought under Fed jurisdiction. The "closely related to banking" test was applied; bank holding companies also had to demonstrate that their subsidiaries were able "to produce benefits to the public, such as greater convenience, increased competition, or gains in efficiency . . . that outweigh adverse effects . . . such as undue concentration of resources."[17]

Even though more controls had been added, the next decade was an active period for bank holding company formation; limited product diversification was soon within reach of most bank companies. At the time of the 1970 amendments, there were just 121 bank holding companies, owning 898 banks; by 1984, there were 5,395 holding companies, owning 7,710 banks. These bank holding companies controlled nearly 75% of total bank assets.[18]

In the mid-1970s, segmented markets for bank services began to erode. Inflation and high interest rates forced many bank customers to become more sophisticated with respect to management of their savings. Before long, depositors (earning 4% on their savings) realized they were missing out on substantial income, available from money market funds paying 8%.

Convenience and declining costs stemming from technological advances were changing the way in which financial services could be delivered; they were also changing the "package." A veteran bank regulator offered a perspective on the declining cost curve of technological progress:

> This old order is being torn apart . . . and probably the most important element is the rate of technological improvements in transmitting, processing and storing information. In the last 15 years, the cost of processing data has declined by a factor of 10; the cost of storing information has declined by a factor of 50. Or, to put it in somewhat different words, now you could do with a $20 hand calculator what it cost $1 million to do in the 1950s through a giant computer. Or yet a third way, computing costs have been declining at an average annual rate of 25%; communications costs at 11%; and memory costs at 40%.[19]

Technology had reduced many of the cost barriers that prevented entry in the financial services marketplace. As a result, almost any entity with access to a large computer, either through ownership or time sharing, could become a potential provider of deposit and/or credit services, whether its traditional product base was insurance, manufacturing, retailing, or securities investments.

But it was the securities industry, with its money market fund, that first appealed to customers of bank services. Merrill Lynch's Cash Management Account accentuated the new delivery trend in financial services. This account tied together an individual's bond account, stock account, and money market fund with check-writing privileges; through its daily electronic account "sweep," funds could be supplied to meet individual transactions while also maximizing savings and investment gains.

Deregulation of trading commissions, which began in 1975, had exerted downward pressure on securities industry revenues, forcing brokerage houses to seek new sources of earnings. Since brokers had cultivated customer relationships and possessed electronic transactions capabilities, there was a strong inclination to broaden their product base. Unlike banks, securities firms were not subject to such strict pricing requirements and they could operate anywhere in the country. Over the past five years financial powerhouses, including Prudential/Bache and Shearson Lehman/American Express had merged, becoming banks in all but name. Said Citibank's Walter Wriston, "The bank of the future already exists, and it's called Merrill Lynch."[20]

State-chartered banks, not subject to Glass–Steagall restrictions, responded by offering full brokerage services and underwriting corporate securities. Until recently, that gap in the act had been of little consequence because other regulatory constraints made securities trading relatively unprofitable. That changed as a substantial segment of the market demanded "one-stop" financial shopping. Within the past three years, a number of national banks had entered the securities business by acquiring discount firms; the purchased companies were legally organized into separate subsidiaries. BankAmerica/Charles Schwab & Company, Security Pacific/Commission Discount Corporation, and Chase Manhattan/Rose & Company were but a few among many mergers that had occurred. For banks, securities transactions represented an opportunity to more fully utilize its substantial "back office" capabilities. In addition to providing banks with a broader range of services, these acquisitions helped banks defend against losses in the "high value" segment of the market.

Both commercial bankers and securities brokers believed they could offer an attractive array of services to consumers, arguing that their participation in one another's market was efficient and beneficial to the financial system. The traditional division between banking and securities was further blurred by the entry of some major insurance companies. John Hancock, Equitable Life, and the Kemper Group had each purchased a broker. The insurance industry had also encroached on the bank market, selling money market funds and stressing the earnings potential inherent in some of its insurance policies.

But it was the large nonfinancial corporations that especially alarmed commercial banks. These "non-banking-based" firms had entered the market, provided many "bank-like" services and prospered. The banking business had become crowded with industrial corporations, such as Gulf + Western, National Steel, General Electric, and General Motors; diversified financial concerns like American Express; insurance companies such as Prudential and Aetna; and a host of retail companies, including Sears, Montgomery Ward, Kroeger, K Mart and J.C. Penney.

The financial activity of Sears underscored the overall trend favoring "financial supermarkets." The giant retailer—with outlets spread across the country—held a significant stake in most segments of the financial services market: It had twenty-four million credit card customers and owned companies engaged in insurance, real estate, and securities brokerage. All these services were easily accessible at any Sears store.

The ten leading non-banking-based firms had been steadily increasing their financial services earnings. In 1972, these ten firms had combined financial earnings totalling over $600 million. By 1983, these firms had earned almost $3 billion from their financial-related ventures—about the same as the total worldwide earnings of the six largest bank holding companies ranked by earnings. This group excluded American Express, Prudential, and Merrill Lynch, whose combined 1983 earnings were also about $3 billion. [21] The finance subsidiaries of several companies such as Borg-Warner and Westinghouse were almost totally devoted to the financing of goods and services, unrelated to their parents' operations. They had become highly effective and direct competitors of commercial banks, at least on the asset side of the balance sheet.

Thrift institutions were also proving to be nimble competitors in bank markets. The thrift industry, which had experienced an unprecedented number of failures due to persistent inflation, was given increased powers with passage of the Garn–St. Germain Depository Institutions Act of 1982. Aside from lifting interest-rate restrictions, the act permitted lending for purposes other than hous-

Table 2 Estimated Financial Earnings of Nonfinancial-Based Companies

	1972		1982	
	Dollars in Millions	*% Total Earnings*	*Dollars in Millions*	*% Total Earnings*
Borg-Warner	6	11	39	21
Control Data	56	96	30	19
Ford Motor	44	5	292	20
General Electric	41	8	271	13
General Motors	96	5	1002	26
Gulf + Western	29	42	87	*
ITT	160	34	405	60
Marcor	9	12	68	126
Sears	209	34	703	52
Westinghouse	15	8	62	14
	665		2959	

*Gulf + Western reported a net loss for 1983.

Source: Board of Governors of the Federal Reserve System.

ing; specifically, authorizing loans to corporate customers. The legislation also provided for merger-related assistance to prevent closing or to reopen any insured institution when threatened by severe financial conditions. A number of banks, securities firms, and retail companies had already stepped in to buy up some of these ailing savings and loan associations.

Bank customers could now obtain financial services from a wide variety of intermediaries, including thrifts, securities firms, and insurance companies. Non-bank providers such as general merchandise stores, supermarkets, computer firms and industrial companies also offered products and services similar to banks. These competitors not only provided banking services directly, but also provided a variety of financial services that substituted quite favorably for banking products. In the view of the comptroller of the currency, "The public wants financial services, but it couldn't care less whether it gets them from banks."[22]

Proposals to ease line-of-business restrictions on banks had spurred great controversy. Proponents argued that economic efficiency would be increased by permitting banks to engage in a wider range of financial offerings. Product-line diversification could generally promote economic efficiency in two ways. First, it would reduce the total cost of marketing and delivering multiple services by consolidating their provision within one operation (most permissible nonbanking activities were performed by separate subsidiaries of the bank holding company). Savings could result from spreading fixed costs over a wider customer base. Second, customers would benefit from added convenience and increased competition.

Opponents responded that these changes would increase the overall riskiness of banks and lead to an unacceptable concentration of market power, thereby damaging smaller competitors. Deregulation of product offerings raised a number of issues with respect to the stability of the financial system. The existence of deposit insurance provided insured institutions some room to take undue risks in the hope of earning higher than normal returns. As a result, most of the bank supervision effort was designed to minimize speculative banking practices. But as the range of permissible banking activity increased, it could well become much more difficult to police the stability of the nation's banks.

GEOGRAPHIC REGULATION

Historically banks had been subject to a number of federal and state laws that restricted entry into new geographic markets. These barriers included the McFadden Act of 1927, the Douglas Amendment to the Bank Holding Company Act of 1956, and state branching laws.

The McFadden Act limited branching to state boundaries and delegated control of intrastate branching to state law. It was clear, particularly in the debate over McFadden, that Congress feared that the consolidation brought on by branching and holding company acquisitions would destroy the existing system of independent banks, resulting in an unhealthy concentration of financial resources. That neither disintegration of existing banks nor substantial banking concentration had occurred was testimony to the protections built into the regulatory framework. The number of banks had remained stable and concentration actually declined since the Depression. In 1940, 56.7% of deposits were held by the top 100 banks; by 1980, their share had declined to 45.5%[23]

Until enactment of the Bank Holding Company Act of 1956, banks used the holding company to skirt existing branching laws. The bank holding company could be used to aggregate within one enterprise the powers of both a state and national bank, allowing it a multiple-state presence. Pursuant to an amendment offered by Senator Douglas, the 1956 Act prohibited bank holding companies from acquiring any futher interests outside its primary state of business.

Intrastate branching of both national and state-chartered banks was controlled by state law. State legislators enacted tough geographical restrictions on banks for two primary reasons: First, it was thought that such branching limits would prevent the outflow of funds from rural areas to large money centers; second, it was believed the laws would help preserve local management and ownership of banks. Most states had restricted branching, either by prohibiting it altogether, known as "unit banking," or by limiting branches to a particular city or county. By the mid-1980s, many states had relaxed their restrictions; about half permitted statewide branching.

Most of the largest banks, however, were able to establish some form of interstate presence, notwithstanding the constraints imposed from the state-by-state banking regime. Banks cultivated corporate loans through Loan Production Offices (LPOs) and serviced international credit demands through "Edge Act" offices. Cash management could also be performed on a national basis. Banks

Table 3 State Restrictions on Intrastate Branch Banking (Number of States)

CLASSIFICATION	1929	1951	1961	1983
Branching prohibited............................	28	17	16	8
Branching permitted but geographically limited	11	14	15	18
Unlimited branching	9	17	19	24

Source: American Bankers Association and Board of Governors of the Federal Reserve System.

could lend nationwide by distributing credit cards and soliciting consumer loans through retail lending offices. But deposit-taking was still strictly prohibited.

The success of automatic teller machines (ATMs) had created a new trend in banking, with ramifications for interstate branching. Instead of building large, full-service branches that were personnel intensive and very costly, many banks were replacing these structures with satellite branches, which were small-scale, highly automated branches. ATMs, for the most part, replaced the teller. National or "shared" ATM networks enabled users to obtain cash at locations that could not be served directly by the finanacial institution holding the account. Moreover, funds were available around the clock.

ATM deployment had increased nearly 35% per year since being introduced in the early 1970s. Some states had established very strict, off-premise deployment laws; the question of whether an ATM or a POS (point-of-sale) terminal was legally a branch was under judicial review. Other states encouraged their use and some permitted interstate deployment of ATMs. The New England states even allowed deposit-taking on the ATM networks within the region. Automated transactions were projected to climb rapidly; experts projected that the number of ATMs would more than double to 77,000 units by 1990.[24]

Some recent changes in federal and state banking laws had affected the so-called "interstate banking" issue. The 1982 Garn–St. Germain Depository Institutions Act, passed to relieve the thrift industry crisis, allowed banks and others to cross state lines to rescue unstable savings and loan associations. Sears and Citibank were among the most aggressive suitors; they gained by legal acquisition what was unavailable under existing statute—a source of interstate deposits.

Twelve states (clustered in New England and in the Southeast), had passed national or regional interstate banking laws. These laws permitted interstate banking on a regional, reciprocal basis only. Regional banking "compacts" would allow cross-border mergers with banks in other states that had similar laws giving smaller banks a chance to combine and grow stronger, to prepare for the full advent of nationwide banking. The New England banking pact, which deliberately excluded New York State—and its large money-center banks—was being challenged before the Supreme Court of the United States. The New York City banks were eager to expand outside their home markets, which were saturated with competition; they considered the regional compacts to be "anticompetitive."

A few states passed special legislation that encouraged out-of-state entry.

Chart 7 ATMs in the United States

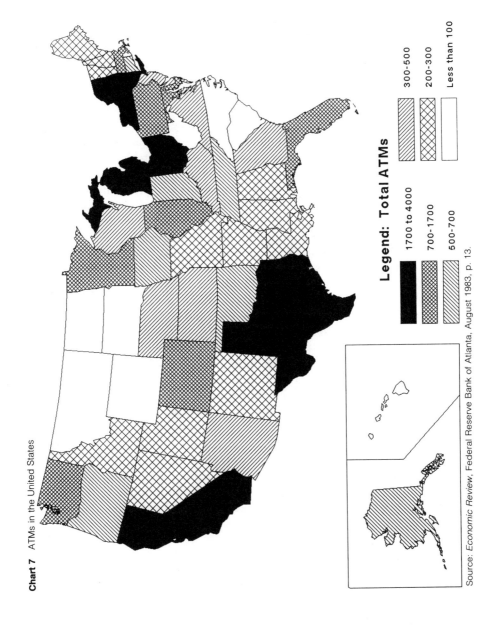

Legend: Total ATMs

1700 to 4000

700-1700

500-700

300-500

200-300

Less than 100

Source: *Economic Review*, Federal Reserve Bank of Atlanta, August 1983, p. 13.

419

South Dakota enticed Citibank to establish a limited national bank in the state; this allowed the bank to escape New York's state usury ceiling and provided an economic stimulus to the state. But as part of its charter Citibank agreed not to compete against in-state rivals. Delaware passed similar legislation, offering itself as a base for money-center expansion in return for the promise of economic development. In addition, some states had permitted "toehold" investments by out-of-state bank holding companies, contingent upon the repeal of interstate banking prohibitions. But state authorities were not uniformly in favor of more interstate activity; in fact, when the conditions appeared to be imposed by the federal government, they resisted fiercely.

A number of large bank holding companies were trying to establish interstate networks of limited-purpose, "non-bank banks." These banks circumvented the definition of a bank (skirting regulatory jurisdiction of the Bank Holding Company Act) by performing only one-half of the regular functions of full-service banks. Non-bank banks would either make loans *or* take deposits—but it would not do both. The comptroller of the currency, who had to review hundreds of non-bank bank applications, had so far withheld the granting of charters, pending congressional legislation.

Those advocating geographical deregulation believed the banking system could become more stable with some form of nationwide banking. Banks located in declining markets could look elsewhere for earnings opportunity and would be less vulnerable to local swings in the economy. The advantages of diversifying economic risk across geographic markets was a major incentive to interstate expansion. A bank that could serve the needs of the agricultural market in the Midwest, export financing on the West Coast, and consumer lending in the East could better balance its lending risks. There were also certain economies of scale that could be realized by interstate expansion; those electronic economies could usually be appreciated once a bank grew to $100 million in assets.[25]

Relaxation of geographical restraints was likely to reduce the number of small "independent" banks; but it would probably increase the number of branches in a given community. Strong local banks would continue to prosper, benefiting from long-standing ties to their community. Although some institutions, particularly the less well managed, might disappear, it was quite likely they would be acquired by more efficiently run organizations. But these geographic barriers retained "an almost mythical significance" to their supporters.[26] Any attempt to deregulate would be met by a well-organized, politically-astute opposition.

DEREGULATION RECONSIDERED: ARE BANKS SPECIAL?

While few doubted that the business of banking had undergone revolutionary changes, some questioned the ramifications for public policy. While many advocated continued deregulation, there was a considerable body of opinion that urged regulatory restraint in the name of "safety and soundness." There had been a large increase in the number of bank failures in recent years. Much of this increase could be attributed to the severity of the recent recession which exacerbated problems of mismanagement and mismatched assets and liabilities. Nevertheless, changes in the risk characteristics of financial institutions could have a significant effect on failure rates in the future. In 1984, the banking system had been jarred by the collapse—and subsequent government rescue—of Continental Illinois Bank, the largest single bank collapse in U.S. history. Although some blamed deregulation for this failure, others argued that excess regulation caused the problem.

Reflecting on the competitive situation facing most banks, a governor of the Federal Reserve System asked for a reconsideration of financial market deregulation. He questioned the popular view of the financial marketplace, and rested his case on the "special" nature of banks.[27]

> The recent evolution of the financial structure in the United States has produced two competing points of view regarding the proper direction for further change. On the one hand, there is the view that the "financial services industry"—encompassing banks, thrifts, brokers, investment banks, and insurance companies—should be looked at as a single entity. According to this view, efforts to distinguish among kinds of institutions are both futile and unnecessary. This view of the financial services industry is based on the belief that many financial services offered by various classes of institutions are so complementary to (or such close substitutes for) one another that institutional distinctions are rendered useless. Implicit in this view is the assumption that banks are not special.
>
> The competing, if not opposing, view is that banks are indeed special. This

Chart 8   Banking Failures

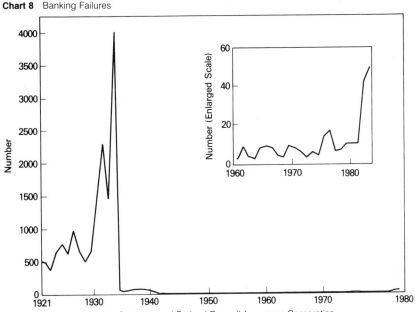

Source: Comptroller of the Currency and Federal Deposit Insurance Corporation.

view holds that specialization of financial institutions has worked well and, at least in some cases, specialization may still be more efficient and also better serve the public interest. This view is associated with the historical separation of banking from commerce and from investment banking. In general, this "separation doctrine" in banking grew out of concerns about concentration of financial power, possible conflicts of interest, and the appropriate scope of risks banks should incur in the face of the special trusteeship falling on institutions that engage in the lending of depositors' money. In a shorthand way, as pertains to banks and the banking system, these concerns are typically captured by the phrase, "safety and soundness."

These two points of view do not necessarily represent mutually exclusive approaches to financial market structure. For example, in the context of a large financial services holding company, banks could be legally separated from non-banks, but it is not clear that such separation would necessarily provide the kinds of protection that are currently built into federal banking laws.

Thus, assessing the merits of these two competing views must start with some very basic questions: Are banks "special" or are they simply another provider of financial services? Does it matter what kinds of risks banks incur? Does it matter who owns banks? Is "safety and soundness" a cliché, or should it have a genuine and substantial meaning for banks, for bank regulators, and for the public at large?

NOTES

1. *Report of the Committee to Investigate the Concentration of Money and Credit*, 62nd Congress; 3rd session. 130 (1913) ("Pujo Report"), p. 152.
2. Roger T. Johnson, *Historical Beginnings...The Federal Reserve* (Federal Reserve Bank of Boston, 1982), p. 25.
3. American Enterprise Institute for Public Policy Research, *Proposals to Deregulate Depository Institutions* (Washington, D.C.: American Enterprise Institute Legislative Analysis, 1984), p. 4.
4. *Hearing Pursuant to S. Res. No. 71 Before a Subcommittee of the Senate Committee on Banking and Currency*, Part I, 71st Congress; 3rd session, p. 1001 (1931).
5. Stephen Koepp, "Banking Takes a Beating," *Time*, December 3, 1984, p. 48.
6. "The New Shape of Banking," *Business Week*, June 18, 1984, p. 104.
7. *Blueprint for Reform: The Report of the Task Group on Regulation of Financial Services*, Vice President George Bush, Chairman of Task Group (Washington, D.C.: Government Printing Office, 1984), p. 103.
8. Ibid., p. 20.
9. Council of Economic Advisers, *Economic Report of the President (1984)* (Washington, D.C.: Government Printing Office, 1984).
10. Board of Governors of the Federal Reserve System, *Flow of Funds Accounts, Assets and Liabilities Outstanding (1960–1983)* (Washington, D.C.: Government Printing Office, 1984).
11. *Effects of Information Technology on Financial Services Systems* (Washington, D.C.: U.S. Congress, Office of Technology Assessment, OTA-CIT-202, September 1984).
12. George Eccles, *The Politics of Banking* (Graduate School of Business: University of Utah, 1982), p. 115.
13. Ibid.
14. Ibid., p. 116.
15. Ibid., p. 119.
16. *The Bank Holding Company Movement to 1978: A Compendium (A Study by the Staff of the Board of Governors of the Federal Reserve System)* (Washington, D.C.: Publications Services, Board of Governors of the Federal Reserve System, September 1978), p. 46.
17. Ibid., p. 61.
18. *Blueprint for Reform: The Report of the Task Group on Regulation of Financial Services*, Vice President George Bush, Chairman of Task Group (Washington, D.C.: Government Printing Office, 1984), pp. 21, 104.
19. *The Future of Commercial Banking (Proceedings of the 1982 Political Economy Research Institute Conference on Banking and Financial Institutions)* (Santa Fe, N.M.: 1982), p. 54.
20. Stephen Koepp, "Banking Takes a Beating," *Time*, December 3, 1984, p. 50.
21. Harvey Rosenblum, "Banks and Non-banks: Who's in Control?," *The Bankers Magazine* (September/October 1984), p. 13.

22. Stephen Koepp, "Banking Takes a Beating," *Time*, December 3, 1984, p. 50.
23. *Blueprint for Reform: The Report of the Task Group on Regulation of Financial Services*, Vice President George Bush, Chairman of Task Group (Washington, D.C.: Government Printing Office, 1984), p. 21.
24. *Effects of Information Technology on Financial Services Systems*, (Washington, D.C.: U.S. Congress, Office of Technology Assessment, OTA-CIT-202, September 1984), p. 118.
25. Ibid., p. 263.
26. *Geographic Restrictions on Commercial Banking in the United States*, The Report of the President (Washington, D.C.: Government Printing Office, January 1981), p. 1.
27. Federal Reserve Bank of Minneapolis, *Annual Report (1982)* (Washington, D.C.: Government Printing Office, 1982), p. 5.

The Comptroller and Non-bank Banks

The U.S. Comptroller of the Currency, C. Todd Conover, did not particularly enjoy standing in line. "I hate to be kept waiting. I thought by now I would be able to obtain new products and services at my local bank. But if I want to obtain the full range of financial services, I still have to do business with Sears." As Conover scanned Congressman St. Germain's letter, it was apparent the wait was over; after eighteen months of prodding, Congress—or more precisely, the House of Representatives—had "failed to step up to its legislative responsibilities for modernizing the nation's financial system."

The news from Capitol Hill was disappointing, but not a total surprise; banks had come out empty-handed. As a result, the comptroller—regulator of all nationally chartered banks—would have to deal with the crumbling regulatory structure of commercial banking. The "non-bank" or so-called "loophole bank" was the largest and most controversial issue. Non-bank banks were a means by which securities, insurance, retailing, and other non-banking companies had circumvented regulation to enter the banking business. More recently, bank holding companies had formed limited-purpose banks to establish an interstate presence, skirting long-standing geographical limitations.

These roundabout developments hardly disturbed the nation's chief bank regulator; in fact, Conover, who served as President Reagan's "point man" for bank deregulation, openly embraced non-bank banks as good public policy. But the much-revered and all-powerful Federal Reserve Board adamantly contested the rise of non-bank banks; they were "illegal," threatening the "safety and soundness" of the financial system. State banking commissions argued forcefully that non-bank banks impinged directly on their "states' rights" and would irreparably harm the "dual banking structure." Small bankers warned of a banking system that would lose its "independence" and become "dangerously concentrated" in the hands of a few money-center institutions. Congress had been outraged.

Conover branded these views "arcane, alarmist and anticompetitive." But in order to foster a full debate over bank public policy, he had twice delayed approving charters by imposing moratoria on non-bank banks. The comptroller had cooperated with banking committees in both the Senate and House with

---

This case was prepared by Research Associate Dekkers L. Davidson, under the supervision of Professor Richard H.K. Vietor, as a basis for class discussion rather than to illustrate either the effective or ineffective handling of an administrative situation. This case was developed from material available in the public record.

Chart 1

U.S. HOUSE OF REPRESENTATIVES

COMMITTEE ON BANKING, FINANCE AND URBAN AFFAIRS

NINETY-EIGHTH CONGRESS

2129 RAYBURN HOUSE OFFICE BUILDING

WASHINGTON, D.C. 20515

September 20, 1984

Honorable Jake Garn
Chairman
Committee on Banking, Housing
 and Urban Affairs
U.S. Senate
Washington, D.C. 20510

Dear Mr. Chairman:

Congratulations on your passage of S. 2851. Your handling of S. 2851 over these two sessions of Congress should leave no doubt in anyone's mind of your ability to fashion a legislative package which the Senate will adopt overwhelmingly.

As I stated to you in my letter of August 9, 1984, "There simply is no consensus on the subject (about how the financial community can be structured to best meet the needs of the nation), and a comprehensive banking bill, expanding the powers of depository institutions, could not pass our Committee or the House at this time."

Having checked with a number of members of our Committee and others in the leadership since passage of your bill, it appears the above observation regarding the lack of time is still correct given the extensive nature of your bill, and the commitments for consideration of necessary appropriations and other legislation on the House Floor during the closing weeks of this session.

Please be assured the subjects contained in your S. 2851, along with other necessary matters, will be considered by our House Committee on Banking, Finance and Urban Affairs at the beginning of the next Congress.

Again, I commend you and, in conclusion, again raise the question contained in my letter of August 9, 1984. Should we at this time consider perhaps not a permanent closing of the so-called bank loophole, but rather a Joint Resolution directing the Comptroller of the Currency to continue the moratorium.

With best regards.

Sincerely,

Fernand J. St Germain
Chairman

hopes for establishing a framework for broad financial services deregulation. Conover also tried to cultivate relations with key committee chairmen, but the results had been mixed. Conover and Senator Garn shared similar philosophical views but differed over legislative detail; Representative St. Germain, however, was a nemesis.

St. Germain's letter provided formal notice of the legislative stalemate; the "perceived non-bank bank crisis" had not stirred the hoped-for congressional reaction. Conover's moratorium was due to expire at the end of the current legislative session—less than two weeks away. There was, however, an outside possibility that Congress would return after the election for a "lame duck" session. And then there was that curious last sentence in St. Germain's letter mentioning a "Joint Resolution"—which was a bill so far as the processes of Congress were concerned. Such a resolution had the full force of law, once signed by the president.

THE DEFINITION OF A BANK

The term "bank" was defined in the Bank Holding Company Act to mean "any institution organized under the laws of the United States, any State of the United States, [or] the District of Columbia...which (1) accepts deposits that the depositor has a legal right to withdraw on demand, *and* (2) engages in the business of making commercial loans."[1] A "bank holding company" is any company or other business entity which controls a "bank," as that term is defined in the Bank Holding Company Act.

> The purposes of the Act . . . are to provide federal regulation and supervision over bank holding companies, to prevent the undue concentration of commercial banking activities, and to maintain the traditional separation between banking and [commerce] in order to prevent abuses in the allocation of credit.[2]

Bank holding companies are subject to extensive regulatory supervision by the Board of Governors of the Federal Reserve System, and, as a general matter, are prohibited from engaging in non-banking activities or owning non-banking-related subsidiaries. All bank holding companies must register with the board, and board approval is necessary prior to the formation of a new bank holding company, or the acquisition of additional banking or non-banking interests. Finally, the Douglas Amendment to the Act prohibits a bank holding company located in one state from acquiring a bank in another state, unless allowed in the second state. The Act, however, did not preempt state banking law.

The current two-pronged definition of a bank had not always been a feature of the Bank Holding Company Act. The original Act of 1956, defined a bank to mean "any national banking organization or any State bank, savings bank, or trust company."[3] A chartering test was then applied: If the financial institution was chartered as a bank by either the comptroller or state, it was considered a bank for purposes of the Act. It included savings banks within its definition of a "bank," despite the fact that these banks were generally considered to be "thrift" institutions.

In 1966, the Act was amended, narrowing the definition to include only those institutions which accepted demand deposits (the first half of the present two-part test). The change was made in order to limit the scope of the Act to commercial banking; savings banks were thereby excluded. However, even this definition was considered too broad since it could also include institutions which were not in fact engaged in the business of commercial banking.

The additional requirement of "making commercial loans" was added in 1970. At the time, however, the Federal Reserve Board indicated that "this amendment would have a very limited application. . .possibly affecting only one institution [Boston Safe Deposit and Trust Company]."[4] Boston Safe was an institution principally engaged in a trust business, but it made a limited number of loans on an occasional basis and as an accommodation to its established customers. But Boston Safe's loan activities, along with its purchases of money market instruments (such as certificates of deposit, commercial paper, and bank acceptances) were exempted from the Act and Fed supervision pursuant to a special exclusion authored by Senator Edward Brooke (R-Massachusetts). Congress instructed the Fed to construe this "exemption. . .as narrowly as possible in order that all bank holding companies which should be covered under the Act in order to preserve the public interest will, in fact, be covered."[5]

During the 1970s, the Federal Reserve Board, which had statutory authority to administer the Bank Holding Company Act, constructed a number of administrative definitions of a "bank." These opinions, usually issued in the form of regulations and orders clarified the terms "demand deposit" and "commercial loan." This was highly important in determining a workable definition of a bank.

In 1971, the board decided that credit balances maintained by an investment company were incidental to the business and not equivalent to demand deposits. Banks, noted the Fed, were "those institutions that offer to the public the general convenience of checking account facilities."[6] A few years later, the board reaffirmed its position with respect to the nature of credit balances in an order approving the operation of an investment company as a non-banking subsidiary of a bank holding company. It was apparent that the Board of Governors considered the acceptance of demand deposits as one of the critical elements in determining whether an institution was a bank; but it was clear they would look beyond the "technical relationship" between depositor and depository.

The Federal Reserve Board had also issued several opinions with respect to the commercial loan aspect of the definition of a bank. In 1971, the Board was asked whether a commercial bank would continue to be a bank under the Act if it terminated its commercial loan business. The Board concluded that such a bank would not be covered under the Bank Holding Company Act. In its ruling, the Fed explained its view as to the scope of commercial loans:

> Commercial loans are considered all loans to individuals or businesses, secured or unsecured, other than a loan the proceeds of which are used to acquire property or services used by the borrower for his own personal, family, or household purposes, or for charitable purposes.[7]

In 1976, the board was asked its opinion as to whether a "broker call loan" would constitute "commercial lending." The board concluded that it was not, because it was a passive medium of investment that did not "have the close lender-borrower relationship . . . characteristic of commercial loans."[8]

WHEN IS A BANK NOT A BANK?

"When it is an abomination," proclaimed the headline on one *Wall Street Journal* article.[9] A bank could become a non-bank by intentionally restructuring so as not to meet the technical definition of bank under the Bank Holding Company Act. Non-bank banks circumvented regulation from the Federal Reserve Board by performing only half the normal functions of a bank; they could either "accept demand deposits" *or* "make commercial loans," but not both.

A non-bank bank looked just like a bank, a fact that infuriated its critics. Sniped one Washington lawyer: "They have tellers and officers on the floor and gold letters on the windows. You can even hire an overweight old person to be a guard."[10]

Linguists, who abhorred the expression "non-bank," dubbed these limited service institutions "semibanks" or "demibanks." Nobody was sure who to blame for the phrase. "We suspect it comes from the Federal Reserve Board because it's so negative," sniffed a lobbyist for non-bank banks.[11] Negative or not, the Fed said "it would never stoop to such a linguistic low as 'non-bank bank.'"[12] Banking experts trace the term to a 1980 article by John D. Hawke, a prominent Washington, D.C. bank attorney, in which he first posed the question: "When is a bank not a bank?"[13] Hawke acknowledged using the term but couldn't recall having consciously invented it.

"There is, of course, the possibility that whoever invented it has already been shot," ventured one bank consultant. "For anyone who cares about our precious language, the expression 'non-bank' is surely provocation enough." The consultant suggested a substitute, "loophole banks."[14] But that, he conceded, wouldn't sit well with deregulation advocates, who blamed archaic banking rules for the whole mess. Indeed, "only regulation could spawn a nonanything anything," observed a non-bank bank advocate. "The non-bank bank deserves a better birthright."[15]

THE FIRST NON-BANK BANK

In June 1980, Gulf + Western's subsidiary, Associates First Capital Corporation (Associates) announced its intention to acquire the Fidelity National Bank, located in California. Associate's application noted that it would acquire 80% of the bank, and then divest its commercial loan portfolio—thereby removing itself from jurisdiction of the Federal Reserve Board. But it was the comptroller of the currency, and not the Fed, that had statutory authority to review the merger application of the nationally chartered bank. Associates filed its application with the comptroller's regional office in San Francisco.

Upon receipt of the application, a director in the regional office immediately alerted his counterpart at the Federal Reserve Bank of San Franscisco that the Associates acquisition raised "substantive policy and legal questions under the Bank Holding statutes."[16] A week later, the Reserve Bank replied: "We agree with your statement, but believe that the nature of the questions suggest that it . . . be resolved between our respective Washington offices."[17] Because of mail delays, it took nearly two months for the Fed's Washington office to receive the Associates application.

On August 12, 1980 the comptroller of the currency indicated it had no objection to the acquisition of Fidelity by Gulf + Western's Associates; the merger was approved.* A few months later, the Fed reluctantly concluded that Fidelity was no longer a bank within the meaning of the Bank Holding Company Act. In reviewing the legislative history of the Act, the board noted that Congress "intended to exclude those demand deposit-taking institutions engaged solely in noncommercial lending from the definition of a bank."[18] The non-bank was born.

TESTING THE NON-BANK WATERS

In November 1980, Wilshire Oil Company of Texas announced that it would transform its banking subsidiary (Trust Company of New Jersey) into a non-bank bank by reserving the right to require fourteen days' notice prior to permitting a withdrawal from its checking accounts. (Wilshire had been ordered to divest either its non-banking interests (such as its oil business) or banking subsidiary by the end of the year.) The 1970 amendments to the Bank Holding Company Act allowed bank holding companies ten years to separate through divestiture their commercial business and banking operations. With the divestiture deadline just a month away, Wilshire argued that its trust company was no longer a bank since it no longer accepted deposits that the depositor had a "legal right" to withdraw on demand.

Even though Wilshire publicly announced it would no longer treat deposits as "payable upon demand," it had informed existing bank customers (but not new customers) that it had no intention of exercising this right. The Federal Reserve Board charged that Wilshire's quasi-NOW (Negotiable Order Withdrawal) accounts evaded the Bank Holding Company Act, since its fourteen day notice requirement served no banking purpose other than to remove the trust company from the technical scope of the Act. Its administrative decision against

---

*Non-bank banks, when chartered as limited service "national banks," came under the regulatory jurisdiction of the comptroller of the currency. Chartering was purely an administrative process, whereby a set of preestablished standards were routinely applied. If it could be demonstrated that the applicant had adequate capitalization, well-trained management, and proper facilities for banking, the charter was granted.

Wilshire apparently focused on the practical aspects of the account. But according to leading bank experts, there was a strong flavor in the ruling hinting that if Wilshire had limited NOW accounts to individuals (excluding businesses), it might have been allowed to retain the trust company.

In May 1981, the Federal Reserve Board not only sanctioned the formation of a limited-purpose state bank by Chrysler Corporation, but granted it access to Federal Reserve System services. The board, in passing on the Chrysler application, acknowledge that Chrysler's case was an exception, not because the bank was organized to bypass "normal banking channels," but because Chrysler was unable to obtain the collection services used by the automotive industry from normal banking sources and "no other viable alternatives existed."[19]

By 1982 non-bank banks started to multiply. Household Finance and Avco Financial Services, both large finance companies, bought small California banks. Parker Pen Company joined the list by gaining control of a small New Hampshire bank, and then divesting its commercial loan portfolio. Each of these acquisitions was approved by the comptroller on the condition that they confine their business to retail lending. In short, the comptroller would allow commercial corporations to become "consumer banks," but commercial lending was still off limits. The non-bank vehicle allowed non-bank financial and commercial companies access to the Fed's system of payments (which facilitated checking transactions) and provided access to the FDIC's insurance (which facilitated deposit taking).

Citicorp, the nation's largest bank holding company, had taken note of these developments and was rumored to be considering the "option" of spinning off its national bank. According to Walter Wriston, the holding company's chairman, a bankless Citicorp would then "start a consumer bank in every state" using the loophole in the bank Holding Company Act definition of a bank.[20] In fact, Citibank did acquire a limited-purpose national charter to conduct its credit card business from South Dakota, which allowed it to move away from New York's restrictive usury laws. Citibank's thinking with regards to "debanking" further underscored the dramatic amount of "legal experimentation" then underway with non-bank banks.

According to one former Fed official, the Fed had been "asleep at the switch." More often than not, it was the flow of paper that determined how a regulatory issue was decided. The Fed's primary mission was monetary policy; bank regulation was a "weak sister" at the central bank, rarely receiving the attention accorded questions of monetary supply. Lacking a staff director for regulatory policy, there was not an effective mechanism for developing a real policy on interstate banking. "The regulatory attitude centered on stopping any evasion of policy, no matter what. . .no one really ever bothered to ask whether a particular development, evasive or not, was good or bad public policy."

THE RISING NON-BANK TIDE

By the end of 1982, increased utilization of the two-pronged definition of a bank to create non-bank banks prompted the Fed to question whether a "de facto" repeal of the Bank Holding Company Act was underway. This concern led the board to expand its definition of demand deposit. The Fed held that a NOW account was functionally equivalent to a demand deposit, since the full notice period (fourteen to thirty days) was rarely required. This position was applied to thwart the takeover of Beehive Thrift and Loan Company (an industrial bank) by First Bankcorporation of Utah (a bank holding company).

Based on this administrative decision, it appeared the board considered the acceptance of demand deposits as the critical element in determining whether an institution was a bank under the Bank Holding Company Act. But the "practical aspects" of the account were considered more relevant than technical or legal distinctions.

> The Board attached great weight to: (1) the manner in which the account was advertised; (2) the manner in which the account was used by the depositor; (3) the historical treatment of the account by the financial institution; (4) whether funds were solicited for the account or were merely incidental to other dealings; (5) whether other laws treated the account as a demand deposit; (6) whether other regulators treated the account as a demand deposit; (7) whether the account was created to evade the Bank Holding Company Act or for a legitimate financial purpose.[21]

The Fed's concern with the rapid increase in non-bank banks was heightened by two transactions initiated by the Dreyfus Corporation, a mutual fund advisory firm. In December 1982, Dreyfus acquired Lincoln State Bank, an existing New Jersey-chartered bank* (now Dreyfus Consumer Bank) and formed the Dreyfus National Bank and Trust Company. Dreyfus received approval from the FDIC to make the acquisition. The Fed objected to the FDIC's jurisdiction by asserting that Lincoln State was a bank subject to the Bank Holding Company Act's approval provisions since the bank would engage in commercial lending. The Fed asserted that the Dreyfus purchase of commercial paper, certificates of deposit, and the extension of broker call loans could *now* be interpreted as commercial lending.

The FDIC concluded, however, that it has regulatory jurisdiction for approving the merger because Dreyfus promised to sell the bank's commercial loan portfolio. Lincoln would cease to be a bank under the Bank Holding Company Act. In a subsequent letter, the FDIC noted with some irritation that the Fed had "dramatically recast the definition of commercial loan by including within it certain activities that clearly had been excluded from the definition in

---

*The FDIC had regulatory jurisdiction over all state-chartered banks that were not members of the Federal Reserve System.

the past." The comptroller quickly came to the aid of the FDIC by declining to honor the board's request that the issuance of a charter to Dreyfus *National* Bank & Trust be denied.[22]

The Fed subsequently issued an order adopting the new commercial loan definition as developed in the Dreyfus case. Dreyfus' application to establish a national bank, which by law had to be a member of the Federal Reserve System, presented the board with an additional opportunity to block the acquisition. As the banking agency responsible for enforcement of the Glass–Steagall Act, the Fed indicated that it would make its "own determination" about the legality of the bank-securities merger when the national bank subscribed to Federal Reserve Bank stock. Notwithstanding the board's objections, Dreyfus proceeded to acquire and operate the bank.

Shortly thereafter, the comptroller approved an application by the J. & W. Seligman Company to charter a new national bank. Seligman, like Dreyfus, was engaged in investment advisory services and had subsidiaries that distributed securities. To avoid Bank Holding Company Act coverage, the trust company announced it would neither make commercial loans nor accept demand deposits. The comptroller, citing the Dreyfus case, approved Seligman's consumer bank application on February 1, 1983. The Federal Reserve Board indicated it would consider Seligman in violation of the Glass–Steagall Act as soon as it applied for membership in the Federal Reserve System.

On February 4, 1983 the comptroller approved the application of the Citizens Fidelity Corporation, a Kentucky holding company, to charter a limited-service national bank in Ohio. This new national bank would conduct the credit card operations for the parent bank holding company, allowing Citizens to take advantage of Ohio's 25% rate on revolving credit and lack of limits on annual fees. The Fed, which had authority over the bank holding company, refused to grant approval until it had issued a new series of regulations with respect to the Bank Holding Company Act. This application gave "the Fed staff fits" and convinced them of "the critical need for legislation to close the non-bank loophole," noted a former Fed lawyer. Within three months, the Fed was nonetheless compelled to approve Citizens' credit card bank.

In March 1983, Dimension Financial Corporation filed thirty-one non-bank bank applications with the comptroller. These non-bank banks, planned for twenty-five states, would concentrate on providing trust services and large consumer loans, but eventually would engage in brokerage services, certain insurance activities, tax planning, and provide other financial assistance. The banks, however, would not engage in any commercial lending, thus avoiding the restrictions of the Douglas Amendment and the need for regulatory approval by the Federal Reserve Board. But the large number of applications was "blatantly greedy" and "scared a lot of people and mobilized Congress," noted a Capitol Hill staffer.

By this time, a number of other bank holding companies were beginning to follow the lead of the securities and nonfinancial companies which had already entered the non-bank bank business. But most holding companies were not particularly enamored of the non-bank bank approach; "the last thing this country needs is *more* banks," growled the president of one large New York bank. But these banks, contemplating the eventual arrival of interstate banking, were lined up at the comptroller. One congressman likened non-bank banking to parking in downtown Washington, D.C.:

> At 6:30 it becomes legal to park on the street, but if you wait until then, all of the desirable spots *will* be gone, and all of the legal spots *may* be gone. Therefore, what people do is they arrive downtown about fifteen minutes early and cruise around until they find a choice spot. Then, they sit there until it becomes legal to park.[23]

FIRST MORATORIUM

On April 5, 1983 the comptroller of the currency, in a letter to the chairmen of the House and Senate Banking Committees, announced a limited moratorium on the chartering of new national non-banks, in order to help Congress "foster free and open debate" over the wider issues of financial services deregulation. Conover urged legislators to lift some of the product and geographical restrictions which handicapped banks in the competitive marketplace for financial services. The moratorium would apply only to new applications and would expire on January 1, 1984.

As Conover announced the moratorium, the Reagan administration unveiled its legislative proposals for revising the structure of the financial services industry. In its key provisions, the bill would allow bank holding companies to engage in a variety of *new* acitivies:

> Broader securities activities: Sponsor, manage, advise, and control mutual funds, and underwrite and sell fund shares; deal in and underwrite a broader range of state and local government debt securities, including limited authority for tax-exempt industrial revenue bonds; conduct a government and municipal securities business; engage in full-scale securities brokerage activities.
> Engage in real estate investment, development and brokerage, including the management of properties. But no more than 5% of the holding company's "primary capital" could be devoted to real estate investment and development activities.
> Engage in full-scale insurance underwriting and brokerage.

The administration's bill would also have closed the non-bank bank loophole by expanding the definition of a bank. Both Todd Conover and William Isaacs, the FDIC chairman, actively supported this bill in testimony before Congress. And both spoke out against the Fed's legislative proposal for a permanent moratorium on non-bank banks. But this bill was soon bottled up by opposition from the securities, real estate, and insurance industries. Bankers were also divided among themselves about the scope of "new powers;" small bankers were reluctant to see bank holding companies widen their advantage through an increased range of products and service offerings.

Senator Garn, chairman of the Senate Banking Committee, was not deterred by the rough reception given the president's bill; he proceeded to introduce legislation that went beyond many of the administration's proposals for expanded bank holding company powers. The Garn bill would allow holding companies to underwrite and deal in mortgage-backed securities; permit regional banking compacts with reciprocal laws and provide a federal "trigger" to spur nationwide banking; allow consumer banks, like the Dreyfus bank, to operate outside the scope of the McFadden Act and the Douglas Amendment. Garn's bill, however, "grandfathered" the non-bank; divestiture would be required of any non-bank bank chartered after June 30, 1983.

As the Congress conducted lengthy hearings on the subject of new bank powers, the focus of public attention shifted to the states. A number of New England states passed reciprocal banking laws, allowing interregional bank mergers. But the New York money-center banks, eager to expand beyond their local, highly competitive market, sued to stop these compacts from engaging in "anti-competitive behavior." The suit, filed by Citibank, argued that these regional compacts were exclusive, since they prohibited entry by New York banks.

REVISING THE DEFINITION OF A BANK

In December 1983 the Fed performed "a bit of regulatory 'legislating' wherein it sought to curtail the proliferation of non-bank banks."[24] After eight months of intensive work, the Fed revised Regulation Y—the statutory license in the Bank Holding Company Act used for exercising authority over acquisition of banks, non-banking activities, and change in control of banks. The board changed the definition of bank under the act by expanding the definitions of the terms deposits and commercial loans. Regulation Y was written to encompass, relative to the earlier definition of deposit, a variety of transaction accounts (excluding money market funds) and relative to commercial loans, an assortment of asset and liability activities. There was a clear intent to legitimize its earlier decisions with respect to the Beehive and Dreyfus cases; it also reflected nagging concerns that Congress would fail to close the non-bank bank loophole.

Notwithstanding its aggressive regulatory stance toward non-bank banks, the Fed could not legally prevent approval of U.S. Trust's non-bank bank application on March 23, 1984. U.S. Trust, a New York bank holding company, was the 19th largest commercial banking organization in the United States, with total consolidated assets of $1.9 billion. U.S. Trust of Florida's activities would include the acceptance of time and demand deposits, including checking accounts, and the making of commercial loans. As part of its application, U.S. Trust agreed that its Florida subsidiary bank would not make commercial loans within the meaning of the Fed's revised Regulation Y.

In approving the application, the board stated that, although it believed such approval "presents a serious potential for undermining the policies of the

[Bank Holding Company Act]," it was constrained by the definition of bank under the Act to approve the application.[25] The board also stated:

> The requirement of Board approval of this application under the provisions of existing law is one of a number of recent developments that underscore the critical need for Congressional action on legislation to apply the policies of the Bank Holding Company Act to institutions that are chartered as banks and that offer transaction accounts to the public.[26]

The board, in effect, sanctioned the use of a non-bank bank by a bank holding company to establish an interstate deposit-gathering and a consumer-lending presence. The Fed was internally divided over the wisdom of this decision; it also faced strong opposition from the State of Florida, the Conference of State Bank Supervisors, and the Florida Bankers Association.

In late March, all three federal bank regulators testified before the Senate Banking Committee; each offered his agency's view toward the non-bank issue and the wider policy question of bank deregulation. Todd Conover urged the committee to focus on the benefits that would accrue to consumers as a result of more vigorous competition. Some likely consumer benefits included: "one-stop shopping for financial services, a more varied menu of products, new product innovations, lower cost insurance and real estate products, increased flow of housing credit, better services for small businesses, and stronger community institutions."

The comptroller strongly supported "the comprehensive approach" because it "would not cater to special interests." But resistance, he cautioned, was to be expected.

> Because of its comprehensive and objective approach, it has opposition, especially from those who want to protect their own markets from outside competition. This is inevitable as we emerge from a heavily regulated environment to a more competitive one. We are all familiar with securities firms complaining about banks entering the brokerage business and banks decrying the efforts of others to offer close, but unregulated, deposit substitutes. Representatives of the insurance industry and independent real estate agents warn of inferior service or an ominous trend toward concentration any time an outsider attmepts to enter into their line of business. These objections mask the real reason for their opposition—they don't want competition.

"Inaction by the Congress," warned Conover, "would mean sanctioning a financial services industry characterized by legal inconsistencies and market inefficiencies."[27]

William Isaac, chairman of the Federal Deposit Insurance Corporation, also spoke of the need for wide-ranging regulatory reforms:

> We believe banks should be authorized to engage in a broader range of financial activities for two principal reasons. First, it would be procompetitive. The Ameri-

can public—including consumers, small businesses, and farmers—would be given a broader range of financial products at more competitive prices. Second, it would strengthen the banking system by allowing banks to be more competitive in the financial marketplace and develop new sources of income to help offset the cost of liability deregulation.

"Except for moratorium legislation," he concluded, "it is hard to imagine the Congress adopting any bill that would be worse than the *status quo*. The marketplace is deregulating, and, try as one might, it cannot be stopped."[28]

The Senate hearings culminated with the testimony of Fed Chairman Paul Volcker. He spoke of the need for regulatory prudence:

> We take as a point of departure, of course, the idea that there is something unique and special about banks that has been reflected in the Federal protections, the so-called safety net around the banking system, for which a certain amount of regulation and insulation is necessary. I think that broad philosophical concept is pretty well accepted and that's what we're dealing with in the definition of a bank. Our concern is that the regulated banking sector would inevitably wither and much of the banking business would take place in institutions not subject to all those policy restrictions incorporated in the act about risk, conflicts of interest, and concentration of resources. We're already beginning to see that kind of migration today into unregulated forms. . .Almost half the number of commercial banks. . .could, with some minor restructuring. . .escape policies of the [Fed].
>
> As things stand now, many of these specific issues will be decided on a case-by-case basis in the courts—but we cannot expect those decisions to be guided by a policy perspective on how the financial system as a whole should evolve. That, in the end, is the task of the legislature, not the courts, which must struggle to adapt today's circumstances to yesterday's laws.

"If Congress does not decide," the central banker predicted that the "decisions will be made. . .but they will be conflicting. One clear risk is that the overriding public interest in a strong, stable, and competitive financial system will be lost."[29]

SECOND MORATORIUM

On May 9, 1984 the comptroller extended the moratorium on non-bank banks to the end of the congressional session. Non-bank bank applications would still be accepted, but would not receive attention until the expiration of the moratorium. Conover went on to point out that non-bank banks were "definitely legal" and that he would have no choice but to "proceed accordingly" if Congress failed to enact changes in banking laws. The number of non-bank bank applications had swelled to 230.

Both Chairmen Garn and St. Germain expressed pleasure with the comptroller's moratorium extension. Senator Garn assured Conover that he was committed to enacting broad-based legislation; he also promised that he "would neither ask for nor support any future extension of this moratorium."[30] In somewhat of a paradox, however, the comptroller approved four non-bank bank applications just as he announced the extension. "This was designed to signal our intent to proceed, if Congress balked at broad-based legislation," noted a top advisor to the comptroller. A former staffer at the comptroller put it more plainly: "We just wanted to assure everybody we were not wimps."

Through the spring and summer, both the Fed and the comptroller continued to wage an aggressive lobbying campaign in Congress for bank legislation. The comptroller, with his blunt criticism of the House bill, did little to endear himself to the House Banking Committee; he complained that the legislation would "turn back the clock in a way that would weaken the banking industry and be detrimental to consumers." St. Germain's bill was much narrower than the Senate legislation and led Conover to assert that "when you reduce competition in the marketplace, the customer is the one who suffers." Obviously provoked, St. Germain shot back: "That is a generalization . . . banking is different . . . for that reason, I say to you, don't give us generalizations, give us facts."[31]

The May 1984 failure and subsequent federal rescue of Continential Illinois Bank, the seventh largest bank in the U.S., diverted attention and undermined much of the support for broad bank deregulation. The FDIC was criticized for rescuing Continental when many smaller banks were routineely allowed to fail. A furor ensued when Conover volunteeered that a "double standard" in the treatment of large and small banks was inevitable.

St. Germain contended Continental's rapid growth should have been a signal to the Comptroller's office that "it was time to move in, to demand a tough internal system of review and to make certain that management at all levels could qualify for jet-age lending."[32] The banking chairman said that if Continental's managers did everything the Comptroller's office told them to do "and still failed, then maybe the handbook needs to be revised."[33] St. Germain also used the occasion to upbraid the comptroller for curtailing the size of the bank supervisory staff. The Continental Bank failure exposed the "fantasy" that big banks were infallible, observed one House staffer. It turned the debate from bank deregulation to the "safety and soundness" of the financial system.

Conover would later concede that "the collapse of Continental worked against new powers, and for all the wrong reasons." He blamed much of Continental's problems on excess regulation; the bank was restricted to the downtown Chicago area by unitary branching laws. As a result, the bank had become heavily dependent on brokered deposits—a costly and relatively unstable source of funds relative to customer demand deposits.

On September 13, 1984 the Senate approved S. 2851, "The Financial Services Competitive Equity Act" by an eighty-nine to five vote.[34] "The size of the margin," said Garn, "reflected the Senate's recognition of the pressing need for legislation to address the competitive issues, the consumer protection issues and the regulatory issues being raised by the ongoing rapid changes in our financial services industry." Garn attributed the large consensus to "the extensive hearings held in 1981, 1982, 1983, and 1984."[35] The act was an amalgam of more than a dozen bills introduced by various senators to address issues facing the financial services industry; according to most bankers, the outcome provided for some modest bank deregulation.

In contrast, the House could only agree to close the non-bank bank "loophole." The Banking Committee was still debating various aspects of more than a half dozen bills circulating within the committee; there was not even a hint of a legislative consensus. To a certain degree, the difficulty could be traced to the disparate committee membership; each segment of the industry (large money-center banks, small independent banks, the "financial supermarkets" such as Sears and Merrill Lynch) was represented by strong-minded and effective legislators. St. Germain claimed that Congress needed more time to weigh carefully the changes necessary for the financial system; he described his reaction to the Senate action:

> The Senate, while recognizing our initiative in closing the non-bank bank loophole. . .adopted what can only be accurately described as a Christmas tree festooned with brightly colored ornaments of all shapes and sizes—credit union amendments, export trading company provisions, a basket of new powers for bank holding companies including new securities activities, consumer leasing amendments, new rules for brokered deposits, preemption of state usury laws, green-mail, golden-parachute provisions amending securities statutes, regional banking compacts which raise signficant constitutional questions, new powers for savings and loans. . .the list goes on and on. The implications of these provisions won't be known for months, and, in some cases, years.[36]

The Senate legislation was "so far ranging and so broadly drafted" that St. Germain had taken the unprecedented step of including two other House committees in the debate over bank policy. But it now seemed clear that the House would adjourn without passing a broad-based banking bill; S. 2851 would die at the end of the congressional session.

The Comptroller's Decision

Todd Conover was confronted with the most important policy decision of his three-year tenure in the Office of the Comptroller of the Currency. Although he had not desired it, his name was inextricably linked to non-bank banks. It was an odd development given the fact that non-banks had their birthright when he was in the private sector, engaged in building his management consulting firm. But upon moving to Washington, Conover quickly realized that non-bank banks could be the lightning rod needed for stimulating a full public debate over banking policy. His admirers believed he "had been exemplary for taking the heat;" critics labelled him an "outlaw" for allowing non-bank banks to proliferate.

His most vociferous critic was the Independent Bankers Association of America, a trade group representing about 7,700 small and rural banks. For the

IBAA, there was no greater "old-time religion issue" than interstate banking; the group fought it every step of the way. The association's president described the view of small bankers: "It's not interstate banking we're talking about, it's interstate ownership. The real tragedy is when a small town bank loses its decision-making process to an out-of-towner."[37] Empirical studies, however, suggested that bank expansion, on balance, could result in greater proportion of loans to locally limited customers where expansion is limited. Moreover, there was no evidence to support the claim that banks were using outlying branches to transfer funds to head offices in urban areas; rather banks transfer among rural offices as dictated by needs.[38] Even so, small bankers had stirred concerns about a banking system that would become more concentrated by virture of the non-bank bank.

The Conference of State Bank Supervisors, representing banking commissions in all fifty states, complained that non-bank banks not only circumvented the Fed, but also escaped any meaningful state supervision. The Bank Holding Company Act specifically reserved to the states the right to preempt federal regulation. In a letter to Congress, CSBS claimed the non-bank bank "lays waste to an entire body of public interest determinations made by those who previously walked the halls of Congress." It continued:

> Through the non-bank bank mechanism, the Bank Holding Company Act of 1956 is being used to achieve exactly what it was designed to prevent. As the United States Supreme Court recently set out, the Act was enacted to accomplish two primary objectives: ". . .It was designed to prevent the concentration of banking resources in the hands of a few financial giants. . .," and "it was intended to implement a Congressional policy against control of banking by. . .a single business entity." As the court noted, ". . .underlying both objectives was a desire to prevent anticompetitive tendencies in national credit markets."[39]

The state regulators had urged Congress to "restore some sanity to the regulatory process, before it is too late."[40] They also claimed the non-bank bank was illegal since it went far beyond the single "Boston Safe" exclusion provided by the Brooke amendment. The comptroller interpreted this exemption much differently; non-bank banks were "definitely legal," since it was unconstitutional to apply general legislation to one entity.

Todd Conover would have to consider the nature of the opposition to non-bank banks before making a final decision. Congress was still being deluged with mail from small bankers, farmers, small businesses urging the loophole be "corked." Congress' "grandfather" provision (which mandated divestiture of non-bank banks formed after mid-1983), could render meaningless any action by the comptroller with respect to non-bank bank charters. And then there was the Fed, which had fought non-bank banks through every regulatory device imaginable. Since most recent non-bank bank applications had been filed by bank holding companies, the Fed would have the final word.

For the moment, however, the decision was entirely in the hands of the comptroller. He had to decide whether to lift or extend the moratorium and when to announce his decision. Congress would be in session for two more weeks, but might be reconvened after the election for a brief "lame duck" session. Senator Garn and Representative St. Germain had already announced that banking legislation would be a "top priority" in the next Congress. Conover wondered if it would be worth waiting; the marketplace certainly would not stand still.

Exhibit 1 Biographical Profile

NEWS RELEASE

Comptroller of the Currency
Administrator of National Banks

Washington, D.C. 20219

C. Todd Conover

C. Todd Conover was sworn in as 25th Comptroller of the
Currency on December 16, 1981. In that capacity, he is the
chief executive officer of the agency responsible for
regulating 4,700 national banks. He directs a staff of nearly
3,000 and is responsible for an annual budget of $165 million.

His term has covered one of the periods of greatest change in
financial services in our Nation's history. During that period
banks have struggled through a long recession, confronted new
competition, and begun offering new services in wider
geographic areas and through new types of outlets. A strong
advocate of bank deregulation, Mr. Conover actively supports
giving banks more power to compete effectively in the
marketplace. Among the new powers authorized by the
Comptroller's Office under Mr..Conover's leadership are
discount brokerage and investment advisory services,
underwriting credit life insurance, establishment of futures
commission merchant subsidiaries, leasing space on bank
premises to insurance agents, providing common trust funds for
the collective investment of IRA contributions, and offering
plain English trusts.

Mr. Conover's experience in banking and management consulting
has included the areas of strategic planning, financial
management, and operations improvement. That background has
been helpful in streamlining the Office's Washington and
regional operations and making organizational and operational
changes to prepare the Office for the future. He has reduced
the number of regional offices and has simplified and
decentralized many of the processes for approving national
banks' corporate applications.

Conover, who holds a B.A. from Yale University and an M.B.A. in
finance from the University of California at Berkeley, came to
the Comptroller's post from Edgar, Dunn & Conover Inc., a
general management consulting firm in San Francisco. Before
helping to found that firm, he was with the management
consulting group of Touche Ross & Co., San Francisco. He was a
principal and national services director for banking for that
firm from 1974 to 1978.

Prior to that, Conover served as vice president, corporate
development, for U.S. Bancorp in Portland, Oregon, and a
management consultant with McKinsey & Company in San Francisco
and Amsterdam, The Netherlands.

Exhibit 2 Summary of Non-Bank Bank Applications

NON-BANK APPLICATIONS (WILL NOT MAKE COMMERCIAL LOANS)

American Security Corporation	Washington, D.C.	2
Bank of Boston Corporation	Boston, Massachusetts	3
Bank of New York Company, Inc.	New York, New York	13
Barclays American Corporation	Charlotte, North Carolina	1
Central Bancshares of the South, Inc.	Birmingham, Alabama	24
Chemical New York Corporation	New York, New York	15
Commerce Bancshares	Kansas City, Missouri	5
Comerica, Inc.	Detroit, Michigan	1
Dominion Bancshares	Roanoke, Virginia	4
Equitable Bancorporation	Baltimore, Maryland	4
Fidelcor, Inc.	Philadelphia, Pennsylvania	2
First Atlanta Corporation	Atlanta, Georgia	1
First Bank Systems, Incorporated	Minneapolis, Minnesota	3
First Chicago Corporation	Chicago, Illinois	5
First Delta Corporation	Helena, Arkansas	1
First Interstate Bancorp	Los Angeles, California	12
First National State Bancorporation	Newark, New Jersey	4
First Railroad and Banking Company	Augusta, Georgia	3
First Union Corporation	Charlotte, North Carolina	7
First Virginia Banks, Inc.	Falls Church, Virginia	1
Fleet Financial Group, Inc.	Providence, Rhode Island	10
Hongkong and Shanghai Banking Corp	Hong Kong, British Crown Colony	6
Marine Midland Banks, Inc.	Buffalo, New York	14
Maryland National Corporation	Baltimore, Maryland	3
Mellon National Corporation	Pittsburgh, Pennsylvania	15
Midlantic Banks, Inc.	Newark, New Jersey	2
NCNB Corporation	Charlotte, North Carolina	1
Suburban Bancorp	Bethesda, Maryland	1
Union Bancorp of California	Los Angeles, California	11
U.S. Bancorp	Portland, Oregon	4
Washington Bancorporation	Washington, D.C.	1
		176

NON-BANK BANK APPLICATIONS (WILL NOT ACCEPT DEMAND DEPOSITS)

AmSouth Corporation	Birmingham, Alabama	9
BankAmerica Corporation	San Francisco, California	13
Chase U.S. Consumer Services, Inc.	New York, New York	21
Citicorp	New York, New York	10
First American Corporation	Nashville, Tennessee	2
First Commerce Corporation	New Orleans, Louisiana	2
First Maryland Bancorporation	Baltimore, Maryland	4
International Central Bank & Trust	New York, New York	1
Irving Bank Corporation of New York	New York, New York	13
People's Bancorporation	Seattle, Washington	2
Rainier Bancorporation	Seattle, Washington	9
RepublicBank Corporation	Dallas, Texas	16
Security Pacific Corporation	Los Angeles, California	20
Sovran Financial Corporation	Norfolk, Virginia	1
		123

Exhibit 2 (continued)

AMENDMENTS TO ARTICLES OF ASSOCIATION OF LIMITED POWER TRUST BANKS

(NO COMMERCIAL LOANS)

Bank of Boston Corporation	*Boston, Massachusetts*	1
Bank of New York Company	*New York, New York*	1
Chemical New York Corporation	*New York, New York*	1
Comerica, Inc.	*Minneapolis, Minnesota*	1
First Bank Systems, Inc.	*Minneapolis, Minnesota*	1
First National State Bancorp	*Minneapolis, Minnesota*	1
J.P. Morgan & Company, Inc.	*New York, New York*	1
Key Banks, Inc.	*Albany, New York*	1
Manufacturers Hanover Corporation	*New York, New York*	1
Manufacturers National Corporation	*Detroit, Michigan*	1
Marshall & Ilsley Corporation	*Milwaukee, Wisconsin*	1
Mellon National Corporation	*Pittsburgh, Pennsylvania*	1
Midlantic Banks, Inc.	*Edison, New Jersey*	1
National City Corporation	*Cleveland, Ohio*	1
NBD Bancorp, Inc.	*Detroit, Michigan*	1
Northeastern Bancorp, Inc.	*Scranton, Pennsylvania*	1
R.I.H.T. Financial Corporation	*Providence, Rhode Island*	1
		17

AMENDMENTS TO ARTICLES OF ASSOCIATION OF LIMITED POWER TRUST BANKS
(NO DEMAND DEPOSITS)

Chase Manhattan Corporation	*New York, New York*	1
	TOTAL	317

	INTERSTATE NONBANK BANK CHARTERS		EXPANSION OF TRUST COMPANY POWERS	
State of Non-Bank Bank	*Will Not Accept Demand Deposits*	*Will Not Make Commercial Loans*	*Will Not Accept Demand Deposits*	*Will Not Make Commercial Loans*
Alabama	2	2	0	0
Alaska	0	0	0	0
Arizona	7	3	0	0
Arkansas	2	1	0	0
California	7	4	0	0
Colorado	3	2	0	0
Connecticut	4	4	0	0
Delaware	0	2	0	0
Florida	3	6	1	16
Georgia	6	11	0	0
Hawaii	2	0	0	0
Idaho	2	0	0	0
Illinois	4	3	0	0

444

Exhibit 2 (continued)

State of Non-Bank Bank	INTERSTATE NONBANK BANK CHARTERS		EXPANSION OF TRUST COMPANY POWERS	
	Will Not Accept Demand Deposits	Will Not Make Commercial Loans	Will Not Accept Demand Deposits	Will Not Make Commercial Loans
Indiana	1	3	0	0
Iowa	0	0	0	0
Kansas	0	1	0	0
Kentucky	0	0	0	0
Louisiana	3	3	0	0
Maine	0	0	0	0
Maryland	2	3	0	0
Massachusetts	4	6	0	0
Michigan	0	0	0	0
Minnesota	3	0	0	0
Mississippi	2	0	0	0
Missouri	2	1	0	0
Montana	0	0	0	0
Nebraska	0	0	0	0
Nevada	2	0	0	0
New Hampshire	1	1	0	0
New Jersey	3	6	0	0
New Mexico	4	1	0	0
New York	3	5	0	0
North Carolina	4	4	0	0
North Dakota	0	0	0	0
Ohio	3	3	0	0
Oklahoma	3	1	0	0
Oregon	4	1	0	0
Pennsylvania	5	9	0	0
Rhode Island	0	0	0	0
South Carolina	1	5	0	1
South Dakota	0	0	0	0
Tennessee	2	5	0	0
Texas	12	17	0	0
Utah	3	0	0	0
Vermont	1	0	0	0
Virginia	4	14	0	0
Washington	1	9	0	0
West Virginia	1	0	0	0
Wisconsin	0	0	0	0
Wyoming	0	0	0	0
District of Columbia	1	6	0	0
TOTAL	123	176	1	18 = 317

NOTES

1. 12 U.S.C. s.1841 (c).
2. *H.R. Rep. No.* 84, 609, 84th Congress, 1st session (1955).
3. Public Law 84-511, 70 Stat. 133 (1956).
4. One Bank Holding Company Legislation of 1970, Hearings Before the Senate Committee on Banking and Currency on S. 1052, S. 1052, S. 1211, S. 1664, S. 3823, and H.R. 6778, 91st Congress, 2nd session, 137 (1970).
5. Philip C. Corwin, " 'Consumer Banks' No Solution to Regulatory Impasse," *Legal Times*, November 21, 1983, p. 34.
6. 63 *Federal Reserve Bulletin*, pp. 595, 597–98 (June 1977).
7. "What is a Bank?," *Federal Reserve Bank of Chicago: Economic Perspectives* (January 1983), p. 20, 24.
8. Letter from Baldwin Tutle, Deputy General Counsel, Board of Governors of the Federal Reserve System to Michael A. Greenspan (dated January 26, 1976), p. 2.
9. "Just When Is a Bank Not a Bank? When It Is an Abomination," *Wall Street Journal*, January 30, 1984, p. 2.
10. Ibid.
11. Ibid.
12. Ibid.
13. Ibid.
14. Ibid.
15. Ibid.
16. Letter from John C. Beers, Regional District Director for Corporate Activities (Comptroller of the Currency) to John J. Balles, President of the Federal Reserve Bank of San Francisco (dated June 13, 1980), p. 1.
17. Letter from Harry W. Green, Vice President of the Federal Reserve Bank of San Francisco to John C. Beers, Regional Director for Corporate Activities (Comptroller of the Currency) (dated June 19, 1980), p. 1.
18. Letter from James McAfee, Assistant Secretary of the Board of Governors of the Federal Reserve System to Thomas F. Bolger, President of the Independent Bankers Association of America (dated March 11, 1981), p. 1.
19. "Developments in Bank Expansion During the Second Quarter," *Bank Expansion Quarterly* (31, 3), p. 2.
20. Ibid, p. 3.
21. Raymond Natter, "Nonbank Banks Under the Bank Holding Company Act: A Legal Analysis" (Congressional Research Service, Washington D.C.: The Library of Congress, 1983), CRS-12.
22. Joseph Diamond and Robert M. Kurucza, "Interindustry Developments: Limited Purpose Banking Operations" (Second Annual Financial Services Institute; Practicing Law Institute, 1984), pp. 14, 15.
23. "Remarks of Representative Chalmers P. Wylie (R-Ohio) Before the Banking Law Institute" (October 1, 1984), p. 1.
24. Harold P. Reichwald, "Expanded Activities Under Revised Federal Reserve Board Regulation Y," *ALI-ABA Course of Study Materials: Financial Institutions - Current Issues*, (New York: American Law Institute/American Bar Association, 1984), p. 80.
25. Brian W. Smith, "Nonbank Banks," *Executive Enterprises: Expansion Choices Towards Establishing an Interstate Presence* (October 1, 1984).
26. Ibid.
27. Hearings Before the Committee on Banking, Housing, and Urban Affairs, United States Senate, 98th Congress, 2nd session (March 21, 1984), Testimony of C. Todd Conover, Comptroller of the Currency, pp. 1221–28.
28. Hearings Before the Committee on Banking, Housing, and Urban Affairs, United States Senate, 98th Congress, 2nd session (March 21, 1984), Testimony of William M. Isaac, Chairman of the Federal Deposit Insurance Corporation, pp. 1274–87.
29. Hearings Before the Committee on Banking, Housing, and Urban Affairs, United States Senate, 98th Congress, 2nd session (March 27, 1984), Testimony of Paul Volcker, Chairman, Board of Governors, Federal Reserve System, pp. 1583–92.
30. "News Release: Statement by C.T. Conover," Comptroller of the Currency (May 9, 1984), p. 2.
31. Hearings Before the Committee on Banking, Housing and Urban Affairs, House of Representatives, 98th Congress, 2nd session, (June 12, 1984), Testimony of C. Todd Conover, Comptroller of the Currency, p. 1635.
32. "House Opens Hearings on Continental Bank," *Washington Post*, September 19, 1984, p. D1.
33. Ibid., p. D14.
34. "News Release: Senate Banking Committee Chairman Announces 1985 Agenda," Senate Banking, Housing & Urban Affairs Committee, (March 29, 1985), p. 1.
35. Ibid, p. 1.
36. "Statement of Chairman Fernand J. St. Germain on the Floor of the House of Representatives" (September 21, 1984), p. 1.
37. "After Half a Century, IBAA Is Alive and Kicking, and Mostly It's Kicking About Interstate Banking," *American Banker*, March 4, 1985, p. 10.
38. *Geographic Restrictions on Commercial Banking in the United States*, The Report of the President of the United States, (Washington, D.C.: Government Printing Office, January 1981), p. 15.
39. Letter to Congress from the Conference of State Bank Supervisors (dated February 22, 1985), p. 2.
40. Ibid., p. 2.